Strategic Transformation and Information Technology

Paradigms for Performing While Transforming

Marilyn M. Parker

PRENTICE HALL, Upper Saddle River, NJ 07458

Parker, Marilyn M.
    Strategic transformation and information technology : paradigms
for performing while transforming / Marilyn M. Parker.
        p.   cm. -- (William R. King series)
    IBSN 0-13-190794-8
    1. Management information systems.   2. Organizational change-
-Management.   3. Information technology.   I. Title.   II. Series:
William R. King series in information management.
HD30.213.P37   1995
658.4'038'011--dc20   95-18153
                                                                       CIP

Executive Managing Editor: Fred Bernardi
Editorial/Production Supervision
    and Interior Design: Susan Rifkin
Acquisitions Editor: PJ Boardman
Cover Designer: Karen Salzbach
Manufacturing Buyer: Paul Smolenski

© 1996 by Prentice-Hall, Inc.
A Simon & Schuster Company
Upper Saddle River, NJ 07458

Printed in the United States of America

10 9 8 7 6 5 4 3 2 1

ISBN 0-13-190794-8

Prentice-Hall International (UK) Limited, *London*
Prentice-Hall of Australia Pty. Limited, *Sydney*
Prentice-Hall Canada Inc., *Toronto*
Prentice-Hall Hispanoamericana, S.A., *Mexico*
Prentice-Hall of India Private Limited, *New Delhi*
Prentice-Hall of Japan, Inc., *Tokyo*
Simon & Schuster Asia Pte. Ltd., *Singapore*
Editora Prentice-Hall do Brasil, Ltda., *Rio de Janeiro*

To Virgil

PRENTICE HALL SERIES
IN INFORMATION MANAGEMENT

William R. King, *Series Editor*

Contents

FOREWORD
Dr. Richard L. Nolan, Harvard Business School   xi

PREFACE   xiv

ACKNOWLEDGMENTS   xviii

Part I.   Assessing New Marketplace Dynamics   1

    1.   GLOBAL TREMORS, LOCAL QUAKES   3

    Looking Back Before Moving Forward   4; Global Markets   7;
    Emerging Global Organizational Models   10;
    Shifting Economic Bases   12; Customers Define
    Markets   15; Individuals in a Knowledge Society   16;
    Information Technology Comes of Age   18; Where We're
    Going   20

Part II.   Enabling Enterprise Transformation with Information Technology   25

    2.   ANYWHERE, ANYTIME WORKPLACES   27

    Virtual Offices   28; Electronic Immigrants   35;
    Office Meetings   37; Voice Mail   39; Exchanging
    Business Information   41; Role of the Fax   42;
    Imaging   45; Observations   46

3.   *INFORMATION EMPOWERMENT*   48

Empowering the Consumer-Customer   49; Empowering the
Organization   52; Intelligent Systems   53; Executive
Information Systems   59; Sales Force Automation   60;
Knowing What to Know   62; Empowering Corporations
Through Information Partnerships   65; Observations   66

4.   *NETWORKED ENTERPRISES*   69

Networks and Electronic Messaging   70; Business Network
Redesign   72; Diversity of Change   85; Managerial
Themes   86; Observations   87

5.   *MASS CUSTOMIZATION*   91

Mass Customization Concepts   92; Mass Customization as
a Business Strategy   94; Putting the "Custom" Back Into
Customer   108; Observations   111

Part III.   Emerging Venues for I/T Leadership   113

6.   *STANDARDS, SERVICE, AND QUALITY INITIATIVES*   115

Emerging International Standards   117; International
Organization for Standardization   121; Total Quality
Management and Its Leaders   124; Crafting a Quality
Program   131; Value and Service   131; Adding Value to the
Product   132; Adding Value to the Service   133; Help Lines
for Customers   134; Service as a Primary Business   135;
Restructuring Service   137; Observations   139

7.   *BUSINESS PROCESS REDESIGN*   141

Business Process and Enterprise Focus Change   142;
Redesigning Collegial Relationships   143; Redesigning the
Business Process   145; Redesigning Employee/Employer
Relationships by Empowerment   150; Redesigning Supplier
Relationships   152; Redesigning for Lean Manufacturing   153;
Redesigning With Benchmarking   156; Technology
Fusion and the Paradigm Shift   158; Redesigning with
Environmental Quality as the Catalyst   160; Observations   162

**8.   *ORGANIZATIONAL RESTRUCTURING
AND TRANSFORMATION***   164

Corporate Culture Reengineering   165; Boundaryless,
Borderless Networked Enterprises   169; Strategic Alliances

and Joint Ventures 172; Mergers and Acquisitions 174;
Outsourcing and Downsizing 177; Management and
Employee Buy Outs 179; Restructuring or Transformation:
Four Examples 179; Observations 188

Part IV. Transforming I/T   189

  9.   *EXPANDING THE I/T CHARTER*   191

Core Competencies 194; Learning Organizations and
Managing Surprise 198; I/T as Innovator, Change Agent,
and Positioning Agent 202; Observations 211

 10.   *REENGINEERING THE I/T INFRASTRUCTURE*   213

Consequences of Change for I/T 215; Realities of Downsizing and Outsourcing 225; Realities of Rightsizing I/T
Products and Processes 229; Realities of Decentralization
and Recentralization 234; Observations 236

 11.   *DELIVERING BUSINESS VALUE*   239

Business-I/T Credibility Gap 241; Business Value of
Information 242; Structural Change and Business Value 246;
Businesses Face New Performance Measures 249; Indicators
of Financial Value Undergoing Structural Change 249;
Stakeholder Values and the Information Age Economy 251;
Observations 254

Part V. Planning I/T and Enterprise Transformation   257

 12.   *IDENTIFYING TRENDS AND BUILDING SCENARIOS*   259

Political Realignment as a Driving Force for Growth and
Constraints 260; Demographic Shift as a Driving Force
for Growth and Constraints 262; Environmental Quality
as a Driving Force for Growth and Constraints 268;
Impact of Environmental Concerns on the Energy
Industry 271; Observations 283

 13.   *CREATING A TRANSFORMATIONAL
       PLANNING CONTEXT*   285

Seven Questions Methodology for Transformation
Planning 287; Observations 304

14. IDENTIFYING NEW VALUE AND RISK CRITERIA 308

Taxonomy of Transformation-Based Value and Risk
Criteria 311; Financial Values 313; Strategic Values 317;
Stakeholder Values 321; Competitive Strategy Risks 325;
Organizational Strategy Risks and Uncertainties 327;
Tailoring the Taxonomy 329; Observations 330

**15. DEVELOPING NEW JUSTIFICATION AND
MEASUREMENT PHILOSOPHIES** 332

Information Economics and Justifying Transformation-Based
Investments 333; Value, Risk, and Performance Indicators
(The Management Dashboard) 340; Stakeholders and
Business Values 345; Stakeholders as the Key to I/T
Business Value 347; Indicators of Financial Value 350;
Indicators of Strategic Values 351; Indicators of Stakeholder
Values 353; Indicators of Competitive Strategy Risks 356;
Indicators of Organizational Strategy Risks and Uncer-
tainties 357; Observations 359

Part VI. Performing While Transforming 363

**16. DISCOVERING NEW PARADIGMS WHILE
REVISITING REVOLUTIONS** 371

Paradigm Blinders 365; Recognizing New Paradigms 371;
Reengineering the I/T Infrastructure and Processes To Support
the Transforming Enterprise 372; Enterprise Transformation
with I/T as a Business Partner 378; Guiding I/T To Create
the Future 383; What Business Is I/T In? 385

Appendix I. Commentary Articles 389

Part I. Assessing New Marketplace Dynamics 389

**CORPORATE TRANSFORMATION: AMALGAMS
AND DISTINCTIONS** 391

Dr. Barbara Blumenthal, Temple University and Dr. Philippe
Haspeslagh, Professor of Business Policy, INSEAD (France)

**MARKET FORCES SHAPING THE COMPETITIVE
ENVIRONMENT** 402

Marilyn M. Parker, Managing Director, Key Strategies and
Solutions, Inc. (United States)

Part II.   Enabling Enterprise Transformation With I/T   425

COPING WITH BUSINESS AND TECHNOLOGICAL CHANGE   427

Michael L. Mushet, General Manager, Power Systems
Management Division, Southern California Edison (United
States) with Marilyn M. Parker

Part III.   Emerging Venues for I/T Leadership   451

VALUE AND SERVICE IN THE RETAILING INDUSTRY   453

Marilyn M. Parker, Managing Director, Key Strategies and
Solutions, Inc. (United States)

Part IV.   Transforming I/T   459

ORGANIZATIONAL RESTRUCTURING AND PROCESS REENGINEERING   461

Lynwood Walker, Director, Community Ministries, The
Salvation Army, Grande Prairie AB (Canada)

BUSINESS VALUE   488

Dr. Robert J. Benson, Professor of Information Management
Washington University (United States)

Part V.   Planning I/T and Enterprise Transformation   503

MANAGING CHANGE IN A PERFORMANCE-DRIVEN ORGANIZATION USING INFORMATION ECONOMICS   505

Lynwood Walker, Director, Community Ministries, The
Salvation Army, Grande Prairie AB (Canada)

STAKEHOLDER VALUES AND STRUCTURAL CHANGE   518

Marilyn M. Parker, Managing Director, Key Strategies and
Solutions, Inc. (United States)

EVERGREEN ENVIRONMENTAL CONSULTANTS   528

Marilyn M. Parker, Managing Director, Key Strategies and
Solutions, Inc. (United States)

Part VI.   Performing While Transforming   537

      NEW TECHNOLOGIES AND NEW SERVICES   539

      Dr. Jon Thorhallsson, Associate Professor of I/T, The
      University of Iceland, and Managing Director, SKYRR,
      The State and Municipal Data Centre (Iceland)

      NATIONAL DEFENSE AND THE AGE OF UNCERTAINTY   545

      Lt. Col. Robert T. Morris, United States Air Force Colorado
      Springs, Colorado and Garden City, Kansas (United States)

      APPENDIX II   553

      NOTES AND SUPPLEMENTARY READINGS   567

      INDEX   597

Foreword

Strategic Transformation and Information Technology is an important book for both the business and I/T professional. In a blink of the eye, I/T has emerged from a bit part in the company to the leading role. Unlike any other functional area, many I/T professionals that were there when I/T was a bit part are still working in the area now as I/T is, and has become, strategic. Marilyn Parker has observed, studied, and researched the best-of-the-best management practices for transforming the business, for managing I/T to enable business transformation, and for transforming the I/T organization so that it can contribute to the extraction of the strategic potential of I/T. These best-of-the-best management practices support new business themes and create new "rules for success."

Technology changes fast; humans and their organizations change slowly. Organizational inertia is one of the greatest problems that business organizations and humans are currently facing in terms of catching up to the potential strategic value of I/T. Most IS (Information Systems) Departments in large organizations are in jeopardy of becoming isolated or extinct. The role of I/T has moved beyond building applications portfolios of systems that automate business transactions. Microcomputers and user-oriented software have put computers in the hands of professionals that can use them without custom-developed "systems" or the use of intermediary programmers. Corporate, industry, and public networks are connecting professionals that are now more accurately described as knowledge workers, resulting in the leveraging of knowledge insofar as managers are learning to act on information on the basis that "you know everything about everything, now." These later trends are resulting in business transformations, and the emergence of I/T as a major player with a strategic role.

Many IS Departments initially saw microcomputers as a threat to be slowed down. Microcomputers spread like wildfire anyway, and now often account for twice the expenditure of traditional transaction processing. Networking in the form of object-oriented development and client/server architectures are having a similar unstoppable surge in the Network era as microcomputers had in the Micro era. There is a real urgency for the message of Marilyn Parker, and to listen to her advice on what to do. It's not built around "business as usual" but is an analysis of the new business realities and their consequences for I/T, requiring rethinking old paradigms and discovering new ones for both business and I/T.

There are few books today written for both business and technology audiences. *Strategic Transformation and Information Technology* can and should be read by both to assist in the development of shared vision and joint execution that's necessary to carry out tomorrow's business strategy. It exposes the business executive to a broad array of successful (and not so successful) technology-based business solutions to gain a better understanding of what technology can contribute to business. This increases business expectations of what technology can do, and requires shared business/technology vision and planning. At the same time, the I/T professional gets exposed to many new business realities. Globalization, changing organizational models, and new distribution channel relationships have profound consequences for I/T—its technology and organizational models, and its planning, development, service, and delivery processes. The book clearly illustrates the challenges of the new charter for I/T, which is to simultaneously transform itself—its organization, people, technology, and processes—and at the same time enable the business functions in its transformations and act as a positioning agent (through technology and platforms) so that the business becomes agile enough to exploit new and currently unforeseen opportunities.

What's important is not the technology per se, but the combined result—the new business strategies and solutions achieved using technology. Successful development and delivery of a business application by I/T, coupled with the successful use of the application by the business, enhances business value—and that successful use involves corporate culture, management attitudes, and customer/user "comfort level" with technology and change as the enterprise simultaneously performs and transforms. This requires new mindsets for everyone involved, including business and technology professionals, customers and suppliers.

I first met Marilyn Parker when she studied and taught information economics in IBM's executive education programs. I had the pleasure to work with her and Professor Robert Benson (Washington University) during their research project on information economics and enterprise-wide information management a decade ago. Surrounded by technology gurus, she never gave an inch in her insistence that there had to be a business reason for investing in new technology and applications, and that the staff of IS Departments had to understand the business they were supporting as well as the technology they were employing. Her study of European businesses and the influence of recent trade agreements provides new insights into the impact of technology in a global business environment. I think that Marilyn has developed into one of the leading applied researchers on information technology planning and management. She has made an important contribution by constantly challenging the artificial barriers erected between business and technology functions, assisting I/T professionals in improving their practice and growing in their profession, and helping business professionals to better appreciate and realize the potential of new technology contributions.

Richard L. Nolan
Harvard Business School

Preface

Today, many U.S. businesses serve as world role models, creating new best practices and new world standards, while still other U.S. businesses have lackluster performance and fail. The same is true for Japan, Germany, and U.K. businesses. All operate within competitive cultures that have evolved over time and in competitive contexts that provide only limited shelter from political and social changes. Each country's legal code defines, supports, and reflects their respective past competitive culture—ones that flourished until enterprises began competing in an expanding, global marketplace.

The four major competitive models—those of the United States, Germany, Japan, and the United Kingdom—are imperfect in the global market, and each country's business leaders study their world-class competitors to learn new paradigms for success.

- Japanese shareholders receive little payout for investments, and workers want a better quality of life. Japanese manufacturers, with their traditions of lifetime employment, begin to abandon these social contracts to sustain global competitiveness and, in this aspect, move closer to the U.S. model.
- Because of high labor costs and strength of labor unions, German manufacturers are moving production out of the country to remain price-competitive. Germany, whose traditional economic model favors tight linkages with government, banking, and labor unions over those with stockholders, finds that it must rethink this emphasis if it wishes to have access to a strong equity market—as exists in the United States—for funding economic expansion.
- Examining British competition, we find similar dissatisfactions. Its Cadbury

Committee recommends new rules for the competitive game. The United Kingdom continues to struggle under the burdens of a costly social system that hinders global competitiveness, while debating the ethical role of the enterprise in society, in search of its own solution.

- In the United States, disenchanted shareholders no longer believe that the boards of directors are adequately representing their interests and believe that executive management is putting personal interests above those of the other stakeholders of the enterprise, including the other employees. Executives and workers alike worry about staying competitive. Despite a competitive model that reflects an adversarial relationship between employee and employer, many businesses adapt the Japanese teamworking concept to improve quality and maintain competitiveness. At the same time, its government ponders a new role of establishing a national agenda to create a world-class information superhighway—not unlike Germany, Japan, and Canada.

As the era of globalization proceeds and enterprises begin competing for the same customer, these competitive cultures will become remarkable in their similarities rather than in their differences as each borrows ideas from the other.

Globalization forces a redefinition of markets, customers, and suppliers. It also forces a redefinition of the enterprise—what it does, how and where it does it, who does it—to compete in the new environment. The enterprise must validate current assumptions, discover and develop new best practices, and search for new success paradigms. Today's competitive enterprise transforms itself by redefining its paradigms for continuous creation of business value through some combination of mass customization, value and service, standards and quality, business process redesign, organizational learning and information empowerment, and organizational restructuring. However, recognizing and redefining the new success paradigms are just the first steps of the transformation strategy. Planning for and actually implementing the necessary changes require the adoption of new planning philosophies, recognition and acceptance of new value and risk criteria, and development of new justification and measurement criteria. In this new environment, it is no longer sufficient for the information technology (I/T) organization, together with its technologies, to align itself to the business strategy. It must become an integral part of the business strategy.

Information technologies, in combination with the organization that supports it, play a vital role in enabling the enterprise to transform itself into a new, more competitive form, and in positioning the enterprise to sustain its transformational activities. However, I/T must transform and reposition itself before it can become a full business partner—sharing both the rewards and the risks in the new competitive environment.

Strategic Transformation and Information Technology: Performing While Transforming has, as its objective, to influence both business and technology professionals in their thinking about the future. Designed for both audiences, it has the following goals:

- To provide the information technology (I/T) component of the business enterprise with a new perspective and appreciation of the massive changes and new paradigms that are just beginning to impact the enterprise, the I/T profession, and the individual in society.
- To develop a new mind-set for the I/T professional that involves a shift from technology-driven rationale to business-driven rationale and an accompanying contextual shift in role definition and participation from technology support to business partner.
- To provide the I/T professionals in a business enterprise with guidelines and methodologies to support, enable, and position the enterprise as it undergoes its business transformation.
- To provide the I/T professional with new expectations and guidelines for transforming themselves into full business partners.
- To provide business and I/T professionals with new perspectives on their roles and responsibilities in jointly transforming the enterprise by information empowerment, by adopting mass customization concepts, and by creating and supporting a learning organization.
- To encourage the business executive to have higher expectations regarding the role of I/T, a greater appreciation of the areas of possible participation and potential value of I/T, and how I/T should contribute to enterprise transformation.

Part I (Assessing New Marketplace Dynamics) identifies major uncertainties (market dynamics) that the enterprise must face and the resulting new business paradigms required that imply new directions, responsibilities, and environments for I/T, and thus successful business transformation. Part II (Enabling Enterprise Transformation with I/T) and Part III (Emerging Venues for I/T Leadership) discuss the impact of new business paradigms and initiatives surrounding enterprise transformation and the consequences for I/T applications and activities. The focus of Part IV (Transforming I/T) is the identification of new responsibilities and roles for I/T and its accompanying change of charter and organizational infrastructure. Key to transforming I/T is the necessary delivery and subsequent measurement of information technology's contribution to business value.

Part V (Planning I/T and Enterprise Transformation) has a planning focus and introduces a three-phase strategic transformation methodology. Phase 1 of the methodology focuses on establishing the correct context in which planning should take place, driven by scenario planning. A Seven Questions Planning Methodology (Phase 2) supports planning for I/T transformation integral to business transformation. The methodology includes adaptations of scenario planning and options pricing, necessary elements to achieve strategic transformation in the enterprise. A discussion of forecasting (e.g., estimating) future business value links with a discussion of a financial justification methodology in Information Economics (Phase 3). Because forecasting is likely to be suspect if no subsequent measurement action occurs, we introduce a measurement approach, compatible with the Information Economics methodology for use in measuring achieved business value. This approach involves developing a management dashboard and using the Balanced Scorecard.

The concluding section (Part VI) is Performing While Transforming. Strategic transformation requires of I/T continuing transformation (change) and contribution to the creation of business value while maintaining a dynamic stability (equilibrium) of the enterprise through well-managed and supported technology deployment. We identify and discuss new business paradigms and the resulting change of I/T paradigms and the interlocking action plans and critical skills necessary for the new business environment. The operative word for this section is *action*!

This is not a theoretical book. Many examples show how companies all over the world adapted these new ideas and give any reader a greater appreciation of the talent and effort involved. Along with the examples in the text, we include one featured Commentary Article in Appendix I for each of the sections. These commentaries offer the reader unique insights into the topics discussed and are based upon the personal experiences of leading business and I/T professionals worldwide. Additional background material and case studies also appear in the same Appendix.

Strategic Transformation and Information Technology highlights the significant changes in the competitive environment and within the enterprise. It illustrates how each directly impacts I/T and how I/T can impact the enterprise change mechanisms. It is not a debate of the ethical issues surrounding full employment, universal health care, or sourcing work to Third World countries. Although these are certainly valid discussion points, they are left to others to debate. Instead, the focus is on the realities of global competition and the impact on businesses and information technology and its organizations.

Acknowledgments

Dr. Robert J. Benson	Washington University
Dr. Barbara Blumenthal	Temple University
Mr. Kevin Brown, I.S.P.	Edmonton Power and Canadian Information Processing Society (Canada)
Mr. Pierre deLasalle	Gemeentekrediet Van Belgic (Belgium)
Prof. Dr. Guido Dedene	Leuven Institute for Research on Information Systems (Belgium)
Mr. Pierluigi Feliziani	Banca Agricola Milanese (Italy)
Dr. Robert E. Fidoten	Slippery Rock University
Mr. Mark N. Frolick	University of Memphis
Dr. Phillipe Haspeslagh	INSEAD (France)
Mr. W. C. Harenburg	Triadigm International
Mr. D. John Hughes	University of Auckland (New Zealand)
Mr. McCurtis Kelly	Moda Espana
Ms. Barbara McNurlin	Consultant
Lt. Col. Robert T. Morris	United States Air Force
Mr. Michael Mushet	Southern California Edison
Dr. Shafiq Naz	Management Centre Europe (Belgium)
Dr. Richard L. Nolan	Harvard Business School
Dr. David P. Norton	Renaissance Strategy Group
Dr. Bridget O'Connor	New York University
Mr. H. Virgil Parker	Key Strategies and Solutions
Dr. Richard Pascale	Stanford University
Mr. Edward M. Peters	Integrated Learning Systems
Dr. Elod Polgar	IBM Suisse (Switzerland)
Dr. Elizabeth Regan	Massachusetts Mutual Life Insurance Co.
Dr. Pieter Ribbers	Katholieke Universiteit Brabant, Tilburgs Instituut voor Academische Studies (The Netherlands)
Ms. Dolly Samson	Weber State University
Dr. James Senn	Georgia State University
Dr. Jon Thorhallsson	The University of Iceland and SKYRR (Iceland)
Mr. Lynwood Walker	The Salvation Army (Canada)

Part I

ASSESSING NEW MARKETPLACE DYNAMICS

New economic and competitive forces create a business environment in which budget reductions accompany management demands to deliver more product, quality, and service. To remain competitive, the enterprise must undergo a transformation. This new form of enterprise is defined by:

- The interrelationship of new stresses, including market forces, changing economic bases, and demographic shift.
- The increased focus of enterprise activities to develop more appropriate organizational models, redesign business processes, and supply chain relationships.
- The growing influence of information-related technologies as an enabler of organizational transformation.

These stresses, activities, and influences coalesce to create a new enterprise and information technology transformation model, introduced in Chapter 1.

Appendix I contains contributed articles from professionals in the field for this and each of the subsequent sections of the book. The featured article for Part I is "Corporate Transformation: Amalgams and Distinctions," by Dr. Barbara Blumenthal, Temple University, and Dr. Philippe Haspeslagh, professor of business policy at INSEAD, the European Institute of Business Administration (Fontainebleau, France). Citing well-known examples, they provide the first steps in conceptualizing the transformational enterprise and its competitive strategies.

A second article, "Market Forces Shaping the Competitive Environment," provides a view of three conflicting forces (political realignments, demographic trends, and environmental awareness) and the impact of each on the competitive cultures in North America, Greater Europe, and the Pacific.

1

Global Tremors, Local Quakes

Global forces impact the way we do business by changing our relationships with suppliers, markets, and competitors. We examine the interrelationship of global forces to changing organizational designs, economic bases, social issues, and the maturation of information technologies, and their effect on today's business environment. These interrelationships shape and form the new competitive environment and cause the competitive enterprise to transform itself.

In 1989, the Berlin Wall came down. The 1990s ushered in the unification of East and West Germany, the break up of the Soviet Union and Yugoslavia, and the velvet divorce of Czechoslovakia. Simultaneously, other European countries (including the now unified Germany) worked to make the European Union (EU) and European Common Market a strong economic trading block. BMW announced that it would build the first German automobile manufacturing facility outside Germany; GM announced it would source globally for manufacturing supplies and parts; and Hewlett-Packard set up a programming center outside Bombay, signaling the possibility of India becoming the world's most proficient producer of computer software.

For much of 1993, the U.S. newspapers focused on the North American Free Trade Agreement (NAFTA), and whether Congress would ratify it. Parties favoring protectionism claimed that whole industries would move south to Mexico if approved. Meanwhile, continental trade advocates focused their campaign on the jobs created resulting from increased trade among the members, and the necessity of forming an effective economic trading bloc to pit against the EU and Japan. Within a week after the signing of NAFTA, front-page newspaper coverage in the United States shifted to highlight globalization issues and focused on negotiating a new trade agreement with

Japan and on the General Agreement on Trades and Tariffs (GATT). GATT, the precursor of the World Trade Organization (WTO), represented the result of negotiations that spanned several years, involved 125 countries, and surpassed 20,000 pages of agreements.

These aren't isolated events that we can simply ignore. They, along with more subtle events, are signals for political and business leaders, warning them that current organizations, political structures, and markets are undergoing rapid and permanent change. There are simultaneous political trends supporting ethnic unity (Germany) and diversity (the EU), yet the strategic intent of both is to improve global economic strength. Significant demographic change is also occurring in the populations of the three leading economic and industrial powers (United States, Japan, Germany). These nations are graying rapidly, while a massive global teenaged population lives in Third World countries. As consumers, this emerging population will change current market definitions and market demands. As workers, they represent a massive future labor force ready to fill positions of retiring Westerners. Here, there are two possible alternatives: either governments will change immigration policies to permit sufficient shifts of worker population, or business organizations will restructure to facilitate remote and global workplaces. No one has all the answers, but business and industry leaders can no longer assume business as usual. This more global view of business, government, environmental concerns, and culture requires new paradigms for business and political policy, for industry and enterprise strategy, and for information technology (I/T) systems, applications, and staff.

LOOKING BACK BEFORE MOVING FORWARD

Not too long ago, an enterprise could, for the most part, initiate its own agenda of change. If an enterprise decided to expand its market, it did so by making incremental, planned modifications to its organization, strategy, and technology support. When it modified organizational design, it considered and managed the impact on customers and employees in an attempt to maintain the enterprise's equilibrium. Strategies and operational planning methodologies focused on change management, based upon the assumption that the enterprise could anticipate, plan for, and methodically integrate any change into its already existing structure. When considering the development of a new product line or expanding an already existing one, go or no go decisions were based on a few relatively simple questions:

- Core competencies: Do we currently possess the necessary core competencies to produce the product; must we develop them internally; or should we buy them from someone else?
- Organizational structure: Given our current (hierarchical) organization, should the function responsible for producing this product be at headquarters (centralized) or in an appropriate line of business (decentralized)?
- Enterprise operating environment: Is this compatible with our current family of

products? Will our current cost structures allow profitability? How easily can we offer this product as compared to our competitors?

- Market environment: Who are our customers? Our competitors? Do favorable distribution channels currently exist?
- Global environment: Are there any existing regulatory agencies or tariffs and trade agreements that might inhibit our entry and competitiveness in this market?

As long as the rate of change didn't accelerate too rapidly, this approach worked for developing a product strategy (see Figure 1-1). Businesses had yearly strategic planning sessions to plan incremental changes for the next year, and every two to five years developed (or updated) a long-range plan. What impacts the effectiveness of this approach is a group of fast-converging revolutions that impose forced change, requiring transformational rather than incremental strategies and solutions for business. To enable these new business strategies and to position the enterprise to exploit future opportunities demands a similar transformation of the I/T function.

Revolution, according to Webster, is a sudden, momentous change that causes a forcible substitution or basic reorientation, and transformation is the resulting new nature, form, appearance, and function. Today, businesses—and their supporting I/T functions—are simultaneously facing six converging revolutions that force them to reinvent and transform itself to remain competitive. They are the following:

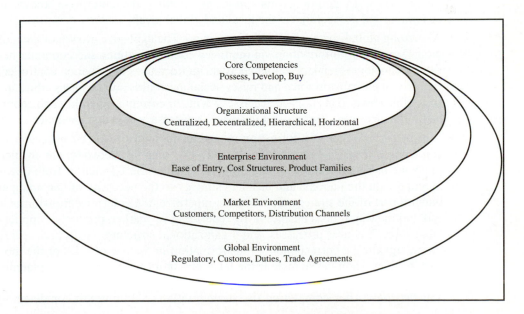

Figure 1-1 Enterprise Planners' View.

- A redefinition of markets: Moving from regional and national markets to continental and global markets, as a result of interlocking trade agreements, simultaneously expands the potential market and increases competitive action. This lays waste any previous assessments of current global and market environments, and introduces a new set of planning dynamics.

- A redesign of organizational structures using new models: As enterprises move from hierarchical organizations (with a focus on management control) to horizontal organizations (built around teamwork and empowerment), it changes how and where work is done, and who does it. The move towards strategic alliances and virtual enterprises increases the importance of strengthening organizational core competencies, innovation, flexibility, and agility. This compromises any previous assessment that assumed a hierarchical model or didn't consider temporary alliances.

- A restructuring of national and global economic bases: Moving from an industrial to an information-based national economy changes the nature of jobs, products, services, and organizational form. This determines if an enterprise is in a sustainable business with favorable and long-term global opportunities.

- A shift to customer-driven planning: Moving from a producer focus to a consumer focus shifts the intent of service and quality programs, changes the direction of research and development, and creates the potential for distribution channel restructuring and market redefinition. This shift compromises much previous planning by questioning whether an enterprise has the core competencies to develop, or the organizational structure to deliver, a product that the customer wants. In addition, this questions whether the enterprise knows its customers and competitors at the local and global levels.

- A growing global society and social awareness: The explosive growth of the individual's access to information via improved communications and computer network technologies renders national borders ineffectual as information controllers. It creates a global workforce and raises social awareness and business ethics to a new, global level. This impacts the assessments of current availability and continued future access to workers that possess the necessary core competencies.

- A growing influence of information-related technologies in the business and social environment: The recognition that I/T and computer networks are enablers of social and organizational transformation changes the I/T charter from one of aligning with the national and business strategy to the necessity of becoming an integral part of the strategy. To remain competitive, the enterprise transforms itself and the way it does business—by redefining its market, products, suppliers, labor force, business processes, and organizational structure—with each redefinition signaling a corresponding transformation in the use of I/T. For the most part, business didn't even include the I/T group in its previous strategic planning sessions. Instead, it often advised the I/T organization on a need to know basis and that only after completing the strategic plan. A litmus test for detecting whether an enterprise is transforming—as compared to making incremental improvements—is if I/T is a true business partner.

Every enterprise is struggling with questions about how it should transform itself to compete in this new environment, and the answers aren't obvious. Each of the six revolutionary forces has its unique timeline and growth curve as each enterprise is unique in how it defines its market, products, and customers and what assets it deploys. While the realignment of trade agreements may seem to occur overnight, marshaling the enterprise to exploit newly opened markets takes longer. Changing in-place I/T systems and effectively redeploying the efforts of individuals, or planning and implementing national access to an information superhighway, is a long-term effort. Significant culture shifts are necessary for all enterprise stakeholders when an organization empowers its workers, adopts new customer-service attitudes, or attempts to keep abreast of technological advances.

Moreover, each of these revolutionary forces has some relationship to and interacts with each of the others, creating an environmental web that entangles and stresses the enterprise, and complicates any efforts to transform and reinvent itself (see Figure 1-2). Because every force is either accelerating, reinforcing, exacerbating, or delaying the impact of the others on existing business and related I/T strategies, the enterprise is subject to constantly differing combinations of discontinuous change. Responding to this discontinuous change by formulating business strategies around incremental improvement is a futile exercise.[1] Not only does planning for the future become more uncertain, but management becomes more difficult, and any success more elusive.

GLOBAL MARKETS

If present trends continue, the world economy will grow 50 percent or more over the next two decades, with international trade a key segment. The dynamic Asian economies are likely to continue expanding, with China emerging as the world's largest economy. (According to some estimates, if the current growth differential between China and the United States continues, Chinese total output will exceed that of the Americas in 2005.[2]) New markets may open up in the countries of Central and Eastern Europe, where the first stages of economic reform are already underway. Poland and Hungary are continuing to make great strides into the world of free markets with their economic and democratic reforms and vast privatization initiatives; and after dismantling the old economic structure, Russia is trying to transform a centrally planned economy to a capitalistic one.

In Europe, continuous development of the EU heads the business agenda. Completion of a single market, progress toward economic and monetary union, and institution of a single currency are just a few of the milestones that will transform European business in the years ahead. Similarly, Latin America shows visible signs of economic growth and stability with increasing levels of capital inflows and investment. The

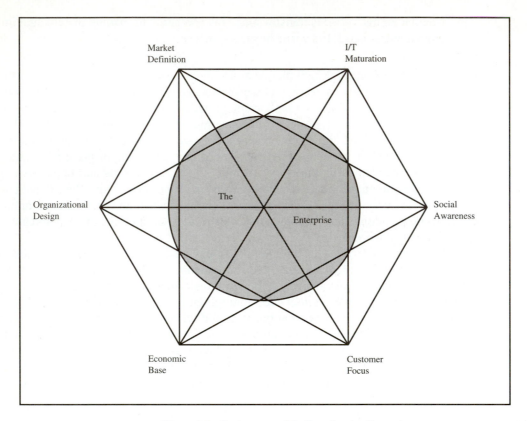

Figure 1-2   Environment of the Transforming Enterprise.

gradual expansion of NAFTA to Central and South America is a milestone for the United States as is the increasing participation in GATT's successor, the WTO.

New economic systems and economic policies of governments are evolving apace, presenting new challenges and opportunities for businesses. Combined with the rapid breakthroughs in a variety of technologies, these evolving economic systems and policies further the present trend towards globalization of businesses, requiring today's business leaders to have an informed awareness of the changes that are likely to effect their companies and prepare to act on them. Developing and continuously updating business strategies against the background of a rapidly changing economic environment is one of the new rules for survival.

Redefining Globalization

With the shift of many national policies from protectionism to continentalization and globalization, the traditional views of defining and measuring markets and market penetration have moved from domestic to broader scopes. The removal of trade barriers through agreements such as NAFTA and the EU provide a two-edged sword—new markets open for our own goods and services, yet we expose ourselves to increased competition in previously protected jobs, services, and markets. Only a few years ago, globalization meant making forays abroad from a strongly defended home market. Now, as the boundaries to commerce and international communication disappear, foreign rivals attack home markets as aggressively as we attack theirs. A strategy of staying domestic has no value when a foreign competitor enters the market with a better product at a better price, therefore products need to be measured against a yardstick of global excellence to maintain domestic market share. Today, the revised strategy of a Miami-based business to serve a Ft. Lauderdale-based customer may be a response to a competitive strategy shaped in Mexico City or Munich.

U.S. businesses, just moving into the NAFTA environment, can benefit from the experience of its European counterparts with the EU. There, a continental transformation is underway. European businesses are creating a new business architecture based upon global competition, with the capacity to cope with cross-cultural issues, to generate global synergistic results, and to be local in every market. Because the world's larger firms do the most international business—due in part to the ability to create and sustain the necessary critical mass—the industries within the EU are looking at mergers, acquisitions, and alliances to leverage combined competitiveness, both for the unified market and the world beyond Europe. In marked contrast to the hostile takeovers in the United States during the 1980s, these European mergers reflect agreement and alliance between partners.

Europeans are also expanding their businesses into the United States. To many of them, the United States is a collection of fifty states, each with different laws and regulations, but with a single language. They are sometimes unprepared for the market, culture, and language differences, for example, between Miami and Jacksonville, or Northern versus Southern California, or of the differing environmental codes between counties within the same state. Conversely, while the assumed homogeneity is misleading to the European attempting to do business in the United States, the assumed heterogeneity is misleading to the U.S. enterprises attempting to do business in Europe. The most significant impact on international trade may prove to be the EU common body of standards. This common set of standards increases trade among its own members, and it forces conformance for those in other trading blocs who wish to penetrate the EU market. If ignored, this could eventually make EU standards *de facto* world standards, to the potential detriment of all other trading blocs.

Decision-Making in a Global Market

The charter of a global manager is to enhance worldwide corporate performance, which requires a conceptual shift for the manager from a mind set of domestic competition and feelings of nationalism to one of global competition and contributing to the global good. Both global and local managers seek higher profits, enhanced market leadership, and improved stock price—all of which have been tenets of the U.S. brand of capitalism. While a local (or national) manager may be loath to close down a plant because of the consequences to the community and may explore other possible alternatives, the global manager will have little allegiance to a small town facility that has outdated equipment, stringent environmental quality regulations, or a highly paid workforce. Paradoxically, while the global manager commits to enhanced worldwide corporate performance, he must also concern himself with the preservation of economic competitiveness of any country or region that provides a major source of revenue. Thus decision-making at any level becomes neither obvious nor intuitive, but will be determined by the unique enterprise-defined economic playing field and its set of stakeholders and values.

Enhancing worldwide corporate performance isn't an easy balancing act. Global competitors in the EU, United States, and Japan are facing some formidable problems at the domestic level. There is evidence of high economic stress resulting from heavy debt loads, increased global competition, vulnerable central banking systems, deferred costs of a decaying infrastructure, and environmental cleanup.[3] The restructuring now going on in most national economies reflects a combination of the necessity to accommodate intense international competition and the transition from military to economic dominance of global affairs. The California economy, for example, is a microcosm of many national economies. For decades, it led the nation in economic growth, but it suffered a disastrous few years in the early 1990s from the simultaneous combination of unemployment caused by cutbacks in defense weaponry spending and the closing of three large military bases, by the flow of low-tech manufacturing employment to Mexico, by an increased social cost due to illegal immigration, and by the loss of business associated with stricter environmental regulations. Reductions in manpower committed to the defense industry and military will require time to redirect and absorb productively into regional or national economies as will the gradual migration of industries searching for new competitive advantages, from one country to another.

EMERGING GLOBAL ORGANIZATIONAL MODELS

The shape and form of the competitive enterprise are changing. Replacing the hierarchical organization built around the principles of mass production is a flatter, horizontal organization built around the concept of a high involvement workplace with self-managing teams and employee empowerment. This new organizational form focuses on managing business processes and accomplishing a strategy (a horizontal flow of work), rather than on functional departments focusing on control (a hierarchical control of work).[4] For some enterprises, the phenomenon of the flatter organization is the accidental result of cost-cutting measures and downsizing, where fewer people with better communications (primarily the use of e-mail) discover they can get their work done with less confusion by personal networking. For the more forward-looking enterprises, this new organizational form is something that they have planned and have been achieving in bits and pieces over the last decade. They have been gradually optimizing and focusing information systems investments that effectively aggregate and distribute operational information.

Unlike the more rigid hierarchical model based on the principles of mass production (whose products require a sustainable, homogenous, well-defined customer set), this new organizational focus supports the flexibility and agility necessary to respond to changing requirements. (These changes come as a result of new customer requirements, whether domestic or foreign, changes in social or political policies, availability of labor, etc.) It creates the organizational environment in which the business can better serve its customers through more customized products and services, and eases the introduction of innovation and change. In it, employees group to accomplish a complete piece of work and have information available when needed, unfettered by a hierarchy and free of unnecessary filters imposed by management. The fundamental role that management plays shifts from controlling the hierarchy to nurturing and enabling learning and change to continually improve the business. Performance measures—the measures of success—also change. The new measures focus on continuous improvement of the business strategies and processes designed with the customer in mind. These newer, more flexible organizational forms have (and require) the support of I/T systems that distribute the needed knowledge to achieve accountability and results anywhere and anytime.

Globalization, by its very nature suggests work—and customers—spread across multiple time zones and countries involving different languages and cultures. The explosive growth of portable personal computing and communications devices and networks allows individuals to travel all over the world, continuing to transact business. It allows business professionals—both providers and consumers of the product or service—to be in their virtual office anywhere, anytime. An information-based product or service like a hotel reservation system with a toll free number has electronic bunkers linked to the reservation database with staff around the clock, located anywhere. Catalog sales organizations, reached through toll free numbers, provide overnight delivery via United Parcel Service or Federal Express. Located in remote areas with a favorable cost and tax base and a pool of workers, they do millions of dollars of business each year. These technology-intensive enterprises begin to suggest new organizational prototypes and models for the global business.

Globalization also introduces a new diversity of workers, management, ethics, and cultures into the domestic arena. In 1988, 3.7 million Americans worked for foreign subsidiaries in the United States. By 1991, that number grew to 4.6 million, and it continues to grow. Although the Japanese get more publicity in the United States, companies from Britain employ twice the number of workers, and Canada and Germany also rank ahead of Japan.[5] The Great Atlantic & Pacific Tea Company (German), Nestle Enterprises and Carnation (Swiss), and Shell Oil (Netherlands) have been part of the U.S. economic landscape for so long, they rarely provoke even an occasional "Buy American" campaign, as do the Japanese Bridgestone/Firestone, Sony, Toyota, or Komatsu. This serves to point out a relatively new kind of problem confronting American employees in the global economy—how to live with management and work ethics alien to them. When Americans join Japanese companies, they find management philosophies and methods that are alien. The Japanese tradition emphasizes collective values over individualism, worker participation (empowerment), and investing for the long-term—whereas the Europeans generally share cultural and political traditions closer to those of the United States that stress shorter-term results and hierarchical management control philosophies.

SHIFTING ECONOMIC BASES

Consider the following scenario. Restless Eastern Europeans, working for the West, worry about the wide wage gaps between VW plants separated by a drive of two hours. In Mlada Boleslav (Czech Republic), workers in the former Skoda Automobile Company's plant, although getting three wage increases from VW in less than two years, can't keep abreast of the price increases that have come with Czech economic liberalization. Even worse, West German counterparts make wages ten to fifteen times higher.[6] As a result, many Czech workers feel they have gone from scrimping inside the Communist zone to scrimping inside the low-cost zone of a capitalistic empire.

We could just have easily substituted Eastern and Western Europe with Mexico and the United States, or paired China and Japan. Economists would argue that the problem isn't that the pay is so low in Eastern Europe (or Mexico or China), but that the pay is high in Western Europe (or the United States or Japan). This wage differential threatens the international competitiveness of labor-intensive industries in the West—particularly those industries requiring few skills and little education. In 1992, DRI McGraw-Hill estimated that wages and benefits add up to $21.30 an hour for the average German worker, compared with $12.84 for a Japanese worker, and $14.83 for a U.S. worker. (In this same period, other sources cite 70 cents an hour for Mexican workers and 8 cents for Chinese workers.) Two years later, Morgan Stanley estimated that German workers cost $25.50 an hour, Japanese cost $19.30, and U.S. $16.70. Although everyone expects Eastern European, Mexican, and Chinese wages to rise, the gains will come gradually and won't match the highest European wages and benefits. To keep up with its global competitors, VW and other European industrial companies must look for sites with low-wage bases for its industrial growth—one of the reasons why BMW built a manufacturing facility in South Carolina and Mercedes-Benz is in Alabama. This is also the reason why the increasing economic competition from the rest of Asia is forcing such wrenching change within the Japanese manufacturing giants.

Now, consider the following flow of jobs, from a U.S. worker's perspective. Some analysts say that while the United States may lose 190,000 jobs to Mexico as a result of NAFTA and the WTO—low-technology, low-skill jobs primarily from the Southeast-based textiles—the economic drain to protect these jobs is too high to sustain. The tariffs and additional cost to the domestic economy to protect each of these 190,000 jobs runs $170,000 a year—a $32.2 billion annual cost.[7] Yet while the Southeast suffers the loss of textile mills to Mexico, involving low-technology, low-skill manufacturing, it benefits from the inflow of work involving higher-technology manufacturing from the German auto industry. The United States has a skilled workforce both *available* and at a *cost significantly less* than Germany. By employing the U.S. workforce, BMW and Mercedes become more cost-competitive in the global market. This suggests that perhaps a better investment of the $32.2 billion is to attract new industry to the United States by improving specific skill levels of displaced workers.

Finally, consider the following statistics. In 1993, the U.S. economy increased its employment base by about 2 million, 60 percent of which were so-called white collar jobs, requiring education and professional skills. In January 1994, the unemployment rate in the inner cities among minorities—the population possessing the poorest education and skill levels—was 11.5 percent, as compared to the overall national unemployment rate of 6.4 percent. Even with some loss of manufacturing jobs to countries with qualified workers at lower pay scales, the number of people employed grew, but growth was disproportional, favoring those with greater skills and education, emphasizing the importance of having a well-educated, emerging workforce.

The annual 1994 U.S. Consumer Electronics Show provides a final example of this new job flow. There it was evident that the domestic information and electronic technology-based industries are poised to exploit the new information superhighway. (The information superhighway—the convergence of computer, cable, programming, and telephone technologies delivered to every household—is the electronic equivalent of the U.S. transportation system of interlinking superhighways.) The United States has the potential of becoming the world leader of information superhighway development because it can immediately apply the necessary highly skilled labor force. This being the result of the information and other high-technology professionals mentioned earlier whose positions (largely in California) disappeared due to reductions in national defense spending. Recognizing that it will trail behind in advanced information and communications services unless it promotes infrastructure improvements and relaxes the regulatory environment, Japan began nurturing the multimedia market as a key sector for the future Japanese economy, a sector that could create 2.4 million domestic jobs for it by 2010.[8]

What is the impact of this gradual shifting of industry siting to improve global competitive position, and what does it foretell political and business leaders?

- Over time, the dominance of postindustrial economies will shift from its predominately manufacturing industries to industries focusing and depending on information, knowledge, education, and services.
- Businesses, organizations, and individuals must be readily adaptable to exploit the shift.
- Time—the window of opportunity—is a critical factor.

Peter Drucker observes that organizations—society, government, community, and family—all function as conserving institutions, trying to maintain stability by managing, slowing, or preventing change.[9] This is not to say that conserving law and order or promoting ethical behavior, for example, is bad—it's just that the legal and ethical codes are reflections of yesterday's society. Consequently, the natural inclination of these institutions is to exacerbate the problem, since the fundamental nature of today's knowledge embodies rapid change. For example, yesterday's military strategy focused on the use of massive force against a known enemy, while today's strategy focuses on rapid deployment of small, highly mobile multinational groups armed with specialized weaponry. Although the titles of rank remain the same, the organizational structures, command structures, and inter- and intraservice relationships and responsibilities are quite different. If the military, with all of its tradition, recognizes and acts on the need to transform itself, so must enterprise.

An inherent danger of transformation for the enterprise and its I/T professionals is that yesterday's perfectly executed information systems become roadblocks to today's rapid organizational redirection. Drucker suggests three factors necessary to insure institutional survival:

- Build around the concept of continuous improvement.
- Exploit knowledge and expertise successfully.
- Possess the capacity to innovate and be able to build the ability to innovate into the processes so that transformation is sustainable (give attention to continuing education, reinventing the business organizational model, and reengineering business processes).

While these qualities improve the ability to be rapidly adaptable, they also tend to destablize everything and everyone around them, which is exactly what makes transformation and its associated changes so uncomfortable. This is as true for government and its institutions and policies as it is for enterprises with their business processes, organizations, and strategies, and for the individual attempting to intelligently manage his or her career.

The ability to sustain global leadership, then, stems ultimately from the ability to selectively abandon conserving institutions (e.g., trade embargo's, restrictive tariffs, labor laws, corporate cultures, organizations, technology, and software) to establish a truly stretching strategic intent and to transform and mobilize the entire organization in achieving it—whether it is a trading bloc, nation, enterprise, or individual. The organization achieves maximum competitive advantage from its resource base by exploiting the most fundamental resource—its portfolio of core competencies. The successful nation, enterprise, or individual is a bundle of resources and capabilities, some unique and some not. If its resources and capabilities are scarce, durable, defensible, or hard to imitate and can be mobilized to align with the future key success factors of the world economy, they can form the basis for sustainable world-class competitive advantage and economic strength.

Resources and capabilities, however unique, are to no advantage if unaligned. This is just as true for I/T and the business it supports as it is at a national or global level. For example, China may not be able to utilize its natural resource of coal due to increasing global environmental hazards, and the cultures of both Germany and Japan may inhibit its ability to influence any shift in its economic base. Germany's factories employ nearly three times as many workers proportionally as in the United States, however, high severance expenses keep companies there from changing as dramatically through downsizing manufacturing activities or growing its service economy.[10] Japan, with its tradition of lifetime employment and massive post-World War II investments in building factories, faces a similar problem. As a result, currently industrialized economies (and its domestic enterprises) may have greater difficulty establishing leadership in technological change resulting from future breakthroughs that could be expected in information sciences, space technology, automation, and instrumentation because of past investments in infrastructure.

CUSTOMERS DEFINE MARKETS

The customer of today expects diversity of choice. A few years ago, a friend was visiting Southern California. A trip to the local grocery store provoked the amazed comment "It's just like walking through a huge duty-free shop!" With the diversity of cultures in Southern California, the supermarkets carry a vast variety of ethnic foods to attract and keep their customers. Exotic fruits and vegetables with unpronounceable names are in the produce section, along with potatoes and carrots. Imported spices and specialty canned goods are, more often than not, integrated with the more traditional offerings. Pet (United States) and Carnation (Swiss) condensed milk appears side by side with coconut milk (Thai) and goats' milk (United States). This is not just the result of recent immigration and the associated introduction of new cultures—it's that through television and travel, and through political debates about NAFTA and GATT, the population is growing more globally aware. The customer wants to express their personal freedom of choice by purchasing a Japanese pear rather than one from Oregon. It is this global customer that demands the right to buy exactly what he wants, no more and no less.

In a *Harvard Business Review* editorial, Rosabeth Moss Kantor observed that global business involves thinking like a customer, and not like a producer—a thought surprisingly alien to many hierarchical organizations.[11] Moving from a producer focus to a consumer focus causes a shift in the intent of service and quality programs, the impetus for product development, and the structure of the organization itself. Initially, success in a global market comes to those who make their product *local,* that is, to tailor products and services to local customs, language, and culture. This is a difficult task for traditional organizations that are built around mass production techniques and management principles designed to support domestically based business strategies. Organizations built around the newer forms of mass customization—putting custom back into thoughts about the customer—provide avenues for rethinking and reforming business processes, markets, and customer relationships.

Kantor posits that producers worry too much about visible mistakes, while losing customers because of the invisible ones—the difference between counting what you have versus not knowing what you don't know. Early quality programs were often narrowly producer-oriented, focusing on reducing the costs of visible mistakes. This was only natural, because the first quality initiatives were in support of improving a mass-production, manufacturing-based environment. However, *failing to take risk, failing to innovate* to create new value for customers, and *misunderstanding the real requirements* of the customer are the invisible mistakes that don't show up in organizationally inward-focused quality measurements that evaluate improvements of internal efficiency. Perhaps they shouldn't (from the perspective of the producer), but customers will determine what additional values they receive by choosing one supplier over another.

In the past, producers created products driven by their own technologies (e.g., the number of VCRs in homes still flashing 12:00, 12:00, 12:00). The reality should be that customer needs and desires should set the priorities, rather than the customer being asked after the fact or demonstrating an unwillingness to use the product or product features once on the market. The problem with producing anything is that its production is a result of a perceived market at a single moment—and that moment is past by the time the producer delivers the product to the customer. Consequently, everything we deliver is in some degree less than satisfactory to the marketplace—even if we asked the customer beforehand. This wasn't too bad in the days when there were only 300-plus products to choose from in a country store and the pace of change was slow, but today's supermarkets—like the one in California—must be quick to recognize new food trends or risk losing impulse sales. A state-of-the-art, just-in-time delivery and restocking system is of little value if the item the customer wanted to buy wasn't on the shelf initially. Today, the pace continues to accelerate and without a quick response to the marketplace—whether in foodstuff, hardgood, or information product—a generation of customers becomes lost to the enterprise.

Ultimately, "what makes a company manageable [what the producer wants] may detract from serving the customer"—for example, having the best service manager working Monday through Friday, when most of the difficult problems occur for the customer on weekends. The advent of suppliers being furnished facilities by its customers for better quality control (automobile paint manufacturers working on-site with automobile assembly, or a pharmaceutical supplier locating and managing inventory in hospital clinics) and of manufacturers working with its customers and its customer's customers to design products (airline personnel and frequent fliers participating in determining design requirements for the next generation airplane), forces new thinking. It forces a simultaneous reevaluation of the traditional supplier-customer relationship, organizational form and location, market and service requirements, definition of markets and economic base, and structure of distribution channels—exploiting I/T capabilities as the vehicle for converting many of the new ideas into action.

INDIVIDUALS IN A KNOWLEDGE SOCIETY

Burt Nanus, in his book *Visionary Leadership,* suggests a number of forces shaping the twenty-first-century organizations (business, political, social) and its capabilities to sustain viability.[3] He foresees the erosion of confidence in all institutions, including governments, families, and religion—perhaps due to Drucker's observation on institutions getting in the way of rapid change—resulting in a search by the individual for self-sufficiency and meaning in work. Nanus anticipates demographic and sociocultural shifts toward more diversity, creating a fragmentation of values, life-styles, and tastes. Finally, he predicts that the individual will experience a relative affluence in material goods coupled with new scarcities (e.g., job security and parental time for children), and increased personal risks from crime and environmental pollution.

What is the role of the individual in the midst of this political, business, and social change? Is Nanus correct? Certainly, the bonds between individual, company, and country appear weakened. Today, individuals seek out mutual funds based upon global diversity to better balance personal investment portfolios; company's seek out cross-border alliances (and ownership) to better represent its products in new and expanding markets; and nations seek better ways to understand, evaluate, and exploit its own economic and intellectual wealth. With the wave of corporate downsizing and outsourcing activities in the late eighties and early nineties, corporations under the stress of increased competition abandoned long-held paternalistic policies regarding employees. As a consequence, employees became largely responsible for their own career management, social well-being, and retirement planning. Thus all of those institutional and individual traditional borders—intellectual, physical, geographical, and emotional—become blurred and less defensible.

Temporary (just-in-time) employment, variable work schedules and workplaces, and the loss of separation of work and home now define the new professional workplace. Taking the responsibility for securing one's own continuing income, education, career, and comfortable retirement is hard work. It takes time away from family and from social activities; it requires time to manage the fluctuations of income and benefits effectively; and it requires time to constantly question one's own values and change them to adapt to the environment—time that we partially try to recapture through the improved use of technology.

No longer are we sanguine about leaving technology in the workplace and leading the simple life. TV commercials integrate now common icons and computer screen formats into its messages, cellular phones save an extra trip to the store for a forgotten item, home computers send and receive faxes and answer the telephone when we're not there, and computer games occupy our children while we're working in our office at home. If we consider the number of mips (millions of instructions per second executed by a computer) installed as a measure of success, the popularity of Nintendo games among the teenagers makes it one of the world's leading computer companies. We may not consider this goodness, but it is reality!

Individuals have, for the first time in history, the opportunity to truly develop close relationships with others beyond their personal surroundings by using the telephone, the fax, and the myriad subscription communications networks where information flows from individual to individual, without an intermediate stop to clear international customs. Information, whether via television, fax, or telephone, suddenly exposes everyone, everywhere, to people and ideas they didn't have access to before, and threatens to destroy the last vestiges of cultural and national isolationism.

The explosive growth of the individual's access to information via improved communications and computer network technologies not only renders national borders ineffectual as information controllers—it also creates a global work force and raises social awareness to a global level. Examples of the phenomena are obvious—the information superhighway, which requires development and availability of both a physical network and software support; the rapid growth in popularity of personal portable communications devices, enabling the anywhere, anytime office; reliable global information networks (like Internet), satellite communications and transportation systems, allowing work to be done by (and for) an enterprise in Bombay, Singapore, or San Juan. These technology-related developments make work easier to move than the worker.

As industries gradually move from country to country searching for labor and investment economies, enterprise policies become less paternalistic. Workers learn to become more self-sufficient and take responsibility for strengthening their own skill base to improve their competitive positions in the job market. Enterprises can no longer count on any long-term employee loyalty; they can, however, count on greater personal initiative and independence and try to find ways of using these traits to improve corporate competitiveness. These are assets in the high-involvement workplace but were liabilities in the traditional hierarchical organization, unless tucked away in a research and development function.

How these forces play themselves out in the leading industrial economies largely depends upon the stakeholder values of the national culture as well as the unique stakeholder values within each enterprise doing business there. Germany, with its strong labor unions, and Japan, with its tradition of lifetime employment only beginning to weaken, will undergo the same kinds of stress on the individual as is the United States but it will be more gradual. In the long run, this might be easier on its workers, but poses more difficulties in keeping the domestic economies globally competitive.

INFORMATION TECHNOLOGY COMES OF AGE

In the 1990s, the business executive has an agenda full of things to worry about. We all recognize the increasingly global business environment and the increased emphasis on shortening business cycles and improving customer service. From this perspective, it seems that the relatively simple role that I/T played in the past (e.g., altering strategic plans or aligning itself to support the business organization) becomes significantly more complex with the demands forecast for the future global business. Furthermore, because of I/T's enabling power for new ways to do business, it becomes possible to imagine new tenets that, in this decade, will fundamentally change the way businesses operate. In short, I/T, linked with vastly dynamic business requirements, will result in enterprises that look quite different from today's business organizations.

Consider the previous discussions:

- Market definition: When any enterprise decides to exploit a global market, *a worldwide communications network becomes essential.* This is the best way the local nationals can stay current on the latest products and technologies—and the off-site personnel apprised of product or marketing related problems. This is an essential part of employee empowerment.
- Organizational design: Whether the organization planned for it or not—I/T, through the proliferation of e-mail and the ability to increase the availability of operational information—was the enabler of the more horizontal organization

and the changes it caused. Conversely, the traditional I/T systems that already exist may impede necessary new organizational forms and change.

- Economic base: Development and exploitation of technology of all types become vital to the shift of the economic base of any industrialized economy. The German, Japanese, and U.S. labor force has become too expensive on a global level to compete with similarly trained workers available in Mexico, India, or China. For current industrial nations to maintain economic leadership in the world economy requires them to shift from industrial leadership to technology and services leadership, similar to the shift from the agrarian to the industrial society that took place a century ago. Exploiting the current leadership in information and communications technology is key to future successes.

- Customer focus: Redefinition of the supplier-customer relationship, particularly at a global level, and conversion of new ideas into action often depends on exploiting current I/T capabilities. A key precept of global customers is that customer service is equally important around the world. It doesn't matter about the location of corporate headquarters—it's where the customer is that counts.[8] While customers need equivalent access to local telephone numbers and service personnel that speak their language, no matter where they are, local employees (nationals) must maintain access to the latest information, thus requiring global communication networks. To get the best from local organizations requires a constant flow of information so that they know they are part of a larger organization with greater responsibilities. This encourages and facilitates regional and global thinking (translating customer requirements into product improvements on a broader scope) and enhances global performance.

- Social awareness: Information-related technologies have spread from the workplace to the home, with teenagers often more comfortable in integrating it into daily life than parents. Public and private schools have computer labs, and computer technology and proficiency have become a requisite for further education. A decade ago executives *didn't type*. Today those same executives are busy using portable personal computers in airports, in hotel rooms, and at home. As the structure of competition and enterprises change, individuals are expected to become more self-sufficient. Some workers will be equipped to do so and others will not. Poor schools have less access to new technology than do their better-funded counterparts; current *information haves* are those family units with medium to high skill sets who are affluent enough to access the information superhighway. Conversely, to grow and improve their job skills, *information have not's* will be dependent upon a social net that still lacks definition and funding.

Businesses are finding ways of substituting investments in I/T networks—intellectual assets—for investments in physical assets like warehouses and inventories. And as the current economic industrial powerhouses discover the less costly well-trained work force in other countries, they begin to build foreign manufacturing facilities, gradually moving toward an information-based home economy. Global communications and information networks are key enablers for supporting global competition and improving competitiveness through its support of the customer focus. The various Information-based technologies are both the cause and effect of new organizational designs, of an increasing global awareness by the individual, and of increased social and economic restructuring.

Future competitiveness for an enterprise becomes increasingly dependent on a strong, competent, flexible, forward-looking I/T organization as a business partner. To adequately service customers over larger and larger geographical areas requires up-to-date information technology and computer systems, along with empowered workers that can make decisions and execute them on the spot. It takes the networks to distribute the information to allow continuous improvement—whether the customer product is a result of physical or intellectual manufacture. Information technology becomes an enabling force for exploiting far-flung markets; it enables the move from hierarchical organizations, focusing on management control, to smaller, horizontal organizations that enable change through empowerment; and it improves current products and services by improving information availability.

WHERE WE'RE GOING

In January 1994, Los Angeles suffered its own brand of transformation when it sustained an earthquake measuring 6.6 on the Richter scale. Water and natural gas transmission lines broke, freeway overpasses collapsed, and buildings and homes crumbled. What was remarkable about the damage was the difference between what withstood the tremor and what became rubble. Since 1971, local building codes required *passive* quake-resistant systems that include specially engineered connecting joints, reinforcing supports, and isolation mechanisms that absorb the energy of an earthquake vibration. Newer buildings and pre-1971 buildings retrofitted with these mechanisms held up well compared to those that didn't have them. However, structures need to be pliable as well as strong. When they are too stiff, they are unable to flex with the movement of the ground and collapse, as some buildings did. The new solution is the use of active technologies and smart materials that allow future structures to respond with flexibility to counter the ground forces and that have the strength to maintain structural integrity. Although more expensive than passive technologies, the active systems offer significantly better protection against earthquakes, making them the system of choice in strategic infrastructures like bridges and pipelines.

There are some valuable parallels here on the urgency of transforming enterprise infrastructures, making them more likely to survive earthquake-like jolts of rapid change in the competitive environment. Many of today's organizations followed the success of Henry Ford, copying his mass production techniques, and hierarchical organization. When the competitive arena began to change in the mid-1980s, some organizations were proactive and began to downsize and search for a better, more flexible organizational model. They focused on the enterprise equivalent of the engineers' active technologies and smart materials by introducing employee and information empowerment, by reducing management hierarchies and modifying corporate cultures to improve productivity, and by listening to customer concerns about product design, service, and quality. Others downsized without organizational change or redirection, introducing internal quality programs and measurements. Structurally, they tightened the screws and didn't reduce the already existing organizational overhead. By taking the passive approach, they became less able to respond to rapid change. Still others made only cosmetic changes, expecting to ride out the storm with its existing organization and culture. Today, we are beginning to see the fallout of these managerial decisions. Companies who made cosmetic changes fade; those slower to change, like IBM, are no longer the leaders they were a decade ago; and the active and smart like Nordstrom, Microsoft, and Motorola have become new role models. To create leadership enterprises, business and I/T professionals (like the engineers trying to minimize earthquake damage) must focus on enabling concepts for flexibility, change, and transformation when envisioning and reinventing infrastructures and organizations.

Common sense says that to win or maintain this leadership, a nation, enterprise, organization, or individual must act like a leader. However, the rules have changed—especially since domestic markets are taking on the characteristics of global ones—and following old principles, old rules, and old practices no longer works. Change is so profound on so many fronts that it defies the use of the orderly, comprehensive, and systematic approaches previously used, since they were based on managing incremental, planned change. Discontinuous and forced changes characterize current business environments in which organizations and national economies behave erratically in attempts to maintain competitive position. To compete effectively in this age of revolutions and transformations, the enterprise must adopt new strategies, organizational forms, and practices that support its transformation. To increase enterprise agility, it must initiate a new life cycle based on discontinuous business vision harmoniously coupled with evolutionary business process and technology change. The substantive questions involve how to start and how to do it, and every move becomes an organizational experiment in learning how to change faster and better.[12]

To this point we have discussed, perhaps idealistically, the potential of I/T. We now need to realize it's potential. This requires rethinking, just as business process redesign and organizational change require rethinking. It takes a redefinition of the I/T charter and a reengineering of the infrastructure from this new business perspective. It takes a rethinking of what delivering business value by I/T constitutes. It takes a new planning and implementation philosophy for I/T that enables the enterprise to better react to risks and uncertainties in the business environment. Finally, it takes a paradigm shift of I/T thinking to match the paradigm shift of business thinking to reformulate the concepts of I/T services in the context of mass customization, business process and organizational redesign, and service and quality to the customer. Rather than simply aligning its activities with an already existing business strategy, it requires that the I/T organization become a business partner.

I/T professionals must identify and understand the major uncertainties (market dynamics) the enterprise must face and the resulting new business paradigms required for successful business transformation. They must identify, understand, and prepare for the impact of enterprise transformation on I/T application areas and on the I/T organization, focusing on its delivery and subsequent measurement of business value. They must focus sufficient attention on planning to continue performing while transforming. For I/T, strategic transformation requires continuing transformation (change) and contribution to the creation of business value, concurrent with maintaining the harmony of the enterprise through well-managed and supported technology deployment. The objective of these combined activities is to position I/T to fulfill its role as a full business partner in carrying out the enterprises' jointly crafted and implemented

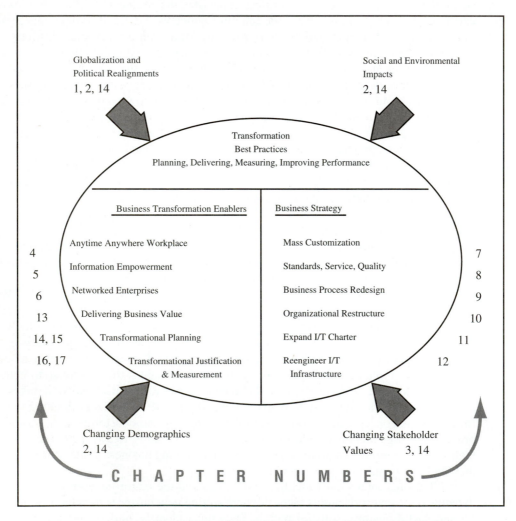

Figure 1-3   Enterprise Transformation and Information Technology Model.

business and technology strategies. These strategies, conceived and executed together, will create the new rules of global competition for transforming enterprises.

This book provides an analysis of the economic and business trends that are underway or in prospect and considers their significance for those in top management of the business and technology functions. The objective is to provide a better understanding of the implications of the climate in which businesses will be operating, thereby helping the enterprise create the best business and technology strategies. These forces, trends, and strategies fit together to form the new rules of global competition for the transforming enterprise (illustrated in Figure 1-3) and provide the basis of discussion for the remaining chapters.

Part II

ENABLING ENTERPRISE TRANSFORMATION WITH INFORMATION TECHNOLOGY

As a result of enterprises attempting to transform themselves to achieve new competitive vigor, new I/T application concepts will gain significant attention from business management. In its effort to implement and strengthen new strategies, business will expect I/T to direct its development, delivery, and support to the new organizational focus.

Four business strategies are of particular importance to I/T. They include the following:

- Anywhere, Anytime Workplaces—requiring a redefinition of the office, work, and the worker (Chapter 2).
- Information Empowerment—providing more, and higher quality information to support enterprise collegial relationships, including employee-colleagues, suppliers, and customers (Chapter 3).

- Networked Enterprises—using I/T to revolutionize not just the internal structures and control systems of the enterprise, but, through network linkages, the enabling and reshaping of external constituency relationships (Chapter 4).
- Mass Customization—applying technology to support new processes, products, and markets necessary to respond to the global marketplace (Chapter 5).

The contributed article in Appendix I to complement this section is "Coping with Business and Technological Change" by Michael L. Mushet. Mushet, as general manager, Power Systems Management Division, Southern California Edison Company (SCE), provides an insight into the evolution and future direction of the I/T function within a business dominated by a management that prizes leadership skills. Becoming an equal partner in planning the business strategy, and being given the responsibilities for the management of a new and vital business initiative, are goals already achieved by the SCE I/T function. This article provides an insight into why this I/T organization is so different from most and its vision of the future.

2

Anywhere, Anytime Workplaces

Portable personal communications devices contribute significantly to the redefinition of what kind of work is done, where it is accomplished, and who does it. New solutions to existing business problems occur through the integration of multiple information-based technologies, creating unique end-user information systems, and new, nontraditional work performed in nontraditional environments impacts both I/T and business reengineering.

Many corporations share a common dilemma: its operations, whether national or global, have grown in response to a business strategy in which information technologies played little part. The result is often a collection of incompatible computers and software, along with other office technologies that should, but don't, link together. The slow but inevitable convergence of computing and telecommunications is providing the motive force for an implosion of new information processing practices and technologies that are revolutionizing the workplace, wherever—and whenever—it is.

The anywhere, anytime workplace, facilitated by a fusion and integration of portable and fixed information technologies, erases the physical and temporal boundaries of information work. Now, traditional work can be done in a nontraditional environment: *hotdesking* reduces business overhead; *homework* replaces office work via telecommuting; and *groupware* reduces the costs of business meetings. Although these are interesting applications of technology, they tend to focus on incremental change/improvement. Nontraditional work in a nontraditional environment—creating sustainable global competitive advantage through business transformation—is also occurring. Banks and other financial institutions offer a full array of services via financial kiosks installed in airports—manned around the clock via electronic bunkers located anywhere; a railroad and a hospital use imaging to completely transform its customer interfaces; physicians do off-site diagnosis, bringing specialized health care to remote locations; and robots in operating rooms perform simple surgical procedures[1]. These innovative applications require custom blending of office, telecommunications, robotics, and multiple computing technologies to meet unique business needs and to create new competitive advantage. In this chapter we highlight some of the major people and corporate culture issues involved in rethinking, reformulating, and supporting the concepts of how and where work is accomplished. New enterprise concepts involving office, office work, office and field workers, and customer interfaces target improvements in productivity, information flow, cost, and revenue structure, to create sustainable competitive advantage through process and organizational transformation.

VIRTUAL OFFICES

There are some social consequences of portable micro-miniaturized personal entertainment, information, and communications technologies. The physical locations we traditionally associate with work, leisure, and similar pursuits rapidly become meaningless, and the time boundaries traditionally assigned to such activities disappear. As a result, several important social boundaries in our lives become very blurred.

One social change resulting from the emergence of portable communications devices is a reduction of privacy, and when people confront previously agreed upon (conventional) boundaries, old rules or paradigms get broken and new ones are made. Today, people receive telephone calls from anyone, almost anywhere. Salespeople, for example, call clients from carphones with increasing regularity, and carrying cellular telephones and personal pagers is commonplace among many working professionals. This practice is convenient for some, and annoying to others—so much so that some restaurants and private clubs now ban the use of cellular telephones.

The proliferation of information and communication technologies also tends to shatter conventional meanings and limitations of time and space of information work, again creating new paradigms. United Parcel Service (UPS) packed business documents into mule pouches to deliver them at the bottom of the Grand Canyon, and a Cincinnati advertising executive received a status report from her agency while scaling Mount Everest. At an altitude of 17,000 feet, she received the report on her laptop computer, utilizing a satellite over Australia and telecommunications equipment at a Tibetan mountain camp in the Himalayas. Although these may be considered extreme examples by some, the result of this information availability is that location and schedule of the workplace no longer frame the schedules of individual lives. This requires more self-discipline about time for work and time for a personal life, as well as a complete reformulation of the concept of work and the role of the worker.[2]

Workspace 21

The forecasts of a decade ago—that computers would increase office productivity, reduce white-collar payrolls, and help the remaining staff work better—proved much too hopeful. Why have the huge sums of money spent on office automation produced such disappointing results? One reason is that we installed technology before we reformulated the concept of the office.

Workspace 21, a two-year study sponsored by Cornell University and funded by firms in America, Japan, Britain, and Holland, predicts how the office of the future will look. Technology, better communications, rising inner-city land costs and the difficulties of commuting, will prompt more workers to split time between a central office, a computer-equipped home office, and perhaps a satellite office in a suburban business park. The central office will become mainly a place where workers from satellite and home-based offices meet to discuss ideas and to strengthen relationships with fellow employees and the company. Those few workers based at the central office will be more mobile, moving between different work stations as tasks change and taking mobile telephones with them. This cuts the amount of wasted office space, and improves communications among employees by pushing them out of the unchanging circle of people sitting nearby. Finally, managers will abandon the long-cherished notion that a productive employee is the employee he or she sees working—because being punctual and looking busy becomes irrelevant. Technology and new patterns of office use will make companies judge people by what they do, not where they spend time. Consequently, offices become places for group interaction rather than solitary concentration, more space-efficient and adaptable, and smaller and nearer home (or in it) while being a part of a global communications network.

Some enterprises are already incorporating these ideas. In California, TRW and GTE established satellite offices and expect employees to increase their efficiency as a result of working closer to home. As an added benefit, the move to satellite offices will reduce the Los Angeles traffic problem. Other examples include Digital Equipment Corporation's subsidiary in Finland. It equipped offices with reclining chairs and stuffed sofas to make the environment more comfortable and conducive to informal conversations and the swapping of ideas. Companies such as Apple and General Electric are also experimenting along similar lines.[3]

Hotdesking

The fortifications around the private workspace are collapsing as property prices and the quest for greater efficiency batter traditional ideas of office organization. Open plan offices started it, where workers owned their desks, but shared a communal working space. Now, a number of companies are beginning to implement the concept of hotdesking, where workers own neither desk nor workspace but make use of any desk that is free during visits to the office.

It is a concept suited to organizations in which staff spends appreciable amounts of time away from their desks and where office space is at a premium, and it is dependent upon technology. A hotdesk normally has a personal computer connected to a corporate network, a place to plug in a portable computer, and a telephone handset. When staff visit the building, they find an empty desk and key into the computer system that automatically sends their own e-mail and telephone messages to that workplace. Each staff member has their own secure locker for personal effects. There are larger, lockable filing cabinets for documents and records used by work groups. Pioneers in hotdesking in London are the large multinational computer companies and management consultants who set up offices in leased buildings that are convenient to their field staff. The concept has proved so popular that one company has specifically built a new office complex designed around the hotdesking concept, with open plan offices around the periphery of the building and open spaces in the center that provide communal dining and recreational facilities.[4]

Homeworking

During the industrial revolution in Britain, families boosted their incomes by working in their homes. Now, some are trying to repeat the success of homeworking by substituting desktop computers and sophisticated telecommunications facilities for the handloom of the last century. Computers and electronic communications are allowing many people to use their homes as offices.[5] In the United Kingdom, managers at British Telecommunications can apply to work at home. Up to 8,000 junior managers and clerical workers are potentially eligible under the scheme. This is not an unusual practice in the United Kingdom. Currently, more than 500,000 Britons work remotely—supported by telecommunications—on a full-time basis, with a further 1.5 million doing so part-time. Some analysts estimate that by the year 2010, at least 20 percent of nonmanual workers in the United Kingdom will be working from or near home.

In the United States, businesses are also turning to telecommuting, driven by shrinking real estate budgets, the need to comply with the Americans with Disabilities Act (which became law in 1992), and the press to keep good employees. At the beginning of 1994, about 6 percent of the U.S. labor force were spending at least a few days a month working at home during traditional business hours, and some experts estimate that between 10 and 20 percent of the U.S. work force will spend a significant amount of time working at home by the end of the decade. This increase will be due to the trend of business adopting telecommuting for its professional, white-collar workers. In 1993 alone, the work-at-home salaried employees' population grew 21.5 percent, representing 5.1 million of the 7.5 million telecommuters.

Mobile Workers

Increasingly, the office is where the worker isn't, and not all workers are fortunate enough to be able to perform their work at home. It's estimated that an additional 45 million U.S. workers spend more of their working time on the road than at their office. This segment of workers—including nonretail sales, service, and technical representatives from such diverse organizations as IBM, the advertising agency of Chiat/Day, and Sears, Roebuck & Co.—are professional, message-intensive, workers. They require message-based, linked technology that allows them to stay in touch in any way—telephones, computers, faxes, pagers, videoconferencing—while they are mobile as well as linked to more sophisticated computer-based applications from off-site locations.

Technical representatives and other professional categories—the so-called road-warriors—are, however, just a small part of the mobile workforce, and portable computers will move into jobs that by their very nature demand constant mobility. With field workers, it's the fundamental business of the organization, which means a direct justification for any capital dollars spent on hand-held devices for those workers. Driving many business initiatives is a growing awareness of the value of information in low-technology jobs. Information about a package is nearly as critical as the package itself for United Parcel Service of America.[6] The company uses a system of electronic clipboards that are carried by every UPS driver in the United States, and can tell customers the exact status of a package at any point in the delivery process.

Extensive use of portable computers means not only more information, but the ability to do more with the information. When Chicago gave its parking-enforcement officers handheld computers—complete with miniature printers to produce parking tickets—it found itself in possession of a new source of data on parking scofflaws. Boot crews, using their portable computers, now operate in real time. The crews canvass the streets of Chicago, entering license plate numbers to see which cars have outstanding tickets. When they find one that does, they immediately install a boot on the wheel to prevent anyone from moving the car. To Chicago, more information means better law enforcement and increased revenues from parking fines.

The real cutting edge for portable development is the link to the office computer. Advances in wireless technology allow an increasing number of portables to stay in touch throughout the day. Information becomes more readily available at the main site and to people in the field. Despite advances in communications technology, portable computers will probably remain best at eliminating errors by standardizing the data-collection process. That quality is vital for companies looking for ways to become more competitive. Everyone wants 100 percent customer satisfaction, but that is impossible without 100 percent quality data at the bottom of the entire process.

Mobile Workforces

The archetype for what characterizes early adopters of portable computing is that its workers are mobile, intensive users of forms not previously automated. Two examples are the international courier and the utility worker.

International Couriers. To provide high-quality service, couriers have adopted package tracing systems. One of the most advanced is the Federal Express (FedEx) system, which supplies its drivers with handheld computers called Dads (digitally assisted dispatch systems) to deliver from two to three million items every day in the United States.[7] The system directs FedEx drivers via the easiest route to their next pick-up using the Dads display. The advantage of this system is that ad hoc collections are possible throughout the day. After collection, the driver scans the computer bar-code label on each package and enters the details of the final destination into a handheld computer. A satellite link transfers the information to the mainframe computer in FedEx's Memphis headquarters, which is then accessible to FedEx bases throughout the world.

UPS, based in Atlanta, calls its device DIAD (delivery information acquisition device). As with the computers carried by other delivery-service drivers, DIAD records the time and location of each collection and delivery into an international mainframe. It also keeps an electronically recorded copy of the recipient's signature. UPS plans to implement a system in which a rack in each truck transmits data back to the office between stops, allowing customers' access to information about their packages in real time.

DHL Worldwide Express has the largest global network and employs a similar system that assists in the delivery of more than 60 million shipments annually. DHL provides customers the option of linking into the network from their own offices, and its EasyShip gives high-volume users the added option of having a system installed on the premises—consisting of a personal computer, two printers, an electronic weighing scale, a barcode scanner, and a modem.

Utility Workers.   One utility company provides electricity to 1.9 million customers spread out over 7,600 square miles and many of those miles have trees with limbs that, if not trimmed, fall and damage power lines.[8] It wanted to better manage the crews of tree trimmers and decided pen computers offered the company a way to do it. The crews spend their day out in the woods, away from their trucks, so they needed something small and lightweight to carry with them. Information from the pen computers feeds into a personal computer database and the Detroit Edison mainframe system. It saved $1.6 million—more than its purchase cost—in the first year of use. The savings came from improved efficiency of its foremen by reduced paperwork and savings in payments to independent tree-trimming companies.

Tracking Systems and Active Badges

Olivetti Research Laboratory in Cambridge (England) developed what it calls the Active Badge, a clip-on badge about the size of a standard security pass, which emits infrared pulses to wall-mounted sensors throughout a company. The sensors, in turn, link to a computer, which collects the information and distributes it over a network. Within 15 seconds of departure of an individual wearing the badge, any colleague who checks the employee-tracking database at the lab will discover the departure. Anyone using Internet, the worldwide computer network, has access to the same information.

These badges (and similar devices) will find a place among the growing array of technologies that label and track people in their daily activities. Global positioning systems already monitor cross-country trucks, and cellular phone systems act as tracking systems, since they must pin down the approximate location of every customer in order to deliver incoming calls via the closest antenna.

Active badges can make life at work simpler. By knowing when someone is in a meeting or out, for instance, colleagues avoid interrupting each other or making wasted phone calls and trips to empty offices.[9] At Olivetti's Cambridge Laboratory, wearers of the active badge have incoming calls ring on the phones nearest the wearer, wherever they happen to be, and at the Media Laboratory of Massachusetts Institute of Technology, electronic doors unlock automatically for privileged badge wearers.

On the Road With Satellite Tracking

In war, the best weapon is often a map, but in the modern office, maps are normally for decoration. This is because today's maps are static. While a picture of a bank's branches is not very informative, imagine what the bank's managers could do with a computerized spatial database showing their customer's homes (highlighting those with mortgages and overdrafts), the location of the bank's ATMs, its competitors' branches, perhaps even the route and location of its security vans.[10] The thought of such a demographic treasure trove is driving the geographical information services (GIS) industry—an umbrella term covering businesses that stretch from computerized in-car navigation to those that plan sewers, reapportion political districts, and measure climatic change.

The key technology in this industry is the global positioning system (GPS), developed by the U.S. Pentagon at a cost of over $3 billion (including the launching of satellites) to help pinpoint the location of its armed forces anywhere in the world. Now, this same technology is affordable for everyone from police departments to boaters. All GPS portable handheld devices work the same way. The unit locks onto any satellites in its range. Then it calculates the longitude and latitude, usually within twenty-five meters. It can also determine the speed of movement, the direction to reach a destination, and how long it takes to get there. With all twenty-four satellites in orbit, it provides information about altitude as well, a useful feature for mountain climbers and pilots.

Most of the new receivers can link to a laptop computer. That way, progress is displayed via a scrolling map appearing on screen. Today, the scrolling map feature and GPS unit is available in rental cars in areas with a thriving tourist population. (Agencies in Orlando, the home of Disney World, were one of the first to offer this option.[11]) Similar navigation systems may become a frequent sight in cars over the next few years.[12] Hardware companies such a Phillips Electronics NV, Pioneer Electronic Corporation, and the Blaupunkt car-stereo unit of Robert Bosch GmbH, are supporting significant technology efforts, while software concerns are rushing to provide electronic maps that can direct drivers to the nearest gas station—or to a three-star Italian restaurant—no matter where they are.

A bit further in the future handheld (and lightweight) devices will perform many of the same functions. Sony Corporation, Trimble Navigation, Magellan Systems Corporation, and others already make models for hikers and sailors. Detailed electronic maps will be on portable compact disks or in central databases accessible by wireless communication. Ultimately, navigation may become just another feature in multipurpose handheld gadgets that millions of consumers will carry wherever they go.

The most promising service industries for future application of GIS/GPS are banking, insurance, and transport. These industries are already feeling the influence of the technology, which can tell an insurer how close a prospective customer's house is to a fire hydrant or to a police station and can calculate how far he drives to work and through which areas, enabling the insurer to offer appropriate rates.[10] Fast food chains like McDonald's and Dunkin' Donuts use the technology to determine where to locate restaurants. Hertz uses it to direct car renters to particular destinations, and police use it from patrol cars to more accurately report accident positions. In Japan, they are installing the sensors-transmitters beneath sidewalks to test their effectiveness in helping the disabled. There, the Inductive Radio Information System (IRIS), working in combination with personal portable communications devices and the installed sidewalk sensors-transmitters, audibly gives the visually impaired their current location and other important information, such as traffic conditions and the color of traffic lights. Similarly, any wheelchair-bound citizen would get directions to the most accessible entrances of buildings.

Personal Communications Networks

The age of the wireless, pocket telephone has also arrived. The lightweight, portable telephone, linked to personal communications networks (PCNs)—systems of satellites, radio waves, and wires—opens the door to a host of remarkable innovations. Unlike cellular systems, PCNs use digital signals that are less subject to interference, and because numerous small PCN transmitters can be located in a given area, wireless phones need little power.

In just a few years, we will carry a wireless phone in our pocket and when we make a call, it will be to a person, not a place.[13] By 1997, as many as 23 million people in the United States will use PCN networks, and subscribers will receive a single telephone number for life if they wish. The wireless phone will function like a conventional cordless instrument, running on a base station plugged into an in-wall telephone jack at home. In the car, the phone keeps the same number and will automatically switch to a cellular phone network. At work, it functions like a portable office phone, connected by radio waves to a desktop.

Office in the Sky

Increasingly, we find it more difficult to insulate ourselves from business communications.

- A recent advertisement for Singapore Airlines opened with the following idea: imagine being able to call anywhere in the world from anywhere above it.[14] It continued by announcing its Global Sky Telephone Service, CELESTEL, for its MEGATOP 747 long-haul passenger aircraft so that passengers may telephone anywhere, anytime they wish.
- Japan Air Lines is one of the leading innovators in offering business services. It provides in-flight mail service, along with personal video screens and satellite communications to support in-flight telephone and fax services.

Walking down the aisle of an airliner, one discovers that laptop computers are almost as much a staple of business flights as attaché cases and carryon luggage. Future flyers, however, will find enhanced technology already onboard for their use. To respond to future demands for technology, Boeing Company's 777 jets offer fiber-optic computer networks as sophisticated as the most advanced ones in today's offices.[15] United Airlines, one of the first to take advantage of the networks, ordered thirty-four of the new planes and plans to offer a computer to everyone on board. A 386 microprocessor in each bank of seats controls three six-inch computer screens, one for each seat. Passengers can use them to call up computer games and other software from a central computer, movies from six VCRs, or even updates on the flight's progress. The network will also carry digital telephone calls, e-mail, and faxes from the passengers own laptop.[15] In the next generation of in-flight service, airlines will do whatever is necessary to keep the business executive in contact with his or her office. From take off to landing, flying time becomes part of the ordinary working day.

Banks Move to the Customer

As banks confront intensifying competition from mutual funds and other nonbank suppliers of financial services, bankers are concluding that free-standing branches are too expensive to build and operate. Worse still, many of the most desirable customers use automatic teller machines and rarely set foot in a branch bank. The obvious solution is to offer banking services where the customers are. One approach has been to open mini-branches in supermarkets, and by mid-1994 there were over 2,000 supermarket branch banks in the United States.

Another approach has been to develop and place financial kiosks in locations with high pedestrian traffic. At the computerized finance center in Pittsburgh International Airport's new terminal, a traveler can sit down at a machine, talk by telephone to a representative whose picture flashes on a telephone screen, and apply for a car loan. The traveler can also buy and sell stocks, cash checks, withdraw money, and get the latest news from the financial markets. Bank analysts say such sophisticated remote centers will spread around the country.[16]

Using the new technology, banks follow customers, rather than wait for them, and traditional bank branches may become increasingly obsolete. The next obvious question—with no answer at the moment—is how does a branch or main office of a bank look in the twenty-first century? With the combination of technological mobility and worker population, the human financial services provider(s) may be operating out of an isolated electronic bunker located anywhere, providing around-the-clock, multilingual service.

ELECTRONIC IMMIGRANTS

Electronic immigrants could become a sensitive international trade issue by the late 1990s. These new service workers telecommute across borders via computers to perform a variety of services electronically and compete against workers in affluent countries.

Offshore Workers

Data processing and other back-office jobs are moving offshore to places where wages are cheaper, where people speak English, and where state-of-the-art telecommunications facilities allow instantaneous links to the company's host computers. Barbados, Jamaica, the Philippines, Singapore, and Ireland have emerged as the most popular back-office locations for the United States. The jobs range from simple data entry to accounting, medical transcription, telemarketing, and technical support for high-technology products.

American computer-based workers could have their work moved halfway around the world, since U.S. companies tend to outsource for purely economic reasons. This would be a blow to U.S. cities that are data-processing centers, including Omaha, Des Moines, Sioux Falls, and Tampa. This trend, particularly in the case of Ireland, is due to planning. Ireland invested $3.5 billion to upgrade its telecommunications network, first with sophisticated satellite technology, and later by laying fiber-optic cable from one end of the country to the other.[17] Ireland also attracts foreign investment through tax breaks and employment, training, and construction grants. A final factor pulling U.S. companies to Ireland is the ability to spread the workforce over different time zones, since an Irish office places demands on expensive mainframe computers at off-peak hours, when most U.S. computers are underutilized.

Airlines Shift Operations Abroad

Most air travelers don't realize that the flight coupons from their tickets probably travel farther than the fliers themselves. American Airlines, for example, processes the tickets it collects throughout the world in Barbados or the Dominican Republic, and Swissair processes its flight coupons in Bombay. Cathay Pacific Airways moved its revenue accounting operations to Guangzhou, China, and its mainframe computer center to Sydney, Australia; and Singapore Airlines (SIA) shifted airline computing operations to Bombay, recruiting programmers and moving some software development, revenue accounting, and other functions. This represents a trend among cost-conscious carriers to move back-office jobs offshore. When underutilized equipment, rising personnel costs, and expensive real estate squeeze airline revenues, the low-cost offshore services producers benefit.

American Airlines.   American Airlines (AA) was the trailblazer. In 1983, the Dallas-Fort Worth-based airline set up a data-processing center in Bridgetown, Barbados. An AA subsidiary, Data Management Services (DMS), employs more than 1,500 people in Bridgetown and in Santo Domingo, Dominican Republic. DMS handles all of American's revenue accounting. (Revenue accounting is a labor-intensive task that involves entering the information printed on flight coupons into computers as a way of calculating revenue to the airline, of settling and clearing payments to and from other airlines, and of deriving information for marketing purposes, including its frequent-flyer program.) About 60 percent of the DMS business isn't for American—it processes medical claims for insurance companies, credit-card applications for banks, and membership applications for a variety of vendors.

Swissair.   Swissair was the next to go offshore. It set up a data entry office in Bombay in 1987. Indian workers rectify errors in reservation bookings made by other airlines and transmit the corrections back to the Swissair main computer in Zurich. Encouraged by the success of this operation, Swissair moved most of its revenue-accounting to a joint venture company in Bombay and hopes the joint venture will attract other clients, much as American's DMS does.

Saving on costs is the paramount goal. An Indian clerk, with computer and supporting software, costs only 25 percent of the expense of a comparable Swissair employee. American Airlines has shaved 30 percent or more off its costs for revenue accounting by sending the work abroad, and that doesn't include the profits made by doing data processing for other companies.[18]

OFFICE MEETINGS

Meetings consume huge amounts of time. According to the New York-based American Management Association, executives spend at least 50 percent of their time in meetings.[19] What's more, many organizations are moving toward more team-oriented management as well as reorganizing the rank and file along team lines. That means more meetings than ever before—and more people attending them. For many, meeting management is a core aspect of ongoing total quality initiatives or teamwork research. How to get the most from these meetings is critical to productivity, quality, and the strategic transformation process. It's not only the time spent in meetings that is important—conservative corporate travel budgets focus on the issue of expense control. As a result, *groupware* and *videoconferencing* become valuable tools to improve overall corporate effectiveness.

Electronic meetings have two key elements: the software support and the meeting manager or facilitator. The electronic meetings use decision rooms—conventional meeting rooms equipped with personal computers and software—allowing people to present ideas, rank action items, and document the meeting electronically. Some also provide for a virtual meeting enabling people to tap in from various locations to attend electronically. In both cases, the tools allow anonymous input, which is a critical factor in getting more honesty and more ideas from the meeting.

Formal and informal research at user companies shows the potential benefits of this approach. The Seattle-based Boeing Company, for example, conducted a nine-month study in which sixty-four groups used meeting software. In a paper submitted to the Institute of Electrical and Electronics Engineers, the company reported 1,773 calendar days saved during the period, a figure based on estimates of group time had they conducted conventional meetings.[19]

Groupware

Just as a spreadsheet organizes and harnesses the computational power of the personal computer, groupware is a category of software that brings out the potential of a computer network for communications and cooperation on shared tasks. E-mail, a process which sorts, stores, and sends typed messages between computers across a network, is a rudimentary form of groupware. So are most electronic bulletin boards, which function something like electronic conference rooms in which many conversations can take place at once.

At some companies, groupware brings subtle cultural changes and, at the least, a better understanding of how a particular corporate environment operates. Groupware forces the organization to make explicit in software the way people in the organization relate to each other. With groupware, for instance, companies have to decide who reports to whom, or who has the authority to change, add to, or approve a co-worker's report. Then it's comparatively easy to diagnose whether an organization values openness or hierarchy, privacy or sharing, cross-functional collaboration or rigid departmental lines of authority.[20] Thus, bringing groupware into an organization isn't as simple as installing new software. It is either useless or a powerful new impetus to team productivity. Groupware encourages more direct communication across organizational boundaries, flattening an organization and making hierarchies vanish. For some few companies, groupware just doesn't fit—they find they can do things just as well with conventional tools, or their culture is too hierarchical.

Continental Insurance Company.   The Information Systems director at Continental Insurance Company, New York, didn't see much use for groupware (in his case, Lotus Notes) the first time he saw it. A few months later, though, his group needed to develop an account-management software package to track such large, complex risks as oil refineries, airlines, or rental-car companies. To do the job, he budgeted $350,000 and planned for at least a year's work by a team of four in-house software developers. The plan was to write an automated checklist to track on a day-by-day basis the more than 170 tasks, some dependent on the outcome of others, that a typical account required—time-sensitive jobs such as inspections, safety reports, regulatory filings, and price estimates. As the team began its work, it rediscovered Notes. The director was able to take Notes and tailor it to his own needs, rather than have his programmers spend a year developing a custom version. They started in September 1991 with a pilot, finished it in three weeks, and had it running in Dallas by December. At a final project cost of $130,000, the director saved more than $200,000 and, even more importantly, got the job done in a third of the time.

Dell Computer Corporation.   Dell Computer Corporation, the personal-computer maker, uses groupware—again, Lotus Notes—to speed up and personalize its response to customer orders and to shorten the manufacturing and design cycles. Testing a prototype product, for example, requires as many as 1,500 separate quality tests for things like software compatibility and stability. It requires dozens of people to work closely together on an extremely tight schedule. At Dell, the engineers had daily meetings to sort out minor problems. Now, with Notes, it's similar to having a continuous meeting going on, except employees don't have to leave their desks to join in. Whenever the employee shows up at the electronic meeting, they're discussing the subject he or she needs to talk about. Also, people who might otherwise not get involved can participate. For example, an employee fielding complaints on Dell's toll free phone line can send redesign suggestions directly to engineering. At Dell, while face-to-face meetings still take place, they are fewer in number and tend to focus on broader issues, not the mundane day-to-day details of getting out a product.

Telephone—Video—Personal Computer Hookups

The long-anticipated fusion of personal computer, television, and telephone is a reality. Whether these combinations of technologies present important new business tools or merely usher in convenient new ways to communicate, they will dramatically change the way we live and work.

IBM Japan and GC Technology built videoconferencing functions into a personal computer. Besides transmitting live images, the system lets users color video data into text messages.[13] This type of technology fusion allows physicians to have instant video access to medical experts and databases around the world and allows businesses to exchange data through interactive systems that are faster and more sophisticated than fax machines.

Telemedicine.   Telemedicine is an emerging hybrid of telecommunications and patient care in which people in medically underserved areas use ordinary telephone lines to consult with highly trained specialists whom they could not otherwise see. U.S. doctors via satellite have diagnosed conditions in patients in Armenia, the Philippines, and in the Near East during Operation Desert Storm. The state prison systems of Texas, West Virginia, Georgia, and Florida have networks that allow doctor and patient to sit down face to face electronically to review symptoms, diagnosis, and treatment for inmates. With the network, consulting specialists guide the doctor or nurse on-site through a physical exam and discuss the results. Less sophisticated methods relying on still photography are in use in Iowa, North Carolina, and Nevada.

Specialists in radiology, cardiology, and neonatology, whose highly skilled services are in great demand in rural areas of the United States, were quick to take advantage of the new technology. These doctors do much of their diagnosing with tests such as echocardiograms, CAT scans, and fetal monitoring—tests easily displayed and transmitted electronically. We can even glimpse the future of global telemedicine in an experiment combining satellite transmission and high-definition television. Doctors in Boston used these technologies to study patients in Belize suffering a parasitic skin disease.[21] While the costs of setting up these systems using satellites, high-definition television, fiber-optics, and digital compression are high, eventually the projected savings from telemedicine—up to $1,500 for every patient who doesn't require transfer to an acute-care hospital—are likely to outweigh the price.

VOICE MAIL

In its basic form, voice messaging is merely a computerized answering service that records and replays telephone messages. However, the latest systems integrate voice with fax and e-mail, transforming the telephone into a multimedia communications terminal. Voice mail is a technology that many hate—but are using—in ever-increasing numbers. An estimated one-third of all large and medium size companies in the United

States already use voice messaging and many residential telephone users have access to voice mail services provided by regional telephone companies.[22]

International Differences

The experience of the United States does not apply in Europe and Asia, however, where sales of voice messaging systems have been slower to take off, in part, it seems, because there is more resistance to talking to impersonal machines. In Europe, there are also regulatory hurdles. It takes about six months and costs about $500,000 to obtain approval from a European PTT (national telephone company) to connect a voice messaging system to the phone network.[22]

While voice messaging systems manufacturers step up their international marketing efforts, voice mail appears set to become more widely accepted. Voice mail is increasing in Europe as a service for users of car phones, where the system picks up messages while the user is not in the car or when the telephone is switched off. U.S. companies view voice mail primarily as a productivity tool, especially among the many companies that are downsizing and cutting support staff. With smaller support staff, voice mail systems ensure that calls get answered.

The full potential of voice messaging is just emerging with the introduction of voice processing systems that allow users to access a wide range of services over the telephone. The caller can tap into broadcast news services, retrieve and update computer database records, initiate or receive fax and e-mail messages, and have them read by a computer-generated voice. Interactive voice response systems, enabling the caller to speak directly to a computer and to be understood, also promise to broaden the applications of voice processing. Although manufacturers of voice processing systems claim that their products are complementary to computer network systems, it will take time to develop standard interfaces. At the same time that voice processing systems are beginning to access data processing systems, computers are acquiring many of the attributes of voice processing, including business audio features that enable the user to record spoken messages and incorporate them in text and graphics documents.

Voice Mail for the Hearing-Impaired

Many office phone systems automatically answer calls and take messages when a phone is busy or unattended. However, none of these voice mail systems can take calls from telecommunications devices for the deaf (TDDs), the terminals that the hearing-impaired use with telephones. While some may consider this a minor inconvenience, it could give large corporations a problem in complying with the Americans with Disabilities Act.

The PhoneMail system from Rolm Co. is the first to address the problem. New software determines when an incoming call contains the distinct tones that TDDs generate and then answers with an appropriate invitation to leave a typed message. Persons wishing to read the message would then use a special TDD-equipped phone. Enhancements include the ability to translate TDD messages into computer text, e-mail, and other formats.[23]

EXCHANGING BUSINESS INFORMATION

Some people define electronic data interchange (EDI) as the computer-to-computer exchange of business information in a standard format. This definition includes companies that might electronically receive, for instance, purchase orders but then follow a paper-based process to complete the transaction. A more advanced definition of EDI is the exchange of business data among application systems in a standard electronic format, allowing, for example, one company's purchase order system to communicate with another company's order processing system.

If it were easy and inexpensive to move business data among companies, everyone would be using EDI. It is not, the difficulty being that exchanging business data mandates a review and redesign of the participants' business practices and processes, and company's find that they have to *change the rules*. When federal agencies tried to adopt paperless business practices using EDI, they experienced conflict with its own regulations because many of the government's internal regulations require the use of handwritten signatures on paper forms. In a 1992 study, the U.S. Food and Drug Administration (FDA) found that its regulations call for signatures in no fewer than 132 different sections. Consequently, the FDA asked for public comment on how to revise its regulations to accommodate electronic records and alternative forms of human endorsement and would evaluate the legal acceptability, integrity, and security features of all sorts of alternative signature schemes, including smart cards, biometrics devices, passwords, encrypted digital signatures, and pen-based computers.[24]

Despite the difficulties of business process redesign, companies implement EDI because it offers significant cost savings and could even be considered necessary for implementing business processes such as just-in-time inventory, total quality management, and zero-defect production. It is the very basis for exchanging electronic mail and implementing supply chain management between trading partners.

Electronic Data Interchange

Large-scale EDI users (or EDI hubs) typically have hundreds of EDI trading partners (or spokes) and plan to add hundreds more in the upcoming years. The first and most pressing problem for hub implementation is the cost of adding trading partners. While the median cost in out-of-pocket expenses and personnel per new trading partner is only about $200 for hubs, it is still a significant expense and a potential barrier to implementation when the number of new trading partners is large.[25] For inexperienced companies, the barrier is most often the technology. It's difficult, it's expensive, and things move very slowly as the companies try to learn how EDI works and negotiate the necessary inter-company legal agreements. Furthermore, there's often little or no pressure forcing them into EDI until they recognize it as a competitive advantage or necessity.

EDI and The Freight Industry.   Access to electronic trading systems for such purposes as e-mail, bulletin boards, and data interchange is increasingly important for many business sectors. For Europe's smaller players in the freight industry, it is a question of survival due to the single European market reforms.

The freight industry is a classic example of a sector in which electronic trading can produce more efficient links between shippers, forwarders, carriers, traders, and consignees. The British International Freight Association (BIFA) and General Electric Information Services (GEIS) jointly developed an electronic trading service called BIFAnet to better control the flow of information between the freight intermediaries.[26] Freight forwarders have to communicate with all members of the supply chain and move information around for every shipment. Because half of the 900 BIFA members employed 10 people or less, the members looked to the association for a modern electronic solution. With the development of BIFAnet, if members had no computer technology before, they now have access to one of the world's largest EDI networks for less than about $3,000 for hardware and software. Cooperative ventures like BIFAnet make state-of-the-art technology available to the smallest of companies.

Electronic Mail and Collaborative Working

Electronic mail (e-mail) is changing fast. A few years ago, it was largely the preserve of mainframe-based systems and notoriously difficult to install and manage. Today, an increasing number of large corporations are downsizing to local area networks (LANs) and are phasing out host-based e-mail systems in favor of LAN systems.

There are now approximately 10 million e-mail users worldwide, of whom around half are using a personal LAN-based system.[27] The applications vary significantly in their level of sophistication. For example, sales representatives use pen-based portable PCs in the field to fill in electronic forms and send the information back to the office LAN for automatic routing and processing, using a wide area radio network. This type of application takes the emphasis away from simple messaging and into the area of workgroup computing. Here, groups of users can work collaboratively on shared information to create a form of e-mail conferencing. Another example of a sophisticated e-mail application is work flow automation, where the system filters electronically created expense forms, automatically routing them to a manager for approval if the total exceeds a certain amount.

The problem with this vision of collaborative working is in the lack of a standard covering how the mail-enabled applications communicate with the messaging back-end, and how that back-end controls the addressing and routing of calls. In fact, few of the several hundred e-mail standards currently in existence even agree on the definition of a message, let alone a common way of addressing and routing calls.

ROLE OF THE FAX

Since the facsimile machine first started to become a popular business tool in the early 1980s it has changed out of all proportion. Once a slow and limited form of sending documents from one place to another over the phone line, it has become the heart of many office data and telecommunications operations. Offices use the fax for corporate document management, telephone management, personal photocopying, and personal computer connectivity. These computer interfaces allow personal computers to control the operation of the fax machine and hook up via a parallel or serial port. The software that usually comes with such PC connections allows the fax machine to act as a printing device so that anything generated on the PC's screen is transmittable via fax. Anything received on the fax can either be printed out or saved as an image file on the PC.[28]

In many cases, computers and fax machines are converging into one single system eliminating the need for a dedicated fax machine altogether. The simplest example of this is a fax machine that uses PC and laser or ink jet technologies to produce plain paper faxes. These are ordinary fax machines with slightly more processing power and the ability to produce faxes on plain paper rather than on the thermal paper used in most machines.

Corporate information systems (I/S) departments often ignore this low-end communication technology, with its distinct competitive advantages. Fax technology isn't really managed in corporate America and I/S department managers ignore the fax as they did the growth of personal computer usage a decade ago. While the same person that buys the office photocopier probably buys the fax, the I/S department will have a role in integrating fax technology with the corporate information network. Whether I/S managers like it or not, fax technology is becoming intertwined with a variety of technologies they already control. Computer-based fax products allow companies to generate faxes from LANs of PCs and from mainframe-based applications such as EDI.

With the worldwide installed base of facsimile machines approaching 30 million units and the volume of fax transmissions doubling every three years, the market might appear to have reached saturation point. Far from it. The number of new technologies, services, and products being announced almost daily gives only a hint of what the future holds for the fax. At the low end of the market (the small office and home-based office), low-cost ink jet technology predominates the developments, along with new, innovative applications of home shopping, reservation, and order confirmation services.

Enhanced fax services are only in their infancy. With developments like the incorporation of optical character recognition for remote access to fax mailboxes and computer databases, voice annotation and speech-to-text conversion, store-and-forward fax, pay phone fax, networked fax and integrated voice-fax-electronic mail, an entire new realm of applications and services not yet envisaged are possible. Though the industry still lacks internationally recognized computer-fax message communications standards, the U.S. market is a key indicator of future potential.

Integrating the Fax

Those I/S departments that have made automated faxing an integral part of the way they do business often find that it provides a competitive advantage. For example.[29]

- A Canadian insurance operation uses a LAN-based fax server to distribute 20,000 faxes per month to insurance brokers. The faxes include such critical documents as price quotes, policy terms, invoices, and confirmations.

- A cruise line, based in Miami, transmits reservation information, fare and itinerary changes, and marketing information to 3,000 travel agents using computer-based fax technology. Competitors are building similar fax systems.
- A Miami-based company that promotes travel regularly uses enhanced fax capabilities to send information on new travel promotions to 20,000 travel agents.
- A logistics company sends thousands of fax orders electronically to warehouses and suppliers, and another service provider now broadcasts orders placed previously by phone or mail.

In at least one industry niche—issuing truck permits—automated fax technology is a competitive necessity. A unit of Cummins Engine Company, Cummins Cash & Information Services, has a network of 3,000 fax machines at North American truck stops and uses it to send truck permits to truckers—sometimes while the driver is still on the phone with Cummins. Previously, they telexed, but the fax put Western Union out of the business of transmitting trucking permits for Cummins.

Automating faxing creates a rudimentary EDI-like network. The ability to send faxes from e-mail and EDI systems makes it possible for small customers or suppliers that lack computer resources to be a part of a corporation's communications universe. For example, Citgo Petroleum Corporation in Tulsa uses a fax system to send information to about 100 small distributors that do not participate in its EDI network. Ideally, Citgo would like all the business partners to be part of its network, but because they are customer service-oriented, they don't force it.

Remote and Mobile Faxes

Along with the increasing use of fax to create business networks, including all those individual faxes installed in home offices and satellite work locations, are the fax machines for the home. Their subscribers can receive news summaries, updates of stock portfolios, credit ratings, and weather reports. With close to 30 million fax machines in the world and with sales growing at about 15 percent annually, the medium is a natural for information dissemination. Some experts estimate spending on fax information services to grow from $.6 billion in 1993 to $1.2 billion by 1995.[30] The growth of the fax market and its related information services adds to its almost universal appeal as a simple way to exchange written material.

Faxing From a Remote Location.   It is difficult to send a fax from remote places where there are unreliable or non-existent communications. There is now a fax machine for the globetrotting executive. Inmarsat C mobile satellite earth stations work with portable personal computers and use the geostationary Inmarsat satellites to provide two-way telex and fax from anywhere in the world. The machine—about the size of a briefcase—takes just minutes to set up using its directional antenna.

Mobile Faxes.   The market for mobile communications devices that integrate fax with cellular phone, modem, and pen-based computer technologies led Eo Inc. to set up a partnership with AT&T, Matsushita, and Marubeni to design, build, and market a new generation of personal communicators. Even though experts believe the market will probably be worth $20 billion by the year 2000, Eo ceased operations three years after its founding. Its two personal communicators proved too costly for the slow-growing market.[29]

IMAGING

In a world that produces 92 million original paper documents every year and doubles corporate files every 3.5 years, document image processing appears to be the answer to every office manager's dream of reducing the mountain of paper in circulation. Many firms are attracted to imaging by the promise of smaller staffs, quicker customer service, reduced transcription errors, fewer lost documents, and reduced paper storage. Banks, insurance companies, and railroads have led the move towards imaging—all paper document–intensive industries.[31]

Imaging and Redesign of Business Processes

Similar to other technologies discussed in this chapter, imaging can be introduced to do a single application, but to achieve maximum benefit from imaging requires review and redesign of the business processes. Because imaging is a component part of the corporatewide document and information processing and management requirements, key questions about redesign must include how one department's image-enabled applications can successfully integrate into existing workstations, networks, and applications elsewhere in the company to achieve planned benefits.[32]

Document Imaging System

Memorial Sloan Kettering Cancer Center (MSK) is renowned as the world's largest cancer treatment facility, but its pioneering use of document imaging systems has also led the hospital to the forefront as one of the top I/T users in the health care industry. The hospital admits more than 18,000 patients each year and processes more than 1 million pages of medical claims, bills, and other administrative paperwork annually. It saw imaging as a strategic technology for the future, yet could find no role models in the hospital industry, so it began to study what banks and insurance companies were doing to see how they were using imaging systems to unclog the paper bottlenecks in their industries.

The system, phased in over a two-year period beginning in October 1989, enables MSK administrators to react to medical claims in a more timely manner. Besides productivity gains of 18 percent to 20 percent, the imaging system yields significant dollar savings for MSK. The hospital saves $85,000 per year in media costs once associated with the eliminated paper and microfiche copying, $55,000 annually in microfilm costs and 2,000 square feet of floor space once occupied by file cabinets housing 90,000 file folders. MSK also eliminated eleven staff positions supporting file library functions for paper and microfiche. The system paid for itself in twenty-two months.[31]

OBSERVATIONS

Most of the technologies discussed in this chapter were introduced into the office environment to solve a single problem and grew over time. Employees brought PCs from home to make life easier at the office, and commuters spending long periods of time in their automobiles bought cellular phones and took them into their offices. Others, who had answering machines or message services at home, wondered why they didn't have them at the office, and still others, weary of air travel looked for better ways to manage meetings. In each of these instances, the technology moved into the office in isolation and proliferated throughout the office environment.

Other more sophisticated technologies like the fax and imaging came along and were introduced by the office manager. At the same time, combinations of existing technologies, such as LAN-based fax generation, were introduced by the information systems or office systems manager. The I/S or I/T managers, in efforts to support remote company offices and workers and to support new business initiatives involving customers or suppliers, implemented networks for information communication and exchange. The application of the various technologies concentrated on automating isolated tasks rather than on reexamining the whole process. The office manager, the I/S manager, and the office systems or office technology manager all automated different aspects of the office and office work in isolation, only to find that the pieces of technology don't fit together, much less achieve the level of benefits expected.

All of this was done to provide the best technology in the work environment to support the way we conduct business. However, what many really wanted to do was to work at or closer to home whenever possible. The productivity of offshore offices proved that many kinds of office work could just as easily be accomplished in a satellite or home office. The experience in setting up remote linkages with employees led to setting up the electronic bunker to provide services to customers—anywhere in the world.

The discussions involving telemedicine and the financial benefits of using imaging for administrative record keeping provide a window into one possible future of health care aided by new, uniquely integrated technologies. Smart cards for capturing patient medical records, smart ID bracelets for hospital patients, and wireless measurement devices for patient monitoring integrated into global information systems are just a few of the technologies that show promise to improve the quality of health care delivery. In 1994, satellites, facilitated by GPS technology, guide ambulances to accident victims in the United Kingdom, and a robot controlled by surgeons from a remote location successfully performs gall bladder operations on patients in Canada, presaging an era of long-distance surgery as an extension of telemedical consulting and changing the who, how, and where of health care delivery.[33]

Today, the major players in the U.S. health care industry—the various insurance companies including the Blue Cross/Blue Shield organizations, and hospitals—are heavy users of I/T, accounting for an administrative load on health care of 25 to 40 percent of the total cost. The management and end results of these and other technology investments by the industry cause national concern on inefficiencies, ineffectiveness, and costs—and demonstrates that technology alone cannot solve the more serious underlying structural problems.

The conclusion is clear: We can no longer afford to accept the perceived limitations imposed by technology about how we do work and how we reach people, nor can we afford to ignore the issue of delivering value to the business through the application of technology. The anywhere, anytime workplace is the workplace of the future. Fulfilling the role of a business partner, I/T must step back and understand how work gets accomplished and how to improve it. I/T must reconceptualize, reformulate, and refit the workplace environment for the enterprise it supports, whether at the local level or global—facilitated by networks, integrated systems, and technologies over multiple time zones in many languages. For I/T, this will raise new issues relating to interoperability, nonstandard interfaces, consistency, and information quality as it attempts to provide customized solutions to unique business problems. They must be promptly addressed and resolved. Only then can work, business processes, and organizational structures successfully continue to undergo their necessary redefinition, redesign, and strategic transformation.

Reformulate the concept of the workplace and workers. A wiser choice of technologies will result, and technology compatibility requirements will be discovered before, rather than after, any technologies chosen and implemented in isolation.

3

Information

Empowerment

Information, when organized and readily available, is power. Empowering systems frees its users to get on with the job at hand without distractions because information by itself doesn't create the value—people do. Specifically, it is the knowledgeable relationships between people that generate value within the enterprise and improve relationships with suppliers and customers. This chapter discusses a series of technologies and systems that have the potential to enhance corporate knowledge—including executive information systems, sales force automation, and a range of intelligent systems.

Information, when organized and readily accessible, is power. William the Conqueror knew this, when, in 1086, he sent clerks out to survey the land he had conquered from the Ribble to the Tyne. This mammoth public-sector information-gathering exercise told the government who owned what property, thus enabling it to collect taxes.[1] It also produced the Domesday Book, the principal source of information on post-1086 history. Now, more than nine centuries later, society is still struggling with issues surrounding the power of information and who determines its availability.

In today's environment, *information empowerment* is the transparent access on demand to data, resources, and collaborators for every user or workgroup in an organization.[2] The contemporary term of *workgroup* is an indicator that people today usually work in collaboration with others. Empowerment involves both the individual user and the group or team within which the individual is working.

Empowering systems have to free its users to get on with the job at hand without distractions because information by itself doesn't create value—people do. Specifically, it is the knowledgeable relationships between people that generate value within the enterprise and its supply chain. It is important to strike a balance between the information imperatives of an organization and the collegial relationships that really make it run. Instead of simply asking what the critical information is that people need, and determining how to deliver it as swiftly and efficiently as possible, designers of empowering systems must determine what the key relationships are, both inside and outside the firm, and how information technology can augment them.[3]

Information matters but quality relationships—relationships that generate innovation and ideas—matter more.[3] If efforts focus on managing information, the resulting business processes do a good job of managing information, but the design implicitly states that the organization values information management over people management. If, however, the design of business processes explicitly encourages and supports productive relationships between informed colleagues, instead of between people and information, then the organization will likely tap new and previously unknown talents and capabilities.

Given the thrust of these ideas, we approach the discussion of the variety of technologies employed in information empowerment from the perspective of how they can change collegial relationships, both inside and outside the business organization. These changes occur within the organization along with business process redesign, organizational restructuring, and transformation and the changing nature of the working environment. External relationships with suppliers and customers improve with more knowledgeable, empowered employees. We begin by focusing on the future information empowerment of the individual in his or her consumer-customer role, creating a paradigm by which we view subsequent new forms of business organizational information empowerment.

EMPOWERING THE CONSUMER-CUSTOMER

Everyone—and every business organization—is a consumer. However, not everyone is an informed consumer. In 1800, a typical American had access to fewer than 300 products and the products were in a single establishment of about 500 square feet—the country store. Choices, if any, were easy to make. Contrast this with today, where the typical American in a metropolitan area of a million people has access to more than a million products, thousands of merchants, and 15 million square feet of selling space.[4]

Due to the sheer volume of alternatives, choices for the individual are much more complex. Anyone who has recently tried to select a mutual fund for long-term investment or differentiate between fifty plus stereo systems at Circuit City, the U.S. consumer electronics chain, will immediately grasp how many purchasing decisions we base on hunches, sales pitches, brand reputation, or sheer fatigue rather than on genuine awareness of quality and value. Given this scenario, it's possible that many superior products won't get produced because potential customers have no feasible way of distinguishing the superior from the average. Venture capitalists frequently comment that the wreckage of fine companies that build great products covers our business landscape. The reason they fail is that the customer didn't have the information available to distinguish its unique qualities from its competition.

The typical American consumer spends 9 percent of nonworking, nonsleeping time in gathering information about products—that is, about 950 hours per year per family and about four hours of information gathering for every $100 expenditure.[4] The consequences of the quality of the information gathering can have a profound consequence on daily life, for example, an untimely death due to inadequate, incomplete, or incorrect labeling of drugs or the suffering of constant pain due to poor information flow between doctor and patient.

Resolving the advanced industrial world's consumer-confusion problem requires a paradigm shift in thinking. One authority suggests it will require recognizing the existence and extent of the problem—the loss of money, time, and energy that results from making uninformed buying decisions.[4] Additionally, it will require an Information Age consumerism based on a high-quality information infrastructure that will revolutionize the private-sector economics of selling information to consumers. The significance of the new information infrastructure—*New Consumerism*—is that it becomes profitable for independent information sources to provide high-quality, convenient, and affordable information to consumers, thus becoming the critical arbiters in the consumer's day-to-day decision-making. Potential customers will control their information intake and will be able to rely on its objectivity, as contrasted with today, when consumers face a barrage of mass-media advertising over which they have little control.

New Consumerism has three tiers: technology, agents, and clearinghouses. The *technology* to support it requires a fiber-optic network reaching into every home; the reallocation of the airwaves to support digital, interactive, and cellular broadband services; and a high-definition television standard that has sufficient flexibility to achieve magazine-quality images. The *agents* would express frank but verifiable product evaluations, thus rendering obsolete the brands, advertising, occupational licensing, institutional certification and consumer-protection agencies. The databases for the *clearinghouses,* for the most part, already exist in governmental agencies.

What is holding the New Consumerism back is lack of vision, not technology. Government regulation requires change, and government policy requires reformulation. Liability legal code requires change to allow the agents to express evaluations with relative impunity. A system of government-sanctioned information clearinghouses composed of certified information agents would then access basic data about products and purchases of goods and services.

Domesday 2000 and New Consumerism

Domesday 2000 is a private sector-backed operation to pull together a host of different sources of information about land ownership, use, and value to create a computer-based databank for England.[1] A user would then be able to find out, for example, who owned a particular property, how much land was in the parcel, and whether there was any contaminated land within a five-mile radius of it.

The first problem the project encountered was in getting the information to build the database. The United Kingdom opened the Land Registry for England and

Wales to the public in December 1990 after nine decades of secrecy when the 1988 Environmental Protection Act required local authorities to compile lists of contaminated land. The lists were available to the public in 1993, but some of the data is incomplete or confidential—such as Britain's Sites of Special Scientific Interest. If enough information is available, the Domesday 2000 project will decide whether there is a market for it. Property developers and home buyers are the most obvious potential buyers, but the system could have a much wider range of uses. Marketing companies might welcome a way to avoid deluging apartment dwellers with mass mailings for lawncare, for example.

In Sweden, where a similar system is available, 60 percent of the inquiries come from people with interests other than property sales. Mass mailings using the system in Sweden are four times as effective as mailings that do not.[1] Austria, Australia, and Canada all have similar kinds of central data registers. In these countries, the information bank exists as a result of national (or state) government initiatives. These countries had a vision of the requirements and implemented them, despite the lack of other elements of New Consumerism, for example, the fiber-optics and high-definition television technology for delivery. They ensured wider access to official files, providing the information necessary for setting up the clearinghouses. In the case of the latter countries, they created the information database.

New Consumerism and the Business Organization

The Domesday 2000 project is evidence that some elements of New Consumerism are viable on a limited basis today—without sophisticated technology. Magazines like *Auto Trends, Consumer Reports,* and *Money* offer unbiased comparisons and reports on automobiles, electronics, appliances, and investment services. However, this is at the very end of the customer-consumer food chain. Tens of thousands of buyer-seller relationships occur before producing the automobile, appliance, or investment service.

If the typical consumer spends 9 percent of his or her nonworking, nonsleeping hours in gathering information to make better buying decisions, how much time do business organizations spend in gathering information for decision-making? How can organizations best inform its employees, suppliers, and potential customers—everyone with whom it has a collegial relationship—so that each can make better, more informed decisions? This is the mandate for information empowerment.

Businesses today can't wait for the availability of the New Consumerism information database to identify its best possible suppliers. Nor can it postpone establishing strong customer relationships until it can contribute information describing its products to a nonbiased database targeted to potential customer subscribers. Thus it is necessary to focus on how business organizations can facilitate the necessary information empowerment for its internal and external relationships.

Be alert to subtle moves toward the New Consumerism concept. Know how your organization can benefit from it.

EMPOWERING THE ORGANIZATION

Key to carrying out information empowerment is the character, attitude, and policies of the business organization itself. A clear view of *how much* and *what* has to change must exist to provide a supportive environment for information empowerment.

Information Politics

While the information-based organization was one of the most popular concepts in the 1980s, today it is largely a fantasy. Christopher Lorenz, a commentator on management issues for the *Financial Times* says that the rhetoric and technology of information management have far outpaced the ability of people to understand and agree on what information they need, and then to show it.[5] The primary reason for the failure, he believes, is that companies did not manage the politics of information.

Politics come increasingly into play as information and knowledge become more important to a company. This information politician role—not as the owner of information but as the manager with primary responsibility for facilitating its effective use—is still in question for many companies, despite the widespread existence of people with titles like chief information officer (CIO).

Until recently, the basis of selection criteria for most CIOs was technical acumen rather than political skills. However, few CIOs embarked on initiatives to improve the usage and management of information—not just I/T—and fewer still had the political clout to make it happen. At far-sighted companies like Xerox, Kodak, and Merrill Lynch, recent corporate information heads have been fast-track executives with records of managing important nontechnical aspects of the business. Such people have a better chance than most of identifying and managing the politics of information—negotiation, influence-exercising, back-room deals, and coalition-building.

> *Understand the politics involved when attempting information empowerment. Information politics are often more important in determining success or failure than any technology-based issues.*

Information Empowerment and the I/T Department

I/T departments have been pushing computerization upon corporate professionals for years, forcing people to change the way they work and realigning responsibilities in the workplace. Now it is their turn to adapt. Rapid changes in information system technology—open systems, client-server environments, interoperability, etc.—that focus on empowering the user is changing the traditional role of the I/T group. Concurrently, users and customers increasingly challenge the expertise of the I/T department. These issues are prompting a basic reassessment of the I/T function, and in some organizations the centralized I/T department ceases to exist. Timex, for example, is replacing an aging mainframe-based system with new integrated software on an open distributed platform and thinks that ultimately the system will run itself.[6] This option may not be open to many organizations, but doing away with the centralized I/T function is not so different from outsourcing it.

The pressure on I/T to maximize the business value it delivers may be undermining some traditional I/T regimes, but it also coincides with a generation of technology that will not only allow I/T to deliver what it promises, but which on any large scale probably demands more specialized I/T disciplines. It also requires more managing than the technology that it replaces.

Technology leaders must understand that the diversity of the forces of change in I/T departments does not release it from the mandate to maximize the business value it delivers.

Empowerment and Organizational Change

As organizations flatten their pyramids to cut costs, accelerate decision-making, and become altogether more flexible and competitive, they can no longer operate in a hierarchical fashion. Instead of a series of levels that command and control the one immediately beneath them, power and information on many issues become delegated, decentralized, and diffused. Establishing trust between management, peers and subordinates, or colleagues becomes mandatory. Cross-functional teams replace individual effort within narrow departmental boundaries. Instead of information being withheld at each successive level in the hierarchy, it becomes shared or, at least, accessible, through informational networking. All this implies fundamental changes in the way that leaders behave.[7]

Consider how most corporate fast tracks operate. The values and behavior patterns that they promote among today's star middle managers and tomorrow's stars are in direct conflict with the powerful concept of empowerment. Instead of changing the fast-track process to encourage empowering behavior in the company's central nervous system—its star managers—many of today's leaders are still cloning themselves. The command and control manager will not be comfortable with information empowerment and its collegial relationships.

There are not many renaissance executives in top management positions who are versatile enough to do it all. All managers must get the maximum out of the existing organization. However, improving organizational performance incrementally compared to transforming the organization to make quantum leaps in performance requires significantly different skills. Business and I/T leaders must make clear to the organization what the strategy is, and be sure that the skills are in place to lead it.

INTELLIGENT SYSTEMS

Thanks to expert systems and artificial intelligence and their merger with existing systems, a number of companies are, in effect, cloning their best employees and spreading them throughout the corporation. Applied intelligence systems, like automated bureaucrats, search a book of rules to decide what to do in any given situation. Because machines don't forget, they can manage more rules more consistently than people. Workers in these corporations view themselves as users of widely accessible intelligent systems that integrate the best efforts and intelligence of the best employees.

A group of computer tools is gaining recognition as part of the information empowerment movement. These tools require complex and subtle interactions between machine and humans, with each teaching and learning from each other. They include the following:[8]

- **Expert systems:** A computerized decision-making technique that embodies knowledge gleaned from experts. It helps users sort through myriad factors and choose the right option.
- **Artificial intelligence:** Software systems that attempt to replicate aspects of human intelligence.
- **Neural network:** A more sophisticated system that tries to mimic human brain processes and learns from the mistakes it makes.
- **Chaos theory:** A theory proposing that seemingly random events, such as stock prices, have patterns that computer programs can detect.
- **Fuzzy logic:** A mathematical method that deals with approximations or gradations.

Expert systems can assist in dealing with an avalanche of minor decisions that workers must make daily, while more advanced systems, such as neural networks, can learn by themselves from their mistakes. For example, one California county uses an expert system that scans some 6,000 government regulations to determine if applicants qualify for benefits and, if qualified, authorizes how much and what type. The process is faster for both the applicant and case worker, and the results are consistent. Not only does it save the county money, but, if adopted statewide, could save taxpayers approximately $400 million a year. Neural networks are also used by business. An example is Spiegel, who uses neural nets to fine-tune its direct-mail operation, saving about $1 million annually by targeting its 200 million catalogs and brochures to those most likely to be repeat buyers.

These management sciences aren't new—they have been around for a number of years and are quite robust in their techniques. Their lack of widespread use in industry today is due in part to the reticence of many executives to discuss successful applications creating competitive advantage for their enterprise. It is also due to the complexity and mathematical bases of the technologies themselves, causing senior management to not take the time to understand, and thus not accept and support, the application of these technologies to resolve a wide range of operational problems.

Expert Systems and Artificial Intelligence

Expert systems provide the intelligence for American Express's knowledge highway, used to improve its customer credit management function. Swiss Bank, like many other financial institutions, uses expert systems to help decide what sort of mortgage, if any, is best for would-be clients. Whirlpool, the appliance manufacturer, installed intelligent systems in its customer service department to smooth the repair of appliances by ensuring that the repairman and the required parts arrive at the same place and time. Another Whirlpool system helps troubleshoot problems coming in by telephone, for an estimated saving of $4 to $6 million annually.[9] More detailed discussions of these types of applications follow.

Xerox Corporation and Financial Planning.   Computers have made financial planning much more flexible. Until two years ago, the seven-member sales forecasting team used a variety of methods to do their work, ranging from paper and pencil to computer spreadsheets. They started on the 1991 forecast in mid-1990. In 1992, they began using an expert system, which gave them the luxury of waiting until October to start on the 1993 plan. Now they're trading information electronically, instead of passing around pieces of graph paper.[8]

The new system lets Xerox project three years out whereas previously the forecast team could only manage the next twelve months. The system constantly analyzes actual results against the forecast, updating it. Further, the time saved allows the Xerox team to consider scenarios of how factors outside their own company might affect it, such as inflation or rivals' performances. Elsewhere in the company, expert systems give advice on marketing (how new products move versus older ones, how price reductions will impact sales, and how compensation changes can better motivate salespeople), and another estimates costs on piece-part manufacturing, for an estimated annual saving of $20 million.[8]

Frito-Lay and the Pax System.   In Perry, Georgia, Frito-Lay implemented Pax, the Packaging Application Expert. The system automates the production scheduling process for tortilla chips as they come out of the food processors for packaging. The volumes associated with this product are staggering: food processors produce 2,350 pounds of tortilla chips for packaging per hour; Frito-Lay has more than 400,000 distributors; consumers buy an average of 14 million bags of the chips each day.

Tortilla chips have a short shelf life, and the time it takes to get packages out the door, into trucks, and onto store shelves is critical. Demand, on the other hand, fluctuates. Consistency of the scheduling process provided by Pax lets Frito-Lay do logistical planning for the warehouse and trucks. It can now schedule seven days ahead instead of only twenty-four to forty-eight hours, which helps ensure timely delivery.[10] Before the Pax system, plant personnel spent a third of their time scheduling. Since Pax was introduced, they are able to review their schedule in minutes, leaving them more time to devote to the sales community and customer service.

Mrs. Fields Cookies.   Expert systems have proved to be a real time-saver for Mrs. Fields Cookies. District managers for Mrs. Fields used to take four to five hours weekly to gather all the numbers from a single cookie outlet. With ten stores in a typical district, that meant at least forty hours each week. Now, the company's central office gathers all the data, and district managers can spend more time at the stores. Randall Fields believes the highest and best use of technology is to get people dealing with people.[8] As a result, they are trying to eliminate many remaining paper functions.

Fields recognizes that computerization has cost top executives some power. Nevertheless, he applauds the power shift because the organization can respond in an instant. If a problem comes up, his people are probably starting to solve it about the same time as he's finding that a problem exists. Freedom from daily minutiae, Fields adds, could change the role of the chief financial officer (CFO), making it less tactical and more strategic.

American Express and the Knowledge Highway.   One of the most ambitious efforts to employ expert systems is in the credit-card operations of American Express.[9] The firm is building a knowledge highway in which computers assist AmEx customer service representatives with every step of managing credit, from card applications to collecting overdue accounts. The business goal is to use the system to shield both credit card holders and employees from the bureaucracy needed to manage American Express's vast business—and letting employees be free to devote their efforts to building relationships with customers.

American Express Company installed expert systems to help its legions of credit authorizers, who sit at computer terminals and decide whether to authorize a charge. That's a critical function at AmEx, which has no credit limit on its cards. Before using the new technology, an authorizer would look at as many as sixteen screens of data per customer before making a decision. Because the company felt this was cumbersome and because too many errors occurred, AmEx distilled the knowledge of its best authorizers into a program that speeds up and sharpens the process, and saves approximately $1.4 million per year.[8]

One recent addition to the knowledge highway helps with overdue accounts. It still leaves employees in charge of collection, but it protects them from error at every step. The system automatically pulls together all the information needed to analyze an account. Previously, analysts had to make twenty-two queries on the average—to computers spread across the company—each time they looked at a problem account. Now they typically make only one. The system keeps track of which state or national laws might affect the account. It helps to generate a collection letter. It files all the paperwork, and it automatically reminds the analyst if the account needs examining again.

As a result of this automated assistance, American Express is gradually changing the type of people it recruits to manage credit. Instead of hiring financial analysts, it is turning to those who know how to deal with people, and it is giving them more scope to use their skills. Previously, the sheer complexity of the work meant that jobs were narrowly defined to be manageable. With that complexity largely hidden, American Express believes it can define jobs more broadly—giving generalists more freedom to make their customers happy.

> *Information empowerment can (and eventually will) change task-time allocations, necessitating business process redesign and/or job redesign, and requires different skills for the staff. Internal power shifts will occur.*

Neural Networks

Neural networks are also receiving corporate attention. They seek to connect processing elements in different configurations to reproduce certain behavioral patterns. Modeled after the complex pathways of the human nervous system, such nets search for patterns in vast streams of data. In finance, for example, the software can search through information on how a certain bond has performed historically, then look at economic indicators plus the fluctuations of barometer bonds such as U.S. Treasury bills. Over time, it learns how different combinations are likely to affect each bond's value.[11]

Texaco.   Texaco uses neural networks for process control and oil exploration by which engineers and geophysicists trace oil deposits via seismic data. These explorations and the methodology used to support them have a direct impact on bottom line performance. Traditional methods are correct about 80 percent of the time. While the use of neural networks might only improve that number by 1 percent or 2 percent, each percentage point can mean millions of dollars to a company the size of Texaco.[10]

Shearson Lehman Brothers.   Shearson Lehman has been training its own neural net to help its traders forecast market patterns. The software incorporates a decade's worth of historical data. For three years, the program has managed its own small portfolio. Since the software can learn from its mistakes, it gets better over time. The first year, it lost money. It broke even in the second and showed a profit in the third, according to Stephen P. Gott, Lehman's chief technology officer.[11] The next challenge at Lehman is to get nets to understand the significance of news stories. Using an English language-recognition system, neural nets are being trained to read financial news stories and to decide how they affect different investments.

Chaos Theory

Chaos theory is a cutting-edge mathematical discipline aimed at making sense of the indescribable and at finding order among the seemingly random. Chaos theory rejects the traditional financial portfolio management theory that investors act rationally and that markets are efficient. In place of those ideas, it posits a more alluring idea: Investors can beat the market.

Chaos theorists maintain that things often seen as random are really following their own set of rules. One of these rules is that they are *feedback systems*—that is, what happened yesterday is having influence over today and, combined with what is happening today, will influence tomorrow. They are applying the same type of statistical stratagems developed to study social and natural sciences, principles used to gauge the timing of such natural events as overflowing rivers and sunspots. If the market is a feedback system, as chaos theorists maintain, then standard portfolio theory is wrong. Along with investors acting rationally in an efficient market, portfolio management holds that prices reflect all publicly available information, and a change in information causes any change in stock price. However, those supporting chaos theory say that investors interpret information haphazardly and irrationally. Some investment houses are beginning to build portfolio management programs around chaos theory. For example, F. Martin Koenig Advisors, a New Jersey money management consultant, uses chaos theory to construct matched portfolios of long and short positions, a market neutral strategy aimed at gaining a premium over the Treasury-bill rate of return.[12]

Chaos theory has yet to prove itself to the satisfaction of the people who really count—CFOs, corporate treasurers, and the trustees of pension funds. Because little real results are available at this writing, investment houses are understandably proceeding slowly. Fund trustees and managers are unwilling to sink money into chaos-based systems based on theories that they simply don't understand.

Fuzzy Logic

Fuzzy logic is another form of intelligent systems that allows users to build systems by degree instead of the traditional binary logic. Despite its name, fuzzy logic uses crisp mathematical methods to deal with approximations, such as most, many, few, and slightly, by assigning specific numbers to clusters of overlapping gradations or sets. Classical logic represents an attempt to formalize human reasoning and to make it more precise, whereas fuzzy logic accepts that most human reasoning is not precise and tries to conform to it. Lofti A. Zadeh, who developed the concept, says that rather than forcing people to adapt to the way computers work, it imbues products with machine IQ so they can better accommodate human foibles.[13] This technology is popular in Japan, and U.S. companies are beginning to follow suit.

For the Japanese, fuzzy logic has proved invaluable for getting products out faster. Software, typically the main bottleneck in any new-product project, no longer requires programmers to foresee all eventualities in excruciating detail. Instead, problem solutions require a few rules written in everyday terms. The Japanese have spent years developing products that rely on this branch of mathematics called fuzzy-set theory. With new fuzzy automatic transmissions, Japanese cars shift with unrivaled smoothness. Japanese brokers even use fuzzy logic in stock trading programs that outperform American-developed software.

The elevator-dispatch system introduced in the fall of 1992 by Otis Elevator Company using fuzzy logic is a direct response to its Japanese-based competition. Other American companies shift to this approach when they discover that fuzzy logic can sometimes produce better accuracy and reproducibility—and therefore quality—than traditional techniques. This is the reason behind Allen-Bradley Company's new fuzzy-logic controllers for shop floor manufacturing, and General Electric's introduction of fuzzy logic to regulate jet aircraft engines, to save water in home appliances, and to drive 200-ton rollers in steel mills.

A final reason for applying fuzzy logic is that it is often a faster way to achieve results. Ford Motor Company, for example, challenged an engineering team to apply fuzzy logic to controls that keep a car's engine idling smoothly under changing conditions, such as when the air-conditioning kicks in at a stoplight. A month later, the program was ready. With binary logic, another team took three months.[13]

> *Be on the lookout for theories existing in the social and natural sciences to migrate into daily business activities under the umbrella of intelligent technologies. They have the potential of being the force in enabling the next generation business products.*

Making Intelligent Technologies Work

In every case, the key to making these intelligent technologies work is to build them into the structure of the organization. American Express estimates that only 20 percent of the cost of its knowledge highway is due to the expert system—the remaining costs are due to the network and the integration of systems.[9] Only with a well-managed integration can companies redistribute work between people and machines.

EXECUTIVE INFORMATION SYSTEMS

During the 1980s, executive information systems (EIS) grew in popularity as executives wanted more information at their fingertips. In the 1990s, EIS is moving topdown as the demand for information access grows throughout organizations. EIS moves from the executive suite to professional offices as managers and other business professionals become empowered to take real-time management actions in response to changing market conditions.

Operations Management

Corporate and information systems managers build EIS applications to support several key management objectives in information-intensive organizations. EIS applications offer a tool for generating graphic reviews of company information and for e-mail access. An increasing number of executives and professionals are beginning to use their EIS applications to build *what if* analyses. They can use corporate information and spreadsheets, or financial modeling packages, for example, to evaluate the impact of pricing strategies.

The immediacy of EIS information is particularly important when used to view operational information. Operational information can lead to necessary and direct management intervention. For example, a quality control manager in a pharmaceutical company can continuously review results of product sampling and machine performance. The EIS helps spot trends requiring preventative maintenance or direct intervention.

For some organizations, the EIS becomes an integral part of ongoing operations. These EIS applications provide central control management capabilities for day-to-day operations. Highly stylized and color-enhanced displays alert systems managers to potential and actual problems in the network and suggest possible solutions. An international package delivery organization, like Federal Express or United Parcel Service (Chapter 2), for example, might use an EIS application to monitor air traffic patterns worldwide, diverting flights when necessary to maintain delivery schedules.

Quality

The American corporate drive for quality creates a new EIS application area. Statistical quality control procedures generate tremendous amounts of information—information requiring analysis. For example, a typical quality control application maintains databases on machinery production levels, product specification variances, and maintenance schedules.

Integrated with sophisticated statistical and reporting tools, EIS applications permit quality control managers to reduce quickly this huge volume of information. They can easily generate manageable reports highlighting current and potential problems in the production process. The drill-down capability inherent in most EIS applications allows management to determine underlying causes of quality control problems. Trend analysis uses time series data bases and analytical tools. It allows quality control managers to examine quality performance over time, ferreting out incidents of slow deterioration and increasing quality variance.

The potential for EIS applications is immense. Corporate data modeling and repositories, e-mail rationalization, and enterprisewide addressing are simplifying and magnifying the ability of users to extract information from corporate databases. Just as hundreds of failing banks discovered that assets have no real value unless they build corporate revenues, the same is true for EIS in business today. EIS applications offer the critically important capability of converting corporate information assets into bottom-line revenues by being expert systems for business managers. Its value comes not only in its use, but in its development, because the process of building and implementing an EIS teaches managers more about their organizations.[14]

SALES FORCE AUTOMATION

Consider the following:

- The average sales representative devotes nine to eleven minutes per day doing paperwork for each account he or she has. For some sales personnel, this can represent a full day of work each week.
- The average sales call in 1993 costs more than $200, triple the cost in 1975.
- CEOs named sales and marketing among their top concerns for reengineering business processes.

Given these escalating times, costs, and concerns, it is somewhat surprising to find that sales departments, which directly account for the revenues that drive so many companies, are among the last to receive enabling information technologies.[15] This is finally changing as difficult economic conditions force companies to reduce costs, optimize resources, and improve quality and service. Now companies are turning attention not only to sales but to related functions such as customer service. Sales force automation (SFA) includes automated sales support and the integration of sales data with other corporate information. SFA takes advantage of current computing trends, such as open systems, group collaboration, and portable computing, to keep sales people better informed than ever.

Virtual Sales Offices

Enthusiasm for SFA will spread as laggard companies come up against companies armed with a *virtual (anywhere, anytime) office.* The virtual office can be as simple as a portable computer, as long as it contains all the information and functions a sales representative needs inside or outside the office. Portable computers in this environment hold all customer account information, order forms, pricing information, electronic sales presentations, and e-mail access. A modem allows the representative to download or interact with information from the home office.

The concept of the virtual office allows sales representatives to function on a sales call as efficiently as if all their prospects had come to their office. Ultimately, such a properly planned and implemented system will generate more and higher quality sales calls. The anywhere, anytime office implies corporate integration, but corporate integration requires a large investment of hard and soft (time and resources) dollars. There are less expensive, less integrated approaches, but they may be insufficient when applied to a highly competitive situation.

An IDC survey asked sales representatives about their views of portable computers as a sales support tool. Forty-five percent indicated that portables enhance sales performance only if they are part of an automated and integrated sales automation effort. Integration becomes particularly important in a team selling environment. Notably, 40 percent agreed that even using portables as personal tools supporting daily sales-related activities would contribute to increased performance. Many companies choose to start at this personal level. However, it is important that they do not get caught in a dead-end strategy. As the system grows, back-end data servers and integration with other corporate information become more important. Portable computer users must adapt to such changes.

Integration With Other Information

The emphasis on teamwork and team selling, particularly among companies selling into large accounts, is increasing the interest in sales force automation. No matter what the composition of the team, integrating the sales information system with other information systems benefits the overall organization and enables individual sales representatives to simulate the shared-knowledge environment offered by team selling.

Currently, more than 75 percent of SFA systems in large companies integrate with order processing and general accounting systems.[15] Seventy percent of these large-company SFA systems integrate with customer service. Information systems, sales management, and sales representatives all agree that order processing, customer service, and price and specification data are the three most important areas for SFA integration.

Company Experience

FMC.   FMC Corporation is a $3.75-billion global producer of food machinery, chemicals, and defense equipment. Already skilled at producing high-quality, low-cost products, the company now wants to take advantage of emerging, worldwide markets while being its customers' best supplier.[16] To do that, FMC plans to supply the sales force with up-to-date information about the markets, the company's product lines, and product availability across its plants. This allows the sales force to access current information from 112 plants in 20 countries. In addition, sales representatives have tools to analyze available inventory, capacity, cost, and currency considerations to achieve the most favorable economics in delivering products to customers.

The need for SFA varies by company. The answer may be as simple as hooking sales into a corporate electronic messaging system, or as complicated as building a highly strategic sales system that integrates various departments across multinational companies.

Insurance Appraisers.   USAA offers insurance and investment services to its clients. It is the fifth-largest private automobile insurer and the fourth-largest homeowners' insurer in the United States, owning and managing $32 billion in assets. In the late 1980s, USAA began using mobile communications and computing to support its auto appraisers/adjusters. It found that the faster the adjuster appeared on the scene, assessed the damage, and issued a settlement check, the less expensive the cost of the claim, the happier the customer, and the more productive the appraiser. The support for the adjusters includes standard laptop computers, cellular telephones, and portable printers.

> *Intelligent technologies are exciting and sometimes even esoteric. However, management, marketing, production—indeed, all functions of the enterprise—can benefit from information empowerment, and it doesn't necessarily require a high-tech base.*

KNOWING WHAT TO KNOW

The challenge for many organizations today is to become information literate. Most organizations and many executives are computer literate, but few are information literate. They know how to get data, but most still have to learn how to use it effectively to turn it into information that enhances knowledge and action. The basic business value that information technology contributes from this point forward is to empower its users.

Integrating Technologies To Reduce Time and Paperwork

Keeping on top of paper-based information can be a nightmare that may seriously delay a new project's development due to time lost locating information and keeping up with design changes. Problems with the development of the M-1 tank prompted the U.S. Department of Defense to decide in 1985 that all new weapon systems designs are digital.[17] The decision is likely to have implications that go beyond the military sector.

Building a modern weapon system presents a challenge familiar to most commercial manufacturers. It involves correlating hundreds of thousands of physical parts, units of information, and pieces of paper to build specialized equipment in the quickest and most efficient way and to control the materials needed for its construction.

In 1992, a contract awarded to Computer Sciences Corporation (CSC) for the Joint Computer-Aided Acquisition and Logistic Support (J-Cals) links 245 military sites across the United States. The system enables the Defense Department to build, maintain, and support weapon systems without the traditional paper tools like technical manuals and engineering drawings. J-Cals has the following features:[17]

- It establishes a global data management system. It can access data from different islands of automation via a global data dictionary and make it available to engineers, designers, and other staff concurrently.
- It establishes a management system that allocates the tools required to perform a function and works out priorities in a paperless environment.
- It establishes and manages acquisition, bringing together all the data for bidding and purchasing.
- It establishes a single source of technical information, ensuring that everyone has access to changes.
- It establishes logistic support, a process of describing what happens to a part during its lifetime, thus enabling a logistics analyst to decide how to set priorities.

J-Cals blends a number of separate information technologies—computer-aided design and manufacturing (CAD/CAM), data compression, optical character recognition, imaging, distributed databases, graphics, and a global data dictionary. By the end of 1992, CSC had already interfaced and linked forty-two separate software systems packages to provide the integrated environment necessary for J-Cals. Because the Defense Department plans to require its 300,000 contractors to deliver their technical data in a format with J-Cals, the spin-off for the commercial and industrial sector could be enormous. For every dollar spent on conforming to J-Cals by contractors, there could be a return of five or six to one, and even more if the contractors combine implementation with a reengineering of the production process.

American Airlines and InterAAct

Max Hopper, senior vice president for information systems (I/S) at American Airlines and vice chairman of AMR Information Services, believes the heart of information empowerment is new thinking about how technology can free people to spend more time on real work, which he defines as devising new ways to do a better job than your competitor in marketing, serving the customer, and allocating resources intelligently.[2] In a widely quoted article in the *Harvard Business Review*, Hopper detailed the guiding principles behind AMR's $150 million project to build an I/T platform that will give every one of its employees access to the entire system through easy-to-use workstations. Although Hopper concedes that he doesn't know how the platform, called InterAAct, will change the airline's organizational structure and work practices over the next five years, he guarantees major changes.

In 1987, the airline launched a study called "Introspect," bringing in an outside consultant to help it explore how it could become more efficient. At the same time, the I/S group had initiated some requirements studies in the office automation area. Although American put a great deal of time and money into its SABRE reservation system and into its flight operating system, both real-time systems, it invested little effort in support of back-office automation. The studies identified three areas requiring attention. It needed a comprehensive effort to develop better office systems, a method to find and extract data from all its databases, and the ability to upload/download data to/from these databases.

In mid-1987 to 1988, it undertook an in-depth study of seven headquarters and field departments. The study team, made up of user representatives from each of the seven departments, I/S, and outside facilitators interviewed department members, getting their input about what they would like, what would help, and what would make them more efficient. By having the users involved from the very beginning of the study, they bought into the whole process and the need for it.

At the time, American was a distributed paper environment where computer information frequently was hand carried or shipped through company mail and then reentered on another PC—sometimes with a time lapse of as much as eight weeks. The studies indicated that the AMR dependence on distributed paper reports hindered its ability to focus on problems and to make intelligent, informed business decisions. The ability to find data was a constant problem, so it needed a central library to define data and its location. The studies also indicated that any system selected had to be user-friendly—users wanted one easy-to-use workstation that allowed access to all the needed systems.

The user requirements forced a convergence of four technologies: data processing, personal computing, networking, and office automation. Up to this time, they had data processing in a mainframe environment; personal computers, mostly used for spreadsheets in the finance department; networking to support their on-line, real-time systems; and office automation, mostly limited to a group with PCs doing local text processing.

AMR elected to make the costly cultural change in an organization in which, despite its leadership position in reservation systems, many employees had never touched a PC. The conversion calls for every employee to have access to a powerful workstation. Ultimately, some 17,000 workstations will link through a technology platform built to support a vast array of applications as yet defined.

> *Don't erect artificial barriers in your thinking about information empowerment based upon current technology or software constraints. Technologies and software systems are constantly being combined, integrated, and deployed in new ways.*

EMPOWERING CORPORATIONS THROUGH INFORMATION PARTNERSHIPS

At a corporate level, forming information partnerships with other companies occurs through the sharing of customer data. American Airlines has, for example, allied with Citibank. Credit card users receive awards of air mileage credit in AAdvantage, the airline's frequent flyer program—one mile for every dollar spent on the card. American has increased the loyalty of its customers, and Citibank has gained access to a new, highly credit-worthy customer base for cross-marketing. Through information partnerships, diverse companies can offer novel incentives and services or participate in joint marketing programs. They can take advantage of new channels of distribution. Information partnerships, in short, provide a new basis for differentiation.

Konsynski and McFarlan suggest other advantages of information partnering, including lessening financial and technical exposure of the participating companies.[18] "Partnerships allow [companies] to share investments in hardware and software—and the . . . expense of learning how to use both . . . While there is no shortcut to learning, information partnerships provide a way to reduce risks in leading-edge technology investments." Four kinds of partnerships have emerged:

- Joint marketing partnerships offer companies the option to "coordinate with rivals where there is an advantage" to do so or to "specialize where specialization continues to make sense. The effort of IBM and Sears to market Prodigy is an example of this type of effort."
- Intraindustry partnerships occur among "small or midsize competitors who see an opportunity or need to pool resources. They collect capital and skills required to create a new technology infrastructure for an entire industry." An example of this is the ATM banking networks.
- Customer-supplier partnerships sometimes arise from "data networks set up by suppliers to service customers." An example of this is the Baxter Healthcare program (formerly American Hospital Supply, purchased by Baxter Travenol) that evolved and became a single platform for buyers to reach their many suppliers. Participating suppliers now reach new customers at lower costs. (A detailed discussion of this system is in the following chapter.)

- I/T vendor-driven partnerships occur when a technology vendor "brings technology to a new market and provides a platform for uninitiated industry participants to offer novel customer services." An example of this is the General Electric Information Services (GEIS) development of BIFAnet for the British International Freight Association, discussed in Chapter 2.

Information partnerships are an effective business strategy. Most successful information partnerships have a shared vision at the top, reciprocal skills in information technology, concrete plans for an early success, persistence in the development of usable information, coordination on business strategy, and an appropriate business architecture—the same things necessary for any effective business alliance. Konsynski and McFarlan also pose the following questions for the general manager:

- Competitive vulnerability: "Is your company vulnerable to a new information partnering? . . . Are there ways to forge alliances of your own to preempt them?" Timing is everything—start too soon and your partners may get into technical trouble, but start too late and the window of opportunity closes.
- Business strategy implications: "Does your business strategy realistically assess the implications of the transfer of power and authority to partners?" The same issues that surround strategic alliances—acting as equals, negotiate decision-making, trust, maintainence of flexibility—apply here.
- Financial vulnerability: "Are your potential partners financially viable? . . . Do they represent the right collection of players for potential synergy?"
- Technical infrastructure: "Is the technical infrastructure you have in place the right one to . . . manage the kinds of strategic alliances that you are considering?"

Unless there is a positive response to each of these questions, there isn't sufficient synergy to make a contemplated strategic information partnership or alliance successful.

Is your information worthy of becoming an alliance asset?

OBSERVATIONS

Knowledge worker is a vague term, but it generally means pricing analysts, marketing strategists and planners, and product-line managers, people who are really running the business. What knowledge workers need is an easy-to-use environment with access to information, collaborators, and partners both inside and outside the organization. To empower them, we must help them work with others, and we must train our users to become information-literate.[2] To do this, John Rymer, former managing editor of *Computing Decisions,* suggests some reality filters to apply before setting priorities and making decisions about information empowerment. They include the following:[19]

- The state of the networking infrastructure: In most cases it won't be adequate for empowerment goals.
- The state of the user base and environment: Consider the investment in the user environments when relying on any new technology. Critical issues for the user base include user by-in to the plan and sufficient user education and support for any new technologies and applications. How can they move into a world where they must exercise control and initiative over their environments?
- The state of the current critical information applications: Are they modular enough to grow? Are they accessible and compatible? Are they rugged enough to maintain high integrity with high usage?
- The state of in-house development resources: They will require retraining.

These filters focus on the technology aspects of empowerment. We observed in this chapter that although technology is important, the much harder issues are of an organizational nature. They require consideration because they are often the greatest contribution to success or failure—and the most difficult to manage. These include:

- The leadership culture: Do the executives perpetuate a command and control culture while espousing empowerment for others?
- The political culture: Does the CIO have the political power to bring it off?
- The organizational motive: Is the reason for the interest in empowerment due to competitive necessity or nicety?

A flood of recent business literature discusses new organizational models and empowering employees. Empowerment, simply stated, means that employees receive an increasing responsibility and authority to make decisions to resolve problems as they occur. Empowerment, as it relates to business process redesign, occurs most often in the arena of the employee-customer interface. There, the employees are trying to improve customer service and are the most knowledgeable of the customer relationship.

However, there is something else involved: the employee-customer interface has historically been the most data-rich, because of billing and service agreements. In the case of American Express, credit authorizers know what information they need and use for better decision-making, which makes their information empowerment relatively straightforward. In the case of American Airlines, it is moving out of the stage of gathering data into a stage in which it becomes critical to create information from the data that it already has, again a focus on empowering the employee through improved information.

What isn't obvious is the type, quality, and time frame of information necessary for improved decision-making in other, data-poor organizational activities because there isn't a history of data and information captured and used for decision-making. Executives, sales, and field workers are often the last to receive attention from I/T, due in part to the legacy of the hierarchical organizational model in which production and accounting provided the greatest financial leverage. Nor does a history exist of the data and information necessary to build and sustain a learning organization. Yet this is really what information empowerment and empowering the user is all about. We need to assist the business and its I/T users in defining and creating quality information. Only then can we discover the knowledge necessary to make business more vital as it proceeds into the twenty-first century. While intelligent systems and other information empowerment initiatives are still a long way from dominating the strategic arena, they are one more potential solution to ease the recessionary, competitive, and global pressures on today's corporations.

Information empowers. Concomitant with empowerment is the responsibility for taking action.

4

Networked Enterprises

Increasingly, I/T is revolutionizing not just the internal structures and control systems of the enterprise, but, through business network linkages, the shape and nature of long-standing external constituency relationships, particularly as distribution channels undergo radical shifts. Computers and communications networks can change supplier-buyer relationships by eliminating intermediaries and inefficient supply chains, as, for example, when customers use on-line services for airline and hotel reservations instead of travel agents, or when businesses direct customers to predesignated service providers in the insurance and health care industries.

The goal of the transformed or renaissance enterprise is increasing competitiveness in an economy that places a premium on quality, added value, and responsiveness. Effectiveness depends on the twin foundations of, first, an assessment of all existing and potential relationships the company is party to and second, the ability to efficiently capture, manipulate, and exchange information pertaining to those relationships.[1] In Chapter 3 we spoke of information empowerment and of the importance of linking internal functions. Here, we focus on the business network linkages that change the shape and nature of external relationships. The building of links and services to customers and suppliers beyond the enterprise walls has accelerated with advances in technology. These linkages may be the source of a variety of benefits, including:

- Faster response time to customer inquiries and service problems: Implementing customer hot lines is a simple, effective way of reaching a vast number of consumers, particularly when the people that answer the hot line calls have the necessary information at their fingertips. More sophisticated information exchanges are those in which equipment such as elevators link back to the computer-based central diagnostic and service facilities of the manufacturer, enhancing the service relationship between manufacturer and consumer.

• Reduced operating costs and less investment in inventories and facilities: Baxter Healthcare and its development of just-in-time inventory and distribution techniques, an example of which is given in this chapter, uses linkages to other enterprises to help its hospital customers reduce operating costs while at the same time increasing sales for Baxter.

• Creation of services that change the nature of a product: Railroads, by tailoring their schedules and type of equipment to the individual customer, move from being a transportation utility to a custom transporter.

• Creation of cross-industry alliances and joint programs to provide competitive advantage: The cross-marketing program between Citibank and American Airlines AAdvantage frequent flyer program illustrates this possibility. Another example is the BIFAnet, an industry consisting of a number of small companies who could not individually afford the technology, but together could access state-of-the-art technology and be competitive with other larger continental-based European Union enterprises.

• Creation of virtual workgroups and organizations to provide solutions to specific problems: Boeing, discussed later in this chapter, used virtual workgroups and organizations composed of manufacturing partners and customer partners during the design of the Boeing 777, accomplishing its strategy to become more customer-driven.

In Chapter 2, we observed that groupware and e-mail helped facilitate virtual workgroups within enterprises. *Virtual organizations* create new linkages that tend to facilitate corporate strategy. People join teams to work on specific projects regardless of their physical location or organizational/enterprise membership, and once the project reaches completion, the team disbands. The same electronic tools of groupware and e-mail, when used in combination with electronic messaging (electronic mail, facsimile, and electronic data exchange) make possible *virtual enterprises,* changing the landscape of competition and traditional supplier-vendor relationships.

NETWORKS AND ELECTRONIC MESSAGING

Enterprises, in an attempt to become more competitive, are breaking down the walls that separate its own operations from those of its business units, customers, and trading partners. What manufacturers need is the ability to view—as a whole—all the operations that can service the same customers, supply multiple facilities, and be jointly managed for greater profitability. They need access to timely, synchronized data on customer demand, inventory, and capacity levels. They need costs and profitability measures in all the business units deemed part of the enterprise.[2]

For a business to survive, it must transcend time zones, geography, language, and even cultural habits. If the 1980s introduced us to the Japanese brand of just-in-time manufacturing as a strategic business weapon, then the 1990s will show the greater value of just-in-time information. Access to all kinds of information—voice, text, data, image, etc.—becomes increasingly vital to business survival. This is especially true in today's high-speed environment, in which transactions between enterprise networks occur in seconds and key decisions in minutes.

Everyone seems to have their own definition of what a network is and how it operates. In some companies, networks imply a set of external relationships, a global web of alliances and joint ventures. In others, networks mean informal ties among managers—floating teams that work across functions and maneuver through bureaucracy. Still other companies define networks as new ways for executives to share information, using management information systems, videoconferencing, and other such tools.

For some companies, network design builds the central competitive advantage of the 1990s—superior execution in a volatile environment. Ram Charan, in his *Harvard Business Review* article, suggests that for these companies, "no traditional corporate structure, regardless of how [uncluttered or] delayered, can muster the speed, flexibility, and focus that success today demands.[3] Networks are faster, smarter, and more flexible than reorganizations or downsizings." Too often, the reorganizations and downsizings turn out to be "dislocating steps that cause confusion, sap emotional energy, and fail to produce sustainable results."

In this decade of flatter, more decentralized organizations, electronic messaging technology delivers the information when, where, and how it's needed. Messaging cuts across all organizational levels, shortening the line of command as well as the psychological distance between top management and staff. As a result, increased responsiveness to the issue at hand contributes directly to the sharpening of a business's global competitive edge. Businesses are finding that the savings in time and labor are well worth the investment in electronic messaging, while others find that freedom from geographic and time constraints are crucial for competing in global markets. Today's progressive companies use electronic messaging to keep in touch with employees, customers, and vendors, overcoming the barriers of time and distance and enhancing business relationships.

Using messaging to augment and complement voice conversations improves partner relationships and reduces the time and cost of making decisions. Petrochemical companies rely on electronic messaging because of the inherent interdependency of their business—one company alone has 28,000 corporate users that communicate with 12 million electronic mailboxes worldwide.[4] For this company, there was never any question about extending its successful corporate messaging system to the outside, the problem was how to implement it to better serve customers and suppliers.

Electronic messaging is a natural extension of available computer and communication technology. E-mail, initially embedded in some office automation packages designed for internal one-to-one communications, has become a powerful external communication tool as well. Customers, suppliers, and business partners can share and manage information, whatever its form. The various components of electronic messaging—electronic mail (e-mail), facsimile (fax), electronic data interchange (EDI), and telex—provide the flexibility needed in the physical network for conducting truly global business, however, the exploitation of the capabilities of the physical network requires an effective business network.

BUSINESS NETWORK REDESIGN

Most business process redesign discussions and activities focus almost exclusively on improving the firm's internal operations. Although internal efficiency and effectiveness are important objectives, business network redesign—reconceptualizing the role of the firm and its key business processes and practices in the larger business network—is of greater strategic importance.

From the perspective of customers, an external supply network, or key trading partners, the danger in concentrating wholly on the internal processes is simply that business process redesign may have little or no measurable impact on the firm's external market performance. Worse, in some cases, the internally focused redesigns may allocate scarce resources away from company initiatives that could directly affect its external customers. Insofar as many companies still tend to use I/T to automate existing processes rather than to redesign them, investments in I/T have yielded lackluster results. Ultimately, what distinguishes improvements in the efficiency and effectiveness of internal operations from a broader rethinking of the firm's internal processes and external relationships with different markets, trading partners, customers, and suppliers is what Hamel and Prahalad call *strategic intent.*[5] They point out that strategic intent is more about outpacing competitors in building new advantages than about seeking competitive advantages that are inherently stable. The traditional view of strategy focuses on the degree of fit between existing resources and current opportunities, whereas strategic intent creates an extreme misfit between resources and ambitions—thus challenging the organization to close the gap by systematically building new advantages. This is a major element of strategic transformation.

It is fashionable to refer to EDI as an attractive source of strategic advantage, and for many, it is. Astute managers in these organizations recognize that I/T offers the vehicle to redefine market boundaries, alter fundamental rules and basis of competition, redefine business scope, and provide a new set of competitive weapons. Yet gaining strategic advantage with I/T implies a giant leap for most organizations, and, alone, may not prove sustainable.

Changing an Industry

Hospital Supply.   The Baxter Travenol system, ASAP, evolved over decades to become a single platform for buyers (the hospitals) to reach their many suppliers. The system, which traces back to 1957, helped propel American Hospital Supply Corporation (AHSC)—now Baxter Healthcare—from its early 1960s market position as a medium-size, regional supplier of generic hospital supplies to Baxter's current position as market leader in this health care market segment. Short and Venkatraman studied the history of Baxter's system to analyze the interrelationship between business process redesign—the company's actions to restructure internal operations to improve product distribution and delivery performance to the hospitals—and the corresponding reconfiguration of the product and services provided by the major players constituting the larger business network.[6] Their conclusions were twofold. First, a distinctive characteristic of this case was the ability of Baxter to proactively make the virtually hundreds of small, incremental redesigns of internal work processes and information technology necessary to improve its overall service level and business relationships with customers. Second, Baxter could reconceptualize its primary business relationship with hospitals as the market began to move away from purely product/price-based exchange (a rational supplier), to become a value-added partner with a changed business scope.

In 1988, Baxter launched ValueLink for its largest customers. ValueLink is a just-in-time package of services that uses EDI as its backbone, developed in response to customer demand and increasing competition. When rival systems began carrying multiple vendor products, Baxter did the same. It began just-in-time delivery to the points of consumption in the hospitals. While ASAP (it's original system) is batch-oriented and offers the entire range of Baxter products, ValueLink customers send in orders from a set list of supplies several times a day for immediate fulfillment, seven days a week, twenty-four hours a day. Baxter employees no longer drop off their cartons at the loading dock—they move down hospital corridors from nursing stations to operating theaters to stock supply closets themselves. Baxter now has more than eighty distribution centers in the United States and uses its own warehouse and delivery staff to supply hospitals on a daily basis. This led to a just-in-time, or stockless, environment, reducing the need for personnel and storage space at hospitals.

The company makes more than 120,000 health care products, from surgical gowns and syringes to kidney dialysis machines, and the Baxter product line accounts for nearly two-thirds of all products used by hospitals. Baxter established a series of strategic alliances to enhance its abilities to address hospital needs it can't satisfy directly. Examples include an alliance with Kraft General Foods to supplement its own dietary offerings and another alliance with Waste Management to dispose of the hospital's used supplies. In the past, hospitals had arm's-length relationships with their suppliers to drive a hard bargain. Today, many hospitals seek out primary vendors for long-term relationships that can address quality and service concerns as well as costs.

ValueLink represented the first industry move towards bringing quality services to the hospitals at reduced cost. The medical center support service at Vanderbilt University Medical Center in Nashville was one of ValueLink's early adopters. For Vanderbilt, ValueLink simplified its materials management operations. Instead of 2,700 separate contracts for products, nearly everything funneled through ValueLink, and by making the medical center's storeroom unnecessary, Vanderbilt had the option of converting the space into a neurodiagnostic clinic. However, even ignoring the potential revenue generation, ValueLink enabled Vanderbilt to eliminate the central supply facility, close the receiving dock, reduce inventory, and close the storeroom, saving about $1.6 million a year in inventory investments and personnel.

In retrospect, what was Baxter's winning formula? The first phase of the system included *local experimentation* to respond to market needs for efficient distribution with a computerized order-entry system and communication capabilities. Then, the business organization assimilation began, assimilating the system into the business strategy and leveraging it through aggressive penetration and diffusion into the hospital customer base. Competitive jockeying followed. Baxter and its competitors tried to control (limit) the electronic channels of distribution, while the hospitals wanted to move toward a multivendor, universal distribution system.

The characteristics of the second phase of the system involve *strategic transformation,* distinguished by a redefined relationship between Baxter and its customers. ASAP Express (1990) provides multivendor computer-assisted purchasing, with Baxter as the prime vendor. The competitive threat to Baxter's ASAP Express and ValueLink is the strong pressure to reduce the bias in multivendor systems for purely product-based exchanges and to move instead toward a common network infrastructure. Strategic transformation for Baxter involves a shift in business competencies and a shift in business network roles. Because the products ordered through the Baxter system are produced by over 400 manufacturers, Baxter must coordinate an integrated logistics system that synchronizes the flow of products and information between the hospital and provide multiple deliveries to point-of-use in the hospitals seven days a week.

Short and Venkatraman believe that this business program has the potential to re-shape traditional conceptualizations of control and coordination in customer-supplier relationships in areas such as purchase initiation, inventory control, monthly invoicing, and payment.[6] Their assessment was that Baxter shifted away from a focus on economies of scale (i.e., efficient, standardized, low-cost distribution) and toward economics of scope (i.e., customized, materials management services provided through a combination of product scope and information scope).

How would Baxter's competitors respond (Johnson & Johnson (J&J) and Abbott Laboratories, for example, who already have multiple vendors represented in its ordering systems)? Because ASAP and ValueLink now include J&J and Abbott products, how can they differentiate themselves from Baxter? Clearly, Baxter recognized the early signs of cost consciousness in hospitals and used just-in-time techniques for differentiation. Whether that competitive advantage is sustainable, considering the New Consumerism attitude shown by the hospitals in wanting a nonbiased all-vendor common network, provides the next competitive hurdle to sustaining advantage that Baxter needs to negotiate successfully.

Hospitals (the customers) wanted one system for ordering from multiple vendors, and, as a consequence, force its suppliers to differentiate themselves by providing timely information and product delivery (i.e., the economies of scope). Again, Baxter understood the customer message and supported the development of a standards-based on-line ordering system, OnCall EDI, developed by TSI International for the hospital industry. Suppliers adopting OnCall EDI include Baxter (medical supplies), Bergen Brunswig (drugs), Boise Cascade (office and paper products), and Eastman Kodak (medical imaging systems), with suppliers and hospitals sharing the costs of the software.

Migration from Baxter's proprietary ASAP and ValueLink to OnCall EDI will occur upon hospital initiation, and Baxter will gradually phase out its proprietary software and concentrate on the delivery of information and product. Here the competitive hurdle is to get the whole industry to agree on and use one vendor's software package.

There are at least two lessons an organization can learn from Baxter. First, what distinguishes many of the successes from the failures is the ability of an enterprise like Baxter to reconceptualize the role of the firm and its key business processes and practices in its larger business network in a coordinated, simultaneous reconceptualization. While business process redesign creates the necessary organizational capability to compete, business network redesign identifies the avenues to obtain new sources of competitive advantages in the marketplace. Second, reconceptualization becomes infinitely more difficult—and exponentially more urgent and risk-intensive—when the customer- or supplier-industry (in Baxter's case, hospitals as a part of the health care industry) is undergoing its own unparalleled transformational stress.

Evolving business strategies often require new or expanded business competencies. Are the necessary business competencies present in the current core competencies of the enterprise? If not, how will they be obtained, integrated, and managed in the new organization form?

Dispensing Drugs.   Marty Wygod decided to offer an alternative distribution system for prescription drugs. He believed that there could be a significant cost saving if medications were mailed from a central dispensary, eliminating the cost of the distributor who supplies the retail pharmacist and the retail drugstore's considerable overhead. He believed he would gain vast economies of scale by using computer technology to automate the dispensing process. Additionally, by linking with large health plans, Wygod could offer through the mail the drugs for chronic ailments like high blood pressure, accounting for 80 percent of prescription drug expenditures. This strategy fueled growth to five big, automated dispensaries and generated $300 million in revenues by 1987, amid constant outraged protests and lawsuits from retail druggists' trade associations, which claimed without success that sending drugs by mail across state lines was dangerous and illegal.[7] (Wygod's success spawned another prescription by mail business—the filling of disposable contact lens prescriptions.)

Publishing.   At a negligible cost and in the span of a few weeks, an entirely virtual global publishing network involving nearly 150 correspondents formed and produced the *Internet Society News*.[8] The Internet Society has 1,000 plus individual members and 24 corporate members. In 1994, Internet had over 770,000 computer hosts attached, with over 4 million users on 7,000 operational networks and 30,000 registered networks in 107 countries from Afghanistan to Zimbabwe. The 150 correspondents of the magazine are similarly dispersed, including one in Antarctica. Concept development, coordination, information transfer, and editing for the magazine was accomplished on Internet. Articles came by e-mail from around the world. A commercial printer completed the process. Such a (publishing) network in many respects equals the complexity of those of Reuters or *Time* magazine, so the ability to do this with relative ease across the entire globe is a profound statement.

Food Retailers.   The structure of the food retailing industry varies enormously across Europe and is largely a parochial affair. Domestic companies still dominate Europe's food retailing markets, with the possible exception of French hypermarkets in Spain. Northern Europe has a few, powerful grocery chains while the Southern sunbelt boasts highly fragmented regional industries. Although they have similar numbers of consumers, Italy has three times as many food retailing outlets as the United Kingdom, for example. Despite their differences, food retailers across Europe are facing many common challenges—a static and aging customer base, the increased internationalization of the supplier base, and, perhaps most important, increased demands for variety, quality, and choice.

Some observers believe recent technological developments have sufficiently broadened the scope of the traditionally defined grocery industry to force vast structural change across the European grocery trade. Andersen Consulting, after conducting a study of the European market, foresees a major change within the next five years in the way the grocery industry organizes itself.[9] They believe differences in distribution efficiency will mark national industries, with the implication that companies that develop a successful formula will be able to translate their success into foreign markets.

The ultimate dream for retailers is to develop a stockless distribution chain with suppliers that will give them enormous cost advantages by reducing the need for expensive storage space. The report by Andersen Consulting suggests that the two main routes to this are electronic point of sale (Epos), which scans the barcodes on all products sold and records supermarket sales patterns throughout the day, and EDI, which creates an information network between retailers and manufacturers, allowing both to align its operations more closely to sales patterns.

Some of the larger U.K. retailers that employ Epos have stopped direct manufacturer delivery to its stores and centralized their distribution functions. This process has reached the stage whereby Tesco, a large U.K. chain, opened a supermarket in Surrey with no warehouse space in the back. Instead, it receives its goods through a series of meticulously calculated daily deliveries. The Andersen report suggests that such companies have fully tackled only half of the distribution chain. The challenge in the 1990s will be to attack the manufacturing end through speedier exchange of sales information using EDI networks, as Tesco is doing. Tesco will not deal with suppliers who are not part of its new automated system for product ordering and payment, and it exchanges thirteen weeks-worth of sales forecasts with about a quarter of its 1,200 suppliers. To be effective, such partnerships require a high degree of transparency and trust. Retailers have to trust manufacturers with sensitive sales information and be confident of delivery to tight lead times, while manufacturers must open their operating procedures to the retailers' scrutiny.

If the two sides fail to establish such partnerships, alternative scenarios may emerge. For example, if food makers can adopt highly flexible manufacturing methods and create joint distribution networks with one another, entirely new retail channels, bypassing traditional supermarkets altogether, might be created. Stores may simply become compact idea centers where customers select what they want from a display of products and then later collect ready-packaged bundles of goods from a nearby distribution center. Another scenario is the economic feasibility of electronic home shopping and direct delivery.

Despite the problems, suppliers have little choice but to gear delivery to the customers' just-in-time schedules. In a recent study of European firms, McKinsey found that timely and reliable delivery was more important than service, price, or brand.[7] In a bid to cut costs, and perhaps to shift more of the burden of stock control on suppliers, many firms are demanding that deliveries be hyper-efficient. Suppliers to Sainsbury, Britain's biggest food retailer, have to specify when its trucks will arrive at the firm's depots to within an hour. Trucks that arrive even a few minutes late go to the back of the line or are refused. Because of its buying volume, 98 percent of the company's suppliers now meet Sainsbury's daily delivery commitments.[10]

This same approach is evident in European manufacturing also. 3M is adding staff and marketing its array of telecommunication and highway products in emerging markets such as Poland and the Soviet Confederation of Independent States. In Western Europe, 3M is sending $20 million to link its subsidiaries and customers together via computer so it can process orders more quickly.[11] It also plans to build or expand four larger, more efficient warehouses in Europe to replace seventeen mini-distribution centers.

Railroads.   Not so long ago, when Proctor & Gamble managers wanted to send its products to retailers, long-haul trucks were the only option if they wanted to guarantee prompt, damage-free delivery. Today, with improved service, freight is an option. After decades of losing business to trucks, barges, and other freight haulers, the U.S. rail carriers halted its long slide. It has cut inefficient capacity, closed down unprofitable lines, slashed the work force by half, and installed modern information technology to move trains on time.

Customized service is becoming the norm for prized shippers. Burlington Northern (BN), for example, runs a special train from Boise Cascade's mills in International Falls, Minnesota, to St. Paul, carrying paper that then gets transferred to other BN points. To lure that business away from truckers, BN acquired new flatcars and set up computer links with the company, so each now knows what is moving, and where and when it's going. As a result, on-time performance has hit 95 percent.[12]

Better yet, rail carriers embrace quality service. Carriers are managing railcars to suit shippers and offering on-time delivery good enough to mesh with just-in-time manufacturing processes. Railroads are able to tell customers not only when the cargo will arrive but also where it is at any point in transit. Because the nation's rail network is regional, with each region dominated by one or two carriers, cooperation among railroads has become an imperative for quality service. Union Pacific (UP), acknowledged as the leader in computerized tracking and scheduling, routinely grants other carriers access to its computers so that they can seamlessly tie into UP's network when shipments pass from one line to the other. Parenthetically, the UP system was key to successfully rerouting rail traffic during the Midwest flood of 1993, covering an eight-state region, keeping the vast majority of rail delivery delays to under twenty-four hours.

The U.S. railroads have access to an EDI network (similar to the European BIFAnet) operated by Railinc, a subsidiary of the Association of American Railroads, which is an electronic clearinghouse serving some 175 railroads and 50 major shippers. A logical next step for the rail industry is to extend linkages to ocean carriers, thus providing for customers utilizing overseas transportation services. Ocean carriers already have an existing EDI network, OCEAN (the Ocean Carriers' Electronic Access Network). Developed by the same company that implemented OnCall EDI, it tracks at any moment some 500,000 containers on 300 ships worldwide, providing the information via EDI to the carriers' 100,000 customers directly.

Trucking and the Just-In-Time Movement.   When the whole business environment changes almost overnight, an enterprise must change with it or go out of business. For the U.S. trucking industry, the combination of deregulation and just-in-time inventory management was just such an event. The regulatory bureaucracy was no longer the center of its business processes, and its customers were switching to just-in-time inventory management. The big retailers and manufacturers that Schneider National served were resolutely slashing inventory costs by installing just-in-time delivery systems.[7] Without bulging warehouses, customers increasingly needed shipments *now.* In response, Schneider National executed a twofold strategy:

- It began a sweeping cultural revolution, replacing the company's regulated-utility mentality with an urgency to get things done. The organization became flatter and more democratic, calling all employees associates and removing status symbols such as reserved parking spaces. Drivers received a fifth paycheck each month, based solely on performance.
- It invested in the latest information technology, including a constantly updated computer system to keep track of equipment and to make the most efficient assignments of trucks and drivers. Far ahead of the rest of the industry, Schneider outfitted each truck with a computer and a rotating antenna, making sure it is on schedule. More importantly, when an order for a pickup comes in, dispatchers know where the closest trucks are and send the order by satellite direct to the driver's onboard terminal, complete with directions to the destination and information about what gate to use and what merchandise to collect—a system with similar characteristics to Federal Express and United Parcel Service.

This responsiveness is critical for a customer like PPG Industries, the glass, coatings and resins, and chemicals giant, which typically gets orders needing pickup that very day. Within fifteen to thirty minutes of sending an order into Schneider's computer, the PPG plant knows which trucks to expect and when. PPG believes that Schneider is more than leading edge. It believes the trucking company is setting the pace for the whole industry. Now that several competitors whose response to deregulation was merely an evolutionary adjustment of lowering rates have gone bankrupt, the survivors' trucks are adopting similar dispatch and tracking systems.

Consolidation and Synchronization of Delivery.   The previous industry discussions of railroads, ocean cargo carriers, and trucking revolve around the larger industry of transportation—a necessary element in the distribution chain of physical goods—where tracking systems became necessary for industry customers once they adopt just-in-time inventory practices. Additionally, we observed the impact of the evolving just-in-time practices of food retailers on its wholesale distributors and distribution systems. Industry solutions ranged from creating individual company tracking systems, as has rail, trucking, and courier delivery (UPS, Federal Express) in the United States, to mounting industrywide programs such as rail did in Europe via BIFAnet.

International air cargo opted for joint development of a solution.[13] Lufthansa is cooperating with the three other major scheduled global cargo carriers (Japan Airlines, Cathay Pacific, and Air France) to develop a joint, global information network that links many different systems. The first phase of this network, TRAXON, went online in August 1991 for booking, handling, and tracking airfreight contracts. A second form of cooperation is the building of information linkages with integrators (those companies specializing in delivering letters and small packages door-to-door around the world and having comprehensive organizations adapted to the requirements of the countries in which they operate.) Thus, Lufthansa, Japan Airlines, and the Japanese trading company Nissho Awai hold a 57.7 percent share in DHL International, the world's largest integrator. Cooperative effort also led Lufthansa specialists to develop a system for converting passenger aircraft into freighters, or back again, in less than an hour, avoiding the cost of separate passenger and cargo fleets.

The European trucking industry is taking still another tack—it is reconceptualizing its practices to create a distribution system of the future that provides just-in-time delivery to its customers, reduces traffic in already clogged city arteries, and reduces vehicle exhaust emissions. Currently, the French telephone company's 6 million Minitel terminals enable private users (companies or individuals) to place transportation orders on an electronic bulletin board. This allows truckers to achieve increased efficiencies through matching pickups and deliveries according to supply and demand on a particular route. However, even the Minitel system doesn't go far enough. The problem is that as more businesses adopt and increase dependence on just-in-time stock management, deliveries will increase as consignments become smaller, requiring a new approach in distribution. The new approach would have goods consolidated at distribution centers on the outskirts of cities and packaged into consignments for individual recipients using a standard EU goods module based upon International Standards Organization (ISO) standard pallets. Future trucks would be quiet (using a hybrid diesel-electric engine) and flexible enough to deliver standardized modules of goods to urban businesses at night, using unmanned automated reception and storage systems. The loading/unloading system would be capable of operating vertically and horizontally, and the trucks would have computers to perform the electronic paper work via EDI with the business's computer. The delivery trucks would complement larger trucks transporting goods throughout the European Union. This new distribution approach will significantly impact not only the truck manufacturers and the trucking industry but the businesses it serves.

In the United States, although both transportation and retail have EDI links with other industries, efforts to develop common EDI standards with each other are relatively new. The real requirement is to have the various manufacturing, transportation, and retail industries communicating electronically with each other, with truckers using technology to reduce the lead times on both pickup and deliveries. While the requirement is clear, the solution isn't, since it depends upon the definition of industry. The more broad the industry definition, the more difficult it is to develop a common standard.

Enabling a Virtual Enterprise: Logistics Providers

Third-party logistics providers are a fast-growing group of I/T-intensive firms whose activities enable virtual enterprises. In 1990, the U.S. market for logistics services totaled $8 billion; in 1994 it was $50 billion and is expected to be $100 billion by 2000. The industry does much more than fulfill outsourcing contracts.[13] Examples include:

- FedEx Logistic Services, which handles all U.S.-based telephone orders, packing, shipping, invoicing, and accounting for the House of Windsor Collection, a London-based catalog company. Executives from the House of Windsor Collection use data generated by FedEx Logistics as input to its strategic decisions involving marketing, merchandising, and finance in the United States.
- Rodeway Logistics Systems assembles customized computer systems for shipment from Rodeway warehouses.
- Turnstone (a subsidiary of Steelcase, Inc.) markets office furniture and products through catalogs designed and printed by a third party. Customers telephone orders to a telemarketing firm that transmits shipment data to warehouses operated by Excel Logistics, who ships the products.

These logistics providers represent new initiatives of transportation companies that enhanced their I/T capabilities to include global EDI networks, imaging and barcoding systems, and sophisticated inventory management systems. This also represents a successful new species of information systems designed to serve cross-functional teams and to provide an integrated solution to customer problems.

Defining an Industry: Commercial Airlines—
Transportation, Travel, or Entertainment?

In spring of 1992, American Airlines tried to simplify U.S. domestic air fares. The result of this strategic move by American was unprecedented in its effect on business travel, other airlines, and other seemingly unrelated industries.

Chronology.   On April 9, 1992, American Airlines lowered its unrestricted business coach fares an average of 38 percent, offered 49 percent discount fares with 21-day and 7-day advanced purchases, and cut the price of first-class fares 20 to 50 percent. American's intention was to simplify airfare structures—to have the structure stay in place and eliminate the hodgepodge of heavily discounted promotions in the industry, and, as the largest and most powerful U.S. carrier, essentially forced the industry to follow its lead in shrinking the fare structure.[14] Robert Crandall, as head of American, announced a plan to replace the industry's labyrinth of ever-changing fares with a set of only four fares per route. American itself was offering about 500,000 separate airfares ahead of the overhaul. Post-streamlining, this shrunk to about 70,000—a significant cost saving which American estimated at $25 million a year in administrative costs.[15] Predictions were that the simplified system, with sharply lower full-coach fares, would boost travel and revenues.[16] The result was that instead of establishing pricing discipline, the airline set off a free-for-all. Weaker carriers, such as Trans World Airlines, operating under protection from competitors, started undercutting American's fares immediately, and major carriers came under intense pressure to restore corporate discounts to high-volume corporate customers.

Fallout.   On April 20, American scrapped its 21-day advanced purchase discounts in favor of a 14-day version and trimmed the earlier business fare discounts an additional 10 to 20 percent. In addition, the company reduced fares in about 400 mostly Southwest markets to match discounts of America West Airlines and cut fares from 214 Northeast and Midwest cities to Florida, matching USAir.[14] These cuts were in response to discounts offered by Trans World Airlines. When those cuts expired on May 20 and American raised fares 10 to 25 percent in many domestic markets, industry observers thought the last of the summer cuts had disappeared, but they were wrong. One week later the airline cut prices 50 percent on most domestic flights in short-term promotion and temporarily scrapped the 14-day advance fare in favor of the 7-day version. The largest carriers immediately matched American. However, within days, financially troubled carriers like TWA, USAir, and Continental were again undercutting fares.[17]

The consumer rush for half-price airline tickets produced unprecedented network traffic and processing delays for the nation's airline reservation systems. Travel agents reported slowed response time from reservation computers and downed links on American Airlines' SABRE and United Airlines Covia reservations systems. The central computers were running at full capacity, and SABRE exceeded the previous record of 3,100 transactions per second, according to an American spokeswoman.[18]

Meanwhile, Continental Airlines saw American's move as another example of irrational pricing intended to generate bookings at any cost. Nevertheless, Continental said it would match Northwest's move, although it was still studying American's fare structure. (Northwest had countered American's price cuts with a "Grownups Fly Free" program, also designed to spur sluggish leisure traffic.) Some carriers—including the three airlines then in bankruptcy court (Trans World Airlines, America West, and Continental)—may never recover from the discounting.

By June 15, Northwest and Continental filed suit against American, charging the carrier with predatory pricing tactics.[19] American denied the allegations and filed a lawsuit of its own in Chicago seeking to have its pricing tactics declared proper. In a related action, America West asked a federal bankruptcy court in Phoenix to order that the lawsuit filed by American be thrown out of court. Stockholders of America West, which reorganized under Chapter 11 bankruptcy guidelines, earlier filed a motion against American claiming that the pricing tactics would severely impair America West's ability to emerge from bankruptcy court. Carl Icahn, CEO of financially faltering TWA, accused American Airlines CEO Robert Crandall, whose price changes triggered this round of fare reductions, of trying to put him out of business. Crandall denied any such attempt, and said that TWA, Continental, and American West were already out of business—though the bankruptcy courts continue to allow them to operate.[20]

Travel agents were the hardest-hit victims of fare wars. Harried agents exchanged higher-priced tickets for lower-priced ones, reducing their own commissions in the process. Uniglobe planned to send American Airlines a bill for more than $500,000, reflecting revenue Uniglobe lost by exchanging previously issued American tickets for the newly discounted tickets. As a goodwill gesture, Delta Air Lines and Northwest announced a reimbursement plan for angry travel agents who lost money on refunds.

Industry Benefits.   Activity increased in a number of other companies. Anheuser-Busch produced 30 million extra bags of its Eagle peanuts for airlines to use during in-flight drink service. When American announced its new 50 percent-off summer fares on May 27, 1992, four of the top five days for long-distance calls logged by AT&T immediately followed: May 28 (160 million calls), June 1 (177 million calls), June 2 (171 million calls), and June 3 (165 million calls). AT&T's previous record for the number of long-distance calls was December 2, 1991, the Monday after Thanksgiving when most people made safe arrival calls after the Thanksgiving holiday.[21]

Hotels, resorts, and car-rental agencies saw an unprecedented surge in bookings from customers who wouldn't have traveled without the cut-rate airfares that took effect the end of May. Prompted by the cut-rate fares, demand for hotel rooms grew twice as much as had been expected for the summer, growing by 4 to 5 percent instead of 2 to 3 percent.[22] Avis, a leading car-rental agency, set a record for reservations on June 1, taking 100,738 bookings, about 10,000 more than the previous record. Hertz had record books, too. Car-rental reservations on May 30 and 31 were double that of a year earlier. The company had to hire additional reservation agents and work them overtime to handle the load. A company representative said that it always hit a peak going into the summer, but that this was like a high tide with a tidal wave hitting on top. It added 30,000 cars to its fleet.

The ripple effect of airfare discounts boosted attendance at amusement parks and business at restaurants. In Florida, Disney World and its resorts had a record volume of calls for that time of the year. Marriott mentioned the cut-rate airfares in its advertising featuring its own summer rates, and reservation inquiries tripled; bookings at

Holiday Inn rose by 20 percent over the previous week; and Ax'ent, a manufacturer of terrycloth bathrobes for hotels, received substantial new orders from hotel chains.

> *If you define your industry and operating environment too narrowly, you may not see opportunity in time to prepare for, and exploit, it. Defined too broadly, you may lose market focus.*

Revolution on the Runway: The Story of Boeing

A cultural revolution occurred at Boeing. In the past, Boeing felt it knew what was best for its airline customers. Now, for the first time in its seventy-five-year history, the world's leading manufacturer of commercial jets implemented a fundamental change in the way it conducts business. It adopted a more open stance towards the outside world and encouraged airlines, suppliers, and subcontractors to participate actively in the design of its 777 widebody twin engine jet. Boeing talks openly of forging close ties, including equity partnerships, with other companies. The reasons for the change are the huge investments necessary to launch new programs and the market risks that are forcing companies to pool resources. This new attitude reflects both the conditions of the civil aviation market, which still struggles to recover from the worst slump since World War II, and the changing nature of the competition facing Boeing.[23]

Boeing 777.   The strategy of openness, reflecting the marketing and financial demands of airline customers, is most evident with the $5 billion Boeing 777 program. The real difference is the direct involvement of airline customers right at the start of the design of the aircraft. Boeing formed 235 design/build teams grouping together designers and maintenance engineers, suppliers of components, and subcontractors together with Boeing designers and engineers. These teams use powerful computers that enable them to share their designs through a common database. International partners can therefore communicate directly from their headquarters.

Boeing, pushed by competitive Airbus to develop a technically advanced aircraft, is state of the art. The Boeing 777 is the company's first plane designed and pre-assembled digitally, entirely on computers. The three-dimensional digital design system comes with its own computer-generated human model who crawls into the images on the screen to show how difficult it would be for a real person to reach the problem area and make a repair.[24] The system enables Boeing to skip usual paper drawings and full-scale mock-ups, going straight from computer images to building the actual airliner.

The company is introducing more electronics in the 777 than it has ever done on a new aircraft.[23] Boeing is using computer-based training methods to prepare pilots and maintenance engineers. The cockpit has new electronics and liquid-crystal displays that lead the pilot through flight checklists and that carry written messages to and from the airport controllers if the voice channels get crowded.

The biggest group of outsiders at the Boeing plant working on the 777 in Renton are the emissaries of a consortium made up of Fuji Heavy Industries, Kawasaki Heavy

Industries, and Mitsubishi Heavy Industries. Back in Japan, they link directly into the digital design system in Renton. The consortium members in Japan will build the fuselage in sections and ship them to the Boeing plant in Everett for final assembly.

The design teams and computers are not to speed delivery of the 777—the time from first contract to first arrival of the plane will be about fifty-five months, compared with fifty months for the 767. Instead, they are to make a better plane from the outset. By putting in effort and money up front, Boeing hopes to make a plane that is really ready for service when it's delivered. In the past, planes came from Boeing's design engineers. This time the design process reflects the views of the airlines that will fly the planes, the mechanics who will maintain them, and the many others who will help build, price, and market them.

One of the things Boeing is trying to do is to meet customer requirements. This collaborative approach aims at building what Boeing calls a consumer-driven service-ready aircraft. Airlines such as British Airways, All Nippon Airways, and United Airlines, all participated in the final design. The airlines welcomed the change because it helps them to introduce specific improvements—such as the fitting of new overhead luggage bins and better-designed cabin lighting systems—more quickly. It produced the first airliner designed specifically to be reconfigured. (Moving galleys and lavatories to create one, two, or three cabin classes takes only a matter of hours.) Boeing also wants to reduce to a minimum any changes due to design problems during the production of the aircraft and after delivery.

Boeing Jumbo.   Just when Boeing starts delivering the first 328-seat 777 widebody jets to customers in 1995, it launches an even more expensive program to develop its new jumbo aircraft. That aircraft is likely to cost even more than the 777 and will inevitably force Boeing to accelerate its open door strategy.

Boeing offered the Japanese firms of Mitsubishi Heavy Industries, Kawasaki Heavy Industries, and Fuji Heavy Industries, already participating in Boeing's 777, a bigger role in its super-jumbo program. This expanded role makes the Japanese risk-sharing partners in the project. Because the biggest demand for such an aircraft will come from the fast-growing Asia-Pacific air transport market, it makes it all the more attractive for Japanese and other Asian manufacturers to participate in the studies and development of a super jumbo.

It also asked Deutsche Aerospace and British Aerospace—two of the four European Airbus partners—to study the development of a super jumbo. Airbus has been one of the most effective European tie-ups in the sense that it broke America's dominance of the civil-aircraft market. While Boeing has just over half of the market, Airbus has about 25 percent, overtaking McDonnell Douglas.[25] Although Airbus officials sought to play down the implications of the Boeing move at the time, the outcome of any agreement will have an impact on the European aircraft industry. It could lead to a radical realignment of the entire commercial aerospace sector.[26] Boeing timed its super-jumbo move carefully, taking advantage of a moment when moves towards greater European political and economic unity were under strain and the European aerospace industry was undergoing a new restructuring phase. That two of the four

Airbus partners even considered collaboration with Boeing is a sign of the fragility of the Airbus partnership and the press of globalization.

With the prospect of one global consortium monopolizing the production of a future big aircraft, both U.S. and EU antitrust rules are sure to come into play, as are Boeing's strategies to reduce its hierarchy, adopt just-in-time inventory practices, encourage innovation and efficiency, and adopt a greater customer focus. For Boeing, survival as the industry leader will hinge on the ability to absorb and thrive with such change.

DIVERSITY OF CHANGE

Companies look, feel, and act differently when they reconceptualize their business. In our examples, the supplier-customer relationship illustrates the diversity of change that can occur.

- Baxter Healthcare rethought the problems of its customers—the hospitals—and now provides just-in-time inventory delivered to point of use for products from Baxter and other manufacturers ranging from dietary supplies to waste management, shifting its strategy from one of focusing on economies of scale to economies of scope, and its competitive advantage shifts from that of developing proprietary software to that of managing information and product delivery.
- Food retailers in Europe are the engines of change in food distribution. Retailers demand just-in-time deliveries from suppliers to eliminate local warehousing and are investigating alternatives for product delivery to its consuming public.
- Railroads embraced the concept of quality, customized service, and industry cooperation by sharing freight movement information, and are able to ensure on-time delivery for just-in-time manufacturing clients. Truckers faced similar problems after deregulation. This eliminated the central focus of one core competency (based upon regulatory expertise) at the same time that customers demanded just-in-time service, requiring a different set of core competencies.
- Pharmacies and their distribution channels, taken together with the rising costs of health care, drove the reconceptualization of dispensing prescription drugs to a new distribution channel—mail-order.
- Publishing created a virtual global network of correspondents to produce the *Internet Society News*. Perhaps this publishing example will accelerate the reconceptualization of how magazines and books are written, edited, published, and distributed.

The final two enterprise examples are American Airlines and Boeing Airplane Company. The airline is interesting from the perspective of the actions of one airline and how it affects its own industry and those outside the airline transportation industry. The Boeing example is probably the most thought provoking of all. The Boeing state-of-the-art technology, its use of strategic alliances, and its use of on-line systems to link all manufacturers of subassemblies throughout the world, brings home the need for a consistent view of the new rules of global competition.

MANAGERIAL THEMES

Warren McFarlan, on the Harvard Business School MIS faculty, suggests consideration of a number of broad managerial themes.[27] One of the most important is to know your enterprise and what drives the profits in your market segments. Being in the top tier of the industry is far different from being in the bottom. Viable and profitable approaches for American Airlines are far different from a company operating under U.S. Chapter 11 Bankruptcy Regulations. The top companies may be able to develop software and services that dramatically alter and disrupt the channels of distribution. American and the impact of its SABRE reservation system on travel agencies, and its EasySABRE, which allows customers to make their reservations directly into the system, significantly affect the previously normal channels of distribution. The reason why this was a successful move by American was that the customer-supplier relationship—the airline-travel agency relationship—is very information-intensive and the transactions occur frequently.

Planning ahead is also critical. In the early 1970s, many regional airlines had the opportunity to join consortia to fund and develop airline reservation systems. Because existing industry regulatory structures, like our trucking example, had been in place and working for over twenty years, the management then had no experience base to even consider what might happen if deregulation occurred. Nor was it popular to use any formal scenario-planning techniques to even question the basic assumptions of planning.

Business leaders must consider the strengths of consortia for any industrywide development activities. The banking industry considered this approach for ATM implementation, but didn't use it. BIFAnet and the strengths of its European railway consortia demonstrate the benefits this approach brings to all the participants. These joint development efforts benefit all participants, and any common development neutralizes competitive differentiation.

Consider nontraditional alliances and competitors. Explore nontraditional alliances and look for nontraditional competition. The nontraditional alliance of Citibank Visa cards and the American Airlines AAdvantage Program provide unique benefits to both. The General Motors Credit Card that credits a percentage of purchases charged toward the future purchase of a General Motors automobile provides competitive advantage in two arenas—the credit card business and the other automobile manufacturers.

Leaders must avoid short-term economies driving long-term strategic planning. Transformation is all about investing in ways to improve long-term competitive agility. This means looking at the assumptions behind all investment justification in the enterprise. Delaying until a pattern is clear before making a move may result in an impenetrable barrier for the enterprise. Only time will show whether Baxter is correct in abandoning proprietary software in favor of an industry-standard system.

Business must assess the critical skill set of the enterprise. Are the skills in-house to support this new initiative, or will it require outsourcing? Is there an out-sourcer that can create a competitive advantage for one enterprise and not pass it on to others in the same industry? McFarlan believes that increased success or expanded scope in this area may force a major rethinking of past technology strategy—and it can also force major rethinking of associated business strategies.[27] Coupled with the critical skill sets is the funding of pilot projects. Use test markets and pilot projects to try out service and ideas. The earlier the customer involvement, the better the results, and the earlier the enterprise will be able to test its own capabilities. Boeing, by pursuing its new design and development industry partnerships, is simultaneously strengthening supply chain relationships and building a better, more serviceable product.

Finally, it is imperative to understand marketing and purchasing management-orientation to external linkage thinking. I/T started out as an assist to the finance function and gradually moved into other areas of the firm—primarily engineering and production. Marketing and purchasing are not always the logical evolution of past I/T development trajectories, yet the key to success often lies in the practical creativity of these groups and their abilities to reconceptualize processes, products, and external relationships. Increasingly, I/T is revolutionizing not just the internal structures and control systems of the enterprise, but, through network linkages, the shape and nature of external constituency relationships.

OBSERVATIONS

Alvin Toffler, in *Future Shock*, points out that one of the most fundamental yet neglected relationships between knowledge and power in society is the link between how people organize their concepts and how they organize their institutions.[28] He observes that the way we organize knowledge frequently determines the way we organize people and institutions and vice versa. When knowledge was considered specialized and hierarchical, businesses were designed to be specialized and hierarchical. Once a bureaucratic organization of knowledge finds concrete expression in real-life institutions (corporations, schools, or governments), the political pressures, budgets, and other forces freeze the niches and channels into place. These then tend to freeze the organization of knowledge into place, obstructing the reconceptualizations that lead to radical discovery.

This is one of the real problems for today's enterprise—high-speed change requires equally high-speed decisions, but power struggles make bureaucracies notoriously slow. While the competitive environment requires constant innovation, change, renewal, agility, and transformation, bureaucratic power inhibits it and continues to try to impose corporate rules. Today, because environments and events are changing the world so rapidly, it's difficult to know in advance what information is necessary to solve future problems. That's why networks, matrix management, and information empowerment are so important, and why bureaucracies no longer work. Innovative solutions cross the boundaries of yesterday's bureaucracy and organizational lines. Baxter Healthcare crossed internal boundaries to change its internal warehousing and distribution system. It also crossed external boundaries to put its employees on customer sites and to facilitate the sales and distribution of other manufacturers' products.

There is mounting evidence that giant companies—the backbone of the mass production era—are too slow to adapt in today's business world. In many fields, the savings that sheer size once made possible are fading. New technologies make customization inexpensive, inventories small, and capital requirements low. With niche marketing supplanting mass marketing, and customized manufacturing rising to replace mass production in many industries, companies will de-mass. The decentralized business units forming today are probably just the beginning of the evolution towards some new type of organizational form. The French economist, Hubert Landier, uses the term *polycellular* to describe the business of the future, while others describe it as *neural* or *network-like*.[28]

The new enterprise must build around core competencies the enterprise possesses, in terms of people, processes, and products. These core competencies link to business and I/T strategy and customers in a network that informs, directs, supplies, serves, and provides new market indicators. Figure 4-1 illustrates the prototype network enterprise. Davidow and Malone, in thinking about the virtual corporation suggest that it is necessary to begin *thinking in reverse* to discover the essence of the new enterprise. Companies will have to begin with the customer and then determine how to structure the virtual company, where to locate it, and what direction to take for its product development.[29] This is why the prototype network enterprise has the customer and potential market as key elements in its network.

There is another problem, often overlooked, in piloting the enterprise through transformations, and that is the viability of the economic theory that has been the investment paradigm during the Industrial Age. Peter Drucker suggests that in today's economic theory, there is no room for factoring in technology and innovation—the two prime movers of today's global economy.[30] Any functioning economic theory of the future must integrate the macroeconomy of money, credit and interest rates, and the microeconomic decisions about how firms and individuals spend money, as well as the dynamics of entrepreneurship and innovation. He concludes that the new reality means we can no longer control the economic weather of recession and boom cycles, unemployment, savings and spending rates, but only the climate—avoiding protectionism or educating the working population to function in a knowledge society. In short, industry must practice preventive medicine instead of blind attempts at short-term fixes. This means that industry received a low return on its I/T investment when its use was to make the existing process faster, or when little time or effort investment focused on questioning and reconceptualizing the entire process. Speeding up the process doesn't address fundamental performance deficiencies nor does it address the new economic factors of innovation and information empowerment.

A new application of I/T doesn't assure innovation.

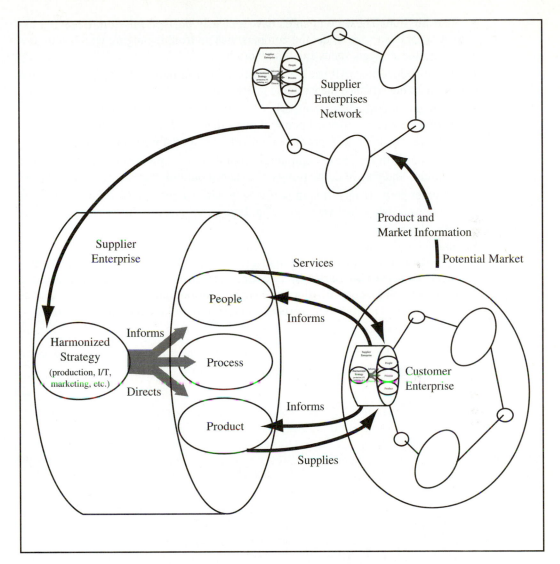

Figure 4-1   Prototype Network Enterprise.

After the companies described in this chapter adopted these new fundamental philosophies, their management fine-tuned and focused on developing the following attributes:

- Sensitive antennae: Revolutionary companies have extremely sensitive antennae for the technological or market forces that create change. It looks beyond what its customer says he wants today to what he will need tomorrow, and what technology will permit him to have.

- Clear mission: These companies have a clearly defined mission. Knowing exactly what it is trying to do, the company has no trouble judging which activities fit with the strategic focus and which don't.
- Disciplined I/T use: All use I/T extensively, but in highly disciplined ways that demonstrably advance the strategic goals.
- Organization embodies teamwork: The organization dedicates itself to accomplishing the sharply focused goals. It plays down bureaucracy and hierarchy and encourages teamwork. It promotes individual responsibility and enterprise.
- Corporate culture: These companies emphasize the importance of the culture: the values, the way of doing things, the shared outlook that enables it to achieve.
- Customer partnerships: It is in partnership with its customers. It knows the customers well, what they want and what their problems are. It stresses the importance of service.
- Challenging boundary assumptions: Baxter challenged assumptions about physical boundaries by placing and managing inventories on hospital sites. It challenged industry boundaries by adopting OnCall EDI. The food retailers like Tesco and Sainsbury challenge distribution boundaries, and the logistics providers cross multiple enterprise boundaries to provide integrated solutions.

Accepting and implementing these philosophies and attributes represent a challenge that will affect the professional and personal lives of everyone.

5

Mass Customization

Customers are demanding customized products and services at mass production prices. Tailoring products to individual consumers or groups of consumers requires new business paradigms *and* business cultures.

Generations of Americans learned to ride a bicycle on a Schwinn. The Chicago-based company, founded in 1895, lost touch with domestic trends and failed to enter the growing market for mountain bikes early enough. As a consequence, it saw its 1950s 25 percent share of the U.S. market plummet to less than 7 percent by 1992 and sought protection from bankruptcy under U.S. Chapter 11 regulations.

While Schwinn was suffering its business reversals, people began to talk about the National Bicycle Industrial Company, the subsidiary of Matsushita. Cited as a leader, it is one of the first to achieve the new (and to many, the impossible) manufacturing paradigm of building every product for the person buying it. At National Bicycle, the process starts with the customer being measured for the bike. The retailer sends to the factory via fax data on arm and leg length, foot size, body weight, and torso length, along with sex and type of bike wanted. Factory personnel enter the faxed data into a computer that produces the blueprint and bar coding to track the pieces. Robots measure each piece of the frame, weld the pieces together, and apply the base coat of paint. From there, skilled workers assemble the bicycle, including the final touch of silk screening the customer's name on the frame. Total time for assembly: three hours. Cost to the customer: $545 to $3,200, just a little over double the price of an off-the-shelf bike. With this personal production method, the customer can choose among 11,231,862 variations of his or her bicycle.[1]

What happened here? If National Bicycle represents success—the Japanese and the rest of the industrial world say it does—then what are the rules of this new game? New paradigms become necessary to make mass production profitable with a production run of one unit. The scientific historian Thomas Kuhn defined a paradigm as an accepted model or pattern that establishes an informational framework and set of rules by which its practitioners view the world.[2] Joel Barker took Kuhn's paradigm principles and applied it to the business world. He understood exactly what National Bicycle was doing. Barker, the consultant that put paradigm into every businessman's vocabulary, identifies *personalized production,* or *mass customization,* as a major paradigm shift in the mid-1990s.[3]

The mass producer must become market (customer)-driven. (This is one of the major revolutions discussed in Chapter 1.) Whether a service or a manufactured product for the customer, achieving some degree of personalization is key to success. How an enterprise begins the business changes necessary to deliver a personalized product via mass customization production techniques is the topic for discussion in this chapter.

MASS CUSTOMIZATION CONCEPTS

The concept of mass customization on a small scale has been around for decades. Who hasn't had a shirt monogrammed or stationery or business cards printed? Who doesn't know someone who went to Hong Kong and had a suit or a pair of shoes made and delivered almost overnight? The concept of mass customization of tailoring became so popular that many large communities (especially the New York and Los Angeles areas) have resident Hong Kong tailors that measure customers and fax the order back to Hong Kong, with a delivery date in the next calendar week. Customization, once a nicety of manufacturing and service offerings for the customer, shows increasing competitive strength. The rules or paradigms for successfully conducting business in this environment differ significantly than those of mass production.

Why Mass Customization?

Think about what happened to manufacturing. Originally, there was the craftsman who delivered one-of-a-kind, quality merchandise that was expensive. The process evolved into manufacturing, where the focus was on quality and repeatability. Next came mass production, where the focus was on low cost and low price, delivering standardized goods to the masses. Some products lost high quality. Others lost uniqueness. The real loss in this process was the skilled craftsman. As mass production reached its zenith, responsibilities shifted. The foreman or manager assumed the responsibility for the skills and knowledge to create the end product. What happened, in many cases was that when de-skilling by machinery occurred, including the application of some information technologies, the loss of the knowledge necessary to change and improve the product also occurred, and the process became inflexible.

This was precisely what the Japanese understood as they translated and projected the mass production principles into the twenty-first century. They understood about quality, and that the worker had to identify with the product to assure quality production. They understood about de-skilling. They knew that machines or robots could do repetitive or programmed things, but it took the skills and craftsmanship of the worker to create a truly quality product with associated processes that could continue to improve over time. The Japanese, with their competitive strategy of assuring market share at the cost of a high profit margin, and with their natural limits on population size and geographical area, needed to focus on a global market. This scale created the potential sales volume necessary to make mass niche markets profitable for them. More importantly, it created a new competitive environment that forced a global reevaluation of best practices for manufacturing.

Mass Customization Paradigms

Demand for many individual products fragmented and became unstable, creating markets that are increasingly heterogeneous. Because profits can't be maintained the old way, the choice—if one wishes to continue in business—is to provide the additional variety and customization desired. This leads to low-cost, high-quality, customized products not producible by the specialized techniques of mass production.

> *The new definition of success becomes the ability to accelerate production of an ever greater variety of customized products.*

When both production and product development time reduce in parallel, products become obsolete faster. Products are continually being improved upon and then replaced. This shortened product life cycle results in less demand for each product, however, it increases the stability of demand for the company and its products compared to its mass production system and its competitors.

There are two important things to notice about this newly defined scenario for success. First, the benefits of low prices due to economies of scale and other cost advantages of mass production are potentially eliminated. A company will be successful if it can retain as many advantages of mass production as possible, while providing the variety demanded by its customers. Second, the niche markets become smaller and smaller, reaching down closer to the individual.

The new paradigms for mass customization must be a synthesis of mass production and customization. At issue is the question of how an enterprise can effectively craft technologies to create new, more flexible processes. How can it apply the inherent flexibility and skills of its workers to quickly develop and manufacture new products—products that more closely match individual tastes? Stan Davis, who coined the term *mass customization,* says that the more a company can deliver customized goods on a mass basis, compared to its competition, the greater its competitive advantage.[4] The new manufacturing paradigms, suggest Garwood and Bane, are the following, with parallel paradigms for services:[5]

- Manufacture only as much as you need, not as much as you can.
- Customer requirements define the economic lot size. It's not what the supplier finds efficient to produce.
- Eliminate steps and move towards a more process-driven flow.
- Lead times are short.
- Measure productivity by total hours and total cost incurred, not by efficiency or utilization. Quality, flexibility, and being on time are meaningful measurements of performance.

This is a new world for manufacturers and service providers. Almost everything about it is substantially different, and it involves business process reengineering, business reorganization, new information systems, and new views of how to justify investments. Bottom line: It requires significant change throughout the enterprise.

MASS CUSTOMIZATION AS A BUSINESS STRATEGY

The market for mass customization is already here, and the growth of this concept is taking off. Davis suggests that this new segmented market is one of a series of niches, where each niche differentiates itself by a number of factors. For example, a market could be young single professionals and female managers within the upper-middle income bracket and living in Southwest Florida. Expanding this local market into a mass customized market becomes the next step. Mass customization of markets means that companies can reach the same large number of customers as in the mass markets of the industrial economy, and simultaneously it can treat them individually as in the customized markets of preindustrialized economies.[6]

Mass customized markets have no predetermined geographical size. What usually changes a geographically smaller market into a larger one (e.g., from a regional to a global market) is the action of a single, major player in an industry. The existence of a global market overcomes one of the traditional problems of mass production. Assumptions were that consumers wanted either low costs or high quality—and they occupied two ends of the customer spectrum, since mass production techniques can't serve both markets equally. Because of simplicity and efficiency, global mass customizers can be both high-quality and low-cost producers simultaneously. The most likely ways that enterprises will enter the arena of mass customization are through the following approaches:[7]

- Standardized products with customized services: The easiest path to mass customization is through already existing or new standardized products with customized services. IBM used this approach with its System/360 and 370 product lines by customizing marketing and support programs to customers' needs. Lockheed, for example, received specified on-site training and staff support during its early conversion and installation efforts for its first 370-based IMS applications.

- Customize through standardization: Use a standardization process to introduce mass customization in development and manufacturing. This is what IBM did with its System/360 and 370 lines. The architecture was modular (standardized) but the total configuration became customized for the individual customer.

- Create products that the customer can customize: The original conception or development of a product or service can allow the individual customer to customize the product. The original AT&T EasyReach 700 Service did this by allowing the individual customer to choose his or her own telephone number and deciding who will or will not get the privilege of reversing the charges. MCI, with its Friends and Family program, did it by allowing each customer to choose who will be in his or her circle of callers. Warner Custom Music accomplished it by offering to create customized cassettes of favorite songs from its inventory of over 1,000 recordings.

- Move final manufacturing function close to the end customer: Accomplish point-of-sale customization by moving the final manufacturing function close to the end customer. American Greetings' CreataCard kiosks accomplish this by moving the manufacturing function directly to the customer. The customer chooses the theme, design, and verse, or writes his own. The Hong Kong tailor does this by allowing the customer to feel the material and choose the style.

- Flexible manufacturing technologies: Manufacturing technologies that are flexible can produce a tremendous variety at relatively low cost. The National Bicycle Industrial Company is an excellent example of this approach. Over 11 million variations of the bicycle are in stock. A further personalization silk-screens the customer name on the frame.

Many industries have already taken the first steps toward mass customization by making it a part of its business strategy. In the following industry examples, we observe remarkably diverse approaches to facilitating mass customization.

Standardized Products With Customized Services

IBM Corporation.   One of the first truly mass customized products in industry may have been the IBM System/360, introduced in 1964. It is certainly one of the most visible and well-known products to have been mass customized. The IBM System/360 revolutionized the computer industry by providing an extremely broad range of computing power under one common modular computer architecture. From the user's standpoint, each System/360 was a completely standardized product. There were no special attachments or RPQ's (Request for Price Quotation) to deal with. They simply chose the capacity and features they knew they needed.

The IBM marketing force worked with specific individual customers or accounts. It helped customers identify their requirements and translate them into the technical building blocks of the System/360. Paper configurators for hardware systems assured that the building blocks would combine properly and create a correct order for each computer. By applying the same configurator approach, software defined allowable options for the operating system. After delivery of the computer, the customer would configure the operating system by doing a systems generation using a paper configurator to choose various options. Once the paper configuration was complete, the customer generated the customized operating system on the computer. Additionally, IBM staffed Field Systems Centers with highly competent technical personnel that helped customers operate systems generation and conversion programs.

Over time, a formal publication was available to assist operating systems configuration. More significantly, the development and availability to the field force of software written in APL, the System/360 Configurator assured correct configurations. A software configurator accompanied the announcement of the System/370. Whenever new (subsequent) models were announced, the configurator was updated. The configurator, which itself employed a modular architecture, was part of the field support system. The modular architecture of the product design combined with the availability of systems configurators significantly facilitated mass customization in the computer industry.

American Express.   American Express has an extraordinary ability to divine the preferences of its credit card members. It accomplishes this by surveying them relentlessly and by extensively refining and test marketing new ideas. It segments its card-carrying universe into groups based on income and lifestyle characteristics and then creates and markets unique services to each—limousine pickup at airports for platinum card members, extra travel insurance for security-conscious seniors, a special magazine for students.

Computers maintain and update weekly a profile of 450 attributes such as sex, age, and purchasing patterns on every cardholder. Careful targeting helps the company avoid mass solicitations. In this way, the company sends out information about home health care products only to people of a certain age and with a certain pattern of medical charges on their bill. AmEx uses its database to accomplish two forms of mass customization. First, it surveys its current subscribers to decide, by segment, what new services might be of interest; and second, it segments its products before solicitation by previous purchase patterns of the individual.[8]

Customize Through Standardization

Using standardized submodules to create unique combinations is another way to provide mass customized products to customers.

Gateway 2000.   At the other end of the computer spectrum, and thirty years later, is the phenomenon of ordering a personal computer (PC) by telephone and having it delivered by United Parcel Service (UPS). Companies like Pfitzer, General Motors, Time Warner, and Lockheed in the United States, and Alberta Government Telephone (AGT) in Canada, routinely use direct marketing houses to get PCs quickly and at a low price.[9]

Gateway 2000 shipped more than 250,000 personal computers in 1991, surpassing Dell Computer Corporation, the long-time mail leader. Major buyers place orders and check on their status electronically. Gateway began as a mass customizer, building each PC to order. With its success, it is turning to some mass production techniques—stockpiling common configurations for the largest customers—to speed shipment and improve service. This is an example of a company redefining its success paradigms to meet customer demands.

Syncordia.   British Telecommunications' subsidiary, Syncordia, competes in the European market with American electronics firms. Currently multinational firms spend approximately $2.8 billion for renting and managing telephone networks that cross country boarders. Traditionally, companies assembled the network themselves, coping with baffling regulations, a multitude of bills, and the ever-evolving tangle of technical standards. For a fee, Syncordia designs and delivers a reliable service from its own network, carrying both voice and data, offering a single bill in any major currency, all business activities supported by its sophisticated (and extensive) information systems.[10]

Create Products That the Customer Can Customize

Many service concerns view mass production techniques as keys to efficiency and growth (e.g., the assembly-line production systems in fast-food outlets). Others tailor new products to serve the individual customer. In the communications industry, CellularOne offers the ability to have a single, virtual telephone number that links up to four real numbers that an individual may possess and automatically forwards incoming calls in a predetermined sequence, for example, office, home, auto, weekend retreat. AT&T's EasyReach 700 Service and MCI's Friends and Family are also services based on demographic change and increasingly mobile customers.

AT&T EasyReach 700 Service.   AT&T offers a service by which subscribers can choose a 10-digit telephone number (which includes a 700-prefix) that can follow them for life.[11] The EasyReach 700 Service allows a subscriber to call a central AT&T number and, using a touch-tone telephone, tell a computer to route calls to another number. Family, friends, or business associates need only know the 700 number. The 700-number becomes a virtual telephone number, assignable to a telephone wherever the subscriber goes.

MCI Friends and Family.   In 1991, MCI unveiled its first Friends and Family program. At the end of its first year, it had approximately 7.5 million subscribers, 5 million new to MCI.[12] These customers call 25 percent more than they did before subscribing and are 20 percent less likely to drop MCI as their long-distance provider. The original program gave MCI customers a 20 percent bonus discount whenever they called the other MCI customers in their Calling Circle. These savings applied to up to twenty members, named by the subscriber to be a member of his or her circle. MCI, with this program, uncovered thousands of supersellers to persuade others to subscribe and join the circle.

AT&T couldn't duplicate the MCI offering because it relied on local telephone companies to calculate and collect its residential bills, so it didn't have access to a centralized database that records when one AT&T customer has called another one. It probably wouldn't want a similar program in any case, since it holds 62 percent of the residential market, and those customers are calling other AT&T customers an equivalent percentage of the time.[12] Discounting these calls would mean a large revenue hit. MCI, however, with its smaller residence share of the market, can discount calls to other MCI customers without such a large revenue penalty and by doing so, significantly increase its customer base.

In 1994, AT&T announced its True Savings calling plan, offering a 20 percent discount on all calls when the monthly total exceeded $25. MCI countered by announcing Friends and Family II, offering 20 percent discount on AT&T calls and a 40% discount on MCI calls to calling circle members. Again, both long distance carriers responded with plans reflecting its unique databases.

Move Final Manufacturing to the End Customer

Another industry, significantly less technology-based than computers, is beginning to adapt the paradigms of mass customization: the printing of business and greeting cards. Unlike the computer industry, the card industry is moving the manufacturing process itself into the marketplace.

Business Cards.   Card vending machines entered the European market in 1988. Over 4,000 vending machine blanketed Europe in the first two years. They are virtually everywhere—malls, department stores, train stations, and airports. The Auto-Print Instant Print Vending Machine was introduced in the United States in May of 1992. Using this machine, the customer designs his or her own card using a variety of logos and three different type faces. Here, the product is the equipment that allows the customer to design an appropriate card. Using the vending machine, the consumer manufactures the product.

Greeting Cards.   American Greetings is in a highly competitive business. Unit sales growth is 1 to 3 percent per year. It has successfully cut costs and improved customer service, so that it doesn't have to compete on price. It is targeting narrow customer segments, such as college students, while continuing to improve services to retailers. American Greetings' recently purchased Custom Expressions, a company that makes kiosks (the CreataCard) where consumers design and print their own cards in minutes. Because of its presumed appeal to nontraditional (male and teenage) card buyers, the company expects CreataCard to reach $500 million in annual revenues within the next ten years.[13] We find CreataCard kiosks next to many traditional greeting card displays as well as in other high-traffic locations like shopping malls and airports.

To keep ahead of competition, the firm has undergone major restructuring. The following moves were part of its restructuring activities:

- It introduced just-in-time processes in manufacturing and card development that reduced inventories and the time to bring cards to market.

- It launched a series of customer service programs to differentiate it from its competitors.
- It formed a new information services department to develop software that analyzes retailers' sales patterns and tracks inventories for many different products.
- It established a new retail creative service department to create seasonal displays throughout retail stores.

As a result, sales of American Greetings cards and related goods grew 10 percent in 1991, compared to its rival Hallmark, who reported a 1 percent increase in revenues of greeting cards and wrapping paper. Continuing emphasis on technology led (in 1994) to the formation of an interactive marketing division responsible for developing a new product line of electronic cards. Customers will be able to create and send these new customized greeting cards by using PCs in their homes.

American Greetings implemented mass customization by two means. First, it provided standardized products (the preprinted greeting cards) with customized services to the retailer through its customer service and creative service departments. Second, through the kiosk approach, it moved the final manufacturing function to the customer by providing the consumer the ability to customize the product.

The near-term threat to future success in this market comes from Hallmark and from Eastman Kodak's launch of its Creation Station. Hallmark entered the kiosk business in hopes of moving closer toward a just-in-time inventory policy that could reduce expenses involved in printing and shipping more than 11 million cards a day. Kodak's Creation Station will not only permit customers to personalize cards but has the added allure of using their own photographs. If retailers are willing to make room for only one or two such devices, it may force the companies to compete for space.

Create Flexible Manufacturing Technologies

Many existing manufacturing facilities and production methods, unable to satisfy global market needs, grow obsolete. Today's marketplace demands a form of manufacturing that is completely different from traditional batch manufacturing systems. Flexible manufacturing technology enables production systems that are capable of creating a wide product variety at prices that approach those of mass production.[14] Many manufacturers will install a sophisticated battery of machine tools called flexible manufacturing systems (FMS), which (in a single factory) turn out immense varieties of product with computer-controlled robots. All companies will have to rethink their information systems, methods of developing new products, and other techniques to respond to customers in a quick, versatile, and economic way.

Deloitte & Touche asked 900 U.S. and Japanese companies to describe their key manufacturing strategies.[15] The key findings were:

- The Japanese stress flexibility: While American manufacturers emphasize product quality—durability, conformance to specifications, and on-time delivery—

the Japanese take these as a given. They focus instead on more and better product features, flexible factories, lower prices, expanded customer service, and introduction of many new products.

- The Japanese rate themselves ahead in nearly all aspects of the game: This includes rapid changes in production methods and the number of new products they can create. This Japanese advantage will grow because they are about a third more likely than Americans to say that increased flexibility is an important part of future plans.

- The Japanese expect to stay ahead through advanced technology: From a list of thirty-eight technologies, Deloitte & Touche found six in which Americans claimed more expertise. Looking toward the future, Japanese companies are 25 percent more likely to emphasize leading-edge manufacturing and have bigger investment plans for thirty-three of forty-two advanced techniques.

Eventually, flexibility means dramatically changing one's ideas about how to run a business. Beyond mass and lean production beckons flexible and agile production. Flexible, agile factories are small and modular, and machinery is reprogrammable to make an almost infinite variety of new or customized goods at a low unit cost.[15] In an age of ever more demanding consumers, mass production no longer works. No one knows how much the Japanese are investing in flexibility, but an analysis by the Tokyo office of A. T. Kearney consulting firm shows that in one area—spending for information technology—three out of four manufacturers cited flexibility enhancement as one of its aims. I/T, in this role, would play a key part in supporting FMS and computer-integrated manufacturing. This was almost twice the number naming the next leading purpose of office automation.

One Japanese company with an emphasis on flexibility is Kao Corporation. Kao is Japan's biggest cosmetics and soap company and is the sixth largest in the world. The goal at Kao is to maximize the flexibility of the whole company's response to demand. The world-class flexibility of its distribution derives from an information system that allows the company and its wholly owned wholesalers to deliver goods within twenty-four hours to any of 280,000 shops, whose average order is for just 7 items.

One system links everything: sales and shipping, production and purchasing, accounting, research and development, marketing, hundreds of shopkeepers cash registers, and thousands of salesmen's handheld computers. Kao boasts that the information is so complete that its accountants can turn out a year-end closing statement by noon of the first day of the new year. Because of its network, it virtually eliminates the lag of an event—a sale—in the marketplace and the arrival of the news at the company. That makes Kao less dependent on sales forecasts and inventory buffers, both money savers.

Flexibility and Economics of Scope and Scale.   Flexibility comes when information feeds the ability to exploit it. A flexible factory is useless if the enterprise doesn't know what's selling, and it doesn't help to know what's going on in the market if the enterprise can't react to it by offering appropriate, timely products.

Investment in flexibility isn't inexpensive, but over time it can save money, something that is counterintuitive for managers who learned to seek economies of scale. Flexibility offers economies of scope, the ability to spread costs across many products. Scale will always matter, but economies of scope sometimes have superior power, because with customization comes unique products that can translate to monopoly-level prices.

In a flexible factory, scale and scope reinforce each other. Japanese automakers are rebuilding factories and systems to become even more versatile and labor-efficient—an effort that could again give them fundamental cost advantages and protect their lead in the time and cost of bringing new cars to market. Nissan describes its strategy as *five anys:* to make *anything* in *any volume anywhere* at *anytime* by *anybody.* As a major step toward accomplishing its strategy, Nissan uses the IBAS (Intelligent Body Assembly System). IBAS is a cluster of fifty-one robots that grasp body parts, line them up within 0.1 millimeter, weld, and inspect them all in forty-six seconds. The company is gearing up to fill market niches with more customized lines. Contrast this with U.S. automakers who contemplate dropping whole car lines.

Flexibility as a Strategy.   The Japanese lead in hardware for flexible manufacturing is, if anything, widening. Okuma Corporation, which makes the world's broadest machine-tool product line, sells fourteen flexible manufacturing systems in Japan for every one it exports to America. Though U.S. purchases of industrial robots are at record highs, Japan has already installed 390,000 to America's 45,000.[15] Unfortunately, having the right machinery available isn't enough. Harvard Business School professor Ramchandran Jaikumar reports that the typical American company with Flexible Manufacturing Systems (FMS) uses it to turn out ten different items, while the Japanese turned out ninety-three. George Stalk, of the Boston Consulting Group, finds the same thing. He observes that when a company spends $700,000 on a big machining center, the factory manager wants to get his utilization rate up so he uses it for his highest-volume products, defeating the purpose of the investment.

That wouldn't happen if U.S. companies saw flexibility as a strategic asset. Most don't. They have a specific project in mind, like a model change, rather than a plan to use robotics to make the whole process more flexible. Capital spending matters less when a factory can change its product line by upgrading and reprogramming existing equipment rather than by replacing it. A prime example of this is the 60 percent drop in the cost of tooling for a new model on Toyota's body assembly lines. The savings appear in lower prices or enhanced features, or can be directed upstream to research and development and downstream to customer service. Japanese manufacturers place more importance on flexibility by targeting product variety, innovation, and technological superiority than do American manufacturers, who are still catching up by emphasizing customer service and reliability. American companies must acknowledge that quality is just a start—the flexibility wars are coming.

Introduce Agility

The theory behind agility is simple. If a company can do all or most of the following, it will be more successful than its competitors:

- Quickly understand what's happening to the market.
- Manufacture many different products on the same line, or deliver many different services using the same staff.
- Switch from one (product or service) to another instantly and at low cost.
- Make as much profit on one product as the other.
- Bring out the new offerings faster than competitors.

Manufacturers and service companies alike must play the game to prosper.

Agile Manufacturing Systems.   Virtually every decision-maker in American business and government grew up believing in the magic of mass production. Mechanized assembly lines spewing streams of low-cost products were the cornerstone of the good life, perpetually generating wealth to support never-ending gains in the American standard of living. For most of the twentieth century, there was no reason to question this wisdom, and each passing decade etched the mass production ideal deeper into U.S. business culture.

Japan, forced to rebuild its industries from meager resources after World War II, rethought the process.[17] It quickly spotted the weakness—by investing huge sums in equipment to turn out enormous runs of the same product, Americans had made their factories inflexible, unresponsive monoliths. With so much capital invested in machinery, management became obsessed with keeping factories humming, even if it meant piling up inventory and parts. Japan's solution—lean production—was a shock to the U.S. manufacturer. Lacking capital, the Japanese began slashing the fat, starting with inventories of finished goods and continuing until they had created just-in-time manufacturing. By the 1970s, they were outperforming U.S. rivals.

Restoring U.S. manufacturing vigor won't come easily, but by rethinking the whole structure of the manufacturing enterprise, there's a chance that U.S. manufacturers can now leapfrog the Japanese system. The United States must rapidly move from mass production to a more agile form of manufacturing, encompassing a number of the concepts discussed in the previous chapters. This form of manufacturing represents a culture change and a new way of doing business. Unlike the mass producers of today, agile manufacturers will build-to-order highly customized reconfigurable products. Under this system an individualized car is upgradeable later when the driver wants to add new features; the price of a small batch of specialized semiconductors is the same as larger lots; or a computing and communications machine programmed to a user's specifications is in the shippers' hands twenty-four hours after the customer orders.

Such service will be possible thanks to highly flexible robotics assembly lines that will be quickly reprogrammable for new tasks. To speed production and aid cooperation, future factories will link by a broadband communications clearinghouse that enables them to locate suppliers and designers and to share information at a keystroke. The network will also facilitate the rapid formulation of virtual, networked companies—joint ventures among multiple corporate units working cooperatively together to seize a market opportunity. Decentralized management and self-managed work teams will be the rule, not the exception, and information will flow freely between research and development, shop floor, and boardroom.

What will the new system look like? The most likely model is agile manufacturing, first outlined in a study by Lehigh University's Iacocca Institute.[16] The age of agility synthesizes the best ideas that emerged from dozens of studies in the 1980s examining the decline of American industry. A blueprint for a fifteen-year plan creates a high-tech infrastructure that could get high-quality, low-cost products to market faster than the competition. It will involve harnessing key U.S. strengths, such as information technologies, and forging alliances among business, academe, and government.

Some American manufacturers are working hard to develop agility. Baxter Healthcare, introduced earlier, is testing an intravenous solution system that it can ship anywhere, assemble in a week, and move anytime. Baxter considers itself to be a leader in rapid prototyping. Using this technology, it makes working prototypes of complex medical instruments for its Belgian design center, shipping them twenty-four hours after it receives the initial specifications.[15] Another example is the prototype factory system developed by Textile Clothing Technology Corporation (TC)[2]. Information taken at point-of-sale (POS) terminals provide manufacturing instructions to computerized sewing machines and assembly line workstations. Within four hours of placing orders, customers receive one-of-a-kind garments, monogrammed to order.

Characteristics of Agile Manufacturers.   Elements of agile manufacturing already exist.[16] Robotics and expert systems are here, and plans for an industrial broadband network are being discussed by industry groups and by the Pentagon, which commissioned the Lehigh study. With the cultural changes that agile manufacturing demands, more electronics companies are joining forces in teaming arrangements not unlike the networked companies proposed in the report. Ultimately, agile manufacturers will share the following characteristics.

- They will link to each other through some kind of a national factory network.
- They will group as virtual companies to seize fast-moving market windows.
- They will deliver customized, upgradeable products.
- They will use easily reconfigured factory equipment and expert systems for fast turnaround.

Agile Manufacturing in Networked Corporations.   Concurrent engineering teams, such as Boeing used in the design of its 777, provide a precursor of virtual corporations by not only cutting across the usual vertical functions but by going beyond the bounds of one corporation to include strategic partners, such as suppliers of critical parts.[17]

Companies use multidisciplinary design and manufacturing teams to develop products that, in theory, meet customer and production requirements. The premise of this concurrent engineering is twofold.

- All sections of a company, and often its suppliers, work in teams to develop new products concurrently, rather than taking on each task in sequence.[18]
- A company that puts more effort into the concept phase of a design reduces the number of problems experienced later, after ordering expensive tooling, components, and equipment. The assumption is that these potential design, manufacturing, and material problems are identifiable early in the process. For many companies, this is still an act of faith—the risk is that lengthening the concept design phase doesn't reduce manufacturing problems, cost, or time-to-market.[19]

Like all techniques—total quality, just-in-time, and so on—badly implemented concurrent engineering will fail. Neither will isolated islands of technology help much. Successful implementation requires linkages between functions—design with manufacturing, purchasing with engineering, and so forth. For peak agility, advanced computer networks will serve as an infrastructure to connect essentially every factory, job shop, and industrial design studio, putting world-class expertise just a computer link away. Companies will concentrate their resources on a few strategic processes and turn to on-line partners for everything else. These electronic linkups would be so tight that a computer-aided design (CAD) system could drive factory tools in another company's factory located hundreds of miles away.[17] The ultimate permutation would be so-called virtual corporations: fluid, on-line partnerships that would be the antithesis of the rigid behemoths of the mass production age. Such ventures would assemble teams of best practice organizations from various companies and use the combined knowledge to speed families of high-quality, low-cost products to market.

Japan and the Three-Day Automobile.   Japan has a similar vision. There, researchers are working with the Japanese auto industry toward the long-term goal of a three-day car. Under this concept, cars are engineered around interchangeable modules: engines, transmissions, bodies, and the like, and consumers could create their dream cars by mixing and matching components. Yet, despite this unprecedented degree of choice, the delivery of the built-to-order car is within three days of ordering.

Along with improving time-to-market and delivery times, U.S. and European automobile manufacturers pursue other competitive edges, such as assuming cradle-to-grave responsibility for its creations. Building cars with easily recycled parts should answer environmental concerns—consumer concerns that will potentially become as important as quality.

Agile Manufacturing Pitfalls and Payoffs.   By 1993, only 40 percent of U.S. manufacturers linked electronically to its suppliers, despite the growing awareness that data sharing is critical to future agility.[16] AMIS (the Agile Manufacturing Information System) is a consortium of twenty-three U.S. manufacturers. They include users of I/T, vendors who provide the necessary technology, and systems integrators whose goals are to increase and coordinate the use of distributed data throughout the emerging manufacturing network. Members of AMIS believe the greatest improvement to future manufacturing will come from new information systems reflecting new manufacturing philosophies involving the adoption of new information systems architectures in place of hierarchical, vertical systems.

The biggest obstacle that agile manufacturing (the virtual corporation) and AMIS members face is the corporate culture—redefining management. The command and control hierarchy will disappear because hands-on supervision becomes nearly impossible as work spreads across corporate boundaries. For example, at the Power Systems Division of AT&T Microelectronics, multidisciplinary teams practicing concurrent engineering have totally replaced the usual departments, resulting in the trimming of management ranks by 40 percent and shrinking the time to develop a new product by 70 percent.

Concurrent engineering already offers a hint of what will follow with agile manufacturing. The biggest payoff is avoiding the rework that plagues over-the-wall engineering. Design itself may account for only 5 to 8 percent of product costs, but decisions made by designers lock in upward of 70 percent of total costs. When management doesn't learn until production is starting that a particular subassembly is too difficult to build, budgets and schedules become meaningless—costs can double and so can time-to-market. When agility expands nationwide, the fruits of cross-pollination and concurrent engineering will bring quantum gains in competitiveness. Using America's superior information infrastructure should yield improvements across the board—in time-to-market, quality, and cost.

Agility in Services

Corporate America needs information technologies that work. It needs systems that can help get closer to customers, create new products and services, and meet global competition.[20] As companies reduce payrolls, its PCs, networks, fax machines, and other information tools must improve productivity.

The dream of every marketer is to develop an interactive relationship with individual customers. Using I/T, companies can now keep track of customer preferences and tailor advertising and promotions to those needs. For example, when AT&T entered the credit card business in March 1990, it had a powerful advantage: it knew millions of its prospective customers by name and reputation because they were already direct-billing customers of AT&T. The results were impressive: Within three months there were over a million Universal Card holders who made more than $100 million in purchases.[21] AT&T was exploiting the freshest option available to marketing in the 1990s—the ability to address each customer personally—with information unique to his or her relationship with AT&T drawn from its on-line database.

The shift from broadcasting to directly addressing customers, according to Blattberg and Deighton, is a subtle change, but quite radical in its consequences for marketing practice.[21] They say that broadcast media currently targets its communications much as a battleship shells a distant island. The new marketing approach creates individual relationships, managing markets of one, and addresses each in terms of its stage of development. Addressability also changes the fundamental marketing rules. They suggest four major shifts:

- A database of transaction histories becomes the primary marketing resource of many firms, determining what kinds of products it can deliver, and what markets it can serve. Customers will shape the firms that serve them.
- Marketing becomes more accountable. New marketing efficiency measurements will relate to changes in the asset value of the firm's customer base, and the unit of measure becomes the lifetime value of each customer to the firm.
- The power of distributors erodes as manufacturers take back functions from other channel members and use information systems to administer them.
- Niches too small to be served profitably today become viable as marketing efficiency improves.

For firms like AT&T, L. L. Bean, and American Express, customer databases containing transaction histories are among its most valuable assets. Other types of service organizations also use frequent customer databases packed with customer preferences to provide better service and to target the marketing of new products.

American Airlines and Hilton Hotels.   Frequent flyer programs like American's AAdvantage Program track flight information, food and seating preferences, and provides upgrades to its best customers. Hilton and its HHonors Program track hotel stays and charges and provides upgrades to its frequent stayers.

Hyatt Hotels.   Hyatt expands this idea a bit farther by improving customer service by shortening or eliminating check-in lines. It lets guests check in by telephone. To do that, Hyatt needed a toll free operator center, datalinks to every Hyatt Hotel, and identical software in each hotel so operators wouldn't have to learn multiple systems. All of this information, now captured electronically, is a basis for building and expanding a marketing database. In 1994, Hyatt introduced—as another expansion of service to clients—the use of kiosks (ATM) check-in devices in its Atlanta and Chicago hotels.

Circuit City.   Circuit City, the home electronics and appliance retailer and one of the fastest growing chains in the United States, envisions computerized files that will contain a complete profile of each customer—the purchases, the charge-account status, the service record. If someone has a problem with a television bought from Circuit City, he calls the company's service representative. A computer screen will show the product's serial number and whether it's still under warranty. The system would then forward the information to a service technician, who could check what parts are necessary and whether they're in stock. The computer would identify Circuit City's best customers, the retail equivalent of frequent fliers, and give them priority service. All this is part of the retailers' effort to improve service while continuing to offer low prices.[22]

Continuous Internal Agility

The idea of maintaining a level of continuous agility for all internal operations is enormously appealing. It means that internal processes, practices, and people are flexible enough to weather any type of competitive challenge, anytime and anywhere. It also means that an organization can't count on anything or anyone being around for an extended time. This affects judgments on how enterprises invest time, money, and effort in its organizations. It discourages both short-term thinking and short-term investments. On the contrary, it mandates thinking about investments from the perspective of supporting long-term agility.

Berghaus and the European Market.   Berghaus has always been a pioneer. Its innovative technical designs and marketing make the 450-person company one of Europe's leading and most fashionable makers of outdoor clothing, including rucksacks, jackets, and trousers.[23] Over the last twenty years this British firm built thriving export businesses in Italy, Germany, Norway, Sweden, the Benelux countries, and Switzerland.

In 1987, it introduced (it thought) a faster and cheaper way of responding to orders from the 500 small family shops that constitute the fragmented Italian market. The company decided that the Italian market required a domestic staging post to hold stock and quickly turn it around. Berghaus exported in bulk, then repackaged in Italy for individual delivery. A vital part of this plan was a new computer system installed in Newcastle in 1989, capable of reserving and allocating stock several months in advance. A second vital element in the plan was a newly implemented two-year redesign and retooling of its manufacturing process, which shifted from mass production to flexible, short runs.

The computer software failed to function as expected, Europe experienced three mild winters in a row affecting sales, and the seemingly ideal location Berghaus chose in Italy, just south of the Swiss border, proved a disaster. The government-promised highway to the town remained unfinished, leaving only twisting local roads, and there were no computer links—a side-effect of Berghaus' U.K. computer problems combined with the Italian telephone system. To solve the distribution problems, it switched to an Italian company that carries out a similar service for the clothing chain Benetton.

The company next prepared to pioneer in a new direction by revolutionizing its relationship with retailers in continental Europe. Until recently, outdoor clothing retailers in continental Europe have mainly ordered stock and taken delivery in two busy seasons, with retailers holding the costly stock for up to six months. Berghaus announced a new rapid order and delivery system for continental Europe that allows retailers to cut stocks drastically. Its stock response system is a just-in-time supply relationship that shifts most of the stockholding risk, and much of the risk of demand forecasting, onto its suppliers and itself.

Christopher Lorenz, a leading business writer for the *Financial Times* observes that Berghaus, by no longer having future orders to rely upon, must forecast better, manufacture speculatively, and take risk on stock.[23] This will severely test its planning, manufacturing, supply, and distribution arrangements.

PUTTING THE "CUSTOM" BACK INTO CUSTOMER

American economic performance from 1970 to 1990 didn't fare too well in the global context. Productivity went down. Quality went down. Innovation slowed or stopped, and imports went up. One reason was that the market changed, and America's system of mass production in manufacturing didn't serve the needs of the changing market. While mass production achieves efficiency through stability and control, the market turbulence encompassed instability, uncertainty, and lack of control. Not a very good match between producer and consumer characteristics.

Another underlying reason for the economic stress was the growing structural shift away from a predominately manufacturing economy to one where service industries gain importance. Today, customers expect more from a product and supplier. Customers of service and manufacturing industries want personalized service, low cost, customized products, and speed-to-market. Customer demands are changing not once, but continuously, and competitors are responding to these new market demands.

The business organization necessary to support mass customization is different from what most of us know today. If a business is to become a successful niche marketer, it will have to expand its operations to a regional or global scale to achieve the volume necessary to create profits. It requires more flexible development, operations, marketing, and I/T support staffs. This staff must operate both synchronously to deliver and support new products, and independently to understand how any change in operations will change the interfaces with other functions within the business operations. At issue is how it responds to the new market demands.

Swiss Swatch

In the early 1980s, the Swiss watchmaking industry was in danger of obliteration by Japanese competition. At the time, conventional wisdom of the watchmaking industry was that Switzerland should retreat to the luxury end of the watch market. The Societe Suisse de Microelectronique et d'Horlogerie (SMH) is the result of a merger of two ailing Swiss watch firms in 1984. Nicolas Hayek became CEO of the new firm. Hayek proposed tackling the Japanese head-on in all segments of the market, including the low-cost end. He argued that a thriving industry needed a mass market to provide the impetus for cost control, technological development, and marketing. The banks (who were shareholders) wanted no part of his plans, so he—with a group of investors—bought out the banks' controlling shareholding in 1985, backing the development of the Swatch with his own money. In the most spectacular company turnaround in Swiss business history, profits soared, debts were erased, and, by sales dollar value, SMH watch sales were poised to overtake those of Seiko of Japan, the world leader in watch sales for the past decade.[24]

How did Hayek do it? He reconceptualized best practices for the watch industry. Swatch slashed the number of parts in a watch and developed a way of assembling them in one operation, allowing fully automated production for the first time in watchmaking. This made Swatches cheap to produce, even in high-cost Switzerland. Due to the high degree of automation, SMH keeps direct labor charges under 10 percent of total manufacturing expenses, in contrast to about 30 percent for most watch-making operations.

Swatch mixes the new automation and information technologies with dazzling designs and clever marketing to project a Swatch lifestyle—youthful, stylish, and provocative. As in couture, Swatch launches a limited collection of sixty stunning watch designs twice a year. Unlike couture, the Swatch combines low cost with Swiss quality and style. There are now close to 1,000 different kinds of Swatches, and roughly 125 new ones each year—the two collections of 60 each plus special, limited edition Swatches. Swatch doesn't repeat previous designs—once the production run is compete, it retires the design.

Early Swatches are now collectors' items, and avid collectors pay thousands of dollars for older models at auctions. In 1983, for example, SMH gave 200 Jelly Fish Swatches to journalists present at its first press conference, and in 1990 a Jelly Fish sold for $17,000. Contemporary Swatch variants like the chronograph are the object of a flourishing black market trade. Crowds gather at stores carrying Swatches at collection introduction time, and limited editions often sell out within hours. There are Swatch Collector Clubs with a worldwide membership of 100,000—10,000 in the United States—where members meet on weekends to display and trade Swatch models. Many members own over a hundred Swatches.

Sales of the basic Swatch remain steady over the years, with sales of its variations including the Pop Swatch, the Flik-Flak for children, and the higher priced chronograph and Scuba diving watches rising rapidly. A Swatch automatic, with a self-winding mechanism that needs no battery, was a 1992 innovation. Some designs were unsuccessful, but continuing innovation and strict cost control (the basic Swatch still sells for its original price of $35) have kept Swatch growing. In April 1992 the 100 millionth Swatch came off the production line, making it the biggest selling watch in history.

Hayek believes other, more dynamic markets are ripe for the Swatch formula—markets involving technological innovation combined with skillful design at competitive prices. Capitalizing on the company's experience with microelectronic and micromechanical devices, it launched the Swatchpager, a paging watch, in the United States in partnership with BellSouth.

The production and marketing skills developed during the Swatch turnaround have helped to revitalize SMH's higher-priced watch brands, including Omega, Longines, and Rado. SMH is now a world leader in luxury watches and generates about half of the company profits. (Sales of the Swatch represent about 25 percent of its profits and half of its unit output.) The company pursues an ambitious strategy of vertical integration, manufacturing its own components including state-of-the-art microchips and batteries. These and some 50 million watch movements sell for assembly by other manufacturers in Switzerland and elsewhere.

There is another, more revolutionary, example for the visionary company that reinvented the watch. SMH and Volkswagen initiated a joint venture in 1991 to develop, manufacture, and distribute the Swatchmobile. Although VW left the venture in 1993, SMH and Mercedes continue to work on the product. The Swatchmobile is an ecological car intended to exploit the huge potential market for nonpolluting vehicles. The rewards could be enormous for an automobile with the right price-performance combination, which has so far eluded the giant car makers. A prototype is under test, and the two companies are hoping to launch the car in 1996. Given the previous success of Hayek, the Swatchmobile may revolutionize the automobile industry. SMH has come up with new solutions to old problems by rethinking the automobile concept from scratch, just as it did with the Swatch.[25]

Swatch Lessons

What did Swatch do to become successful? It took the best paradigms from manufacturing and mass production, rethought the watchmaking industry, and created its own rules. It focused on producing a low-cost, low-priced product using economies of scale (mass production characteristics) and combined them with high quality and continuous technological improvement (automation and information technologies). It significantly reduced time-to-market, producing two limited collections each year, creating its own definition of mass customization and set of best practices. It continues to search for and define new niche markets, such as watches for children and scuba divers. It adopted vertical integration, developing and manufacturing its own components. More importantly, through short runs and limited editions of each watch design, each purchase signifies an expression of individuality by the consumer.

> Mass customization (personalized production) is the major paradigm shift for the mid-1990s and is highly technology-dependent. To be successful, it requires a total reconceptualization of business processes and products and its supporting I/T processes and products. These new business processes demand new best practices.

What does the future hold for SMH? The greatest near-term risk for SMH is its Swatchmobile. Its alliance with Mercedes allows that company to make better use of its excess capacities in production and engineering, while Hayak has expertise at taking a luxury product downscale while preserving its cachet. The strategic risks are whether there is a sufficient sustainable market for the small city car and whether the Swatchmobile can capture an adequate market share.

OBSERVATIONS

The world of mass customizing has some very practical applications, whether we are dealing with a product, a service, a market, or an organization. Both Berghaus and Swatch relied heavily on continuous technology developments to achieve its strategies of mass customization. In fact, one characteristic common to each example of successful mass customization is the continuing thread of the customization being technology-dependent. In *Future Perfect,* Davis observes that there are potentially five types of technologies that will be pivotal in future mass customization breakthroughs. They are holography, parallel processing, customized chips, biotechnology and genetic engineering, and customized catalysts.[26]

Holography.   Holography is an inexpensive and foolproof way to store, conceal, identify, and secure information. Some credit cards and passports use this technology today. Currency is the next likely candidate. Transparent instrument panels, connected to computers could display information so that it would appear to be floating in the windshield of a vehicle, and the driver or pilot would never have to look at the dashboard. Television screens could become three-dimensional holographic stereograms to complement the newer all-around sound systems.

Until some of these or similar products become mainstream, we can't assess the impact on businesses. Nonetheless, we can assume that any business organization, as it embraces this new technology, will change. For example, what would an organizational chart look like if expressed holographically, and what could consultants or managers inside the organization learn from it? The consecutive x-ray images made with a CAT scan and converted into three-dimensional holographic skeletons have become an important diagnostic tool in the medical profession. Similarly, could the application of holography become a major diagnostic tool for business and I/T professionals?

Massively Parallel Processing.   Computer processing makes a contextual shift when it changes from step-by-step sequential processing in a single computer to a simultaneous approach, where many processors handle different parts of the same job. This is parallel processing. As the ability to do faster and faster parallel processing grows, we gain the ability to solve more difficult problems. The financial industry was one of the first to pioneer the use of massively parallel processing (MPP) computing systems. It is using MPP to do complex financial analyses such as collateral mortgage-back obligations analytic applications for itself and its customers.

Today, however, we are still a serial problem-solving world. As new software and hardware become available, we will be able to solve new problems as well as reformulate old problems and come up with new solutions. IBM, Digital Equipment Corporation (DEC), NCR, and Cray Research are among the vendors who offer parallel processing products.[27]

Customized Chips.   Less than a decade ago, the PC was to many a state-of-the-art technology. Today, the PC is a commodity purchased by telephone or mail order. The next step is to mass customize computers-on-a-chip for large customers.

Customized chips represented only 12 percent of the market in 1985, but it doubled by 1990. To dominate the market would require only a small compounded growth. To customize chips, end-customer involvement is necessary. This creates a much stronger supplier-consumer relationship, similar to the relationship the American manufacturers had with its suppliers in the nineteenth century.

Biotechnology and Genetic Engineering. Computer modeling using holographic-like techniques shows researchers how a drug reacts with a body protein at the molecular level. This is the way drug companies can bioengineer new customized drugs. A decade ago, this was a research project at the IBM Scientific Center in Winchester, England. What will occur over the next decade? We may design molecules the same way that today we design automobiles, jet engines, and homes, resulting in customized molecules that are mass produced to fight and prevent disease.[28]

Customized Catalysts. To date, chemistry has been a science of discovery. Over the next decade it could become a science of design. Once scientists understand why catalysts takes place (perhaps using a combination of all four technologies just discussed), they can custom design catalysts to produce specific chemical products, just like the drug manufacturers and genetic engineers. For example, we might create whole new fuels and fibers using this process.

Technology plays a critical part in the mass customization process. As each new wave of technology enters the business world, change will occur. The technology, paired with the paradigm shift to mass customization, will create change in the business organization, the product, and the marketplace. As consumers, we embrace the process that provides the exact product we want. As providers of customized products and services, we are less enthusiastic since it requires radical business change on all fronts.

- Combining holography and geographical information services could create a whole new information industry based upon customized spatial database products.
- Parallel processing could provide the breakthrough necessary to reconceptualize the development of information systems.
- Customized chips could be the new delivery vehicle of mass customized application software to users.

These are all potential breakthroughs that will shape the future of I/T. Unfortunately, breakthroughs don't conform to a predetermined schedule—neither the new technology nor the innovative application of it that creates competitive advantage. The consequence to I/T? To stay competitive in today's environment requires an awareness of the possibilities and the organizational agility to change everything.

Part III

EMERGING VENUES FOR I/T LEADERSHIP

Building upon the market dynamics identified in Part I, businesses are beginning to identify new business paradigms that are necessary for the transformation to a new competitive form and focus. These paradigms involve a reconceptualization of the office, the individual's access to information and the power to use it, eliminating previous enterprise boundaries, and adopting the customer's view. The overarching strategies and initiatives that the individual enterprise invokes to accomplish these changes include:

- Standards, quality, and service (Chapter 6)
- Business process redesign (Chapter 7)
- Organizational redesign (Chapter 8)

These initiatives are translated at the individual enterprise level into strategies requiring innovative and diverse information technology participation and support.

What underlies each of these strategies and resulting initiatives is the issue of quality of results and the role of I/T.

Featured in Appendix I is "Value and Service in the Retailing Industry," which spotlights the Nordstrom organization and its emphasis on customer service.

6

Standards, Service, and Quality Initiatives

In today's harshly competitive global environment, conformance to standards and manufacturing and service excellence is not an obscure technical issue, but a matter of corporate survival. Worldwide, businesses are looking for ways to improve the quality of products and strengthen customer relationships. Product without service and value is no longer acceptable; and value is about real performance, informative advertising, and delivering on promises. To be successful, service organizations must learn to aim and hit a continually moving target. To achieve market supremacy, businesses must plan for customers' current and future expectations, and deliver and support its products worldwide at a reasonable cost.

Worldwide, businesses are looking for ways to improve the quality of their products and strengthen their customer relationships. In today's harshly competitive global environment, manufacturing and service excellence are not obscure technical issues, but a matter of corporate survival. Although price still plays an important role in buying decisions, many customers demand high quality at any price level. As a result of this growing emphasis by the customer on quality, approximately 87 percent of the largest U.S. industrial corporations initiated or expanded existing quality-enhancement programs during the 1989–1990 period and continue to increase spending on subsequent quality initiatives.[1]

What does this emphasis on quality mean to the business that expects to provide it? Throughout the world, businesses are facing a common competitive issue: how to best create new business practices that foster the development and delivery of quality products, whether they are as a result of manufacture or service. An international quality study conducted by Ernst & Young in conjunction with the American Quality Foundation revealed national differences in practices currently applied and planned to improve quality.[2] The survey included 584 companies in the United States, Canada, Germany, and Japan, representing a comprehensive effort to specify why some corporate programs are successful while others falter. The study details experience across a range of quality-improvement programs in the auto, computer, banking, and health care industries.

Two-thirds of Japanese businesses report involvement of only 25 percent or fewer of its employees in quality-related teams, and its management plans to continue employee participation at the same level. Contrast this with businesses in all other countries surveyed. Here, management plans to increase employee involvement in quality-related teams. This is thought provoking, considering that Japan is the only country surveyed to extensively involve employees in regularly scheduled meetings about quality. Taken together, these results challenge the (Western) belief that Japan has organized its entire workforce into quality teams. Because the Western nations plan to increase the use of such teams, this leads us to the following alternatives regarding the differences.

- Quality is so integrated into Japanese businesses that management no longer thinks of it as a separate function.
- Cross-functional (matrix) activity has become so commonplace that these teams become unnecessary.

Whichever is true, it provides an insight into the differences between the organizational and managerial cultures.

Current business practices in North America do not support the claims of its leaders that customer satisfaction is important. This is surprising, given the advantages of integrating customer expectations into early stages of product and service development. German and Japanese businesses place more importance on incorporating the customer's desires into the design of new products and services than do North American businesses. While 58 percent of Japanese and 40 percent of German businesses always or usually translate customer expectations into new business products and services, only 22 percent of U.S. and 14 percent of Canadian businesses do so.[3]

Japan also led the other countries surveyed in the use of technology to support quality improvements. Currently, Japanese companies use technology for this purpose twice as often as done in the United States. Because each enterprise must define its own objectives and its own path for achieving them, applying new technology entails two things. First, it must define the service and quality objectives and a measurement system to support those objectives. Second, it must initiate appropriate changes in management objectives and measurement systems that require an underlying culture shift. Neither change is easy.

Key to many of the issues surrounding the global focus on quality is the setting of standards. Standards assure repeatability of the process and provide a basis for measurement, such as number of defects. The combination of rapid growth of all technology types (e.g., computers, telephones, handheld calculators) and size of the global market demands international product standards. This is the only way to ensure the repair of a product somewhere other than in its country of manufacturing origin, or that it will interface with manufactured products from other countries. Thus, as part of the quality movement, standards have become a part of business strategy, concomitant with the quality-driven enterprise.

Throughout the world, there is intense interest by business to broaden its understanding of the standards and quality practices that most effectively link with financial and marketplace leadership. There are two categories of questions for business when examining current practices:

- Management practices: Do management practices currently in place support this quality and standards emphasis or are changes necessary? What practices are most critical in the quality process? What policies are critical to international standardization? Do the policies and practices conform to current best management practices?
- Business processes: Have the business processes undergone study and simplification before implementing new quality or manufacturing standards or before introducing new technology to support new customer (and management) expectations? Do the management practices support the new business processes and/or new technology? Do the new business processes embody current best practices?

Over time, market leadership will go to those enterprises who identify and make the necessary fundamental changes in current management practice to assure standards and quality conformance, and implement supporting strategies. The cornerstone of global competitiveness is international standardization for manufactured goods, and the quality of both manufacture and service provides the entree to global markets. The successful standards setting, quality programs, and service initiatives are all based upon quality information and systems. The information (and systems) will monitor, measure, support, and validate the accomplishment of business strategy. Increasingly, I/T staff is called upon to contribute to the planning and implementation of these business imperatives.

EMERGING INTERNATIONAL STANDARDS

Standards are a part of daily life, and like many things, we only think about them when problems occur. International travelers constantly experience the frustrations of differing standards for products and services. They often leave hair dryers and electric shavers at home, because standards in other countries render such appliances useless. Alternatively, they buy a set of converters and hope that one in the set will serve their needs.

Imagine trying to get even a simple task accomplished in a business world in which there were no interconnected telephone systems or where countries arbitrarily choose unique calendars. That's why there is international standardization. That's why film manufactured in America, exposed using a Japanese-made camera, and processed in Germany, suffers no loss of quality. It is the existence of international standards that allows anyone to send a fax from Venice (Italy) to Venice (Florida) as easily as sending a fax across town.

Standards are formal agreements that define the contractual, functional, and technical requirements to ensure that a product, service, process, or system performs as intended. Until recently, companies focused its standards efforts mostly on meeting safety and supplier requirements. Standards considerations weren't strategic and were an incidental part of doing business. With the emergence of the global marketplace, that view is changing.

- There is a demand for compatibility from computer users.
- Time-to-market for new products has greatly accelerated.
- A standards-driven single market in Europe is gradually emerging.
- There is a growing need for global environmental standards.

The above unique set of circumstances exist. They combine to make standards and standardization a strategic corporate priority.

Standards-Setting as a Trade Issue

The proliferation of new standards, covering many products never before regulated, raises the hurdles for exporters that have so far been able to tap Europe's market with relative ease. Small exporters may find the price of compliance so high that they stop exporting to some countries. The problem seems to lie mostly with the United States, which has historically taken relatively little interest in international standards because it could prosper in its home market. As the importance of trade to the U.S. economy grows, so have the problems caused by a lack of attention to international standardization. Many U.S. companies, for example, still operate on the imperial system of weights and measures more than two decades after major trading partners adopted the metric system. As a consequence, U.S. enterprises lack the organization and experience to help shape the standards and then respond to new ones. Additionally, thousands of U.S. exporters haven't invested sufficiently in establishing roots in Europe, and the overall American export machine suffers from a lack of coordination among government, industry associations, and exporters.

The European Union is concentrating on approximately 1,500 safety, health, environmental, and quality standards that it wants to make consistent throughout member nations. The Europeans plan to establish upwards of 10,000 standards. These new rules are being drafted by the European Committee for Standardization (CEN), composed of European industry representatives. Some already completed standards went into effect in January 1993. The first 200 highly detailed standards published by the CEN cover everything from tractors to toys. As an example, the rules on a washing machine's electrical system are over 100 pages long.

Some of these standards may evolve into international (world market) standards. This gives added impetus to becoming informed and involved. Large multinationals are represented on the U.S. Department of Commerce advisory committee that monitors the standards-writing process. Large companies have even made direct approaches to the European standards-making bodies, which officially offer no seat to U.S. executives or officials. Smaller companies rely on the U.S. Commerce Department or the private American National Standards Institute (ANSI) to represent its interests to the European bodies.[4]

Standards are an important trade issue. U.S. industries may suffer unless the government gets more involved in the process of setting standards, because more than half of the manufactured goods that the United States exports are, or will be, subject to EU product safety standards.[5] The harmonization of European trade laws and standards may not only make it harder for U.S. companies to trade in Europe, but it could also allow the Europeans to play a greater role in setting international standards.

In every major industrialized nation except the United States, governments view standards and the standardization process as part of the industry infrastructure, and they support it accordingly.[5] Countries of the European Union and Japan already have programs to assist its domestic companies in the use of standards and provide technical standards training to developing countries that could serve as future markets. (As an example, the European Union and Germany provided $16 million in financial support for an electric component test laboratory in India.) In contrast, approximately 400 private standards-development organizations conduct most standards activities within the United States. Many of these private organizations also act as publishers, selling standards and standards services in exchange for developing them for industry or professional societies.

In the United States, the American National Standards Institute (ANSI) provides leadership in strategic standardization activities. ANSI is a nonprofit, privately funded membership organization that administers the U.S. private-sector voluntary consensus standards system and approves American National Standards. It serves as the sole U.S. representative to the International Organization for Standardization (ISO) and the International Electrotechnical Commission (IEC). The IEC sets international standards in electrical and electronic engineering.

In 1992, ANSI focused on the development of an integrated set of standardization policies and strategic services required by U.S. industry to successfully compete in a global economy. A consortium of major U.S. corporations leads this effort, called the Strategic Development Initiative (SDI). This customer-driven research marries the effort to determine the needs of U.S. business with a benchmarking effort to identify best practice in the areas of standards, standardization, and the strategic use of standards. Through this research, SDI expects to better develop the concept of strategic standardization, that is, the use of standards to gain competitive advantage.

Concern for the lack of a concerted voice in the setting of trading bloc and global standards led America's standards organizations to initiate a number of cooperative ventures. For example, NSF International, the leading organization for developing consensus standards in public health and environmental sciences, has cross- registration agreements with A.G.A. Labs and Underwriters Laboratories (UL), who certify and develop American national product safety standards. The UL has published nearly 600 safety standards, the majority of which gained approval by ANSI as American National Standards.

The future effectiveness of this private-sector process is questionable, due to the structural changes in the economy and the competitive environment.[5] These changes include:

- An increasingly competitive global economy that the United States no longer dominates, including the emergence of regional trading blocs.
- The growing importance of multinational corporations and other transnational nongovernment institutions.
- The rapid advance of technology.

Without more government involvement in the standard-setting process, the United States risks the loss of future markets and a weaker international competitive position. It will be up to each industry (or large corporation) to try to influence standards development in other trading blocs if it wishes to maintain international markets.

Standards and Corporate Strategy

In the past, companies traditionally relegated standards to the engineering department because management considered them simply a technical matter. This is no longer true. Many in industry now realize the importance of standardization and the role it plays in achieving success in the global marketplace. To achieve their goals, these senior executives establish strategies to deal with the impact of standardization on their business operations, because it is now a strategic imperative.[6]

Standardization is a strategic business issue that has a direct impact on new product development. Whether developing a physical product or a service, standards increasingly play a key role in helping advance competitive position through quality assurance. Adherence to quality standards reduces barriers to market entry and is important when competing in a global market. Standards go directly to the heart of the quality issue and quality goes to the heart of the competitiveness issue.

Standards Activities at AMP.   AMP, the leader in the worldwide connector market, does business in over thirty countries. It operates with the philosophy that standards are at the forefront of emerging technologies. When the technologies of computers and telecommunications began to overlap and customers began demanding interconnectability, AMP recognized that standards are market- driven. It realized that if it didn't get involved with setting standards, the lack would severely curtail its future ability to do business. Over 300 AMP employees involve themselves in standards work as part of their duties, and the company's standards activities link to the company's overall Plan for Excellence. AMP's goal is to have its new products achieve *de facto* standard status and become the official standard. As a result, managers maintain an active presence in standards bodies to help make that happen, and AMP people serve on hundreds of standards-making committees around the world. Their mission is simple yet strategic: to assure that standards committees hear company, industry, and country voices in the technical deliberations going on every day and to work to ensure that AMP products satisfy the requirements of emerging standards. (Information contained in the preceding three paragraphs was abstracted from a paid advertising section prepared for the November 2, 1992 issue of *Fortune* magazine. All rights reserved.[6])

INTERNATIONAL ORGANIZATION FOR STANDARDIZATION

The International Organization for Standardization (ISO) is a federation of one hundred national standards bodies, publishing more than 9,000 standards since its establishment in 1947. Combined, the ISO and the IEC (the International Electrotechnical Commission), which has forty-two active members, produce about 800 new and revised standards each year. Since 1991, the EU's standards bodies work in parallel with ISO and IEC, producing the same or consistent standards and issuing them simultaneously.

In 1991, ISO compliance became part of hundreds of product safety laws all over Europe, regulating everything from medical devices to telecommunications gear, with ISO 9000 as the subset of standards that address quality. These products account for only 15 percent of EU trade, but German electronics giant Siemans requires ISO compliance in 50 percent of its supply contracts and asks suppliers to conform. For Siemans, this eliminates the need to test parts, which saves them time and money.[7]

Some businessmen think that thousands of U.S. companies will ultimately seek ISO certification, since delay in compliance could keep foreign products out of the European Union, if only temporarily. By the end of 1992, more than 20,000 facilities in Britain and a few thousand more in the rest of Europe received ISO certification. This compares to 400 ISO certifications in the United States and 48 in Japan. Parenthetically, the United States has more to lose than Japan, since 30 percent of its exports go to Europe.

International Standardization of Quality and ISO 9000

The European Union through the CEN established quality standards for its post-1992 common market: the ISO 9000 guidelines from the ISO in Geneva. The ISO 9000 guidelines act as both management tools and trade barriers. Either way, conforming to ISO will be a requirement for any company in Europe, as well as any company outside the European Union that wants to do business there. U.S. companies such as DuPont and Eastman Kodak adopted ISO 9000 in the late 1980s to avoid exclusion in European markets and found that it helped improve quality, and Malcolm Baldrige National Quality Award winners Motorola, Xerox, and IBM require suppliers to adopt it. DuPont only began its ISO drive in 1989 after losing a large European order for polyester films to an ISO-certified British firm.

In 1987, the European Union, through its specialized agency for standardization of quality, defined and published international standards for three levels of quality assurance: EN 29001, 29002, and 29003, equivalent to ISO 9001, 9002, and 9003. They also published EN 29000 (ISO 9000), defining the basic elements of a quality assurance system, and EN 29004 (ISO 9004), providing guidance on applying the appropriate quality assurance level.[8] Together, these standards comprise the EN 29000 (ISO 9000) criteria. Over 50 countries adopted the standards, most establishing national systems to certify companies complying with the ISO 9000 criteria.[7] (See Table 6-1 for a comparative summary of equivalent quality systems standards between ISO, the European Union, and the United States.)

ISO 9000 is a basic, bare-bones quality program encompassing standards relevant to all types of businesses. It does not provide the level of quality assurance found in the leading-edge quality approaches, such as total quality management (TQM), nor does it require continuous improvement. What ISO 9000 provides is a good starting point for introducing and establishing a quality system and, for many companies, it re-instills discipline lost in the 1980s rush toward self-managed workteams.

The ISO 9000 premise is simple—consistency breeds reliability. Two concepts form the basis of ISO 9000 standards:

- Quality systems: The rationale is that if the production and management system are right, the production or service it produces is right. It's based upon building quality in rather than screening errors out.

Venue	Level 1	Level 2	Level 3	Guidelines	
	Quality assurance in design, development, production, installation and servicing	Quality assurance in production and installation	Quality assurance in final inspection and test	Selection and use of quality management and quality assurance standards	Elements of quality management and quality systems
International	ISO 9001	ISO 9002	ISO 9003	ISO 9000	ISO 9004
European Union	EN 29001	EN 29002	EN 29003	EN 29000	EN 29004
United States	ANSI/ ASQCQ 91	ANSI/ ASQCQ 92	ANSI/ ASQCQ 93	ANSI/ ASQCQ 90	ANSI/ ASQCQ 94

Figure 6-1   Equivalent Quality Systems Standards.

- Third-party assessments: Individual purchasers don't assess suppliers. ISO 9000 offers assessment by a third party that all purchasers can rely upon.

ISO 9000 standards prescribe the design, material procurement, production, quality-control, and delivery procedures necessary to produce quality equipment and materials. There is a one hundred-page, five-part ISO 9000 guidebook that directs the preparation of documentation of how workers are to perform every function that impacts quality and requires the installation of mechanisms to make sure they follow through on the stated routine. Internal teams form to verify that the procedures are being followed in twenty prescribed domains, from purchasing to training. Examples of the quality standards for sample domains include:

- Design: Sets a planned approach for meeting product or service specifications.
- Process control: Provides concise instructions for manufacturing or service functions.
- Purchasing: Details methods for approving suppliers and placing orders.
- Service: Gives detailed instructions for carrying out after-sales service.
- Inspection and testing: Compels workers and managers to verify all production steps.
- Training: Specifies methods to identify training needs and keep records.

Companies that implement a comprehensive ISO 9000 quality system find that it improves efficiency and reduces scrap and rework. Periodic internal audits demonstrate its business value to management and enforce commitment to quality. It can also reduce time-consuming external audits by customers, potential customers, and regulators.

If a company doesn't have a formal quality assurance program, the ISO 9000 standards are an excellent starting point for introducing and establishing a quality system. The ISO 9000 program is a foundation for implementing a TQM system. If a quality system already exists, it can be worthwhile to compare the existing system with the appropriate ISO 9000 standard to assure conformance. While registration confirming adherence to ISO 9000 standards may not have the cachet of a Baldrige or Deming award, it will enhance a company's image. Qualifying as a registrant can provide a possible competitive advantage in the U.S. market, or it can be a requirement vis a vis EU directives if competing in the European marketplace.

For all the ISO 9000 benefits, there are some gaps in coverage. Purists define quality as a product or service specification set by customers, but ISO 9000 ignores customer input. It also includes no appraisal of the cost of quality and ignores any need to benchmark performance so that it continually improves. Comparisons show ISO 9000 at best meets 40 percent of the criteria used by the Baldrige Award.[7] As a result, some companies are pressuring ISO to upgrade its quality guidelines by 1996.

ISO 9000 Certification

Although ISO 9000 is a set of quality standards and guidelines born of the European Union, it is of importance to all who do business in Europe. The first U.S. agency to offer registration to an ISO 9000 series standard was A.G.A. Laboratories, the American Gas Association's testing and certification facility. (A.G.A. Labs is the nation's principal agency for testing, certification, and inspection of gas appliances and accessories.) As a certification agency, it helps assess whether a company needs ISO 9000 registration and assists in determining advantages of international agency cross certification. Once a business makes the decision to conform, A.G.A. labs act as consultants to ensure that an ISO 9000 audit runs smoothly. They offer training programs and preaudits as a route to successful registration.[8]

One drawback is that certification still lacks uniformity. Each of the countries that has adopted ISO 9000 interprets it a bit differently, so certification awarded by auditors in one country may not be valid elsewhere. More than a dozen European and four domestic auditing agents operate in the United States, which adds confusion to the process. Some certification agencies have agreements with counterpart agencies in European countries that provide mutual registration recognition, while others don't. Agreement on a system of mutual recognition for ISO 9000 certificates may be years away.

TOTAL QUALITY MANAGEMENT AND ITS LEADERS

Quality is important to competitive survival. Translating the quality ideal into quality production of goods and services to fit the customer's requirement is the challenge, and most Fortune 500 companies are pursuing some form of TQM. Few believe that quality programs are just another management fad. Although many companies improved competitiveness, managers in these same companies are less than satisfied with current quality efforts. What seems to make the difference is the active participation of the chief executive officer. A survey by the Rath and Strong consulting firm suggests the following keys to achieving quality:[9]

- Work with employees to decide what the company should be.
- Focus quality effort on customer service, not on cost cutting.
- Show willingness to change everything.
- Set up pilot programs in which employees learn how to solve problems.
- Let workers make changes they suggest.
- Reward employees when they improve customer service.
- Keep workers informed on the success/failure of the quality programs.
- Stay actively involved throughout the quality effort.

Senior management involvement in the quality program decision-making process is mandatory, since the process involves considerable costs, and revenues from existing and potential markets are at stake.

Total quality management focuses on processes rather than results and products. Get the details of the management and manufacturing or service process right, goes the theory, and the result will be a high-quality product. Intrinsic to all the quality programs and gurus is that quality doesn't happen by accident—quality requires planning. Quality control should be an integral part of management control.

The acknowledged leaders of the quality movement are W. Edwards Deming, Joseph M. Juran, Phillip B. Crosby, and Armand V. Feigenbaum. While they all emphasize management best practices, each has unique views and methodologies. All are U.S.-based, however, Deming (now deceased) and Juran gained world recognition as the leaders of the Japanese quality movement.

Deming and Quality Improvement

Four decades ago Tanabe Seiyaku, a Japanese drugs company, won one of the country's first Deming prizes—an annual award named after W. Edwards Deming, the American consultant who set off Japan's post-1945 quality revolution based upon total quality management. The Deming Prize, awarded to individuals or companies, promotes quality control and companywide quality.

Deming, the father figure of the modern quality revolution, introduced the application of statistical quality control in Japan.[10] He urged managers to focus on problems relating to manufacturing variability and its causes—identifying and separating special causes of production variability from common causes. Special causes are for those effects assignable to individual machines or operators, while common causes (e.g., faulty raw materials) share various operations and are clearly management's responsibility. The primary statistical technique employed for the separation are statistical process control charts. Deming created the following principles and program to transform industry.

- Create constancy of purpose to improve both products and services.
- Adopt a new philosophy for the new economic age by management learning their responsibilities and stepping up to the leadership necessary for change.
- Cease dependence on inspection to achieve quality. Eliminate the need for mass inspection by building quality into the product.
- Stop using price as the single purchasing criteria. Minimize total cost and move towards single suppliers for items in order to have greater quality control over raw materials.
- Improve constantly the system of production and service to improve quality and productivity and to decrease costs.
- Institute on-the-job training.
- Institute leadership. Improve supervision of management and production workers.

- Drive out fear. All employees should have positive feelings about the organization and not be afraid to make suggestions for improvement.
- Break down barriers between departments. Use cooperative efforts between research, design, sales, production, and customer service to anticipate and solve problems in production and use.
- Eliminate slogans and numerical targets for the workforce. Zero defects or new productivity levels divert attention from the real problems, which generally belong to the system and are beyond the power of the workforce. This is the responsibility of management.
- Eliminate quotas or work standards and management by objectives or numerical goals. Leadership, not quota setting, is the answer.
- Remove barriers that rob people of their right to pride of workmanship. Eliminate annual or merit ratings and management by objective.
- Institute an aggressive education and self-improvement program.
- Put everyone in the company to work to accomplish the transformation. Everyone must feel that they share the responsibility for the success or failure of the quality programs.

He also created a systematic approach to problem solving that is cyclical. The PDCA (Plan, Do, Check, Action) cycle is a helpful procedure for improvement at any stage of the quality program and is built into many quality methodologies. Along with the above points and the PDCA cycle, Deming identified a number of deadly diseases that afflict quality programs. These include a lack of constancy of purpose, an emphasis on short-term profits, and management by exclusive use of visible figures with little or no consideration of intangibles, risks, and uncertainties.

Juran and Quality Improvement

The methodology advocated by Joseph M. Juran has a strong managerial flavor. He focuses on planning, organizational issues, management's responsibility for quality, and the need to set goals and targets for improvement, emphasizing that quality control should be an integral part of management control.

Juran sees quality planning as a part of the quality trilogy—quality planning, quality control, and quality improvement. According to Juran, the key elements in implementing companywide quality planning are identifying customers and their needs, establishing quality goals, creating quality measurements, and designing the processes capable of meeting quality goals under operating conditions. Producing continuing results improves market share, commands premium prices, and reduces errors in the office and factory.

Juran's approach to quality isn't as statistically driven as that of Deming's. He is much more customer-oriented, concentrating not just on the end customer, but identifying other external and internal customers as part of the quality process. This affects his concept of quality because it forces consideration of the *fitness of use* of any internal customers' interim product, including product development, operations, marketing, and customers.

Like Deming, Juran identifies the majority of quality problems as the fault of poor management, rather than poor workmanship on the shop floor. He believes that management controllable defects account for over 80 percent of the total quality problems. Thus, he claims, Phillip Crosby's zero defects approach doesn't help, since the premise is that the bulk of quality problems occur because workers are careless and not properly motivated.

Crosby Concepts of "Zero Defects" and "Do It Right the First Time"

Phillip Crosby gained recognition for his concepts of zero defects and do it right the first time. Crosby defines quality as conformance to the requirements that the company itself has established for its products. Like Juran and Deming, he does not believe that the workers should take primary responsibility for poor quality. Instead, it is management that needs to get it right. Management sets the tone on quality and workers follow their example. What *zero defects* means is not that people never make mistakes, but that the company does not start out expecting them to make mistakes.

Like Deming, Crosby also has identified steps to quality improvement. In addition, he identified his Absolutes of Quality Management. They are:

- The definition of quality is conformance to requirements, not goodness or elegance.
- The system for causing quality is prevention, not appraisal or measurement.
- The performance standard must be zero defects and not "that's close enough".
- The measurement of quality is the price of nonconformance, and not indices.
- There is no such thing as a quality problem—there are only management problems.

Not everyone agrees with his approach to quality, but he has created a number of effective quality-enhancing tools. One tool addresses defect prevention in non-manufacturing. Another supports self-examination by managers of their personal qualities, and how this may impact product quality.

Feigenbaum and Total Quality Control

Armand Feigenbaum argues for a systematic and total approach to quality, requiring the involvement of all functions in the quality process, not just manufacturing. His idea is to build in quality at an early stage, rather than inspecting and controlling quality after the fact. He views quality control as a business method, emphasizing the administrative viewpoint. Feigenbaum considers human relations as a basic issue in quality control activities and stresses that quality does not mean best, but best for the customer use and selling price.

The word *control* in quality control represents a management tool with the following steps:

- Set quality standards.
- Appraise conformance to these standards.
- Act when standards are exceeded.
- Plan for improvements in the standards.

Feigenbaum argues for using statistical methods in an overall quality control program when and where they are useful. Statistical methods are only part of the overall administrative quality control pattern. Unlike Deming's work, they are not the pattern itself.

Quality Awards

In the quest for quality, two trophies stand out: America's Baldrige Award and the Deming Prize from Japan. To win either prestigious award, companies invest long hours. Even losers find that the self-examination, new policies, and tough standards needed merely to qualify for these prizes yield a valuable dividend. The exercise often transforms them into more thorough, more profitable, and simply better companies. A third award, Mexico's National Award for Total Quality, focuses on quality improvement efforts in Mexico. Here too, the quality emphasis pays huge dividends to a country that once had a reputation, like Japan, as a producer of inferior products.

Malcolm Baldrige Award.   U.S. Congress established the Malcolm Baldrige National Quality Award to motivate America's companies to adopt total quality as an ethic for improving their products and services.

Data from a U.S. General Accounting Office (GAO) survey from twenty of the twenty-two companies that reached the final round in the first two years of the Baldrige Competition (1988–1989) show that companies with aggressive quality-boosting efforts achieved increases in market share, along with marked cuts in customer complaints and staff turnover. Getting these results took time, however. It took an average of two and a half years, and some as long as five years, before the benefits of a quality management plan became clear. Nor did all areas of business improve. For example, few reported notable gain in retaining customers or boosting the rates of return on sales or assets.[11] The survey reported a market share increase of an annual average of 13 percent, an 11 percent drop in customer complaints, a 6 percent decline in employee turnover, a 12 percent reduction in order-processing time, and a 10 percent decline in defects. The biggest change reported was a 16 percent rise in the volume of employee suggestions. Feigenbaum, the quality consultant who advised the GAO on its study of Baldrige finalists, commented that quality management isn't a short-term, instant pudding way to improve competitiveness—it requires hands-on, continuous leadership, coupled with an appropriate business strategy.

To apply for the award, a company must document and describe, in no more than seventy-five pages, statements such as the following:

- Top executives incorporate quality values into day-to-day management.
- The company trains workers in quality techniques.
- It has systems in place to ensure high-quality products.
- It works with suppliers to improve the quality of their products or services.
- The products are as good as or better than those of its competitors.
- Customer needs and wants are being met.
- Customer satisfaction ratings are as good as or better than its competitors.
- The quality system yields measurable and important results such as gains in market share or reduction in product-cycle time.

After submission of an application, examiners award points for accomplishments in the thirty-two sections of the award criteria. Top scorers receive site visits by senior examiners, who then make recommendations to a panel of judges.

The criteria for the Baldrige Award places great emphasis on improving internal processes, yet comparatively little emphasis on assuring that the improved internal processes actually result in improved quality to the customer. As a result, many Western firms concentrated on improving their quality processes and lost sight of the customer on the way to seeking the prize.

While only a comparatively few companies apply for the Baldrige Award, thousands aspire to win it and use its criteria as a model to improve their products, service, and operations. The Baldrige has become the centerpiece of the total quality management movement as well as a model for other quality prizes.

Xerox.   Xerox was one of the two winners of the 1989 Malcolm Baldrige National Quality Award. Less than a decade ago, Xerox was in serious trouble. The company was steadily losing customers to Japan's Ricoh and Canon. In 1974 it had 86 percent of the global market share in basic copiers. A decade later, it was just 16.6 percent.[1] While Xerox's Japanese competitors conformed to rigorous quality standards, Xerox discovered that it was slowly destroying itself with inefficiency at almost every level. It launched an all-out campaign for quality in 1983, forming employee teams to encourage shop-floor innovation and cooperative problem-solving. Xerox set new standards for every phase of operations, from design and production to inventory management and sales. As a result, manufacturing costs and product defects dropped 50 percent, customer satisfaction increased 38 percent, and Xerox recaptured the lead in moderately priced copiers. While Xerox defined quality as *meeting customer requirements,* it lost sight of its goal. By refocusing on quality in the mid-eighties, it regained its global market share.

Deming Prize.   The Union of Japanese Scientists and Engineers (JUSE) created the Deming Prize in 1951. JUSE designates consultants to help companies implement the strategy called total quality control, and these same experts serve as Deming judges. The directives, plans, and reports associated with participating in the award process runs over thousands of pages, so competing for the prize involves and stresses nearly everyone in an enterprise.

NEC Tohoku.   NEC Tohoku is a NEC Corporation subsidiary that manufactures telephone switches, printers, and computer peripherals. It set about applying the PDCA (Plan, Do, Check, Action) cycle to accomplish three broad policy goals: fill orders on time, improve return-on-assets, and lower defect costs. The printer manufacturing department used a technique devised by Tamagawa University Professor Yoji Akao, called *quality function deployment* (QFD), to determine what customers really wanted from their printers and how they used them. After thirteen months, the printer manufacturing department reported improvements in production flow, clarity of specifications, and number of problem parts. Between December 1987 and October 1991, the defect rate for NEC Tohoku's printer package declined from 26 to 1.2 percent.[12]

Companywide, the quality drive achieved similar results. Customer-reported defects in telephone switches dropped 60 percent. Productivity for telephone switches, printers, and hybrid integrated circuits more than doubled. Pretax profits rose from $6.5 million (1987) to $8.7 million (1989). The company, convinced that quality efforts pay off, set a new goal after winning the Deming Prize in 1989: the next target is the Japan Prize. Only former Deming winners are eligible, and only after a five-year wait.

Mexico's National Award for Total Quality.

Mexico, in its quest to change its paradigms and become a world-class economy, instituted a number of reforms to promote business quality. New laws protect industrial property and copyrights. To improve the skills of workers, the government made fundamental reforms in education. These reforms include compulsory high school, a longer school year, merit pays for teachers, and greater emphasis on basics in the curriculum.[13] Concurrent with Mexico's quality movement is a widespread move into the technology age. Companies and the government are investing so heavily in computers that even though Mexico is the thirteenth largest economy in the world, it is the sixth or seventh largest PC computer market.

Mexico's National Award for Total Quality, given each year to a select group of companies, recognizes products or services that are the best. The award symbolizes a dramatic change in Mexican business and in worldwide expectations for Mexico. Mexico has always been a low-cost producer compared to the United States and many other countries. What's new, and what has been building this past decade, is the world-class quality of Mexican goods and services, coupled with the growth of technological expertise. One winner of Mexico's National Prize is CYDSA's fiber division, Crysel.

Crysel.   Crysel took seven years of quality commitment to win the National Award. Part of the company's total commitment to quality is to create added value for Crysel's customers beyond specifications and technical assistance. (As an example, Crysel consulted with its customers (textile companies) on the design of a computerized information system.) A focus of improved service, quality, and productivity achieved dramatic results. Crysel produced 55,000 tons of fiber with 1,600 employees in 1985. By 1992, it produced 80,000 tons with 960 people. It continues to change by divesting itself of unprofitable operations. It is also building a permanent export base by opening offices in Italy, Spain, Chile, Argentina, and the United States. (Information contained in the preceding three paragraphs was partially extracted from a paid advertising section prepared for the November 2, 1992 issue of *Fortune* magazine. All rights reserved.)

CRAFTING A QUALITY PROGRAM

National boundaries no longer protect market niches. Economic nationalism disappears with the customer's unrelenting demand for access to the best possible products and services, regardless of country of origin. Therefore, many U.S. companies need a clearer focus to generate better products and services in terms of standards and quality.

In an attempt to maintain competitiveness, many managers have jumped blindly onto the quality bandwagon, with the belief that any quality improvement practice is beneficial. The Ernst & Young study disputes that broad-sweeping notion. It finds that the success of certain practices depends on a company's current performance. For example, the formation of employee teams to help identify and solve small problems can help lower-performing companies as they begin their quality improvement efforts. However, teams can ultimately lose value and distract from broader strategic issues once corporate performance improves.[14]

By contrast, benchmarking works best for higher-performing companies. These concerns typically have the knowledge to apply lessons from studying recognized quality improvement leaders. For lower performers just starting a quality effort, however, benchmarking may create unreasonable goals, potentially frustrating the entire quality program. The study identifies a handful of practices that consistently benefit every organization. These universal truths include:

- Explain the corporate strategic plan to employees, customers, and suppliers.
- Improve and simplify production and development processes.
- Scrutinize and shorten cycle time (how long it takes to get something done from the design to delivery of a product).

The new American commitment to quality comes at a time when competitive challenges from abroad are growing rapidly. An increasing number of foreign-owned plants are based in the United States. Japanese and German competitors, joined by new rivals from Asia, the European Union, and Latin American countries like Mexico, provide new competitive arenas. The rules of the game will keep changing, and the standards will keep getting higher. After winning the Baldrige Award, the Xerox chairman compared quality to a race without a finish line—as a company improves, so does its competition. To many, this is disheartening, but the true competitors find it invigorating.[1] That is the kind of ambition needed to survive the global marketplace and its competitors.

Customers demand quality and service, and the standards for both are continuing to rise.

VALUE AND SERVICE

Customers are demanding the right combination of product quality, fair price, and good service: they want value. Value means not overpaying for quality. Value is about real performance, informative advertising, and delivering on promises. Value can be a $42,000 Infiniti Q45 from Nissan, a $14,000 SL2 from Saturn, or a shopping trip to a manufacturer's outlet.

The customer's perception of value is important to service industries such as retailing, restaurants, banking, and airlines. It is equally important to service organizations within manufacturing industries, such as automobiles and computers in which the service component lends added value to the product. Service is difficult to define precisely and even more difficult to measure, but to be successful in today's global economy, service and value are important and need planning and measuring to ensure that customers get what they pays for.

There is a tendency to think of service workers as hamburger flippers or janitors, but service quality is just as important to McDonald's as it is to American Airlines. In both cases, managers and workers must be alert to one fact: customer desires and perceptions of service levels and value are constantly changing. To be successful, service organizations must learn to aim at and hit a continually moving target.

> *To achieve market supremacy, businesses must plan for customers' current and future expectations and deliver and support its products worldwide.*

ADDING VALUE TO THE PRODUCT

Why this heightened consumer interest in service and value? Many industry watchers attribute the change to the demographic shift in age.[15] They believe that as the industrial nations' population ages, it creates a market of mature purchasers of the worlds' goods and services. The more mature purchaser shows less interest in flash than in substance. Providers of goods and services find that to be successful in this market they must demonstrate product value through increased emphasis on product performance and service at a reasonable price.

Keys to Value and Service

The keys to successfully marketing a product in this new environment are:

- Offer products that perform: This is the price of entry. Consumers will no longer tolerate poor quality, and fashion won't distract them.
- Give more than the customer expects (but not more than they want): Whether it's providing environmentally sound packaging, including a radio in the Saturn's standard price, or offering air conditioning and automatic transmission in the basic models of the Chrysler minivan, giving more than the customer expects wins customer loyalty.
- Give guarantees: Offering an enhanced warranty and paying full refunds when problems arise can help justify a higher price.

- Avoid unrealistic pricing: Compaq found out about unrealistic pricing when the increasing quality of IBM-compatible PC clones challenged its technical superiority. IBM found out about unrealistic pricing when it failed to see the PC market turn from a specialty market to an off-the-shelf commodity market. Again, this was due to the increased quality of PC clones plus the combination of direct marketing, overnight shipping, and toll free help lines offered by manufacturers like Dell Computer and Gateway 2000.

- Give customers the facts: Use advertising to provide the type of detailed information today's sophisticated consumer demands. Text-rich advertisements for items like pharmaceuticals and automobiles are now the norm.

- Build relationships: Frequent buyer plans, toll free numbers, and membership clubs can help bind the consumer to a product and service. In the era of just-in-time delivery, an out-of-stock condition for even one day of a seven-day promotional sale is a sure way to gain dissatisfied customers.

- Enhance service: Improve service with enhanced guarantees, longer warranties, and toll free information and help lines. Make it easier for a customer to deal with the company.

Saturn and Enhanced Service

A classic example of enhanced service is a story concerning the Saturn automobile. In 1990, Saturn learned that about 1,100 customers received automobiles with an improperly formulated engine coolant. Corporate contacted the dealers who had sold the automobiles. Dealers personally contacted all the customers owning the Saturns and offered the choice of either a new car or their money back. Only thirteen took the money. The rest took new Saturns.[16] This satisfied both customers and dealers.

ADDING VALUE TO THE SERVICE

In the early 1990s, Japan began to emphasize the importance of its service economy, driven by three factors: domestic expansion, deregulation of the telecommunications industry, and the growing role of advanced technology stimulated by falling computer prices.

Japan exports service products in retailing, restaurants, leasing, and travel.[17] Other businesses, including education, advertising, and communications are likely to follow. They are also likely to succeed, because the same factors that gave Japan an edge in producing cameras, automobiles, and VCRs are being applied by companies seeking to provide world-class services. These factors are:

- Customer feedback: Like manufacturers, service suppliers in Japan listen to what users complain about and then design products that solve the complaints. Just as NEC Tohoku employs a technique called *quality function deployment* to determine how customers really use their printers and then apply the results to design a better product, Japanese retailers use customer information to develop new department store images.

- Quality assurance: Again like manufacturing, Japanese service suppliers build customer satisfaction into service products rather than add it as an afterthought. For example, Japan Air Lines trains its cabin crew on etiquette and politeness longer than any other airline. As a result, its customers rarely need an apology or demand a refund, and the company has the reputation of providing quality service. Japan Air Lines, by building quality in rather than screening errors out, became an industry leader.

- Economies of scale: With labor costs high, Japan supports service employees by automation to help them deliver a better product. Instead of having many individual kitchens making meals like McDonald's and Burger King in the United States, Skylark, Kyotaru, and other Japanese fast-food chains use point-of-sale (POS) ordering computers, on-line networks, and just-in-time delivery to serve customers with dishes prepared in vast centralized kitchens. This has proved so successful that many of the large hotels in the United States have subsequently adopted the technique.

HELP LINES FOR CUSTOMERS

One way to ensure customer feedback is to provide a toll free help line. Increasingly, people dial toll free numbers at all hours of the day or night to get consumer and personal advice and quick solutions to an array of problems. Help lines fill a growing need. Consumers today demand more product information, and they expect prompt and focused answers. There is only one thing worse than not having a help line for customers and that is to provide inappropriate staffing for that function.

To the millions of customers who call the help lines, they are convenient, personal links with experts in virtually everything, from using computer software to using a camera. Callers expect informed service. They expect accurate information, given in a timely way. Staffing of the service requires skills greater than the typical order takers that manufacturers and retailers normally use to service telephone sales operations.

For manufacturers and marketers of all kinds of products, help lines represent a two-way street. Callers aren't the only beneficiaries. Consumer services present smart businesses with a wealth of new marketing opportunities and information. While demonstrating a commitment to provide customer assistance through the help lines, businesses collect valuable consumer data and feedback that pay off later. Operators at General Foods, Pillsbury, and General Mills, for instance, extract information from callers that can lead to new or improved products, better packaging, and new advertising approaches. A flood of calls encouraged Dole Foods to expand its frozen juice bars line and to replace a coloring agent some consumers associated with health hazards. Many food manufacturers generate even more goodwill by mailing coupons, recipes, or nutrition information to callers. The General Mills consumer help line receives a half-million calls annually; General Foods receives almost twice that number.

Help lines empower customers, and to a limited degree, employees. More U.S. companies will adopt the concept as the global economy challenges them to work harder for their share of the market. Whether the help lines are a consumer lifeline or business booster, toll free lines are in tune with the trend toward improving service, and the service will continue to proliferate during the nineties.[18]

SERVICE AS A PRIMARY BUSINESS

There are virtually hundreds of different theories about measuring, forecasting, and managing business. Although these theories vary widely, they have one thing in common: they all assume a manufacturing business. Increasingly, however, service is displacing manufacturing as the primary class of business. However, when managers consider such familiar concepts as the value chain, inventory, and delivery from a service perspective, the concepts become complex and ill-defined. One of the biggest problems with managing service industries and service functions today is that many simply do not understand them well enough, and previous manufacturing-based management approaches don't necessarily work.

What Makes Services Different?

How are services different? Services are deeds, performances, or efforts, and are experimental, making it difficult to assign hard attributes to them (and thus difficult to measure). Although tangible items, such as the delivery trucks and airplanes of Federal Express are involved in the service, the purchaser is buying performance rendered by one party for another. Services, as compared to manufacturing, are intangible and represent the closeness of the consumer to the product.

Because services are experimental—either the service or the customer is unique—it is difficult to assign hard attributes to them. Without these attributes, a service provider has nothing to measure. The real issue, from a service point of view, is how a provider knows when the service is adequate.

What Makes Measuring Success Different?

One of the reasons business and I/T have become so good at measuring things from the provider point of view rather than the customers is that the customer really doesn't have a single point of view. Rather, there is no one point of view that fits all customers. Just as real families never have 2.3 children, the sophistication and expectations of a customer group—such as consumers of I/T services—span a wide range. The banking industry illustrates this problem. Almost everyone in the country has some dealings with banks. Some customers have a difficult time opening a checking account, much less balancing it. Others want to check the rate for thirty-six-month certificates of deposit from their car phones.

It is also difficult to come up with a meaningful set of service measures that apply to both extremes of the consumer set. Look within any enterprise and there will be different skill sets, expectations, and aptitudes among internal customers. A sophisticated consumer may be more understanding of limitations in providing service or may be more demanding because they understand the potential of what the provider could (but isn't) delivering. People who have more limited capabilities may have much higher levels of frustration because they feel they have no control, or they may just shrug and accept it. Therefore, when thinking about quality and quality in service, it is important to recognize that customers differ in their ability to assess satisfaction consistently.

Additionally, as a service organization begins to focus on quality and quality in service, it also begins to create new expectations within the minds of those being served. What is excellent quickly becomes the de facto standard, even though there is no change in the actual service level. Subsequently, as an organization begins to measure certain criteria and improves, customers expect continuing improvements. The result is that with service improvements, there is no such thing as being done.

Delivering I/T services and determining the quality of the results suffers the same problems. This is a particularly sensitive issue in organizations that have full-blown quality improvement programs throughout the rest of the enterprise.

Keys To Measuring Quality Service

The Marketing Sciences Institute, a research group in Cambridge, Massachusetts, developed a group of ten categories to measure quality of service.[19] Note that all the category definitions are from the perspective of the consumer. This checklist is a good way to start thinking about the delivery of quality in I/T services.

- Access: Access addresses the availability of the service and the ease of contact from the customer viewpoint.
- Communications: Communication involves keeping customers informed in a language they understand and with clear communications channels.
- Competence: Competence evaluates whether the customer is interfacing with competent people. It assesses whether the customer and/or company interface works smoothly and with few customer complaints about incorrect information.
- Courtesy: Courtesy determines whether the service representatives are courteous, no matter what the level of stress. Again, the measurement base is the customer's perception of the personal interface.
- Credibility: Credibility assesses the customer's view on the credibility of information they receive from the service. Does the customer perceive that the service organization has their best interests at heart?
- Reliability: Accuracy and dependability (timeliness) of the service being performed right the first time is important, again, from the customers' vantage point.
- Responsiveness: Is the service responsive to the customers' requirements, and does it demonstrate a willingness to perform the service from the customers' viewpoint?

- Security: This measures the customers' freedom from doubt about the service. Does the service organization really understand what the problem is? This is the customers' view of their needs and of the service organization's effort to understand them.

- Tangibles: What are the tangible benefits? From the customer's view, does the service save time, or shorten the learning curve? From an operating manager's perspective, is it accurate, timely, or involve cost savings? Can the operating unit achieve operating efficiencies through use of an (internal) service?

- Understanding and/or knowing the customer: Does the provider of the service understand the problem? Does the provider of the service know the customer, or know whether this is a repeat call? What kind of information is available to the service provider to improve the service level to the customer?

Matching the above keys for measuring quality service from the customer's perspective to the current measures of success provides a guide for developing quality service measurements. This same process is useful for uncovering and diagnosing service strengths and inadequacies requiring management attention.

RESTRUCTURING SERVICE

The service industries—as well as service organizations within manufacturing—face massive restructuring. Part of this is due to the press of competition. Bank mergers provide us one example of cost cutting without damage to service.

Global View of Service Productivity

The productivity of many large service industries is still higher in the United States than in other leading industrialized countries. A study by McKinsey Global Institute found that the U.S. advantage is greatest in airlines, retail banking, and telecommunications. The study concludes that many of the most important variations in productivity are due to differences in national regulatory systems and labor market policies. Productivity was highest in those countries in which policy encouraged competition and labor market flexibility. These countries achieved fewer gains by applying advanced technology than by introducing efficient organization and management. The study compared recent international productivity records in a number of service industries. These industries included airlines, retail banking, retailing, and telecommunications.[20]

- Airlines: On a weighted average of six different measures, including such things as ground transportation, in-flight service, and ticketing, European productivity was only 72 percent of U.S. levels. The gap was smallest in airport handling and widest in ticketing, sales, and promotion. Though part of the U.S. airlines' advantage reflected superior scale, geographic route structures, and the mix of services demanded by the market, the biggest reason for their higher performance was efficient organization of labor. The study also found that the hub-and-spoke route structure, favored by large U.S. airlines since industry deregulation, reduced productivity.

- Retail banking: Overall productivity in Britain and Germany was only two-thirds the level in the United States. In Britain, the difference was due to weaker competition. In Germany, the difference was due to the commercial banks' extensive networks of small branches. The study also found that U.S. banks offered customer service in its branches comparable to the two other countries and had invested more heavily in information systems and automated teller machines.

- Retailing: Overall U.S. productivity was narrowly ahead of Germany and almost double the level in Japan. Performance reflected the degree of concentration of the industry in each country, income levels, and industry structure and organization.

- Telecommunications: The U.S. advantage was largely due to superior capital productivity. U.S. telephone networks handled four times more calls per dollar invested than in France and Germany and twice as many as Britain.

Service Sector Restructuring

Service companies, which include health and financial services, wholesale and retail trade, transportation, and a number of other areas, employed about 80 percent of America's workforce in 1992 and, until recently, many service industries enjoyed regulatory protection and faced little foreign competition.[21] The sheltered position of such industries led them to meet any problem simply by adding more people. However, many of these industries have lost this privileged position through deregulation: airlines, trucking, cable TV, telecommunications, and finance are just some of the examples. Additionally, foreign companies have acquired large stakes in U.S. businesses (e.g., hotels, advertising, retail trade, transportation companies, insurance companies, and banks).

As competition grows more intense in today's economy, the quality of service will play a bigger part than ever in determining the winners and losers. The combination of increased competition and major cost problems is forcing the service sector of the United States to restructure. Service companies are doing what manufacturers did earlier—dismissing people—but there is a limit to how far that can go. After all, service companies are people businesses. They have to reduce costs without reducing the quality of their service. Bank mergers, which became popular in the early 1990s, exemplify restructuring with the goal of trimming costs with no reduction of service. Savings from bank mergers accrue by merging back-office operations. Among the methods employed are heavy investments in automation and simply making better use of existing staff.

OBSERVATIONS

Customers are demanding product quality and good service at a fair price. Businesses are looking for ways to improve the quality of its products and strengthen customer relationships. Management is demanding standards by which they can measure improvements in service to the customer, whether that service is in support of a manufactured product or a service product. To fulfill any of these demands, we must clearly define what our service strategy is, not only the elements (e.g., access, communication, customer satisfaction), but how the strategy supports the business mission.

How to do this is not always clear for either the internal or external service organizations, with many lines of service, each with different objectives and performance measures. To provide an overall service quality measure for the entire organization may be impossible or meaningless. However, by concentrating on each line of service (e.g., I/T services, customer help line service, field repair service) to define its service and quality measure is appropriate. This service measure, in combination with the usual cost and performance measures, provides a more accurate evaluation of the contribution of service initiatives to overall business performance.

> *Service and quality are important to the customer. To be sure it is being managed well, measure its delivery from the customer's viewpoint not from the provider's.*

The role of I/T is relatively clear on service and quality. Successful service and quality initiatives depend on quality information being available to track problems from identification to solution. Although there are many philosophical approaches for quality programs, they all rely on the availability of consistent information gathering, comparing, and reporting. Despite this obvious requirement, surprisingly few U.S. enterprises look to the I/T organization as a means to achieve enterprisewide service and quality objectives. Although updated I/T applications provide better management feedback and ensure that all staff know any progress achieved in reaching the service and quality goals, many business executives still view the I/T organization as unresponsive and slow to change. Therefore, they reason, it is inherently incapable of supporting the long-term quality goals of continuous improvement and change. Past performance of I/T organizations and currently restrictive architectures are, consequently, major hurdles for the I/T function to overcome.

The role of I/T in standards initiatives and activities is less obvious to executives, but significant in its business consequences. Tracking conformance to standards to measure defects in manufacturing or service delivery is really a quality issue. However, being aware and influencing or conforming to emerging standards that have a potential impact on I/T applications and service deliveries are different issues altogether. They include:

- ISO 9000 conformance for software development: Organizations already exist to certify that software products conform to ISO 9000 standards—important to enterprises that are in the software development business or expect that the software might have international usage.

- ISO standards for product data exchange: ISO 10303-STEP embodies an international manufacturing and information standard that is a key enabling technology for the networked (virtual) enterprise (Chapter 4).[22] Because the U.S. efforts in product data exchange (through EDI) development already amount to over half of the global activity, any ISO standard on data exchange will affect, to some varying degree, the majority of U.S. I/T organizations.

- ISO standards and current I/T applications: ISO standards have the potential to impact current I/T applications supporting manufacturing and service product delivery, specifically in the areas of product documentation requirements and delivery.

Early NAFTA negotiations attempting to harmonize standards between the United States, Canada, and Mexico proved difficult for even these friendly nations. It also proved the necessity of a common set of standards for promoting effective global competition. I/T, like any other business function, must be constantly alert to the potential influence and impact of outside standards-making bodies.

The impact of current and future ISO initiatives promises to influence, to some degree, all future I/T activities.

7

Business Process Redesign

Business will reinvent itself by reconceptualizing and then fine-tuning its organization and business processes to improve competitive position, fostering greater employee involvement, innovation, and new research and development. This reinvention takes place through business process redesign (or reengineering) and encompasses a fundamental rethinking and radical redesign of business systems, using benchmarking as a tool to identify best practices. Concomitant with business organizational redesign (the subject of the next chapter), business process redesign works to reshape the enterprise for the new competitive environment.

Many existing business processes simply evolved as enterprises grew. Enterprises began automating formal, documented processes in combination with the surrounding informal processes to improve accuracy or reduce costs. Because the automation processes tended to capture the business processes as they existed, automating the sub-processes in place, neither the business processes nor the islands of automation within them underwent any significant rationalization.

Business process redesign or reengineering is a term that encompasses a fundamental rethinking and radical redesign of a business system. It embraces an overhaul of job designs, organizational structures, and management systems. The premise of business process redesign is to organize work around outcomes, focusing on key business processes, not on tasks or functions.

One hotel chain, the ITT Sheraton Corporation, reengineered its operations with impressive results. It decided to discard the old rules and invent a better hotel.[1] The typical 300-room Sheraton Hotel required up to 40 managers and 200 employees. By eliminating narrowly defined jobs and rethinking antiquated procedures, ITT found it could run a reengineered version of 250 suites with only 14 managers and 140 employees—with higher customer satisfaction. It redesigned the processes of the company and eliminated everything it didn't need to do, including unnecessary management reports.

At a time when many companies suffer from cost-cutting obsessions—through layoffs and downsizing—bold ones look for ways to grow by spending on advertising, new products, and acquisitions. When the bold companies cut costs, it's through work redesign and reorganizations that improve, not reduce, efficiency and customer service. Office furniture manufacturer Herman Miller shifted to a more flexible organization led by cross-functional teams in June of 1992. There, the chief executive officer likened its linked business process redesign and continuous quality improvement program to permanent white water and constant turmoil.[2] He believes today's organization must resemble an organism that is fast and adaptable. Similarly, a vice president at Boston Consulting Group contends that at the core of strategy for this decade is the notion that the business processes will differentiate the company, and it is the management and constant improvement of these processes that matters. Reason: Just about everything else—being a low-cost producer or building economies of scale—tends to be a fleeting advantage because it is easy to duplicate.

Business process (or core process) redesign increases market share by serving customers better, identifying opportunities more adeptly, speeding new product development, *and* bringing costs down. For example, Alcoa reduced the time it takes to fill an order in its sheet-can business, which supplies the beer and beverage industry, by about 60 percent. One of the executives observed that in a slow-growth environment, redesigning the organization allows a company to pick off a big part of the market because the company is producing more value with fewer resources.

Companies are finding new markets and redesigning work to serve customers better for less. Executives talk of achieving improved quality, value, and service to the customer to better the competitive position. Business process redesign, concomitant with business organization redesign (the subject of the next chapter), work hand in hand. They reshape the enterprise and its information systems for the new competitive environment.

BUSINESS PROCESS AND ENTERPRISE FOCUS CHANGE

A business process is a grouping of ordered actions and decisions to produce an output that meets a specific objective. The following points are key to the business process:

- Process ordering: The ordering of these process actions and decisions is an important form of knowledge to the organization. Incremental enhancement or reengineering of the ordering increases the process knowledge.
- Process resource: A process transforms raw materials to an output with a specific objective. To a process, raw material can be any resource such as people, capital, information, or facilities.

- Process management: Processes get managed, not the products. People manage results by managing the process by which they produce the results. A process is successful if it meets its objectives.

To fully understand the process, a change of focus within the enterprise must occur. The focus changes from what the firm makes (its products and services) to what the firm does (its processes).

What constitutes the enterprise focus shift from the classical perspective to the new perspective? The financial focus changes from a return-on-investment in products and services to a return-on-investment in the processes and their continuous development and improvement. There is a change in focus from economy of scale (the cost of things you make) to an economy of scope (the value of how you do things). Finally, there is a change in focus from the quality of what you make to the quality of what you do.

Business process redesign is one of two key tools for business improvement. Along with cycle-time reduction (time-to-market), Japan uses process simplification (business process redesign) and is the only major industrial economy routinely employing both of these practices. The international quality study conducted by Ernst & Young, showed that about half of Japanese businesses use these practices more than 90 percent of the time, while fewer than 25 percent of Canadian, German, and U.S. businesses use either of the practices consistently.[3] The fundamental redesign of the business employs change on all fronts: employee-employer and worker-to-worker relationships, supplier-customer relationships, and rationalization of all core business processes. No relationship, process, or work product is sacred during business process redesign.

REDESIGNING COLLEGIAL RELATIONSHIPS

Despite decades of experience with alternative techniques, authoritarian management still prevails in most American organizations. It is a premise of this text that the changing nature of our competition combined with changing technology render authoritarian management inappropriate in the increasingly global enterprise. Although authoritarian management was appropriate for Henry Ford's mass production, it doesn't help with today's management problems. Participative management becomes more appropriate for continuous improvement of quality because it allows for more open systems thinking and teamwork that improves the whole system. We need management practices that support the business purpose (the mission), allow for relationship building, and identify roles and ensure individual accountability. These changes must create value for everyone involved, that is, the stakeholders of the business.

Individual Jobs

How does one begin analyzing the opportunities for work redesign? Hackman and Oldham suggest consulting all stakeholders before expanding job dimensions.[4] Then, when redesigning jobs to incorporate new technologies or functions, they suggest the following strategy:

- Analyze job content: Determine exactly what the individual does—roles, tasks, procedures—within the realm of a given job. A part of the analysis is the identification of the reason why the individual does it. How can we implement improvements, and who are the stakeholders in the decision-making process?
- Combine tasks: Task combination puts fragmented job tasks into new job modules, combining all the tasks required for a given piece of work. There may be times when organizational or technical reasons constrain task combination. Should the physical organization restrict the redesign or should the organization give way to the better process? Determination of whether the constraints are valid—the "why not" question—can trigger group and process redesign.
- Form natural work units: Forming natural work units in conjunction with task combination provide further opportunities for task identity and significance. A *natural work unit* refers to grouping tasks in a logical or inherently meaningful way. Organize natural work units according to groups of customers, types of transactions, geographical distribution, or any other arrangement that makes good sense to those performing the work. For example, Union Pacific organizes its customer hot line answer teams by geographic area. In that way, the team members become familiar with the customers in their area and with the availability of the rolling stock, thus providing better service to their customers.
- Establish client relationships: When forming natural work units around specific groups of clients, it may be possible to put the employee in direct contact with clients and give them continuing responsibility for managing relationships with them. Clients may be customers of a firm, other individuals or departments within an enterprise, or other publics of the enterprise, such as the stockholders, government regulatory agencies. An effective client relationship provides direct contact between client and employee, clearly establishes criteria for evaluating the quality of the product or service, and provides a regular channel for relaying feedback directly to the worker.
- Vertical load jobs: Vertical loading pushes down responsibility and authority formerly assigned at a higher level, thus giving employees more control over their jobs. Giving employees more discretion in planning, scheduling, and checking their work; consulting with others; or giving them the discretion to set one's own goals to accomplish a specific short-term project are ways of accomplishing vertical loading.
- Establish feedback channels: Feedback channels should give workers direct, immediate, and regular information about how well they are performing their jobs. Establishing feedback channels involves removing barriers or blocks that insulate employees from information about their performance. Establishing direct client relationships is one of the most effective feedback channels.

Successful implementation of these ideas requires a supportive organization. Work redesign efforts must have the full support of all stakeholders affected or the intended results won't materialize. Said another way, there must be a culture shift within the management and organization structures.

The objective of a job design program is to organize work and to assign responsibility for completing tasks in a way that creates motivating and satisfying jobs. When the work process changes, the organizational structure, which defines the relationships among jobs, is likely to change. Redesigning work is a complex process, but the payoff for those who succeed can be extremely high.

Self-Managed Work Groups

Although the same principles apply, redesigning work for self-managing groups is more complex than designing work for individuals, write Regan and O'Connor.[5] Redesigning group processes requires addressing not only the issues of motivating individuals but of group dynamics as well. The focus of system and job design encompasses the overall task of the group rather than on tasks of members.

Self-managing work groups are intact (albeit small) social systems whose members have the authority to handle internal processes as they see fit to generate a specific group product, service, or decision. Self-managing work groups include task forces set up to solve specific problems, decision-making committees, and many kinds of management and quality teams. Management considers them successful when:

- The work of the group meets or exceeds organizational standards of quantity and quality
- Group experience contributes to meeting the personal needs of its members
- The social process in carrying out the work maintains or enhances the capability of members to work together on subsequent tasks

Work groups that are self-managed generally have a much greater impact than individuals in the organization and can ultimately cause change in organizational structure and management climate. Increasingly, with participative management approaches, work groups are the norm rather than the exception. As middle management's numbers diminish, ad hoc work groups make decisions single individuals formerly made.

REDESIGNING THE BUSINESS PROCESS

Combining job and work group redesign with implementation strategies for technology initiatives provide new opportunities to rethink the work organization. Due to the influence of the early manufacturing model, most American corporations structure along functional lines. Functional organization optimizes each task and function separately. Optimizing individual functions, however, does not guarantee overall operation optimization. Such segregation of functions often leads to situations in which various parts of an organization work at cross-purposes. Bottlenecks in one area negate efficiencies in others and the interests of clients get lost in the cracks between functional areas. Trade loading, discussed next, is a prime example of how and why this occurs.

Rationalizing Distribution Channels and Trade Loading

A surprisingly common management practice called *trade loading* runs entirely counter to the corporate crusades to become lean and flexible. Manufacturers of automobiles, computers, soft drinks, and many other products load by inducing their wholesale and retail customers, known as the *trade,* to buy more product than they can promptly resell. In the era of just-in-time everything, those practicing trade loading fill warehouses with cases of products that sit. Managers, shareholders, and consumers pay for the indulgence.

The manufacturer stockpiles ingredients and packaging supplies to meet peak production levels, tying up cash in unneeded inventory. The plants prepare huge runs, and scheduling is chaotic, with more overtime and temporary workers. Freight companies charge premium prices for the manufacturer's periodic peak shipments. Distributors overstock as they take advantage of short-term discounts, and cartons sit for weeks in warehouses. At distribution centers, the goods get overhandled, and damaged goods go back to the manufacturer.

Largely due to trade loading, the average grocery product takes 84 days to travel from factory floor to retail store shelf. Approximately $75 billion to $100 billion in grocery products, mostly nonperishables, sit at any one time on trucks, railcars, or in distribution centers. This inventory grew steadily over recent years and adds some $20 billion to the $400 billion that Americans annually spend on groceries.[6] Loading can also steal from long-term profits and mislead investors. Manufacturers often begin loading because management wants to achieve quarterly profit targets. In the short-term, the manufacturer can ship enough extra product to reach the financial goals and perhaps increase stock prices. However, financial health can rapidly deteriorate: to improve or maintain the volume the manufacturer must offer increasingly lucrative discounts to its distributors.

Trade loading is a difficult habit to break, since usually only dramatic action can clean out the excess product. De-loaders must concern themselves with investors' interests in steady, predictable short-term results. Letting customers reduce stockpiles means shipping small amounts of product for at least one or two quarters, which translates into lower revenues and profits. Unfortunately, management must also contend with a backlash from distributors, who no longer have the proliferation of discounts and other short-term buying incentives, and retailers, who must make money from selling and not buying on special promotions. Everyone in the supply chain must think long-term instead of short-term, creating requirements for different industry core competencies.

Shoppers benefit when the manufacturer reduces short-term deals that encourage loading. With this approach, no more panic purchases are necessary for ingredients: the company cuts down on inventories and frees up cash. Factories run on normal shifts, cutting down on overtime pay, and supplemental workers. The manufacturer eliminates peak-and-valley distribution, saving 5 percent in shipping costs. Wholesalers' inventories get cut in half, so that storage and handling cost decline 17 percent. Retailers receive undamaged products, and their perception of the manufacturer's quality improves. The consumer gets the goods in fifty-nine days—twenty-five days earlier—and at a 6 percent lower price. Lastly, information systems for invoicing become simpler due to the elimination of special discounts. Everyone seems to benefit.

Proctor & Gamble.   Proctor & Gamble (P&G) is one of a growing number of companies that is trying to stop the use of trade loading. Believing that it was a bad corporate strategy, management began attacking the problem in 1990 by dramatically reducing the discounts and short-term incentives to the wholesalers and retailers. One dissatisfied retailer likened P&G to a dictator, for spoiling the discount practice, and a handful of chains, including A&P and Safeway, protested the actions by taking some slow-moving P&G items off its shelves.

In the 1990s, value redefines quality, and a good product selling at a low and consistent price will win customer loyalty. By withdrawing the trade money—estimated at $2.6 billion in 1991 paid to distributors in the form of incentives and rebates—P&G discourages forward buying, smoothes out its own operations, and can afford to reduce list prices from 8 to 25 percent. Loaded less, the distributors and retailers pass P&G's lower prices on to shoppers.

The process of reengineering the distribution system requires rethinking of every business process and relationship. This impacts suppliers, shippers, wholesalers, retailers, and consumers. Production, packaging, marketing, and sales require rebalancing. If P&G succeeds in completely eliminating trade loading as a business strategy and practice, it could cause an enormous industry transformation, with consumers benefiting most through the more efficient distribution system, faster-to-market products, and lower prices.

Quaker Oats.   Quaker Oats wanted its managers to develop a no-load mindset to help smooth out its total operations. To encourage management, Quaker modified its compensation practices. The company changed the bonus base of annual sales and operating profits, a base easily manipulated by year-end loaders. Instead, Quaker pays its top managers for efficiency in manufacturing and moving goods to market. Managers earn a bonus if they improve, for example, the production flow of Gatorade, reduce Rice-A-Roni's use of capital, or ship Cap'n Crunch cereal to Kroger in five days instead of six. The design of the new compensation program disciplines management not to load the product at the end of quarters again, and the company saves $5 million to $10 million a year through this action.

R. J. Reynolds and Philip Morris.   Trade loading is particularly prevalent in the cigarette business because manufacturers raise prices each year, encouraging wholesalers to "forward buy" large quantities and hold them for sale until after the price increase. A second factor making trade loading popular is that cigarettes are a declining market in the United States, consequently, suppliers must load the distribution pipeline just to keep shipment numbers steady.

In the past, R. J. Reynolds loaded heavily to forestall market share losses to Phillip Morris. It stopped the practice in 1989, and withstood a $360 million impact on earnings. When it began to trim production, wholesalers and retailers sold billions of cigarettes stored in warehouses. Since de-loading, Reynolds ships almost in line with customer demand. The benefits: smoother production runs, reduced costs for trade promotions, and a cash flow windfall of approximately $50 million annually.

Philip Morris continued to trade load. In June of 1992, following a generous promotion, wholesalers interviewed said they were storing at least four weeks—and as much as nine weeks—of Marlboros, Merits, Virginia Slims, and other Philip Morris brands. For perspective, when Reynolds stopped loading, its management decided that four and a half days of stock at the wholesale level was ideal. Philip Morris's load at the end of that June—conservatively, four weeks of excess product—represented 17 billion cigarettes, worth about $1 billion in revenues to the company and over $400 million in operating revenues. Management at the cigarette company defends loading, arguing that distributors with extra quantities in its storehouses encourage their customers, the retail trade, to expand Philip Morris's shelf space in the stores. Nonetheless, wholesalers disagree, saying that loading the trade generally does not lead to better positioning in the stores.

> *Business network redesign implies both the strength and flexibility to change distribution channel characteristics and intraenterprise relationships as well as the commitment and tenacity to change the internal activities through business process redesign.*

Redesigning Around New Technologies

Business processes are tasks completed through a series of subtasks, known as work flow, that occur in a linear, or step-by-step fashion. Technologies—imaging, networks, and groupware—can transform business processes. Information technologies can automate workflow allowing faster process completion (parallel rather than linear). Assuring the accrual of such benefits requires a technology strategy and infrastructure.

I/T is often a catalyst for business process redesign programs that provide new opportunities for helping people work more productively and creatively. While one generation is still fretting over whether to trust the banks' automated teller machines, a new wave of technology is building that has the potential to fundamentally alter the ways in which we get our work done. The catalyst is digitization, which portends a dramatic reordering of the computer, consumer electronics, entertainment, and information industries.

Most intriguing is the category of digitization-enabled products called personal digital assistants (or PDAs). These hand held PCs are a hybrid: electronic datebook, Rolodex, notepad, and fax machine. For busy managers on the move and industries with staff in the field, the personal communicator—a portable battery-operated device able to send or receive written or spoken messages at any time, from almost any-where—has the potential to trigger major business process redesign, which is why we discuss it here, rather than in Chapter 2.

Imagine being able to write a note with an electronic notepad and transmit it di-rectly via fax or e-mail while in an airport lounge, or retrieving messages left in an electronic mailbox from a hotel without connecting a computer to the telephone sys-tem, or having instant access to remote databases and on-line information systems. (Apple staked out a portion of the PDA turf with its product, Newton. It does calcula-tion, lists telephone numbers, and maintains schedules. The design includes the ability to communicate via modem for sending and receiving faxes or collecting data from computers back at the office.)[7] Later generations of personal communicators will in-corporate graphics and full-motion video capabilities as well as videoconferencing and transmission of high-resolution still images.

As promising as the concept of an integrated wireless personal communicator is, the mass market for this product will be long-term, due primarily to the limitations of (or lack of) the current infrastructure. However, this problem is being addressed. In August of 1994, several companies purchased radio spectrum rights assigned to ad-vanced two-way paging systems in the U.S. that will enable users to send and receive short messages, with these services available within five years. Additionally, at the end of 1994, the U.S. Federal Communications Commission held an auction for li-censes to operate pocket communication service (PCS) networks, which expand on today's cellular telephone services by adding data communications and possibly lim-ited video capabilities to conventional voice transmissions. These PCS networks will cost billions of dollars and take several years to build.

Boeing Airplane Company.   While PDAs are being positioned largely as consumer products, these handheld information tools have obvious business applica-tions, too. Would-be PDA makers are already considering job-specific PDAs, such as one by Apple that would put all the specs for a Boeing 747—paper documents that take up to 10 feet of shelf space—in an airline maintenance worker's hands. The man-ual would always be up to date, due to periodic updates via telecommunications.[7]

Northern Telecom.   Sony's first entry into the PDA area is the Data Disc-man, a hand-held electronic book player. Data Discman's forte is to help find informa-tion in reference books. When a technician from Northern Telecom makes a call, Data Discman goes along, carrying the equivalent of 18,000 pages of manuals on disk. By using keywords, technicians instantly flip to the electronic page describing the repair procedure.

Technology Limitations.   Critical elements of the technology required to make personal communicators live up to full expectations are currently wanting. One fundamental weakness with the device itself lies with the limitations of today's hand-writing recognition programs. Like all pen computers, they are poor at reading the handwritten word, frequently misinterpreting even carefully printed characters. With some practice, users can improve their ability to write clearly on a computer slate, but it takes time. Another weakness (mentioned earlier) is that cellular telephone networks do not yet provide a reliable medium for wireless data communications. Eventually, Europe's digital cellular system and the growth of Cellular Digital Packet Data systems in the United States will provide a more reliable method of sending data, but these are some years off. Finally, the goal of the personal communicator is anywhere at anytime, but airlines often prohibit the use of similar devices during certain stages of the flight. In response, manufacturers suggest that busy executives will be able to prepare notes and messages during a flight and then send them when the aircraft lands. However, even this will depend on the dispensation of the airlines, for some still completely prohibit the use of a PC.

REDESIGNING EMPLOYEE-EMPLOYER RELATIONSHIPS BY EMPOWERMENT

Often, one of the first changes that a business makes in trying to improve customer service is to empower its employees. Empowerment is an overworked word that connotes the giving of legal power or authority. Businesses in the United States have applied the term to a number of dissimilar activities.

Types of Empowerment

After studying a number of companies, David Bowen and Edward Lawler suggest three types of empowerment. They are suggestion involvement, job involvement, and high involvement.[8] McDonald's, the fast food chain, uses a limited form of empowerment best described as employee *suggestion involvement.*

Another, more common type of empowerment is *job involvement.* This entails extensive job redesign, so that employees use a variety of skills, often in teams. They have considerable freedom in deciding how to do the necessary work. Despite the increased empowerment that it brings, the job involvement approach does not change higher-level strategic decisions about organization structure, power, and the allocation of awards. These remain senior management's responsibility.

A third level is what Bowen and Lawler call *high involvement,* a form practiced by Federal Express and the Herman Miller furniture company. Employees become involved not just in how to do their jobs, or how effectively their team performs, but also in the whole organization's performance. Virtually every aspect of the organization is different from one that is control-oriented. Sharing of information on all aspects of business performance occurs horizontally across the organization as well as up and down the (delayered) structure. Employees develop extensive skills in teamwork, problem-solving, and business operations. They participate in work-unit management decisions. High-performance groups focus on relatively tight objectives and get measured accordingly. There is profit sharing and employee ownership. Empowerment at this level carries with it a much greater responsibility as well as the need for higher performance.

There is no single approach that is ideal in every industry, company, function, or situation. Like so many other things in management, the ideal degree and form of empowerment are contingent upon the circumstance. The relative balance between direction, support, and autonomy varies according to each situation.

The fundamental principle of empowerment is radically different from the traditional (Western) one of *command and control,* in which managers transfer their ideas into the hands of the workers. Instead, it rests on Konosuke Matsushita's dictum that the survival of companies today depends on the *day-to-day mobilization of every ounce of intelligence available.*[9] That implies a very different relationship than in the past between leaders and followers, managers and managed. This also explains why many empowerment programs develop problems after a few years. It is far more effective for most companies to introduce empowerment as part of an organizational and business process reengineering program than for management to focus on empowerment as the single vehicle for organizational improvement.

Teams, Teamwork, and Legal Regulation

In the 1980s, hundreds of U.S. companies followed the Japanese lead by reorganizing around teams of workers to tap employees' knowledge. Motorola, Cummins Engine, and Ford, along with others, found that by allowing workers to make key decisions—not just follow management's orders—productivity and quality improved.

Three types of teams evolved:

- Problem-solving teams: Usually five to twelve volunteers meet a few hours a week to discuss ways of improving quality, efficiency, and the work environment. They don't (aren't empowered to) implement the ideas.
- Special purpose teams: These teams may design and introduce work reforms or new technology, or meet with suppliers and customers. In union shops, labor and management collaborate at all levels.
- Self-managed teams: These teams consist of 5 to 15 workers who learn all production tasks and rotate from job to job. Team members do managerial duties like scheduling work and ordering materials.

Japanese business demonstrated the power of the team concept to improve service and quality of manufacturing. U.S. businesses, in their efforts to implement and empower teams, must also conform to an existing legal framework—The Wagner Act.

The National Labor Relations Act of 1935, known as The Wagner Act, set up the National Labor Relations Board (NLRB).[10] The act forbids many work-teams. For example, the act states that it is an unfair labor practice for an employor to dominate or interfere with the formation of any labor organization or contribute financial support to it. It also defines a labor organization broadly and includes any employee representation committee that exists to deal with employers concerning grievances, wages, hours of employment, or conditions of work.

Do teams violate federal labor law? At least one company, Electromation, was accused by the Teamsters Union to have violated The Wagner Act. The NLRB judge upheld the charge. Electromation's committees were the same as those at many companies. One of its basic principles, for example, is participative management, which has grown into a focus on teams. It, along with other companies, based quality initiatives around work-teams—and, as a result, is concerned about any encroachment of its basic quality approaches. If the former (Electromation) are illegal, the latter likely are too. (One of those companies is Motorola, discussed in the next chapter.)

The issue is a dilemma for the NLRB. Even though The Wagner Act seems to prohibit many types of team activities, its original intention was to keep companies from setting up sham unions that undercut legitimate ones, a common 1930s business maneuver. While most business groups don't expect the NLRB to outlaw teams, it might suggest guidelines for when they're acceptable. Either way, an appeal of the board's decision to the U.S. Supreme Court is likely. As a result, U.S. companies with teams may go on worrying for years.

REDESIGNING SUPPLIER RELATIONSHIPS

As U.S. corporations redesign their business processes, they are increasingly turning to just-in-time management approaches. Many use electronic data interchange (EDI) technology to link with suppliers and to ensure appropriate information flow. Others examined Japan's approach to supplier relationships. They found that a major strength of the Japanese *keiretsu* is the intercompany-group relationship allowing access to technology and shared learning and have tried to tailor the Japanese approach to the U.S. market.

Automobile Manufacturers and Supplier Relationships

Automobile manufacturers design supplier relationships to build long-term trust and cooperation. Toyota Motor Corporation, for example, forms supplier improvement groups. Toyota helped a U.S. supplier, Flex-N-Gate of Danville, Illinois, improve its factory operations. After two years of Toyota-led changes, Flex-N-Gate more than doubled productivity while cutting lead time 94 percent, inventory 98 percent, and defect rate 91 percent.[11]

Toyota has at least two long-term suppliers for every part. Those two compete vigorously, but other competitors are not welcome. Toyota does not summarily drop a supplier for a lower price elsewhere. It also takes blueprints from one supplier and shares them with one other supplier. These two then split the business.

Two U.S.-based automobile manufacturers take different approaches than Toyota. Chrysler asks suppliers how it should change to help them hold down costs and prices. Ford's emphasis is on quality. Ford set quality targets for its suppliers in the mid-1980s. From 1992 on, only those suppliers meeting the targets can bid on new business.

A third U.S.-based auto company takes a different tack. In 1992, the General Motors Corporation vice president of worldwide purchasing began offering to supply engineering talent free of charge to help suppliers find ways to reduce cost. The core of his strategy was PICOS, an acronym for Purchased Input Concept Optimization with Suppliers. It involves sending teams of manufacturing engineers into supplier plants. The teams root out waste, help install lean manufacturing techniques, and generally cut costs. The vice president used PICOS teams with great success as head of purchasing for GM Europe and started setting them up immediately upon his arrival in Detroit. PICOS teams in North America, after visits to its supplier plants, have yielded, on average, productivity gains of over 50 percent, reduced space needs on factory floors by 46 percent, and cut inventories by 48 percent.

Reduced to its essence, the technique used is lean manufacturing, a version of the Toyota Motor Corporation's production system that tries to eliminate all wasted labor and material, while maximizing attention to customer satisfaction. Toyota is proof that the combination lowers a supplier's cost—and, in turn, the prices that suppliers charge. Traditionally, American suppliers have calculated what it costs to produce a part, add profit to the cost, and the sum is the price. However, Toyota, and now GM, have a new procedure. First, they determine the amount that represents the lowest price a customer will pay for a part anywhere in the world. To win a contract, the supplier must then reduce their cost below that lowest global price to make a profit.

One supplier, General Safety Corporation, makes millions of seat belts every year for Cadillac, Buick, Pontiac and Oldsmobile.[12] In the case of General Safety, it eliminated and replaced several assembly lines with individual workstations where employees can perform multiple tasks—improving efficiency, saving floor space, and allowing for smaller inventories. Moreover, workers help redesign their own jobs, permitting a dozen or so to move to new positions. It becomes easy for a company that is close to a process for a long time to never step back and make major changes, observed Alfred J. Fisher III, General Safety's president. (His grandfather was a coach builder and a founder of GM.) The changes implemented by General Safety yielded double-digit improvements in productivity.

GM also introduced the practice of strategic insourcing.[13] This practice covers certain high-quality suppliers that GM is willing to offer additional business. These companies get factory space free of charge in underused GM plants, rather than expanding their own facilities. In return, the supplier agrees to employ GM workers currently in the company job bank. The suppliers pay the workers, who remain GM employees, the prevailing GM union wage rates.

REDESIGNING FOR LEAN MANUFACTURING

The Japanese practice a concept called lean manufacturing. To make a shift from mass production to lean manufacturing requires a complete change of thinking. Under mass production the individual is subordinate to the machine. The pace of the machines determined the pace of the worker. In lean manufacturing the worker, not the machine paces the production. Lean manufacturing is people-oriented and provides a favorable environment for mass customization, while the orientation of mass production is to capital and equipment. GM in Eastern Germany and Rover and Unipart in the United Kingdom are three examples of how manufacturing is changing. Each took a different approach and achieved varying degrees of success.

GM in East Germany

Louis Hughes (president of GM Europe in 1992) believes that the mass production of Henry Ford has no future. He thinks that lean manufacturing is the second great industrial revolution, after the invention of the assembly line.[14] According to Hughes, GM has implemented elements of lean manufacturing in pilot projects at European plants, from team working to zero-defect production strategies, just-in-time component delivery, and continuous improvement techniques. When a company combines all the elements of people, materials, equipment, and systems, the results can be staggering. GM would normally need much more than 3,000 people to get the same capacity as its plant at Eisenach (East Germany) with 2,000 people. For GM, the Eisenach plant is a chance to demonstrate that on a *greenfield* site in Europe it can achieve the high quality, productivity, and efficiency of the Japanese *transplants* set up by Nissan, Toyota, and Honda in the United Kingdom, and which have already sprung up across North America over the last decade. For the German government, the Eisenach plant provides a chance to demonstrate the rapid regeneration of East German industry under reunification.

Rover and Team Working

Management at the Rover Longbridge (United Kingdom) automobile assembly plants took lessons from the Japanese and in particular from Honda, which has a 20 percent stake in the company.[15] Rover made a big effort to involve its 34,000 workers more in their jobs and in the company, to increase their training, to improve their work environment, and to ask them what they think. Every manager uses the word *empowerment.*

The work areas are much cleaner than a traditional British factory. There is little surplus stock. Management introduced the concept of lean manufacturing. Occasionally a group of workers gathers together discussing how to improve their own or the company's performance. Workers answer to a team leader, whom they help to choose, and the culture of the team is paramount. Team leaders monitor quality and productivity of the group and keep the team informed. Although elected by team members, potential leaders have to pass tests and gain approval of the company. The only potential losers in the system at Rover are the trade unions. In the past, shop stewards were the main conduits for communication within the company; the team system threatens that role. The union fears that the team system will minimize its power.

Rover's program of change concentrated on the team leaders. Below them, there is apathy and even hostility. One worker sees no value in team briefings and says that although he didn't work hard enough in the old days, now it's gone too far the other way. Another worker applauds the management's emphasis on quality, but is angry that he has to answer to inexperienced team leaders. No one wants to return to the days of strikes and work stoppages, but the agenda has changed. If Rover is to compete with the Japanese manufacturers in the United Kingdom, it must do more than prevent strikes. To stand a chance of eroding the current quality and productivity gap, it must win the commitment of its workers. Although one manager felt they had come a long way, in reality, they have only just started.

Britain's Unipart

When John Neill led an employee buy out of Unipart in January of 1987, the first recommendation of financiers was to abandon manufacturing.[16] Unipart's main Oxford (United Kingdom) factory had drab workshops and old machine tools. The company could have closed the factory and concentrated on its core business—that of marketing and distributing parts and accessories made by other manufacturers.

Neill believed otherwise. He believed the Oxford factory could survive, but only if it adopted the lean manufacturing methods of Japanese producers. The techniques are exportable: the Japanese have demonstrated this by opening automobile and components factories in America and Europe. The Japanese plants are usually new factories built on greenfield sites, and employing newly recruited workers who haven't experienced the restrictive practices common in older, unionized factories. Unipart's sixty-year-old Oxford plant was just the sort of aging factory that greenfield plants mean to surpass and replace. Neill decided the only way to save the Oxford plant was to go directly to the Japanese. In the summer of 1987, Unipart sent a team of shop floor workers to Yachiyo Kogyo to study their manufacturing methods. The workers returned to Britain determined to start an industrial revolution.

The British team discovered its counterparts in Japan had a completely different way of working. Instead of producing large numbers of parts quickly—the British way—the Japanese stressed quality and reducing waste. Unlike the British, the Japanese shop floor workers also assumed far more responsibility for the factory's efficiency. The workers even organized the plant's maintenance, repairs, and training.

When the British team returned home, it tried out the ideas in a corner of the factory. Once the team's members had proved to fellow workers that they could boost quality and output, they introduced the methods to the rest of the factory. They abandoned traditional piecework pay rates in favor of salaries based upon ability. Next, they reorganized production. Instead of being based around function, they grouped machines into cells in which small, flexible teams of employees would carry out a variety of tasks. They cut seven layers of management between the factory's general manager and the shop floor to three. They installed new equipment after winning an order to make fuel tanks for a new Rover automobile model.

The factory's teams of workers devised faster ways to set up existing stamping presses, some of which were fifty years old. Previously, if press modifications were necessary to stamp out a different part, they scheduled the changes only once a week. Now they are able to change the machines up to three times a day. The faster set-up times allow the production of smaller batches of goods to support just-in-time delivery. Inventory turnover increased from three to four times a year to twenty-seven times a year. Such changes shrink a factory: stocks of parts and finished products that once occupied 80,000 square feet now occupy only 28,000 square feet.

The revolution that began in the corner of a single factory is spreading throughout Unipart. *Contribution circles,* initiated by management and employees, have worked on about eighty projects and helped cut Unipart's annual costs by some $3 million. In March of 1992, it ended recognition of trade unions. Unipart now pays all of its 4,000 workers' salaries, just like the company's managers and office staff. Citing competitive pressures, Unipart declines to provide separate figures for the transformed manufacturing division, so it is difficult to estimate savings. However, they are doing comparatively well. While counterparts lost millions in 1991, Unipart increased pretax profits by 18 percent, to approximately $23.25 million on sales of about $849 million.

REDESIGNING WITH BENCHMARKING

Benchmarking is the art of finding out how others do something better than you do so you can imitate—and hopefully improve upon—their techniques. Through research and field trips conducted by small teams, you compare your products and processes with those of competitors, or with those of non-competing companies in your industry or with enterprises in completely different businesses.[17]

Taiichi Ohno reports a brilliant precursor of benchmarking in his book about the Toyota production system, which he created. On a trip to the United States in 1956, he visited the automakers as a matter of course but got his best idea from looking at American supermarkets. They provided an impressive variety of products because they replenished foods rapidly in response to sales. Customers pulled the goods through the stores. Picking up on the practice, Toyota started pulling parts through its production system at precisely the right time and in exactly the quantities needed. That's how just-in-time manufacturing came about.

Ford and Xerox

When Ford decided to build a better car in the early 1980s, it complied a list of some 400 features that customers said were the most important, then set about finding the car with the best of each.[18] Then it tried to match or top the best of the competition. The result was the popular Taurus. Updating the Taurus for 1992, Ford benchmarked again. The result: Taurus was the best-selling car in the United States in 1992, ending Honda Accord's three-year reign as top seller and increasing the company's share above 20 percent as GM's and Chrysler's shares shrank.

Xerox was probably the first in the United States to initiate benchmarking activity. That was in 1979. (Up to that time, the Japanese had been copying assiduously, mainly by traveling around, watching what others did, and checking with related companies in their *keiretsu*.) First, Xerox benchmarked its competition. Its next big step was to look at generic business practices. Like Ohno's imaginative borrowing from the supermarkets, Xerox's benchmarking manager read an article about L. L. Bean, the firm that sells outdoor wear. It has the reputation for fulfilling orders quickly and accurately. A trip to Bean's hometown of Freeport, Maine, revealed that its warehouse worker could pick and pack items three times as fast as Xerox. The secret was not in high technology, but in intelligent planning and the right kind of software. Bean organizes items in the warehouse according to velocity, not category—it shelves items that sell the fastest the closest to the desk where the pickers get their order sheets and the slowest-moving items the farthest away. Orders come in randomly, but software sorts them so that the pickers can combine trips. These and other techniques aided Xerox in its warehouse redesign.

Guide to Benchmarking

Everyone who does benchmarking seems to have their own unique approach to it. There are five basic points of the process, developed by the Strategic Planning Institute Council on Benchmarking, by other groups, and in texts and other business publications. They are:

- Don't go on a fishing expedition: Pick a specific area to improve and do your homework. Study your own procedures thoroughly and choose a company or companies to benchmark that handle the process well.
- Send out the people who will have to make the changes: These people need to see for themselves. It won't help for senior executives to do the benchmarking and then come back and tell the owners of the process what to do. Keep visits short and teams small.
- Be prepared to exchange information: Be ready to answer any question you ask another company.
- Avoid legal problems: Don't anticipate learning about new products or discussing things that might imply market allocation or price fixing. Most benchmarking missions focus on existing products, business practices, human resources, and customer satisfaction.
- Respect the confidentiality of the data you obtain: Companies that do not mind sharing with you may not want the information going to a competitor.

Benchmarking in the British and Japanese Auto Industry

A benchmarking study by Andersen Consulting, Cardiff Business School, and Cambridge University, comparing Japanese and U.K. suppliers provide a chilling insight into how far most of the U.K. industry has to go to match the world class productivity and quality standards set by the best Japanese companies.[19] Average productivity levels inside the benchmarked U.K. companies were less than half those of its Japanese counterparts, and quality standards—measured by rejection rates—were one hundred times inferior. The study monitored eighteen companies—nine in Japan and nine in the United Kingdom. One third, all Japanese, showed outstanding performance in both quality and productivity, while the five worst performers in the group were British.

Mainland European companies would probably do no better, says Daniel Jones, coauthor of *The Machine That Changed The World,* the book that documents the Massachusetts Institute of Technology study into efficiency levels in the world motor industry.[20] It was this study that first coined the term *lean production* to distinguish manufacturing systems (pioneered mainly by Toyota) that use radically fewer resources in people, materials, time, and space than traditional mass production techniques. Jones describes the benchmarking process as the most powerful tool available for assessing industrial competitiveness and instigating change. He notes that after benchmarking one can no longer hide behind excuses or put the clock back. One has to face the facts, however unpleasant, and do something about them.

The best benchmarked companies achieved faster throughput and much higher first-time quality, reduced rework, and required minimal stocks. They worked to stable schedules. The full benefits of such processes, Jones argues, aren't achievable without a complete supply chain organized along similar lean principles. They discovered a tightly integrated world-class chain—integrated between vehicle assembler and even the most preliminary stages of the parts supply chain. The characteristics of the integration included minimal stock, frequent deliveries of small volumes of parts, lack of disruption, and stable supply volumes. The discipline of the system came from the compressed order-to-delivery lead times and from changing the practice of manufacturing to increase inventory to one of manufacturing to fill a customer order. The benchmarking team concluded that such a chain can work only if a partnership relationship exists all along the chain. Implicit in this shared destiny is a clear mutual understanding of the need for a fair reward for each party as well as shared learning.

> *Benchmarking all aspects of the enterprise against world-class generic best practices and improving them ensures at least one necessary element of a world class competitor— a flexible organizational form.*

TECHNOLOGY FUSION AND THE PARADIGM SHIFT

While some manufacturers like Unipart, GM, and Rover learn about quality and new ways to manufacture, and then transplant the techniques into their own organizations, some Japanese companies have quietly undergone a paradigm shift and support technology fusion as a corporate strategy. Most Western companies still have technology strategies that look for the next generation technology and develop migration strategies around it—the breakthrough approach. Relying on breakthrough strategies focuses efforts narrowly and often ignores the possibilities of combining technologies. Leading Japanese companies, however, focus on supporting both the breakthrough approach and in combining existing technologies into hybrid technologies. This hybrid technology approach is technology fusion. By fusing electronic, mechanical, and materials technologies, Fanuc created an affordable numerical controller (NC). It subsequently became the world market leader in computerized NCs and one of Japan's most profitable companies.

From 1988 to 1991, Fumio Kodama directed the research program of Japan's National Institute of Science and Technology. During that time, he observed Japan's commitment to three principles of technology fusion.[21] They are a market-driven approach driven by "demand articulation" which in turn drives the research and development (R&D) agenda; an intelligence-gathering capability to keep track of all technology developments where all employees are part of the collection and dissemination process as active receivers; and collaborative long-term R&D ties with a variety of companies across many different industries. For management, this requires a different mind-set and a new set of management practices.

Practicing technology fusion causes four paradigm shifts, according to Kodama. They are:

- "Manufacturing [as a] . . . thinking organization": The manufacturing company is in the process of being redefined. Economist's view the manufacturing company "as a production function: capital plus labor equals output."

  Because R&D investment of (Japanese) manufacturing organizations now surpasses its capital investment, the corporation shifts from being a place for production to a place for thinking. This shift portends new organizational forms and management practices.

- "Business dynamics . . . [shifts to] multi-technologies": "Technology diversification has progressed so much [in Japan] that it is hard to distinguish a company's principal business from its secondary one . . . Today's leading Japanese companies have entered the stage in which they survive by adapting to the environment, relying on consistent, dependable R&D."
- R&D activities focus on invisible enemies: The basis for making investment decisions is no longer rates of return. "If you miss investing in only one [wave of innovation,] the loss becomes permanent." The pattern of competition is also changing: competitor's formerly came from companies within the same industry. That is no longer true.

  High-tech companies must monitor the competition within its own industry as well as companies in other industries. Because technology alliances can create new markets, new products, and new competitors, companies must, as a result, engage in competitive R&D competition with invisible enemies.

- "Technology development from linear demand to demand articulation:" The norm of Western technology replacement is a linear, step-by-step strategy of technology substitution: from the vacuum tube to the semiconductor or the LP record album to the CD. The "technology strategy traditionally . . . emphasized the supply side of technology development."

  "A need [arises] for a technology strategy that works from the demand side." It must blend incremental technical improvements from several previously separate fields of

technology (the technology fusion) to create products that revolutionize and create markets. The requirements for products that will create the new or revolutionized market are customer-defined and not what the technologist has produced in the lab.

Three of the four paradigm shifts have a direct impact on I/T and its activities. Manufacturing as a thinking organization portends increased emphasis on information empowerment and continuing business process and organizational redesign. R&D activities that focus on invisible enemies suggest the requirement for global scanning of technology advances as well as the requirement for a knowledge base of industry alliances that may lead to new competitive action. Technology development from linear demand to demand articulation requires taking the consumer view—a common thread throughout the topics of service and quality, mass customization, and information empowerment. The common thread of the four paradigms is, however, the vastly increased dependence upon a sustained flow of quality information throughout the enterprise.

REDESIGNING WITH ENVIRONMENTAL QUALITY AS THE CATALYST

Environmental issues are the basis for some global trends, and they could play out at a national level. In this section, we focus on one service industry—fast food—and examine how the global trends influence business process redesign and practice at the enterprise level.

McDonald's and the Clamshells

In 1988, McDonald's, the biggest fast food chain, found itself the target of a campaign by environmental groups. The groups were protesting against the enormous amounts of rubbish McDonald's produced. Although other fast food firms did the same, McDonald's was the target because of its success and visibility.

The polystyrene clamshells in which McDonald's sold its hamburgers became a vivid symbol of the throw-away society. The company had chosen polystyrene, a lightweight plastic foam with good insulating properties because it seemed ideal for packaging fast food. The problem for the environmentalists and McDonald's was that while the company packaged a product that took seconds to consume, the packaging took centuries to decompose. The company realized the problem was a threat to its future: many of its customers and employees were young and interested in environmental causes.

Moreover, packaging is at the heart of the fast food business. The biggest innovation introduced by the McDonald brothers in 1948 had not been to slim their restaurant's menu to fifteen inexpensive items as had others in the industry, but to put the food in paper bags so that people could take it away.[22] Since then, advances in packaging have been as important to the fast food industry as have new recipes.

Recycling the clamshell was the first approach, but it quickly ran into problems. Typically, customers carried 60 to 70 percent of the clamshells out of the restaurants and threw them away beyond the reach of the restaurant's recycling bins. Customers who ate in the restaurants became bewildered by the task of sorting waste into different bins. However, as a number of American cities began to ban the use of polystyrene altogether, it forced local franchises to abandon the recycling effort and to switch to alternative packaging. McDonald's then announced that it would replace the clamshell with a quilted paper wrap made from a layer of tissue sandwiched between a sheet of polyethylene and a sheet of paper. Though the quilted wrap is not recyclable, it is less bulky and takes up only one-tenth as much space in a rubbish dump as the clamshell. Thus the approach became one of reducing waste at its source rather than trying to collect and recycle it.

McDonald's formed an alliance with the Environmental Defense Fund (EDF) to collaborate on ways to reduce the company's solid waste. The alliance resulted in concentrating the company's efforts on a hierarchy of environmental goals—reduce, reuse, and recycle—and, as a result, improved the company's financial performance.

In pursuit of its first environmental goal—the reduction of waste at its source—it is trying to reduce the amount of packaging used. Offering smaller paper napkins didn't, for example, lead to an increase in the number that customers use. It is reducing the amount of chlorine-bleached paper it uses, thus reducing the environmental damage caused by the manufacture of packaging it must continue to use. It's trying to make its rubbish more environmentally friendly by using plastics that are easier to recycle or by using materials that are candidates for composting.

The second goal—reuse—caused more difficulty. McDonald's considered and discarded the idea of providing plates for washing like a conventional restaurant. Washing dishes would turn the economics of its business upside down—coping with dishes would mean more space and more labor. It concentrated instead on reducing transport packaging by, for instance, shipping products like ketchup in reusable crates and encouraging suppliers to buy more durable pallets.

In 1990, 29 percent of McDonald's packaging was already recyclable. The company wants to increase that proportion, although there are legal constraints on allowing recycled materials to touch food. It is also experimenting with composting food scraps and paper, to ultimately create fertilizer.

The partnership with EDF has improved McDonald's environmental image, and the chain has experienced financial savings as a result of its environmental efforts. The quilted wrap is less expensive than the clamshell. The costs of getting rid of rubbish are escalating rapidly, so its emphasis on reducing rubbish has helped to restrain the company's costs. Both suppliers and employees of the chain are more active in suggesting changes that benefit both McDonald's and the environment. More obvious is its educational value: the company's suppliers, its customers, and its staff have all begun to think differently about the environmental impact of business activities.

Why is environmental quality important to I/T? It is important for any I/T organization to fully understand the business goals and to share ideas to attain them—and for the McDonald's I/T function, environmental quality is important. It is just as important for the I/T function to contribute to the constant fine-tuning of McDonald's fast-food business by using point-of-sale (POS) equipment to capture data to pinpoint customer transaction service delays and eliminate them, or enabling customers to pre-order meals via fax or office computers, as it is to support any company environmental initiatives by whatever means it can. It is the synergistic effect of collaboration with suppliers, customers, and staff to achieve a mutual goal that makes many of the seemingly difficult goals in business attainable.

OBSERVATIONS

We have many different definitions of what an office or an enterprise is. Three views exist: the physical view (a physical site); the organizational view (the relationships among people—how coordination of tasks takes place); and the process view.[23] The process view is the view of tasks and activities that need performing if an organization is to exist. Increasingly, managers and information systems professionals are taking the process view of office work, which is increasingly multisite and multinational.

Radically redesigning work, which invariably means simplifying it, is perhaps the best way to ensure getting more work done better, and with fewer resources. When the work process changes, the organizational structure, which defines relationships among jobs, also changes (as it did at Unipart). Organizational changes—the subject of the next chapter—may result in revisions in the formal organization chart or may simply alter communication patterns or power relationships among groups or departments. Changes in organizational structure may take place immediately as part of the planned system changes, it may evolve over time as the enterprise gains familiarity with new technology and its capabilities, or it may change in conjunction with reflecting and executing its business strategy.

> *Business process redesign is a fundamental reconceptualization and radical redesign of a business system and its supporting I/T processes and systems. Radically redesigning work invariably means having the appropriate information available to simplify the process—the surest way to get more work done with fewer resources.*

In today's environment, nothing is constant or predictable. For business and technology, uncertainty clouds market growth, customer demand, product life cycles, rate of technological change, and the nature of competition. The consequence is that new demands are being placed on the enterprise. This market turbulence drives both business product and business process change within the enterprise, changing the focus of the enterprise and its I/T activities.

Unfortunately, business process redesign has one fundamental handicap—it is difficult to put into practice. Management must unite in the decision to redesign and be willing to invest considerable emotional and financial resources in its execution.

Forces outside the enterprise also contribute to the difficulties of changing current practices. These include:

- Existing legislation (for the United States, The Wagner Act)
- Trade unions (for Holland and Germany, a powerful influence in policy making)
- Government interference in the market (Italy and the steel industry, and France and its Air France airline)

Too many existing corporate cultures became insulated from market pressures. Could emerging nations from the Pacific or Latin America, without the baggage of existing corporate cultures and government social policies prevalent in Europe, the United States, and Japan, leapfrog its existing craft-based economies to lean manufacturing? Perhaps—but this scenario doesn't consider the role that technology leadership or technology fusion could play. Productivity-enhancing technological gains coupled with reengineering are occurring in many enterprises, fueled by new software, improved computer networks, and more powerful and widespread hardware. However, creating and maintaining this successful linkage requires every I/T professional to commit and assume a personal responsibility for understanding both information technology and business trends and constantly promoting change in his business enterprise and I/T function. Does this enabling force flourish in your enterprise?

8

Organizational Restructuring and Transformation

Business will reinvent itself both internally, by downsizing and outsourcing, and externally, by mergers, acquisitions, and strategic alliances. It will become borderless and global. The difficulty is to rationalize and renew the physical organization and corporate culture concurrently with rationalizing and renewing its underlying business processes, information systems, and I/T infrastructure.

In the 1990s no company—whether in manufacturing or service—can grow, or ultimately even survive, in the once-comfortable vacuum of a protected national market place. We live in a single global competitive arena. It is an arena increasingly dominated by a few massive players, but one in which the enterprising niche player can still seize opportunities. In this environment, competing successfully requires staying informed on critical economic, political, and technological developments, and on translating the possible implications into management strategy.

Unfortunately, simply identifying critical trends and staying informed about them is not enough. We must change our attitudes, business processes, organizational forms, and corporate cultures and inculcate appropriate new business paradigms. Keeping a company healthy over time requires working continually to improve every relevant aspect of its business system. If a company wants to operate globally, it has to think and act globally and that means challenging entrenched systems and organizations that work against collaborative efforts. In this chapter, we discuss the most difficult of challenges—to successfully rationalize and renew both the physical organization and the underlying corporate culture.

CORPORATE CULTURE REENGINEERING

The culture of a corporation is a powerful influence in its economic performance. Shared values and unwritten rules and assumptions can profoundly enhance its economic success. Conversely, old values and rules can also lead to failure to adapt to currently changing markets, environments, and paradigms. Furthermore, past or current success is no guarantee of future success, because cultures that engendered past successes can undermine an organization's ability to adapt to future change. This is particularly important as we experience the discontinuous market change associated with strategic transformation.

We encounter corporate cultures all the time. When they aren't ours, we recognize distinctive characteristics immediately: the customer service culture at Nordstrom, the greeter at the Wal-Mart door, the conservatively dressed IBM salesperson, or the casually dressed academic. When people talk about corporate culture, they talk about the values and practice that all groups in a firm share, at least within senior management. Creating a corporate culture simply requires that a group of employees interact over a significant period and be relatively successful at whatever they undertake. Solutions that repeatedly appear to solve the problems they encounter tend to become part of their success culture.

Once established, cultures perpetuate themselves in a number of ways. The sales trainee adopts the dress of the successful sales representative. Senior members of the group explicitly teach the group's style—the sales trainee makes practice sales calls on a successful sales representative, who then critiques the trainee's efforts. Successful managers hire and promote someone with similar traits. The longer the solutions or practices seem to work, the more deeply they become embedded in the culture. Kotter and Heskett, in their study of corporate culture and performance, came to the following conclusions:[1]

- Corporate culture has a significant impact on a firm's long-term economic performance.
- Corporate culture will be an even more important factor in determining the success or failure of firms in the next decade. Performance-degrading cultures have a negative financial impact because they inhibit firms from adopting needed strategic or tactical changes.
- Corporate cultures that inhibit strong long-term financial performance are common. They develop easily, even in firms that are full of reasonable and intelligent people.
- Although difficult to change, management can force corporate cultures to become more performance enhancing.

Unhealthy corporate cultures, suggest Kotter and Heskett, tend to originate in the following way. Some combination of vision and luck helps to create and implement a very successful business strategy. Next, the firm experiences much success with growth and profits or it establishes a fairly dominant position (thus experiencing for a time a lack of strong competition) in some market or markets. Gradually, the pressures on managers shift from the market place and competition and come mostly from within the firm. They build and staff bureaucracies; they forget the importance of external constituencies; they begin to believe that they are the best, and top management does nothing to stop it. Finally, the firm requires, hires, and promotes managers (not leaders) to cope with the growing bureaucracy, and senior management gradually allows these people (not leaders) to become executives. The result is an unhealthy corporate culture with some common characteristics:

- A strong, often arrogant, culture develops.
- Managers place a low value on the opinions and wishes of customers and stockholders.
- Managers behave insularly and politically.
- Managers place a low value on leadership and on the employees who can provide it.
- Managers tend to stifle initiative and innovation and behave in centralized and bureaucratic ways.

The unhealthy corporate culture remains entrenched until business becomes unresponsive when challenged by change. At this point, the enterprise must create a new culture or face the business consequences.

To create a new performance-enhancing culture requires leadership from the top. One or two top managers must be excellent leaders and possess an outsider's broad perspective and an insider's credibility. They must provide effective leadership by convincing people that a crisis is at hand, by communicating in words and deeds a new vision and a new set of strategies for the firm. Finally, they must motivate many others to provide the leadership needed to implement the vision and strategies.

From this, a new corporate culture emerges. A growing coalition of managers begins to share the values of top management (the leaders), especially on the importance of satisfying customer, employee, and stockholder needs, and the importance of leadership or the capacity to produce change. Behavior and practices change. The growing coalition of leaders and top management embrace practices that fit the business and provide leadership to change the practices when constituency needs dictate. The closeness to the constituency provides early warning signals to the coalition that change is likely to occur and provides time for proactive strategies and practices. The business experiences improved enterprise performance in those areas in which practices fit all constituency needs.

After creating the performance-enhancing culture, the next step is to preserve it. The actions of top management (the leaders) must clearly differentiate adaptive values and behaviors from the more specific practices needed today. They must show a strong commitment to those core values and behaviors but not allow more specific practices to ossify. They communicate endlessly about core values and behaviors and behave in ways that are consistent with that core. They don't allow new management systems or managers to undermine the core, are intolerant of arrogance in others, and keep their own egos under control. This results in a corporate culture in which managers value all key constituencies as well as leadership throughout the enterprise. When necessary, managers change strategies and practice so that they fit the business context, and they engage in specific practices that fit the needs of the business environment.

Changing corporate culture takes time. In a very large setting, significant time is necessary to move from an unhealthy corporate culture, to create a new culture, and then to preserve it. It can take from five to fifteen years. In those intervening years, the ill-prepared can lose markets and fortunes.

Team Working

Management specialists agree that team working helps Japanese firms develop better products and get them to market faster. In the preceding chapter, we discussed teams, team working, and the legal restrictions imposed on U.S. corporations by The Wagner Act. Even ignoring the restrictive aspects of the legislation, many U.S. firms find team working a losing battle. The reason is corporate culture.

The leader in the use of team working in the United States is the automotive industry. At the Saturn division of General Motors (GM), most of the work force organizes into fifteen-member cross-functional teams, from design studio to shop floor, yet managerial hierarchies imported from the notoriously bureaucratic GM continue to hamstring creativity and efficiency. Even Ford, after a decade of using cross-functional product-development teams, admits that it still has serious problems with the approach.

The structure and composition of Western companies' teams are to blame. Many firms shy away from creating truly cross-functional teams because ingrained corporate hierarchies actively resist. Without broad, companywide support, teams end up being led by junior managers lacking the power to secure the people and resources needed. (These teams are often referred to as *lightweight* because of their lack of senior management participation and influence in the organization.) In an attempt to bolster limited resources, these teams then spawn numerous satellite teams and advisors, a practice that is woefully inefficient.

American automobile manufacturers need an average of 1,500 employees to staff lightweight product-development teams, while Japanese counterparts employ heavyweight teams of 250 workers and managers to produce a more sophisticated design of a comparable product—and complete the task in less time.[2] While the American manufacturers use lightweight teams led by junior managers for new product development, the Japanese heavyweight teams have a senior manager, access to the best of the firm's people and resources, a clear idea of mission, and ownership of the whole project. Ownership encourages responsibility and commitment, which helps the team focus on its goal.

Western firms that have perfected team-base product development, such as Motorola and Hewlett-Packard, use heavyweight teams. Conversely, GM's Saturn teams are relatively lightweight, with less decision-making power. At Saturn, the role of senior management is that of external team advisor—counterbalanced by an advisor from the United Auto Workers Union.

Inflexibility both inside and outside the team causes it to fail—the lack of a supporting corporate and legal culture, no flexibility to determine membership, and no freedom of vision. Teams must be relatively unstructured entities that continually evolve outside the corporate hierarchy and bureaucracy. One expert on team working, Charles Savage, talks of how *virtual teams* should share knowledge, employees and resources as required and break up and form again with new members as the product-development cycle requires.[2] These teams include not only a firm's employees, but also members recruited from customers and suppliers. For example, the team that developed the production facility for Motorola's successful Bravo pager included a software expert from Hewlett-Packard. For teams to be truly innovative, they must be able to break rules.

Stifling corporate hierarchies are not the only cause of inflexibility and failure. Management systems and procedures—another element of corporate culture—also contribute. Incompatibility of a company's various computing systems, or the inability of existing management accounting systems and procedures to cope with cross-functional projects, can be equally damaging to successful team working. Such pressures cause many Western firms to abandon team work prematurely—the existing corporate culture simply cannot tolerate team work. Nonetheless, Timothy Dickinson, a management consultant, views teamwork as the ultimate vehicle for changing corporate culture for the better.[2] He thinks that teams may be the only management remedy for bureaucratic inflexibility. Dickinson believes that they are analogous to a poisonous antibody that the company needs to fight the infection of unchanging corporate culture.

Thinking, Learning Organizations

The enterprise and its corporate culture must organize for constant change. According to Peter Drucker, the enterprise must "organize for the systematic abandonment of whatever is customary, familiar, and comfortable—whether that is a product, service, or process; a set of skills; human and social relationships; or the organization itself."[3] The function of the organization "is to put knowledge to work—[whether that is] on tools, products, and processes; on the design of work; or on knowledge itself". Drucker concludes by observing that it is the very nature of knowledge that it changes so quickly, causing "today's certainties [to become] tomorrow's absurdities".

In the preceding chapter, we discussed the paradigm shifts of the Japanese corporations that practice technology fusion, the first paradigm shift being that manufacturing companies must transform themselves from *producing organizations* into *thinking organizations*. This shift requires new organization styles and management practices, because producing skills change slowly and infrequently while thinking skills and knowledge change constantly, and corporate cultures strongly influence the rates of change of both. The growth and change dynamics of knowledge impose one clear imperative: every organization has to build the management of change into its structure and culture. It must devote itself to creating the new through continuous improvement of its products, exploitation of its knowledge, and continuous innovation. The corporate culture must support a constantly thinking, learning, changing organization.

Global competition turns increasingly on the knowledge of a nation's work force. Most U.S. companies still rely on mass production techniques that require many workers to have, at best, only a high school education. Although many non-U.S. companies embrace tactics that require employees who can solve problems by themselves, only a few trend-setting U.S. companies such as Corning and Motorola have responded to their global competitors with strategies to change the corporate culture. These two companies are investing heavily in training and in restructuring work to give employees more control.

Today's economy requires more education. As a result, much of the urgency about fixing the U.S. educational system stems from the recognition that it must upgrade tomorrow's workers. Competition in a high-tech, global economy stresses quality, service, speed, and innovation. Producing the most at the least cost doesn't achieve it: workers at the point of production must think and act for themselves. Success and prosperity of both nations and corporations depend upon the ability to create value through its people, and not by husbanding resources and technologies. That's why empowerment, total quality management, and team working become the focus of today's proactive managers.

BOUNDARYLESS, BORDERLESS, NETWORKED ENTERPRISES

In an economy founded on innovation, change, and the better educated worker, one of the premier challenges is to design appropriate organizations. Enterprises are replacing vertical hierarchies with horizontal networks. Not only are they linking together traditional functions through interfunctional teams, they are forming strategic alliances with suppliers, customers, and competitors. Moreover, managers are insisting that every employee understand and adhere to the company's strategic mission.

Clear definitions of the roles and responsibilities of departments and individuals and their interrelationships exist in hierarchical relationships, but new technologies, fast-changing markets, and global competition are revolutionizing business relationships. Consequently, as a company blurs traditional boundaries to respond to this more fluid business environment, the formal organizational structure no longer defines the work roles. Managers must break down the boundaries that make enterprises rigid and unresponsive and create a new physical organizational model with a supporting corporate culture. Increasingly, business organizations accommodate this new focus of globalization by becoming a borderless enterprise, using people outside the present organization and enterprise to help. The enterprise accomplishes this through work teams (discussed in Chapter 7), outsourcing or alliances, or through mergers and acquisitions with businesses, often in a foreign country.

Flexible Network Organizations

What should the organizational model of the enterprise look like? The chief executive officer of General Electric described his vision of this new organizational model in GE's 1990 annual report as a boundaryless company. The new model has no walls to separate organizations from each other on the inside or from key constituencies on the outside.

A prime objective that many company's have—and indeed may require for survival—is to get closer to both their suppliers and customers. Some companies have pushed networking to the point at which barriers between the enterprise, its customers, and suppliers almost disappear. Nike, by rearranging what each supplier does on the network, can change product mix almost overnight. This creates Nike's greatest competitive advantage—they respond to fashion change faster than their rivals.

Managers are right to break down the boundaries that make organizations rigid and unresponsive; however they are wrong if they think that doing so eliminates the need for boundaries altogether. Although network organizations are immune to structural problems that vertically integrated conglomerates experience, they also have faults. Most network organizations, because they seek to build close, long-term relationships with its customers, suppliers, subcontractors and distributors, rapidly become part of a stable network. Miles and Snow suggest that the *stability can lead to staleness.*[4] If a supplier or subcontractor becomes too dependent on the core firm in the network (e.g., if General Safety Corporation discussed in Chapter 7 supplied seatbelts only to General Motors), the price and quality of its products remain untested in the wider market. If that happens to several firms in the network, the core company may fail to exploit innovation available elsewhere in the subcontractors' industry. GM, for example, could prevent this by ensuring that those in its network also work for firms outside the GM network.

Miles and Snow think that the principal cause of overdependence is customization.[4] As it tries to get an edge over competitors, a network's core company tends to encourage subcontractors to customize production facilities to its needs. While we focused on the positive aspects of mass customization in Chapter 5, this customization to a single customer strategy becomes detrimental in the following scenario. As a subcontractor draws closer to the core company, it overspecializes and is unable to compete in markets outside the network. Worse, it may lose the innovative edge it gained from working for several, equally demanding customers. With no innovations to contribute to the network, the subcontractor or supplier eventually loses even the core firm's business. Toshiba attempts to avoid this loss of competitiveness and innovative edge by always having two long-term suppliers that compete vigorously.

Too much customization can also threaten a network's core company. As it becomes more deeply involved in specifying subcontractors' operating processes—Motorola, for instance, insists that its suppliers apply for the Baldrige quality award—the core firm runs the risk of managing its subcontractors. This not only stretches the core company's managerial and technical resources, it also turns the network into something resembling an old-style vertically integrated firm.

General Motors and Its External Network

By using strategic insourcing and offering consulting services to improve the quality of its suppliers as quid pro quo for a 20 percent price cut, GM may pose a different kind of threat. Suppliers can't easily ignore GM's business. The corporation spends about $30 billion to $35 billion a year on automotive parts in the United States, and represents the greatest percentage of revenue for some suppliers.[5] GM—or any other company—could face short-term fallout from this strategy, despite suppliers not wanting to lose the business. Some suppliers may say that because its engineers are spending so much time working on new price quotes, it may delay parts (or whatever) for new models. Other suppliers may choose not to comply and risk losing the business, leaving the core company with fewer suppliers from which to choose. Still others will piece together a battle plan to seek out new customers.

IBM and Its Internal Network

Large multinationals trying to turn themselves into internal networks are especially prone to reverting to the old, vertically integrated ways. Consider IBM: Senior management is stage-managing an internal revolution in organizational structure, market orientation, and managerial behavior at a time when the company's competitive environment is in turmoil and its strategy is in virtual tatters. It missed the industry's epochal shift to desktop computing, lost dominance of the computer business, and plunged into the worst crisis in its history. Large restructuring costs in 1991 contributed to the company's first loss. After undergoing five major reorganizations and shedding over 100,000 workers and a quarter of its factories, it still had not transformed itself into a federation of autonomous units refocused on more fertile software and services markets.[6] In its attempts to transform its rigid, centrally planned hierarchy into a cluster of self-managed businesses, free to buy and sell goods and services to each other and to outside clients, it is seemingly unwilling to forego many previous management practices and a paternalistic culture. For example, individual units can't truly have responsibility for its own profits if it can't run the sales team, yet many IBM managers still cling to the concept of a single sales force. The ambitious plan for a federation of autonomous units will succeed only if IBM is able to throw off its top-down corporate culture. Perhaps the only sure way of accomplishing this is for IBM to split itself up, formally severing all its rigid vertical links.

When Enterprise Networks Work Well

Networks work well if the core company transfers technological advances quickly enough from one subcontractor to another, as is the practice of the Japanese *keiretsu*. The danger here is that once the network is working, the core company begins to ignore better ideas from potentially new subcontractors or suppliers.

Networking problems are easier to prevent than to cure. A company can avoid the overdependence of a supplier on a single customer by explicitly setting a limit on the proportion of assets that subcontractors or suppliers should dedicate to the core firm. Contracts between a core company and its network of subcontractors or suppliers should be flexible enough to leave both sides to withdraw. Most important, networking organizations must shed its old, confrontational ways. General Electric's *workout program* brings together not only its managers and subcontractors, but also subcontractors and General Electric's own customers, to help them work as a team.[7] Would-be network members should listen and learn from both the mistakes and successes of others who have tried.

STRATEGIC ALLIANCES AND JOINT VENTURES

Strategic alliances and joint ventures are an integral part of contemporary strategic thinking, due largely to the growing global market place. The rate of joint venture formation between U.S. companies and international partners grew by over 25 percent annually from 1985 through 1992.[8] Although many of the early alliances failed, managers grew smarter about what to expect from this type of linkup and how to craft a winning alliance. As a result, today's corporate partners show less interest in short-term ventures designed to save a few dollars and focus instead on long-term alliances where they can harvest gains for years to come.

Alliances are the coming together of equals to jointly produce some product or service, as compared to a delegation of function to some other activity. They provide flexibility and the ability (organizationally) to respond to abrupt market change. The objective of a business alliance or joint venture is *synergy*. An example of synergy achieved through a strategic alliance is the pact between Motorola and Toshiba, in which Motorola's role is to develop the chip for Toshiba's high-definition television sets.[9] This is a follow-on alliance, by which the same two companies jointly develop and manufacture a microprocessor for Toyota Motor Corporation's next generation of automobile engine.

Sufficiently diversified organizations don't have to go outside their own corporate family to create synergy, however. If a large and diverse enough corporate infrastructure exists, affiliates can often provide synergy. GM, for example, sells cellular telephones and service through its dealers as well as cellular network equipment through its Hughes Aircraft Company subsidiary. International Mobil Machines Corporation, a 6 percent-owned Hughes affiliate, produces the Hughes digital radio equipment.[10] Here, GM is piggybacking on an existing physical infrastructure.

Alliances also improve a company's ability to become a more clearly market-driven organization, with new access to shared technology linkages for supporting the combined product and service mix. Alliance partners should be able to exploit time, product and service mix, or other unique factors as a competitive advantage available only to that alliance partnership. Ram Charan, a consultant whose clients include General Electric, Du Pont, and Citicorp, believes that saving cash alone is not enough to justify an alliance.[8] The reason for an an alliance is to get access to a new market or a special expertise or to beat others to market. If an alliance won't achieve any of those things, his advice is not to do it.

Keys to Successful Alliances and Joint Ventures

Act as Equals.   Alliances and joint ventures are more likely to succeed when the partners behave as equals even when they're not. What is essential is the spirit of cooperation and attention to the ongoing advantage of both partners. If one feels even slightly disadvantaged, the alliance won't last. For some alliances, this translates into a mutual need, in which each partner must take whatever steps it can to ensure that the other continues to need it.

Share Objectives and Risks.   Both parties must clearly agree on what they intend to maximize together, and both must accept the bearing of a considerable degree of shared risk. The risks can be personal as well as economic.

Negotiate Decision-Making.   Acting as equals doesn't necessarily mean sharing decision-making. Partners often try to run their joint ventures together—whether out of distrust of each other or out of a genuine desire to share. Core(s) decision-making, decentralized empowerment, and matrix management across enterprise boundaries often represent the style and shape of management. Often, the result is management gridlock. To solve this problem, alliance veterans suggest two alternative strategies—either give one partner sole authority to run the venture or set the alliance up as a completely autonomous operation answerable only to its board. The basis for the rationale for giving one partner operating control is a superior knowledge or skill.

Don't Have Surprises.   The demands placed upon newcomers to corporate alliances often come as a surprise. The difficulty lies not only in the management of the business but also in less defined areas such as personal relationships between managers from different corporate cultures. When conflicts erupt, they are typically much harder to resolve than in conventional companies, where a top executive can usually end an internal dispute by fiat. The only solutions that seem to work are time-consuming contacts between senior managers at the participating companies. If this organizational cross-pollenization isn't effective, neither is the alliance. The potential damages from these conflicts lessen if the participants carefully craft agreements at the outset. It is possible to craft an agreement for a merger or acquisition in days, because the dominant company imposes its corporate culture. However, a joint venture or alliance can easily take a year to negotiate.

It is also a good practice to define the enforcement of any preexisting limitations or barriers regarding shared skills, core competencies, and so forth, between partners. Formal renegotiation is necessary if any of these limitations or barriers become impediments to the success of the alliance or venture.

Permit Autonomy.   Autonomy is emerging as an important ingredient for success in alliances because it allows a new venture to adapt to its particular market instead of copying the practices of its parents. While the parent corporations typically have a mature corporate culture and management systems and practices, a startup generally doesn't benefit from the predefined structures. Most alliances are better off starting from scratch and designing new systems for themselves.

Trust.   Perhaps the biggest stumbling block to the success of alliances is the lack of trust. The best legal minds can't write trust into a contract: it has to come voluntarily. It's this subtlety of relationship-building that most U.S. companies lack. U.S. companies, unused to the familial relationships between corporations typical of Europe or the Japanese *keiretsu,* act using the mind-set of acquisition and control rather than of collaboration.

Maintain Flexibility.   The most important precept of alliances is to remain flexible. Markets continue to evolve and so should the expectations of alliance partners. While joint efforts need clearly articulated groundrules and goals, they need the flexibility to change direction. Rethinking and reevaluating the direction of the alliance to keep it fresh makes many a questionable alliance successful.

In case the mutual need disappears or the shared objectives change, an exit strategy should be part of the initial negotiations. In this way, both partners understand that this possibility exists if mutual benefits disappear.

Corning and the Role of Alliances

Corning, the $3 billion a year glass and ceramics maker, is renown for making alliances work. Alliances are so central to the Corning strategy that the corporation now defines itself as a network of organizations.

A testament to its success is Dow Corning, a joint venture with Dow Chemical, big enough to be one of the Fortune 500. Corning's success at corporate alliances comes from working with a very long-term perspective. The vice chairman, Van Campbell, looks for what he calls lifetime associations. He reasons that you must constantly nurture the partner relationship, maintaining high-level contacts. Then, when you deal with business items of substance you are dealing with friends, people you understand and respect.[8] A partnership that is going to last only five to seven years, Campbell adds, simply doesn't warrant that kind of investment.

MERGERS AND ACQUISITIONS

Another means of physically restructuring the enterprise is through mergers and acquisitions. When two existing enterprises combine, it is a *merger* if it is a combination of perceived equals and an *acquisition* if one is clearly the dominant enterprise.

Mergers and Acquisitions in Europe

Many enterprises are using mergers and acquisitions to restructure and position themselves for the European Common Market. Some of these activities are subject to the EU merger regulation. Its main provisions are the following:

- The regulation applies to concentrations that involve companies with combined worldwide sales of European currency units (ecu) amounting to 5 billion, and two or more companies with EU sales of ecu 250 million.
- Once notified by Brussels, mergers and acquisitions become suspended for three weeks, or longer if necessary.
- If the task force has serious doubts about a merger or acquisition, it launches a full investigation. The commission then has four months to decide whether to approve it, block it, or insist on modifications.[11]

There are a significant number of cross-border mergers and acquisitions taking place that doesn't require EU approval. These take place on an almost daily basis as companies attempt to establish a presence in another country (see Table 8-1 for an example group of investors, target companies and sectors, and strategic objectives).[12]

Bidder/Investor	Target/Partner	Industry Sector	Comments
PepsiCo (US)	Knoor Elorza (Spain)	Soft drinks	Merger and/or Acquisition (M&A) to double local market share.
Unilever (UK/Netherlands)	Lipton India (India)	Food	M&A to increase stake to 51%.
Waste Management Int'l. (US/UK)	Environment Service (France)	Waste management	M&A to fuel French expansion.
Nestle (Switzerland)	Coca-Cola (US)	Soft drinks	50/50 Joint Venture (JV) to develop ready-to-drink tea and coffee market outside Japan.
PepsiCo (US)	Unilever (UK/Netherlands)	Soft drinks	JV to develop tea-based drinks and distribution of Lipton tea products, initially in US.
PepsiCo (US)	General MIlls (US)	Snack food	Merger of continental European snack food businesses in a 60/40 JV.
Unilever (UK/Netherlands)	BSN (France)	Snack food	JV to make and market worldwide products combining ice cream and yogurt.

Table 8-1   Sampling of Cross Border Strategic Alliances, Mergers, and Acquisitions.
Source: *Financial Times* (New York), November 30, 1992, p. 14, col. 6–8, and January 22, 1993, p. 13, col. 2–6.

Mergers and Acquisitions in the Banking Industry

When business strategies require either a large physical or internal critical mass to be successful, a merger or acquisition is often the only possible alternative. Witness the activity in the American banking system. The dominant strategy is to create a bank that will be competitive in the new environment of national and/or global banking and to cut costs at the same time. The BankAmerica acquisition of Security Pacific positions BankAmerica not only as the leader in the West but as one of the few potential leaders in national branch banking. By pruning overlapping operations (10,000 jobs out of a combined 93,800) the new bank expects to add $1 billion to its annual pretax earnings within the first three years of the acquisition.

Bank of America and Security Pacific Become BankAmerica. The merger of Bank of America and Security Pacific in 1991 created a bank with assets of $194 billion, second only to New York's Citicorp.[13] The new bank, BankAmerica, dominates the western states: from Alaska south to its headquarters in California, and then south and east to Texas. In Texas, its eastern border meets the western boundaries of NationsBank, the giant southeastern bank that is a product of the merger of NCNB Corporation and C&S/Sovran. BankAmerica territory also touches the southern outreaches of Ohio's BancOne, which became one of America's ten biggest banks by spreading steadily through the Midwest in a series of modest mergers. Thus the industry is already organizing the future heartland of America's national retail banking industry.

Many bank mergers aim at cutting costs to boost profit and generate capital. BankAmerica ultimately expects to save an annual $1 billion from the merger by reducing duplicate staff, closing redundant branches, and combining computer systems. This merger has additional logic: BankAmerica's traditional strength is northern California, whereas the Los Angeles-based Security Pacific is strong in the South. The combined bank controls around half of the California retail market and so dominates the state that any potential national rivals will have difficulty getting established.

The new bank is the country's biggest retail bank. It runs the largest network of automated teller machines and originates more home loans than any other competitor. BankAmerica expanded steadily throughout the West, positioning itself to be a formidable leader in national retail banking and quietly built its position in national commercial banking.

BankAmerica is firmly entrenched in commercial banking, due to its technology investment in an international computer network in the mid-1980s. Only it and a handful of other banks—including Citicorp and Chase Manhattan—can offer U.S. companies a host of essential services anywhere in the world, ranging from foreign-exchange trading to deposit and check-clearing functions. BankAmerica has an edge over other rivals domestically because it dominates the highly automated business of check processing, processing nearly one out of eight checks written in the United States.

One post-merger problem was the development of a cohesive strategy for Asia. Both banks were doing business in locations throughout the region before the merger. They had dissimilar business strategies and customer bases, and the breadth and depth of their presence in the region created problems. BankAmerica employed 2,800 people in the region, while Security Pacific had 1,500. Both banks had entrenched business in virtually all major Asian markets.[14] While both emphasized trade financings in the Asian markets, BankAmerica targeted top-tier local clientele and foreign multinationals in Asia, while Security Pacific targeted the middle market, composed mainly of small to middle-size Chinese companies. Even in Malaysia, the business was different: Security Pacific had been developing more merchant-banking business to supplement its traditional trade-financing operations while BankAmerica's primary focus was lending and trade finance.

Six months after the merger, it was still trying to sort out what shape—what culture and business direction—the melded entity would take in Asia. Despite this delay, given the established networks of the two banks in the region and the public perception that Asian interests can best be served by West Coast banks, BankAmerica is likely to strengthen its hold in the region.

Chemical Banking and Manufacturers Hanover Become Chemical Banking.   The merger of Chemical Banking and Manufacturers Hanover created the third largest bank (ranked by assets) in the United States, behind Citicorp and BankAmerica. The new bank was born with a cost-cutting mentality. It adopted the Chemical name partly because doing so required fewer sign changes.

Before the merger, the two banks competed mostly in the New York City metropolitan area. The potential savings from consolidation are enormous because there were so many overlapping operations. They plan to meet their target of $750 million annual savings within the first three years of the merger.

The merger created financial and services synergy. In the first quarter of 1992, the new company reduced expenses by $50 million, which caused higher ratings on Chemical's senior debt. In turn, this higher rating helped produce higher revenues by encouraging safety-conscious customers to use Chemical more often for such services as cash management, letters of credit, and trading. First quarter 1992 trading revenues climbed to $228 million, up 37 percent from the total for both banks a year earlier.[15]

The merged bank also attracted customers with a broader menu of services than its predecessors could offer. Each tended to have its own specialty—Chemical in mergers and acquisitions, for example, and Manufacturers Hanover in international business. The combined bank now has more than half of the New York City area's highly desirable middle market business, lending to companies with sales of $250 million or less. Almost every banker covets these customers. Unlike bigger corporations that issue commercial paper, these businesses still borrow from banks. A good relationship between the two chief executive officers smoothed the path to integration and that cooperation spread throughout the newly combined organization.

OUTSOURCING AND DOWNSIZING

Many U.S. enterprises have fundamentally reshaped their work forces in recent years, establishing a core work force of permanent employees surrounded by a flexible border of temporary and part-time workers. As the economy and business grow, temporary workers fill a significant percentage of added jobs. Employers defer filling permanent positions and keep work forces lean. Companies are turning to flexible staffing to maneuver through the ups and downs of the business cycle. This approach helps to avoid layoffs and transforms fixed costs into variable costs. Temporary help firms are increasingly asked by larger clients to assume charge of entire functions such as the testing and training of office personnel. Expect this trend, while still young, to continue.

Rationale of Outsourcing

The business strategy behind outsourcing should be to keep the best people in the core organization and identify another organization or enterprise that can do the rest of the functions and do them better than the current staff. Note that this is a different business strategy than often practiced, which is to keep the best, let go of the rest, and find an organization or enterprise that can do the work for less. The latter reason for outsourcing is wrong because it's based on cost. Instead, base outsourcing decisions on quality issues for the core business, key business processes or peripheral processes.

Quality performance for both goods and services is the litmus test for the successful global enterprise. In a recent book, Peter Drucker entitled a chapter "Sell the Mailroom: Unbundling in the '90s."[16] He believes that by the end of the century it may be the rule, especially in large organizations, to outsource all activities that do not offer the people working in them opportunities for advancement into senior management. He adds that this approach may be the only way to attain productivity in clerical, maintenance, and support work.

Increasing productivity in such work will remain a central challenge in developed countries. His rationale is that in-house service and support activities are de facto monopolies. They have little incentive to improve performance because they have no competition. The people running in-house support services are also unlikely to do the hard, innovative, and often costly work required to increase productivity associated with service work because, until it is possible to gain promotion into senior management for doing a good job, it won't get done. Using this rationale, productivity won't go up for support activities until separate, free-standing enterprises perform the work. An outside contractor always knows he risks replacement by a better-performing competitor unless he improves quality and cuts costs.

Outsourcing in the Banking Industry

In the early 1990s, cost-cutting American bankers viewed outsourcing as a quick fix to the rising costs of technology. They delegated to specialist subcontractors the data processing, systems integration, and management that accounts for up to two-thirds of a banks' operating expenses not interest-related.[17]

Outsourcing offers obvious gains. It provides instant economies of scale for repetitive operations such as data processing. These yield good cost savings and relieve a bank of the worry of keeping up its hardware and software investment. Additionally, banks can get access to specialist services, including credit card and student loan processing, or, in the case of merged banks, systems consolidation.

The practice also has its drawbacks. Managers lose responsibility for what has become a large portion of the banks' costs. Also, outsourcing leads banks to discard in-house technological expertise just when banking is becoming an increasingly high-tech business. Like other service firms, banks have to be low-cost, high-quality suppliers. Technology now drives both improvements in customer service and new products. Because third-party vendors have little incentive to create strategic advantage for just one customer, many banks are deciding to regain control of the future by terminating outsourcing contracts and revamping current technology. The real question that a bank must answer is whether I/T is—or should be—a core business.

MANAGEMENT AND EMPLOYEE BUY OUTS

Management and employee buy outs prove valuable as a way to restructure companies. Following the current corporate trend to move away from diversification, the business practice popular in the early 1980s, many large companies concentrate on the core business in which the majority of the skills within the company lie. Today, few corporate boards reject out of hand the idea of selling a noncore or underperforming business.

Both types of buy outs are a popular vehicle for moving service and support activities out of the core business. Once the noncore business becomes independent of the parent, it can be refocused and taken forward at a much faster pace. An independent owner-managed company will have greater incentive, shorter lines of decision-making, and freedom to manage and make decisions quickly.

Most buy outs have one thing in common: the participants have never done it before. This makes negotiating a buy out a particularly stressful experience for all involved: the buyers, the sellers, and the financial backers. Financial backers and the sellers want to see a well-balanced group of managers and employees with financial, marketing, and production skills. They want people with senior experience but who have also not lost touch with the realities of doing business. They know that running a small company is very different from managing part of a large corporation with extensive support systems and known cultures in place. The sellers have justifiable concern about the management talent, especially when the buy out creates a service organization to which they will outsource. Buy outs not only arise from corporate restructuring situations and as vehicles to accomplish outsourcing, they can and will continue to assist the succession of ownership of private companies.

RESTRUCTURING OR TRANSFORMATION: FOUR EXAMPLES

The recession of the early 1990s hit the chemical industry hard, both in the United States and elsewhere. Weak demand squeezed profit margins while companies struggled under a burden of overcapacity and excessive costs. These common problems, however, elicited different responses. In the United Kingdom, Imperial Chemical Industries (ICI) announced plans to split off its pharmaceutical businesses and engaged in a program of cost cutting, while U.S.-based Union Carbide spun off its business in industrial gases to create a free-standing company, Praxair. Two other U.S.-based chemical companies—Du Pont and Monsanto—took significantly different approaches to the changes in the global economy and competition. Du Pont chose restructuring while Monsanto Resins, a division of Monsanto, chose to move toward transformation.

It is difficult to transform a division, and the task to transform an entire enterprise seems almost insurmountable. Nevertheless, Motorola, now the global market leader in cellular phones, pagers, two-way radios, and microprocessors, faced the challenge and is one of the few genuine role models for strategic transformation. The fourth example—the transformation of the Canadian national economy—provides an insight into transformation activities that may occur beyond enterprise walls and influence the competitive environment.

Restructuring Du Pont

Du Pont, the biggest U.S. chemicals group, embarked upon the most radical restructuring plan in its 190-year history. The plan, which involves cutting costs, concentrating on core divisions, expanding European and Asian revenues, and disposing of noncore assets, will determine whether Du Pont can stay among the leaders of the international chemicals industry during the 1990s. As the eighth largest of the Fortune 500 companies in the United States, the restructuring is also a measure of how well U.S. industry is adjusting to the international economy.[18]

In the United States, falling demand from industrial customers, especially in the auto and housing industries, adversely affected Du Pont. This caused Du Pont to develop and embark on a new strategy. The Du Pont strategy is simple and straightforward:

- Reduce fixed costs.
- Concentrate on core businesses.
- Expand geographically.

Du Pont's strategy reduces fixed costs by $3 billion (about 30% of the total) by 1996. It involves its principal divisions—chemicals, fibers, polymers, and energy (a division dominated by Conoco, the oil company). The total work force of 130,000 will shrink by almost 12 percent, and there is a plan to eliminate about 3,200 outside contract workers. Du Pont also entered a joint venture (Du Pont Merck Pharmaceutical) between its pharmaceuticals business with Merck, the biggest U.S. drug company. Pharmaceuticals were too small and too costly to operate alone. It sold half of its coal business to Germany-based Rheinbaum, as part of its strategy to dispose of nonstrategic businesses.

Reflecting its strategy to concentrate on the core businesses, it is investing $1.5 billion over a ten-year period to modernize U.S. nylon production facilities. In response to a Taiwan-based company that is building a polyester plant in South Carolina, it is investing $300 million in modernizing its U.S. polyester plants.

Internationally, Du Pont seeks to almost triple its nonenergy European revenues to $15 billion by the end of the decade. It agreed to swap most of its remaining acrylics business for the European nylon holdings of ICI. In Asia, it invested $240 million in a new Taiwan pigments plant, moving the competition into the home territory of its new and lower cost competitors. It plans one or more big acquisitions in Europe.

Along with the numerous disposals and cost cutting, the company's management culture is changing. Executives admit that until recently there was much complacency among the management ranks. Now a rigorous assessment of middle management takes place, removing and replacing those believed to be underperforming. One chemicals analyst at a New York investment house observed that Du Pont historically wanted to be the biggest and the best and would spend the most to get there.[18] Now it has restructured itself into a company that will get there by spending less and spending it more efficiently.

Transforming a Division: Monsanto Resins

Monsanto Resins, the second largest chemical division of Monsanto, moved its headquarters out of the parent company's home country to Brussels. The resins division's largest business is the vinyl that goes into laminated vehicle windshields and some architectural glass. Using the brand name Saflex, Monsanto is twice as large as its closest rival.

Only 40 percent of Saflex sales are in the Americas, against 50 percent in Europe, and 10 percent in Asia—both of which have markets expanding faster than that of the United States.[19] The vast proportion of the division's customers are global glassmakers, most of which are headquartered outside the United States. Due to the German automobile and building industries, and to the Japanese, many of its most innovative customers are also outside the United States. Given the geographic realities of its customer base, the elements in Monsanto Resins' strategy were to:

- Move headquarters closer to the market.
- Create and reflect a global mind-set for planning and production.
- Manage horizontally across disciplines and regions.
- Reengineer management and production systems.
- Provide appropriate training and motivation for the new work ethic.

Until the Brussels move, it had an organizational setup that forced a focus primarily on North America—at the expense of product and market opportunities elsewhere. Because of the Brussels move, the time spent on strategy for North America dropped significantly. With a largely new management team, the head of the resins division is creating a global mind-set in resins. The new attitude is that the division's headquarters might be anywhere—since globalization is a state of mind.[19]

About half of the management team is in Brussels, with the remainder based in St. Louis and Boston. It facilitates communications between these people and their subordinates with extensive in-house video conferencing across the United States, Europe, and Asia. To optimize production on an ongoing worldwide basis, processes for product categorization and labeling, capacity planning, working capital, and production loading are being redesigned to integrate the various plants in Europe, the United States, Brazil, and Asia. Additionally, it plans worldwide consolidation and control of orders, production flows, and inventories.

Perhaps more difficult to accomplish than the technical problems associated with reengineering key business processes is that of changing people's attitudes and ways of working. In the past, everyone identified their interests with their region, discipline, and department, and made decisions accordingly—whether about work on research projects, new product development, production, pricing, or anything else. Decisions and actions that needed coordination went up the vertical hierarchy, and then transferred across to the next hierarchy at the senior level before being referred downwards again. Now the organization is working horizontally as a worldwide team. This involves getting people at all levels to manage horizontally across disciplines and regions. It also requires rethinking and reengineering of each management procedure and system.

Working as a global team also requires retraining and motivation programs so that people at all levels understand their new roles and how they are to relate to each other. Monsanto Resins makes extensive use of team work psychologists to help train its people and influence their real readiness to work in the new style, rather than just their expressed acceptance. One manager observed that the employees are coming over one at a time and starting to think differently about working in flexible, interdisciplinary project teams, emphasizing repeatedly that the human side of going global is at least as important as redesigning systems and procedures.[19]

Transforming an Enterprise: Motorola

Large well-established corporations like General Motors and IBM have been struggling with the failure of management to effectively anticipate and embrace change, or to foster a participative culture, or to organize workers into more productive, smaller work teams. Motorola, however, transformed itself into a stronger enterprise. From a slowly declining U.S. electronics company, it became an industry legend, driven by a corporate culture that embodies decentralization, empowerment, and continuous quality and cycle-time improvements. The corporate culture enables it to continually move out along the curve of innovation, to invent new, related applications of technology (a form of technology fusion) as fast as older ones become commodity-type products.

Motorola is in the top ten companies in the United States for investing in research and development to support technology advancements and manufacturing improvements.[20] Its corporate culture encourages conflict and dissent, finds promising but neglected projects to fund, and generates a constant flow of information and innovation from the thousands of small teams that hold to rigorous, statistically evaluated goals. Elements of Motorola's transformation strategy are aggressive:

- Support a corporate culture that anticipates and builds on change.
- Continue emphasis on quality.
- Support a heavyweight team culture.
- Sustain information and (technology) intelligence flow.
- Maintain a participative culture encouraging freedom to act and to dissent.
- Provide appropriate employee training and motivation.

Creating this type of transformation isn't without a price. Managers burn out, and workers are released as the company changes product direction or replaces them with automation. The combative culture sometimes causes delays. What it buys is priceless: an organization and culture that is good at anticipating change.

Motorola imbeds anticipation in the corporate culture through their use of a technique called technology scanning, coupled with an intelligence department that reports on the latest technology developments. After gathering the information, they use it to develop technology roadmaps that assess where breakthroughs are likely to occur, when they can incorporate them into new products, how much the development will cost, and what the competition is doing. Dissension and conflict are also part of the culture. The benefit is that it results in keeping top managers fully informed— through, for example, the filing of a minority report when an employee feels their idea isn't being supported. Dissension about the quality in its two-way radios provided the entree for a formal quality program at the company.

It announced two productivity goals in 1987: first, reduce manufacturing defects by 90 percent every two years, and second, reduce cycle-time—the time required to develop a new product or fill a customer order—by 90 percent every five years. In 1991, Motorola spent $70 million teaching employees techniques for identifying and fixing problems affecting quality, among other things. Motorola imposes the same performance standards on the outside sources that provide some of its parts.

Extensive team work is part of Motorola's culture, and employees receive training on team working before they become team members. One team, mostly composed of high-school graduates, started using basic industrial-engineering techniques to analyze inventory for Motorola's automotive and industrial group. They reduced average levels of supply from seven weeks to four, saving the company $2.4 million a year. Teams, formed to address specific problems and then disbanded, continue to contribute to Motorola's strength.

During the period 1988–1992, Motorola's work force grew only slightly, while its sales doubled. In 1988, it was one of the first winners of the Malcolm Baldrige National Quality Award. A continuing audit of expenses, such as for factory downtime and warranty repairs, indicates Motorola's 1992 costs are $900 million lower than they would have been without its investments and reorganization.[20] In 1993, the profits surged 77 percent to $1.02 billion and sales grew 28 percent to $17 billion—performance driven largely by its continuing commitment to quality.

Having one of the finest reputations for quality in corporate America, however, doesn't guarantee that success will continue. Motorola's leaders believe that by the end of the century, quality will have changed from a goal to a given, and the next set of crucial competitive weapons will be *responsiveness* (constantly improving cycle-time and time-to-market), *adaptability* (the organizational agility and core competencies to change rapidly), and *creativity* (the thinking, innovative enterprise). To develop these attributes and instill them in the corporate culture, Motorola launched a program built around the concept of lifelong learning, increasing its training goals. (The 1994 average was already forty hours of training a year per employee.) The objective is a work force that is both disciplined (knowledge of procedures and practices) and freethinking—providing the knowledge and independent-mindedness necessary to conquer rapidly changing technologies and markets. With change rendering an engineer's knowledge obsolete every five years—and with Motorola in the technology business—there seems little choice but to begin to inculcate the technology fusion paradigms into the corporate culture.

Transforming a Nation: A Knowledge-Based Canada

Canada has one of the highest standards of living in the world, due to a combination of abundant national resources and native ingenuity. Continued success, however, depends upon the ability to change its economic context to reflect the rapidly evolving knowledge-based global economic environment. Moreover, with capital becoming increasingly mobile and deregulation becoming a global norm, governments are less able to shelter inefficient industries from international competition. Combined with data showing that growth industries from 1973 to 1988 relied heavily on knowledge and innovation, the facts pointed to a requirement for Canada to commit to fundamental economic change.

In 1992, the Canadian Information Technology Sector Advisory Committee of the Information Technology Association of Canada, comprised of members of five of Canada's leading I/T professional organizations, published a comprehensive set of goals, strategies, and actions necessary for a knowledge-based nation.[21] The committee identified four goals in the economic transformation: a competitive national environment, innovation in research and development, effective financing, and work place transformation. The strategies for accomplishing each goal are parallel to strategies that transforming enterprises employ.

Not unlike other nations, Canada's public policy is regulatory in nature and isn't favorable for fostering strategic alliances. Provinces still protect current industry by erecting trade barriers with each other—acting almost like a confederation of independent nations—which makes the establishment of any national critical mass difficult. Additionally, national economic measures don't adequately reflect the true nature of the structural change. This shortcoming contributes to a mainstream Canadian population that focuses on resources, manufacturing, and traditional services.

The strategies identified to accomplish the goal of national and international competitiveness address the necessity to:

- Eliminate all Canadian-made barriers to trade and adopt a common regulatory framework for inter- and intra-Canadian trade.
- Revise Canada's national economic indicators and measurements to reflect the shift towards an increasingly knowledge-based economy.
- Adhere to international standards.
- Foster the use of I/T by Canadian organizations to improve competitiveness.

Canadian research is fragmented among many parties and lacks the critical mass to be world-class. Strategies to improve Canada's activities in innovation, research, and development include initiatives to:

- Realign and refocus university and government mandates to support the new vision.
- Orchestrate one or more national projects that will stretch Canadian capabilities in the development and application of I/T.

Canada lacks a strong venture capital culture, which hinders any significant investment in its technology companies. Strategies to promote a more effective financing environment include government actions to:

- Seed new private-sector technology-focused venture capital funds with government funds.
- Create a more favorable financial climate for high-risk ventures through regulatory change.

A combination of skills obsolescence, limited access to I/T-skilled immigrants, Canadian overachievers migrating to countries offering better opportunities, and an overall lack of appreciation that change is a necessity, create the need to transform the Canadian workplace. Strategies to transform the workplace include actions to:

- Create a skilled work force by improving Canada's school system.
- Promote the concept of lifelong learning.
- Create a national awareness of the necessity to change.

The proposed Canadian strategies tie together a number of themes already introduced—the need for appropriate indicators and measurements, the need for lifelong learning, the necessity of adherence to international standards, and the recognition that these changes impact everyone. These themes, applied at the individual, team, enterprise, or national level are universal to all transformational efforts. Other Canadian strategies involving the role of I/T in the transformation serve as an introduction to the growing importance of the I/T charter in maintaining competitiveness at all levels. By the committees' actions, it initiated what has since evolved into a business partnership between the I/T professional community and the Canadian government.

OBSERVATIONS

Transformation involves not only a discontinuous shift in an organization's capability, but also the ability to sustain that shift, which is substantially harder.[22] Richard Pascale, one of the sought-after American advisors on how to accomplish radical change, points out the difficulty of detecting the need for a transformation even in the midst of success (or excess), starkly illustrated in the mid-1980s. Only five years after the publication of the 1982 best seller, *In Search of Excellence,* all but fourteen of its forty-three *excellent* companies had either grown weaker or were showing warning signs of an impending decline despite managements best efforts to improve things.

Faced with the need for a change, companies come to a fork in the road, argues Pascale. About 80 percent take the easy route, stripping themselves back to basics, searching for the latest tools and techniques—and going on to risk stagnation or decline. Managers in these companies drive change by managing by the financial books. They sell off underperforming and noncore businesses and outsource services and support functions but stop short of addressing the cultural, managerial, and organizational deficiencies that are at the heart of the problem. This approach affords a short financial respite, but does not form the basis of a long-term solution.

Only about 20 percent of the companies take the much tougher, alternative route, illustrated in Figure 8-1. This involves three big steps:

- Inquire into the underlying paradigm: Question the way everything is done—including thinking. Articulate and examine the basis for every assumption.
- Attack the problems systematically: Attack the problems systematically on all fronts, notably strategy, operations, organization, and culture.
- Reinvent to sustain transformation: Reinvent the organization in such a way that the transformation becomes self-sustaining and continuous.

Transformation stands for nothing short of a revolution.

For companies facing the real-world challenge of globalization, what matters are the practical and innovative approaches being formulated and applied to every facet of the strategic management of the global business—areas such as manufacturing strategies, like mass customization and lean manufacturing, and product development, marketing, and distribution strategies. In this and the preceding chapter we introduced two other intertwining facets of the strategic management of the global business—those of business process and organizational redesign and restructuring and human resource planning and development.

For business to successfully plan for and accomplish these strategies requires information and information networks in their most global and local sense—team work

Promise	Management Actions	Enabling Technologies	Enterprise Change
Renaissance Enterprise	Reinvent to sustain transformation	Inter-enterprise computing	Recast external and internal relationships
Integrated / Networked Organization	Attack problems systematically on all fronts	Integrated and networked systems	Organizational and cultural transformation
High Performance Team	Examine and verify all paradigms	Teamworking computing	Business process and organizational redesign

Figure 8-1   Transformation to the Renaissance Enterprise.

computing; integrated, networked systems; and inter- and intraenterprise computing whose design criteria support an implementation that reflects flexibility and the realities of constant change. Business management, in efforts to develop, implement, and strengthen new strategies in support of the transformation of the enterprise, demand philosophically new applications of information technology. They include:

- The support of business reengineering of design, manufacturing, delivery, and service and quality of mass customized products.
- The creation of a seamless global office through integration of multiple technologies.
- The information empowerment of all employees.
- A borderless network of information for flexible organizations.

To create a Renaissance Enterprise requires transformation in three ways. First, the enterprise must recreate the structure through business process and business organization redesign. Second, it must recreate the culture by systematically examining and changing all business and I/T policies, strategies, systems, and people to support the new vision. Third, it must recreate both internal and external relationships to support constant change.

Part IV

TRANSFORMING I/T

As a result of enterprise transformation, management expectations for I/T (current activities, future roles) are changing. This discussion will focus on translating enterprise change into new requirements for I/T, and how current organizations are enabling this change (Chapters 9 and 10). Key to these activities is the ability of I/T—both the technology and the support organizations—to consistently demonstrate the contribution to business value through evolving measurements that reflect the goals and objectives of the transforming enterprise (Chapter 11).

The featured contributed article in Appendix I is "Organizational Restructuring and Process Reengineering," by Lynwood Walker. It constitutes a case study of one company, AGT Limited, and its I/T various organizations and the actions taken to improve market position. Technology downsizing, outsourcing, decentralization and recentralization, and strategic alliances are just part of the I/T activities surrounding the I/T role in facilitating business change. The second article, "Business Value," by Dr. Robert J. Benson, offers an in-depth discussion of the various perspectives of value.

9

Expanding the I/T Charter

Core competencies and learning organizations are critical concepts for transformation. However, core competencies and learning organizations can't thrive without an I/T organization chartered to deliver and disperse information and shared knowledge throughout the enterprise. The emerging I/T charter to support both the enterprise and its own transformation activities include new management approaches and business roles and leaves little room for reticence in adopting the new paradigms.

Up to this point, we have put into a working perspective a number of management concepts: product quality and responsive customer service, mass customization, empowerment, employee involvement through work teams, cross-functional collaboration, and the redesign of business organizations and processes. These concepts aren't really new ideas for management. What is new is the fervor with which executives are attempting to apply them within the enterprise. They do so with the hope of transforming it to maintain competitiveness in the market place.

There are two additional management concepts associated with transformation that we address in this chapter—core competencies and learning organizations. The reason for delaying the discussion until now is that I/T and an appropriate I/T charter within the enterprise are inexorably linked to the successful application of these concepts. Core competencies can't strengthen and learning organizations can't thrive without an I/T organization with a charter to disperse information and shared knowledge throughout the enterprise. A free flow of information across internal organizational boundaries must exist before any information can efficiently and effectively convert to knowledge. This is what enables the knowledgeable decision-making necessary for transformation.

CORE COMPETENCIES

Markets are transitory. Early business law recognized this and provided for a company to form for a particular purpose and then close at task completion. There was no legal intention that companies would last forever, finding new roles after fulfilling their original purpose. Yet despite the uncertainties of the commercial world, some businesses survive not just for decades, but for centuries. A Dun & Bradstreet guide to the largest 50,000 companies in England found 258 businesses over 200 years old and more than 3,200 at least 100 years old![1]

What allows these businesses to survive while the vast majority succumb? The common characteristic they share is that all stayed in the same core sector in which they started, even though they had to adapt to considerable technological, political, and social change. Two examples are Aberdeen Harbour Board and Alldays Peracock. The Aberdeen Harbour Board (the oldest company on the list) began by collecting tithes from shipping in 1136 under the authority of King David I of Scotland. It installed its first crane in 1582, adapted to steam trawlers in the late 1800s, and now serves the oil and fishing industries. Alldays Peracock began in 1650 manufacturing bellows for blacksmiths' forges and foghorns for the British Admiralty. Before mission statements were fashionable it decided that its role was to *move air*.[1] Its current business is manufacturing centrifugal fans for heavy industrial use.

Now, after more than a decade of acquisition-based growth, businesses are getting ready for the future through divestitures and going back to basics—its unique core competencies. Sears, Roebuck announced, for example, that it would abandon its financial services ventures and focus on retailing. GTE Corporation made a similar move when it abandoned its lighting and precision-materials divisions to concentrate activities on communications. This trend towards focusing on core competencies also feeds outsourcing activities, from activities as mundane as mailroom services to tapping specialized contractors for their expertise and efficiency.[2] We need, therefore, to understand the concept of core competency to assess its importance in the transformational process.

Core Competencies: What Business Brings to the Table

In previous chapters, we emphasized the key forces (quality, service, process redesign, and so forth, in the new globally defined market) that are rapidly changing the business environment, impacting every existing enterprise. We discussed various ways in which the enterprise responds to these pressures—downsizing, outsourcing, strategic alliances, mergers and acquisitions, and joint ventures, among others. Behind a decision to implement any of these business alternatives is the rational assessment of the core competencies of the enterprise, where the existing competencies undergo evaluation to develop a best fit business strategy.

Attributes of core competencies for both the business and I/T functions fall into three categories. They are people, process, and product. For the business function, these categories have the following attributes:

- The degree of asset embodied in the intellectual assets of its people: These assets represent the organizational qualities involving such things as vision, skills, capabilities, innovation and new ideas, planning, plan execution, and corporate culture. These attributes represent the ability of the business function to anticipate and rapidly accommodate change, to think and act beyond traditional boundaries, and to sustain an environment of continuous innovation within its existing or transforming corporate culture.
- The degree of asset represented by its current processes: Flourishing work teams, fluid functional and operational organization boundaries, knowledge and implementation of best practices, and a culture base of change and flexibility provide an organizational and functional environment with a culture supportive of continuous change. To achieve strategic transformation, Sumantra Ghoshal, while professor of business policy at INSEAD—the Fontainebleau-based European Institute of Business Administration—further refined this process core competency into those of the *entrepreneurial process,* that drives the creation of new businesses; the *integration process,* that links and leverages the organization's resources and capabilities and builds a new company; and the *renewal process,* that continuously revitalizes the company by challenging existing beliefs and practices.[3] For management, this requires a fundamental change in roles: the front-line manager must become an aggressive entrepreneur, while senior managers become their coaches. The most traumatic role transformation occurs at the executive level. Top management, according to Ghoshal, will need to exercise institutional leadership. Simultaneously, it must create the infrastructure and context for others to assume their new roles as entrepreneurs and coaches.
- Product intelligence: Whatever the product created, the basis for the degree of asset this category contributes is knowledge—knowledge of best of practice, the current and future market, and possible windows of opportunity. This knowledge endows the business function with the necessary sensitivity to outside forces that may possess the potential to change current markets or to create new ones.

These combined core competencies create the unique body of business knowledge that is the construct for focusing both I/T and business strategy. This shared business-technology knowledge base also provides early warning of supplier and customer trends so that I/T can formulate alternative technology responses. Other assessments derived from the knowledge base created by the business core competencies include existing versus future (people) competency requirements, existing versus future (process) flexibility requirements, and existing versus future (product) time-to-market requirements. Drawing upon its unique set of core competencies, the I/T function translates the articulated business requirements into sets of alternative I/T responses. Choosing from the menu of alternatives becomes a joint business-I/T activity (see Figure 9-1 for an illustration of this relationship).

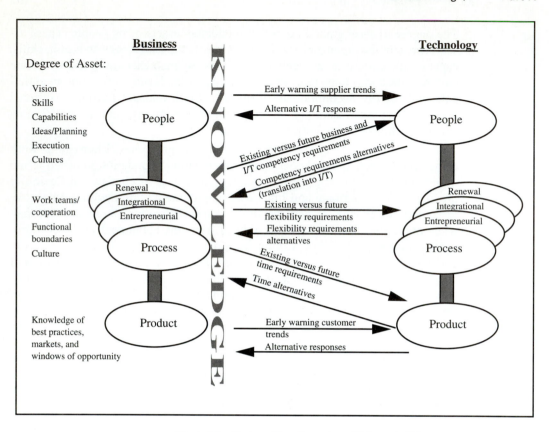

Figure 9-1   Business Core Competency Linkages to I/T.

Core Competencies: What I/T Brings to the Table

Like the business function, the I/T function has a similar set of core competencies that create a technology-oriented intelligence base.

- The degree of asset embodied in the intellectual assets of its people: Specifically addressed is the knowledge of technical capabilities and the ability to envision and create viable, often innovative, alternatives by its technical and management staff. These attributes represent the ability of the technology function to translate business requirements into business solutions through the application of technology.
- I/T has a set of core capabilities relating to process: This includes such capabilities as creating, managing and working in a team environment, cross-functional (business) knowledge, knowledge and implementation of (process) best practices and systems analysis, design, and implementation. These capabilities create the culture for initiating and sustaining transformational change.
- Product-related core competencies: Intimate knowledge of supplier, enterprise,

and customer skill-base through, for example, electronic data interchange (EDI), and knowledge of (product) best practice provides the business function with another view of the outside world, as well as an assessment of its own internal functions.

The degree to which each of these core capabilities is a fully developed asset contributes to the overall makeup and unique characteristics of the enterprise shared knowledge. It provides the technology view of the outside world to the business function for its analysis and action. It is the construct for the technology alternatives available to create business solutions, supporting information empowerment activities for the business people, organizational and process redesign for the business process, and contributes service, quality, and value to the business product (see Figure 9-2).

It is obvious, as we reflect back on some of the industry examples in previous chapters, that each enterprise has a unique set of competencies whose character gradually shifts over time. Competencies may languish and die as a result of outsourcing. Others become redundant or meaningless during mergers or acquisitions or are out-

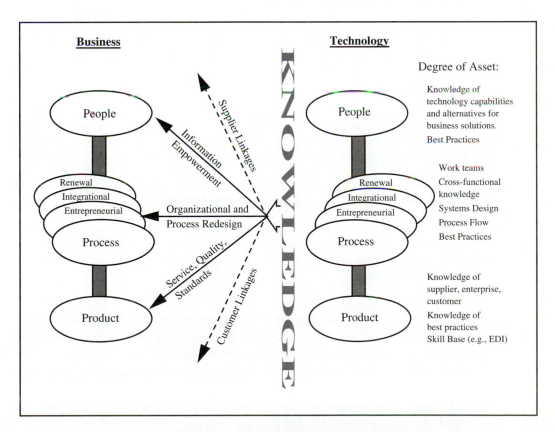

Figure 9-2   I/T Core Competency Linkages to Business.

dated by a changing market. Conversely, each can gain a new importance if the competency is necessary to successfully implement a new business strategy.

Identifying and assessing the unique profile of business and technology core competencies is necessary. It is *not* just another interesting academic exercise. Assessing core competencies is of significant strategic importance when confronting the task of developing the enterprise transformation strategy. Additionally, from a competitive perspective, a company's profile of competencies, however strong, is of little value unless it is so distinctive as to be virtually unique. Otherwise, it is an enterprise indistinguishable from its other *vanilla* competitors.

Without assessing the strength of core competencies, how can one determine if the enterprise has sufficient competency to successfully execute a proposed strategy? To answer this question requires knowledge of both the individual enterprise and its competitors' competencies. How can one know whether it is safe to abandon a current competency to outsourcing? Can a strong technology competency strengthen a weak business competency—or better yet, can a strong technology competency strengthen an already strong business competency to create competitive advantage? *The only way to know is to do the assessment!*

> *Identifying and assessing core competencies of the enterprise is fundamental to business survival. Core competencies hold the key to developing and implementing viable business strategies for strengthening product lines, creating new markets, and strengthening or exiting old ones.*

Additionally, core competency assessment of current or potential suppliers and customers is useful for considering the capabilities of suppliers to meet new requirements or for assessing the market readiness by potential customers to demand and use new products.

Business-Technology Core Competency Linkages

There are four general areas in which technology core competencies can enhance, or to a limited extent, substitute for weaker business core competencies—or the reverse, where the business core competencies strengthen or substitute for technology core competencies. They are:

- Shared vision, skills, and execution, linking business people to technology people.
- Organization and process redesign, linking business process to a technology process that utilizes both business and technology people.
- Information-infused end product, linking business product to technology product.
- Information empowerment, linking business people, process, and product to technology people, process, and product.

Consider the following set of business competency assessments, and the I/T strategy in response.

Business Assessment and I/T Strategy #1.   The people and product competencies are excellent, but the process is weak. As an example, think about oil exploration. The I/T strategy is to place emphasis on deploying I/T design skills (if available) within the enterprise. In the oil exploration business, I/T might deploy efforts to improve site and drilling data analysis to decrease the number of dry wells.

Business Assessment and I/T Strategy #2.   The product and the process competencies are strong. People—the intellectual assets—are most vulnerable due to downsizing activities. Consider as a context, national demographic and lifestyle change. The I/T strategy might be the following. For the internal business organization, emphasize information empowerment to leverage the people still remaining, increasing their productivity. Facilitate off-site, off-hour computer usage from home, creating an appropriate anywhere, anytime office. For the external (supplier and customer) linkages, enhance intelligence-gathering, if possible.

Business Assessment and I/T Strategy #3.   The people and process competencies are strong, but the product isn't competitive due to extended emphasis on improving the first two competencies. The I/T strategy could emphasize information-infused end products linked with mass customization of information. For example, drug chains may prevent a loss of business due to increased prices by employing I/T to implement a customer profile that checks for possible drug interactions. I/T might also print the price of the generic alternative below the price of the requested name brand or ensure through the customer profile that the customer over sixty years of age receives all available discounts. Another strategy might be to place additional emphasis on information empowerment, especially intelligence gathering through supplier and customer contacts.

Admittedly, these examples take a one-sided view with the implication that it is the business core competencies that are consistently insufficient and technology can always come to the rescue with a technology-based solution. More often than not, it is just the opposite. If technology doesn't have the sufficient competency to provide the appropriate business solution and the solution is sufficiently important, business will outsource despite the possible consequences to I/T. However, business might not outsource if there is sufficient understanding between business and technology management built through the joint assessment of core capabilities that it is necessary for I/T to experience a particular learning curve (deprived through outsourcing) to remain viable for the future (see Figure 9-3). The difficulty that most enterprises encounter is a lack of a supportive corporate and management culture that enables the sharing of skills and talent and the joint (business and I/T) development of strategies and solutions. This brings into play the final management concept necessary for transformation—the development of the learning organization.

LEARNING ORGANIZATIONS AND MANAGING SURPRISE

Only a few years ago, most managers thought that their biggest problem was management of change and searched for a process that would make change orderly. Today, most managers would probably say that their biggest problem is the management of surprise—surprises that disrupt or destroy relationships with customers and suppliers; surprises that suddenly change the definitions of the market (thus changing the concepts and measurements of market share); and surprises that create generational leaps rather than incremental moves in all sorts of technologies—surprises that lay waste the carefully crafted but vision- or knowledge-deficient strategic plan.

Learning more and learning more quickly becomes necessary for the organization if it is to adapt faster and better. Edgar Schein from MIT Sloan School suggests that organizations tend to have three distinct types of learning requirements, each having different time horizons.[4] They are:

- Knowledge acquisition and insight: Acquiring additional knowledge often gives new insight and direction, but it doesn't automatically change behavior. If learn-

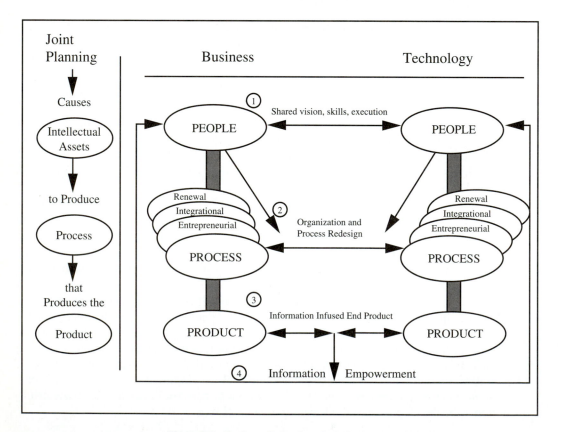

Figure 9-3   Business-Technology Core Competency Linkages

ers perceive new knowledge as being difficult or disruptive, they block its assimilation. This is why leaders often have difficulty in implementing their new vision, even after communicating it widely.

- Habit and skill learning: This learning is slow because it requires practice and a willingness to be temporarily incompetent. Lack of a safe environment in which to practice and to make errors constrains acceptance.

- Emotional conditioning and learned anxiety: This is learning through punishment. The basis of behavior patterns stems from avoiding punishment in the past. The most common defenses against this learning are to not hear the message, to deny that the message applies, or to rationalize that the leaders don't understand the problem. This type of learning occurs quickly. It is the unlearning that is slow.

To improve any of the organizational learning skills for transformation requires overcoming the negative effects of past penalty boxes—the historical reward for making mistakes. This necessitates creating a new culture that makes people feel safe in learning: they must have a motive, a sense of direction, and the opportunity to try out new things without fear of punishment.

Organizational learning occurs through the sharing of insights, knowledge, and mental models—thus organizations learn only as fast as its slowest link learns. Change remains blocked until everyone learns together, shares the beliefs and goals, and commits to taking the actions necessary for change by committing the new concepts to organizational memory. The tools of organizational memory are the institutional mechanisms—the policies, strategies, information systems, and explicit models—used to retain knowledge.

Peter Senge's 1990 book, *The Fifth Discipline,* focused on the formidable topic of *systems thinking,* as part of a broader concept of how to turn one's company into a learning organization capable of adapting to—and even anticipating—change in the competitive environment. In it, he suggests the five disciplines of a learning organization.[5] These disciplines are:

- Building shared vision: This is the practice of developing shared pictures of the future that foster genuine commitment.

- Personal mastery: Personal mastery is the skill of continually clarifying and deepening a personal vision and the capacity to see reality objectively.

- Mental models: This is the ability to uncover personal internal pictures of the world, to scrutinize them, and to make them open to the influence of others.

- Team learning: Team learning is the capacity to think together. Accomplishment occurs through mastering the practice of sharing ideas, dialogue, and discussion.

- Systems thinking: Systems thinking sees **wholes** not **parts**, and patterns of interdependency, not just isolated events. This is the discipline that integrates all the preceding disciplines by showing their common emphasis or interdependency and change.

Building, refining, executing, and evaluating scenarios is a natural process for the learning organization. Learning organizations become predominately learning-oriented and idea-sharing rather than controlling, and action—a learning by trying—increases both knowledge and the capacity to learn.

I/T and the Learning Organization

In 1989, Ray Stata, as chairman of Analog Devices, became an outspoken advocate of the learning organization. He made a compelling argument that the U.S. industry's most serious competitive problem lies in a declining rate of innovation—and that this decline is traceable more to a lack of management innovation than to weak product or technology innovation. He believes that the preceding organizational learning disciplines are the key to successful management innovation.[6] As part of his discussion of management innovation (or the lack thereof) he suggests the importance of the role that information systems play in a learning organization. His key observations are that *old systems enforce old cultures; information systems have inherent biases; and presentation formats may be critical.*

Old systems enforce old cultures.   Old systems, though they still work, can thwart the success of new organization forms and new strategies. Initially, Analog used a network of trading companies and representatives to distribute products internationally. Its product divisions sold to the trading companies, who then resold at the highest price the local market would bear. Over time, it replaced the independent agencies with wholly owned sales affiliates, but kept the accounting practice and information system that handled the transfer pricing intact for over twenty years *because it still worked.*

Stata discovered that as competition intensified, management spent more and more time haggling over the transfer prices between divisions, instead of figuring out how to retain market share in a competitive world. The information system unintentionally encouraged division managers to hide facts and play games to increase their share of the profit and subsequent bonus. Consequently, Analog introduced a new information system designed to enforce cooperation between divisions and to make decisions based upon improving company performance rather than improving the performance of one division at the price of another. The new information system now helps divisional managers understand their individual businesses better and to make better decisions for the company as a whole.

> *Business leaders must be wary of aging information systems that "aren't broke." They may need "fixing" to enforce the desired culture changes. It is also dangerous to assume that I/T will recognize the situation. It is the responsibility of business management to identify the problem.*

Information Systems Have Inherent Biases.   Information systems report financial information to stockholders and government agencies—creating a strong bias towards financially-based performance measurements. Stata observed that unless quality improvement and other more fundamental performance issues become elevated to the same level of importance as financial measures, financial considerations will always win out when conflicts arise. To get around this problem, Analog instituted a division scorecard that reports the barest of financial information and places the greater emphasis on quality improvement goals. The scorecard—not the financial statements—is the basis for evaluating division performance and structuring division bonus plans.

> *Both business and I/T are grappling with the same problems of effectively living with financial (quantitative) measurements and managing and motivating with value (qualitative) measurements. The organizational elements must learn together to create meaningful measures to support the desired corporate culture.*

Presentation Formats May Be Critical.   The format for presenting information has an impact. Analog changed its practice of circulating pages of information summaries to managers. Now, everyone receives a single-page summary chart of on-time delivery information. The previous reports—a separate one for each division—were missing the most crucial information for management: the half-life trend of the product. In the new one-page summary, the trends are readily discernible due to a switch to graphical format. Just as important, by displaying all divisions together on a single page, Analog increased motivation. By changing the information presentation format, Stata harnessed a high level of internal competition existing between product groups to generate the fastest learning curve. Without saying a word, he made it obvious (and embarrassing) to other managers when a group was not performing.

> *I/T won't intuitively know what's important to business management and how to best motivate the business organization. It is the responsibility of the business leader to tell them.*

He concludes that the challenge is in deciding what information and knowledge—and in what form—the company needs. Both business and I/T are more likely to generate the information and knowledge that managers need to take effective action if they have the mind-set that organizational learning is a goal of information systems design.

I/T Embodies the Core Values of the Enterprise.   While I/T and its networks are essential—and justified as such—for decentralizing hierarchies, empowering workers, and downsizing, state-of-the-art systems frequently can have astonishing perverse impacts. For all the promise of increased productivity, technology has a way of reinforcing an organization's cultural weaknesses. Analog recognized this phenomenon and took action to ensure that I/T design criteria included enforcing the desired corporate culture. Yet even the recognition of desired corporate culture in I/T systems design doesn't ensure success.

A network intended to flatten the corporate hierarchy can mutate into a medium that reinforces autocracy. Schrange at the MIT Sloan School states that organizations that run on power and influence do not take the *participatory management pledge* simply because they've invested a fortune in network technology.[7] The individual must change, too. Precisely because network technology blurs traditional organizational boundaries, top management can use it as a vehicle to project their personalities and impose power.

> *I/T networks and systems don't destroy organizational hierarchies; they reshape them.*

Enterprises cannot simply look to I/T as its tool for transformation and expect success. However, technology can reinforce new ways of doing things when business process and organizational design and I/T implementation design are concurrent and jointly executed. Technology can help provide the free information flow necessary to develop and support a learning organization. What technology cannot do is operate in a vacuum. Neither can the leaders of the enterprise. Transforming the corporate culture to enable the organization to successfully manage surprise is the responsibility of everyone. Schrange concludes that companies must design their technology systems and networks as much around their understanding of the enterprise core values and how to transform them as around their critical information. Negotiating that relationship will be the management challenge of the decade.

> *I/T is the delivery vehicle for information and the capture of subsequent knowledge. If jointly envisioned and supported by the people and the culture, it will run as smoothly and seamlessly as the Swiss train system. If not, it will be like the preliminary trials of the Soapbox Derby—untested vehicles, inexperienced drivers, and little in common except the soapbox.*

I/T AS INNOVATOR, CHANGE AGENT, AND POSITIONING AGENT

In the coming decade, I/T leaders must broaden their responsibilities and recast themselves as effective change agents. A 1992 JC Penney initiative, involving a $200 million replacement of 42,000 electronic cash registers with networked point-of-sale (POS) systems for marketing and reorder analysis, was a sweeping change in business procedure proposed to executive management by I/T. At the Burlington Coat Factory, something similar occurred. The I/T group provided the impetus for a shift in distribution procedures from a drop-ship strategy to funneling most shipments through a Burlington distribution center.[8]

Both POS and EDI implementations exemplify passive I/T projects that have, in turn, positioned many companies to become more proactive. Many POS installations started out as vehicles for managing inventory, then turned into a demographics-generating marketing tool creating increased revenues. New areas of opportunity could, for example, focus on the blends of technology—voice mail, e-mail, fax, and seamless handover digital (wireless) telephone service, or it could exploit the modularity of client-server architectures, allowing I/T to make changes to existing processes in more granular pieces.

Users making up wish lists tended to stifle I/T innovation in the past. These wish lists put I/T in an order-taker mode rather than one that structures an approach to improve business processes. While some business managers could argue that the I/T group had insufficient knowledge of the business to do effective business process redesign in the past, they can no longer ignore the development of this resource.

Any new I/T charter must focus on the broader role that I/T must play and the greater responsibilities that I/T must assume in the success of daily business activities. This emerging role of the I/T professional in the enterprise includes a range of new career paths, new competency requirements, and new functional responsibilities. It also extends the role beyond the traditional enterprise boundaries to encompass industry-wide activities and strategic enterprise activities involving supply chain relationships.

I/T and School-Industry Networking

Earlier, we discussed industry-based networks of the supplier-consumer variety in which information linkages occur through EDI networks, e-mail, and fax. In discussing the types of enterprise core competencies, we observed the linkages beyond the physical boundaries of the enterprise. Here, the members of the organization through their informal and formal business activities exchange information with suppliers, consumers, and other business-related professionals. Anything they find of interest to others within the organization passes along via e-mail—particularly if more than one individual or department would find the information of interest. A new area of cooperative exchange to emerge is that of school-industry networking, and it has the potential of profoundly affecting the social charter of the business enterprise and, specifically, its I/T function.

Part of the new corporate social responsibility growing in the United States is school apprentice programs. This is in response to the rising concerns about young workers' technological skills. Of the estimated 24 million jobs created by the year 2005, over 20 percent will require specialized computer or health care skills.[9] Because the workplace is evolving so rapidly half of all Americans don't have the training to keep up with changing technology in these fields and others. Large corporations as diverse as McDonald's and Motorola have set up their own internal universities to ensure that current employees have the necessary skill levels, with I/T playing a major role as the delivery vehicle. Outside the enterprise, university faculties constantly review and revise curricula, author new texts and revise current ones, and actively consult in their fields in attempt to keep up with change. Left out of these activities is the emerging work force.

The background for many training-related discussions are the apprentice programs in Europe. Britain guarantees two years of training for sixteen- and seventeen-year-old dropouts, and Germany provides an elaborate training program for 375 occupations.[9] Germany provides three-year apprenticeships during which most trainees from the age of sixteen work three days a week and attend vocational school two.[10] Contrast this with the United States, where in 1992, only 3,500 high-school students in twenty states participated in formal apprenticeship programs. Links between schools and employers are common in countries like Germany with a strong tradition of youth apprenticeship. However, these links mark a profound change for the United States, where most parents want their children to have a university education. This forces schools to rethink their purpose and methods, now that there is a scarcity of well-paid jobs for those who do not enter postsecondary education. The result is a sharp increase in local experiments that try to provide a coherent strategy for the 84 percent of U.S. pupils who do not go to a university.[11]

There are two difficulties with such efforts. One is that they require the kind of links between employers and schools common in Europe, but that are virtually nonexistent in the United States. The second is that parents are reluctant to select skilled employment rather than university studies for their children. Until parents and students start to see the value of an alternative to university education, many in the United States will remain loyal to a form of schooling originally built to serve the interests of all, but is increasingly failing the majority.

Successful job-preparation programs require the collaboration of schools, government and industry, and while they are not necessarily costly, they do require active business participation. As examples:

- Volunteers from the corporate world can directly influence programs. In Corpus Christi, Texas, schools replaced welding classes with courses for computer-aided design after business executives told school officials that welding is largely a seasonal job.[9]
- In Fort Worth, Texas, students intern with local businesses.
- In 1993, the Office Systems Research Association (a national association whose primary membership are university academics in the related fields of business, office, and information systems) held its annual conference jointly with the Information Management Forum (a national association of business professionals in the management-related fields of business, technology, and human resources) with the specific objective of identifying new requirements for curricula.[9]

School-industry networking will profoundly change the social charter of the business enterprise. Stepping up to the demands of these new social responsibilities will be part of the I/T charter. This is a natural consequence of I/T experience in in-house educational and information-based delivery and the growing knowledge-based economy.

Recognizing I/T as a Business Function

One of the major differences between the I/T function in the United States as compared to Japan is that the Japanese place greater emphasis on its information specialists—the information integrators, librarians, business analysts, and writers. An Ernst & Young report, "Information Management and Japanese Success," assesses the information business practices in eight of Japan's largest firms and points out a second major difference: It suggests that the Japanese devote much more time and effort on information management-related issues rather than on information technology-related issues.[12] They simplify their business first, and then they automate. This tends to reduce the number of islands of information that aren't optimally used. They view the information integration function as a proactive, preventative function, rather than the U.S. approach of trying to reactively, after-the-fact, reduce the number of islands of information.

The Japanese style of rotational management also impacts the I/T function. As employees move up the corporate ladder in Japan, they move from function to function, and from division to division. By the time a Japanese employee becomes a general manager, he or she has a better overall understanding of the businesses' informational needs. Additionally, instead of having the chief information officer function viewed as a career path for the I/T professional, information management responsibilities rotate among all company managers every three to five years. This allows each manager to learn the information's use and value as well as the economics of providing it.

This integrated business approach is seeping into progressive U.S. businesses deploying a matrix style of management under which each executive's success depends upon the success of all other business units. I/T executives in any organization—whether matrix or not—can initiate this process by building strategic alliances with other informational functions within their firm.

Leading the learning organization requires a rudimentary set of I/T skills and knowledge. Rotational assignments of business managers into the I/T function accomplish this objective, but not overnight.

Business Value of Rotational Assignments Out of I/T

Some of the earliest work to understand Japanese business practice, culture, and management identified the Japanese practices of non-specialized career paths and holistic concern as being totally opposite of the American practices of specialized career paths and segmented concern. This is critical in differentiating the two organizational models.[13] The top officers of American businesses average working in less than two different functions. If they were in charge of either finance or personnel in their company, they had typically never worked in any other specialty. This practice continues to be a potential threat to the future of American industry because other research suggests that workers at all levels who continually face new jobs are more vital, more productive, and more satisfied with their work than those who stay in one job. This is true, even when the changes in job do not include a promotion but are entirely lateral.

Rotational Assignments in Japan.   Contrast the typical functional specialist within the U.S. enterprise to what happens at Sony. Behind the success of Sony is its product development. Each year the company produces about 1,000 new products—an average of four every business day. With a track record of innovation like this—a key outcome of a learning organization—Sony creates about 800 products based on improvements of earlier devices. The remaining 200 products aim at creating whole new markets. While Sony culls the major universities in Japan for its talent, just like its competitors, it doesn't necessarily seek out the top students in each discipline. Instead, it prefers well-rounded generalists.[14] Sony looks for people who are *neyaka*—which translates roughly as optimistic, open-minded, and wide-ranging in their interests. According to Minoru Morio, a senior managing director, they move their people into a variety of functions during their working-life in the belief that having continuous success in the same area narrows employee perspectives and lessens creativity.

Sony and Rotational Assignments for I/T.   Could I/T professionals benefit from rotational assignments in other business functions? Consider the career path of one Sony software engineer, Tomoshi Hirayama. After five years as a programmer in Sony's home computer product group, he decided that he needed to learn more about how the computer market place really worked before he could realize his dream of creating a successful Sony product. Hirayama persuaded his product group's marketing division to send him to Britain in 1986 to work as a technical support specialist for Sony's home computers. For two years, he helped customers and dealers with their problems and suggested modifications and enhancements to the product development team back in Japan.

During Hirayama's return flight from Britain to Japan, he began to crystallize an idea. Once back in Tokyo, he made a formal product proposal that caught the attention of Sony's top management, and the concept became a product. Thus Tomoshi Hirayama, who began his career with Sony as a programmer, became the *intellectual father* of a successful product. That product is the Sony PalmTop—the pocket-size note pad computer that reads hand-printed Japanese writing and Roman characters and keeps track of appointments, addresses, phone numbers, and personal memos. While business can't expect to achieve this level of success with every rotational assignment, the example supports the premise that I/T specialists may have the capacity for significant business contribution when provided the opportunity.

Rotational Assignments Through Decentralization.   Over the past few years we have seen the centralized I/T function of many large corporations disappear. Often, its members joined a smaller line of business organizations dedicated to local technology support, product groups, and single function organizations. These same I/T professionals are a potentially rich, in-house source for the generalist professional. They can, at a minimum, contribute to the broader views necessary to successful business process redesign.

> *Provide rotational assignment opportunities for I/T professionals into business functions if this hasn't already occurred as a by-product of decentralization and downsizing. Everybody benefits.*

I/T Charter for Information Integration

There is an allure about bringing in a consultant to assist during difficult times. After they leave and things don't work, the business can blame the consultant. Unfortunately, after the consultant leaves, the expertise disappears. One critical area to the new I/T charter that the organization should keep internal is the function of information integrator.

Role and Responsibilities.   The key responsibility of the information integrator is deciding where and how to deploy systems to optimize business processes and to get data to the people and functions that need it. This includes identifying technologies that can ease communication across organizational boundaries and providing access to data held in several different databases that may or may not be under the control of a central I/T organization. It also involves coordinating in-house and external experts to turn integration plans into realities. The information integrator must have an intimate knowledge of the enterprise organization, its culture, and its existing resources and talents.

Organizations like British Petroleum Australasia and PacifiCare Health Systems implemented the role of information integrator internally rather than focusing on an outside consultant to provide the services. Their idea is to buy help but cultivate their own strategic integrators. What these organizations gain with an information integrator is a strong, well-entrenched leader to give users quick and accurate access to the full range of the organization's information resources. Typically, someone in this position reports to a chief information officer or its equivalent and acts as consultant on all projects related to making systems work together.[15]

The information integrator reviews existing practices and work processes and suggests changes to them if necessary—therefore he or she must be well versed in not only the information processes but in the business processes as well—and acts as project facilitator.

Skill Set.   The basic skill set of the information integrator includes:

- A thorough knowledge of the business and all its processes.
- Vision and creativity, with the ability to devise and develop an I/T systems strategy.
- Strong project management and leadership skills.
- Political skills.
- The ability to gain the confidence of a diverse set of clients.
- The ability to work as easily with the business professionals as with the I/T professionals.
- A thorough knowledge in both voice and data communications, a working knowledge of the various office systems technologies, and of the business product itself.

• The ability to have learned from the past and a sense of the future while dealing with the present.

In many I/T organizations today, this skill set is largely incomplete. It is critical for those organizations to begin to build these skills, because only then can I/T begin to produce sustaining answers to business needs. If this individual exists in the I/T organization, he or she may also be of significant value in addressing interoperability issues relating to quality and integration of data.

> *Information integration is a key function within the learning organization, requiring a combination of business and technology expertise. Nurture and protect this expertise every way possible.*

I/T and the Charter for the Chief Information Officer

In 1981, William Synott coined the title *CIO* for chief information officer and envisioned a dynamic and creative function.[16] A decade later, CIO—for some—stands for Career Is Over and the individual holding that position faces a future that is perilous in both title and function. Observers today acknowledge it as the most difficult position in the company to staff and to carry out, combining technical competence with general management abilities.

CIOs emerged in the 1980s as the realization grew that I/T could have an influence well beyond cutting administrative costs. I/T budgets increased sharply on the promise of computer-based competitive advantage and the CIO charter was to manage and exploit the technology. Over time, some CEOs became insecure with the position because they couldn't find effective ways to measure the CIO business contribution—and ultimately confined the CIO to technology-based decision-making. Other CIOs became integrated into the business strategic planning activities as active participants. Still others became rather silent observers. While not contributing to business strategy, business management expected the CIOs to quietly deliver technology support at the appropriate time. Some CIOs came from one of the business functional areas—often times from strategic planning—and had to learn the technology, while others came from I/T, not understanding the nuances or politics of the business. As a result, some CIOs have enjoyed enormous success, and others have experienced just the opposite.

A 1993 study by the London Business School revealed five significant differences between the CIO survivors and those who left the position.[17] They had to do with political relationship building, the relationship with the CEO, sharing an I/T vision, and personal characteristics involving sensitivity and credibility.

Relationship Building.   The chief information officer is not a job but a series of relationships. Survivors actively build relationships with peers and superiors, enabling them to gain support for I/T within the organization. This takes both time and effort—one survivor claimed it took two years to interest and educate a new senior executive. (This is a situation in which rotational assignments can benefit everyone involved.) The nonsurvivors were not relationship-builders and admitted that they didn't like the diplomacy and politics required in a corporate role.

CEO Relationship.   In many organizations, there are only monologues, and for senior executives, they are usually about the economics of I/T investments. Survivors were close to the CEO and enjoyed their support for I/T investments. Nonsurvivors had a poor or nonexistent relationship with the CEO. Typical comments from this group involved problems of lack of support, clash of personalities, and obsession with costs.

Shared I/T Vision.   The vital ingredients for any business to succeed are clarity of business vision, product differentiation, customer service, and agility. Using I/T will not automatically guarantee success; however, creative application and ingenious use will continue to provide opportunity for competitive advantage. Survivors worked to create a vision for the I/T contribution to the enterprise and made sure the top executives understood and shared it. Nonsurvivors either had an unshared vision—or complained about the lack of one—coupled with a short-term mentality.

Sensitivity.   Survivors seemed to have an intuitive feel as to which battles to fight. Nonsurvivors were often at odds with other senior management over important policy shifts.

Credibility.   Never promise more than you can deliver. Survivors fulfilled their commitments. Nonsurvivors often missed both financial and performance targets.

Nurturing Business Management Exposure to I/T.   The interesting conclusion of the study is that CEOs should treat I/T as a *nursery* for the company's best talent and seek to develop young executives' I/T expertise by a rotational assignment in I/T—but not necessarily in the role of the CIO. This would eventually broaden the base of technology appreciation throughout the executive level and make the roles of both the CIO and business executives easier. There are too few people who can weave technology throughout the business *and* manage the restructuring of the business at the same time.

If we think back to the qualities necessary for the internal information integrator we see an interesting parallel in the qualities that make a successful CIO. This suggests that the role of information integrator is an excellent training vehicle and testing ground for potential CIO candidates.

> *The role of the CIO continues to be a difficult one to staff and carry out. It requires technical competence, business knowledge, general management skills, and relationship-building skills.*

Management Competencies.   The management competencies required for the CIO are not so different from those required from business management today.

As a result of delayering hierarchical organizations into horizontal ones that require some form of matrix management, functional business managers are being replaced by general business managers. IBM UK, for example, chooses and measures the performance of its senior business management using six management competencies: intellect, tenacity, vision, impact, skills in active management, and skills in general management. Perhaps the gradual evolution of a set of common management competencies between business and I/T will lead both to some form of rotational assignment at the senior management level.

I/T Charter for Positioning and Change Agent Activities

Recently, General Motors paid fines for not meeting federal mileage, emissions, and safety standards.[18] This came as no surprise to its executives, because they had included this possibility in their budget. They understood that with today's cost to build automobiles, its often cheaper to pay the fines than to meet the standards within the mandated time-lines. This results in a budget that includes the fines. This money can't be returned to the shareholders in the form of dividends, reinvested in the business to improve future performance, or passed on as savings to its customers—the fines become a cost of doing business.

Changing the View That I/T Is a Cost of Doing Business.   Today, many I/T organizations represent a cost of doing business rather than representing an investment in the future. Not so many years ago, I/T was an investment in the future—organizations invested dollars in I/T to save dollars elsewhere. The gradual accumulation of systems requiring maintenance resulted in fewer resources to spend on developing new applications. Demand didn't slack off, and as there were fewer resources to spend on new applications, the backlog grew as did precious resources spent on backlog management.

How does an organization that is trying to transform get around this cost of doing business? I/T can focus on cutting those costs by outsourcing anything that isn't strategic. There is an increasing interest and activity by business in outsourcing many I/T functions. The reason: Businessmen feel that outsourcing is a tool to control direction and control costs of I/T activities. In this context, outsourcing becomes a tool to make the problem someone else's concern—while keeping costs fixed and predictable for the near-term future. What is missing, when outsourcing in this context, is the opportunity to redirect and refocus the I/T group, giving it a direction and management structure that can bring maximum benefit to the company, that is, to transform the I/T function into effective positioning and change agents for the business.[19]

Cost and High Quality as a Rationale for Outsourcing.   In 1987, John Dearden argued that users would soon control individual systems and that outside software specialists would do most systems development.[20] In essence, he predicted the demise of the in-house information systems department because the costs of services from a software specialist would be lower and the quality higher than that developed internally.

Costs and high quality are one issue. Outsourcing makes sense for I/T development activities that don't involve core competencies vital for the future of the business. However, the idea of outsourcing requires the business to invest not only the money but the necessary time to impart the business information and direction, thus providing the basis for an outside software specialist to proceed. Often, outsourcing decisions overlook this investment.

Outsourcing is reasonable, logical, and generally cost-justifiable for nonstrategic activities. For more than two years, Deere & Company (the tractor manufacturer based in Moline, Illinois) outsourced a portion of its mainframe software development to Satyam Computer Services in Madras, India. Because Madras is ten and a half hours ahead of Moline, Satyam's daytime development crew accesses Moline's mainframes in the middle of the night, when its computers are relatively idle. Response time was better at the workstations in Madras than in Moline during the headquarters' normal working hours. Consequently, the development in India proceeded more quickly than it in Moline.[21] This saving in time accompanied a saving in cost of labor, since labor costs in India are lower.

Core Competencies and Strategic Intent as Outsourcing Considerations.   I/T skills necessary for competitive advantages and for improving business processes are also issues. Noted earlier in the discussions of banking industry outsourcing activities (Chapter 8), technology drives both its improvements in customer service and in its new products and forces the industry to question whether technology is (or should be) one of its core businesses. We also note that strategic intent is more about outpacing competitors in building new advantages—something that is impossible to do without a fast-paced learning organization. We have, in some respects, completed the circle by coming back to the issue of core businesses and core competencies and the necessity of understanding, evaluating, and growing them to ensure business viability. This emphasizes the I/T roles of positioning and change agents. Here, dollar cost is not so much the issue as it is the contribution or value to the business.

I/T outsourcing criteria must balance cost and quality with strategic intent.

OBSERVATIONS

In his 1993 book on the post-capitalist society, Peter Drucker talks about how the capitalist society of the mid-1800s to mid-1900s had two forces dominating it: capital and labor. Now, and increasingly over the next two decades, he believes we will move rapidly into a knowledge society in which the most vital part of production will no longer be natural resources, capital, or labor—all obtainable with relative ease today. Knowledge dominates this new society.[22] He predicts that by the year 2000 there will be no developed country in which workers making and moving goods account for more than one-sixth of the labor force. Instead, the two key classes of society, with a grayer line between them than there has been between capital and labor, will be knowledge workers and service workers. Drucker argues that the main economic and social challenges will be, respectively, the productivity of the former and the dignity of the latter, whose numbers will be slightly greater.

His view assumes the free market as the only proven economic mechanism, albeit some of its institutions will redefine their roles. Commercial banks, for instance, will make money by receiving fees for information rather than by earning a return on money. Schools and colleges will be open to all ages to support lifelong learning and will be more competitive and accountable for their performance. Education moves out of the traditional classroom setting through the application of technology.

Already, there is evidence of this shift. Libraries, the repositories for the accumulated information and knowledge of the world, are starting to create limitless digital bookshelves. This foretells vast changes in academic research, where scholars of the next century access the world's finest libraries from their desktop computer, with sound from the oral history collection available through earphones. It also changes the role of the library from one of collecting and preserving books to one of electronically storing and disseminating information.[23] The electronic library can share its books with other libraries through networking, thus avoiding redundant efforts across the entire population of libraries. It can eliminate dozens of copies of reserved texts since many students could read them simultaneously from a desktop computer. While institutional and ergonomic pressures will keep the all-electronic library away for the next few decades, today's library buildings may ultimately become museums of old books.

In this new age, literacy consists of reading, writing, and arithmetic plus new demands on understanding and a fluency in science, technology, and foreign languages.[24] Most important of the new knowledge skills will be such things as learning how to be effective as a member of an organization, and process knowledge, knowing how a process works (such as learning how we learn) rather than knowing traditional (but quickly outdated) subject-specific knowledge. Yet the value of knowledge, despite its importance, remains difficult to quantify. There is no economic theory of knowledge, even though knowledge is at the center of the new wealth-producing process. If one cannot quantify the value of knowledge, one cannot calculate a return on it.

Those in business and information technology organizations may have experienced a certain amount of *deja vu* while reading this section. In a few short years the transition from data processing to information systems to systems and applications embodying knowledge occurred. They witnessed the increasing emphasis on productivity improvements for the knowledge workers within the enterprise and recognized the upsurge in end-user computing and information empowerment with the weakening of the centralized information systems department and its glass house. They both observe and experience the redirection and redeployment of those possessing I/T skills critical to the enterprise. Moreover, few in business possess any immunity to the financial justification disease of trying to forecast future benefits or measure past ones attributed to technology deployment. None of these past experiences came without pain and the changes necessary to accomplish strategic transformation are no exception. Despite an expanding I/T charter, these same areas of applications redirection, productivity, functional redirection, and financial evaluation continue to be vital to enterprise (and professional) survival.

10

Reengineering the I/T Infrastructure

Companies are abandoning vertical integration in favor of an agile structure centering on core competencies. As part of the process, they begin to question the I/T function—its role, organization, systems, and deliverables. Modular corporate forms demand that I/T play a different role than in collaborative enterprises, changing economic and industry structures place still different demands, and differing core competencies impact the I/T response. Appropriateness of information systems construction, content, and delivery are in question, along with the organization that delivers and supports it. Shared vision between business and I/T is key in this new environment and mandates that I/T be as audacious as business in its transformational thinking.

As more companies shun vertical integration in favor of a lean, nimble structure centered on what they do best, the role of I/T and the appropriateness of its infrastructure becomes an issue. This new breed of corporation avoids the kind of bureaucracy associated with the glass house surrounding technology and adopt streamlined structures to fit today's fast-moving, tumultuous market place. It outsources noncore activities to hold down unit costs and investments needed to turn out new products, freeing them to direct scarce capital to where it holds, or where it can develop, competitive advantage. These new modular corporate forms typically invest in market research and new product design, getting and keeping the best engineers and product developers, and in training the sales or service personnel. Going beyond janitorial and mailservices, these enterprises outsource previously internal service organizations and, as a consequence, improve financial performance.[1] (The four services most frequently outsourced are trucking and delivery, catering and food service, data processing, and accounting.) These modular corporations slim down to unique core competencies and tend to be complete enterprises from the perspective of producing the product and getting it out the door. Because the business didn't perceive I/T as a consistent contributor to business value, it gets lumped into the other services considered by management as being peripheral to the core business and becomes an outsourcing candidate. Whether it did or did not contribute value isn't the issue.

A somewhat slimmer version of corporate form is the virtual, extended or collaborative enterprise. This is a temporarily networked group of independent companies that come together quickly and exploit fast-changing opportunities through highly selective strategic alliances.[2] It will have neither central office nor organization chart, no hierarchy, and no vertical integration. These companies tend to have one or more core competencies that represent best of practice, for example, world-class, but network with other similar companies with different core competencies that, in combination, produce a world-class product or service. Integral to making this type of alliance work is the ability to quickly establish a business network between the participants. Electronic data interchange (EDI), e-mail, local area networks (LANs), and standardization of common communications among participants—all I/T-based functions—are key to the success of this type of company. Through I/T, this collaborative enterprise shares skills, costs, and access to each others' market.[3] Until national and international networks and standards allow corporations to easily communicate with each other, I/T must ensure a level of electronic communication between current and potential partners. By accomplishing this, the I/T function becomes the enabler of the collaborative, virtual enterprise.

This later type of enterprise form works equally well at both the local (national) and global level. Additionally, the collaborative enterprise avoids the problems that many of today's international companies have—that of having a home-base. For example, during periods of scarce capital, global firms tend to protect home markets at the expense of developing untapped markets overseas; anti-trust laws limit the ability of global firms to expand through takeovers; and insofar as global companies have a home country, other governments will treat them as foreigners, placing them at a political and competitive disadvantage. A multinational alliance of independently owned firms overcomes these home-country biases. However, as businesses become increasingly global, nations and trading blocs polarize (Chapter 1) and develop inter-trading bloc standards (Chapter 6).[4] An I/T organization in this type of collaborative enterprise requires a knowledge of regional differences in communications interfaces and EDI standards and a reconciliation of the differences.

The shift to cross-border collaborative enterprises triggers a cascade of activities. Governments redefine the rules of competition, shifting them from a national to a global level. When the rules of free enterprise and competition change, market and industry definitions change, triggering a change in the strategic vision of the enterprise. When business strategy changes, the business processes often require redesign. The resulting restructuring of key business processes and different organizational forms often change information systems construction, content, and delivery. For example, quality programs involving an international collaboration may require a global network for e-mail, a reconciliation of national quality and product standards, and a system of cross-certifications, all opportunities for I/T innovation and support. The competitive nature of business mandates that all of these changes are cost-effective.

Along with the changing markets and organizational forms, there is the gradual shift in economic structure. The United States, along with other leading economies, is slowly evolving from a manufacturing-driven economy to a technology-driven economy whose growth is largely knowledge-based rather than capacity-based. Replacing the manufacturing infrastructure that required highways, airports, and telephones, is a new technology infrastructure that requires telecommunications, satellites, and fiber-optics. These are the enablers of this new economy.

Why is this long-term shift in the makeup of economic growth and the shifts in organizational forms important in considering a restructuring of the I/T infrastructure[5]? Because these are two of the four major forces that define the context for I/T infrastructure transformation. (The other two major forces are existing core competencies, discussed in the previous chapter, and demonstration of business value, the subject of the next chapter.) The gradual withering of the manufacturing economy will not promote a sustained atmosphere of innovation, change, and transformation at a national level, thus providing even greater challenges regarding the form and scope of I/T infrastructure transformation, especially within the low-tech manufacturing industries.

Organizational forms have a similar liberating (or limiting) role in defining the context for I/T restructuring. For the modular corporation, core competencies are of paramount importance. If I/T didn't demonstrate its value in the past—and gain recognition as a core competency—it is unlikely to gain stature and attention soon. For the collaborative or virtual corporation, there is a growing recognition that I/T is one of the enablers of collaboration and necessary to business success. To accommodate either of these scenarios requires changing the I/T infrastructure:

- How it gets staffed and organized.
- How and what it delivers as its product.
- How it demonstrates added value.

The first step for any I/T organization is to identify the probable range of parameters for its transformation context. The next step is to identify the right set of questions to explore before seeking any solutions.

Industry sector, existing core competencies, emerging organizational form, and demonstration of business value define the enterprise context for reengineering the I/T infrastructure.

CONSEQUENCES OF CHANGE FOR I/T

This theme of change jeopardizes the equilibrium between the I/T infrastructure—its processes and products—and the dynamically changing enterprise it supports. I/T or-

ganizations strive to keep their strategies in balance with the business strategy—and
the I/T organizations and architecture to the business organizations—with all their
cross-linkages. When it doesn't, the enterprise operates less efficiently. This suggests
that the better long-term business strategy requires coordinating business transformation with new I/T platforms and capabilities, whether that I/T capability is outsourced
or kept as an in-house activity.

This also requires I/T to create a new mind-set and organizational infrastructure
to carry out the responsibilities associated with its role, along with new success criteria. Establishing the new criteria must precede the development of any strategies for
developing strategies and scenarios to choose and implement the next-generation I/T
infrastructures and architectures. Through their actions today, I/T organizations must
provide the leadership and planning necessary to avoid the consequences of becoming
the limiting factor to future business success.

I/T and the Global Enterprise

As we move steadily toward a world economy, what does this mean to the various I/T-
related organizations? How can it best prioritize the people and dollar investment opportunities across the myriad alternatives represented by application development,
end-user computing, training, help-desks, maintenance, new tools and technologies,
architecture and blueprints, business and data models? How can it best get ready to do
business in this new world?

Borderless Organizations.   Borderless is a key word here for both business and I/T functions. I/T must be able to move and adapt systems easily and support them as the enterprise creates alliances and collaborative relationships with
others.

How does I/T do that? Is I/T designing systems and procedures today in a way
that sufficiently supports future flexibility and mobility? Is I/T providing access to information that supports the concept of single owner and multiple user, or do applications and systems design accommodate possible alliance partners, collaboration,
shared responsibility, and matrix management? Too often, the answer is the former,
whereas new enterprise organizational models require the latter.

Global Support.   Is expertise available to the I/T function that can, when it
becomes necessary for strategic planning, deal with global or trading bloc economic
models? Are these professionals able to work with the business strategist responsible
for global scanning and translate the findings into new opportunities, challenges, and
business requirements for I/T?[6] Some enterprises already have technology scanners in
place, responsible for identifying new technologies to improve business performance.
The I/T global challenge is twofold:

- Expand the technology scanning to a global scale.
- Begin business scanning at a global level for improved business performance
  through innovative I/T applications incorporating world-class best practices.

What are the consequences for I/T on the level and type of service it provides? A global view of service will, by definition, provide multiculture, multilanguage, and multitime zone support to its users. This also suggests multistandards and rule sets, interoperability, mobility, and portability, things that many large-scale I/T organizations are already facing.

> *Competing in a global economy requires performing technology scanning and providing technology support at the global level.*

I/T and Enterprise Restructuring

There are political problems associated with getting things done in an enterprise, and the emergence of steering committees represents a first step to remedy this situation. Currently, these committees tend to focus attention not on getting things done, but on the collection and coordination of activities that have to occur across many functions (and in the future many more linked enterprises) to produce a key result for an enterprise. The issue for future organizational forms also has two critical parts:

- Will steering committees or some other organizational group emerge to manage relationships?
- What role will I/T play in facilitating enterprise collaboration and consensus?

Organizational Interdependencies.   There are interdependencies among enterprises occurring every day. The airline that serves an in-flight meal depends upon the catering company to deliver what it promises. What happens when the flight is late because the catering company fails to deliver on time? The airline incurs additional costs associated with the flight crews, the flyers are unhappy and miss connections, and the catering company probably pays a penalty to the airline. Given a similar scenario, what happens (between I/T and its internal customer) when the business is late in announcing a new product when I/T fails to deliver? Business management is unhappy, perhaps a competitive window of opportunity closes, potential profit is unrealized, and business chastises I/T for failing again to provide timely support.

Now consider what might happen if the business is unprepared when I/T fails to deliver in a collaborative relationship. What happens to the relationship? Who is responsible for the management of the relationship? What if the I/T development itself was a collaborative effort?

From a business management and strategic planning perspective, and from an I/T perspective, new governance and planning forms—similar to steering committees—are emerging for lines of business and key business processes. New value and measurement systems for collaborative efforts are also emerging. When there are no best practices, what are the practices for managing interdependencies across enterprise boundaries for shared systems and responsibilities between I/T organizations? It becomes requisite for I/T to tailor its management structure to echo the flexible style of the enterprise management structure and is not a trivial task.

Managing Outsourcing.   Earlier, we discussed the role of two types of power shifts in the future business enterprise (Chapter 8): outsourcing and alliances. These two business strategies add significantly to the ability to seize the moment and gain competitive advantage and to add product and/or service line offerings. Some business literature views these two approaches interchangeably. However, they are not interchangeable when considering the impact of these business approaches and the associated planning and support required by the I/T organization.

When the enterprise decides to outsource some required function, the I/T organization must raise some challenging questions on the quality and level of support for this outside organization doing inside work. For example, where are the business (project) champions for the I/T support? Is the champion the inside manager managing the interface or contract? Is he or she fully aware of the needs of the outside organization to perform as its qualified representative? Can he or she represent and describe the function that is being outsourced to someone responsible for redesigning the business process in which the outsourced work is an integral part?

Managing Security.   Security is another important issue. If a project is strategically sensitive, where do the loyalty and dedication of the (outside) workers lie when they are doing the work? Does the sensitivity of the project demand additional security measures be implemented by I/T? Is the system easy to use? Are there good help-screens, so that the outside-worker training and support are relatively easy? If the outside-worker needs access to current systems or needs to update current databases, is I/T able to quickly provide the access necessary while maintaining necessary security? Security needs must address outsourcing of work at the line of business or functional level as well as outsourcing I/T development activities.

Managing Heterogeneity.   I/T must ask itself how well it knows its future customer. More importantly, how well does it know what its future customer requires. I/T must face the issue of planning for heterogeneity and plan for even greater dissimilarities than what business forces it to do today. It must think in terms of planning systems, services, and products using mass customization, just as its business counterpart (Chapter 5). The ability of the I/T organization to identify and support multistandards and rule sets, and security and training levels, is key in establishing the I/T *value add* for any enterprise that is outsourcing. Projects integral to risk management, productivity, and change and flexibility in support of outsourcing both business and I/T functions become part of the standard I/T portfolio.

Managing Alliance Relationships.   Alliance relationships place a unique set of requirements on I/T, due to the implications of shared or joint responsibility, the transitory nature of the relationships, and the financial justification of applications.

Shared Responsibility.   Business alliances bring with them some of the same I/T problems as outsourcing: identification of the business (project) champion for I/T support; security, training, and parceling access; and heterogeneity of data, systems, and information. What is different about alliances is that I/T must provide service to collaborative departments, sharing responsibilities across multiple organizations. Flexible, loosely coupled organizations require flexible, loosely coupled systems. This may mean a mingling of systems and data with shared responsibility for its integrity and security. How do the two I/T organizations work together in this situation? At this point, there are few role models as exemplars of best practices.

Transitory Nature.   Alliances by their very nature are temporary. An example: Borden's marketing marriage with Meiji Milk lasted twenty years, but when the market share for Lady Borden ice cream dropped in Japan, Borden decided to break away from its Japanese partner.[7] These fluid business organizations require the development of new views of how I/T should provide support. How does one justify and develop I/T applications that are robust enough to last up to twenty years (in the case of Borden and Meiji Milk), yet independent enough to discontinue at a moments notice?

The implication of the transitory nature of alliances for I/T is staggering. Some I/T organizations have yet to define a single business model for its enterprise. I/T will need to define and support multiple business models in the future. These models include the business model of its home enterprise and a business model of each of its alliances. Additionally, because the business reason for having alliances is to seize the moment by exploiting a competitive opportunity rapidly, the I/T organization will have the same charter. I/T must be able to seize its own moment and instantly (relatively speaking) restructure the relevant business models, systems, services, and products it supports. Unfortunately, these business alliance models may be ill-identified and ill-defined, because the business enterprise will create the alliance and not necessarily advise or consult I/T. Who is the customer for the I/T organization now? How does I/T support multiple matrix-managed teams across multiple organizations and enterprises?

I/T must make it easy from an information access perspective, for forming, operating, and dissolving business alliances if its enterprise host is to remain competitive.

Financial Justification.   There must be new types of financial justifications and guidelines developed to apply to I/T as a result of alliances. The new bottom-line will be the ability to contribute value and demonstrate the contributed value to the alliance(s). The information assets necessary for alliance support require:

- The ability to mingle data, systems, and information.
- The ability to do instant restructuring of the business model(s) and the systems.

- The ability to develop and maintain multiple business models with a new view of investment prioritization.

This, however, necessitates creating whole new definitions and profiles of value for the financial investment and justification process.

By delivering increasing flexibility in support of collaborative efforts, I/T contributes value to the enterprise.

I/T and Mission-Based Performance Imperatives

A critical issue for business and I/T on outsourcing and alliances is the *performance imperative*. There will be a greater emphasis on the measurement of past accomplishments and a greater emphasis on predictive tools to link to subsequent accomplishments, for example, harvesting the benefits. Both quality and productivity improvements must occur for I/T and the business. User empowerment, user training, security, and flexibility will be key, and most especially knowledge-worker empowerment. The new view of planning for I/T must encompass planning to measure, planning for quality and productivity (reengineering), and planning for building the asset base. I/T must both produce and prove.

Earlier we discussed, from the enterprise perspective, the issues surrounding quality (Chapter 6), and why outsourcing and alliances are occurring with increasing regularity (Chapter 8). I/T management faces the same issues as business management when providing service to its customer—the enterprise and the enterprise alliance. They include contract management versus shared responsibility, quality, loyalty, training and ease-of-use, security, and anywhere, anytime offices.

Focus on Key Business Processes

The role of I/T and its connection to managing and controlling the enterprise seems fairly obvious. Now, the problem of sources and uses of information becomes global. More profoundly than that, the real implication of I/T is to allow business to assess the goods and services it provides to its customers and to manage the production of those goods and services through key business processes (KBPs). The planning consequences of KBPs for an enterprise are to consider again from the customer view the key deliverables, and then consider the KBPs that produce them with an eye toward both effectiveness and productivity, quality, and service.

An example of a key business process for the MassMutual Life Insurance Company is the New Business function. The objective for MassMutual's New Business Model Office was to streamline the entire application processing, risk assessment, and policy issue process, providing faster service to clients (agents and policyholders). This included issuing policies more quickly. The emphasis was on minimizing the number of times work passes back and forth among individuals and departments. It's noteworthy that after the work and procedure transformation, the underwriters felt that the process had taken a step backward, because the paperwork was staying on their desks longer. This was true. However, the total elapsed time for issuing a new policy dropped by 50 percent.[8] What does this demonstrate?

- Improvements are a matter of perception!
- Measurements are important!
- Communicating the results of change to those who feel the effect is mandatory!

We now have two threads of ideas going in parallel. The first thread is I/T—with proper approaches to analysis and design, it becomes possible to imagine radical reorganization of KBPs. The other thread is to imagine KBPs crossing boarders—national lines, continental lines—and the implications of competitiveness from a global perspective.

Why should a business and its I/T group worry about it from the market (market-driven) perspective? Answer: In the past, a company could produce domestically and be moderately efficient and be successful. It could be moderately good at whatever standards it might choose—cost, quality of product, time. This is no longer true. With increased levels of competitiveness made possible by global markets, the number of competitors in any given area has the potential for increasing and that increased competitiveness raises the stakes concerning what is necessary for success. (U.S. television manufacturers discovered that—and the United States doesn't manufacture televisions anymore.) *Every* enterprise has the prospect of facing increased levels of competition.

It also becomes more important to be best as a provider of products or service. Why? Now it's easier for customers to identify the alternatives—competitors that have chosen to have a global view of the market. It is this combination of factors—the playing field, the global competition, the new business organization, the consequences for the KBP's through outsourcing and alliances—that mandates the reconceptualization and reengineering of the I/T infrastructure.

Enterprise-wide Information Management Model.   In 1985, the IBM/Washington University Joint Study on Enterprise-wide Information Management (EwIM) published a view of Information Systems and the Organizationally Driven Enterprise as shown in Figure 10-1.[9] (The author and Robert J. Benson were the directors of the study.) Here, the emphasis was on developing the technology-to-business linkages.

After examining a number of case studies over the ensuing decade, it was obvious that simply applying the concepts implied by the model and ensuring the presence of strong business-technology linkages were insufficient to predict the level of success for any enterprise and its I/T organization. (The model did, however, effectively support linkage and strategic alignment of the I/T functions to the bottom-up/top-

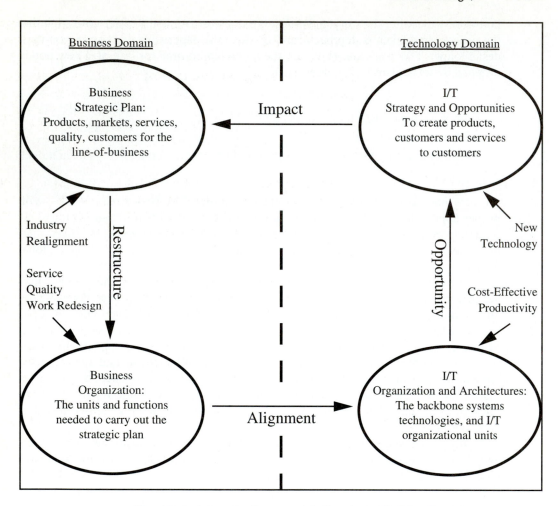

Figure 10-1   Information Systems and the Organizationally Driven Enterprise.

down strategic planning approach appropriate for the hierarchical business organization. The value of this planning approach for flat or collaborative organizations is questionable.) This meant that either the business strategy with the I/T supporting strategy wasn't appropriate, that the business organization with the I/T supporting organization wasn't appropriate, or some combination of both was the problem.

    Business Process-Driven Enterprise Model.   What was missing from the EwIM model was a focus on key business processes. The KBP, not the product, gets managed (Chapter 7).[10] People manage results by managing the process that produces these results, and a process is successful if it meets its objective. This approach changes the role of I/T. I/T in the KBP-driven enterprise places emphasis on:

- Service, wherever the service points occur.
- Identifying and supporting the key business processes, whether in-house, through alliances, or through outsourcing.
- Enabling business improvement and change through constant improvement of KBPs, with I/T as the improvement and change agent.
- Enabling strategic business opportunities by exploiting flexible infrastructures and architecture, with I/T as a positioning agent.

In using I/T to change the KBPs of the business, technology impacts business performance. If I/T has inhibited change through, for example, inappropriate standards, poor quality and/or usability of the deliverable, or lack of timeliness, it has a negative impact on business performance. If I/T has facilitated change through, for example, capacity planning, appropriate use of outsourcing, implementing flexible architecture that supports business redesign, and constantly assessing the effectiveness and applicability of its infrastructure and architecture, it contributes to the ability of the business to react quickly to changing market conditions. It has a positive impact on business performance.

Figure 10-2 illustrates I/T and the business process-driven enterprise. Here, we include the diagonal linkages between the I/T Infrastructures and the business strategic plan, qualifying the effective employment of I/T as the positioning agent for the business strategy. We also see the diagonal linkage between the I/T opportunities and the KBPs, for the effective deployment of I/T to become a change agent.

Conceptually, the model begins to shift from a vertical axis to a more horizontal axis, dividing the enterprise into two functional activities—creating the shared vision and operationalizing the shared vision to produce the product. With the better business strategy building around the coordination of business and I/T transformation, the challenge for I/T becomes the creation of an infrastructure that facilitates coordination and maintains optimum equilibrium.

Focusing on I/T Investment Priorities

Organizations must prepare for the simultaneous execution of two or more distinct strategies: the short-term (transitional) strategy(s) and the long-term strategy(s). Obviously, there must be funding for both the development and implementation of these strategies. While new product and platform announcements may drive down costs for existing functionality, any temporary recessionary pressure on the budget could lead to giving these dividends away. Bruce Rogow of Gartner Group warned of this as early as 1991. He believes that industry will need that (dividend) and much more to build (or continue to rebuild) the I/T infrastructure of the future, based upon learning curves and critical skill availability.[11] A case in point: one company set up a standards group to support worldwide business activity to build open systems implementation over the next decade. It started early because of the learning curves associated with the new set of requisite critical skills.[12]

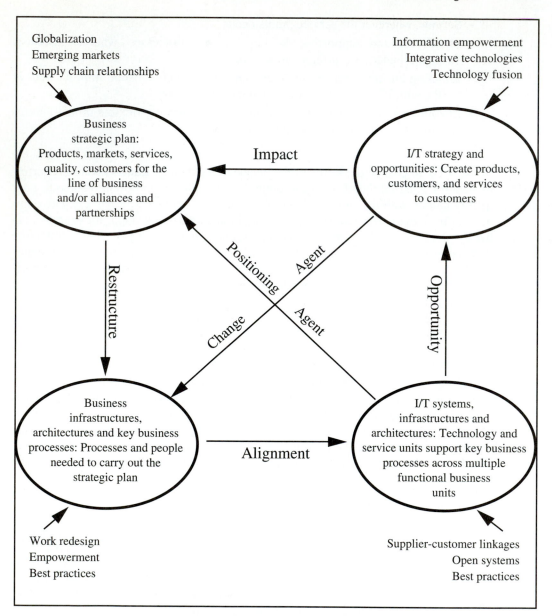

Globalization
Emerging markets
Supply chain relationships

Information empowerment
Integrative technologies
Technology fusion

Business strategic plan: Products, markets, services, quality, customers for the line of business and/or alliances and partnerships

Impact

I/T strategy and opportunities: Create products, customers, and services to customers

Restructure

Positioning

Agent

Change

Agent

Opportunity

Business infrastructures, architectures and key business processes: Processes and people needed to carry out the strategic plan

Alignment

I/T systems, infrastructures and architectures: Technology and service units support key business processes across multiple functional business units

Work redesign
Empowerment
Best practices

Supplier-customer linkages
Open systems
Best practices

Figure 10-2   Information Systems and the KBP Driven Enterprise.

The consequence? The successful I/T executive must have a detailed analysis of the new master platform as part of the strategy and business plan. The new platform makes technical uncertainty, risk, exposure, and opportunity major issues again (just as in the S/360 and 370 days). I/T must create these timelines, risk assessments, and scenarios for each major part of the business, requiring a constant dialog with senior business management. Can I/T do this, given the current state of I/T planning methodologies?

Translating the Early Warning Signals into Appropriate Action

Today, the formidable task for the business and I/T professional is to take the key forces and concerns and translate them into a set of early warning signals for I/T. These early warning signals indicate that a major change is about to occur within the enterprise. Currently, the enterprise reacts and accommodates itself to the outside forces by changing its business strategy and its interface (its business organizations and architectures) to the market. This often necessitates new I/T support requirements and results in enterprise inefficiencies. Ideally, the presence or occurrence of the early warning signals should trigger previously defined and developed I/T action scenarios that support, through planned infrastructure change, the business enterprise as it adapts to the changing business environment.

> *I/T must create scenarios for the future now, to avoid becoming an inhibitor of change.*

REALITIES OF DOWNSIZING AND OUTSOURCING

The press is full of news about downsizing, outsourcing, networking, and rightsizing. The problem is that few writers (or business executives) bother to define exactly how they are using the terms. We use the terms *downsizing* and *outsourcing* the way the business executive often does—meaning the reduction of personnel assigned to perform a function and moving functions outside the traditional organizational boundaries for others to accomplish. We use *rightsizing* to describe the movement of information processing to smaller (equipment) processors—often onto systems located outside the normal purview and control of the typical centralized information processing organization. Unfortunately, because there is no generally accepted alternative, we fall into the same trap as others when using the term *networking*. Networking refers to the intellectual and social activities of sharing information and establishing relationships with others. It also refers to the physical architecture and systems that establish the electronic network to facilitate the intellectual and social activities. Despite the terminology used, the overriding concern for I/T professionals should be to contribute value in providing the needed information for effective business operations and decision-making.

Market forces drive outsourcing and downsizing of staff. The need to maintain competitiveness also drives rightsizing—the mixed environment of many different-sized machines—driven by the business needs of smaller units but logically related to the bigger organization. The need for highly integrated information structures occupies one end of a spectrum and is most often served by an information utility infrastructure. At the other end are totally unconnected (information) parts, most often served best by local solutions with local support. The issue is whether today's downsizing, outsourcing, and rightsizing activities provide any assistance toward developing the skills and core competencies necessary to support the new business scenarios. It's the business and I/T visionaries that make this determination, given their organizations' current core competencies and the business scenario of the future enterprise.

This means that there is no best practice that every enterprise should follow in shaping its view of the I/T infrastructure.[13] The break up of the centralized glass house for data processing was critical to integrating I/T with business strategy. Establishing client/server systems and stand-alone processors in the lines of business accomplished only part of information empowerment. Now, however, some companies find major cost savings and new strategic benefits from recentralizing operations—particularly those related to setting up and managing networks to share information across traditional organizational boundaries. These new I/T organizational forms are a mix of centralized and decentralized functions, and the specific best form is dependent on the corporate technology culture.

Setting technology and architecture standards, approving major purchases, and identifying cross-functional systems opportunities are candidate functions for centralized management. Business application development is a candidate function for the business units, where I/T and line managers can work together in response to customers and markets. No matter what structure seems to be appropriate at the time, the most important thing is to continue to be flexible—business conditions change and as they do, the organization must continually adapt itself to new organizational, architectural, and technology demands.

Downsizing and Outsourcing I/T Functions

In an uncertain business environment, an enterprise wants to be able to control its costs. That's difficult to do when a company has money invested in multiple mainframe computers and systems, representing fixed costs, when outsourcing allows a company to pay based upon the amount of processing data. Companies also save on taxes—while hardware gets depreciated over three to five years in the United States, outsourcing fees are deductible as a current business expense.

Corporations see other benefits besides costs. Many companies decide they lack the resources to keep up with new information processing technology. If they have no core competencies in the area that they wish to protect or grow, they align themselves with outsourcers to benefit from economies of scale. Outsourcers save money by using a single mainframe for data from several companies, and its customers gain access to a pool of experienced technical staff.

The strategies for outsourcing I/T activities vary with the enterprise. For example, National Car Rental carries its outsourcing activities further than most companies. It outsources its corporate data center, its reservation system, the terminals at the service counters, and its 200-plus employees who program and run the machines to Electronic Data Systems (EDS).[14] National believes it understands what it wants from technology and can direct EDS to implement it, freeing it to concentrate on how to launch new products and deliver improved services critical (and core) to its business.

Others take a more conservative approach to outsourcing than National, outsourcing only generic tasks (mainframe operations and maintenance of standard software applications such as payroll) while retaining people who are particularly skilled at applying technology to the business. When a company outsources its very best technical people—the ones who should be developing strategies for the company to extend technology—it is analogous to outsourcing its business strategic planners.

Core Competencies and Outsourcing

Business organizations, through long-range strategic planning processes, identify core competencies and invest to keep them viable. Additionally, they identify the core competencies necessary for the future and plan and invest in their development. It is critical for I/T organizations to do the same thing.

From an I/T perspective, the key decision filter for whether to outsource I/T functions should evolve around growing and maintaining core competencies within the organization. As the business organization becomes more turbulent and business functions more dynamic, the architectures and platforms employed today become inadequate. I/T must envision a series of transition architectures that keep the current business enterprise competitive and, at the same time, position it to be competitive in the future. This results in the I/T organization embracing multiple learning curves at every turn. It also requires the I/T organization to:

- Understand the business strategy (or possible alternative strategies) and its resulting impact on the information technology strategy (and its possible alternative strategies).
- Make informed decisions (about alternative I/T scenarios) in time to support the business.

Outsourcing will probably become more prevalent in many I/T organizations. However, it must be wary of outsourcing functions that will deprive it of experiencing the learning curves necessary to get from its *as is* state, through multiple transition states, to its future state.

Balance maintaining the integrity of core competencies against possible short-term savings.

Outsourcing I/T Offshore

Outsourcing I/T related functions is not a new trend. In 1986, about 70 percent of I/T support operations in the United States were internal. Five years later (1991) that figure dropped to 45 percent.[15] Serving Fortune 500 companies primarily, the offshore I/T industry supports banks, magazine and book publishers, insurance companies, airlines, hospitals, and data banks. Originally, back-office activities used offshore sourcing, primarily routine data processing, involving payroll, accounting, billing, and mailing lists. However, offshore sourcing now includes a wide variety of information services such as systems design, testing, maintenance, conversion, and software development. In addition, some offices perform word processing, order processing, transcription of dictation tapes, coupon sorting, and other manual clerical tasks.

Language and education often present no problem. Many Caribbean countries have a high literacy rate, a holdover from their British colonial past. Other nations, such as India, the Philippines, and Ireland, have a surplus of college-educated people, often graduates in information systems. Surprisingly, even in Asian nations with quite different languages and alphabetic notation, the lack of English-speaking data-entry operators isn't an obstacle. Offshore Asian offices cite the principle that the Oriental operator will key what they see and are quite adept in character recognition.

What does seem to be a problem is potential inconsistencies between corporate and community culture of the offshore site as compared to a U.S. or European outsourcer. Corporate culture, which includes a range of items from personnel metrics and rewards to a corporate code of ethics, creates potential barriers to productivity. As an example, although overtime is legal in the Dominican Republic, employees of one company refused to work extra hours on weekdays and Sundays, preferring leisure time over money. Another company who had offshore workers in St. Kitts and Jamaica, bought uniforms for both locations, since its St. Kitts employees expected them—only to find that its Jamaican employees refused to wear them.[15]

After initial successes in outsourcing data entry, companies now consider I/T applications development as a candidate for outsourcing. Low-cost, highly productive, quality international competition now forces members of the U.S. I/T infrastructure to reexamine their effectiveness. Key comparisons between the world-class software organization and the run-of-the-mill software organization are those of staff cost (salaries and benefits), staff productivity, and quality of the systems developed.[16] Costs can be lower and productivity and quality higher for some types of programming done outside the United States, especially when productivity becomes influenced by common, rigorous use of a standardized development methodology. Here, the United States tends to be at a disadvantage, since its programming culture tends to make hotshot programmers into idols. As long as any programmer culture supports individuality to the extreme, standards suffer. European and Asian business managers are more focused and comfortable in standards-driven environments, which makes them more competitive than U.S. managers in a global market place. The same holds true for the U.S. I/T manager and programmer. When this culture holds sway, any U.S. I/T organization is vulnerable to exporting and outsourcing of programming development activities.

Outsourcing International Networks

Outsourcing international networks is an option many companies exercise when going international.[17] Local knowledge is essential when dealing with the various regulatory bodies and it takes time to become an expert on, for example, pan-European telecommunications. An important trend is putting service-level and quality guarantees into international telecommunications outsourcing contracts. This is often as important as cost in negotiations.

REALITIES OF RIGHTSIZING I/T PRODUCTS AND PROCESSES

Rightsizing is a term used to describe the trend toward moving information processing away from a central processing function to smaller processors (and organizations). The traditional styles of computing—multiuser mainframes and standalone PCs—are being replaced by new client-server technologies that combine the best of both. In the client/server model, the network becomes the system. Instead of residing on the mainframe, applications get distributed across multiple computer platforms or servers. Intelligent workstations, or clients, access any server system on the network to get the data or resources needed. The end user sees a common, graphical interface that provides integrated access to all necessary business applications.

Client-Server Environment and Technology

Client-server technology allows companies to redistribute the work out of the centralized information processing function to the desktop or department where it is most appropriate. This movement acts as a catalyst for the fundamental redesign of mission critical business processes, facilitating decision-making, and providing improved customer service. Using these networks of personal computers and workstations instead of mainframes, client-server projects get created faster and with smaller hardware budgets.

While the initial motive for moving to a client-server model is often financially based, other maturing technologies such as low-cost networking, groupware, customizable workflow software, multimedia capabilities, and easy-to-use application development tools are combining to enable real process improvements.[18] With careful planning, these new tools and techniques vitalize redesigned business processes while leveraging investments in existing technology.

Planning Is Key.   To set the stage for discussing the planning issues around client-server, W.C. Harenburg of Triadigm International uses a diagram similar to the one shown in Figure 10-3 to describe the client-server environment.[19] This environment has five major components: databases, a connectivity tool, a workstation tool, a dictionary, and a directory. The components in the figure are conceptual, but a list of

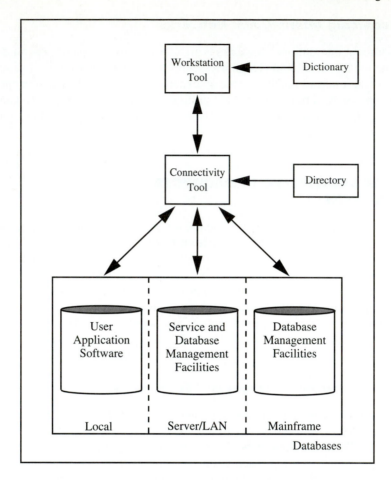

Figure 10-3 Client-Server Environment.
Source: W.C. Harenburg, Triadigm International 1993.

products (installed or under discussion) within each classification is possible. These represent the applications and systems software components operating within the client-server environment.

Harenburg uses a second figure similar to Figure 10-4 to represent and discuss the hardware components of client/server. Here, one can substitute mainframe or mini hardware boxes and add servers and local area networks (LANs) to match installed or proposed configurations for the enterprise. This diagram often helps to draw out and create a mind-set for discussing some of the complex problems encountered with shared data in a distributed environment.

Once this phase of planning is complete, the organization can formulate a migration plan.[20] One successful approach is to:

• Establish a baseline workstation infrastructure.

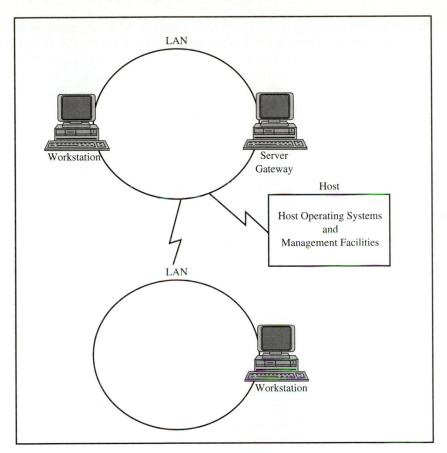

Figure 10-4   Client-Server Hardware.
Source: W. C. Harenburg, Triadigm International, 1993.

- Model and implement the users' task environment.
- Use encapsulation to integrate existing systems.

This structured evolution to client-server makes implementation feasible, since all-encompassing implementations tend to fail most often due to lack of needed skills, culture shock, and inappropriate up-front expenditures.

Contributing Value (and Risk) with Rightsizing

While the technology scanning activity in the enterprise often identifies the client-server model as a technology with possible merit, the organization must determine the value of client-server rather than blindly accepting and applying the technology. How an organization handles legacy applications usually indicates whether its development is technology-driven. In these organizations, the I/T developers often ignore systems still in use, where data is entered or calculated and placed in databases for sharing and use by others. Here, the company invests valuable resources to capture and enter data that represents the best information available. Managers in this environment must be wary of recommendations to discard data and applications without an accompanying analysis that includes a determination of the current value and the identification of the value contributed by the new technology.

New technology by itself does not necessarily contribute value.

I/T professionals tend to forget that many organizations still have what Harenburg calls *Sneakerware* as a networking protocol, where files get shared by running from office to office with a floppy disk. Some portables still don't have an electronic connection to get shared or corporate data, so these users will still trade floppy disks to share data. As a result, many of the issues regarding the success or failure of client-server relate to:

• Understanding the quality of the data.
• Using encapsulation to integrate existing portable and standalone systems.

Rightsizing is the appropriate concept—using the right size tool to meet the needs of the organization. This could be either hardware or software. In one situation, the best solution might be to replace the entire suite of applications with a client-server solution supplied by a software vendor. In another situation, the solution might be to modify the mainframe with a graphic user interface (GUI) or GUI front-end (sometimes called a screen scraper) to fit it within a GUI workstation standard. This allows a seamless interface for the user to switch between applications.

One of the benefits of client-server is the modular I/T components to fit the modular business approach. Modular client-server solutions more easily support shedding or absorbing business units. Not only should the conversions and interfacing required by the mergers and acquisitions of the 1980s become a thing of the past, but as businesses form new alliances, they will benefit from using the modular client-server model because the components are smaller and more functionally oriented.

As the business organization evolves into the more modular, compact form, the smaller client-server solutions become more responsive to the business needs. The old monolithic organization structure of the past required large teams of software developers to identify and support the complex business requirements. With the more modular form, capturing and supporting those requirements requires a smaller team and less time.

One way to accomplish an easier transition from traditional development approaches to client-server is to take advantage of the 80/20 rule. In software development, the rule refers to the 80 percent of the requirements that take 20 percent of the time to identify, while the remaining 20 percent of the requirements take 80 percent of the time. One item that usually takes excessive time for requirements' definition is that of report design. In the client/server environment, it is possible to give the basic data to the users so that they can easily incorporate it into their favorite workstation tool—usually a word processor or spreadsheet package. The user takes the data and formats it to their liking. Subsequent report creation can take advantage of the software remembering the source of the data and create the new report automatically.

What are the risks in rightsizing and the client-server model? (A necessary part of any value contributed analysis is addressing the associated risks.) Beyond the obvious general technology risk of moving too quickly or too slowly, the client/server model has its own risks. If the organization is not ready, costly design errors often occur. Additionally, client-server involves more than a learning curve for a new technique. While simple or complex techniques for exercising a new software tool or hardware feature are skills easily transferred through the standard training methods, what is of concern here are the design options and architecture issues inherent in client-server design and implementation that require learning through experience. Any inappropriate solution could result in a business loss. Use of outside consultants can reduce some of this risk, but in the rightsized business, costs are being watched closely and consultants may not seem cost-effective for such a small project.

A major risk relates to the fact that in the client-server model the network is the system. The major hardware vendors of the 1980s spent considerable time and effort to develop reliable communications capabilities and purchasers usually bought from those vendors. Now, the I/T organization is the creator of the custom network to fit the organization. The risk comes in the stability, flexibility, maintainability, and resiliency of the uniquely mass customized network. Has the vendor had experience in similarly configured networks? Can the technical people detect problems early enough to fix them? Is there sufficient redundancy built into the critical components? How does the network perform under an unusual load?

Rightsizing, Core Competencies, and Key Business Processes

If the business core competencies are identified, applications to support them should get special attention. This does not mean that those applications will continue being developed and maintained in the same fashion as in the past. Rather, cost-effective solutions in these areas are more critical to business operation than those in some peripheral business areas.

The core applications will have value in data collected that will need to be maintained. The data needs to be maintained, but not necessarily the application. The tendency for I/T personnel is to start from scratch with an application design effort. The emphasis in rightsizing is to pick the right solution for the need. In existing applications supporting a core business process, the need developed over the years, resulting in a finely tuned application creating business value. It may be worthwhile to use the client-server model to further fine-tune a portion, but perhaps it may not be wise to discard the entire application and start over.

The client-server model allows the maximum modularity and flexibility to mix and match the solution and the problem. When the modular business expands, merging new components require less investment than the more traditional business environment. It remains for the I/T function to construct the applications in a modular fashion so that when the business needs to divest or outsource marginal areas, I/T is the facilitator—not the bottleneck.

Client-Server Application Examples

Who uses the client-server approach? United Airlines uses it for crew scheduling.[21] It changed the crew-scheduling process from a mainframe-based system to one using a client-server application for data entry, editing, and file management on the client system and a FORTRAN-based model on the server. By doing so, United expects to save between $1 million to $1.5 million annually just by having more efficient schedules for its 8,000 pilots and 17,000 flight attendants. While the final flight schedules aren't available any faster using the client-server approach, each of the scheduling analysts has his own dedicated processor so they have more elapsed time to perfect them. United spent a little less than $1 million on labor and hardware for the new system it calls Paragon.

Computer-systems integrators often do the initial installations of client-server applications. For example, Bell Canada not only outsourced its data center operations to Systemshouse, but it formed a joint venture with them to meet its systems-integration needs and to sell similar client-server installation and application services to other telecommunications companies.[22] (Systemshouse, besides its Bell Canada connection, is developing an Express Mail tracking system for the U.S. Postal Service and provides technical and marketing support for IBM's RISC System/6000 in Canada.)

REALITIES OF DECENTRALIZATION AND RECENTRALIZATION

Decentralization and centralization for I/T functions are not mutually exclusive. Decentralization—often associated with downsizing, outsourcing, and flattening the enterprise through business divisional and user empowerment—is often the first move in dismantling the I/T glass house and establishing the autonomy of business units. Most enterprises base this initial move on cost containment and savings. For some, steady decentralization continues. For others, there is a move towards highly selective recentralization, based upon a refocus (or reassessment) of business strategy.

Transforming I/T to better support the changing enterprise isn't straightforward at all, and distributed computing (like client-server) is not a simple cure-all.

Often, I/T best practices, security, and back-up procedures suffer, causing chaos, re-dundancy, and confusion. Many companies find after decentralizing its I/T func-tions that it inadvertently destroyed some function critical to business strategy. For example, one company whose business strategy espoused an increasingly global presence found those core applications that bridge worldwide geography's and cross-match data aren't possible within its decentralized model.[23] Additionally, re-ducing duplicated efforts, establishing standards, and maximizing the effectiveness of technology investment's companywide are difficult goals to achieve without some centralized effort.

What functions fit nicely into the decentralized environment and what are can-didates for centralization? Again, there are no perfect or universal answers. Each enterprise is different—guided by its core competencies and business vision. Notwith-standing, the following are some general guidelines for I/T functional placement.

- Operations: Consider centralizing or outsourcing computer operations. Make the decision based upon cost and quality service criteria.

- Network management: Consider centralizing network management, when the network is across conventional company boundaries, for example, an intraenter-prise network. Consider decentralizing local area network management at a business unit level, however e-mail, electronic data interchange (EDI), elec-tronic funds transfer, and interfaces with other local area networks increase the need for tighter, higher level, control and security.

- Systems and applications development: Large systems that cut across conven-tional company boundaries work best as centralized activities. Examples of this type of activity include the intraenterprise sharing of data, a system requiring in-teractions between two or more divisions, or an application shared by multiple functions where no one function has sufficient critical mass and resources for implementation. Consider developing (or purchasing) division-base applications at the local level, from the perspective of defining and fulfilling user require-ments. Straightforward systems or applications that are not strategy-sensitive can be outsourced. (Remember that if outsourced, managing the interface is important.)

- Systems and applications maintenance: Perform systems maintenance at the same level as the original development. An exception is for business applica-tions developed centrally but used by a single company unit or function. In this case, consider doing applications maintenance at the business unit level where changes in business requirements can be tracked, and implemented when necessary.

- Development of standards, tools and techniques: Better located at a centralized function if it has the potential of impacting multiple functions. This reduces costs by eliminating redundancies and incompatibilities between packages.

Don't expect to avoid all redundancies and incompatibilities caused by decentralization. Concentrate instead on eliminating the most costly 20 percent.

OBSERVATIONS

Realities for Systems Delivery

Redesigning I/T systems and their delivery is a major process change that is strategic in nature and requires significant senior management involvement. Business and I/T leaders must jointly understand their current enterprise capabilities and envision future needs. In this joint effort, both must envision the company's future business environment before either can begin to envision the I/T systems environment in support of the shared business vision. The strategic vision of the systems environment determines the projected I/T development environment—the portfolio of delivery mechanisms that enables the delivery of systems to meet the needs. These delivery mechanisms include the tools, methods, and approaches employed by I/T to develop, deliver, and support its products.

The characteristics of the I/T systems environment and the types of systems it supports both change when there is:

- A business emphasis on business process and organizational restructuring to improve customer service and quality while reducing time-to-market.
- An emphasis on interdependencies and empowerment (whether within the organization or outside the organization as a result of collaborative business relationships).

Process-oriented, interdependent organizations need supporting cross-functional transaction systems, where the focus is on satisfying end-to-end business events or service strategies rather than on discrete activities. Empowerment activities require a new level of information-richness for decision support systems, executive information systems and other similar application groups.[24]

To respond to these business actions means that any new I/T delivery infrastructure needs to deliver systems quickly—a focus on assembling rather than on developing internally built or purchased standard components. It also means that new transaction systems are flexible, integrated, and span across traditional business boundaries and represent current business best practices, providing companywide and alliancewide access to consistent, reliable information. Common to its business functions, few I/T functions have the necessary core competencies (knowledge or experience) to get from today to tomorrow in one giant step—thus most enterprises and their I/T organizations must go through a transformation process involving a difficult transition phase to get to a new cultural, organizational, and technology environment supporting constant change.

Realities for Transforming the I/T Business

In the past, the use of I/T did not necessarily ensure the reshaping and improvement of business processes. After sometimes extensive development efforts, significant business improvements were difficult to find. The failure, for the most part, of the new technologies and products was due to not making the necessary changes in individual and organizational habits to obtain the sought after business benefits. Technologists and business executives wanted to introduce change with the least amount of impact on the status quo—and this meant that a company never got the real payoff from the investment in I/T. Today, this means that when change to the status quo is at a minimum, the enterprise will not achieve the necessary breakthroughs in productivity, service, or time-to-market.

I/T is one of the principal enablers of business change based on reengineering business processes. Once business commits to business change, it can leverage the capabilities and the power of I/T to support business change and to accomplish the breakthroughs necessary to improve competitiveness. After observing many efforts to institute the business transformation process, we can define *reengineering for business transformation* as any initiative meeting the following six criteria:[25]

- The initiative has highly aggressive business goals in terms of current productivity or results, or in creating new business.
- It uses technology as a major vehicle for rethinking the business.
- Its goal is a radically new business design.
- The solution requires *both* non-incremental thinking and new business paradigms.
- The initiative has existing business champions.

Remember also that the change agent is not exempt from change. The same new levels of competitiveness force I/T to reengineer and change itself. While I/T makes possible radically new paradigms for performing and organizing work, the I/T organization must rethink and redesign its own infrastructure and create a new operational charter for itself. I/T must do some audacious thinking about its role and contribution to business value, and the preceeding criteria for redesigning its business are reasonable ones for I/T to apply to its own redesign for the future.

What does this portend for the I/T function?

- It forces and focuses I/T to examine its past, present, and future contribution to business value.
- It requires I/T to evaluate its own core competencies and activities considering the business goals and objectives to create an appropriate infrastructure and portfolio of services. (This will include outsourcing of some activities and a redirection of others.)

• It requires a redefinition of the role that the I/T function has traditionally played in the enterprise (from order taker to initiator; from service staff to business partner).

In short, I/T must redefine itself in terms of quality, service, core competencies, competitive advantage, and contribution to business value.

To have shared vision requires I/T to be equally as audacious as business in its transformational thinking.

11

Delivering Business Value

Business, with its supporting I/T organizations, can't compete effectively in this new market environment without interlinking strategies and support groups. Key to implementing this effective linkage is the ability of I/T to demonstrate its understanding of what constitutes business value and what its contribution is.

Not all I/T organizations link closely to improvements in business performance—or to what many of its users would believe are their needs. These I/T organizations are similar to other service functions found in traditional hierarchical organizations. Over time, management practices evolved that placed more emphasis on the efficiency of the function (because management considered I/T a cost of the enterprise) rather than on its level of service effectiveness delivered across the entire enterprise. Consider the following story about one service organization, a company cafeteria—its underlying management philosophy and practices and overall contribution to the enterprise.[1]

Imagine that this is the first day that Robert is working in his new office. He is hungry and decides to take a lunch break. Robert considers the company cafeteria, but the selection isn't quite what he wants, and co-workers tell him that the price is high. He considers ordering by telephone—there are restaurants that specialize in serving the food he wants—but this is also against policy. Robert considers his only remaining option—going off site—but finds that company policy prohibits him from doing so. He has to pay the high price for food he doesn't really want.

He visits the company cafeteria. Signs direct him to get in a single queue. If he wants to go directly to the head of the line, the rest of the people in the queue (other managers) must vote to accept his higher priority. When Robert arrives at the order point, another sign instructs him to fill out an order form. He then joins another queue to consult with the specialist in cuisine and diet, who tells him what would be good for him, and places the order. The cuisine specialist informs Robert that preparing his order will take some time, so he should be patient. When Robert asks the price, he finds that the price depends on the time it takes the chef to prepare his dish—the price of ingredients is of comparatively little consequence—so he really won't know in advance how much it will cost.

Will Robert be happy with the service offered by the cafeteria? No, because (without breaking the rules) the alternative is to do without. Will he feel that the price of his lunch was fair? No, because no estimate is available to him before the chef prepares the dish—and even automobile repair shops and doctors will do that! Would the cafeteria management feel it is offering a quality service? Yes, because unlike most other company cafeterias, it furnishes personalized menu planning designed to improve the health of the employees. Would the cafeteria management believe it is charging a fair price? Yes, because each dish gets priced according to (labor) preparation time, the largest factor in the overall price of the dish.

Robert finds out later that the cafeteria reports to the purchasing department, and its management tends to get the better service and on a schedule tailored to its needs. Robert plans to host a customer visit next week, but is told that he must keep his request consistent with meeting the needs of others. He insists on something special—a birthday cake—because the visitor is his biggest customer. Raymond, the cafeteria manager, informs Robert that this really doesn't matter, because the policy is to treat everyone equally (although purchasing sometimes has a head start).

Will Robert be happy with the arrangement? No, because the cafeteria rules are getting in the way of the customized lunch he wants to provide his customer. Will he value the cafeteria as being especially important to him? No, because it was unable (or unwilling) to provide the timely assistance he needed to achieve his business objectives. Would cafeteria management feel it was providing the best service it could? Yes, because once management makes exceptions to anyone other than purchasing, it begins to lose control of its budget, and maybe even its facilities.

The following month, Raymond, the manager of the cafeteria comes to see Robert. It seems that Raymond's facility is aging; he needs cash invested in the cooking and service area to keep up with cafeterias in other organizations, and he wants to prepare for future growth. He wants to create a state-of-the-art food service, but plans no new customer services. Raymond asks Robert to support his request to have the funds allocated to his projects. (In other words, Raymond wants Robert to allocate a sizable percentage of his departmental budget to cafeteria improvements.) He also wants to raise his prices to cover the additional costs of upgrading and operating his new facility.

Will Robert support Raymond's request? Probably not, because of the track record of inflexibility in helping him meet his business objectives, and because now he brings his lunch from home. When he wants to do something special for his customer, he works at the customer site all day and chooses his favorite restaurant to host lunch for the two of them. Robert doesn't see the cafeteria providing any competitive advantage. Moreover, Robert may consider bringing up the matter at the next managers' meeting and suggest asking for food service bids from outside vendors. Would cafeteria management believe it was making a reasonable request? Yes, because the employees will continue to have an eating requirement, and because it takes time to order, install, and train the cafeteria staff in the use of new equipment and in recent changes to the nutrition guidelines.

Now let's think of another investment request, only this time it comes from the I/T organization, and you are the manager that must make the funding decision. I/T has a legacy of management policies, procedures, and pricing somewhat similar to the previous service organization (the cafeteria). Even though you didn't develop effective measurements of the value that I/T delivered to the business in the past, you know that technology probably has a role to play in your future business transformation, so begin to ponder the wisdom of the request.

You ask the following (or similar) questions of your business associates. Are we getting our money's worth from the current investment in I/T? What are we getting from the information systems group that is helping us to build today's business to better withstand tomorrow's challenges? Is the money for I/T purely for overhead of current business operations, or is it an investment in the future viability of the enterprise? These are familiar questions to anyone who is in business today. Unfortunately, few businesses or I/T executives have any ready answers.[1]

BUSINESS-I/T CREDIBILITY GAP

Business executives have a full agenda: the increasingly global business environment, the necessity to reduce product time-to-market, and the demand to improve customer service. At the same time, many of them face downturns in revenue and profit, reductions in headcount and budget, and increased performance and productivity objectives. Is it any wonder that the I/T executive without solid evidence of the technology contribution to business value faces an increasingly unreceptive business audience?

For five decades, I/T promised to change how business operates. The point of emphasis has shifted from time to time—from cost-saving automation to management information, from customer-focused information to customer and supplier electronic highways—but the central problem remains the same. How can an enterprise best take advantage of its I/T opportunities, and how can management best cope with the resulting aspects of technology and business change management?

Technology Management

Compounding the problem is the way I/T gets managed. From the very beginning, a gap existed between business managers and I/T managers. Technology applications attempt to bridge the gap with initiatives such as systems development methods and high-level languages. Today, management innovations such as linked business and technology planning processes attempt to close the gap. However, modern technology, especially communications-based technology intended to change business practices throughout the enterprise, represents further management hurdles that need attention to achieve real business value.

Business and I/T managers have to learn how to manage, measure and justify technology as a business matter.

It would be catastrophic if business permits the next generation of information technologies—especially those with such large opportunities as inter- and intraenterprise communications and enterprisewide computing activities in support of reengineering processes—to suffer the same hurdles and barriers that past generations did. For I/T—computing and communications in particular—offers dramatic new ways to add value to the enterprises that are able to successfully employ them. Whenever management raises questions about the levels and value of I/T investments, the heart of the matter is usually the identification of business value. Some straight talk about the questions of business value, what it is and who is responsible for its generation, is in order. Only then can management address what I/T functions must do to fulfill its role in the enterprise.

Issues That Won't Go Away

In today's competitive environment, more is being demanded of individual business investments. Without a bottomless bucket to dip into for funding, excessive research and development budgets get cut, and new plant and equipment expenditures get postponed. While the apparent benefits of spending on plant and equipment are both visible and tangible, executives frequently doubt the existence of similar tangible evidence of the value received for I/T spending.

   A great deal of the pressure for business value, and the confusion in determining it, stems from the intermingling of operational, management, and strategic issues by I/T executives when talking to their business counterparts. Exacerbating the confusion is the current literature and the authors who have yet to agree on a common definition and then use it.[1] To provide a base for this chapter as well as the remainder of the book, it is important to define *business value* and what it means for the business executive.

BUSINESS VALUE OF INFORMATION

The word *value* means something different from cost or benefit. When managers talk about the value of information, it suggests that information is worth something, that information has value in the way that tangible assets do, and that management should be willing to pay for information, invest in it for the good of the company. What is it that makes information valuable, and what is the consequence of attributing value to information?

Linkage to Business Purpose

Many I/T professionals assume that the production of information is the main purpose for information systems. This is an incomplete view, for information alone has no value. Information has no value except as it is useful for a business purpose—it is the linkage between specific business purpose, and it is the use that makes information valuable. Intrinsically, it has no value—when linked to some business purpose, information has value.

The key words are *business purpose,* for not just any purpose will do. An enterprise is a success when it delivers services and products to customers so that it satisfies its customers and achieves its financial objectives. The enterprise sets business objectives and manages to them, measuring progress along the way. Information is of value to the enterprise when it contributes to the achievement of the measurements based upon business purpose. The important idea is the linkage.

Information that has some linkage to one of the following three basic measurements has business value.

- Customer choice (that is, market share, or other indicators of success in getting customers to choose the product or service over other offerings).
- Quality of the enterprise performance—or product—once the customer makes the choice (i.e., error rates, or customer complaints, or product returns).
- Financial consequences of the performance (i.e., the cost of producing the product or service and the revenues derived from it).

From an I/T perspective, I/T contributes value by altering customer choice, by improving business performance, and by improving the financial performance of business units. That is, I/T contributes value when information systems, the information I/T manages, contributes to the ability of each strategic business unit to improve customer choice, business performance, and financial performance. I/T contributes value by improving the performance of the business in ways determined to be important by the business unit.

Well-Managed I/T May Not Generate Business Value

I/T professionals must also recognize that well-managed information systems operations may not generate any business value. Conversely, the lack of it can impede an enterprise in its pursuit of a competitive strategy. A well-managed I/T delivery function is, however, the first step toward creating business value.

> *The ability of the business organization to use and exploit the capabilities and capacities that I/T creates is necessary to create business value.*

Business value isn't a matter of how much the firm spends on systems and people, or even how good the systems are. It's what the firm does with the capabilities that it creates. The performance of business activities creates the business value of I/T. This means that the generation of business value is the responsibility of the business executives, and that business value creation occurs outside the I/T function. It is the responsibility of the I/T executives to both deliver the technology (creating the potential for value) and prepare the business organization to exploit the capabilities (creating business value).

Consequences of Business Value

For some, this is a new mind-set for I/T organizations to think about purpose. Instead of focusing on serving user needs, I/T must focus on contributing value to the strategic business unit—to improve the functioning of every department, including those internal to the enterprise as well as those that deal with customer matters.

I/T generates business value when, for example, it will:

- Create new business opportunities that build volume.
- Enable the firm to access new geographical markets.
- Enable new segments in an existing market.
- Expand the firm's product line or its ability to deliver more product or service without increasing the investment in human or physical resources.

Productivity enhancements, whether realized through structural alignment or not, are different from generation of business value. They are not repeatable, and they focus on internal efficiencies rather than on a competitive repositioning in the external market. They are worthwhile efforts and contribute added value to the enterprise. However, they do not create business value. Creation of business value occurs when I/T activities support the building of the business.

There are other consequences to this idea of business value. One important consequence is that each I/T organization has to understand how it intends to contribute business value through information, but only after it understands how to measure that value. It isn't enough to assert that there can be business advantages derived from the use of information. I/T has to be capable of knowing how improvements in performance create that value, and how much it might create. Once having taken this perspective, it can now define, more effectively, how to approach business management. By describing information to support decisions, the ability to respond to customer needs more rapidly and by creating new business opportunities that build volume (through anticipated movements in the measurements of business performance), information systems and I/T become an asset of the enterprise to exploit, rather than a cost to control or reduce. For enterprise resources that contribute value (e.g., a product technology or a new manufacturing plant), business management attributes real value and considers them an asset of the enterprise. Information is no less an asset when linked directly to improving customer choice, quality, and financial measures.

I/T creates business value when it contributes to the improvement of the business unit performance measures over multiple measurement periods.

Another consequence to the idea of information value is the necessity for I/T staff to have a thorough understanding of the business and to select tools and skills appropriate to solving the business problem. Many I/T organizations view systems planning as a software engineering problem, relying on tools of structure, data flow, and similar systems-oriented views of the user organization needs. The use of software engineering-based approaches are important, but tend to overlook basic business understanding—the dynamics of both the business organization and the business process dynamics. Another planning approach is necessary along with software engineering and structured development.

The I/T role is to manage the information necessary to contribute to business performance. The I/T organization not only has to concern itself with understanding the business it serves, and add value to that business, I/T must also be capable of creating the conditions under which its users can effectively and efficiently use the information for its intended purposes. The information has to be accessible, but even more important the users themselves have to share the same view of importance and purpose and be capable of using the information. Users demand productive I/T services and appropriate information for decision support, with appropriate responses to their needs. The I/T organizations must be efficient, provide the right information, and have the capacity to respond to user demands for services.

- I/T must understand both the technology and the business—and understand the basis of each strategic business unit and its measures, the conditions that define its success, and the basis for value of information.
- I/T must create the appropriate environment so that the business unit can effectively use the information.
- I/T and the business unit must share the same view on the value of the information.

It's a difficult agenda, but one that's required for the future.

Business Value and the Impact on I/T

It is relatively easy to express the need to link information to change in business performance, but considerably more difficult to define exactly how this should occur. Obviously, management wants to find strategic and business advantage and have information contribute to business improvement. Logically, the next question involves how to proceed. The best way is to conduct I/T planning with business, not technology, methods. The most important questions—for both business and I/T management—are to determine what business it is in, and what problems it has in the business. For it's the answer to these questions that will help identify the way in which information, and I/T, can make the difference. When information does make a difference, the measures of performance for the business will reflect it.

The I/T function must undergo a fundamental change to survive. Too many I/T

organizations have lost sight (if, indeed, they ever had it) of business management fundamentals. By not changing the organization to be responsive, cost-effective, and
aligned with the business vision, it dooms any I/T initiative to failure. I/T management itself, must also change. It must learn how to build better support organizations.
It must empower both technical specialists and users in the business to provide input
to and make technology and budget decisions. I/T must adopt the mind-set of a *culture
maker*—building an environment in which people can make the best decisions.[2] This
requires a distinct business perspective for the I/T organization. It adds new responsibilities to the I/T group: it no longer is enough to provide information, to manage and
acquire it. Rather, the I/T group has to get into the business of providing access to
information—the right information that contributes to business success. This means,
too, that the users have a similar perspective.

This new mind-set focuses on leadership—I/T leadership. It requires energizing
and motivating each I/T professional to better understand the business itself. It is not
just the job of the CIO. It's the job of every I/T professional to develop the vision and
see the *business purpose*—meaning the linkage to improvement in business performance—for every information system.

> *It is not enough to merely respond to technology trends and user needs, which are essen-
> tially reactive postures. Rather, it's a proactive responsibility to link technology opportu-
> nity to business opportunity.*

Linking the user requirements for value-contributing information with the I/T organization requirements that effectively develop and deliver technology is a formidable
task. It's one of leadership, a new I/T role for many enterprises. While some I/T organizations are more able than others, every I/T organization faces the same challenge,
to understand exactly what the role entails.

> *I/T can no longer view itself a being in the technology management business—I/T is in
> the business success business.*

STRUCTURAL CHANGE AND BUSINESS VALUE

In early 1993, there was talk about whether the United States was in the recovery
phase of its recession. This discussion took place not only between political nominees,
but among economists, business school professors, and by business leaders in their
boardrooms. The basis for much of the controversy centered on the fact that traditional
economic measures, the leading economic indicators, displayed the characteristics of
an economic recovery, while the rate of unemployment, considered one of the key
economic indicators, remained high, which normally signals a lack of recovery. This
wasn't a onetime anomaly, as some claim, but an indication that structural changes
were taking place in the economy and the business and government leaders—not to

mention their economic advisors—had yet to develop an adequate set of measures to appropriately reflect these new dynamics.

Consider the just-in-time philosophy that is becoming increasingly pervasive in the manufacturing and retailing industries. Low inventories no longer automatically trigger a bulk purchase by the manufacturer or retailer, nor do they necessarily trigger an overtime and new hiring cycle by the producer. Distribution channels today are becoming simpler, cleaner, and quicker. Nonetheless, many experts still cite inventory levels as one of the leading economic indicators of economic health—we hear about them during the evening news or we see them highlighted in leading financial journals.

New housing starts are another one of the often referenced leading economic indicators. In 1993, the United States experienced the lowest interest rates in a decade, along with a low inflation rate. Both of these conditions would—even a decade earlier—support a healthy housing market. Yet this indicator remained relatively stagnate, due in some part to the unemployment rate, but due in a much larger part to changing demographic patterns. The baby-boomer generation that kept its parents moving up from one and two bedroom homes in the 1950s through 1970s left home. They rent instead of buy, due in part to wages not increasing as fast as rents, making it difficult for the potential first-home buyer to save enough money for a down payment. Additionally, this demographic group marries later and has fewer children. Meanwhile, parents retire, live in their original homes or retirement communities, and are less likely to move again. Unless there is a growing population of young adults (which the United States, Germany, or Japan do not have), combined with robust employment opportunities (which come and go), housing starts are not necessarily a key indicator of a nation's economic growth. Other factors further exacerbate the problem: There is no new geographic frontier to populate, a relatively stable native population mix, and an increasing sensitivity to unchecked immigration. New housing starts are increasingly unlikely to regain their former level of importance to anyone other than construction-related industries like lumber and plumbing.

While the manufacturing industry embraced just-in-time philosophy and adjusted to changing demographics, other industries restructured and introduced new products to maintain competitive positions. For example, banks in the United States responded to the competition from brokerage firms and other financial institutions selling mutual funds to the public by offering similar funds to its depositors. Since depositors often fund these purchases through bank deposits, offering mutual funds keeps a greater percentage of bank assets intact. Now, banks are better able to serve the depositors who choose to move their savings from bank certificates of deposit to proprietary mutual funds (managed by the banks themselves) and nonproprietary mutual funds. Yet at the same time that the banking industry pursued this perfectly logical competitive move, the Federal Reserve continued to define the U.S. money supply to include bank certificates of deposit and to exclude mutual funds. Insulating economic measurements from financial industry strategy forced the Federal Reserve to describe the growth of U.S. money supply as sluggish. With the growing tendency of savers to shift money out of bank certificates of deposit into mutual funds, and with banks abetting the process, the Federal Reserve faced a decision. Should it redefine its key measure—the money supply—to restore its usefulness as a meaningful link to economic activity, or should it assume that the popularity of mutual funds is a temporary aberration and not change its measurement definition?[3]

Businesses today face similar questions. While the economists don't have a way of describing and measuring the robustness of the national economy as long as they continue to use—to the exclusion of all others—measures developed over time to track and diagnose what was going on in an economy driven by a manufacturing engine, neither do business executives. Current measures don't reflect what's going on in this new economic and competitive environment. Whether we call it knowledge-based, information-based, service-based, or technology-driven, business needs new ways to describe and measure progress in maintaining and improving competitive position in the new economy.

Although these examples focus on leading economic indicators and measures at a national scale, the issue is even more relevant for businesses. It accomplishes little to celebrate an increase of domestic market share if management doesn't look at the whole picture.

- Is the increase due to a better product and service than provided by our competitors?
- Is the increase due to some competitors going out of business because the domestic market is disappearing (like the buggy whip market at the turn of the last century) or is no longer as profitable?
- Is the increase based on governmental protectionist policies that may change in the future?

New business value descriptors and measures must, therefore, reflect the enterprise position relating to global competitors, global markets, and product alternatives. And, just like governments and economists, business enterprises today don't have solidly established criteria—quantitative or qualitative—based upon this new type of competitive base.

Both government and industry leaders are uneasy with the current criteria and realize that this new competitive environment requires new measures of progress. The electric power industry, for example, began using the *negawatt* as a measure of number of *watts not produced* for consumption as a result of introducing energy saving programs. While the negawatt may not be a perfect measure, it reflects the industry effort to express progress towards new environmental goals. Equally important, it reflects a positive measure to counterbalance the accompanying revenue reductions.

Business and I/T leaders must also accept that there is no proven set of best measures that are equivalent to the constantly evolving industry best practices to apply and accept instantly. We must begin to jointly develop new best practice performance measures, measuring progress towards accomplishment of strategies that prepare the enterprise for changes in the competitive environment.

BUSINESSES FACE NEW PERFORMANCE MEASURES

Businesses are becoming besieged by guidelines and measurements. Not only are they having to develop new measures to express new conceptual assets to stakeholders—such as the negawatt to express value in energy conservation—but they are having to develop new ways to effectively express competitive position or strength as competition and market scope evolve from local to global. PPG Industries, for example, uses a form of business array in its annual report to present this type of information to its stockholders. For each of its major businesses (coatings and resins, glass, and chemicals) it includes their annual sales and operating earnings. It then describes each of the business areas in terms of worldwide size, annual growth rate, major products and uses, global competitors, and PPG's competitive position in the global market.

The U.S. Council on Competitiveness takes another approach.[4] It recommends the evaluation of investment programs rather than evaluation of discrete projects, separating the determination of the asset position from the evaluation of the means of achieving it. Along with the current quantitative measures of investment, the council recommends the addition of qualitative measures such as the skills of its work force (intellectual assets) and the sophistication of technology employed (technology assets). Bottom-line: It recommends the development of a standard way to evaluate investments in intangibles, so that one can report and compare between similar enterprises or between differing industries.

Who can argue with a recommendation to assess the intangible assets of, for example, the core competencies of people, process, and products within a corporate culture of one enterprise to compare it with the strengths and weaknesses of another enterprise? Business leaders constantly struggle to discover the underlying formula that ensures future business success. However, just as one set of paradigms seems to offer that assurance, the business environment changes. The validity of recently learned paradigms (with accompanying measurements and ratios) becomes of questionable value.

INDICATORS OF FINANCIAL VALUE UNDERGOING STRUCTURAL CHANGE

Every financial magazine seems to have its own list of best and biggest as a way of ranking and comparing one enterprise to another, or one industry to another. Today, there are lists of the fastest-growing, the most profitable, the greatest revenue-producers, and the most admired. Accompanying these lists are similar least lists, slowest growing, least profitable, and so forth. The problem is that when comparing these best or worst lists, there isn't a consistent set of companies. This is due to the peculiarities of accounting practices, the unavoidable differences in the cost of capital, and the way each company accounts for it, affecting simple profitability.

For example, a comparison of Bethlehem Steel (a U.S. steel maker) with Colgate-Palmolive (a producer of consumer goods), shows that their 1989 profit and turnovers were quite close. The return-on-sales comparison ranked them side by side. However,

Bethlehem Steel required 50 percent more capital than Colgate, and a return-on-capital ranking would have shown Bethlehem well behind.[5]

Ranking by return-on-capital favors labor-intensive companies over capital-intensive ones. It also favors companies with old capital over those with new capital. This is as a result of accounting practices based upon, for example, what equipment cost in the past as compared to what it costs to replace it. Additionally, the methods used for financing the purchase by the various companies influence the results.

To get around these problems, the London Business School (LBS) in conjunction with *The Economist* developed a new measure intended to reflect the quality of the added value of a company. The LBS version of added value measures how much more a firm's output is worth than all its inputs of materials, capital, and labor. It is an output-based added value (OVA) analysis.

OVA is excellent for comparing capital-intensive and labor-intensive industries because it treats all financing the same (by applying an especially developed capital charge of multiplying the enterprise's total current-cost capital employed by the interest rate on risk-free bonds in its home country). To find out a firm's added value (or corporate quality), the LBS approach starts with the operating profits, adjusts for the differences in accounting approaches for dealing with depreciation (they also have a formula for this), and subtracts its capital charge. The remainder represents the added value for the shareholders. Oil giants like Shell, Exxon, and British Petroleum dominated the top ten lists for about 2,000 publicly quoted companies drawn from a number of international databases for the years of 1981–1990. Companies cited as examples throughout the book who made the top thirty list (in absolute terms) include Royal Dutch Shell, IBM, General Electric, General Motors, British Telecom, Phillip Morris, Du Pont, Ford, Matsushita Electric, Texaco, AT&T, Toyota, and Sears, Roebuck.

It's obvious that the OVA approach (if it stopped here) has one remaining bias—that of size. Some companies earning large added value at low margins do so because they are in highly competitive markets like the automobile industry, while others chose that route as a conscious business strategy. However, others may earn large amounts of added value at low margins because they are big bureaucracies in a temporarily easy market. To remove the bigness bias, the LBS expresses its added value calculation with percentage of sales. Now, the industries that dominate the top ten are pharmaceutical and utilities, and no oil company even makes the top thirty. If we look at the best of the big (annual sales of more than 1 billion ecus (European Currency Units) where the ecu was worth $1.27 in 1990), only British Telecom survives the previous list, with a 17.9 percent added value as a percentage of sales. Joining it are others we cite, including Southern California Edison (SCEcorp.) with 19.3 percent, Detroit Edison (16.3%), and McDonald's (16.3%).

Finally, if we focus on the added value of companies with smaller revenue streams than our aforementioned global giants (annual sales of .5 million to 1 billion ecus), three of the top ten are computer services (Autodesk in the U.S. with 33.9% and Volmac in Holland with 32.4%) and computers (Cray Research in the U.S. with 25.6%). An additional four represent service organizations (communications, health care, financial services, and transportation). This list may or may not foretell the giants of tomorrow, but it does present a clear picture of a potential infrastructure shift from a clearly manufacturing-based economy (the biggest by revenues) to one based upon information and services (the best by added value flow to the stockholders).

While the LBS calculation for corporate quality only purports to measure the added value available to the stockholders, *it does not measure the overall wealth created by a company.* A firm may create wealth very efficiently, but instead of making it available to the stockholders, it may pass it on to its employees in the form of high wages (as in Germany, with its combination of high wages and high output). It may also pass it on to its customers, accepting lower prices and lower returns to achieve long run market share and growth (as has been the practice in Japanese companies).

Other performance indicators similar to OVA are also gaining new advocates as management tools. Economic value added (EVA), an annual figure based upon a company's net after-tax operating profit minus the capital employed in the business, measures a company's success over the past year.[6] Market value added (MVA) is forward-looking and reflects the market's assessment of a company's prospects by combining all the capital that is in the company (shareholder investments, loans by banks, retained earnings, etc.), and subtracting the current value of the company's outstanding stock and debt. If the enterprise's market value is greater than all the capital invested in it, it has a positive MVA. If the MVA is negative, management has destroyed wealth. If, for example, a company has a negative EVA and a positive MVA, it reflects past difficulties for a company that now has a potentially bright future. Used in combination, these indicators focus on management's performance as stewards of capital.

While we don't have calculations to measure the added value flowing to stakeholders other than the stockholders today, these measures will surely follow. The reason is that today's market share is apt to be tomorrow's business value. British and American companies may be reaping the competitive rewards of past competitive battles, but losing today's battlefields to the Germans and Japanese. Until we start developing, tracking, and validating new performance indicators and measurements that accurately reflect all competitive cultures, we can't detect competitive shifts until it's too late.

STAKEHOLDER VALUES AND THE INFORMATION AGE ECONOMY

To this point we've said:

- Different competitive cultures have different stakeholder values. Until there is a common way to measure all business value generated, it is difficult to compare any performance shifts between like industries operating in different competitive cultures.
- Traditional leading economic indicators are of questionable value in reflecting the power or scope of structural shifts at a national level.

- Industry is creating new measurements to reflect intangible, other than financial, activities and progress towards achievement of goals.
- I/T has difficulty in measuring business value contribution and getting business management to believe it.

There is some good news in this! For the first time, understanding the impact of investments in technology (of all forms) on business performance is important to global competitiveness. The result is that others outside the I/T profession recognize and are working on solving the problem.

Nuala Beck, a Canadian economist specializing in the structural changes required to move from the manufacturing to the information economy, undertook extensive research to discover how to facilitate this change. She set out to develop a set of ratios to assess the level of robustness of the new information age competitive environment. She believes, like Porter and the Council on Competitiveness, that the nature of value has changed and that you can't measure new wealth (or assets) with old tools.[7] Beck set out to develop a series of financial ratios that would address this new nature of economic value and how we might measure its growth. Her initial efforts focused on statistics associated with knowledge-intensive employment growth and on measuring Canada's high-tech trade balance.

Beck's ratios assess the full range of technology at a (Canadian) national level. This is more good news for I/T, because it represents the first step toward the development of standard industrywide and nationwide business measurements for technology and its level of contribution to business success. Some companies already find a variation of them valuable in assessing their own investments in I/T and other technologies.

Ratios that directly link to the effective use of information technologies in the enterprise include:

- Technology spending ratio: This is the ratio between the amount of current investment in technology and total investment.
- New technology-to-technology spending ratio: More often than not, in companies with technological edge have the advantage in the market place. As a consequence, one often needs to better understand the investment patterns of the technology dollars within a company. This second ratio assesses the level of investment dedicated to innovative and sophisticated new processes (e.g., groupware) as compared to replacement processes (e.g., a combination of voice mail and e-mail to substitute for a switchboard). and is an extension of Nuala Beck's technology spending ratio developed by this author.

Key to making these measures meaningful is not only the effective development and transfer and subsequent support of the tools that I/T delivers to the business organization, but the receptivity and preparedness of the business culture (the people, processes, and products) to embrace them.

While these (previous) ratios address the current level of investment in technology and indicate the level of industry leadership in technology, the following ratios indicate how knowledge-intensive the industry, company, or organization is.

- Knowledge ratio: This ratio expresses the number of knowledge workers as a percentage of total employment in an industry, individual company, or organization. High knowledge-intensive industries have knowledge ratios of 40 percent or higher and tend to include the leaders of the new knowledge-based economy including consulting, engineering and architecture, commercial research, and development. Moderate knowledge-intensive industries range from 20 to 40 percent and tend to include members of the mass manufacturing economy. The low knowledge-intensive industries, according to Beck, fall below 20 percent and most of the lower-paid service sector workers, including retailers, beauty salons, and barber shops. This ratio measures the *corporate IQ*.
- Return-on-knowledge assets: The number of knowledge workers to profit earned (analogous to the current return-on-assets calculation). This measure helps evaluate whether a company is using its brain-power productively.

Taken together, the set of four ratios provides an insight into the importance of knowledge workers and their productivity within the current environment. The investment pattern to leverage the knowledge workers over time gives a clear indication of future competitive strength or weakness. Knowledge-based industries require constant monitoring of these ratios. They are also useful to compare the knowledge effectiveness of internal functions and departments in evaluating their evolution into agile, learning organizations.

A second group of Beck's ratios targets the issue of how well enterprise management has managed the company's current product lines in anticipation of changing market demand and how well the company has positioned itself to develop and produce new products. These include:

- Peak-to-growth ratio: Revenues from product lines sold to industries that have not structurally peaked expressed as a percentage of revenues from its businesses that are on a downward slope. This shows how well the company's management is managing the current product line to growing markets from stagnating ones.
- Patent-to-stock-price ratio: The ratio of the number of patents divided by the price of a company's stock. This is a gauge to assess the company's value based on its potential to develop new products for the market place.
- Research-to-development ratio: The ratio of research dollars spent to the development dollars spent. If all the money is for development and marketing, there is no money left for new research. A balance between the two efforts is necessary to both incrementally enhance old products and to create new ones.

- Research and development-to-patent ratio: The ratio of research and development investment to number of new patents issued. This ratio, in combination with the research-to-development ratio, illustrates the level of effectiveness of product innovation, given the investment level.

These ratios are indicators of future enterprise success through new product development. They offer a measure of how much business value is being contributed to effective research and development (R&D) through I/T development and support activities.

Underlying these R&D ratios is the problem that every I/T manager faces for their own venue—how much effort to spend on maintenance versus new development; how much effort to expend on prototypes versus the real product; how much effort to spend on chasing new technology versus implementing new technology; and how to prioritize the support among functions to maximize the delivery of business value to the enterprise. With minimal effort, I/T can develop a set of parallel ratios that will be invaluable as input for future managerial decision-making and tracking of results.

A final group of Beck's ratios address enterprise funding patterns. These ratios measure the vulnerability of the company to domestic upheavals and changes in interest rates, the level of financial commitment that management has made to the success of the company, a measurement of the total market share worldwide, and the degree of (voting) control the shareholders have over the revenue streams flowing into the company. While the development of these ratios was for application at the enterprise level, they, too, have principles applicable to I/T. What I/T group doesn't worry about funding issues? This is particularly true as more companies establish a global presence. When I/T depends on funding through a transfer of payments between subsidiaries involving foreign currency, it must be aware of the volatility of foreign exchange. Additionally, domestic sources of funding may disappear in the face of rising interest rates, when internal stakeholders compare the perceived return on investment from I/T to alternative investments. Being aware of the degree of vulnerability for funding contributes to better I/T resource management.

OBSERVATIONS

Consider the massive structural shift from the agrarian to the manufacturing economy that began almost a century ago. Eventually, everything changed—economic, business, and social structures—including the concept of the farm. Today, even farming is big business, adapting mass production paradigms and measurements of success to its own operations.

Now, economists and industry leaders alike are observing the beginnings of another massive structural change from manufacturing to an information-based and technology-based economy, requiring another set of paradigms, measurements, and accounting practices to reflect success. Enterprises are abandoning practices like standard costing, developed in the 1920s in support of mass production, and adopting activity-based costing (ABC) to better reflect the cost structures of mass customization.

Similarly, some I/T groups in networked enterprises are abandoning price/performance numbers based on hardware benchmarks for cost-to-use analysis.[8]

As business continues to adopt new paradigms, it must search for new performance measurements and I/T as a business partner must do the same. While some of the new business value measures may be directly applicable for I/T use (e.g., efforts to measure intangibles), others require examination to see if there are underlying principles that will affect I/T practices. There is no assurance that any of the emerging I/T performance indicators will be right the first time or will even be in use five years from now. In fact, many of them probably won't be. They will take time to fine-tune and that will happen as business fine-tunes its success paradigms.

I/T has been the most obvious standard-bearer of the information and technology structural shift within the enterprise. As such, it is the one that is invariably asked "Why are we doing this?" As a consequence, it is also the professional group that has probably thought the most about the impact and accommodation of change and the consequences of not investing in technology. These are assets taking on new value and importance in the business-I/T partnership.

> *It is the responsibility of I/T to be aware of the volatility of what business value means to business management and be able to speak and support this new measurement language.*

It is also necessary for I/T leaders to remain abreast of new developments in the measurement of technology and in its link to possible change in competitive position. Effectiveness of use, acceleration of change, and pervasiveness within the business remain important internal measurements; however, changing technology investment patterns of competitors provide early warning of structural change at the industrywide level.

Part V

PLANNING I/T
AND ENTERPRISE
TRANSFORMATION

New methodology is necessary to accomplish the planning and implementation for the strategic transformation of I/T and its enterprise. This section discusses the necessity for methodology change and presents an effective approach, that of scenario planning, to develop the contextual framework within which transformation planning must occur (Chapter 12). The discussion includes the recognition and subsequent definitional development of transformational value and risk criteria as well as justification and measurement criteria. These approaches employ the use of the Seven Questions Methodology for Transformation Planning (Chapter 13) and Information Economics (Chapter 14). Justification criteria are linked to the development of new measurement criteria and systems (Chapter 15). Thus we link the establishment of the mission and strategy to the justification and funding of specific action plans and the justification process to the development of appropriate measurement systems.

In *Managing Change in a Performance-Driven Organization Using Information Economics* (Appendix I), Lynwood Walker concludes his description of what happened at AGT Limited. It focuses on the introduction, use, and fine-tuning of Information Economics at AGT during a time that the enterprise was experiencing significant turmoil involving its strategic transformation. *Stakeholder Values and Structural Change* is a supplement to Chapter 12. *Evergreen Environmental Consultants* (a fictitious name) is a case study of an I/T organization as it becomes a full business partner and an enabler of change in a professional services enterprise. It is a supplement to Chapter 13. Both are found in Part 5 of Appendix I.

12

Identifying Trends and Building Scenarios

Key to the success of any planning process is the validity of the assumptions upon which the plan is built. Here, we discuss the concepts and philosophies of scenario planning and its appropriateness for use in developing the context to plan for transformation.

Every person has their own view of the world and makes decisions daily based on that view. The collective views of management shape and define the view of their enterprise and its role in the competitive world. If an enterprise hopes to thrive in the next decade and beyond, its management must constantly seek out new perspectives. Today, too many enterprises base decisions on outdated interpretations of the world, its inhabitants, its social structures, and the ways that markets behave.

Wedded to today, governments, companies, and individuals are invariably hopeless at predicting what will happen tomorrow. This inability has two main causes. First, most people are comfortable with the status quo and want to deny that tomorrow will be anything different. Second, if they do dare to make a guess at the future, they will select just one option and stick to it, no matter what. Unfortunately, neither approach works when attempting to effectively plan and invest for future success.

One approach does work—that of scenario-based planning. The starting point is to draw up, and develop consequences from, a handful of possible alternative futures. The idea is to free the mind to admit that tomorrow might not be like today and to consider what might happen if the unthinkable occurs. The purpose of the scenario is not to predict the future: it is to think about alternative business strategies and actions when world truth and market definition change occur and to initiate planning in that context. Scenario-based planning posits that all the clues to the future exist—they simply need identifying and monitoring for change.

Peter Schwartz, in his 1991 book, suggests a series of driving forces, including technological change, perception-changing events (such as global warming), and popular culture, that he uses as elements to begin the construction of scenarios.[1] In parallel to his thoughts, in Part I we discussed political realignment and explored some of the social and economic shifts. We did this to create a new mind-set for thinking about the role of business and the I/T functions within it.

Now, we begin the process of building scenarios. The intent of any scenario is to stimulate thinking about the potential (business) consequences and alternative strategies in response to new and alternative competitive environments. The initial scenarios suggest possible economic, political, demographic, and environmental change within each trading bloc, and subsequent scenarios propose alternative shifts in the relationships. We close the chapter by examining how one enterprise uses scenarios and scenario planning to drive its strategy development and business plans.

POLITICAL REALIGNMENT AS A DRIVING FORCE FOR GROWTH AND CONSTRAINTS

The three dominant trading blocs (North America, Greater Europe, and The Pacific) are undergoing stress in dealing with a number of pressing issues, including its aging work force, immigration policies, and concerns for the environment. Each feels the press of competition from other trading blocs as well as from members within its own economic bloc. The first set of scenarios admittedly is rather benign but furnishes a starting point to think about possible future competitive environments.

Political Realignment Scenarios

North America.   The United States, Canada, and Mexico all have bright futures.[2] The United States-Canada Free Trade Agreement (NAFTA) broke down the business and economic barriers between the two countries. As a result, a political realignment occurs, fueled by the desire to improve economic position in a global economy. Canada fails in its attempts to eliminate existing trade barriers between provinces, causing increased political divisiveness. Fueled by economic concerns, Quebec, as prosperous as Switzerland, becomes independent before the turn of the century. More importantly, two Canadian provinces initiate the move to become new stars in the flag of the United States. Mexico, too, experiences prosperity. It overcomes its problems with pollution, the overpopulation in Mexico City, and the badly deteriorating infrastructure through extensive use of privatization of government functions and massive investments in communications technologies.

Greater Europe.   The European Union has a more difficult time than North America. Reunified Germany overcomes the economic imbalances caused by former East German Communist control. Unemployment disappears as a result of a combination of economic growth and the restructuring of social services to the point that labor shortages begin. True prosperity arrives by the year 2000, and Germany becomes the recognized economic leader of the EU. Very gradually, the emerging democracies of

Eastern Europe strengthen ties with the EU, providing a long-term growth market and work force for further EU economic expansion.

The Pacific.   The Pacific, dominated by Japan, is the regional powerhouse of the twenty-first century. Japan loses some of its productive dominance, but improves its economic strength through international acquisitions and consortiums and strengthens its economic ties with the West Coast of North America. North and South Korea reunite. Hong Kong and Taiwan become economic partners with Mainland China and promise to be an economic force equal to Japan by the year 2010.

Some "What If" Caveats Involving Political Realignment

Now that management is able to visualize what role each power bloc will play, they begin to consider how enterprise strategies might change to profit from new market opportunities and customer-supplier relationships. The business picture looks positive. They begin planning, based upon this single vision of the future.

This, however, is not what managers who use scenario-based planning do. They go a few critical steps farther before beginning to plan. They look at other, sometimes equally probable scenarios, reflecting differing combinations of events, trends, and time-lines. Consider the following alternative scenarios and think about how the competitive environment changes as the balance of power shifts. Consider whether strategies developed as a result of the initial vision would be successful. Finally, consider how business planners might develop flexible strategies that allow the business to maximize the benefits of change.

North America.   The individualistic approach that the United States applies to business and policy making is no match to the teamlike communitarian approach of its European and Japanese opponents. By the end of the twentieth century, America cedes world economic leadership to Germany or Japan. Adding to its economic woes, a major earthquake occurs along the San Andreas Fault, devastating much of the Silicon Valley. Damage in varying degrees in San Francisco and Los Angeles causes massive economic disruption throughout the country. National focus necessarily becomes one of internal rebuilding rather than international trade and investment.

Despite Latin America's wealth of natural resources, the region continues to suffer from poverty, overpopulation, and social division between the wealthy minority and the poor majority. These problems invite social unrest. Military coups occur in countries south of Mexico and Belize, wiping out the initial economic synergism created by NAFTA.

Greater Europe.   Reunified Germany has a difficult time overcoming the economic imbalances caused by former East German Communist control. Problems with unemployment take longer than expected to resolve. The restructuring of social services necessary to maintain economic balance is not complete until the year 2000. Only then does Germany take an active leadership role in the revitalization of the EU.

The imbalance among the three power blocs and the rest of the world grows. Europe becomes the confrontational crossroads for economic and political imbalance. Terrorism and chemical or biological weapons give the have-not nations disruptive powers, and the EU considers reactivating its border checks.

The Pacific. Japan's history includes devastating earthquakes occurring about sixty years apart, the previous one occurring in the 1930s. In July 1993, an earthquake measuring 7.8 on the Richter scale, accompanied by 10 to 30 foot tsunamis and killing close to 200, destroyed villages on the northernmost of Japan's main islands. The Hokkaido quake proves to be a fore-shock of an even larger earthquake involving Tokyo. This quake occurs along the major fault that lies beneath Tokyo, home to some 60 percent of Japanese gross domestic product (GDP), and significant damage results. To rebuild, Japanese investors sell holdings in U.S. commercial real estate, entertainment, and banking industries. They terminate costly joint ventures in the European Union involving automobile and light manufacturing and cease additional new investments in Eastern Europe. This creates economic disturbances throughout the world, due to the disruption of current industry and the time and financial investment necessary for rebuilding. It also gives Japan's Pacific partners an unprecedented opportunity to emerge as a new economic power bloc.

At this point, business strategists can begin to identify the possible range of change in its market and the possible range of change in global competitors and trading blocs. Strategists would also identify the early warning signals to indicate that a possible change in any of these market dynamics is about to occur.

DEMOGRAPHIC SHIFT AS A DRIVING FORCE FOR GROWTH AND CONSTRAINTS

Perhaps by now, managers have an idea of a highly probable, probable, and least probable political and economic environment in which their future enterprise must compete. However, this isn't the only factor to shape and influence market definition—population change also contributes its own market forces. They investigate two facets of demographic change—those of aging and immigration—and posit another set of scenarios for the trading blocs, again contributing to the shaping of the enterprise market and market definition.

Aging as a Constituency

In the late 1950s, Perry Mendel recognized that the baby boom produced an abundance of preschool children.[3] He knew that many of the mothers wanted to return to work. Seeing a growing need for quality child care, Mendel founded KinderCare Learning Centers. KinderCare's past success in capitalizing on a major demographic shift is a valuable lesson. It's an example of new business opportunities in the next major demographic shift, the aging society. However, unlike preschool children, the aging society is far from a homogeneous group. Mature consumers are highly heterogeneous, differing by family and marital status, ethnicity, geography, education, and social class. These factors combine to create needs for differing products and contribute to the accelerated destruction of the mass market.

The Center for Mature Consumer Studies (Georgia State University) uses combinations of two criteria for understanding older consumers: health and extroversion-introversion.[3] Some seniors' interests are socializing and traveling, while others are private and center their activities around the home. This results in four types of older consumers.

- The healthy indulger is healthy and active. Members of this group are likely consumers of financial services, clothes, entertainment, leisure services, and high-technology items. Health club memberships and products that mask or retard aging such as cosmetics, hair coloring, and skin moisturizers are of interest. They travel. As a result, there will be great opportunities for hotels, travel services, restaurants, and entertainment and hospitality services offering services designed for the growing senior population.
- Healthy hermits are in good health, but spend a great deal of time at home. They are consumers of home entertainment, security systems, domestic and financial services, home conveniences, and do-it-yourself and maintenance items. Exercise equipment and prepared foods low in cholesterol or salt interest this group.
- The ailing outgoer is active but ailing. Conscious of health problems, this group's interests are retirement housing, and health and financial services. They have an increasing need for corrective devices, such as hearing aids, walkers, etc.
- Frail recluses center most activities around the home and are often in failing health. They are consumers of domestic assistance, home and health services, adult day care, respite care, nursing care, and home-based entertainment.

Aging Fragments the Financial Services Market

After examining the lifestyles of each group, it's obvious that a single, mass-produced product won't serve them all. Consider financial services, a service that everyone in the aging population uses. The healthy indulger will likely use credit cards, lines of credit, ATMs, travelers' checks, and managed investment funds, while the healthy hermits probably prefer home banking and a more hands-on participation in managing their investments. They may use home computers and Internet to gain access to financial data and their investment and stock brokers. Meanwhile, the ailing outgoer prefers to bank by mail or use a home computer. They switch from self-managed or aggressive investment funds to funds offering safety, and most of their financial transactions are home-based. Finally, the frail recluse market splits into two groups: self-managed and caretaker-managed. If self-managed, all financial transactions are home-based. The availability of quality financial service via telephone is key, along with service for the hearing-impaired. Computer-based financial services must be designed to accommodate ease-of-use characteristics and to consider limited dexterity and impaired eyesight. This group switches to trusts and reverse mortgages. The caretaker-managed financial service takes on the character of ease-of-use and ready availability.

For the financial services business, the connecting theme to all the groups is that customers will not be on-site. They will not present themselves in the bank, brokerage, or insurance office to be sold or to have the product serviced. Technology will be the link between the service provider and the service consumer.

Future success in financial and investment services depends upon how mutual funds, stockbrokers, and other financial institutions package their products. These institutions will get the economies of scale through mergers and alliances. This allows investment in computerized telephone systems and data imaging like Fidelity and Twentieth Century, who are already using these technologies to lower costs and improve services. This also allows the traditional retail brokers like Merrill Lynch to reengineer their operations. (Merrill invested more than $200 million over a three-year period into a retail information management and trade execution system for its financial consultants.[4]) As in any other retail business, the winners will be those who deliver the highest service the customer desires and at the lowest cost.

Immigration and Consequences for Two Cities

Los Angeles.   The Los Angeles Basin is a laboratory of the American Metropolis, about 100 miles in diameter. In 1990, the five-county area's gross product was $360 billion, larger than all but eleven of the world's largest economies. The Los Angeles (LA) garment industry will soon overtake New York as the country's biggest production center, and it is already the leading exporter. The region's population of about 13.5 million will grow to 18.4 million in 2010 to challenge New York.[5] New Americans—Hispanics, Asians, and Armenians, among others—contribute to the city's economic strength, remaking its culture.

Freeways are a way of life in LA, however that's about over. Without major changes in travel patterns, rush hour traffic in 2010 may be at a standstill on a third of its freeways. Air pollution, the nation's worst, will deteriorate after the turn of the century. A regional agency proposes drastic steps to cut smog, but the key components require further legislation, technological improvements, and public support.

The city faces an era of economic contradictions. The problems stem in part from its crumbling infrastructure and school system. Well-paid union jobs continue to disappear, housing costs soar, and public aid to education falls behind inflation. Gang violence is so widespread that teenage killings are the staple of local television news. Stray gunfire plagues parts of the city. Americans, drawn to the area for decades, are leaving.

Only sixty years ago, the LA Basin was America's biggest agricultural producer. Now, one in every fifteen manufacturing jobs in the United States is there. It is America's manufacturing center, home to about 1.2 million jobs, employing about 20 percent of the region's work force. However, manufacturing firms are starting to leave the area, complaining about the state's anti-business environment, congested freeways, and high prices. Light manufacturing jobs may drift south of the Mexican border as a result of NAFTA.

It is difficult for immigrants to work their way up into middle class via service and tourism jobs, because many of these positions demand language skills that new immigrants don't have. Since factories provide many immigrants with their first jobs in the state, a rapid decline in the manufacturing base could leave behind a dangerously polarized society. This would set a rich, mostly white, class against a poor class of recently arrived immigrants.

Yet even the most pessimistic forecasters think that the LA area will outperform the rest of the United States over the next decade because of its location. No other American city location is better to benefit from the growth in both Pacific and NAFTA trade. Los Angeles and Long Beach ports are now larger than the New York-New Jersey port.[6] Economic growth will create more service and tourism jobs, and even though people and manufacturing jobs move out of the area, population growth continues due to high birthrates and immigration.

Miami.   Miami is emerging as a thriving and sophisticated mecca for international trade, where bilingual phone messages and business cards are commonplace. Building on its deep Hispanic roots and proximity to promising markets in Mexico, the Caribbean, and South America, Miami is attracting investors and traders from Europe and Asia. Miami is also seeing new investment by American businesses. American Telephone and Telegraph (AT&T) and Texaco expanded their Miami offices in preparation for the new business opportunities in the telephone and oil industries of Latin America. Hewlett-Packard relocated its Latin American headquarters to Miami from Mexico City because it offered a more diverse Spanish-speaking labor pool and better telephone and airline connections throughout the region.

About 25 percent of Miami's economy ties directly to international commerce and tourism. Today, only New York's John F. Kennedy International Airport moves more foreign passengers and cargo than Miami International Airport. Miami, along with a few neighboring ports, moves more containerized cargo to Latin America than any other U.S. harbor.

Miami is also a communications hub. AT&T laid the first undersea fiber-optic cable to South America, connecting South Florida to Puerto Rico, Jamaica, the Dominican Republic, and Colombia. It's working with Spain, Italy, and Mexico to complete the fiber-optic link between those countries, the Caribbean, and Florida.

Both Europeans and Asians are arriving, drawn to the markets in the Caribbean and southward. To tap the Latin American market, DTK Computer, based in Taiwan, opened offices in Miami in 1988. Now DTK has two computer assembly lines in Miami devoted to manufacturing thousands of machines to be sold in the United States and Latin America. However, Miami is not attracting manufacturing investment as much as it is emerging as the administrative and managerial hub, a point of access at which companies are moving decision-making for the region. Trade is also building between Miami and the Caribbean islands as well as Central American countries that have preferential trading rights with the United States. It will be the first to reap both the rewards and problems of a reopened Cuba.

Historically, the large Cuban population dominated Miami's strong Latin character. Now the demographics are changing. In 1990, the Hispanic population accounted for nearly half of the metropolitan area's population of 1.9 million. Cubans make up two-thirds of the Hispanics. The remaining one-third of Hispanics consists of Nicaraguans, Colombians, Venezuelans, and Brazilians. Because this group is growing at a faster rate, the Cuban dominance may lessen over time.

Miami today is still very much a segregated community. Without Spanish, language can be a barrier to employment. This makes it difficult for the black work force—particularly in tourism—since the Spanish-speaking majority dominates it. That creates friction and that friction occasionally erupts in violence, where the foreign businessman or vacationer becomes an easy target.

Miami has its unique set of problems. It started with theme park construction in Orlando in the 1970s. That siphoned off tourist trade, hurting Miami's domestic economy. A glut of office space created more local economic woes. Additionally, crowded schools and traffic snarls are common. This caused the county to tighten controls on auto-exhaust pollution: it worries about Los Angeles-like smog. High unemployment (about 9%) fuels racial tensions and crime, and arms and drugs are the staple of its gray economy.[7] Yet despite these difficulties, Miami is rebounding with its global connections, because cities need to be part of both the domestic and global economies to remain prosperous and to grow. The city's social ills become of secondary concern to a new population mix as business connections and a communications infrastructure, rather than a dependence on tourism, turn Miami into one of North America's most dynamic cities for business.

Demographic Scenarios

Two aspects of demographic change, the aging of the industrialized nations' population and immigration patterns, predominate the following scenarios. The passage of time will show how these shifts affect a nation's economic growth and the international balance of power. Evidence of the trends is here today, offering the opportunity to plan for change—change to create economic and business advantage.

Will aging and immigration policies require changes to business strategy? They will, because availability of a work force, the stability of a market, and the opportunity to identify growing markets are key to business success. The first set of scenarios reflects a positive and open attitude of industrialized nations regarding immigration. The second set represents a more pessimistic attitude. Either attitude is possible, and any change can cause a shift in the economic balance of power that impacts global and local competitiveness.

North America.   The United States becomes more selective in its immigration quotas. Young immigrants with advanced degrees and skilled labor from Central and Eastern Europe receive preferential treatment. Extension of preferential treatment to Latin America and the Caribbean solidifies the NAFTA accord. As a result, the economies of the Southeastern states, especially the cities of Miami and Atlanta, prosper. Miami, with its state-of-the-art fiber-optics communications base, becomes the hub of international commerce and industry activity in Latin America and the Caribbean.

Greater Europe.   The EU reaches an accord on migrant labor and immigration control. A provision of the accord allows proration of migrant and immigrant-related expense among EU members. This benefits Germany, who bears the brunt of Central and Eastern European migration. Another provision sets percentage quotas for immigrants possessing special skills to receive preferential treatment. The purpose is to balance immigration from Central and Eastern Europe to allow relocation for other reasons, such as alleviating economic hardship and reuniting families.

The Pacific.   Japan modifies its position on immigration. It seeks a limited number of immigrants from Asia and the Pacific with outstanding business and scientific skills. They also recruit second-generation Japanese-Americans from California universities and from Seattle high-technology companies. The strategy is to create a brain trust in Japan that will lead the world in scientific and technology development for new products and markets.

Some "What If" Caveats Involving Demographic Change

In the preceding set of scenarios, each power bloc takes a rational and practical view of the issues surrounding its aging work forces and develops new immigration policies to reflect national requirements. Each power bloc sets aside its cultural differences and creates a new vision of itself. North America and Greater Europe both take a middle-of-the-road approach, expecting its business cultures and strategies to undergo a moderate change. Japan, however, takes a comparatively radical approach and pursues a new national strategy for protecting technical dominance by creating the brain trust, based in Tokyo.

However, what if each bloc reacts a bit unpredictably? A business planner must evaluate each possible scenario change, and assess how cultural differences could impact the best of business strategies and consider the consequences.

North America.   Cuba reopens, and 250,000 Cubans arrive in Miami during the two months when all Caribbean immigrants received automatic amnesty. An additional 12,500 Haitians come during the same period. Miami, and Dade County, still recovering from the economic devastation caused by Hurricane Andrew in 1992, ask for federal relief funds to cope with the costs associated with the flood of immigrants. They receive fewer funds than requested, hampering the relocation efforts. Relocation of earlier immigrants to Atlanta failed due to cultural differences, and to the Midwest, due largely to climate differences. Relocation to the states of Texas and California is impossible, due to the influx of Mexican workers there. The state, along with California and New York, sues the federal government for reimbursement of state funds spent on federally mandated services for immigrants, forcing Congress to initiate hearings on immigration policy. The three states, because of their deepening financial crisis and newly enacted stringent business tax laws, see already-established foreign businesses flee to neighboring Caribbean and Latin American countries offering tax incentives.

Canada, the U.S.'s NAFTA partner to the North, is successful in its attempt to re-focus its immigration policy. It offers preferential treatment to young professionals with business and technology skills who would otherwise immigrate to the United States. As a result, Canada builds to a critical mass a new R&D Center for Technology Fusion and begins a global intellectual competition with Japan's brain trust.

Greater Europe.   German pensioners demand pension increases to bring them to the level of economic support granted to the immigrants. The German econ-omy is under stress, and immigration processing ceases. Germany expels illegal mi-grant workers from the country and begins to regroup and reorganize its economy around its aging work force. Other European countries follow the lead of Germany.

The Pacific.   Japan succeeds in nurturing the brain trust. It targets the United States and Canada as it initiates the first deployment of businesses based upon newly developed technology. They consider the Los Angeles area but decide against it, due to the deteriorating quality of life, the lack of quality infrastructure, and the predomi-nant Hispanic population. Instead, they choose Vancouver/Bellingham because of its already existing economic ties with Japan and its close proximity to the Hong Kong Chinese population in Canada.

Here, the business strategists begin to address and assess the effects of shifts of foreign capital, the stresses of aging citizenry and immigration on local and regional economies, and the interrelationships of economies within the same trading bloc in devising an appropriate business strategy. Again, the strategists will identify the fac-tors that provide early warning signals of impending change.

ENVIRONMENTAL QUALITY AS A DRIVING FORCE FOR GROWTH AND CONSTRAINTS

The need for energy pervades human life. This is especially true in the Western coun-tries, where the day normally begins with the clock radio signaling that its time to get up and take a hot shower before breakfast. The day ends by turning out the lights, setting the alarm for the next day, and using the sleep timer to turn off the TV automatically.

The use of energy proliferates as the population increases and standards of liv-ing rise. Only 150 years ago, the world consumed about 8 million barrels of oil a day (about 1 million less than the consumption of present day Japan).[8] In 1992, the world used about 161 million barrels a day of delivered energy. By 2010, the population in-creases by an additional 2 billion, and energy use grows by another 50 to 60 percent.

Increasing energy consumption at this rate has three disturbing consequences.

- Environmental damage: The world can't afford to burn all the fossil fuel now known to be economically recoverable, because producing, transporting, and consuming this energy source often leads to permanent environmental damage. No one needs to look very far to find examples: Chernobyl, the Exxon Valdez, urban smog, deforestation, and the thinning ozone layer.

- Technology can't fix everything: Existing technologies won't necessarily fix it. Some are cost-prohibitive, while others are still in experimental development. Additionally, many underdeveloped countries don't have an alternative for coal as fuel.
- Time: By the time scientists can accurately measure and predict the damage due to the thinning ozone layer, many more tons of unrecoverable pollutants will be in the atmosphere.

Considering this, it is logical to conclude that a combination of wise use, conservation, and governmental regulation is in the future for everyone. The consequence that does not follow is that what's good for the environment is necessarily bad for the global economy—even though it would have a profound impact on the energy industry itself. Products that protect the planet will earn big profits in the future. Electric cars, solar cells, and other environmentally friendly products represent a global market estimated to be more than $200 billion a year—a market that has just begun to grow.[9] Barring a conflict, the twenty-first century consumer will increasingly favor— and governments will mandate—technologies and products that preserve and protect the environment.

Concern for the environment will cause other changes, too. Environmental controls in cities encourage new work patterns and lifestyles. Changing public attitudes about the conservation of energy and the protection of the environment create a new set of political, social, and business responsibilities. Fortunes of companies and nations will rise and fall on how well they answer the call to save the environment.

What is fueling this environmental economy is a combination of forces. Leading-edge technologies and engineering and marketing skills are part of the answer, but perhaps just as important is the enormous influence that government leaders contribute. Michael Porter, Harvard's expert on international competitiveness, argues that well-designed regulations can foster technological advance and restrain the cost of meeting green goals.[10] In his view, a country may gain competitive advantage through high, not low, environmental standards, because others will eventually follow. He argues that environmental regulations, judiciously applied in Japan and Germany, allowed those countries to dominate world markets for pollution-control equipment to the detriment of the United States and Canada.

Energy and Environmental Scenarios

The intent of the following alternative scenarios is to stimulate thinking about the potential political and business consequences and possible business strategies in response to energy and environmental policies and events. The initial scenarios suggest economic consequences of poor environmental management. The caveats introduce alternative shifts in environmental policy and shifts in the economic relationships among the three trading blocs. Again, the purpose of the scenario is not to predict the future. The purpose is to stimulate thinking about alternative actions when long-run environmental well-being conflicts with relatively short-term economic well-being.

North America.   The federal government orders the closing of all (or some particular design) nuclear power plants in the United States. This results in major technical and financial implications for the entire U.S. electric utility industry, including higher electric prices, mandatory energy conservation measures, higher oil and gas prices, and a negative impact on the economy. Oil is available in plentiful supply from the Mid-East, but at a high price. Due to the severity of impact on the national economy, the federal government suspends some environmental enforcement procedures for the interim.

Greater Europe.   The flourishing economy in Western Europe creates additional employment and spreads to the East. This results in more cars, more commuting, and more air pollution. Within the EU, Germany mandates the use of zero-emission automobiles and trucks. The imposition of much more stringent environmental restrictions increases the cost of power generation. Severe restrictions on energy created using fossil-based units become mandatory.

The Pacific.   As China and India dramatically grow their manufacturing capacities, pollution from their coal-burning facilities begins to impact the catches of the Japanese fishing industry. Japan's Pacific trading partners experience reduced air quality. Pleading atmospheric contamination, they ask the United Nations Security Council to support an international economic blockade against China and India.

Some "What If" Caveats for Energy and the Environment

The second set of scenarios offers equally plausible views of the future. Does the U.S. energy shortage accelerate the movement of manufacturing outside the country, or can the United States find an alternate source of energy? Business strategies associated with capital investment would certainly be different under the two scenarios. Europe and Japan also face some hard choices.

North America.   Major new sources of clean and inexpensive energy become available from a variety of external sources. Canada creates hydroelectric power, and Mexico exploits a major geothermal discovery. Available transmission capacity exists to bring the power into the United States after purchase.

Greater Europe.   The initial design of four nuclear facilities in Eastern Europe has proven faulty. No accident occurs, but the potential is there. Eastern European recovery is dependent on the energy produced by the facilities. If they close, 20 percent of the energy sources fueling the EU economy diverts to Eastern Europe on an emergency basis.

The Pacific.   Japan successfully concludes its experiments to commercialize the manufacture of hydrogen. The cost of energy from manufactured hydrogen is 50 percent higher than the cost of oil. For developing nations such as India and China, low cost labor and untapped natural resources still support the use of coal as the primary energy source.

Environmental and energy issues are not casual ones to be dealt with and disposed of easily. They involve every business. Manufacturers must have the energy available and must maintain its facilities to conform to the now gradually more restrictive emissions and toxic waste disposal mandates. Service providers must manage its work force to more restrictive regional controls for commuters. Although the impact of these constantly changing regulations must be factored into all enterprise business plans, they have the greatest impact on the energy industry.

IMPACT OF ENVIRONMENTAL CONCERNS ON THE ENERGY INDUSTRY

Oil

How does an enterprise even begin developing a set of relevant scenarios for its business planners? In particular, where can an enterprise start if it is part of the industry contributing to the problem? One oil company looked at all of its operations—oil exploration, well management, tanker operations, and refinery management—and initially developed scenarios around two alternative concepts.

The first scenario assumes a sustainable world, in which the world would find peaceful solutions to any major economic disputes. The strategic consequence for oil was clear: with no economic wars to fight or physical borders to defend, nations would concern themselves with becoming good global neighbors. There would be an emphasis on the conservation of energy and protection of the environment. This would translate into new emission standards for automobiles, manufacturing facilities, electric power generation, and so forth. This would also cause an increase in regulation and regulatory agencies. If uninterrupted by periodic global conflicts, it would cause a major restructuring of the entire worldwide energy industry.

The second scenario assumes global mercantilism, in which intermittent regional conflicts threaten to destabilize the world. There would be trading wars and strong trading blocs. More significantly, the lack of global unity would cause a lack of any environmental consensus. The strategic consequences for this scenario are also clear. There would be less regulation, greater energy (oil) consumption, and at best only a regional approach to environmental issues.

Obviously, there are many gradations between the two extremes, and the company gradually expanded its portfolio of relevant scenarios to create the context within which it could do its strategic planning. Over the last decade, variations of the sustainable world scenario have held center stage, and the consequences are being played out daily by the entire energy industry. In the following section, we examine an electric utility and observe how the economic conditions reflected by the sustainable world scenario forces it to change its strategies and operations.

Electricity

Concern for the environment drastically changed the functioning of the electric power generation industry. Before 1970, it had marketing programs dedicated to selling electrical use over other alternatives. New homes featured all electric kitchens and central electric heating and air conditioning units, rather than natural gas. This changed in the early 1970s when the industry discontinued marketing programs and initiated conservation and cleanup programs. As the pollution regulations became more restrictive, regulatory agencies became more innovative in supporting demand-side management. Regulations changed, making it more profitable for a utility to invest in conservation instead of supplying more power. The focus of planning has, by necessity, changed from predicting future growth requirements to one of responding efficiently to change.

Southern California Edison

Environmental Leadership.   California has the most restrictive and all-encompassing environmental legislation of any state in the United States. Southern California Edison (SCE) supplies power to ten million people in 50,000 square miles of central and southern California and is the second-largest electric utility in the United States. SCE promotes conservation with demand-side management and has set up a special division to do research into technologies that may solve customers' energy problems. Examples of some of the conservation activities as a result of this initiative includes the following:

- To customers, the most visible examples of demand-side management are special promotions for compact fluorescent light bulbs, selling in stores for $13 to $18 each. SCE offers a $5 rebate to any customer who buys one and has provided over 1 million bulbs to poor households at its own expense. The bulbs last about nine times longer than standard incandescent bulbs and use only 25 percent as much energy. SCE calculates that each bulb saves the equal of one barrel of oil over its lifetime.
- SCE provides financial incentives to industrial customers enabling its customers to buy efficient motors and pumps.
- SCE researches potentially energy-saving technologies, such as low-frequency radio-wave curing ovens for commercial bakeries.
- To support mandated battery-powered zero pollution vehicles, SCE is exploring a strategy by which it may open service stations for motorists to swap exhausted batteries for charged ones, a process that would take no longer than filling a tank with gasoline. SCE would own the batteries, which would be earning the allowable rate of return.
- SCE has its own fleet of electric vans used by employees to go between various company locations. From these vans, they are experimenting with usage patterns.
- The company's Welcome Home program offers building contractors rebates of $5 to $15 per square foot. All the contractor has to do is exceed state energy-efficiency standards by 10 to 30 percent for such things as heating and cooling

systems and the thermal envelope, which includes a building's insulation and windows. The program now covers about 25 percent of new home construction in Los Angeles. The utility hopes to increase the coverage to 50 percent.

- SCE and Texas Instruments are jointly developing a new solar cell design. By 1995 the developers expect to sell the ten-foot-square panels for about two thousand dollars each. They would mount on the roof of a home. In sunny California, each panel would generate power to help meet peak electricity demand for a typical household. Homes with more panels could generate excess power to sell back to the utility.

- SCE developed energy-saving ways to dry paint and lacquer coatings used in the huge Los Angeles furniture industry. The utility sees it partly as a way to stop the region's tough air quality laws from driving the furniture industry, with its predictable base-load of demand, out of the LA Basin.

- SCE and the Los Angeles Department of Power and Light both announced in 1991 that each was setting its own targets for reducing carbon dioxide, targets much more aggressive than required by the state.

Nationally, about 200 utilities invested $2 billion into 1,300 conservation programs during 1991.[11] Southern California Edison with its CEO John Bryson is an industry leader in this energy turnaround.

History of Planning.   All the above initiatives have a single, common thread—that of managing demand.[12] SCE, like other electric utilities, is in the business of manufacturing on demand electricity for immediate delivery. It has huge investments in its electricity manufacturing sites and delivery systems. SCE has no in stock inventory of the product it sells—its inventory consists of equipment to service its manufacturing and delivery systems. To serve its customers, SCE must have the capacity to deliver on peak demand. Every nuance of resource planning becomes key to success.

Three decades ago, resource planning was easy for the utility. A utility made projections on population and industry—a simple forecast of future load and resource requirements. This single-load forecast defined the resource requirements necessary to meet the load with an adequate safety margin. The process worked well during the decades of steady growth and few surprises.

Then business and the environment began to change. In 1965, the Northeast blackout demonstrated the importance of power reliability. Havoc reigned in New York City, since it was the financial and commercial business center most affected by the blackout. The years of 1969 and 1970 saw the enactment of both federal and state environmental legislation. This ushered in the environmental movement of the seventies.

The early seventies saw a rapid growth of the area's economy, and SCE planned to service the growth through construction of nuclear facilities along the California coast. It became a predominately summer peaking utility due to the growing use of air conditioning. SCE discontinued its air conditioning marketing efforts as an attempt to manage down the peak. The era of environmental impact reports began, making it difficult to site future nuclear facilities, and the first (Arab) oil embargo occurred in 1973. In 1975, the California Energy Commission became the state-level energy and conservation policy agency.

The late seventies saw even more change. SCE adopted a new energy conservation ethic, directing attention to conservation and load management programs. SCE began to reduce its vulnerability to oil supply interruptions; and it introduced lifeline rates to protect low-income customers. The passage of The Air Quality Act in 1976 placed additional stringent requirements on emissions in the LA Basin; a legislative bill on nuclear waste disposal made it impossible to build another nuclear power plant in the state; and the second oil crisis, this time Iran, began in 1979. The National Energy Act of 1978 included The Public Utilities Regulatory Practices Act (PURPA) and The Fuel Use Act, changing the nature of the electric utility business over time.

If SCE management had any doubts that planning for the future included uncertainty and unpredictability, they abandoned them in the 1980s. Economic growth was slow. SCE focused on capital cost minimization strategies and decided to put its corporate resources behind the rapid development and deployment of renewable and alternative energy resources. The plan focused on energy from wind, solar, geothermal, small hydroelectric, fuel cells, cogeneration, and synthetic fuels. The unanticipated events that changed the business environment in this period included spot oil prices reaching an all-time high in 1981 following the outbreak of the Iran-Iraq war. The economic slowdown of 1979–1982 resulted in the shutdown of five of SCE's largest industrial customers, accounting for 3 percent of its sales. The relicensing of hydroelectric permits became a hotly debated issue. One mixed blessing occurred: the identification of long-term Qualifying Facilities (QFs), small-power producers who qualify under PURPA regulations to sell electricity to utilities. The planning focus for SCE shifted from a concern for identifying and developing enough QF's, to one of integrating excess QF sources into its resource plans.

The 1985 business plan had the benefit of incorporating the new realities of energy conservation and efficient energy utilization that started in 1973. Gone were the days of mammoth coal or nuclear projects, or ownership in renewable and alternative energy resources. At the same time, it was becoming clear that electric utilities were a mature industry with low demand growth and increasing costs. Success in that environment depends on being the lowest-cost supplier. Consequently, management focus shifted again to a new set of issues: competition, industrial cogeneration, minimum load conditions, and what to do with excess generation during off-peak periods. Then the bottom dropped out of the oil prices in 1986, and the Chernobyl accident occurred.

SCE managers, looking back at their plans, discovered the underlying theme of why their single-load forecasts missed the mark. In each case, a number of unforeseen events changed the basic assumptions that went into the forecasts, rendering them inaccurate. No one could have predicted with any degree of accuracy the nature or timing of the events. Even if they had anticipated the events, they couldn't have foreseen the full impact on their business environment a priori. SCE planning staff felt that current predictions of the future wouldn't be any more accurate than those in the past and that the only certainty about the future was change. Because the future was so uncertain, it was futile to tie future plans too rigidly to a single projection or forecast, no matter how sophisticated the forecasting technique.

They had three ideas on how to develop future plans.

- Separate the forecasting from the planning, in the sense that even if the forecast is off the mark, the planning won't be.
- Prepare for future uncertainties by considering a number of alternative scenarios and preparing response strategies for each.
- Understand the options, so that today's planning focus keeps future strategies unencumbered.

It was this vision that became the cornerstone of the new planning philosophy at Southern California Edison.

Enterprise Planner's View of the World

Few enterprises remain untouched by global concerns and trends and both leaders and planners at SCE felt the increasing impact of this change on future plans for business and I/T infrastructures. The scope of change was so large that it seemed to defy the application of even the most flexible of current planning methodologies. It was necessary, therefore, to construct a new view of the world from the perspective of the enterprise and its planners. This new, conceptual view had to address the interrelationships between changes in the global and market environments and how these changes affect enterprise competitiveness. It had to also address various interrelationships within the enterprise itself—including I/T and business infrastructure change, business process change, and the enterprise core competencies. Only then could the company begin to exploit any advantage it would seek through the recognition of impending change and its early warning signals.

The conceptual model of the enterprise and its environment is similar to an onion, with the source and timing of early warning signals in its various layers. Imagine, for a moment, that the enterprise consists of its key business processes and is at the very center (see Figure 12-1).

- The (Level 1) Core Environment is the source of the specific processes supported by I/T. Examples include marketing planning and marketing.
- The key business processes are used within, and supported by, the (Level 2) Organizational Environment, the source of the specific physical business and I/T architecture (organization). Outsourcing relationships, alliance structures, service and quality structures, and product/service product mixes are part of the business architectures.

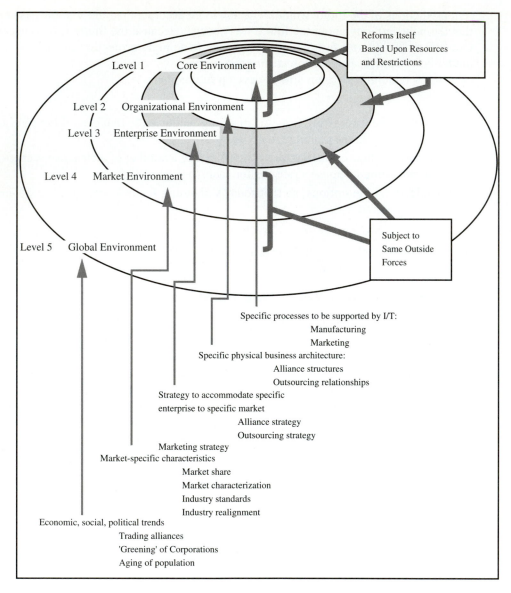

Figure 12-1   Planning View.

- The Organizational Environment is a result of the (Level 3) Enterprise Environment. It reflects the business strategy and plans that accommodate the enterprise to its market environment and is the source of early warning signals to accommodate an enterprise to a specific market. It is also a source of business strategy alternatives and subsequent specific business strategies. These strategies may include alliance strategies, outsourcing strategies, service and quality strategies, product/service product mix strategies, competitive strategies, marketing strategies, and key business process identification and restructuring strategies. They evolve as a result of the enterprise specific view of its market.

- The (Level 4) Market Environment is outside the enterprise structure. The Market Environment is the source of early warning signals involving market-specific characteristics, including market share, market characterization, industry standards, and industry realignments. The market environment includes suppliers, competitors, customers, and scope, as determined by the global environment.

- The final, outside layer is the (Level 5) Global Environment, representing the external forces on the enterprise at the macroeconomic level—the economic, social, and political forces. This is the source for early warning signals involving government regulations and policy and social and economic trends. Global Environment planning drivers include broad trends or specific occurrences in the global environment that may ultimately impact the enterprise: its form, function, and strategies. Government regulations and policy as well as social, demographic, and economic trends are in this group.

The greater the level number in the model, the more profound the effect the forces described within it will have for I/T and the enterprise. Each enterprise in a market (Level 3), is subject to the same outside forces (Levels 4 and 5), however, each will reform itself based largely upon the resources and restrictions it perceives (Levels 1 and 2), including corporate culture, current organizational form and staffing levels, skill set, and so forth. All of these elements must be applied in a planned, cohesive way to create the business scenarios that serve as the drivers for business and I/T strategy and plans. The scenarios, early warning signals, the business and I/T strategies and plans, would repeatedly undergo review, refinement, and reevaluation.

Planning for Uncertainty

Because experience shows that long-term forecasts are more often wrong than right, the focus of SCE's future plans is on the identification of alternative futures, using the approach called scenario planning.[12] Scenario planning postulates a set of plausible futures, each of which is possible but not assured. This spreads the risk by ensuring that a business is not planning for something that is essentially unknowable. SCE was the first in the electric utility industry to use the approach. Some of the key features of scenario planning are:

- It encourages examination of underlying assumptions. The mere act of identifying the assumptions opens the door for discussion and challenge.
- It permits planners to change their assumptions and to examine the resulting changes. As a result, both the planners and the plan are more receptive and adaptive to change.

- It allows management and staff to ask what if questions and to get better answers.
- Because the process is one of visualizing and examining alternative futures, those participating in the process have their own horizons expanded. For some, these new horizons change reading habits, television viewing habits, and lifestyle.
- The process promotes evaluation of alternative options. In the development of a flexible strategy, the goal is to keep options open. When an option doesn't exist, it should be the result of a decision, not an oversight.
- It allows an examination of robustness of different plans under alternative futures.

It's important to remember that scenario planning is only a tool and its usefulness doesn't extend beyond the imagination of those applying the technique and interpreting its results.

Scenario Development: It became clear in the early stages of analysis that many alternative scenarios (i.e., combinations of primary driving forces of growth and constraints) resulted in very similar net consequences relative to the need for new resources. That is, even though different factors were the cause, the end result on SCE's resource requirements was quite similar. Since SCE's charter is to have the capacity to deliver electricity to satisfy peak demand, this reinforced the importance of focusing on the consequences of scenarios to the business as opposed to the cause of the scenarios themselves. As a result, SCE planners grouped the scenarios into a smaller subset based on its consequences regarding demand patterns, pricing, and degree of regulatory freedom. The final outcome of this consolidation process was a set of a dozen scenarios that encompassed a wide range of potential futures and set reasonable bounds on what SCE might expect over the next decade.

Briefly, the scenarios cover the entire range from extreme low to extreme high growth rates. They include:

- No surprises, a scenario that best represents SCE's view of the future, and with a higher likelihood to occur than other scenarios.
- Economic bust, the low-growth scenario.
- Oil crisis revisited, the high-fuel cost scenario.
- Clean air at any cost, the scenario representing extreme environmentalism.
- Big customers vanish, where large industrial and commercial customers satisfy their own energy needs and SCE's role becomes one of providing backup.
- Deregulation postulates a number of assumptions on the speed of deregulation and the mandated wheeling of power. (Wheeling is the industry term that describes the process whereby private-party facilities that generate excess electricity have open access to the electric utility transmission system to sell and deliver its excess.)
- Economy imports, a scenario in which major new sources of inexpensive energy

become available from a variety of external sources and transmission capacity is available to bring it into the power grid.

- Competitive rate-making, where the energy prices are specifically set to discourage cogeneration.

- Facility shutdown assumes that an unforeseen event occurs, isolated to a given site or plant-type and not affecting the rest of the system or other utilities. It causes a loss of 2,100 megawatts of base load capacity over an extended time.

- Global tension—analogous to the global mercantilism scenario of the oil company—postulates a large military buildup with a corresponding boom to the southern California defense industry, SCE's service area.

- Nuclear phaseout is based upon on the unlikely event that the federal government orders the closing of all (or some particular design) nuclear power plants in the United States, affecting not only SCE, but the entire U.S. electric utility industry.

- Economic boom, the high-growth scenario, assumes strong economic growth and migration into SCE's service area, high levels of employment and income, resulting in substantially higher electricity consumption.

Note that each of the scenarios has a very brief, but highly descriptive name. This creates an instant picture in the minds of the planners or managers of the scenario under discussion and supports better (and faster) communication. By examining this wide range of possible futures and the impact of each on the utility systems requirements, SCE gained a wealth of insight and expanded its horizons far beyond any previous planning exercises.

Strategic Elements.   Plausible combinations of parameters comprise the SCE scenarios, and each leads to a set of outcomes affecting economic growth, employment, income, housing, trade, financial services, industrial activity, and so forth at a regional level. Because the demand for energy is a derived demand, the consequences to SCE and the rest of the energy industry members are a function of the scenario outcomes. Industrial activity, for example, could significantly increase its demand for electricity as a result of increased production of consumer goods (economic boom) or as a result of a large military buildup (global tension), and the net increase in demand to SCE could be identical. Conversely, an equivalent drop in demand for electricity could be caused by either the low growth of the economy (economic bust) or by SCE's large customers satisfying their own energy needs (big customers vanish).

Because SCE didn't know which one, if any, of the plausible scenarios would happen, it focused its resource planning process on developing a flexible business action plan that would cover the entire set. To achieve this objective, the resource plan consists of a number of strategic elements that can be rearranged in a variety of ways to accommodate any plausible future scenario and its associated demand articulation. These elements fall into three general categories—the facilities (and backup facilities) that generate and deliver the product, the potential new resources for power generation and delivery, and the strategies and programs that can influence the demand. The strategic elements include extended or shortened use of oil and gas units, the existing and planned transmission network, the resource of power generated by independent entities, active (customer-side) load management using time-of-use differentiated pricing and marketing strategies, passive (supply-side) load management via participation in promising energy storage technologies, and conventional and non-conventional new resources that are modular and brought on-line quickly.

For I/T, there was a similar set of strategic systems elements whose importance linked to the strategic business elements and scenarios. Two examples follow:

- Transmission network management system: Various scenarios affect the complexity of the transmission network system. Economy imports require the ability to interface and manage delivery from non-U.S. sources; deregulation requires the ability to interface with many small independent private-party facilities; facility shutdown and nuclear phaseout require the continued management of the current domestic interfaces with other regional power grids (to have access to back up energy) and a new rationing of delivery of scarce energy.
- Pricing management systems: Different scenarios also place a different emphasis on these systems. Time-of-use pricing plays a role when consumers receive incentives to manage their consumption, whether caused by a shortage of source energy (facility shutdown, global tension, and nuclear phaseout) or by increased consumer demand (economic boom). If energy prices are intentionally set to discourage cogeneration (competitive rate-making) or if the pricing structure remains a regulatory body issue (deregulation), each generates its own unique systems support requirements.

From a planning perspective, both business and I/T focused on the business consequences of the scenarios. Business took the demand articulation that was the consequence of each scenario and created a plan—using its business strategic elements—for producing the product, tempered by active (customer-side) or passive (supply-side) strategies to manage its impact. I/T took the demand articulation that was the consequence of each scenario, along with the applied business strategic elements and applied its own I/T strategic elements—those systems (hardware and software) that link to and support each of the businesses strategic elements, identifying new requirements, possible limitations, and options.

Planning Philosophy.   To make planning successful at SCE, it adopted a new planning philosophy to complement and implement the scenario planning technique. The seven basic elements of the planning philosophy are:

- Focus on the consequences of events: Scenario planning is a self-defeating exercise if undue emphasis is placed on the events and scenarios compared to their consequences. Scenarios are important because they expand one's horizons and allow the luxury of imagining the unimaginable. Beyond that, the focus of scenario planning should be on the business impact, dealing with the consequences and preparing for contingencies.

- Scrutinize assumptions: Assumptions are the fundamental driving force behind any forecasting exercise. Place heavy emphasis on examining the robustness of the assumptions and their validity under different conditions.

- Stress fundamentals: Scenario planning isn't productive unless you go behind the scenario facade and examine the fundamentals: What drives growth in energy consumption? Who are the customers? What are their basic energy service needs? Even though historical relationships are sometimes misleading, there is momentum and inertia there that needs consideration. Are there self-sustaining mechanisms in the system?

- Question trends and consensus: Economic growth and energy consumption grew in lockstep fashion for so long that many analysts took the relationship for granted. For the energy industry this relationship terminated in 1973. Don't place too much confidence in industrywide consensus. It gives a false sense of security. Sometimes the odd-sounding ideas are the ones worth examining.

- Examine the impact of new technologies: In the electrical energy industry, as in others, technology-based innovations change the nature of business and the competition over time. For this reason, examine the impact of new technologies as an integral part of future scenarios.

- Monitor actual versus predicted: Early identification of deviation from the predicted course is important because it allows an examination of the reasons for the discrepancies. It also provides time to react to the new business environment.

- Be prepared to change the course: The plan and the entire process of planning should be fluid, flexible, and responsive to change.

This planning philosophy, along with scenario planning, helped SCE managers expand their horizons and gain additional insights to the future and its direction.

Reflections on the Energy and Environment Scenarios.   To remain a dominant force in the energy industry, SCE senior management must continue to nurture its industry foresight. Senior management must continue to re-conceive the corporation and the industry in which it competes, and question all assumptions and givens. Simply understanding the trends in technology, demographics, regulation, and lifestyles isn't enough. The understanding and insight needs harnessing in order to rewrite industry rules, transform industry boundaries, and create new competitive space, requiring creativity and imagination.

Senior management and staff must continue to use whatever tools and techniques they find useful—such as technology forecasting, market research, scenario planning, and competitive market analysis—to improve their foresight and to better communicate their foresight to the rest of the company. This is the only way they can meet the two-fold challenge of creating and maintaining industry foresight and achieving operating excellence.

> *Scenario planning, technology forecasting, and market research aren't substitutes for industry foresight—they are tools that assist in the subsequent validation, communication, and operational planning to support it.*

How will the future unfold for SCE and the energy industry? Alternative economic conditions, growth rates, and regulatory, environmental, technological, social, political, and business environments are part of the considerations. Alternative actions by SCE itself are another part of the consideration. For example, the regulatory environment constantly changes. If regulatory agencies encourage alternative energy suppliers to increase output by assuring them access to transmission networks, will regulators force SCE to buy the alternative energy at a higher cost than if it produced it itself? Alternatively, will regulators create a level playing field and impose the same environmental mandates and fixed return-on-investment on the alternative energy suppliers as they have on SCE? Should SCE, as an energy producer facing an increasingly hostile regulatory environment, pursue any or all the following strategies?

- Concentrate on lobbying to change the regulations.
- Pursue a long-term plan to essentially abandon its energy production in favor of energy delivery management.
- Pursue research and development activities targeted toward the consumer market involving household solar cells and zero pollution vehicles.

Alternatively, should SCE, as an energy producer facing an increasingly benign regulatory environment, pursue any or all the following strategies?

- Lobby to increase regulatory control of the qualifying facilities (QFs).
- Stay in energy production and build new facilities as necessary, mount an aggressive expansion of energy production capacity, or phase out all energy production.
- Abandon or pursue consumer market product development.

Adopting any of these strategies redefines both the market and SCE's future in it.
 The scenarios at SCE focus on identifying trends that impact all business to some degree. If ignored, these trends could mean the end of local, national, or even

global competitiveness, as we know it today. Some of SCE's customers initially ignored the environmental trend. By the time they felt the full impact of the movement, it was too late: they had to cease operation. Some closed their doors permanently. Some moved their operations out of the state, while others moved to Mexico. To avoid their fate, it is necessary to think through alternative strategies and actions and to initiate business planning in that context. The next steps, that of rehearsing for the future (e.g., planning for it) and developing appropriate implementation vehicles are the central themes for the remaining chapters.

> *Incremental change is no longer the basis for the development of effective business and I/T strategy and subsequent plans to carry it out. The strength of the scenario planning technique is the ability to develop, in an orderly way, effective strategy and plans for an environment of discontinuous change.*

OBSERVATIONS

In the past, forecasting accuracy was the measure of success for any planning activity. Today, the most significant measure of successful planning is the anticipation and responsiveness to change, the linchpin of scenario planning. Scenario planning requires imagination and hard work to get the most from the process. Simply identifying the trends and translating the consequences into alternative scenarios isn't sufficient. It takes a planning philosophy that has the seven basic elements of SCE.

- Focus on the consequences of events. It may be intellectually stimulating to discuss possible political realignments or the potential impact of immigration restrictions, however, it is a waste of time if the possibilities don't translate into business consequences.
- Scrutinize the assumptions. Are we sure enough of the characteristics of the aging market in industrialized economies that the products and services we offer will fulfill their individual needs? Are we sure enough of the characteristics of the global teenage market to develop profitable niche markets for our products and services? Assumptions resulting from experience with the KinderCare generation don't necessarily translate into facts about this emerging market.
- Stress the fundamentals of identifying the customers and needs, growth assumptions, and level and required core competencies of the enterprise.
- Question trends and consensus. Are we sure that everyone will want their personal telephone number, and always carry a telephone with them? Are we sure that everyone will become (to some degree) computer literate? Are we sure that everyone will want to shop by computer, TV, or catalog?
- Examine the impact of new technologies. Meters that read themselves replace the utility meter-readers. E-mail and the fax replace postal workers. Who—and what industry—is next?

- Monitor actual versus predicted. This means the development of new measurements and indicators. How long has it been since there has been a change in internal performance measurements?
- Be prepared to change the course.

Because scenario building and scenario planning are of growing importance in transformational planning and involve systematic thinking, business planners should consider the integration of graphical, modeling, and quantitative tools into the process. There is a currently evolving category of software tools that support systems thinking—whether a management, social, or economic system.[13] These software tools build around the assumptions that changes in one part of a system will have intended and unintended consequences upon other parts of the system and that these consequences occur over time. Thus business planners could build and evaluate a model of a business strategy or scenario by running a simulation using many different variables.

Finally, if the reader has yet to explore the Commentary Articles contained in the Appendix, the article entitled "Coping with Business and Technological Change" offers further insight into the innovative, leading-edge I/T function at SCE.

13

Creating a Transformational Planning Context

The use and relevance of I/T to the corporation are undergoing a basic change in the nineties. Now, it is mandatory to have an appropriate application and architectural strategy to successfully assimilate the new waves of technology into an increasingly dynamic business environment. Tied to these strategies is the imperative for I/T to be the equilibrium tool during enterprise transformation. Organizational fit, business value measurements, and understanding and translating the nuances of business strategy into I/T requirements—along with the current support, future platform, and equilibrium imperatives—requires a different planning philosophy. The Seven Questions Methodology for Transformation Planning provides this contextual framework.

Successful chief information officers (CIOs)—and the organizations they lead—realize that virtually all aspects of the environment in which they operate are changing. The very nature of the enterprise, the role and relationships of I/T to the rest of the organization, the measurements used to assess the I/T contribution, and the architectural platform upon which it operates, must adjust to today's economic, business, and technology pressures. The I/T organization, with its CIO, faces the realities of recalibrating strategies, plans, agendas, and courses of action to best navigate through unprecedented change.

The use and relevance of I/T to the enterprise are undergoing a basic change. Now it is mandatory to have both an appropriate application strategy and an appropriate architectural strategy to successfully survive the dynamics of the business environment. Success goes to the I/T organizations whose leaders read and interpret business and technological change and react by constantly recalibrating paradigms and management agendas. The challenge is to find and adopt ways to develop strategies and action plans flexible enough to meet the new business expectations. Practically, this translates into identifying new strategic planning and financial justification methodologies to help create and sustain business transformation.

In 1984, the IBM Los Angeles Scientific Center and the Center for the Study of Data Processing and the School of Technology and Information Management (STIM) at Washington University, launched a multiyear study devoted to the effective use of I/T in the business environment.[1] The two directors (Parker representing IBM and Benson representing Washington University) quickly discovered that the issue was not a technology problem. Instead, the real I/T problem was all the business issues related to the use of I/T in the organization: the planning and working relationships between business and I/T and the justification, measurement, and communication of the I/T-contributed business value to the enterprise.

Tradition dictated that information systems be built around the information flow between organizational subunits of a business. When the organizational structure changed, as it inevitably did, the information system built around it required change. Systems concerned themselves with the nonstatic elements of the business with the express purpose that they outlive future organizational changes. I/T planners counted on the business process being less dynamic than the organizational form surrounding it, mainly blaming size and complexity of the enterprise for the inability to understand the entire organization.

Of the more popular planning methodologies, none reflected the interactive quality of entities influenced by dynamic forces. They didn't easily answer the "what if" questions posed by top management or view the enterprise as a totality and go on to identify the critical elements. While they went a long way in analyzing the business or subenterprise, the approach was empirical, reflecting the status quo. To become a business partner, I/T needed a new approach to planning that more accurately reflected the realities of the present and future business and technology alternatives.

What I/T planners require is a methodology to provide an active representation of the enterprise reflecting the dynamic nature of its current strategies, organizational forms, and critical business processes and how they fit when applied to future business conditions. Additionally, this methodology must produce results that translate into I/T requirements to form a direct linkage between business strategy and action plans, and I/T strategy and action plans.

With this as a focus, the products of the study included the development of new concepts for strategic planning (the Seven Questions Methodology) and an approach to formalize the quantification of intangible benefits (a justification technique called Information Economics). Both effectively linked I/T to the creation and delivery of business value and incorporated a modular design easily tailored to an individual enterprise.

Throughout the Joint Study, Corporate Affiliates of Washington University and the Beta Group (a consulting firm) evaluated and adopted many of the ideas. At the conclusion of the study in 1991, the study directors began developing extensions to the planning and justification approaches for strategic transformation. Key Strategies and Solutions, a firm specializing in transformation planning, reflect these extensions in its consulting practice methodology. The discussions of the Seven Questions Methodology and Information Economics, in this and the following chapter, include the approaches developed during the Joint Study, combined with methodology enhancements for a Strategic Transformation Consulting Practice. Because long-term business value contribution—as opposed to short-term financial gain—is the core concept of the Seven Questions Methodology and Information Economics, the techniques easily suit planning and monitoring transformation.

SEVEN QUESTIONS METHODOLOGY FOR TRANSFORMATION PLANNING

Any kind of business planning consistently suffers from two major impediments.

- Successful planning has management support; however, getting that support is particularly difficult in situations characterized by management disinterest or misunderstanding of the planning objectives.
- Most managers perceive successful planning as complex and overwhelmingly detailed.

To simplify understanding of strategic planning (and the approach to linking business and I/T planning) and to provide a planning tool requiring a relatively small time commitment, any organization can use seven questions to form a new planning process, or validate the current one. The questions permit the planner to quickly identify contextual base-points before any actual planning begins for the line of business or enterprise. The answers to the questions help focus the more detailed strategic planning process, whether it is for the entire enterprise, a business function, a department, or I/T. The questions drive toward explicit answers involving strategy, strategic planning, and action planning, establishing feasibility and priorities.

The seven generic questions are:

Strategic Planning Issues
- Question 1: What business(es) are we in?
- Question 2: What problems, forces, and critical success factors do we have in this business?
- Question 3: What are our strategies in the business?

Action Planning Issues
- Question 4: How can we contribute business value?
- Question 5: How can we change (improve) the strategy or basic business plan?
- Question 6: How can we organize to best accomplish the business goals?
- Question 7: What Action Plan supports the answers to questions 1 through 6?

Feasibility and Priority Issues
- Planning Results and Outcomes
- Justifying the Results; Making the Decision

While the questions might appear simple at first glance, developing appropriate answers isn't. Because the purpose of I/T is to add business value to the enterprise, there is an important link between business performance and its uses—its application must produce improvement in business performance. This requires an understanding of the factors that impact business performance, as compared to merely linking to business planning.

The questions create a simple planning process without having to add any more complex or detailed steps. Ideally, the first iteration of the Seven Questions focus on the enterprise strategy, and the outcomes establish the contexts within which the business planners develop the lower-level enterprise strategies, including I/T, also driven by the Seven Questions.

Originally, the impetus for the development of the seven questions was to provide a vehicle for facilitating strategic planning. Over time, and as more clients faced strategic issues directly related to enterprise transformation, refinements focused on transformation strategy and support. Although grouped under the umbrella of the seven questions methodology for facilitative and discussion purposes, they are not secondary issues. They are critical to the development of the transformation strategy. The expanded sets of questions apply, starting at the enterprise level. They carry through the strategy and operational planning at the functional and departmental level, as well as I/T. The following discussion, however, covers only I/T (see Table 13-1).

What Business(es) Are We In?

What kind of business is the I/T function supporting? Is the I/T organization a centralized or decentralized function and is it supporting a single line of business, multiple lines of business, or an extended enterprise with multiple strategic alliances? If I/T has no clear view of the organization and its intent, it can't develop effective strategies to support it.

Pretransformation Issues.   What business(es) are we supporting? What business(es) should we be in? What services business(es) are I/T in? If the I/T organization is supporting multiple lines of business (even though the physical business organization may not reflect this reality), the business strategies for the lines of business are probably unique to each. If this is the case, a single I/T strategy is inadequate. Therefore, the first question determines whether the I/T organization must develop single or multiple interlocking strategies to support all lines of business.

If the answer to this question is satisfactory, the more challenging question is: What business(es) should we be in? Here, the focus is much different. Together, busi-

STRATEGIC PLANNING ISSUES

1. What business(es) are we in?

        What business(es) are we in?

        What business(es) should we be in?

        What services business(es) is I/T in?

        What business(es) are we likely to be in?

2. What problems, forces, and critical success factors do we have in this business?

        What problems, forces, and CSFs do we have in this business?

        What forces are changing the business environment?

        What are the early warning signals?

3. What are our strategies in the business?

        What are our key strategies in the business(es)?

        What strategies are we applying to support the business(es)?

        What action plan(s) are we following to support the business(es)?

ACTION PLANNING ISSUES

4. How can we contribute business value?

        How can we contribute business value?

        How can we improve business performance?

        How can we better deploy technology?

        What new technologies can I/T deploy?

        What are the critical skills?

        How can we measure contributions to business value?

5. How can we improve the strategy or basic business plan?

        How can we improve the business strategy by creating new opportunities?

        How can we improve the basic business plan (new product, customer or
            market) by creating new opportunities?

        How can I/T 'change' the business?

        How can I/T employ infrastructures/architectures to increase enterprise
            mobility?

        What new technologies or platforms should we employ?

        What are the critical skills?

        How can we measure the improvements?

6. How can we best organize to accomplish the business goals?

        How can we organize the business to most effectively achieve its goals,
            business strategy and plans?

        How can we organize I/T activities to best support the business goals?

        What is the best I/T organizational form to support the business organization?

        What are the critical skills?

        How can we measure (improved) organizational effectiveness?

7. What action plan will support the answers to questions 1 through 6?

        How can I/T implement change to maximize enterprise equilibrium?

        What are the critical skills?

Table 13-1   Seven Questions Methodology for Transformation Planning

ness and I/T management plan the future of the business, addressing issues such as product, customer, and market development and improving performance. When developing strategy for the I/T function, it is important to devote an appropriate level of attention to this first set of questions.

Transformation Issues.   What business(es) are we likely to be in? In the current business environment, with disappearing time and space buffers to protect the enterprise from market dynamics, it is critical to understand the alternative courses of action, the strategies business might employ when facing new market conditions. This is particularly true for the I/T function, who, like the End-User Information Systems group at Evergreen Environmental Consultants, must simultaneously maintain the past and provide current support with the perspective of building an infrastructure and architecture capable of sustaining tomorrow's possible requirements.[2] (See Appendix I for "Evergreen Environmental Consultants.")

This will never be a straightforward, fill-in-the-blanks task. However, when the enterprise employs scenario planning, the business forecasters and planners develop likely market and business scenarios, and planning for I/T becomes an exercise—still nontrivial—in ensuring that future infrastructure and architecture investments accommodate the defined business scenarios.

An important part of the exercise is understanding and communicating to enterprise management the price the business must pay to keep various options available. This is where the existence of an option pricing procedure, understood and adhered to by both business and technology management, becomes pivotal. Although most business units have an option pricing approach, it's rarely used consistently. This lack of consistency isn't acceptable for I/T, because business units competing for centralized or shared I/T support must understand and follow some uniformly applied logic for its investments.

What Problems, Forces, and Critical Success Factors Do We Have in This Business?

What problems do we have in this business? What forces are affecting this business? What are the critical success factors (CSFs) for the business? These are all business-based questions, whose answers are key to the I/T planning process.

Pretransformation Issues.   Do the industry and market characteristics change rapidly? If so, this places additional demands on the I/T organization to develop systems and support quickly and to provide a significant level of flexibility for architectures and applications.

What are the things that absolutely must go right for the business to prosper? For a courier delivery service, it is dispatching pickups, tracking parcel movements, fleet maintenance, and on-time delivery. For a hardware store, it is determining and maintaining breadth of inventory, maintaining minimum stock levels, and training and monitoring staff. For a hospital emergency room, it is breadth and depth of the staff's medical specialties, determining recruiting and scheduling requirements, managing facility utilization, and managing drugs' inventory and control. These are critical success factors and are unique to each business.

I/T development and support plans must recognize and reflect the CSFs of the business. If these functions go unmanaged (or are poorly managed), the company won't be successful. We would expect, then, for the I/T plan to reflect greater emphasis on management and operational support of the business CSFs, as compared to other functions such as personnel and accounting.

Transformation Issues.   What forces are changing the business environment? What are the early warning signals? In the opening chapter, we likened some long-term changes in the competitive environment to incremental shifts of the San Andreas Fault. Business becomes so desensitized to the gradual shifts that they can no longer see and act on them. Long-term demographic trends, along with changing market demands, require competitive businesses to change business processes and organizational forms. The response time to recognize impending market change, to translate the change into new business requirements, and to institute the appropriate change into new business practices, processes, and organizational forms, becomes critical to enterprise survival.

> *The ability to correctly anticipate possible market dynamics and initiate the appropriate business flexibility before a competitor does, creates competitive advantage.*

Obviously, the keys to recognizing impending market change are to identify what the combined factors and events are that might precede it, to continually verify that they are the appropriate factors and events, and to *constantly monitor them* in the context of current strategy. This is the essence of scenario planning as practiced by Southern California Edison (Chapter 12). While we can express the concept behind scenario planning fairly easily, everything else requires time and a talented staff.

- Build and validate the scenarios.
- Identify and track the early warning signals of each scenario.
- Continually retest and revalidate the scenario assumptions.

It takes significantly more effort than just a casual focus at the beginning of each traditional planning cycle. While many planners believe that they are already doing this, the ramifications of simply not questioning current or past assumptions creates potential strategic time bombs, and it is an easy trap to fall into.

American Educational System.   At the conclusion of World War II, American universities initiated an investment in expansion of facilities that was to span over three decades, fueled initially by pent-up demands of returning veterans and supported by the subsequent generation of baby boomers. Generations of university planners faced a constant shortage of facilities to service the growing demand, and few ever considered a strategy to protect them if demand dropped. As a consequence, in the 1990s, when planners faced declining enrollments caused by a declining birthrate, it caught them by surprise, even though the trend began two decades earlier. Many of these same universities began closing schools, discontinuing programs, and consolidating faculty to compensate for underutilized facilities and faculty. While some universities continue on this downward spiral, others redefine product offerings to include professional education—recapturing former graduates who require new skills—and still others redefine the scope of its customer base from national to global, going to Europe and the Far East to recruit superior students.

Although this is a quick analysis of a trend that impacts American universities today, it suggests a whole new set of strategic issues, time-lines, and relationships that its planners must understand and track. When the continuously declining birthrate signaled a constantly smaller pool of 18-year-old potential applicants, how many university chancellors factored it into the (domestic student) strategy? For those universities that recruit globally, how many actively recruit students from other, even more rapidly aging nations like Japan and the EU countries? While going global is an effective short-term strategy, is gaining market share in an irrevocably disappearing market (as defined by the populations of the current industrialized nations) a successful long-term strategy? The last buggy-whip manufacturer in the United States could probably provide some valuable insights to the problem.

While expanding curricula to include professional studies is an effective strategy to fill empty lecture halls, other parts of the university business process remain, for the most part, untouched. For example, the educational delivery system remains largely unchanged over the past five centuries. In the fifteenth century, before Gutenberg invented moveable type, students gathered around a single copy of a book, held by the teacher. Later, as German universities gradually shifted from educating gentlemen to educating the mercantile, specialized schools within the university developed. Today, although each student has his or her own book—sometimes even an electronic copy—and perhaps a chosen area of specialization, the organizational hierarchy with the educational delivery system remains virtually the same. Consequently, while university strategies focus on increasing the number of students (its customers) through globalization and product diversification (through professional programs), the true strategic breakthrough will come when university faculties apply the various information technologies to create worldwide electronic universities and offer just-in-time delivery of education.

Elementary education, on the other hand, seems more adaptable to change. Voice mail, on-line services, and interactive videos in the home, narrow the gap between home and school. Parent-teacher voice mail has spread in the past few years and is a boon for separated or working parents who want to keep track of their child's progress—a reflection not only of the changing family unit but of the broad base of familiarity with the technology.[3] However, these new technology links to the home and in the classroom aren't the only changes. Some school systems are moving from the nine-month school (defined by the agricultural economy of the past) to year-round schools, thereby achieving improved utilization of physical facilities and staff, while others are instituting magnet schools for specialized education. Elementary education is clearly trying to match its changes to the movement of its economic and demographic base.

What Are Our Strategies in the Business?

Michael Porter defines the generic business strategies as cost leadership, differentiation, and focus. Whatever basic strategy the enterprise adopts will determine, to a large extent, the direction of the I/T strategies.[4]

Pretransformation Issues.   The investment strategies for I/T resources for a low-cost producer focus on systems associated with cost displacement, cost avoidance, or cost reduction. For an enterprise with a strategy of product differentiation, investment of I/T resources focuses less on cost issues and more on factors that create a unique, customized product. Examples are special customer services of home banking and automated teller machines in the banking industry, and frequent flyer programs in the airline industry. Focus strategy selects a market segment to serve, to the exclusion of others. A medical supplies firm may choose to participate in the home health care market to the exclusion of institutional health care. Here, investment strategies dedicate I/T resources to better meet the special needs of the target market segment.

Transformation Issues.   What strategies are we applying? What Action Plan(s) are we following? It is critical for the I/T organization to fully understand and appreciate the nuances of the business strategy. To enable the desired flexibility of the business organizational structure—the alliances, joint ventures, work teams, and any-where-anytime offices—in conjunction with enhancing the agility factor to quickly redesign or re-configure business processes, elevates the I/T architectural platform and application prioritization to a critical success factor for the transforming enterprise. This translates into a redefinition of the I/T charter and the redesign of the entire I/T delivery and support infrastructure to both assure the timely and effective support of the business strategy and to effectively deliver—and subsequently measure—business value. It is here that the I/T and business spirit of partnership become a reality, and the successful chief information officer is one who operates equally well in both the business and technology arenas.

> *The I/T architectural platform and application set are critical success factors for the transforming enterprise.*

How Can We Contribute Business Value?

How can I/T improve the functioning of the business and achieve success in its strategies and critical success factors? Key to these answers is moving the I/T performance measures from a cost basis to a basis of value.

Pretransformation Issues.   Because I/T wants to gain positive management attention and action, it needs business performance measurements that signify a contribution to value. These measurements must represent the true value of the I/T services and allow both I/T and business to chart the improvements.

A classic measurement within I/T is machine utilization, and it was meaningful when machines were more expensive than people. Businesses such as Evergreen Environmental Consultants (Appendix I) usually find these measurements useless in making decisions about future business plans. If I/T thoroughly considers what and how to measure, it will probably end up discussing the measures with a controller, a vice president of finance, a person or group responsible for logistics, I/T peers, and the ultimate end user of the services. All will have very different views of what the I/T service is and how to measure its value. This poses the questions of what I/T is trying to deliver, and what business we are in, the first question of the seven questions.

The implications for I/T are clear. I/T groups get accused of trying to create and enforce standards on the business users that inhibit freedom of choice. (The business managers of one enterprise the author is familiar with refer to the CIO as Dr. No—an indication of the level of frustration within the organization.) Some I/T organizations may negotiate contracts stating what it will provide the user, what the internal client will receive, and when it will happen. Often, these contracts, though conceptually strong, are weak in implementation because they don't cover the quality issues. Thus, there are problems defining the mutual expectations of the parties, often leading to misunderstanding and disappointment.

Executive management is putting demands on I/T to come up with solid numbers to measure the effective use of its resources. I/T is trying to make progress in quantifying and measuring service success and service quality—added value to the enterprise. The key is to clearly define what the I/T service strategy is, not only the elements (e.g., access, communication, customer satisfaction, etc., discussed in Chapter 6), but the level of the strategy element. That is, has I/T accomplished the strategy from the provider's perspective if the consumer views the service level as poor, mediocre, or superior? The cost to place emphasis on an element of service quality that moves the customer's perception of the service from acceptable—being just-good-enough—to exceptional may simply not be justifiable.

Given that we have identified what business we are in (or want to be in), what the problems and CSFs are, and what the strategy of the line of business is, we have now established the context for I/T to improve current business performance. Evaluation of this improved business performance occurs using business values and added values that the enterprise defines. To do this, linkages between the mission, the organization, and the measurements must be complete. There must be interlocking planning strategies that answer the how questions. Internal operating measures must relate to the efficiency of the operation. Interlocking measurements must answer the "how much" and "how well" questions to provide the effectiveness measures and to translate operational results back to the strategic goals.

How to do this is not always clear to the I/T organization, with its many lines of service, different objectives, and performance measures. To provide an overall service and quality measure for the entire organization may be impossible or meaningless.

However, concentrating on each line of service to define its service and quality measures deserves attention. These service and quality measures, in conjunction with the usual cost/performance measures, provide a more accurate evaluation of the contribution of I/T to overall business performance.

> *I/T organizations must dramatically increase their demonstrated business contribution to become strategic components of the business. For an organization that doesn't will become a cost-sensitive support function similar to transportation or facilities and a prime target for elimination through outsourcing.*

Transformation Issues. How can I/T improve business performance? How can I/T better deploy technology? What new technologies can I/T deploy? What are the critical skill sets? How can we measure contributions to business value? For I/T organizations, the key to delivering business value is the ability of I/T to demonstrate its understanding of and contribution to the new—and evolving—business values associated with transformation. This includes developing and supporting new business measurement systems that reflect the corporate vision and stakeholder values so perfectly that the measures become routine input to business decision-making. More importantly, it demands that I/T understand the business processes being measured and how I/T (organizationally and technologically) might improve them, resulting in improved business performance. The answers may lie, for example, in information empowerment, or in increased information integration and team learning.

While there is an increased emphasis for I/T to thoroughly understand the business to better support and improve its processes, there is also a commensurate increase in emphasis for I/T to be better versed in technology alternatives to support current business processes and/or products. Bottom-line, the I/T contribution to business value involves assessing and strengthening both the I/T and business core competencies, and it involves the evolution and maturation of the learning organization. The resulting free flow of information and knowledge in the organization enables the knowledgeable decision-making necessary for sustaining transformation.

How Can We Change (Improve) the Strategy or Basic Business Plan?

What new uses of I/T can change the business strategy, or change the basic business plan (new product, customer, or market)? Here, we are focusing on opportunity planning. Given the current level of technology expertise within the line of business and I/T organization, the issue is how to leverage that expertise to create new, leading-edge, business opportunities.

Pretransformation Issues. Consider American Airlines and how it answered these questions a few years ago. Can new products or new services be developed? The data entry services offered by American Airlines' AMR Caribbean Data

Services is an example of a new product or service based upon its existing organization. Can a use of I/T expand the current customer set? The Citibank AAdvantage Card creates new customer alliances by linking American's frequent flyer mileage program to Citibank Visa and MasterCard credit lines. Finally, can an I/T application create a new market? The SABRE reservation system, used by professional travel agents, is the base for EAASY SABRE, the personal reservation and information system. Here, I/T creates information and reservation linkages between the airline, hotels, and car-rental agencies from the user's home.

Transformation Issues.   How can I/T change the business? How can I/T employ infrastructures/architectures to increase enterprise mobility? What new technologies or platforms should we employ? What are the critical skills? How can we measure improvements? While maintaining the current enterprise and product line is important, it is imperative to improve current products, drop outdated products, and—most important for the future of the enterprise—successfully develop and market new products. The focus on opportunity planning involves leveraging current I/T expertise to create leading-edge business opportunities.

It is difficult enough for businesses to effectively (or accurately) forecast their future competitive role and reinvent their strategy and structure. Unfortunately, in the early 1990s, I/T compounded the problem. Like the former planners for American universities, I/T built its current infrastructures based upon a scenario of continuous business growth—not a scenario based upon global competition and economic downturns. When enterprises attempted to put out local fires caused by global competitors, they dramatically reshaped business architectures. Downsizing, outsourcing and restructuring, rather than a newly conceived business strategy, drove this reshaping of the interim business architecture. I/T responded to the business organizational change by tying together disparate architectural platforms never designed to work together. The business restructuring strained the existing I/T architectures to the point that few I/T organizations were making the necessary new platform and technology investments to ensure future business competitiveness.

As new business architectures emerge with myriad organizational variations, each will depend on functional characteristics of its I/T platform. Businesses attempting reengineering or transformation can reduce the transformational stress by synchronizing the I/T and business architecture changes.[5] Choosing which of the new technologies, platforms, and concepts to adopt is critical, because short-term, I/T-based business transformation based upon existing I/T platforms creates little sustainable advantage. It is the crafting of and the movement to the new I/T platform that changes the competitive playing field—based upon the critical decisions related to capability implementation time-lines. Each major part of the business must develop time-lines, risk assessments, scenarios, and appropriate measurement schema, and senior management must evaluate the risk relationship to business plans. Given the lead times required and the way the technologies affect the transformation time-line, I/T and senior business management must maintain ongoing dialogs to ensure the availability of critical skills.

Long-term business strategy must include the coordination of business transformation and new I/T platform capability.

Thus, I/T executives must prepare their organizations for two distinct technology strategies. The first strategy involves the exploitation of the current platform, leveraging existing systems wherever possible for benefits. This strategy contributes immediate business value (Question 4). The second strategy focuses on the new (future) I/T platform, involving pilot programs and experimentation, organizational learning, and technology transfer. This is the strategy that leverages enterprise transformation through the application of new I/T resources and skills (Question 5).

How Can We Organize to Best Accomplish Business Goals?

How can we organize the business to function most effectively achieve its goals, business strategy, and plans? How can we organize I/T activities to best accomplish the business goals? The function of the I/T organization is to support the line of business and enterprise strategy. It is the means to sustain and improve business performance.

Pretransformation Issues.   Organizational design is a problem for I/T management because criteria for optimizing the management and structure of I/T are vague, at best. Even worse, signals that existing management structures fit poorly may lie hidden in poor morale, application development cost overruns, or deficient application portfolios.

For I/T, there are costs associated with an inappropriate organizational structure. While using the appropriate structure may have some direct impact on the organization's ability to attain its goals, its biggest impact will be on the adaptability of the organization and the behavior of its managers.[6] Indicators of dysfunctional organization design may include:

- I/T decision-makers may not be able to anticipate problems before they occur. The organization may have a tendency to wait until problems are critical and then react.
- I/T decision-makers may err in trying to predict trends in their decision environment. Without proper coordination across groups, the organization may lose control over the relationship between its internal functioning and its environment.
- The I/T organization may not be able to get key information to the right place for effective decision-making.
- The I/T organization, having identified a problem concerning its strategic portfolio, may not be able to take corrective action quickly enough.

These data are generally available from simple personal observation to formal surveys that monitor the organizational climate.

Transformation Issues.   What is the best organization? What are the critical skills? How can we measure (improved) organizational effectiveness? While much of the recent rhetoric surrounding the appropriateness of the I/T organizational structure seems to focus around the centralized versus decentralized debate, there is much more to the issue than that. This becomes obvious when an I/T organization—whether centralized or decentralized—confronts the issue of how to best organize to support a business organization that uses matrix management or self-managed workgroups. Organization structure is more than boxes on a chart. It is a pattern of interactions and coordination that links I/T technology, application development, and human components of the organization to the business organizations, functions, and processes that accomplish management's goals of delivering business value. Organizational structure links the strategic enterprise resources through channels of communication. The key question for I/T management is what organization structure to choose.

Functional Organizations.   When a business organization's environment is relatively simple (e.g., a stable balance of power in supplier relationships or new product generation), there are fewer factors to consider in competitive decision-making, and a functional organizational structure may be appropriate. One characteristic of the functional organization is specialization by functional area. As a strength, functional organizations support in-depth skill development and a simple decision-communication network. However, when disputes or uncertainty occur among managers about a decision, they get pushed up the hierarchy for resolution. A primary weakness of the functional organization, therefore, is that when the organization's environment becomes more dynamic and uncertainty tends to increase, many decisions move to the top of the organization. Lower-level managers do not have the information required for decision-making, so they push decisions upward. Top-level managers become overloaded and are thus slow to respond to the environment. With the move toward flatter, more horizontal business organizations, previously effective I/T functional organizations often become inappropriate.

Decentralized Organizations.   For a business environment with a high degree of change, I/T organizations tend to become decentralized and develop lateral relationships with the business organization to increase the amount of information available for decisions. A decentralized organization is possible whenever an I/T organization's tasks are self-contained. Decentralized organizations typically support I/T products, support applications, or markets. In the decentralized organization, managers only have to worry about their own products or services; they have the resources to carry out these activities, and they don't have to compete for shared resources. There is also a full-time commitment to a particular product line. The decentralized structure is particularly effective when the business organization's environment is very complex, that is, when there are a large number of factors to consider in decision-making and when the environment can segment into I/T product or support areas around which it can structure itself.

Decentralized organizations face several problems. For example, it is sometimes difficult to decide what resources to pool in a corporate staff used by the entire enterprise. If the business groups are very different from one another regarding products, customers, technology, and so on, it becomes difficult to staff a corporate services unit with the diverse knowledge needed to help other groups. Restricted innovation is another problem decentralized I/T organizations may encounter. Because each group organizes around a particular product or geographic area, each manager's attention focuses on his special area. As a result, I/T innovations focus on the particular specialties of each manager, and managers don't have the diverse information needed to produce enterprisewide innovations.

A major liability of decentralized I/T organizations is their relative inability to provide integration-coordination among the groups, even when their interdependence increases. When groups are relatively autonomous and have only pooled interdependence, there is not much need for coordination. However, when uncertainty increases and they must work together due to increased interdependence, decentralized I/T organizations have no formal mechanisms to coordinate and resolve the increased needs for information.

As today's organizational environment becomes more complex and interdependent, large decentralized enterprises find the need to integrate increases for at least four reasons.

- The increased level and complexity of government regulations require more coordination across organizations to be sure that all regulatory requirements are being met.
- Organizational environments are changing, leading to a requirement of more coordination across internal organizational boundaries as well as across the enterprise boundaries for strategic alliances, joint ventures, and other consortia.
- Technological changes place more emphasis on increased interaction among organizations. Increasingly, organizations share computer systems and R&D services, compelling the organizations to interact more with one another.
- The cost of poor strategic decisions increases for both sunk costs and losses because of failure to get market share. Because poor decisions sometimes result from lack of contact between organizations, they emphasize the need to have better coordination across the organizations and more sharing of I/T services.

All the above reasons demonstrate a need for increased I/T coordination among decentralized organizations. Given the communication weaknesses of a decentralized organization, good I/T organizational design must maintain information flow to reduce decision uncertainties.

Lateral Relations.   Lateral relations are processes overlaid on an existing functional or decentralized structure. They push down decision-making to the level in the organization at which the problem occurs and differ from decentralization in that there is no creation of self-contained tasks.

There are four basic types of lateral relations: liaison, integrator, task force or team, and matrix. From liaison to matrix, each of the lateral processes becomes increasingly complex and costly in implementation. For example, an enterprise might use matrix management for I/T development if the department serves a strategic role and maintains a large portfolio of applications. Competitive analyses dictate the appropriateness of using one or more of the lateral processes.

Creating the role of liaison, for example, can occur by physically locating a member of I/T development among production people, thereby providing a communication link. Such roles provide impetus to direct contact among different staff personnel. When differences between groups in an organization become more complex, the use of integrators may be appropriate.

The integrator could be a systems manager or a group executive whose additional function is to coordinate and integrate the diverse units (or groups) in ways that meet the organization's common objectives. To be effective as an integrator, a manager needs to have certain characteristics.

- The integrator needs wide contacts in the organization so that he or she possesses the relevant information about the different integrating groups.
- The integrator needs to understand and share, at least to a degree, the goals and orientations of the different groups. He or she cannot favor one particular group's perspective.
- The integrator must possess broad technical training and speak the language of the different groups. Able to demonstrate some expertise in each area, the integrator is credible dealing with each group. Since the integrator is trying to facilitate information flow and cooperation, the groups must believe that he or she is working toward a solution acceptable to all.

Because differences exist between the units or groups, conflict is inevitable, and confrontation is the conflict resolution style. By confrontation, the intent is that parties to the conflict identify the causes of the problem and commit to adopting a problem-solving approach that leads to a mutually acceptable solution.

When coordination involves working with six or seven different groups, the enterprise often establishes task forces or teams. Task forces involve a group of managers working together on the coordination problems of their diverse groups. In a manufacturing organization, for example, the marketing, production, I/T, finance, and engineering managers may meet twice a week to discuss problems of coordination that they may have and which require cooperation to resolve. In this use, a task force is a problem-solving group formed to facilitate coordination.

The matrix is the most complex form of lateral relations and is typically a formal structure in the organization. It is not a structure added temporarily to an existing functional or decentralized structure. The most salient characteristic of a matrix structure is dual authority, and both the heads of functions and the matrix manager have authority over those working in the matrix unit.

The matrix structure developed initially in the aerospace industry, where the organization had to be responsive to products and markets as well as technology. Because the matrix focuses on a specific product or market, it can generate the information and concentrate the resources needed to respond to changes in that product or market quite rapidly. A variety of business, public, and health organizations use the matrix approach.

Matrix organizations, however, are difficult to manage. Because both project managers and traditional functional area managers become involved in matrix organization, personnel in the matrix have two managers, creating an inherent potential for conflict. As a result, the use of the matrix form of lateral relations occurs in those situations in which an organization faces a unique problem in a particular I/T product or business market area.

Lateral relations in I/T management require a certain organizational design and special interpersonal skills if this process is for reducing I/T project uncertainty. This necessitates the presence of four factors:

- The organization's reward structure must support and reward cooperative problem-solving that leads to coordination and integration.
- In assigning managers to participate in some form of lateral relations, it is important that they have responsibility for implementation.
- Participants must have the authority to commit their business units to action.
- Lateral processes must integrate into the vertical information flow.

Lateral relations as used in organizing I/T development, then, are processes that overlay onto the existing functional or decentralized organizational structure. Lateral relations require various skills, so it is imperative that an organization never adopt this approach without training the participants. Before implementing lateral relations, an enterprise might use team building to develop the interpersonal skills of the relevant managers.

Critical Skills.   Although the emphasis to this point has been on organizational structure, choosing and implementing a new organizational structure is pointless if the organization doesn't have the set of critical skills necessary to carry out the business goals. One of the reasons for using scenario planning to establish the context for both business and I/T planning is that it forces the issue of identifying the appropriateness and availability of skill sets across multiple business alternatives.

While the importance of individual (common) core competencies can vary within scenarios, it is the identification of a unique competency or skill to individual scenarios that is critical here. Is the scenario (business or technology) even a viable option if the potential source for a critical skill isn't identifiable? How long would it take to recruit an individual with the specific skill necessary or to identify an individual to develop the necessary skill? In this later case, how early (and how reliable) are the early warning signals for this scenario? The early warning signals might occur too late to obtain the necessary critical skill—or create the necessary critical mass of the skill—rendering the scenario alternative meaningless.

The learning organization demands a constant emphasis on specific skill improvements and the determination of these specific skills is a necessary by-product of scenario-driven planning. Any strategic (or long-term) planning and subsequent investment of resources by the I/T organization that does not directly support these business goals are questionable.

What Action Plan Supports the Answers to Questions 1 through 6?

Pretransformation Issues. Most strategic planning presentations appear long on concept and short on execution. It is one thing to talk about Michael Porter's Value Chain and quite another to use it in a planning process in a real enterprise.[4] (See "New Technologies and New Services" in Appendix 1.) One reason strategic planning processes tend to overlook process is the wide spectrum of differences among enterprises. It is very difficult to specify a general process that applies to many types of enterprises.

On the other hand, a contingent approach to planning processes is both feasible and effective. The Action Plan (Question 7) represents the key ideas of a contingent planning process. To do the strategic planning is the goal of the action plan and activated through the Seven Questions. Its purpose is to apply the insights and learning from the experience of organizations doing strategic planning and to create a state-of-the-art methodology.

Three ideas stand out.

- First, enterprises are different. Accordingly, a generic action plan has to provide diagnostic steps to permit fitting the planning process to the requirements and circumstances of the specific enterprise. Hence, a contingent approach to planning is reasonable, where the planner can define the suitable approach most likely to bring success. Enterprises and its lines of business are unique. The idea of diagnosis is central to planning. Consequently, a planner should orient the Seven Questions to determine the character of the enterprise and line of business and to then apply the appropriate planning tool and planning approach for best effect.
- Second, enterprises consist of one or more lines of business. The resulting planning process might apply in one of them but not likely all. Planning, in this sense, is bottom-up; the focus is on one line of business and not on the enterprise as a whole.
- Third, a large number of tools already exist for planning. A generic planning methodology should not invent new ones but rather should identify where existing tools apply in the lines of business studied.

Planning, fundamentally, is an exercise in persuasion. Accordingly, a plan has to be contextually appropriate *and* convincing and effective in communicating its value and worth. This requires an effective measurement of cost and value against the yardstick of stakeholder values and corporate vision. The resulting Action Plan provides for enterprise processes and line of business processes and concludes with an application of Information economics.

Transformation Issue.   How can I/T implement change to maximize equilibrium? Key to successful transformation—and certainly to maintaining transformation—is the ability to maximize equilibrium between the functioning parts of the enterprise. We stated earlier that organizational structure was more than boxes on a chart—that it was the pattern of interactions and coordination that links technology, application development, and the individuals within the organization to create and deliver value to the business. ("Evergreen Environmental Consultants" in Appendix I provides a clear illustration of this.) The I/T organization, combined with the technology it delivers, becomes more critical to the daily functioning of the business as the enterprise becomes:

- Increasingly mobile through anywhere-anytime offices (Chapter 2).
- Smarter through information empowerment (Chapter 3).
- More flexible internally through physical organizational redesign and restructuring and business process redesign (Chapters 7 and 8).
- More ambiguously defined through the establishment of network linkages supporting external constituency relationships (Chapter 4).

I/T, as a consequence, creates whole new waves of business dynamics. As the various organizations employ I/T, they change business processes and organizations to first accommodate (although not working very efficiently) and then exploit (working very efficiently) the new capabilities and create new requirements. Whether the function is working very efficiently or not, it impacts the productivity of the rest of the functions in the enterprise. Additionally, these other functions are going through similar transformational changes, resulting in a potentially dysfunctional enterprise.

Therefore, I/T has an additional charter in transformation: it must reduce the potential dysfunction of the enterprise by the judicious planning, implementation, and deployment of I/T to the business functions to maintain a level of equilibrium between the functions.

I/T strategy must accomplish three things: First, it must exploit the current technology platform to produce business value; second, it must leverage enterprise transformation through new technology platforms; and third, it must focus on maintaining equilibrium among the enterprise functions.

OBSERVATIONS

Tools and Methodologies In the Seven Questions

Consultants and companies use a variety of tools and techniques to support the Seven Questions.

- The facilitator of discussions involving questions surrounding the first question group (what business(es) are we in, what business(es) should we be in) might use Porter's three generic strategies, the Porter Value Chain, or corporate values as the focal point.
- For discussions involving the second group (what problems do we have in this business; what forces affect this business; what are the CSFs for the business), the facilitator might choose to focus on the three questions themselves. An analysis of competitive strengths, weaknesses and forces, and matching the CSFs to the Action Plan inventory are also effective techniques.
- The third question (what are the strategies in the business), lends itself to choosing the appropriate focus using a discussion of the strategies themselves, cost-benefit analysis and risk assessment, and technology and opportunity scans.
- An analysis of how the application of I/T can improve the business and achieve success in its strategies and critical success factors (the fourth question), involves not only the organizational structuring, behavior and culture touchstones, but an analysis of how effectively—and how quickly—internal organizations supported past strategy, with measurement systems as the focus. Organizations, like people, need measurement systems to excel because they need to know how well they are doing. Until new measurements—such as performance measures linked to compensation—support the new strategies, organizations will lack direction.

Knowledgeable, quality facilitation is necessary for getting all of these activities started off right in the enterprise. If an enterprise doesn't have someone on staff highly skilled in these areas, consultants are available. Two consulting groups, the Beta Group and Key Strategies and Solutions, participated in the actual development and application of the concepts. A complementary consulting practice, the Helix Group, developed HelixPLAN, a management team planning and decision-making methodology that applies to any combination of planning frameworks and/or issues (e.g., scenario planning, the Seven Questions Methodology, and Information Economics).[7] Other consulting groups, such as Global Business Network, specialize in developing scenarios for subsequent use in scenario-based planning; still others, like Renaissance Strategy Group, possess particular expertise in the development of measurement systems. Key to selecting the right consultant to assist your organization is experience and in-depth knowledge of appropriate planning methodologies combined with the facilitative skills to engage the organization to come to conclusive, appropriate decisions.

This gives the reader a general idea of the range of consultative skills available and the flexibility and ease of tailoring this approach to specific organizational planning activities. While not complete, it serves as a starting point for discussion and application of the ideas using techniques easily configurable to any planning situation. It also provides a valuable insight into the multidisciplinary characteristics of transformation planning.

Using the Seven Questions To Create Project Methodologies

While the Seven Questions are the focus of any transformation planning process, they are also a vehicle for the creation of the context for all enterprise strategic planning. It is possible to flesh out the questions into a complete planning process by the addition of conceptual tools to help derive complete answers to each question. Ultimately, the successive uses of the Seven Questions move from developing strategic action plans to developing operational action plans and methodologies. (See Table 13-2 for an example of an end-user information systems project methodology that might result from successive applications of the seven questions for a particular enterprise.)

The Seven Questions approach to strategic planning is not traditional portfolio management. The approach doesn't focus on what business we should be in to the detriment of successfully supporting today's business. Rather, the focus is how to make the current business more successful—now and in the future—through the development of an Action Plan. For I/T, this means keeping all scenario-identified options open, while finding the most important investment opportunities for each line of business, organization, and product to move it from today to the twenty-first century.

Project Steps	Job Performance	Work Process	Business/Management Control	Technology Design
1. Define Project Scope Establish clear understandings or problems to be addressed, boundaries (scope) of the project, expected benefits, and resources required. Obtain project sponsorship (funding).	Identify number of workers affected. Identify levels and types of jobs affected. Establish individual performance objectives.	Identify business departments affected. Identify and describe specific business functions and tasks affected. Identify high-level data subjects and information needs. Develop work process objectives.	Select business sponsor(s). Define business objectives. Identify expected benefits. Identify critical success factors (CSF). Identify all stakeholders (those who have most to win or lose by maintaining or changing current procedures, functions, organizations). Assess project priority based on preliminary cost/benefit analysis. Establish target date.	Define system objectives. Define expected results. Define system benefits. Obtain preliminary agreement on approach. Estimate development/implementation on time. Estimate cost range.
2. Plan the Project Establish project organization. Make initial assessment. Develop a detailed workplan and assemble project team.	Establish approach for work process redesign.	Relate functions to current organizations. Relate functions to data subjects. Relate functions to information needs. Determine dependency among functions.	Establish project review board/steering committee. Define management control measures. Assemble project team. Assign roles and responsibilities. Develop initial project workplan with tasks, target dates, and responsibilities.	Establish project methodology based on scope, objectives, approach, and time. Train and educate project team and managers on the process and methods.
3. Assess Requirements Understand and document the structure and purposes of the current system. Determine requirements for a new system. Evaluate alternative solutions and recommend the preferred solution.	Identify knowledges, skills, and abilities of users. Collect current job descriptions. Determine current performance criteria/measures. Do a cost-benefit analysis for individual workers. Document what changes are needed and why.	Perform a task analysis. Document current work processes. Document current procedures and workflows. Identify major inputs and outputs for all affected work processes. Document what changes are needed and why. Develop business models.	Define mission of all functions/departments to be impacted. Assess impact on organization structure. Identify internal and external clients. Obtain organizational charts of affected departments. Identify CSF's for business. Develop more refined cost/benefit analysis. Develop vision statement linking business goals and technology plans. Assess organizational culture. Assess climate for change. Obtain sponsor approval to proceed to next phase.	Analyze current system (manual, mechanical, or automated.) Determine technology requirements of new system. Identify need to interface with other systems. Assess available technology environment. Estimate capacity requirements. Study alternative solutions. Design a prototype. Define system tactics and alternatives for achieving EUIS objectives.
4. Design: Describe the System in Detail Develop detailed specifications for the proposed project solution.	Develop skills inventory. Define instructional strategies. Identify skills, knowledges, and information required for different positions.	Identify tasks that can be streamlined, eliminated, combined with automation. Document proposed new work processes design. Document proposed new	Conduct client survey (to determine service/quality factors from client perspective). Define quality. Define "best practices."	Determine system requirements. Document existing systems. Define specifications for proposed system or system alternatives.

Phase	(Training)	(Procedures)	(Organization / Change)	(Hardware / Software)
(continued)	Analyze job design. Develop new job descriptions.	workflows. Define business requirements for all applications to be automated. Define requirements for help systems.	Develop proposed organization charts. Define requirements/objectives for organizational restructuring. Set up model office, if needed.	Develop RFP for systems/work to be contracted/purchased. Evaluate alternative proposals. Conduct benchmark testing.
5. Select or Develop Solution Bring a working version of the system to a usable stage. Write and test all customized software, applications, procedures, documentation, and training materials.	Develop training program. Develop cross-training plan. Develop documentation. Develop help systems. Develop CBT. Develop job aids.	Develop and document new procedures. Develop conversion plan. Create test cases and procedures. Develop training data base, if needed.	Develop change management strategies. Develop new management measures. Develop quality control measures and monitoring procedures. Create physical site plans. Create detailed implementation plan.	Select application software. Select hardware, system software, communication network. Modify/customize software as planned. Construct software applications, menus, interfaces. Secure needed contracts.
6. Implement Solution Implement all necessary steps to convert from existing operating environment to the new system.	Train software skills. Train EUIS application development skills. Train new job skills or crosstrain. Maintain business activity as training is conducted. Provide hotline and other support.	Install new procedures. Convert all work to new systems/procedures. Eliminate tasks/procedures replaced by new.	Implement model office activities. Make adjustments based on model office experience. Prepare facilities. Cut over to new systems or implement all planned installations. Implement new measurements. Implement change strategies. Install backup and security procedures.	Install pilot locations. Make adjustments based on pilot results. Install hardware and software at all locations. Resolve any technical problems.
7. Evaluate Results Determine if new system meets performance criteria, satisfies defined project objectives, and meets client expectations. Identify additional action (steps) to be taken.	Identify any performance problems. Identify additional training needs such as problems with tasks, and the use of system features. Identify where users are in the learning curve. Assess level of needed behavior changes.	Identify bottlenecks. Resolve problems with new processes. Respond to new ideas/new insights for additional improvements. Assess user problems, acceptance, applications.	Assess actual results against planned results. Assess client satisfaction with new system.	Assess system performance. Troubleshoot problems with hardware or software.
8. Institutionalize Results Provide reinforcement needed to sustain workplace changes. Capitalize on new learning and insight to improve results.	Deliver remedial training. Deliver advanced training. Reinforce/reward desired new behaviors.	Modify work processes as needed. Implement additional/more advanced applications. Provide additional business training.	Refine business criteria and success measures. Develop new measures if appropriate. Reinforce organizational changes. Bring benefits to bottom line.	Make any needed system modifications. Develop any needed enhancements. Acquire additional hardware/software.

Table 13-2 EUIS Project Methodology.

14

Identifying New Value and Risk Criteria

Each enterprise stakeholder has a unique set of values that, taken with others, form the basic business measures. When stakeholder power shifts or the stakeholders themselves change, so do the value criteria and value systems they represent. The problems arise as we try to focus on identifying specific values and risks that are critical to industry, enterprise, or department success and then translate them into criteria for determining new investment agendas. To successfully support a newly developed enterprise vision requires a close mapping of the resource investments that recognizes the new values and risks involved in the business strategy. However, simply recognizing them isn't enough—they must translate into criteria to judge the contribution of each investment initiative in an equitable way, along with the continuing financial realities of cash flow, limited resources, and profitability.

Enterprise stakeholders have different values that form the basic business measures, and when stakeholder power shifts from time to time, so do the value criteria and value systems they represent. Not only are there a number of stakeholders in the enterprise, each having a different set of values and criteria for success, the same set of stakeholders likely has different values and criteria for success from industry to industry. Added to this complexity are the differing attitudes of stakeholders in different parts of the world. Thus global competitors, investors, and customers also shape stakeholder values.

While each nation seems to have its own approach to creating and maintaining its corporate value systems, the common value and success criteria for enterprise stakeholders include the following:

- Employees (including managers), who want to excel in compensation-base measurements, and thereby enhance their income base and job security.
- Stockholders, who search for some combination of growth and income (short-term or long-term) and accept varying degrees of risk.
- (Family) owners, most often found in Europe and Canada, and to some degree in Japan through the *keiretsu,* strive for growth and income in perpetuity.
- Lenders, such as banks, pension funds, or *keiretsu* members, require various levels of financial integrity.
- There are always regulators, who demand conformance (at any price).
- Customers seek service and quality at a reasonable price.
- Competitors demand market share and conformance to business ethics.
- Suppliers constantly seek predictable orders, paid on time.
- National and local governments, and to some extent, trading blocs, monitor and formulate policies to foster a favorable economic and competitive environment for new job generation and a growing economy.

Through the formalization of stakeholder relationships in the business value definition and measurement process, I/T is theoretically able to measure its contribution to business value. Today, the process is difficult, and it's not just that the I/T portion of the contribution to business has too few good measures. It is that many barriers hinder the creation of a consistent justification and measurement base for the enterprise as a whole, and these barriers subsequently impact the internal functions and measurements.These barriers include:

- Whenever the business environment changes, some previously valid justification and value measures may become obsolete: Even though the enterprise may not have a global presence, it can have global competitors enter its domestic market. As a consequence, the definition and measures of its market share must undergo change to remain meaningful. New value measures must reflect the enterprise position with global competitors, markets, and product alternatives.
- Enterprises go into new businesses, offering new products and services that require new measures of justification rationale and success: In Chapter 11, we mentioned how the U.S. banks responded to competition from brokerage firms selling mutual funds by offering similar funds to its depositors. The competitive response of the banks compromised one of the leading economic indicators tracked by the Federal Reserve Board because the design of the measurement insulated it from changes in financial industry strategy.
- Industry best practices constantly evolve, necessitating an evolving justification and measurement base: The measurement of negawatts—the watts that, through industry action, remain unused (e.g., saved as compared to projections

of normal consumption)—was the result of the energy industry searching for a way to express to its various stakeholders that a drop in revenues (since revenues link directly to the consumption of energy) was a positive rather than negative indicator of long-term success. A second example of evolving industry best practice involves the just-in-time philosophy. Just-in-time inventory practices may initiate radical change (shift or reduction) in the inventory levels of an industry. Continuing to use inventory levels as an indication of economic health without a change in interpretation is at best, a waste of time, and at worst, misleading if used for decision-making. Similarly, generalizing about inventory levels is misleading when an industry's traditional distribution channels are in the process of changing. A final example is the American Customer Satisfaction Index (ACSI), a U.S. national economic indicator that made its debut in late 1994. It balances economic output quality with economic output quantity for seven industry sectors and forty industries within the sectors.[1] Think what the U.S. auto industry could have learned, given the information ten years ago, that as its customers became increasingly dissatisfied with product quality, sales went to foreign competitors offering higher quality products at a comparable price. Think of how the Federal Reserve might use the index, for example, to help decide if there was an impending inflationary cycle. (If satisfaction and price rise at the same time, the customer gets an improved (noninflationary) product; however, inflation threatens when more than one major sector has reduced customer satisfaction coupled with rising prices.)

• Markets are eroding at a faster pace, so that current products become obsolete faster, requiring greater attention to developing future products: No longer isolated in domestic markets, enterprises must pay more attention (thus make greater investments) to creating a steady stream of emerging products. As a result, R&D investment levels get more coverage in the various financial publications. However, heavy investment in R&D doesn't necessarily guarantee new competitive products. This places more emphasis on developing measures linking R&D investments to time-to-market (getting products to the market earlier), R&D investments to number of new products (converting the R&D into real products for the enterprise), and R&D investments to success levels of new products (measuring the quality of the new products developed through R&D efforts). Concurrently, there is a reduced emphasis on the more traditional measurements of R&D investments as a percentage of revenues, profits, or total investment.

• A justification and value measurement developed for the hierarchical organization supporting mass production doesn't necessarily serve the team-driven flat (or matrix) organization supporting mass customization or information-based products: Just as the paradigms of mass production (built around homogeneity) don't work as paradigms for heterogeneous mass customization, many of the justification approaches and value measurements aren't transferable either.

If we are investing time and money in organizational restructuring and business process reengineering, how do we know if we invest in the best projects? How do we know if we are successful? Alternatively, given our current level of success, should we be even more successful? These are critical questions—they focus on identifying specific values and risks that are critical to industry, enterprise, or department success and translate them into criteria for determining investment agendas. To do this effectively requires some form of scenario planning to develop the initial planning and strategy contexts and the Seven Questions Methodology to drive the strategy and action planning. To successfully support this new enterprise vision requires mapping the resource investments to the new values and risks involved. Simply recognizing these new values and risks isn't enough—they must translate into criteria to judge the contribution of each investment initiative in an equitable way, side-by-side with the continuing financial realities of cash flow, limited resources, and profitability.

In this chapter, we cover some of the salient ideas in traditional resource investment planning (based on cost-benefit analysis using tangible, measurable benefits). From there, we move to some of the softer benefits that most businesses are comfortable with. We then discuss some of the recurring new values and risks that face transforming businesses and suggest approaches for reflecting them in investment strategies.

With these values and risks, we introduce the idea that we judge (or score) all investment initiatives using the same criteria or yardstick. Some initiatives will be strong revenue generators, but won't create new markets; others will create new markets but won't return a quick profit; still others will reduce time-to-market for the major product line, creating competitive advantage but also running the risk of failing if strong competitors force distribution channel restructuring. Each of these initiatives has merit, but each also has weaknesses and risks. A successful investment strategy is one that blends a variety of initiatives into a support structure that maintains the enterprise performance today while it builds and transforms it for a successful tomorrow. Defining and developing criteria to compare the potential value contribution and its associated risks and uncertainty for each (alternative) initiative is key to the enterprise justification process.

TAXONOMY OF TRANSFORMATION-BASED VALUE AND RISK CRITERIA

Many important values get ignored in financial quantifications like return-on-investment (ROI) or net present value (NPV) calculations. Some are unique to the technology domain while some are clearly in the business domain. In *Information Economics* and *Information Strategy and Economics,* we proposed a series of approaches to estimate and combine the tangible and soft measures.[2] Additionally, we proposed an approach to include those innovative applications in a justification methodology, so that enterprise planners, strategists, and managers could review highly strategic initiatives with currently unpredictable outcomes for funding in a rational, even-handed way. Since publication, this approach has gained worldwide recognition and application, especially in the European Union countries and the Pacific. As a result of many global speaking and consulting activities, clients began identifying new issues surrounding investments in transformational initiatives and began refining the existing categories and adding new ones that were pertinent to their organizations.

The emerging generic set of values and risks fall into five categories: financial, strategic and stakeholder values, and competitive and organizational strategy risks and uncertainties (see Table 14-1).

- Financial Values: These are the benefits that are measurable using current accounting practices. These values exist at the enterprise (business-based financial values) and I/T levels (I/T-based financial values).
- Strategic values: These are enterprise product-based, externally focused strategies to produce value for the enterprise. They include strategic match, competitive advantage, and competitive response. Additionally, management information for critical success factors focuses on the internal activities that directly affect the externally delivered product and the external customer. This is the bridge between

Business	Technology
Financial Values:	
• Business-based financial value	• I/T-based financial value
Strategic Values:	
• Strategic match	• Strategic I/T architecture
• Competitive advantage	
• Competitive response	
• Management information for CSF's	
Stakeholder Values:	
• Service and quality	
• Environmental quality	
• Agility, learning, and empowerment	
• Cycle time	
• Mass customization	
Competitive Strategy Risk:	
• Business strategy risk	• I/T strategy risk
Organizational Risk and Uncertainty:	
• Business organizational risk	• I/T definitional uncertainty
	• Technical and implementation risk
	• I/T services delivery risk

Table 14-1   Generic Categories of Value and Risk.

the externally focused customer and product strategy and the internally focused organizational strategies.

- Stakeholder values: Stakeholder values represent a blend of broad internal and organizationally focused strategies to support external, customer, and product-focused strategies. The presence and blending of these strategies is unique to each enterprise. These include (but are not limited to) service and quality; environmental quality; agility, learning, and empowerment; cycle-time; and mass customization. Also included is the I/T strategic architecture, which supports the dual strategies of supporting the internal customer set and the externally based business or customer-consumed products. Generally, each requires business process reengineering and organizational redesign to enhance stakeholder value.

- Competitive strategy risks: These are external risks with an external focus. For the enterprise, business strategy risk focuses on the long-term risk involved with political realignments, demographic change, and so forth. For I/T, I/T strategy risk focuses on the risk involved with the resulting changing business structures, including alliances, joint ventures, virtual corporations, and work teams.

- Organizational strategy risks and uncertainties: This category has an internal enterprise focus. Business organization risk focuses on the short-term risks inherent in business process redesign and organizational restructuring, while the I/T group focuses on implementation and delivery risks including I/T definitional uncertainty, I/T technical and implementation risk, and I/T services delivery risk.

We discuss each of these value and risk criteria and suggest a generic scoring system ranging from 0 (where no relationship exists between a particular initiative and the value or risk) to 5 (where there is a significant relationship existing between a particular initiative and the value or risk). This creates a consistent approach for comparing the attributes of unlike initiatives. The next steps—topics in the next chapter—are those of determining which of the factors are important to the enterprise and how comparatively important they are to each other.

FINANCIAL VALUES

In the early 1900s, Pareto theorized that when evaluating the worth of alternative choices in public projects, one project was superior to another when the net benefits were larger.[3] Pareto's work was the basis for original cost-benefit analysis development. Those in management science, economics, accounting, operations research, and other disciplines refined and reworked the original Pareto optimality criterion to suit their own needs. Thus accounting practices developed and emerged as a discipline in business schools after World War II. These practices focus on measuring and reporting after-the-fact financial performance in a standard way—and for an environment dominated by mass production paradigms.

Within a short time, business managers found that assessing future impact on financial performance required different tools than those in use for measuring financial performance. Translating line of business (LOB) or enterprise strategic direction into financial goals and balancing the supply and demand for corporate funds is a question of assessing alternatives, which is different from measuring outcomes. Although inadequate, traditional cost-benefit analysis techniques are still the common financial bridge or language between assessing alternatives and measuring outcomes. For this reason, traditional cost-benefit analysis is the starting point for the discussion of value and risk.

Business-Based Financial Values

There are two types of costs and benefits. They are tangible, characterized by a known and subsequently measurable dollar impact on cash flow, and intangible, characterized by having a difficult- to impossible-to-measure dollar impact on cash flow.

Certain assumptions are inherent in any cost-benefit analysis. They are:

- Components of any initiative affecting costs and benefits are definable. They include costs and benefits controlled or managed by the I/T function, and costs and benefits associated with initiatives and impacts on other functional organizations. Using current (generally mandated) accounting practices, they become quantified.
- Estimates of scope, size, type, and timing of costs and benefits for both I/T and LOB organizations is complete and agreed to by all management involved (sponsor, user, strategic planning, I/T management).

To determine tangible costs and benefits require the following steps:

- Break down the effort using the work functions affected by the initiative.
- For each function involved, identify alterations, additions, or deletions associated with the specific job processes.
- Determine the cost of performing the job process involved. Cost categories include labor, contract, equipment, facilities, material, and supplies. Cost sources include organization and function budgets or projections using time, volume, and labor rates.
- Determine the effects on indirect costs caused by the change, such as inventory carrying costs and property taxes.
- Determine the changes to the job processes because of the new initiative.
- Determine the cost of performing the process after modification.
- Determine where additional costs will occur in the future if no change occurs in the job process. Categories include (but are not limited to) additional volume re-

sulting in more labor, equipment, and material or supplies; new or modified facilities; and additional indirect costs.

- Calculate the difference between performing the process the old way and the new way. The result of this calculation is the expected tangible benefit or an added cost of doing business.

After determining the expected benefits and costs of the implementation of an initiative, the relationship of benefits to costs requires definition. There are several approaches for developing the cost-benefit relationship; however, it requires a common method for the decision-making process to maintain equity among investment priorities. These approaches include:

- Simple Return-on-Investment or the accounting rate of return: Simple ROI is the ratio of the average annual net income of the project divided by the internal investment in the project. Analysts plot the implementation and operating costs and the expected benefits. The point at which accumulated benefits exceed accumulated costs establishes the point where the base ROI occurs. Use of this method assumes that funds are available within the organization to support implementation as well as any other cost-justified projects. Because the existence of unconstrained resources is more theory than fact, this method is not viable as a standalone justification method when competing for investment dollars.
- Discounted rate of return, or discounted cash flow method, or internal rate of return (IRR): Discounted rate of return is probably the most widely used of all the analytical techniques. It determines the discount rate at which the present value of cash receipts equals the present value of cash expenditures.
- Net present value: This method uses a discount rate determined from the company's cost of capital to establish the present dollar value of a project. The discount rate determines the present value of both cash receipts and cash outlays. It is possible to adjust the discount rate to reflect other criteria set by management, such as an adjustment to compensate for perceived risk.
- Profitability index or present value index: The profitability index creates a ratio, which results from dividing the present value of cash receipts by the present value of the cash outlay. Applying a discount rate determines the present value of the cash flow and outflow. It is not as popular as IRR or NPV.
- Payback period: A commonly used but technically deficient method, payback period determines the amount of time required for the cumulative cash inflow from a project to equal the initial investment.
- Present worth: Businesses use this method because it provides an accurate picture of profitability. This method assumes that the funding required to support some or all of the cost-justified activities is borrowed or acquired through the sale of stock. The costs and benefits get plotted over time as in the simple ROI

calculation. Analysts discount the cash flow for future periods, based upon the enterprise's cost of acquiring funds (normally available from the treasurer's office in the company).

- Probability of attainment: This method is an expansion of either simple ROI or present worth. It describes varying levels of confidence within the expected benefits. Using this technique results in three sets of benefit values. The first set of numbers represents the benefits that are certain of achievement (generally, 80 percent confidence level and above). The second set represents the benefits that are probably achievable (50% confidence level and above). The third represents any benefits realized if all goes well. Analysts set and summarize the probability for realizing the benefits related to each job process and to indirect costs. The middle figure is the generally used basis for ROI and present worth calculations.

Other methods of developing a cost-benefit analysis use techniques that require more sophistication. These include decision analysis, structural models, and break-even analysis. Decision analysis applies game theory to business decisions; structural models use models for the line of business and impact of change; and break-even analysis applies subjective assessments of benefits to objective assessments of costs.

A significant problem associated with any of the above methods is the concept of risk. The methods by themselves (with the exception of probability attainment and net present value) do not consider any type of risk. Other factors ignored by these methods include, for example, definitional uncertainty (the lack of specificity of definitional scope by a project proponent) and any strategy match (the degree to which a proposed project is consistent with the strategy of the enterprise). Other critical factors that may result as project benefits but that are not apparent to the typical financial analyst are similarly ignored.

I/T-Based Financial Values

By far the easiest I/T application with which to calculate the costs and benefits is one that is substitutive by nature, because it substitutes *machine power* for *people power*—and both are easy to measure. Examples are payroll, accounting, and billing applications—all alignment in nature. While estimating and subsequently measuring these benefits is easy, the size of the total benefits is generally low in today's organizations, unless linked with business process or organizational redesign, which in turn, complicates the calculations.

Complementary applications focus on increasing productivity and employee effectiveness for existing activities, for example, a marketing network and terminals for order entry or query by customers in their offices. These applications link to the bottom-line performance of the enterprise directly (through revenue acceleration and increased customer retention) or indirectly (through increased productivity resulting from restructuring). These types of applications generally contribute more to improved business performance than do the substitutive applications, but both prediction and subsequent measurement of benefits are more difficult to do because they generally involve both business process and job and/or organizational redesign.

Innovative applications are those designed to maintain or improve competitive position by, for example, creating a new market or creating differentiation through operating cost reductions that flow through to the customer. While potential value to the business is high, the prediction and measurement approaches are speculative. This is due to the nature of creating entry barriers and having to be both *first* and *right* at the same time. Being first causes a problem in estimating both the costs and benefits, because there are few precedents to follow. Being right brings up the issue of estimating the risks associated with failure.

It is unfortunate for the cost accountants and financial analysts in the industry—and staff dealing with them—that innovative applications are the bedrock of strategic transformation as are the complementary applications linked to process and organizational redesign. These applications are the ones that provide intangible benefits through added value to R&D activities, improved time-to-market, and enhanced customer service and quality. They contribute efficiencies in business processes and support effective organization restructures—critical elements in creating and sustaining transformation.

Intangible benefits, then, are the reasons for an enterprise taking actions that immediately or directly measurable benefits can't justify. Certain assumptions are also basic to the identification and development of intangible benefit estimates:

- Estimates of scope, size, type, and timing of all benefits associated with the initiative for both I/T and the LOB organizations are complete and agreed to by management (sponsor, user, strategic planning, I/T).
- The types of intangible benefits included in the decision-making process are components of, and further characterize the overall, overarching business strategy, and are applied cross-organizationally.

The sponsor of a proposed initiative has the responsibility to relate intangible benefits (which we call strategic values and stakeholder values) to costs. They must convince the decision-makers that other factors are equally important, or of even greater importance than measurable costs and benefits. Motivating groups behind these initiatives may include regulatory agencies, shareholders, customers, employees, and the financial community—all stakeholders of the enterprise.

STRATEGIC VALUES

Strategic values flow from initiatives that contribute to the accomplishment of the externally focused stated goals of the enterprise. These values are market and product oriented, often described as market share, market creation, product differentiation, customer relationships, and so forth. They focus on the achievement of specific market, product or customer strategies (*strategic match*), the creation of new markets or the increase of current share (*competitive advantage*), and the protection of current market share (*competitive response*). Additionally, this group of values includes the availability and quality of information used in any decision-making processes regarding the execution of these strategies (management information for CSFs). Together, these four strategic values represent the *strategic face* that the enterprise presents to the market and to its outside stakeholders.

Strategic Match

Strategic match focuses on the degree to which an initiative supports or aligns with the enterprise or LOB stated strategic goals. This value provides an avenue for enhancing the scores of innovative applications that are in direct support of achieving business goals. We assume that a strategy is in place for the enterprise or LOB and that the participants in the planning process sufficiently understand the strategy so that they can agree upon the specific contribution level of the initiative. For an I/T initiative, this category emphasizes the close relationship between I/T planning and business planning, and it assesses the degree to which a potential initiative contributes to the accomplishment or enhancement of the business strategy. (For example, a university may base its strategy on the recruitment of students, and an I/T initiative that improves the successful recruitment of quality students becomes especially valuable.) For purposes of the scoring process, the strategic planning department will identify the allowable strategic goals contained in the current plan for use by those scoring this category.

Initiatives that form an integral and essential part of the corporate strategy deserve a higher *strategic match score* than those projects that do not, regardless of the economic impact (e.g., ROI, NPV) calculation. Obviously, there are many ways to obtain a favorable short-term economic impact. However, it is generally more desirable to obtain the desired economic impact and simultaneously move toward a broader corporate purpose. Strategic match assesses the value of moving toward that long-term goal (and requires its expressed existence).

The scores range from 0 (having no linkage to stated business strategy goals) to 5 (having a direct linkage). Each enterprise should develop its own unique descriptors. (For illustrative purposes, a sample set follows for Strategic Match. A generic set of descriptors for each of the remaining factors appears in Appendix II.)

0   The initiative has no direct or indirect relationship to the achievement of any stated enterprise, LOB, or departmental strategic goals.
1   The initiative has no direct or indirect relationship to the achievement of any stated enterprise, LOB, or departmental strategic goals, but will achieve greater operational efficiencies.
2   The initiative has no direct or indirect relationship to the achievement of any stated enterprise, LOB, or departmental strategic goals, but the initiative is a prerequisite to another initiative (or initiatives) that achieves a portion of an enterprise, LOB, or departmental goal.

3   The initiative has no direct or indirect relationship to the achievement of any stated enterprise, LOB, or departmental strategic goals, but the initiative is a prerequisite initiative (a necessary precursor) to another initiative (or initiatives) that does achieve an enterprise, LOB, or departmental strategic goal.

4   The initiative directly achieves a portion of a stated enterprise or LOB strategic goal.

5   The initiative directly achieves a stated enterprise or LOB strategic goal.

Because the strategic match score depends on the degree to which the proposed initiative corresponds to established strategic goals, initiatives that are integral and a critical part of the enterprise, LOB, or departmental strategy receive a higher strategic match score than those that support the strategy to a lesser degree.

Competitive Advantage

There are three basic objectives that a company must strive for if it expects to gain *competitive advantage:*

- It must position itself to alter the industry structure. The enterprise must support initiatives that will change the degree to which buyers, suppliers, new entrants, and substitutes or rivals influence competition.
- It must improve the organization's position in its existing businesses. The enterprise must support initiatives that can differentiate a company's products or services or change the competitive scope of its business.
- It must create new business opportunities. There are several ways an initiative can contribute to competitive advantage, including I/T initiatives to sell or use information as a by-product of the current business or to use internal information processing capabilities to start a new line of business. Airline reservation systems are examples of this kind of value.

The assessment for competitive advantage considers the major strategy being followed by the business. Using Porter's (1985) terms, this would be an implementation of cost leadership, differentiation, or focus.[4] The assessment mechanism to support cost leadership converges around cost avoidance, cost reduction, and identification and exploitation of any sources of cost advantage. Differentiation strategy assessment converges around a scale focusing on those factors that would make the product unique, and the uniqueness must be one valued by the customer. Finally, focus strategy rests on the target segments of the enterprise as a subset of the total market potential.

   To include competitive advantage as a strategic value, the enterprise must develop assessment descriptors that accurately reflect the chosen strategy and the potential contribution to its support. Competitive advantage scoring depends upon the degree to which the proposed initiative directly or indirectly provides the enterprise or line of business (LOB) with an increased ability to compete for market share. For example, initiatives that provide information to increase the area sales staff's ability to measurably increase sales will receive a high competitive advantage score. In addition, initiatives that measurably reduce the cost of sales in markets where price is an important factor, also score high. Strategic planning would normally provide to those scoring the initiatives a list of market or product segments in which competition is a significant factor.

Competitive Response

Competitive response measures the degree to which failure to successfully address the initiative will cause competitive damage to the enterprise. Although similar to the concepts of opportunity cost and competitive advantage, this category includes the risk of losing market share that, once lost, may be difficult or even impossible to recover. This can occur because competitors already provide the service, product, or data exchange, or the industry requires the capability, or some authority mandates the initiative as a condition of continued business activity. Examples include the installation of automatic teller machines at one bank, which forces competing banks to offer the same service, or when one major airline introduces a special promotional fare and others quickly follow to maintain current market share.

For I/T initiatives, competitive response looks at the timely implementation of projects as a possible preemptive move to prevent the competition from gaining a foothold. The assessment of value ranges on the low side (a score of 0 or 1) if postponing the project for a year won't compromise competitive position. On the high side (a score of 4 or 5), postponement of the project will result in competitive disadvantage to the enterprise, a loss of competitive opportunity, or curtailment of existing activities. Intermediate values reflect the more balanced potential.

Competitive response provides the avenue for expressing the specific window of opportunity for an innovative application in the overall economic assessment. It acknowledges the element of time as an overriding imperative for implementing strategic business initiatives.

Management Information for Critical Success Factors

The ability of management to consistently make an informed decision is important to all companies. *Management information for critical success factors* is an assessment of an initiative's contribution to management's need for information on critical activities, for example, activities directly involved in the realization of the enterprise mission, as distinguished from support and accounting activities. Support functions supply resources to the critical activities, such as a spare parts inventory, truck maintenance, and so forth, for a trucking company, while accounting activities translate the critical and support functions into financial terms.

Assessing an initiative's contribution to critical activities of the business requires that the enterprise identify its critical success factors. Information in support of the business CSFs reflects the degree to which the initiative provides management information on the key activities of the enterprise or LOB. As an example, a natural gas utility selling and delivering product to domestic households includes the following activities:

- Providing service to customers.
- Scheduling and dispatching field personnel and equipment.
- Safety monitoring.
- Market demand and market share forecasting.
- Financial statement forecasting.
- Equipment servicing.
- Regulatory filing support
- Legislative analysis and lobbying.

The scoring in this category depends on the degree to which the initiative provides management information that allows decision makers to assess operations and to make them more effective, materially benefiting the enterprise. The score also depends on the extent to which the management information supports the predefined key CSFs and key activities. Specific CSFs might be in planning (facility forecasting, production capacity planning), in management control (service performance, quality control), or in operations control (facility scheduling, customer services, claim processing). The definition of specific core activities for an enterprise and its associated CSFs is necessarily unique to each organization. As a consequence, although the core activities will be different, the assessment descriptors applied against the core activities will not be. This value factor provides an avenue for championing initiatives that provide better management information and systems to support the business strategy.

STAKEHOLDER VALUES

Stakeholder values flow from initiatives that contribute to the successful execution of enterprise strategies that enhance broad stakeholder interests and represent directional or transformational change. As noted in the chapter introduction, while each stakeholder has a different view of value, there are some common themes. All express interest in environmental quality, but each place a different value or priority on its importance. The same is true for service and quality, and the other stakeholder values that enhance the ability to adapt quickly to new competitive environments and opportunities. These values and value systems tend to be difficult to initiate and execute in isolation because they affect and pervade the entire enterprise. As a result, the enterprise must weave these values into the entire fabric of the enterprise strategy and culture to have any hope for achieving them—which tends to require jointly executed business process reengineering and organizational restructuring, jointly planned by business and I/T. These values also tend to create long-term enterprise viability rather than any short-term revenues.

Restructuring business processes takes many forms. Essentially, it enhances the ability to get a new product or an improved one to the customer expeditiously, incurring the lowest costs to produce the quality and service the customer expects. Service and quality programs are an element, as are initiatives involving information empowerment, work team support, R&D-to-product and time-to-market processes and procedures.

Organizational restructuring has some consistent themes, too, and many overlap with business process reengineering—it is difficult to imagine significant business process restructures not requiring accompanying organizational restructures. Likewise, it is difficult to imagine a corporate goal of information empowerment if there is no associated effort to change the form of the organization or to change the business processes and the way the business physically works to make it more agile. The concept of the anywhere, anytime workplace, placing great emphasis on mobility, may change where or how people get their work done without ever changing the business process itself, but it has a great impact on organizational form and issues involving supervision, staffing, and training.

As a consequence, the value lies in the identification and development of the overarching business strategies (such as environmental awareness or service and quality) and the specific business strategy (such as redefining the distribution channel between the enterprise and the consumer) and the cumulative and synergistic effects that the techniques applied to execute the strategy may have on the enterprise. Likewise, implementing the concept of the anywhere, anytime workplace is of little value unless it is of strategic importance—such as improving the service level to the customer for a company whose strategy is differentiation, or by significantly reducing overhead costs for an enterprise whose strategy is cost leadership.

In this section, we introduce six stakeholder values—*service and quality; environmental quality; agility, learning, and empowerment; cycle-time; mass customization;* and *strategic I/T architecture.* These transformational values represent broad-based, long-term themes for change within the enterprise and often appear as isolated fragments rather than strategic themes in the current planning processes. Each has the quality of time sensitivity. That is, if they are important at all in driving industry or enterprise change, they require timely initiation and implementation to maintain or improve current market position. We do not suggest that these six themes are all necessary for every strategic transformation, nor that they represent all the possible strategic themes. They are simply the frequently recurring strategic themes for enterprises committed to transformation.

Service and Quality

In the early 1990s, there was a spate of books on the importance of *service and quality* initiatives. While the volume of new books on the subject has lessened, the importance of the topic has not. Within any enterprise, initiatives purported to improve service and quality levels are plentiful. The problem is that they often suffer from a lack of co-ordination. They often appear isolated to a single function or department, and there is no linkage between the expected results and a measurable improvement in the end product that the *customer cares about.* This is not to say that they are not worthwhile efforts. Rather, the improvement of service and quality levels are an enterprisewide issue, and should, therefore, have a focused, enterprisewide strategy. Additionally, the strategy should be a recognized investment priority, and any individual initiative, al-though perhaps limited in its initial impact, will have a cumulative and synergistic ef-fect on the overall success of the enterprisewide strategy.

Service and quality initiatives, as noted in Chapter 6, have a synergistic effect enterprisewide and require a long-term continuous commitment to improvement. Ini-tiatives are significantly less successful when limited to a single department or prod-uct line.

Environmental Quality

Environmental quality has become a common rallying cry to many corporate stake-holders. Regulators insist on it, employees want to work in a nontoxic environment, customers express concern about the safety of the product in use as well as the safe disposal of any by-products, and investors express concern about potential liability as a result of the product's production and use.

Environmental quality will remain a recurring strategic theme. While legislation sets limits and standards, simply being a good corporate citizen requires early and vol-untary conformance and participation. Being an industry leader demands it, and per-ceptions of external stakeholders are critical.

Agility, Learning, and Empowerment

Agility, learning, and empowerment focus on making both employees and business processes more flexible and more quickly adaptable to change. It makes them smarter through employee and enterprise investments in continuous, life-time learning. It also empowers, by giving those closest to the problems the necessary information, respon-sibility, and authority for decision-making. It can (and eventually will) change task-time allocations, necessitating business process redesign and/or job redesign, and require different skills for the staff. Agile, flexible, learning organizations of the future build on the empowerment initiatives of today, enabling employees and business proc-esses to be more adaptable.

Cycle-Time

Improving *cycle-time* is a competitive necessity. Cycle-time focuses on all elements in the process, from establishing an innovative culture that stimulates new product ideas through its successful development and production and delivery to the customer at a time that meets or establishes a new industry standard or best practice. This translates into moving products from R&D into production faster, moving products from the producer through the distribution channel to the consumer faster, and responding to specialized customer requirements via mass customization techniques faster than competitive suppliers. All are elements of focusing on cycle-time as a competitive strategy.

Mass Customization

Mass customization requires the ability to more quickly produce an ever greater variety of products through customization. Niche markets and a flexible product line require business processes, organizational design, and information systems—all designed with heterogeneity in mind.

While we think most often of mass customization for production of consumer goods, mass customization principles are applicable to the personalization of services. As such, mass customization principles and strategies are a necessary part of internally and externally focused strategies for I/T involving information empowerment, stakeholder services, and accommodating information sharing via electronic data interchange (EDI) networks, strategic alliances, and virtual corporations.

Strategic I/T Architecture

Until recently, many businesses treated and evaluated I/T initiatives independently. However, the technology, by its very nature, may impose an ordering and urgency for initiatives that go beyond the economic impact of the business domain. Database systems, relational databases, and distributed systems often have an inherent implementation sequence or relationship.

Strategic I/T architecture evaluates the degree to which the initiative aligns with the overall I/T strategies. This alignment reflects in the I/T plan (or blueprint), which provides the structure into which future data, systems, and initiatives fit and identifies priorities. For example, enabling a variety of other application initiatives may initially require a project involving bar codes in a library. Hence, its value derives from its role in contributing to the architecture and infrastructure learning curve. Projects that are an integral part of the plan earn a higher value on this evaluation than projects that are not, ensuring that the viability of the I/T strategy is considered at every application review.

Of all of these values, the business domain values of strategic match, competitive advantage, competitive response, and management information for critical success factors, and the technology domain value of strategic I/T architecture were in our original writings.[2] With an increasing emphasis on initiatives supporting strategic transformation, we—along with our clients—discovered the necessity to rethink previously defined strategic values. We also had to add more explicit, more definitive strategic values (e.g., service and quality; environmental quality; agility, learning, and empowerment; cycle-time; and mass customization) to provide proper focus for strategic planning and subsequent resource allocation. Without the added focus on the creation of long-term values, they were quickly becoming risks for the enterprise.

COMPETITIVE STRATEGY RISKS

While many people use the terms risk and uncertainty interchangeably, never differentiating between the two, we do not. *Risk* occurs when the (planned or assumed) outcome of an action, situation, or initiative is not certain, but where the range of possible outcomes is known and the probabilities associated with these outcomes are known or estimated with some degree of accuracy. *Uncertainty* relates to those actions, situations, or initiatives when the range of outcomes is known, but where the probabilities of outcomes are impossible to accurately estimate, or—in the extreme case—where even the range of possible outcomes is unknown. Elements that contribute to both risk and uncertainty for an enterprise include such things as changing technologies, long-term trends, competitive actions, governmental actions, differential inflation, unexpected labor disruptions, supply and distribution channel changes, market redefinition, and the like. In addition, time can affect some of these risks and uncertainties.

Efforts to cope with these problems include using scenario planning to develop a portfolio of business strategies. By developing and evaluating market scenarios, an enterprise reduces uncertainty. By developing business scenarios that address the outcomes of the market scenarios, the enterprise is able to identify and address risks, thereby reducing or containing some of them, and to develop strategies to avoid or eliminate others. This is done in conjunction with other techniques, such as developing more accurate forecasts of cash flows, making consensus-developed subjective adjustments to some of the factors influencing the outcome of an initiative, establishing a high rate-of-return standard for potentially risky projects, or developing risk management programs. It is necessary to be as clear as possible about the objective and subjective elements that enter into assumptions, projections, and weightings.

Perhaps most important, top management must define their attitude towards risk and uncertainty and communicate this position to the rest of the enterprise, because some risk will impact the economic well-being of an organization and yet lie outside the purview of most of its employees. These risks or uncertainties are, unfortunately, often the very ones affecting or determining the success of the overall strategy.

Business Strategy Risk

Business strategy risk reflects the level of the success of the business strategy itself, given the market dynamics, enterprise dynamics, and timing. For I/T, initiatives associated with a risky business strategy are also at risk, a factor to consider in assessing the viability of an initiative. For example, the application of robotics and flexible manufacturing may reduce costs, but whether a strategy of reduced cost will produce additional business is another question. If the risk has a primary impact on the measurable (financial) benefits, it is possible to address it as part of the economic impact calculations. If, however, the risk is associated with the intangible benefits or values, address it as a separate factor. One manufacturing organization uses the following descriptors to classify the Business Strategy Risk and is sufficiently unique to include here. (Reminder: The compete set of generic descriptors is in Appendix II.)

0   The initiative reflects a strategy that is successful for the industry leaders. It is an industry standard practice and a necessary cost of doing business. No long-term external force (e.g., political realignment, regulatory group, demographic shift) will affect the initiative.

1   The initiative represents a level of change accepted as incremental improvement by suppliers and/or consumers. No long-term external force is likely to affect the initiative.

2   The initiative represents differentiation from industry leaders. Although initially disruptive, suppliers and/or consumers will recognize long-term benefit. No long-term external force is likely to nullify the long-term benefit of the initiative to the supplier and/or consumer or the short-term benefit to the enterprise.

3   Medium risk requires moderate change in supplier and/or consumer relationships. The relationships are strong and a well-defined product or market exists. A long-term external force is likely to nullify the long-term benefit of the initiative to the supplier and/or consumer but not the short-term benefit to the enterprise, which, in turn, may weaken the currently strong relationship.

4   The initiative will require a moderate change in supplier and/or consumer relationships that are weak or relatively new. It is a moderately defined market, but new to the enterprise. A long-term external force may nullify any benefit of the initiative. Alternatively, a market may develop, but not sufficiently enough to sustain the initiative.

5   A high risk requires significant competitive strength to force change associated with supplier or customer relationships, supplier and distribution channels, ordering or inventory or pricing practices, business and industry practices. Alternatively, no clearly defined emerging or existing market collapses due to a previously unrecognized long-term external force, or the initiative may exacerbate long-term external force, forcing withdrawal from market.

Business strategy risk focuses on the long-term risk surrounding competitive strategy and change in the market environment due to changing supplier-consumer relationships, political realignments, demographic trends, or regulatory trends.

I/T Strategy Risk

I/T strategy risk focuses on the competitive strategy risk involved as a result of changing business structures, including alliances, joint ventures, and virtual corporations, and the necessity to support the enterprise as it adjusts to the new demands of the market place. It reflects the level of potential impact on long-term I/T strategy as a whole, including architecture and platform (e.g., closing off future options), systems interdependencies (e.g., incompatible but similar systems in other business functions), business strategy (e.g., mergers, acquisitions and divestitures), business environment change (e.g., industry restructuring, deregulation), equilibrium, and critical skills. This dimension focuses on the volatility of the industry environment and the accommodations the enterprise must make when being forced by others or by its own initiatives.

ORGANIZATIONAL STRATEGY RISKS AND UNCERTAINTIES

While competitive strategy risks focus on externally based risks, organizational strategy risks and uncertainties have an internal enterprise focus. They include *business organization risk, I/T definitional uncertainty, I/T technical and implementation risk,* and *I/T services delivery risk.*

Business Organization Risk

As organizations and business processes evolve, the actual existing skill levels may not match the level anticipated (or required). *Business organization risk* focuses on the short-term risks inherent in business process redesign and organizational restructuring. It reflects the level of sophistication of the various business organizational components involved. These include in-place business plans, business and change management systems, contingency plans, processes and procedures, critical skills and training, management champions, and well-defined and well-understood market needs.

     For an I/T initiative, business organizational risk is an assessment of how much an I/T project depends on new or untested non-I/T corporate or LOB skills, management capabilities, or experience. For example, a business unit that installs on-line terminals to interface to its customers runs the risk of lack of acceptance—upsetting (or further upsetting) the current degree of equilibrium between the organizational units. (Is the receiving business unit ready? Is the off-site customer ready? If not, what are the consequences to the enterprise?)

     While an initiative may look attractive and the technical skills may be available, it may still have an unacceptable level of risk if other required skills are missing. This category also focuses on the extent to which the organization is capable of carrying out the changes required by the initiative, that is, the user/business requirements. This does not include the I/T technical organization, measured under the category of I/T services delivery.

I/T Definitional Uncertainty

I/T definitional uncertainty, along with the remaining I/T technical and implementation risk and I/T services delivery risk focus on implementation and delivery risk and reflects the level of stability (or lack of volatility) of the receiving environment. Generally, definitional uncertainty assesses the specificity of the enterprise (user or business) objectives communicated to the I/T project personnel. When the user cannot properly describe a problem, or the problem consistently changes, the I/T group is hard-pressed to supply an appropriate answer. Essentially another measure of risk, this dimension relates an initiative's potential to reach objectives to the degree to which they can be specified.

I/T Technical and Implementation Risk

I/T technical and implementation risk focuses on the short-term organizational risks evolving around existing skills, hardware and software dependencies, application software dependencies, and application implementation dependencies. It assesses an initiative's dependence on new or untried technologies that may involve a single technology or a combination of new technical skill sets, hardware, or software tools. For example, a mainframe staff designing and building a complex personal computer application can face major difficulties in implementation. An initiative may be inherently risky if it requires the introduction of an untried technology.

Technical and implementation risk reflects five risk components in any I/T project:

- Skills required, reflecting the critical skills level necessary versus available for management and staff.
- Hardware dependencies, reflecting the hardware necessary versus what is currently available and/or in use.
- Software dependencies (other than application software), assessing straightforward versus significant advances in state-of-the-art technology and/or associated software.
- Application software, reflecting commercially available or currently existing versus new state-of-the-art technology and/or associated software, even if accomplished through subcontracting.
- Application dependencies, reflecting the level of complexity of implementation, including the length of the project, new technologies, accuracy of estimates, and complexity of the implementation organization.

The business may (or may not) wish to include these risks as part of its decision-making criteria for funding and strategy development. Whatever the business decision, the I/T organization *must* include these assessments in its strategy development.

I/T Services Delivery Risk

I/T services delivery risk focus is on the short-term organizational risks for the computer service delivery. The assessment is essentially an environmental assessment, involving such factors as data administration, communications, and distributed systems. It reflects the level of change required by the delivery organization, including up-front costs, integration, management training, reorganization requirements, and threat to the current equilibrium. It assesses the degree to which the entire I/T organization is both required to support the project (e.g., the degree of nonproject technical support investment necessary) and the degree to which it prepares to do so. An initiative that requires the support of several functional areas is inherently more complex and difficult to supervise and depends on factors that may not be under the control of the I/T project manager.

Employment of, for example, a relational database or a new client-server system as part of the I/T strategy to improve performance is an example of investment in I/T services delivery. Although relational databases or client-server systems are not risky in and of themselves, the first application developed within an enterprise that depends on this new technology may represent significant risk. This is due to the requirement for the application of new skills, training, and technologies.

TAILORING THE TAXONOMY

All of these factors have some level of importance in strategy development. Nevertheless, focusing the same degree of effort to score each potential investment initiative on its contribution to the full eighteen factors is unproductive. To determine the best I/T investment strategy to support the enterprise strategy, some factors will demand intense discussion of the nuances of contribution, using the scale of 0 to 5. Others may only justify a 0 for no contribution, a 2.5 for moderate contribution, or dependence, and a 5 for high contribution or dependence. Still others may justify only a 0, signifying no contribution or dependence or a 5, signifying high contribution or dependence.

Furthermore, we strongly recommend combining or eliminating factors to tailor the investment profile to the enterprise in order to provide a clearly focused investment strategy. It's better to concentrate on only about half a dozen factors. This approach contributes to a clear articulation of the business strategy and investment rationale and communicates to everyone what is important and how important it is to the enterprise. For example:

- Financial values (business-based financial value and I/T-based financial value): Instead of treating the business and I/T values separately, the enterprise may wish to combine them into one calculation per income- or profit-related initiative.
- Strategic values (strategic match, competitive advantage, competitive response, and management information for critical success factors): Planners could group and address these characteristics as a single category. In this case, the definition of strategic values would be essential and vital support for a strategic business initiative, including regulatory requirements, organizational requirements, and competitive pressures.
- Stakeholder values (service and quality; environmental quality; agility, learning, and empowerment; cycle-time; and mass customization): These factors are not easily combined into one all-inclusive group, nor should they be. Each has a unique characteristic: after the initial successful execution of the strategy (or initiative or group of initiatives), it tends to move from being a specific, bounded initiative to one of becoming an integral part of the continuing business operations and a strategic value. That is, once successfully inculcating service and quality into the organizational culture, continuing it (e.g., improved product to the customer) becomes a competitive necessity to maintain market share. (Note

the example of Motorola in Chapter 8.) For most enterprises, environmental quality also falls into this same category. Agility, learning, and empowerment, although three distinct objectives, tend to be highly interdependent. It is difficult to empower staff without also providing continuing access to the information and the education necessary to make appropriate business decisions. Likewise, it is impossible to create an agile, innovative enterprise, able to recognize and change direction to achieve competitive advantage if staff is lacking an appropriate culture. That culture must sustain the information and learning environment necessary for innovation and responsibility-taking. Cycle-time improvements and mass customization may require an already existing culture of agility, learning, and empowerment and/or service and quality. The specific interdependencies and interrelationships are unique to each enterprise.

- Competitive strategy risks (business strategy risk and I/T strategy risk): These two risks combine into strategy risks as a matter of course when business and I/T develop strategy jointly.

- Organizational strategy risks and uncertainties (business organization risk, and I/T definitional uncertainty, I/T technical and implementation risk, and I/T service delivery risk): Even with a combination of jointly developed business and I/T strategy and distributed computing, these are less likely to collapse into a single category, due to the differing outside influences. However, planners can easily collapse them into the two categories of business and I/T. Outside business influences include unanticipated market or channel restructuring, level of extent of involvement in strategic alliances, outsourcing, and so forth. Outside I/T influences also include the use of outsourcing as well as receiving market dynamics, hardware and software vendors, and unexpected technology-related learning curves.

Thus an enterprise doing joint business and I/T strategy development may have a set of straightforward investment value and risk criteria, consisting of financial values; strategic values; agility, learning and empowerment; cycle-time; strategy risks; and organizational risks. These can effectively express—once weighted to show relative level of importance—a strategy as complex as Motorola, or as relatively simple as Manpower Temporary Services.

OBSERVATIONS

Searching out and investing in initiatives that produce transformation-based value is somewhat analogous to the planning and investment in a college education. For the individual without one, employment opportunities become limited, as are lifetime earnings, with few exceptions. The college graduate invests four years of study in anticipation of a lifetime of exercising professional alternatives at the behest of parents or other stakeholders providing the financial support. Unfortunately, neither the college degree nor the investment in enterprise transformation comes with any guarantees of future success.

Successful transformation requires more than simply developing a transformation strategy. It takes consistent review of the strategy, examining the underlying assumptions for any change, setting appropriate priorities and executing them in appropriate time frames, and measuring accomplishments to validate progress.

In the prior chapter, we introduced the Seven Questions Methodology to help develop appropriate transformation-based scenarios, strategies, and action plans. In this chapter, we developed a blend of traditional value and risk criteria with new criteria appropriate for strategic transformation that provide a basis for introducing a level of objectiveness and consistency into previously subjective and often emotional discussions and comparisons of alternative enterprise initiatives. The next step, and the subject of the next chapter, is to develop and adopt appropriate investment and measurement methodologies.

15

Developing New Justification and Measurement Philosophies

A new corporate consciousness, shaped by the stresses of transformation, defines and sizes new values and risks associated with decision-making. Based upon tangible and intangible criteria, the value and risk factors associated with information economics and transformation provides a framework for I/T value measurement, linking the forecast of business value with the subsequent achievement of business value. By developing and using a management dashboard, we create new measurements of business value.

Previously, we observed that enterprise stakeholders have different values that combine to form the basic business measures, and when stakeholder power shifts, so do the value criteria and value systems they represent. A new corporate consciousness, shaped by the stresses of transformation, increasingly employs largely intangible criteria to define and size new competitive values and risks. New value and risk criterion, once identified, become integral to the enterprise justification and measurement philosophy. However, how to develop and integrate the new measures is at issue. Organizations already recognize the following:

- Measurements are important.
- It is extremely difficult to motivate an organization without an expressed, defined goal.
- It is equally difficult to quantify any progress toward that goal without some kind of yardstick, or measurement, that describes success.

We know from past experience that good measurement systems take time to develop, install, evaluate, validate, and fine-tune. This experience, however, is largely gained from organizations whose initial design criteria reflect the industrial model of mass production and hierarchical management. We also know—through past experience—that staffs tend to ignore bad measurement systems or (worst case), if believed, they begin to mislead not only management, but entire organizations.

Today's organizations have neither the time, money, nor expertise to develop and introduce full-blown operational measurement systems to measure transformational activities at the same time as they tries to make the transformation happen. Driven by these business realities, we offer a set of management or organizational indicators, similar to the dashboard of an automobile—a management dashboard—that indicates, through a variety of measurements, lights, signs and symptoms, the health and progress of the organization. Information economics and its associated value and risk criterion for transformation provide:

- A framework for developing a management dashboard.
- An indication as to which measures are most critical to the business.

The dashboard contains a set of indicators that, taken as a group, point toward successful strategy implementation. Once the initial management dashboard indicators prove valid as correct reflections of the accomplishment (or failure) of strategic direction, we successively link the forecast of business value (from the information economics justification process), with the management dashboard indicators and then with I/T business value measurement. In conjunction with already existing financial measurements, these measurements will link and translate into further business value contributions through updated operational measurement systems.

We can't expect these justification and measurement systems to be right the first time or to be obvious and easy to implement. This task is just as difficult as that of introducing scenario-based planning into an organization still comfortable in its domestic market, or that of reengineering a hierarchical organization, designed around mass production paradigms, into a horizontal one that produces customized products.

INFORMATION ECONOMICS AND JUSTIFYING TRANSFORMATION-BASED INVESTMENTS

We note a twofold problem in justification and measurement. First, we have I/T functions that have no process in place to justify their proposed investments or to subsequently measure the effect of its actual investments on the business values or outcomes of the I/T actions. Second, enterprise transformation depends upon developing and justifying I/T investments that anticipate and support the various business strategy scenarios. To accomplish either requires significant change by the I/T organization.

- I/T organizations must constantly be with, rather than one step behind, the business as it plays out its strategy.
- I/T must be anticipatory in resource allocation by becoming part of the business strategy process.
- I/T and business must both be comfortable with business and I/T intangibles.

In Chapters 12 through 14, we examined new methodological approaches to apply during the enterprise planning efforts. In this chapter, we address the issues of justification and measurement. The theory and a complete case study behind the justification approach that follows appear in the books *Information Economics* and *Information Strategy and Economics.*[1]

Philosophy

The problem that we were initially trying to solve with information economics was, first, that any firm has a limited amount of funds, whether it is operating budgets, or capital money. Second, in determining where to put those funds, return-on-investment (ROI) is helpful but insufficient, due to the inadequacies of dealing with important elements not yet credibly measurable. Third, we want to make decisions among alternatives. We needed to design a vehicle for making decisions about I/T initiatives that answers these concerns:

- It gives us the wisest allocation of our least, or scarce, resources.
- It takes into account any important considerations that are not yet financially credible.
- It allows us to make decisions.

Information economics evolved from its origins as a capital-budgeting tool and exists today as a *process to decide* and a *method for evaluation and assessment.*

Practice

As a method, there are some built-in additions to the traditional financial justification calculations; however, the process perspective is probably more important. The process requires the following:

- Business must clearly state its strategies and priorities.
- Business and I/T must educate each other on any alternatives.
- Business and I/T must communicate and reach consensus.

The information economics process works to build a consensus across all the participating factors in assessment and decision-making. It is of no value for the financial and I/T analysts to be in the corner doing computations if they are not credible to those who must make the final decisions. The process is to get the decision-makers to make the assessments also, or at least concur in them. Consensus, on an individual project, which involves the end user, also involves the business manager and the financial manager, the chief executive officer, and the I/T group.

Consensus is crucial for decision-making among projects and in showing the relative ranking of each project. It requires shared vision.

The information economics process model allows us to define our goals (established by some previous strategic planning process) for the business activity (the shared vision). It also allows us to describe how each project enables success in achieving the objectives and critical success factors (CSFs). The process is as follows:

An enterprise (or line of business) decides what particular combination of factors is important to the definition and accomplishment of its specific business strategy and develops its business investment profile (see Table 15-1). The business investment profile includes criteria such as financial contribution, supporting current strategy, creating competitive advantage, and reducing business risks. The I/T portion of the business investment profile includes building or improving the strategic I/T infrastructure (people, platforms, architectures) necessary to support current and future business strategy and reduce I/T risks if this is important to the enterprise. We characterize, or describe, each potential project using a relative scale based upon enterprise-dependent descriptors that reflect the contribution level of that initiative to the business investment criteria.

Every business enterprise develops its own unique business investment profile that reflects their specific strategies and the comparative importance (or weight) of each.

Business and technology management choose the descriptor that best characterizes the contribution level of the initiative to the business objective, along with input from potential users, business finance, and strategic planning. All concerned parties must come to a consensus using the language descriptors to describe the risks, benefits, and contributions associated with the initiative. After reaching consensus, each of the language descriptors (or characterizations) converts to a numeric scale. (We use 0 to 5, where 0 represents no contribution or relationship to achieving and supporting the specific criteria. A 5 represents a significant dependence on the initiative to achieve the business goal. Only after achieving consensus is the project included in the list of potential projects for funding. (See Table 15-2 for an example of a set of initiatives that went through the process.)

Likewise, every business enterprise will tailor the specific descriptors of each investment decision criterion, based upon its own unique requirements.

Factor	Weight
Financial Value (FV)	10
Strategic Value (SV)	7
Stakeholder Value:	
Service and Quality (S&Q)	1
Strategic I/T Architectures (S(I/T-A))	2
Business Organization Risk (R(B))	1
I/T Risk (R(I/T))	6

This enterprise is pursuing an investment strategy with equal emphasis on financial viability and pursuit of strategy, and is very risk averse regarding any inherently risky I/T initiatives. The investment strategy reflects the enterprise objectives of insuring shorter-term cash flows (a weight of 10 for financial values), and strengthening longer-term competitive strategies (a combined weight of 10 for strategic and stakeholder values).

ABC Corp. recently invested heavily in establishing itself as a major EDI hub in its industry. The success of its business strategy—using EDI to further strengthen supply chain relationships—is highly dependent upon its I/T organization delivering no risk, fail-safe I/T applications for its supply chain partners to use. Although the business enterprise itself was technologically adept, it was unsure of the technology skills of all of its EDI supply chain partners. Thus, it reflected a minimal concern for its own business organizational risk (a risk of 1) while significantly concerned with avoiding risks associated with its trading partners' volatility, skills, and expectations (a combined risk of 6).

Table 15-1   Sample Business Investment Profile for ABC Corp.

The participants assessing strategic (business) values are from the business domain. I/T management doesn't interpret the business strategy and decide what is (or is not) in support of it. Those discussing and scoring strategic value are those who understand the nuances of the business thrust. User department management, finance management, and corporate planning management (or their equivalents), although initially scoring the initiative from their own respective views, negotiate with each other to develop a final value that is acceptable to each. Table 15-3 illustrates the relationships of the participants and their roles in the process.

Senior business management (generally a management steering committee or equivalent) will, in the interim, fine-tune the weights for the weighted business investment profile that determines the relative importance for each of the criteria.

A member of the steering committee or staff converts the weighted business investment profile to reflect its numeric proportions. (We convert the profile so that the combination of all the positive criteria combines to equal twenty and express risk as a negative in Table 15-4 (top line). This results in a perfect project scoring a 5 for all values with no associated risk and a score of 100. (Alternatively, we could

Evaluator	Business Domain				Technology Domain	
(Factor)	FV	SV	S&Q	R(B)	S(I/T-A)	R(I/T)
Customer Billing:						
Business Domain	1	4	3	0	xxxxxxxxxxxxxxxxxxxx	
Technology Domain	xxxxxxxxxxxxxxxxxxxxxxxxxxxxxx				2	3
Driver Dispatch:						
Business Domain	5	4	4	1	xxxxxxxxxxxxxxxxxxxx	
Technology Domain	xxxxxxxxxxxxxxxxxxxxxxxxxxxxxx				4	2
Parcel Tracking (Barcode):						
Business Domain	4	4	5	2	xxxxxxxxxxxxxxxxxxxx	
Technology Domain	xxxxxxxxxxxxxxxxxxxxxxxxxxxxxx				5	3
Parcel Tracking (EDI):						
Business Domain	3	5	3	4	xxxxxxxxxxxxxxxxxxxx	
Technology Domain	xxxxxxxxxxxxxxxxxxxxxxxxxxxxxx				4	3
Customer Analysis:						
Business Domain	1	5	0	0	xxxxxxxxxxxxxxxxxxxx	
Technology Domain	xxxxxxxxxxxxxxxxxxxxxxxxxxxxxx				0	2

Where:

FV	Financial Value
SV	Strategic Value
S&Q	Stakeholder Value - Business - Service and Quality
R(B)	Risk - Business Organization Risk
S(I/T-A)	Stakeholder Value - Strategic I/T Architectures
R(I/T)	Risk - I/T Risk

Table 15-2   Sample Set of Initiatives after Undergoing Contribution Assessment.

use a different set of descriptors and express risk as a positive factor, which also requires a concurrent assessment of the effectiveness and cost of risk management programs.)

By multiplying individual scalars of each project by the appropriate factor weights in the investment profile and summing them, we develop the project score. Next, we order the projects by their scores. The project with the highest

Participant in Process	Value	Investment	
Business Manager(s)	Business Domain Feasibility	Technology Domain Viability	
Financial Officer(s)			
Corporate Planner(s)			
I/T Manager(s)			Agreed Ranking
Consensus: Agreed Values and Evaluations			

Table 15-3   Information Economics Initiative Assessment.

score represents the initiative that contributes the most to achieving the overall business strategy; the project with the lowest score represents the undertaking that contributes the least. The basis of funding decisions is the consensus-supported evaluations. Table 15-4 illustrates the weighted business profile applied to the previously scored set of initiatives and the relative contribution (total score) of each to the business strategy.

Obviously, for this approach to work, we must be secure in the knowledge that:

- We have the best potential initiatives, given the business strategy.
- The business investment profile truly reflects the business strategy.
- I/T has a set of scenarios for the continuing evolution of its architectures based upon alternative business strategies and architectures.

Once capturing all the information, doing "what if" analyses become an almost trivial exercise in support of evaluating the potential effects on I/T due to changing business conditions or shifts in business strategy.

The process of information economics establishes the relative contribution of (I/T) projects to the achievement of a predetermined (business) strategy.

Evaluator	Business Domain				Technology Domain		Total
(Factor)	FV	SV	S&Q	R(B)	S(I/T-A)	R(I/T)	
Weighted Business							
Investment Profile	+10	+7	+1	−1	+2	−6	
Driver Dispatch	+50	+28	+4	−1	+8	−12	77
P'Track (Barcode)	+40	+28	+5	−2	+10	−18	63
Parcel Track (EDI)	+30	+35	+3	−4	+8	−18	54
Customer Analysis	+10	+35	+0	−0	+0	−12	33
Customer Billing	+10	+28	+3	−0	+4	−18	27

Where:

FV	Financial Value
SV	Strategic Value
S&Q	Stakeholder Value - Business - Service and Quality
R(B)	Risk - Business Organization Risk
S(I/T-A)	Stakeholder Value - Strategic I/T Architectures
R(I/T)	Risk - I/T Risk

Table 15-4   Sample Assessment and Ranking of Initiatives.

Information economics helps to effectively communicate:

- The potential value of I/T to business management.
- It provides the basis for going back and measuring the actual impact of I/T actions on business performance.
- It helps establish the direct linkage between I/T and the accomplishment of business objectives.

It is also an extension of management planning for a business function or line of business because it is a tool to address what I/T can do to collapse business cycles, integrate business functions, improve quality and productivity for the business unit, or prepare itself to support future business change. The approach works well for this last function because it forces the identification of specific business objectives and the role I/T plays in achieving those objectives. It forces managers to determine the business-based reasons for funding I/T projects that are most likely to move the business (unit) forward.

This is linkage: initiative objectives are business-driven, and priority decisions are business management-driven. However, many of the business objectives addressed in solving linkage are soft—customer satisfaction, service and quality, management information—though necessary elements in determining future competitiveness. Experience shows that the prioritization processes and value determination schemes of information economics, which are detailed to a level predetermined by the business organization and include relatively soft (although consensus-driven) judgments, may not persuade senior business management unless they fully understand and participate in at least some portion of the process.

In summary, the following are the salient features of information economics:

- All initiatives are measured with the same yardstick: Senior business management determines the strategy mix and the importance of each element, creating the weighted business investment profile. They are the only ones that can modify it.
- Eliminates hidden agendas and misunderstandings of strategy: The business investment profile, in combination with the discussions surrounding the actual scoring process, communicates clearly to all what the strategy is.
- Consensus-driven process: Consensus not only eliminates the squeaky wheel funding phenomena, it broadens the participants' perspective and knowledge of the business and its processes.
- Ability to completely tailor to each enterprise: Each enterprise determines its own investment profile and weights and modifies them when business conditions dictate.
- Creates a structure where intangibles get treated in a predetermined and consistent manner: Whether ignored, simply acknowledged, assessed for strength, or assigned a relative range of future value contribution, all important intangible benefits get equitable treatment.

Since the basis of information economics is to establish and evaluate the linkage between I/T and the accomplishment of business objectives, it is the bridge that connects future systems and I/T scenario planning.

VALUE, RISK, AND PERFORMANCE INDICATORS: THE MANAGEMENT DASHBOARD

Every company has its own set of measurement systems that it deems appropriate and that it uses as a yardstick to measure and report various changes and accomplishments. Flash measurements, or indicators, present a quick picture—like a Polaroid—of the state of the business at a particular moment, and it is often up to each manager to interpret the results and make them meaningful as input to their short-term future decisions.

Management Dashboard

A few years ago, Pierre deLasalle (Gemeentekrediet Van Belgic, Belgium), Dr. Elod Polgar (IBM Suisse, Switzerland), Professor Guido G.M. Dedene (Katholieke Universiteit Leuven, Belgium), and Pierluigi Feliziani (Banca Agricola Milanese, Italy), spoke of their ideas on the necessity to develop the same kind of performance indicators for I/T—a kind of automobile dashboard—whose dials and gauges would give early warning that I/T was about to experience some malfunction. The problem was that every I/T department was different, each had different strengths and weaknesses, development philosophies, and operational charters from business management, but more significantly, each played different roles in the development and support of business strategy. In the ensuing business cycles, these differences seem to have become more acute, while the need to develop some set of indicators, particularly considering transformation activities, has escalated.

Increasingly, I/T is becoming a part of the business strategy, rather than simply being aligned with the strategy after the fact. At the same time, no one can easily demonstrate and prove that one strategy is universally more valid than another for accomplishing a successful transformation of either business or I/T. These two observations lead away from the idea of an automobile dashboard's standard instrumentation and toward a concept that creates a set of management indicators tailored to reflect the strategies embodied in the information economics investment profile. The indicators may change over time to reflect shifts in strategy; they may require elimination because they prove invalid, not useful, or even misleading; or they may require enhancement because they prove more useful than originally conceived. We call this dynamic set of performance indicators the management dashboard.

This leads to the question of when and what performance indicators included in the management dashboard need institutionalizing through the creation of a formal, operational measurement system. Unfortunately, when times are good, taking time to develop measurement systems (and validate the measurements themselves) seems somehow less strategic than investing that same amount of time in creating more product or service for which there is an immediate demand. Equally unfortunate is the consequence: when we don't measure, we don't detect subtle change until it is too late.

Companies often focus new measurement systems on measuring what it should have measured to prevent past problems. Instead, it should focus on creating new measurement systems to complement and measure the effectiveness of new management practices, organizational structures, and business strategies in the context of changing market and competitive structures, shifting stakeholder values, and demographics.

Every company must abide by (at this point, country by country) standard accounting practices to report financial performance to stakeholders outside the enterprise. However, little else is standard or common between companies when performance indicators relate to effectiveness of management or managers, manufacturing techniques, execution of strategy, deployment of core competencies, flexibility of production, quality programs, or energy conservation. Some of these effectiveness indicators are important to decision-making and communication among internal stakeholders, while others are important as communication vehicles to the external stakeholders and trigger decision-making. What is most important, however, is that all of these effectiveness indicators are vital to successful enterprise transformation activities. Accordingly, these indicators require special attention—both at the time of new initiative justification and during the implementation process—because they are useful indicators of progress towards future success.

> *Measurement criteria, however defined, are important because stakeholders—employees (both individual workers and managers), functional organizations, and outsiders (both critics and customers)—pay attention to them.*

Individual workers and managers may view measurements as goals to work toward to achieve promotions or special compensation, and functional organizations may reorganize or reengineer their activities to meet financial or production targets. Stakeholders outside the organization may use them as yardsticks to compare their enterprise performance and activities with their competition. This means that there can, and probably will be, a number of different indicators and measurement systems related to the same activity, but designed to communicate, motivate, or assuage different stakeholders.

Consider, for example, the desire to be a good corporate citizen through a demonstrated contribution to environmental quality. Reduce, reuse, and recycle becomes measurement criteria integrated into daily activities—for example, reduction of raw material waste, percentage of recycled paper used, percentage of rejects reworked and used or recycled. (These same environmental quality measurements may also be part of service and quality measurement systems.) Functional organizations may translate financial targets into specific operational and financial objectives such as cost savings through waste reduction, cost savings through use of recycled paper (or sale of paper products to a recycler), or reduced production time and cost through improved quality of manufactured components. When the enterprise reports its environmental activities to various external stakeholders, each type of stakeholder will receive a different report (and message). Regulatory agencies will get the facts they require, and no more. Stockholders, potential investors, and environmental groups will probably receive progress reports detailing reduced emissions or reduced toxic waste and energy saved. They may also receive plans for the future that specifically demonstrate good corporate citizenship combined with the ability to sustain and improve corporate competitiveness.

The point of this discussion is simple. If something is important, we should measure it. These measures may take a variety of forms and be used in a variety of ways—and all are necessary. Portraying a good corporate image to potential investors is just as important as demonstrating a sound financial structure. Communicating a strategy through enunciated goals and measurements to an organization is just as important as being able to report the progress towards achieving those goals to investors and regulators. Using financial accounting measures of return-on-investment (ROI) and return-on-gross-assets (ROGA) will continue, so we can't ignore them—thus our emphasis on the I/T organization and its responsibility to deliver and measure its contribution to business value. However, when using these same measurements in isolation, they often provide misleading signals about activities involving, for example, innovation and continuous improvement—two activities necessary to sustain competitiveness. Consequently, there are multiple (and sometimes overlapping) performance indicators in the enterprise—each designed for a specific purpose, but linking as contributors to (and receivers of) other performance indicators that may eventually evolve into institutionalized measurement systems.

> *Some of the indicators for the management dashboard may involve measures that are financial in nature, while others may be highly subjective. Similarly, some of the measures have an internal focus, while the design of others suggests (or requires) communication with an audience outside the enterprise.*

Balanced Scorecard

Although the factors making up the information economics investment profile are useful in defining and communicating the enterprise strategy with its financial and broad strategic goals for financial justification, the management dashboard provides initial indicators that attempt to reflect progress toward that strategy. Both require a translation into operational factors (and measurements) as the enterprise attempts to reform itself and begin to execute the strategy. A highly compatible approach with information economics and the concept of the management dashboard is the balanced scorecard.[2] This approach, developed and documented by Robert Kaplan and David Norton, provides a balanced presentation of both financial and operational measures. The scorecard "includes financial measures that [reflect] the results of actions already taken. Measures also show the operational aspects of how the financial measures were achieved, along with operational measures that are the drivers of future financial performance" (e.g., customer satisfaction levels, innovation and continuous improvement activities, and internal business process reengineering).

The balanced scorecard, along with investment profile factors and management dashboard indicators, focus on strategy rather than on control. It employs measures that move companies forward in the successful accomplishment of the strategy. The scorecard uses goals and measures developed from four perspectives: financial, customer, internal business, and innovation and learning. Translating and migrating the justification-based factors of information economics to the balanced scorecard is relatively straightforward. (See Table 15-5 as an example.) Some investment factors may appear in more than one balanced scorecard perspective but that is because the factor may involve both internal and external stakeholders. For example, I/T Services Delivery Risk may require measurement perspectives for both the internal users or stakeholders in production scheduling (internal business perspective and an automated order entry system) and external users or stakeholders (customer perspective and an automated order entry system linked to the customer via EDI or to suppliers who do just-in-time deliveries).

New Information Economics	Balanced Scorecard Perspective	Intellectual & Financial Accounting for I/T-based Projects
Business-based Financial Values	Financial	Financial, Structural
I/T-based Financial Values	Financial	Financial, Structural
Strategic Match	Customer	Structural, Customer
Competitive Advantage	Customer	Structural, Customer
Competitive Response	Customer	Structural, Customer
Management Information for CSF's	Internal Business	Structural, Human
Service and Quality	Customer	Structural, Customer
Environmental Quality	Customer	Structural, Customer
Agility and Empowerment	Innovation and Learning	Structural, Human
Cycle Time	Internal Business	Structural, Human
Mass Customization	Internal Business	Structural, Human
Strategic I/T Architecture	Internal Business	Structural, Human
Business Strategy Risk	Customer, Internal Business	Structural, Customer
I/T Strategy Risk	Customer, Internal Business	Structural, Customer
Business Organization Risk	Innovation and Learning, Customer	Structural, Human
I/T Definitional Uncertainty	Customer, Internal Business	Structural, Customer
I/T Technical & Implementation Risk	Customer, Internal Business	Structural, Customer
I/T Services Delivery Risk	(Internal) Customer Perspective	Structural, Human

Table 15-5   Migration of Investment Justification Factors to the Balanced Scorecard and Intellectual Accounting.

Employing the investment profile factors to establish justification and investment priorities for new initiatives only ensures that investments will support the stated strategy. It does not, however, guarantee a winning strategy. Neither does employing the Balanced Scorecard and developing an excellent set of accompanying indicators and measures assure success. However, used together, the tools can translate a company's strategy into rational investments in initiatives and into specific measurable objectives.

Intellectual Asset Management and Reporting

Another approach—a blend of measurements for internal management use and external stakeholder reporting—focuses on intellectual assets.[3] The premise is that managing intellectual capital improves financial performance. Dow Chemical uses intellectual asset management for its patent management, ensuring that Dow realizes maximum business benefits from the patents it holds.

Two financial services companies—Skandia Assurance & Financial Services (AFS) and Canadian Imperial Bank of Commerce (CIBC) apply the approach more broadly.

- Managers at Skandia Assurance & Financial Services distinguish between human capital (the source of innovation and renewal) and structural capital (information systems, knowledge of market channels, and customer relationships). Innovation asset reporting includes business development expenses as a percentage of total expenses and production and sales from new products. I/T asset reporting includes I/T investments as a percentage of total expenses (similar to the technology spending ratio in Chapter 11), and I/T employees as a percentage of all employees (similar to the knowledge ratio in Chapter 11). The company devotes one page of its Annual Report to its intellectual assets.

- Canadian Imperial Bank of Commerce takes a similar view. They define intellectual capital as human capital (the individual skills needed to satisfy the customer) plus structural capital (the organizational capabilities needed by the market, e.g., I/T) plus customer capital (its strength of franchise). They manage the flow and linkages from human capital (e.g., number of new ideas generated and implemented) to structural capital (e.g., dollars per transaction, improved cycle-time, costs of key processes), resulting in customer capital (e.g., improved customer relationships, faster complaint resolution).

There are common classes of activities, or indicators (discussed in the next section) that provide initial yardsticks for measuring improved management of intellectual assets and progress toward enterprise transformational goals. Some focus on detecting incremental change, and others focus on detecting and indicating the discontinuous change most characteristic of transformational activities. As a result, some are financial in nature, while others are operational, customer-oriented, or innovation-based and changed-based. While none are perfect or complete, they suggest new ways to justify, indicate, and measure progress towards the enterprise's transformational goals.

> We *must prepare for both thinking about and implementing new ways to measure and be measured.*

STAKEHOLDERS AND BUSINESS VALUES

An interesting parallel exists between business value and quality. Not that many years ago, business managers said they couldn't possibly measure and manage quality. Quality was something that happened during the production process, and if there was a subsequent problem, the service organization took care of it. Consequently, many large service organizations did nothing but rework defective products and try to keep the customer happy. Today, we know that the quality of any product starts in the design phase, and we must manage and measure it throughout production and delivery. We also know that we can design quality into, produce and deliver, and manage and measure, service products. The measures probably won't be right the first time, but by attempting to measure quality, an organizational awareness of quality develops. This new quality mind-set provided the base for better quality measurement programs and better quality products, and as measurement programs improved, management's business decisions based upon the measurements improved, leading to higher product quality. As elusive as the measurement of quality and industry best practices seemed even five years ago, organizations made great strides in the measurement arena because they adopted the quality mind-set. Now, both business and I/T organizations must adopt a business value mind-set because stakeholders demand it.

Changing conditions and relationships outside the enterprise walls create new questions for product line organizations regarding levels of efficiency and effectiveness. Outside stakeholders—the company stockholders, for one—are asking what executives are doing to deserve their high compensation packages, how current investments are going to increase enterprise levels of productivity and innovation, and how future (planned) investments will increase the overall agility of the company. Stockholders ask how the company will transform itself to be competitive in the information or knowledge era without a plan and measurements to track accomplishments.

While the corporate balance sheet is important, the basis for establishing corporate reputation and achievement of future success isn't one of spotting short-term opportunities for high profits. Instead, enterprises are looking at new ways to work towards and achieve long-term goals, including exerting influence on government economic policy. Obviously, it needs new measures to chart the progress along the way, and these measures go far beyond the Balance Sheet or Profit and Loss Statement found in most corporate Annual Reports.

Some companies discussed earlier already reflect this new focus in corporate vision and carry it into the Annual Reports. As early as the 1991 Annual Report, SCEcorp, the parent company of Southern California Edison (Chapter 12) announced its commitment to a new corporate vision and set of values.[4] Its vision builds on the SCE (utility) role as part of the vital infrastructure for every business and citizen in one of the world's largest economic markets. Its values include a commitment to constantly improve performance, to constantly renew its understanding of its changing business, and to conduct all relationships with honesty and openness. It commits to value for customers, leadership in the community and environment, team excellence, shared purpose with regulators, and value for shareholders. This new vision responds to increasing competition, expanded customer choices, and the changing regulatory climate. Along with the traditional financial reports, the reader comes away with a sense that SCEcorp is exerting leadership in its community through energy-saving programs, promoting clean air, advancing electric technologies, and being a good neighbor—and can cite examples of how SCE did it. Clearly, SCEcorp positioned itself as a major global competitor.

An even earlier example of this new definition of corporate success—and the accompanying vision—is the PPG Industries' *Blueprint for the Decade 1985–1994*, published in 1985 in a small eight-page pamphlet and used by the author as a model for a Statement of Direction in a previous book.[5] In it, PPG pledged to support the private enterprise system, to be an outstanding corporate citizen in each country it does business, and to participate only in businesses that contribute to excellence of performance, as measured by long-term benefits to shareholders. Guided by the blueprint, PPG became a global company, placing priorities on leadership in technology, environmental protection, worker safety, and on-going quality and productivity programs. During the blueprint period, PPG attained an average annual return on equity of 17 percent, an annual productivity increase of 4 percent, and an annual real sales growth of 2 percent. Not so incidentally, the performance of the PPG stock over the blueprint period surpassed the leading industrial indices—the total return to investors (including reinvested dividends and stock appreciation)—was about 23 percent a year, compared with 17 percent for the Standard & Poor's index of 500 publicly traded stocks.[6]

Observe that both SCEcorp and PPG Industries have corporate visions and values that explicitly address its stakeholders. In Chapter 14, we introduced the idea of the external stakeholders—such as governmental agencies, regulatory commissions, environmental activists, labor unions, investors, current and potential customers—and their role in establishing the financial goals and ethics of the company. For I/T, however, its contribution to business value gets judged by its own set of stakeholders—the internal stakeholders of the enterprise—and how this I/T-contributed business value enhances the value that ultimately flows to the external stakeholder.

STAKEHOLDERS AS THE KEY TO I/T BUSINESS VALUE

A recent article reported on a poll taken among top executives regarding their attitudes toward I/T.[7] The executives said that I/T was either critical or very important to them for improving company quality (89%), reengineering business processes (83%), reducing cost (68%), and improving productivity (90%). This is a strong indicator that I/T is recognizing and defining the critical needs of the participants in the business value process. The players in today's business environment have always been there, but now it is imperative that each of these business value stakeholders be defined according to their specific roles in the value process. It is necessary to define business values with associated measurement criteria for each stakeholder.

In general terms, the stakeholders in the business value process include the following:

- I/T, which delivers automated business function to the business process.
- Business process owners and users, whose output is in production terms, or whose production is used by the customer or consumer. Production criteria usually characterize the values and measures.
- The ultimate green dollar customer or client who uses or consumes what the business process owner or user produces. The values and measures are expressions of quality and productivity as the customer defines it.
- The final stakeholder in the value process is the enterprise, the strategic business unit, or the collaborative relationship that derives its value from its rela-

tionship with the customer or client. The value here is a measure expressed in financial terms.

There are value interrelationships that occur between stakeholders as well as *upstream values* (e.g., from I/T up to the business process owner or user, up to the customer or client, up to the business unit or enterprise). While the degree of interrelationship between stakeholders is important and is a measurable benefit of partnerships, the focus for this discussion is the upstream benefits and relationships.

In today's business processes, the relationship between process production and customer consumption gets defined and measured with infinite precision. Sophisticated models build in business and economic factors and attempt to define and measure the relationship between these two stakeholders. Yet, with the huge budgets and personal commitments by the corporation and I/T, the relationship between I/T and its upstream stakeholder is left almost to chance.

Viewing the general model of stakeholder relationships (Figure 15-1), we observe the external forces (global and market) that influence the enterprise value strategy. The enterprise responds to these outside forces by producing a value flow to satisfy its external stakeholders. To produce this external value flow (the interorganizational value flow), the enterprise must create an internal environment (the culture) that supports the intraorganizational value flow among its people, processes, and products. We can apply this model in an abstract way to discuss the general characteristics of value flow between internal and external stakeholders. Unfortunately, no all-inclusive specific model relationship between I/T and its stakeholders—complete with accompanying measurement guidelines—exists.

Building the model requires work—much trial and error—to make it explicit. The reasons vary.

- Most of the important business measures have imperfect definitions and lack clear ownership by any functional area of the business. For example, key business processes typically cross multiple organizational lines. Although the contributing portions of the overall business function may be able to measure its individual performances, an overall measure that all business stakeholders agree to may be difficult, and in some cases, impossible to define.
- Because there are different types of businesses, there are different types of business measures. For example, the attributes for a successful advertising agency would spell trouble for accounting firms. Values and measurements differ for different businesses, yet there is an overall consistency for business of a similar industry type. Likewise, I/T system values should, but do not always, depend on the particular values of the lines of business served. The choice of measurements of business performance—and consequently the contribution of I/T to its improvement—focuses on the characteristics of the business or lines of business for each enterprise, not the I/T systems values.[7] To be meaningful to

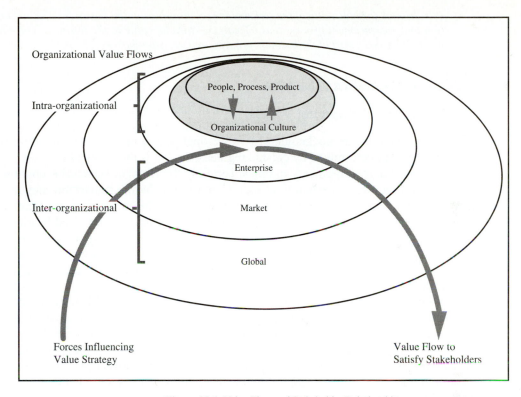

Figure 15-1 Value Flow and Stakeholder Relationships.

an industry or individual enterprise, the model must be explicit, making each unique.

- Participation in building the model must occur at all levels of the enterprise, and the participation must be predefined and agreed to. This participation definition process will be the most difficult, because this is where operationalization of measured business value attributable to I/T will come as a cultural shock to the organization. There may be considerable resistance to this concept, since it has been very easy in the past to lump I/T costs into one bucket and view them as a cost with little relationship to the outside world. Now, we are asking the enterprise to include I/T as a measured partner in the complete business process.

I/T organizations must understand and explicitly define their stakeholder relationships. To define and measure I/T value, this explicit stakeholder relationship, in conjunction with the business value definition and measurement, must be part of the I/T discipline and be included in the design of every business process involving automation.

*It is through formalization of the stakeholder relationships in the business value defini-
tion and measurement process that I/T can measure its value to the business. Once in
place, it becomes part of the business process, and decision-makers rely on it.*

INDICATORS OF FINANCIAL VALUES

Business-Based Financial Values

How do we look to our stockholders? Are we operating within the previously proscribed venues as determined by outside regulators? This is the focus of the vast majority of financial measurements and most certainly the focus of standard accounting
practices and the Securities and Exchange Commission. While important, they only
reflect past performance, or in the case of estimates used for investment justification,
the probable future performance based upon past experience. Discussed briefly in
Chapter 14, these measurements (return-on-investment, earnings-per-share, price-
earnings' ratio) represent at best, historical trends of business performance. Because
many of the financial reports are mandates from outside regulatory agencies, they—
and the supporting measurement systems—will be slow to change.

Similarly, there are certain aspects of business-based financial success criteria
that remain unchanged, even though the market structure, product base, or way of
doing business, may change. Every enterprise must maintain and monitor cash flow to
survive. To flourish, it must increase market share and return-on-equity. While the
measurements themselves won't change or disappear, the interpretations require constant monitoring for validity—especially the definitions involving market that doesn't
reflect a global scope.

New financial measurements and ratios will gain acceptance as indicators of
changing enterprise funding patterns to support transformational and global activities.
Vulnerability to currency fluctuations and changing interest rates become a necessary
part of the financial indicator portfolio for global activities as do the investment patterns of technology spending.

I/T-Based Financial Values

A key role for I/T is ensuring that information technology is cost-effective: it should
be driving down the cost of doing business, not just the cost of I/T.[8] It should be driving down that cost today and in the future (generally, substitutive and complementary
applications as discussed in Chapter 14). It should contribute to that part of the business infrastructure that enables change, learning, and adaptability—generally, the innovative applications. While it is often times difficult to get agreement or gain
consensus on the outcomes, these measures still rely, to a large degree, upon standard
financial practices.

Some organizations employ new financial ratios as indicators of the effective
use of technology in the enterprise. The technology spending ratio (measuring the
amount of current investment in technology—specifically I/T—to total investment),
paired with the new technology-to-technology spending ratio (assessing the level of

investment dedicated to innovative new processes as compared to maintenance and replacement processes), provides two new performance indicators. They indicate how effective I/T is within the enterprise, and, when compared to competitors in the same market, whether the enterprise is creating a potential technological edge in the market place.

INDICATORS OF STRATEGIC VALUES

Who determines what is strategic and whether one thing has greater strategic value than another? How well has management translated potential change into change in the current (and near future) product line, or in anticipation of changing market demand? Top management determines these answers, right or wrong, when it participates in the establishment of the information economics business investment profile. Whether it is the right strategy—given the customer preferences, economic climate, market structure, and core competencies of enterprise—is another issue.

Strategic Match

In Chapter 14, we employed internally focused descriptors for strategic match—that is, we supported stated strategies of any enterprise, line of business, or departmental strategic goal (the internal business perspective of the balanced scorecard). Contributing to manufacturing excellence reducing unscheduled downtime or by improving manufacturing yield through better management of raw materials inventory, are examples of possible measurable actions. The same descriptors suffice for any strategy with a focus strengthening the customer relationship—the customer perspective in the balanced scorecard, or customer capital as a part of intellectual assets. Examples include on-time delivery as defined by the customer, frequency of down-time of EDI linkage, and frequency of trouble calls relating to EDI interface.

Competitive Advantage

The ability to alter the industry structure, the differentiation of product offering, and the ability to create new business opportunities, creates competitive advantage for an enterprise. Changing channels of distribution by becoming the owner or manager of the industry EDI network is one example. Another is to differentiate products and services by providing more product imbedded information. Examples include the on-board computers in automobiles that log usage characteristics between service appointments and the portable diagnostic equipment that service managers use for test drives. These competitive strategies use technology to assist and enable the enterprise strategy in creating competitive advantage for its products.

Since it is the customer that determines the market, any goals or measures of competitive advantage are from the customer perspective. While improvements in on-time delivery, productivity, and manufacturing quality are significant factors, they don't automatically translate into improved financial position or increased market share. Current customers can become more demanding and when marketing efforts focus on increasing the customer base to the detriment of maintaining the current one, no one wins. In this case, it is important to focus on the activity factors—and subsequent measures—that the customer deems vital. It may be technology leadership, requiring the supplier-enterprise to focus on innovation, learning, and time-to-market, or it may be manufacturing leadership, requiring the supplier-enterprise to focus on productivity, capability, and customization. Creating a new market requires activity factors and related measures associated with innovation and vision, organizational flexibility and adaptability, and a risk-reward environment.

Competitive Response

Competitive response addresses the negative aspect of competitive advantage. Some other enterprise recognized and exploited an opportunity for which we failed to recognize and plan. Here, we address the possibility of losing market share and/or revenues that, once lost, are costly, difficult, or even impossible to regain. Definitions for competitive response are most often in terms of the effort necessary to regain lost market share, and measurements generally reflect the customer perspective. Activity factors and measures involving customer satisfaction, joint development, marketing, manufacturing or distribution efforts, or the percentages of commodity versus customized product line are common indicators (or measures) for demonstrating the ability to develop a timely response to previously unplanned-for markets.

Competitive response may also involve activity factors defined from a purely financial perspective. Southern California Edison, as a utility, is subject to regulation of its retail rates. During the last week of one December, when nearly every enterprise is understaffed or closed in observance of the Christmas and New Year holidays, the California Public Utilities Commission granted permission for a retail rate increase that was effective immediately. Because regulations prohibit retroactive billing for the utility, the invoices prepared and mailed to customers at month-end had to reflect the rate increase or the revenue would be unrecoverable. The I/T department, through previous design, had billing systems with enough flexibility to respond to the change, and the company experienced no revenue loss.

Management Information for Critical Success Factors

We care about better management information regarding the enterprise critical success factors because, as internal stakeholders, we need the information to better manage and accomplish the key internal activities of the enterprise. These activities will, in turn, accomplish key goals, materially benefiting the enterprise. While most of these measurement factors revolve around internal business activities (e.g., manufacturing efficiencies, costs, and time to reconfigure), others may include developing or emerging capabilities (e.g., activities relating to understanding and exploiting new technologies). Also included are the activities to improve the total time-to-market cycle for a new product (the linkages and flow between pure research, patent activity, applied research, product pilot programs, and technology transfer activities between laboratory, testing, pilot production, market introduction, and full production).

INDICATORS OF STAKEHOLDER VALUES

Although all stakeholders may subscribe to enterprise strategic themes (e.g., service, quality, environmental protection, financial integrity, manufacturing or service excellence), each class or set of stakeholders place different emphasis and value on them. Stockholders may prize environmental protection, but not at the cost of reduced dividends or the stock price. Employees may prize environmental protection, but not at the price of closing aging, polluting manufacturing facilities and eliminating jobs. A city may prize environmental protection, but not at the cost of eliminating a manufacturing facility that provides a large percentage of its tax base. Consequently, in justifying, indicating, and potentially measuring the delivery of stakeholder values, it is important to know who the major stakeholder is and have the primary indicators or measures of the activity link to the primary customer for this value—in this case, the regulatory agency. Indicators on the management dashboard and subsequent measurement systems reflecting the values and priorities of other stakeholder groups (e.g., the stockholders, the employees, the city) intersect with this primary indicator and provide secondary views of progress.

Service and Quality

For service and quality, the identification of the champion stakeholder—around whom all the justifications and measurement systems tailoring take place—is equally straightforward. It is the customer stakeholder—the external buyer or consumer of the product in combination with the internal buyer or consumer of internally generated products and services. It accomplishes little when a company invests to improve internal procedures (serving internal customer stakeholders) and external customers receive no real benefit.[9] Thus, defect-free, on-time, and correct delivery of product or service at an appropriate price is the indicator and measurement criteria for any stakeholder concerned with service and quality.

Environmental Quality

The Economist observed that most economists know even less about accounting than most accountants and businessmen know about the environment. The difficulty—after one begins to understand the discipline boundaries among the three professions—is to build the bridge that effectively translates and links environmental impact with economic impact.[10] The real pioneers have been those who have tried to build the linkages between environmental actions and financial or economic consequences.

Two broad styles of measuring and reporting are emerging. The first is an event-counting, regulatory agency driven, approach—the number of unwanted events such as accidental spills, complaints filed, fines levied—and enhanced with details of pollution prevention and safety, targets for future improvements, and progress towards previously set company goals. This is the approach separately taken by Monsanto and PPG Industries, who publishes an annual report listing penalties paid for environmental violations and the amount of hazardous waste it produced. The second reporting style tries to capture the difference between what a company takes in (energy and other raw materials) and what they produce (residual end products).[10] For example, the Danish Steel Works measure and reports the inputs of steel scrap, chemicals, and energy, against the output of pollutants and useful products, and BSO/Origin, a Dutch firm, publishes financial estimates of the damages its activities do to the environment, where it subtracts the total value lost (environmental damage) from its value added.

Internally, some companies use a technique called life-cycle analysis (LCA) to measure how green a product is by evaluating its environmental effects before, during, and after its existence. For example, Proctor & Gamble used LCA to discover ways to reduce the energy consumed in the manufacture of its laundry detergent, Tide, experimenting with different chemical compounds. A life-cycle analysis showed that 80 to 90 percent of the energy use occurs after the detergent left the factory (to heat the water in the washing machine). As a result, the company developed a cold-water detergent to market as a green laundry product.[11] Similarly, when America's biggest fast food chain faced the problem of the polystyrene clam-shells used to package its hamburgers, McDonald's initial answer was to develop ways to recycle polystyrene. Using LCA, the better answer was to reduce waste—and McDonald's abandoned its clam-shells, substituting a light wrap made of paper and polyethylene.

Even among the few early companies that voluntarily issued environmental reports, there are huge variations in the quality and quantity of measurements. Few come from continuous measurement or even frequent measurement—most come from estimating approaches and event-counting.

Agility, Learning, and Empowerment

Measuring the effects of agility and empowerment is difficult because there is little past history of successful approaches. Previous measurements reflect the classical Frederick Taylor management and production philosophy of input-process-output (IPO), where business was a collection of activities by workers, and the manager's job was to optimize the various time and motion functions. In the environment of a shrinking work force, quality circles, constant reengineering, worker empowerment, and mass customization, financial planners find that the new financial overheads are product research and development, targeted marketing, and worker training to strengthen core competencies. These growing overheads represent an increasing proportion of the cost of doing business because they are key to improved competitiveness.[12]

IPO-based management systems are unsuited to this aspect of measurement, causing some organizations to migrate to the work flow concept, supported by work flow software. Companies like Bankers Trust, EDS, IBM, and General Motors Europe are integrating work flow methods into their organizations.[12] The work flow concept views every transaction as a closed loop with four distinct steps: preparation, involving a request from a customer or an offer from a performer to do something; negotiation, allowing the two parties to agree on the work and what constitutes success; performance, doing the work and reporting its completion (the IPO approach); and acceptance, closing the loop with the customer expressing satisfaction that the provider met all conditions. Work flow software helps document the various work flows and keep track of progress (e.g., indicators and measurements including targets and dates) at each stage.

Cycle-Time

An important part of cycle-time is the effectiveness of technology transfer within any organization—the ability of translating the research and development (R&D) investments and efforts into marketable products. When investment moneys are scarce, R&D activities are often the first to shrink, since they are so difficult to value. Yet these are the very activities vital to creating new product streams that fuel future growth—and its appropriate management is vital to getting products successfully and expeditiously moved from the laboratory to the market place. The major problem surrounding R&D funding is that while many of the R&D are commercially relevant, they tend to be premature, given the culture of the parent industry or market place. In the 1970s, Xerox still saw itself solely as a copier company, while rivals were transforming themselves into vendors of information-handling systems.[13] The result was that innovations made at PARC (Xerox's Palo Alto Research Center) made fortunes for others in the Silicon Valley because the Xerox vision and culture weren't ready.

Pittiglio Rabin Todd McGrath (PRTM), a Massachusetts-based consulting firm, uses a benchmark it calls the Index of R&D Effectiveness.[8] This index is calculated by dividing the percentage of total revenue spent on R&D into new product profitability—also expressed as a percentage. When the firm applied this measure to forty-five large electronics firms, PRTM found that only nine of the forty-five, 20 percent, enjoyed a positive payback on R&D. Companies that missed break-even spent 18 percent of R&D funding on products that never got out the door, while the top nine held such losses to 2.5% by frequently checking on products in development versus market opportunities and canceling marginal development activities quickly. These same companies that earned a positive payback on R&D also got new products to the market in half the time as the others, resulting in a revenue growth double the average of all forty-five companies.

Mass Customization

A decade ago, one of the first indications that the Christmas and Holiday Season were approaching was the family visit to the stationers to look through books of sample greeting cards. After choosing something appropriate, the family ordered cards with a suitable inscription. Today, we receive few preprinted cards. Instead, we receive cards containing personal greetings through letters documenting the family progress through the year, handwritten notes, pictures of the growing (or shrinking) family group, new house, or new pet; or we receive the personalized products of American Greetings or Hallmark vending machines. Instead of by just the postman, the delivery of the greetings comes through by fax, e-mail, United Parcel Service, and Federal Express. Customers of every variety of service and product now expect a personalized, customized response to their requirements.

To fulfill this customer expectation of mass customization requires the ability to quickly produce a product or service tailored to specific customer requirements and one that maintains the cost, quality, and service attributes of mass production. Any yardstick for measuring the expectations of providing customized product, or any indicator reflecting the progress towards accomplishing this goal, requires a reflection of each of these elements—elements that must reflect both the customer perspective and the internal business perspective.

Strategic I/T Architecture

As stakeholders, internal users expect to have their future needs met quickly. Justification, goals, and measures for an initiative involving strategic I/T architecture from an internal business perspective involve the ability to maintain a balance between business organizational, managerial, operational, and functional change with that of I/T.

Customers, although they have no active voice in the internal enterprise justification and measurement process, are the second group of stakeholders that require a representation of their perspective. Any architecture (or lack of same) that might negatively affect prompt order and delivery of product, release and service of new product, or accurate product information, requires inclusion in the goals and measures from the customer perspective.

INDICATORS OF COMPETITIVE STRATEGY RISKS

Transformational success largely depends on the knowledge and technology level within the enterprise. How knowledge-intensive is the enterprise (or organization) as compared to the industry as a whole, or its best competitor within the industry? Where and what are indicators of the future direction of the industry, and does the enterprise have the core competencies to succeed in this new environment? Is the level of commitment there by the current management and board of directors to make a success of the strategy and enterprise? These are difficult questions and finding the appropriate indicators for management to apply is equally difficult.

Business Strategy Risk

When I/T and business develop strategy jointly, each share some risk in what the other does. Suppose the business strategy is one based upon least cost: if the enterprise can reduce production costs, it can reduce the price to its customers, thus creating additional business volume. I/T applies a strategy of installing robotics and flexible manufacturing, which reduces manufacturing costs. However, additional volume through reduced costs is not achieved, because the rest of the industry moved at a faster pace than the enterprise—it offers mass customized products at mass production prices, providing higher levels of quality and service. The enterprise required a broader base of improvements to improve market share than simply the one element of reduced cost.

In the preceding chapter, we offered a set of descriptors for thinking about and quantifying the level of business risk. Although a strategy for industry leadership is transformation, this is a venue in which there are few standard industry practices as we currently know them. Few transformation strategies exist in isolation from external forces such as political realignments, regulatory agencies, or economic turbulence. This is the reason scenario planning is so vital in the process of planning for transformation and why constant monitoring for any early warning signals becomes a vital part of any management dashboard.

The road to carrying out any new business strategy, especially that of transformation, is a difficult one, and needs unwavering top management commitment. An indicator of current management commitment is Nuala Beck's Insider Funding Ratio (Chapter 11). Here, we compare the proportion of company financing provided by management and the board of directors to the level of investments from outsiders.[14] This is a telling indicator when thinking about the problems of large companies, for example, IBM (Chapter 8), owned largely by nonmanagement employees and pension funds, who still suffer the effects of predominately risk-avoiding caretaker management as opposed to the change-driven, risk-management, confrontational philosophy of a Motorola (also Chapter 8).

No matter how high the level of commitment, current capability must also be present. How well the company's management is managing the current product line into new product areas through product innovation is an indication of how much business value is being contributed to effective R&D through I/T development and support activities.

I/T Strategy Risk

If I/T strategy, as a result of the enterprise strategy it supports, doesn't contribute any measurable long-term business value, what about the vulnerability of its internal strategy? How does it value and grow core competencies, how does it create flexible information architectures for future exploitation (yet undefined, undetermined, and perhaps not even imagined)? The I/T strategy must focus on the volatility of its own host enterprise, and the subsequent accommodations the enterprise must make as a result of being forced by others (or by its own strategies) to take certain initiatives.

The examples for assessing I/T strategy risk (Chapter 14) suggest the requirement of scenario building, protection and growth of core competencies, and an ability to set a price (or cost) of exercising (or closing off) certain future options. Most industries already have some techniques that they apply in evaluating the exercising or closing of future options. It would benefit I/T management to become familiar with the ones used within its host enterprise and understand their application to any future I/T investment strategies.

INDICATORS OF ORGANIZATIONAL STRATEGY RISKS AND UNCERTAINTIES

Vital to any technology advancement success is the effective deployment, transfer, and subsequent support of the tools that I/T delivers to the business organization, along with a receptivity and preparedness of the business culture (the people, processes, products) to absorb them. How knowledge-intensive is any industry, and what does the future look like? Industry leadership based on technology just doesn't happen—it requires both the recognition and the nurturing of the appropriate core competencies.

An organization can't become smart overnight to improve its position in a knowledge-intensive competitive battle—high-knowledge-intensive industries have knowledge ratios of 40 percent or higher (Beck's ratio of knowledge workers as a percentage of total employment in an industry). To try to grow the current organizational ratio by even 2 to 5 percent generally requires reengineering major business processes, massive retraining of current employees, or recruiting new personnel—all of which disrupt the organization's current production capabilities.

Business Organization Risk

Business organization risk, from an I/T perspective, is an assessment of the degree to which the I/T project depends on new or untested non-I/T-corporate or line of business skills, management capabilities, or experience. Many businesses are sensitive to the problems of technology transfer in taking a product from a research environment into a pilot product environment, into full production. The vast majority of product ideas never make it out of the production door. What business is less inclined to be sensitive to are the issues of I/T-related technology change and the impact of trying to move new technologies into an unresponsive, untrained, or unreceptive business organization. No matter how well entrenched into long-term business strategy, there are short-term risks inherent in business process redesign and organization restructuring—the transformation vehicles.

Deciding whether a project has the potential to produce significant business value requires a set of indicators; however, these indicators are incomplete if the enterprise wishes to make an informed decision about whether it is ready and has the skills and competencies available to apply to make the new initiative a success. Assessment of core competencies (people, process, and product competencies discussed in Chapter 9) is necessary, along with the potential costs of creating and managing a risk containment program appropriate for the initiative.

I/T Definitional Uncertainty

Definitional uncertainty reflects the stability of the delivery environment for the initiative, product, or service. How stable are the drug stores as marketing outlets for American Greeting and Hallmark vending machines or other new standalone customer-operated mass-customizing products? Will the drug store remain a stable marketing environment, or will its traffic patterns and customer sets change significantly as prescriptions by mail order become popular? Will the tellers in the nearby branch bank remain the primary marketing vehicle for new banking products and services and the primary users of funds transfer systems, or will the branch bank of tomorrow become a wall of highly versatile automated teller machines staffed with a single banking concierge, assisting customers when they need specialized service? More importantly, from an I/T perspective, will I/T systems design that supports internal stakeholders remain viable as the enterprise structure reengineers around a core process rather than the current task; as teams begin to manage everything and become accountable (and reap the rewards) for measurable performance goals; as customers drive performance, and as supplier and customer representatives become full working members of in-house teams during product development; and as employees require more information?

How fast any of these changes occur, and how they effect the stakeholder using the product or service is a necessary ingredient in the assessment of risk of any I/T initiative. Here, the dynamics of the receiving environment are the driver and definer of the management dashboard indicators. These indicators must provide assessments of these core criteria, in combination with assessments of potential costs of creating and managing any risk containment program for the initiative.

I/T Technical and Implementation Risk

In conjunction with I/T definitional uncertainty, I/T technical and implementation risk and I/T services delivery risk focus on implementation and delivery skills necessary for a successful initiative. In the preceding chapter, we said that I/T technical and implementation risk reflect five components of risk (skills required, hardware dependencies, software dependencies, application software, and application dependencies). These are all short-term organizational risks and to be both valid and useful, any associated management dashboard indicators must reflect solid, honest assessments of the skills available to apply to the problem, and to project (and track) the potential (and subsequent real) impact of the diversion of these skills from existing activities.

I/T Services Delivery Risk

The I/T services delivery risk is an ongoing assessment of I/T infrastructure risk and the impact of developing and delivering the initiative successfully. This means that other initiatives have the potential of being affected by the activities and resources necessary to make this initiative a success. Elements that the performance indicators reflect include the level of change that is necessary within the development and delivery organization, and how many processes or process teams will participate. Any initiative that involves multiple linkages of teams, processes, or organizations becomes inherently more risky. Effective performance indicators provide these risk assessments in combination with assessments of potential costs and are used to create and manage an appropriate initiative risk containment plan.

OBSERVATIONS

The focus of Part V (Chapters 12 to 15), was to examine new methodological approaches for planning, justifying, and measuring enterprise transformation activities.

However, simply enthusiastically adopting the new methodologies en mass, or gradually infusing the current set of enterprise methodologies in use with appropriate new concepts, solves only a part of the problem—the process part.

What is just as critical is the people participating in the process. Scenario planning won't produce the desired product when:

- The facilitator, whether an outside consultant or an in-house expert, doesn't have the appropriate blend of communication and visionary qualities.
- The participants, who envision the consequences of each scenario shaping the enterprise's competitive environment and strategic response, aren't freethinking, multidisciplinary, questioning, and creative.

There are people dependencies for the Seven Questions Methodology also. Here, the process won't produce any valid results if:

- The facilitator doesn't have the necessary skills or influence to force the investment of the proper level of skills and time to freely explore each question.
- The participants don't have the experience, skills, and influence within the enterprise and industry to understand the possibilities and then translate them into appropriate and effective action plans that the rest of the enterprise will accept.

Additionally, there are people dependencies associated with using *Information Economics* in its original form, and these dependencies become increasingly critical in a transformational environment. Results of the process are in jeopardy when:

- The facilitator can't create and sustain a consensus-driven environment.
- The senior management or the management steering committee hasn't fully participated in developing and supporting the use of the weighted business profile.
- The business and I/T participants that develop the initiative scores can't come to consensus, don't thoroughly understand the underlying business strategies, haven't sufficient knowledge of business and I/T capabilities, or aren't sufficiently knowledgeable of what is possible to ensure that the best set of initiatives (i.e., the best set of possible solutions) is being considered for funding. Another pitfall is when they either lack honest assessments or don't fully appreciate the realities of the enterprise core competencies—both their limitations and the potential.
- The business and I/T nonparticipants aren't sufficiently knowledgeable of the process to understand the business priorities and strategies to accept the results, especially when pet projects fail to receive funding.

People dependencies are also inherent in developing and applying measurements associated with the balanced scorecard or with intellectual assets. Financial measures are easy to do and are precise because they objectively measure past performance using standard accounting practices. The subjective measures are the ones that are critical to leaders that build toward future success—and no standard set or best practices of measures exist for measuring progress towards improving corporate culture, making business processes more open to change, or enabling just-in-time education and empowerment. The entire enterprise must understand that these measurements and indicators aren't perfect and aren't permanent. They, like the enterprise and its strategies, will continue to evolve and focus on the next set of challenges.

Finally, no planning, justifying, and measuring, guarantees product success. It is the innate intelligence, wisdom, experience, inventiveness, imagination, and skills of entrepreneurship possessed and applied by the enterprise leaders that turn an ill-conceived strategy into an organizational learning experience and an appropriate strategy into competitive advantage.

Part VI

PERFORMING WHILE TRANSFORMING

Two themes appear throughout the book:

- Business as usual is no longer possible.
- Business paradigms unchanged or unchallenged are no longer valid as business operating rules that ensure success.

The concluding section identifies some new business paradigms, discusses the consequences for I/T organizations and strategies, and develops suggested Agendas for Action.

New Technologies and New Services (Appendix I), is based upon a presentation given by Dr. Thorhallsson at ALGIS (The Academy of Local Government Information Science), as part of its International Workshop in Marathon, Greece. Dr. Thorhallsson is associate professor of information technology at The University of Iceland and is also managing director of SKYRR, the state and municipal data center in Reykjavik. SKYRR is a member of a group of Nordic Kommunedatas whose sole customer is its own government. This makes it uniquely vulnerable to competition from other Kommunedatas as well as other profit-making data services. Dr. Thorhallsson applies the value chain to define problems and develop solutions for his I/T service organization.

National Defense and the Age of Uncertainty (Appendix I), by Lt. Col. Robert T. Morris, United States Air Force, provides a unique view of the consequences of political and economic restructuring for the U.S. military. Significant downsizing of personnel and organizational restructuring, coupled with a fundamental shift of mission and strategy, required the military to transform itself while it continued to perform its role of national defense.

16

Discovering New Paradigms While Revisiting Revolutions

We are in a period of massive enterprise transformation—whether through improving operations by redefining business objectives and developing core competencies to create and sustain competitive advantage, or by nurturing learning organizations and continuous improvement programs, enabling corporate self-renewal. I/T has a significant role to play—and significant opportunities and responsibilities—in the process. Transformations require the institutionalizing of behavioral change required for long-term success. Many of these organizational behavioral changes require not only the active support of I/T, but require that I/T be the first to change to effectively support the initial business transformation initiatives.

PARADIGM BLINDERS

When Henry Ford's engineers applied the idea of process flow to the Model T production in 1913, the labor spent to assemble a single automobile dropped from twelve hours and eight minutes to two hours and thirty-five minutes. Six months later, the average labor time dropped to just over ninety minutes.[1] The defining characteristics of this new system of mass production included a focus on low-cost, low-priced products, economies of scale, and product standardization—all managed using a hierarchical organization with professional managers. These success characteristics created the paradigms of mass production. They included bigger is better and organize by function. The definitions of productivity involved measures of how busy the equipment and people were.

Consumers accepted these mass production paradigms, too. They accepted standard goods, and this acceptance facilitated price reductions through increasing economies of scale. The gap between the price of mass-produced goods and customized goods further encouraged the clustering of demand around homogeneous products. These same mass production paradigms infiltrated and influenced the services area—from fast food outlets to the traditional church.

The overwhelming success of the paradigms made it extremely difficult for managers over the past two decades to realize that the world was changing. This is the problem with a paradigm—while it is a powerful tool for ordering information and focusing goals, a paradigm will automatically filter out information that is contradictory, thus ignoring any early warning signals associated with change. (This is also the singular most important reason for the use of scenario planning today—to question and revalidate paradigms before planning.)

The seeds for destroying mass production paradigms were there all the time, but the paradigms worked so well that it was difficult to see any change taking place. The Japanese system of lean production, created to produce smaller volumes at lower costs than the American mass producers, was the technology shock that changed the rationale of the mass production process. The second shock came when the American consumer began to diversify its tastes, creating an ever-widening array of demands.[2] These forces of change, along with all the others mentioned in Chapter 1, impact products and markets differently and require each market to develop a different mix of customization and production paradigms to maintain competitiveness.

Market Restructuring

The emergence of NAFTA, the EU and Association of Southeast Asian Nations (ASEAN) foretells of new political and economic relationships between member nations and new political and economic relationships between the trading groups. Trade agreements are forcing, at the very minimum, the continentalization of markets. In this interlinked global economy, the success factors shift from having natural resources to appreciating the market place, in which one must participate to prosper. Knowledge, as the new economic driver in the global market, creates a new long-term leverage point available to upgrade industry and the individual—that of education and training—and companies are discovering that the ability to learn faster than competitors may prove to be the only long-term sustainable competitive advantage.[3]

- Retailing is undergoing radical change. Even twenty years ago, the focal point to any shopping was the downtown department store. Next to appear were the suburban shopping centers with a department store branch as a retail anchor, followed by strip malls populated by small specialty shops and large discount stores. Today, department stores and specialty shops come into the home via the catalog, supported by toll free numbers for telephone and fax orders. Tomorrow, many of these same retailers will migrate their merchandising to computer and television networks and distribute catalogs of new offerings via VCR customer-subscribers. This doesn't mean the death of department stores, but illustrates its current loss of market dominance resulting in a continuing restructuring of the industry.

- Financial services must rethink their strategy and portfolio of products as the population grows older and fragments a previously homogenous market for banking and investment services (Chapter 12).

- The energy industry faces massive restructuring due to the dual (and conflicting) forces of increased regulation due to growing international concern and cooperation on controlling environmental quality, and the trend towards allowing competition from nonregulated independent power producers (i.e., retail wheeling) to use the current system for power transmission and delivery (Chapter 12).

- Media, too, is at a crossroads. With the potential of the information superhighway as a delivery vehicle, the race is on to be the first to identify and capture now profitable niche markets. (See Chapter 4 and the Internet example.)

- Manufacturing—with very few exceptions—is being forced to adopt lean and agile manufacturing approaches and to abandon the hierarchies of mass production paradigms (Chapter 5). Today, Allen-Bradley's automated assembly lines for electrical relays and switches are state of the art—so flexible that the firm pays no penalty for making one of a kind (using mass customization techniques) rather than a large batch (using mass production techniques).

> *"No single technological achievement yields a lasting competitive advantage", "Every industry is at risk for those continuing business as usual", and "The creation of wealth is linked to the knowledge of the individual" become paradigms in this economy.*

As in so many technologies, the U.S.-Japan race in factory automation has mixed results. Japan is ahead in the breadth of applications of plant automation—robots, flexible manufacturing, and advanced machine tools. The United States is ahead in areas of research and in computer-integrated ordering and manufacturing. Japan has more robots, but most run on U.S.-produced software. The most advanced manufacturing plants in the world are probably in the United States—IBM in Austin, Texas, and Lexington, Kentucky; LTV in Dallas, Texas; Allen-Bradley in Milwaukee, Wisconsin— but Japan has more plants at a higher level of automation.[4]

Service organizations look to technology solutions to provide improved services to the customer at little or no additional cost. Approaches vary from enabling a better business relationship as American Express did (Chapter 3) by implementing its knowledge highway, to automating the enterprise-customer relationship as AT&T did. In 1951, AT&T introduced direct-dialed long-distance calling. In 1992, AT&T, America's biggest long-distance telephone company, began replacing up to a third of its 18,000 human operators with computers that understand just enough speech to reverse the charges on a telephone call. This is the start of an era of machines that not only listen but also respond. The machine simply scans through whatever it hears until it spots collect, calling card, person-to-person, third-party billing, and operator and takes the appropriate action. Voice recognition is just one more step down AT&T's chosen technology path.[5]

Both manufacturing and service companies are beginning to reap the benefits of its investments in automation through increased efficiency and reduced costs.[4]

- A General Electric dishwasher plant, for example, increased production 50 percent and reduced labor 30 percent through automation.
- National Steel raised tons-shipped-per-employee 26 percent over a two-year period while reducing man-hours per ton 10 percent.
- A maker of printed circuit boards in Georgia increased output 500 percent and cut design time 400 percent through automation.
- A Motorola plant in Boynton Beach, Florida, uses robots to take orders and assemble radio pagers in 1 percent the time of previous methods, producing pagers within two hours of order time.
- Goodyear used to make 100 tires a day on one line, with 20 percent of the tires faulty. Now robots on the same line make 1,000 tires a day—with almost no defects.

Behind all this activity is the need to invest for the future. Managers realize they can't compete in world markets if they focus only on short-term results and now look farther down the road for ways to increase productivity. One obvious way is to understand what competition is doing and try to do it better. Another way is to understand who has the best generic best practices, and why yours differ. Business process and business network reengineering, benchmarking, and concurrent engineering focus on internal processes and supports the move toward new processes and the new organizational forms that employ them.

Technology and the Transforming Enterprise

The use of technology—as Baxter Healthcare found—changed the face of its business over the past twenty years. Often, however, technology has simply added to the problem. Customers on both sides of the Atlantic bought too much equipment, believing that, for example, computer-integrated manufacturing was simply a case of giving everyone a computer screen, or that sales force automation was simply giving a personal computer, software, and modem to every sales representative. Businesses bought over-sophisticated equipment, failed to understand the cultural implications of a computer investment, or simply bought the wrong system for its needs.

Now, manufacturing organizations are moving towards small, simple manufacturing cells with varying levels of automation aimed at producing truly flexible manufacturing and sharply reducing cycle times. Manufacturers are looking for computer systems that support rather than smother the process. They want a factory in which there is a computer-based, seamless integration of people's functions, I/T, and manufacturing processes that achieve business objectives defined by management goals.[6] At the same time, service organizations strive for similar objectives, achieving flexibility, reduced response time, and integration with other business functions, again, in support of achieving business goals. The trend towards open systems—nonexclusive, nonproprietary standards for computer and communications environments—offers immense opportunities for businesses to create effective interfaces between different elements of its computer systems. This is particularly true for manufacturing, in which such developments address the key challenge for major Western world manufacturers in the 1990s—reducing time-to-market and product development times.

Western companies have traditionally found the people issues surrounding technology hard to handle. Many times it is due to the lack of training or the lack of involvement of the users in the initial purchasing decision. Other times—particularly in union shops—the problem has been the lack of necessary job and business process redesign to make the best use of the technology. Enterprises and its corporate cultures, along with all of its employees, must prepare for an environment of constant change that focuses on increasing the ability of the enterprise to respond to dynamic market conditions, not allowing the foot-draggers and the uninvolved to prevail. Like quality programs, enterprise transformation requires a continuing focus on improvement. Enterprises don't just do quality or do transformation and then move on to the next management tool-of-the-month.

Although we can spot some hearty pioneers, we have yet to identify the global experts of sustaining transformation and all of its underlying principles, tools, and techniques. Certainly, benchmarking is key to identifying who has the world-class best practice for a particular internal business process. Today, business process and business network reengineering, fueled by benchmarking and designed and implemented by appropriate forms of workgroups based on concurrent engineering principles, provide a beginning set of tools to achieve the business transformation necessary for tomorrow's world class competition.

However, tools are only a part of the story. Transformation also requires leadership. It takes a leader to envision how it might be possible to change an industry and then communicate that mental model to the rest of the agile organization. Only then can members of the enterprise contribute to its fulfillment.

Managing the resources to accomplish transformation is more difficult, more expensive, more time-consuming, and more challenging than that of managing them to improve quality, and requires new leadership skills.

Challenging Paradigms

Many rules of work design still have invalid assumptions about technology, people, and organizational goals. This results in work processes and organizational structures that have not kept pace with the changes in technology, demographics, and business objectives that require new, discontinuous thinking. "Quality, innovation, and service, for example, are now more important than cost, growth, and control." Michael Hammer, the author and lecturer on reengineering, believes that unless we discard those old paradigms, "we are merely rearranging the deck chairs on the Titanic."[7]

Business can't achieve breakthroughs in performance by cutting fat, because little remains after downsizing. It can't by automating existing processes because they aren't flexible enough and require too much overhead. Finally, it can't be by spending time looking for a quick fix because there are none that address the type of discontinuous business, social, and economic change that we are experiencing. Instead, leaders "must challenge old assumptions and shed the old rules that [initially] made the business underperform."[7] The enterprise has some transformation alternatives:

- The reengineered or redesigned enterprise requires fundamental rethinking and radical redesign of a business organization and its business processes built around producing global quality and constantly improving cycle-time. This often results in a series of discontinuous business visions. It represents an enterprise transformation based upon evolutionary improvements of operations and involves a reconceptualization of the enterprise structure, forcing managers to think broadly about the organization and how tasks, people, and formal and informal structures fit together. Strategic alliances, virtual enterprises, networks and networking, workteams, and groupwares are often outcomes of this thinking.

- Sustainable competitive advantage admits that nothing guarantees competitive advantage forever. No single technological or intellectual breakthrough will do it. The alternative is for the enterprise to attempt to sustain competitive advantage by redefining business objectives, creating new core competencies, and stretching old ones to its limits and by focusing them on new market opportunities. This approach represents an enterprise transformation based upon strategic transformation and also requires continuous improvement in quality, innovation, core competencies, product, and time-to-market. It requires a constant focus on the exploitation of I/T to enable enterprise agility, communication, and knowledge-flow. It also requires constant focus on strategic intent. One strategy might be for an enterprise to focus on time-based competition by which management adopts the belief that time is the equivalent of money, productivity, quality, and innovation. Time, like costs, is then manageable and a source of potential competitive advantage throughout every process in the organization.

- Self-renewal addresses the issues of change—both incremental and discontinuous—and focuses on creating the ability within the organization to anticipate and cope with change so that any significant operational gaps in the reengineered enterprise, or processes or strategy gaps in the quest for sustainable competitive advantage, don't develop over time. Learning organizations, continuous improvement programs, fast decision-making coupled with responsibility-taking, empowerment (both information and decision-making), and open communications, all contribute to create a new way of managing to stay ahead of competition. It also requires I/T to be the enabler.

There are two additional interdependent concepts: those of the learning enterprise and core competencies. A conceptual framework for the organization of the future is that continuous learning is central to success. Everyone needs to see the bigger picture, to escape linear or incremental thinking, and to understand subtle interrelationships. This involves information empowerment, scenario planning, and open organizations. Companies must also identify and organize around what they do best—their core competencies. Corporate strategy based on competencies that give a company access to several markets, is difficult for competitors to imitate.[8]

None of these concepts are compatible with the traditional (and incremental) change management philosophies, by which it is the enterprise itself that determines the calendar for change. Today, market forces mandate change. However, technology realities and business audit trails require evolutionary change processes. As a consequence, discontinuous business visions and strategies, harmoniously executed using evolutionary business processes and technology, require something new. It requires adopting new—often previously untried management approaches. (Tom Peters, for example, draws inspiration and new paradigms from Percy Barnevik.[9] Barnevik cut Switzerland's Brown Boveri corporate staff from 4,000 to 200 after the company merged with Sweden's Asea. The end result is a series of more nimble companies that are closer to their customers.) Viewing every business process and technology as a transition process or transition technology is a first step toward achieving these new goals.

RECOGNIZING NEW PARADIGMS

The concurrent revolutions identified in Chapter 1—the globalization of markets, the new organizational models, a shifting economic base, the consumer-driven focus, a growing global and social awareness, and the impact of information-related technologies—present a broad agenda of change for every enterprise. This set of common action agendas includes:

- Smaller, more flexible workgroups given greater responsibilities for producing a quality end product, whether the product is of manufacture or service—representing a behavioral change for the individual. The enterprise has fewer layers of management, and supports fewer physical boundaries, whether they be internal (functional, departmental) or external, separating the organization from suppliers, customers, or joint venture partners, representing a required behavioral change for the enterprise and the associated corporate culture. Cross-functional teams and empowerment are critical here.

- The importance of developing and maintaining personal, professional, and enterprise core competencies grows. The identification of emerging requirements, the nurturing and growth of current competencies, and the recognition and abandonment of competencies no longer relevant becomes the norm. This requires a transition mind-set and a behavior change by managers and strategists.

- Independence and responsibility for oneself. Responsibility for career management, continuing education (increasing depth of knowledge in current skills), lifetime learning (broadening scope of skills to improve cross-disciplinary knowledge), and retirement funding become an increasing responsibility for everyone. By placing the responsibility on the individual, so that they become and remain socially responsible throughout life, requires significant behavioral change. It requires building a personal and professional network and contributing to it.
- Continuing improvement—in the product and the process by which it is produced, in the individual and the growth of personal competencies, in the enterprise and its ability to predict, recognize, and react to change, and in building the strength of resources to initiate industry change on its own timetable. Business process and organizational reengineering provide the context in which continuous improvement programs, innovation, learning organizations, and risk-allowing and responsibility-taking environments can flourish.

Note that continuous improvement, individual responsibility, core competency relevancy, and empowerment all require the majority of individuals within the enterprise to change their behavior—the way they relate to other people and organizations, the way they interact with coworkers, the way they perform their jobs. To succeed at transformation, management must commit itself to it and must visibly demonstrate that commitment through personal leadership.[10] At the same time, the organization and its workers must have the tools that will support them in their attempts to perform their jobs differently. This is where I/T becomes a catalyst and enabler of transformation and contributes business value, and the chief job for I/T management is to participate in developing business strategy while keeping the technology engine running smoothly.

REENGINEERING THE I/T INFRASTRUCTURE AND PROCESSES TO SUPPORT THE TRANSFORMING ENTERPRISE

Smaller, More Flexible Workgroups

First, the I/T organization must understand what the characteristics are of the new, transforming enterprise. Only then can it begin to understand how to redesign itself and assess its infrastructure and process redesign to support the enterprise. The following group of new paradigms, for example, include both the anticipated business actions (the new business paradigms) and the resulting I/T impact that supports the smaller, more flexible workgroups.[11]

- The business will organize itself around the process, not the task. It will base the new process and its performance objectives on the customer needs, not on organizational convenience or custom. For I/T, this means significant application and data integration around the newly defined business process that will undergo continuous refinement as a result of continuous improvement programs. It also means that the requirements process will be customer-driven—not I/T-driven or business organization-driven—and because the business process now reflects the (end) consumer focus, business staff will be uncompromising in the demand that customer requirements and I/T commitments be met.

- The business organization will flatten the hierarchy through minimizing any subdivisions of process. From a business perspective, it's better to have a larger team responsible for an entire process, rather than a series of smaller teams that risks losing the customer focus. From an I/T perspective, it means dealing with more (internal) business opinions, but by maintaining a singular view of the business customer, it reduces the number of differing views in the requirements process, thus reducing definitional uncertainty and business ambiguity.

- Business will give senior leaders responsibility for processes and process performance and empower them to make the decisions and live with the consequences. This forces business management to change its focus from control to one of promoting and nurturing the capacity to improve and innovate. It also forces I/T to do the same for its management, and it provides the one thing I/T always searches for—the business process champion.

- Business will link performance objectives and evaluation of all activities to customer satisfaction. An enterprise is successful as long as it continues to satisfy its customers. Any measurements or objectives that don't specifically link to maintaining and improving customer satisfaction detract attention from them. This means that I/T must redesign and link all of its performance objectives and evaluations to its stakeholders—the business process team and the business customer it supports. This is the reason for the lengthy discussions regarding new business values in Chapters 1, 11, 14 and 15, and the discussion of standards, service, and quality initiatives in Chapter 6. Without a clear understanding of the new business values and how they drive business strategy, I/T will not be an effective change agent for business transformation, nor will it be an effective positioning agent for future business opportunities.

- Business will make teams, not individuals, the focus of organization performance and design. Individuals, working alone, don't have the objectivity, capacity, and influence to continuously improve work flows—objectives of both business process redesign and enterprise transformation activities. I/T must reengineer its own development and delivery processes and focus on teams. The day of the single systems analyst, working alone until midnight, is over. If this happens, either the team hasn't taken responsibility for the problem, or the lone systems analyst doesn't want to share the glory of solving the problem with teammates. In either case, I/T management has a significant problem that requires immediate attention. Business will, however, recognize and reward individual skill development and team performance rather than individual performance alone. If the basis of performance measurements and rewards is on improving personal skills and team performance, that's what will happen. As long as the reward base is individual performance, team performance pays the price. I/T management must review and revise its performance measurements and reward system to reflect this philosophy.

- Business will combine managerial and nonmanagerial activities wherever possible. This reduces the hierarchy and empowers the workers simultaneously. It can also overload them with the immediacy of work to do, so that I/T may get less devoted, thoughtful attention when staff need guidance. Occasionally, it will confuse the issue when decisions are necessary on expenditure of I/T resources.

- Leveraging future business opportunities requires every employee to develop several competencies. The prized workers in the future work force will have cross-disciplinary training and experience and will be multidisciplinary in thinking through and solving problems. Most workers today don't contribute new expertise—they execute expertise learned from a small group of state-of-the-art thinkers. While specialized knowledge is important, it is the ability to translate the knowledge into skillful execution, and the transfer of that knowledge into other processes, subprocesses, products, or prototypes that is critical. I/T professionals face the same mandate. Transfer of knowledge and transfer of skills is increasingly important as is the development of technology visionaries that are business literate and thus able to translate emerging technologies into an enhanced competitive position. This also emphasizes the importance of the performance measurement and reward system that encourages the individual to take the responsibility for expanding their skill set without simultaneously inhibiting team performance.

- The business will inform employees on a just-in-time, need-to-perform basis with data that is unfiltered and unshaped by management. When the business performance measurements link to customer satisfaction, the empowered employee (or team) knows how to improve its performance. For I/T, the emphasis is on substantial information empowerment (Chapter 3). The quality and reliability of the information and its ready availability become vital to daily business activities—thus gaining increasing visibility and importance to all employees. Ease of use and training of non-I/T staff become critical to leveraging the I/T contribution to business value. Anywhere, anytime offices require unique solutions, often involving rogue hardware and a Sneakerware networking protocol or software (Chapter 10). This creates new challenges regarding balancing flexibility, interoperability, standards, and quality. No matter how good the system, it doesn't contribute value if staff have difficulty using it.

- Business will maximize supplier and customer contact with everyone in the organization. If staff doesn't know the customer, it doesn't know how the customer uses the product—a key factor in improving customer satisfaction. Participation in joint problem-solving teams (customer or supplier) is the enterprise window to the real world and will be kept open. I/T has a critical role here. Managing EDI hubs and supporting network linkages to customers and suppliers provides business a unique window into the other organizations. (This I/T opportunity appeared in Chapter 9 as an I/T core competency.) Networking enterprises, virtual enterprises, and agile enterprises are highly dependent on I/T services—again raising the visibility of I/T and its contribution (or lack of contribution) to business value through ease and reliability of linkage (Chapters 4 and 5).

- Business will recognize the role and importance of I/T in the horizontal organization. The hierarchy was the defining and controlling force for the vertical organization; I/T, through its networks and the information it carries, becomes the defining force in the smaller, horizontal organization. Business can't have self-managing teams, empowered workers, and satisfied customers without it. However, with increased business recognition come increased I/T visibility, increased (sometimes unrealistic) expectations of performance, and increased risks relating to nonperformance and unreliability. For I/T, this is the price of becoming a true business partner.

- Management will create future small enterprises with a clear set of customers, markets, and performance measures with few internal boundaries. This means that sets of customers or customer needs define the business units, and the people and processes necessary to serve them group into businesses. For I/T to maximize its contribution to business value, it will require an infrastructure that can share common skills across business units to create a critical mass for developing new skills. It also must somehow recentralize high-risk technology efforts to provide a layer of protection for the business unit, without at the same time losing the close relationship and knowledge of that business units' staff, customer set, and product family.

- Business will place greater emphasis on management of intellectual assets. Intellectual assets are often larger than the physical assets of an enterprise, and this will become increasingly the case for the information-age enterprise. Management performance will require attention to both the current measureables of physical and financial assets and the current unmeasureables of the benefits of education and training, which increases discovery, innovation, and organizational agility. This places greater importance on the ability of I/T to clearly articulate its contribution to business value and on its management as a intellectual (structural) asset.[12]

Importance of Core Competencies

The importance of personal, professional, and enterprise core competencies creates some new paradigms for business that directly impact I/T.

- Business will classify, manage, and measure many of its core competencies as intellectual assets. The I/T department that supports a business core competency will be under constant scrutiny for its role and contribution to leveraging the intellectual asset. The I/T function itself becomes a structural asset (Chapter 15), requiring new management skills within I/T. This translates into a host of new measurement systems.

• Business will apply a new global business logic to assess the core competencies of people, process, and product. The people competencies will be based upon agility—and include empowerment, the smart organization, the capacity to implement change quickly and with minimal disruption, and an environment that embraces risk. Additionally, the people competencies will require innovation—the capacity to initiate product innovation, service innovation, market structure innovation, organizational innovation—and will involve the spread of I/T and computer networks. The process competencies will focus on productivity—continuously improving productivity, improving ratios of cost of labor and overhead to unit-produced from a global perspective, and moving from hierarchical to horizontal organizational forms. Process competencies also focus on service, quality, integrity, value, and the dependence on information availability, reflecting the move from an industrial to an information-based economy and the level of I/T contributions to overall achievement of business value. The product competencies focus on price, serviceability, mass customization, and availability and involve the ability to compete in the global markets.

• Business will, because of its newly flexible characteristics, require equally flexible tools. For I/T, the concept of standalone applications, hardware, and software disappear—replaced by expectations of unlimited interoperability. This interoperability will be between customers, suppliers, and staff in the field anywhere in the world, at anytime. The interoperability will cause mass customized solutions to unique problems, creating competitive advantage for the business and unparalleled risk for the I/T department that supports it. Issues regarding security, reliability, and ease of use become competitive issues and require completely new strategies by I/T. So does the rogue hardware and Sneakerware protocol and software, mentioned earlier.

• Businesses will, through cross-functional team-building, enable new, flexible career paths. This not only becomes a by-product of the flatter organization, it becomes a requirement to perform well in the future. Rotational assignments become the norm, rather than the exception, especially for I/T professionals, as false organizational barriers disappear.

Few I/T professionals will be able to afford to build a career on superior technology knowledge alone.

Self-Responsibility and Continuous Improvement

Independence and responsibility for oneself create new paradigms on business expectations. The central one is that:

- Business will expect staff to identify, develop, and take responsibility for new core competencies and new business initiatives and to become anticipatory of business change along with technology change. The I/T role of order taker disappears, replaced by a new role of business partner, accepting the risks with the rewards. Innovation, initiative, and self-improvement programs become a part of everyday performance expectations, with the consistent exploitation of I/T capabilities to improve business performance and competitive position.

There is also a theme that bridges the ideas of self-responsibility and continuous improvement and that is the learning organization.

- Businesses will expect staff to detect relevant external information and use it to add value to the internal organization. Both business and I/T staff must learn how to turn signals (the early warning signals associated with scenario planning, for one) into knowledge that benefits the enterprise. Business will develop new mental models for processing and sifting information, creating new knowledge for dissemination throughout the organization, and embodying it into products and services. I/T will learn to create systems to capture and disseminate the information in new ways to better enable the mobilization of knowledge and to foster collaboration between people of diverse disciplines and ways of thinking.

Lastly, the theme of continuing improvement creates additional paradigms and for I/T the important one is that:

- Business will expect continuing improvement in business processes, organizational efficiencies, and tools to work with—ease of use, ease of change, speed of delivery. I/T will play an increasing role in all facets of business organizational and business process improvements. It will be contributing to, and ultimately leading, service and quality initiatives because these initiatives are so dependent upon quality measurement systems. It will contribute to business process redesign initiatives because I/T has unique knowledge of cross-functional linkages. Finally, it will be expected to enhance organizational restructuring. Any previously developed I/T applications that enforce the rigidity of organizational architecture must change.

Choosing which paradigms to adopt is determined by the unique core competencies within the business, combined with the specific strategy that the enterprise wishes to pursue. There is no one right answer or one correct set of paradigms that will ensure success. Each enterprise will determine its future by the paradigms it chooses to follow, and each has significant ramification for the future roles, responsibilities, and strategies of I/T.

ENTERPRISE TRANSFORMATION WITH
I/T AS A BUSINESS PARTNER

Enterprises focus on transformation in three ways.[10] They improve operations by reengineering business processes, restructuring roles and responsibilities, and redefining performance standards and measurements. Alternatively, they may focus on redefining business objectives and creating new competencies that support the strategic intent. A company may focus on self-renewal, a final alternative, creating the ability to anticipate and cope with change so that operational and strategic gaps don't develop. Whatever the route to enterprise transformation chosen, a shift in relationships occurs among the four enterprise functions (business strategy, I/T strategy, I/T organizations, and business organizations). (See Figure 16-1.) Current business and technology boundaries blur and disappear, and the enterprise emphasis shifts to create the vision (strategy) and create and deliver the product in partnership.

As an enterprise undergoes the transformation process, so does the emerging partnership role of I/T. Strategy development and business process improvements become joint efforts of business and technology. The emphasis becomes:

- Service, wherever and whenever it's needed.
- Identification and support of business processes, wherever and whenever it happens.
- Enable business improvement and change through constant improvement of the processes, with I/T as the improvement or change agent, wherever and whenever the opportunity occurs.
- Enable strategic business opportunities by exploiting flexible I/T infrastructures, platforms, and architectures, with I/T as the positioning agent, however and wherever it possibly can.

The opportunity for I/T to contribute to building an environment to create future business value is unprecedented in a transforming enterprise. Improving customer service points through the application of I/T can create business value. Improving a business process through the application of telecommunications can enable a firm to access new geographical markets. Open architectures can provide a firm with the technical flexibility necessary to support a new business strategy that exploits new markets or dominates old ones.

How can we ensure a future environment both rich in the ability to create business value and able to efficiently perform during change? Maintaining dynamic stability—or coordinating the chaos—among the four enterprise functions is critical as each is undergoing its own transformation. Maintaining dynamic stability requires a well-run, just-in-time, I/T function to maximize operational capabilities and efficiencies. It also requires that future business and I/T strategies build around the coordination of business transformation with I/T transformation. Ensuring this strong linkage

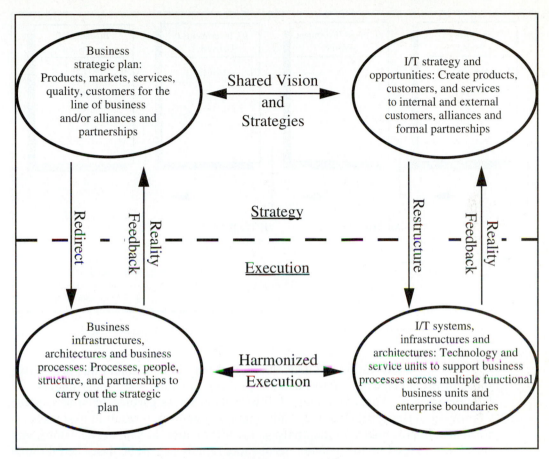

Figure 16-1   New Enterprise Partnerships.

between I/T and corporate strategy needs special attention because the impact of I/T is inseparable from the business opportunities that create the I/T-related business value.

There is no guarantee of receiving the rewards of transformation efforts. One of the major problems confronting business today is that few companies have an effective strategic planning process that produces linkage to business performance measurement other than financial and management compensation plans. The first level of the solution aims to convince top management that they should include a well-designed, integrated, and consistent value definition and measurement process to make strategic planning more effective. This requires the active involvement of both top business and I/T management. Once management becomes convinced, it is then possible to get on with the larger problem of developing an effective strategy for business value measurement and a plan for implementation of the strategy (see Figure 16-2).

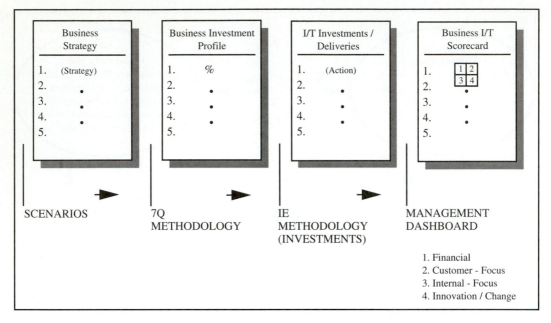

Business Strategy

1. (Strategy)
2.   •
3.   •
4.   •
5.

Business Investment Profile

1.   %
2.   •
3.   •
4.   •
5.

I/T Investments / Deliveries

1. (Action)
2.   •
3.   •
4.   •
5.

Business I/T Scorecard

1.   [1][2][3][4]
2.   •
3.   •
4.   •
5.

SCENARIOS

7Q METHODOLOGY

IE METHODOLOGY (INVESTMENTS)

MANAGEMENT DASHBOARD

1. Financial
2. Customer - Focus
3. Internal - Focus
4. Innovation / Change

Figure 16-2   Visible Strategy + Visible Actions = Visible & Measurable Results.

For I/T organizations to understand how they intend to add business value through providing automated business process function, they must understand how business measures that value. I/T, with its business partner, must be capable of proving (quantifying) that these information systems will result in business performance improvement. Productivity gains, information to support decisions, and the ability to respond to customer needs more rapidly can all be described through anticipated change (plus or minus) in the measurements of business performance. By improving the business intellectual assets of the enterprise, and by developing information systems that become business structural assets, the issue of I/T cost disappears.

Building an I/T Strategy to Capture Business Value

Identifying the business value of I/T requires a strategy in the same sense as any business proposition (it *is* a business proposition). Many firms question the I/T value today simply because such a strategy has previously been absent. It is never too late to start establishing credibility for today and the future—in fact, it is imperative if I/T is to become a true business partner in the future enterprise. A strategy for capturing business value in today's enterprise includes the following components:[13]

- Make the decision to start. Begin a program of assessing information technology value.

- Raise the visibility of I/T capabilities to business. Publicize the value dependencies through whatever means the firm uses to disseminate ideas (e.g., newsletter, sales meetings, bulletin board posting). Inform the users and management of what is going on in other companies that might be applicable and solicit ideas for improvements and innovations. Focus especially on keeping visible the world-class best practices.

- Raise awareness of I/T capabilities to business. Place I/T on the operating committee's agenda to demonstrate I/T capabilities for reaching markets, interconnecting with customers and suppliers, and producing extensions to the product service line. Have the inherent capabilities discussions led by a functional or divisional manager. Educate and inform at every level, constantly.

- Recognize the dependencies between the knowledge level of the user and the sophistication of the I/T product that is delivered; the dependencies between the business pressure on the user and the I/T management of the product and its delivery to the user. Separate the assessment of the value of I/T from determining the quality of I/T management. Likewise, separate allocation of infrastructure cost from assessment of its impact. Then examine how one influences the other.

- Make monitoring of business value a senior management responsibility. Better still, make the monitoring and achievement of business value the responsibility of everyone—users, management, and I/T should all have input into the process. Whoever gets assigned the responsibility of making the final, business judgment must have a vantage point from which to view business strategies, I/T strategy, and the link between them.

- Separate investment and expense components. Fund (and manage) I/T infrastructure costs separately from application costs. Because they are expensive, are shared across applications, and are multiyear in impact, treat them as capital investment, according to organization policy, and not as an expenditure. Understand what's being invested in transformation-based activities, what's being invested in creating a new infrastructure, and what's being invested to keep the business running in the interim. In other words, separate the performing expense from the transforming investment.

Early stages of transformation are designed to be disruptive to business as usual and, as a consequence, exacerbate declining performance and subsequent performance measures.

- Develop a tracking system. Identify those opportunities captured or lost because of a firm's prior investment in I/T (e.g., the network, the responsiveness of the database system, etc.). Failures are just as important as successes because both are valuable as learning experiences.

- Track new measurement activity in the business and in the industry group, as well as in I/T. New measurements by the business or industry could give early warning to new expectations of business for I/T. New I/T measurements could point the way to new or improved I/T management practices that create new or additional business value.

A successful measurement program must have strong, dedicated support from senior I/T and business management. It must be renewed, revised, and refocused constantly to maintain its business value relevance and to provide meaningful business measurements to management.

Building a Strategy To Create Business Value

As we execute the strategy for capturing today's business value, we must also establish a strategy to ensure that I/T positions itself to create opportunities for business value in the future enterprise. Building on the strategy for capturing business value, the strategy for creating opportunities for new business value includes the following additional actions:[13]

- Begin global technology scanning and global business scanning. Technology scanners would be responsible for identifying I/T technologies to help improve I/T business performance. I/T professionals must adapt current technologies and anticipate, and even create, future technologies so that the enterprise can stay aligned with business conditions. Business scanners would be responsible for identifying and translating enterprise and market early warning signals into meaningful alternative scenarios for I/T to follow. Both functions must scan globally.
- Focus on the new terms of competition: quality, low price, speed-to-market, mass customization, and service. What can I/T do to better support the enterprise in this new competitive environment? Where can I/T create new or enhanced current business value?
- Be a partner in business process reengineering and organizational restructuring. The I/T organization is a source of one of the key skills necessary for business process reengineering and organizational restructuring. That key skill is systems analysis and design. No other function in the business has the unique license to cross functional boundaries to drive change. However, realizing the potential of I/T occurs only when that technology is integral to the strategic vision of the organization and when its use redefines and enables job structures, processes, and lines of authority.
- Review service principles. Rearticulate service and quality principles in the context of maintaining dynamic stability during transformation. Understand that I/T business value flows from appropriate tool availability as well as from a receptive, well-trained, enthusiastic business user.
- Review investment and performance measurement strategies. Rearticulate the

investment strategy in the context of transformation. The development of a new master platform will make risk, technical uncertainty, exposure, and opportunity major issues for I/T. Begin linking these with the improvement of new business performance measures based upon the concept of intellectual assets.

- Develop an options pricing procedure. Begin by establishing the potential value to the business. Then establish the cost for I/T to keep the technical options open that are necessary to support future business options. This is mandatory for joint business and I/T strategy development and future interoperability requirements.

- Identify and nurture the I/T critical skills set. New skills will be necessary within the I/T function—such as technology scanning and translating business product and organizational strategic options into I/T ramifications—and others will become less valuable.

GUIDING I/T TO CREATE THE FUTURE

There are five recurring themes throughout the discussions that I/T must address if it is to fulfill its role in business transformation. They include:

- Linking to Business Value: I/T has the capacity to deliver real value. The challenge of survival for organizations in the postindustrial information age lies in large part upon the organization's ability to improve customer service, product, and quality while at the same time make money. Historically, while most technology installations have succeeded in improving customer service, they have not enhanced the installing organizations' ability to make money. They forgot the all-important value capture portion of the exercise. I/T must be able to demonstrate a linkage between I/T investments and business value. If, in the long run, the I/T investment doesn't facilitate improved business performance (improved profit picture, improved service and quality to the customer, improved ability to react to market changes), there is no justification for the investment. The process illustrated in Figure 16-2 will help develop and demonstrate that linkage. Does the current justification approach provide the same linkage? Will the current approach provide the ability to justify next-generation enterprise infrastructure investments that encompass technical uncertainty, risk, exposure, and opportunity?

- Rapidly Changing Business Environment: Business change is coming in more ways than we can count: globalization, outsourcing, alliances, and management and organizational styles, causing changes in products, markets, customer sets, and suppliers. At the same time, to support these new business organizations and products I/T is relying on architectures and concepts that are often decades old. Should it? What are the alternatives?

- Coping with I/T lead time: *Webster defines agile as marked by ready ability to move with quick easy grace* and by *being mentally quick and resourceful.* Successful enterprises, as they transform themselves, will adopt these characteristics. Today's enterprises must become agile enterprises that can move quickly and efficiently to take advantage of market place change. Because I/T has a longer lead time to develop support for a business transformation than does business to change/transform its strategy and organization, I/T logically must be ahead of business planning. It must anticipate alternative paths that the business might take and then translate these alternatives into I/T scenarios for action. Can it? This also means that I/T should adopt scenario-based planning even if the enterprise hasn't. Has it?

- Maintaining dynamic harmony: When one or more of the elements of the business transformation model (business strategy, business organizations and architectures, I/T organizations and architectures, I/T strategy) are out of phase with the others, the remaining elements operate less efficiently. I/T must adapt new ways of doing business so that business views it facilitating, rather than inhibiting, change. This is taking the issue of coordination of chaos and trying to maintain dynamic stability one step farther—it is trying to establish a harmony of relationships between the parties. Has it?

- Identifying, maintaining, and growing the I/T critical skill set: Due to rapid advances in technology and rapid changes in business environments, it must nurture a core staff that can truly negotiate the rapids. Through some type of scenario planning it must identify the critical skill sets and people that are necessary for the future survival of the fittest enterprise competition. Has it?

Put another way, I/T has a problem with business dynamics. The problem won't go away if ignored—only the competitive advantages will. What should an I/T organization do about it? An initial seven-item agenda for business and I/T organizations to pursue in concert follows:

- Introduce global technology scanners for I/T responsible for identifying I/T technologies that can assist in improving the I/T performance. Optimally, I/T needs global business scanners responsible for scanning and translating the enterprise early warning signals into meaningful alternative scenarios for I/T to follow. In other words, I/T needs to gear for action and get ahead of the (business change) curve now. It may be the only chance.

- Focus on today's terms of competition: quality, low price, time-to-market, customization, and service. Given these competitive evaluators, rearticulate the strategic planning approach to balance planning between transition strategy and long-term, transformation strategy. Include in the strategic plan an identification of current core competencies and the critical skills to protect, as well as those to develop, for the future. Adopt scenario-based strategic planning to have a better understanding of the skills and talents needed for the future as well as for the alternate futures.

- Rearticulate the criteria for investment in I/T. Anything that can be perfectly sized in hard dollars for costs and benefits probably isn't worth investing in because it's either not transformation-based or it doesn't reflect the necessary investments to leverage the intellectual assets. Crisp criteria needs developing:

    1. to reflect transitional and long-term, transformational strategy
    2. to reflect key business process investments
    3. to develop new long-term business strategic factors
    4. to reflect I/T infrastructure investments
    5. to develop a viable investment profile for the next generation enterprise, focusing on the business managers' assessment of I/T contribution

    Use information economics criteria as the concept and framework within which to drive the transformation process.

- Rearticulate I/T service principles for migration to the transitional and new business organizational forms.
- Identify the enterprise key business processes and the enterprise critical success factors. When used together with the balanced scorecard and intellectual assets to create the management dashboard, the enterprise has a tool to assess the effectiveness of the strategy. Given the strategic intent expressed by the management dashboard, review the previous steps for purposes of modification and fine-tuning.
- Rearticulate the terminology so that technology planners are able to discuss and contribute to the resolution of future business issues. Make sure everyone is using the same terms to mean the same things. Don't let semantics hinder effective communication with other organizations within the enterprise. For example, the practice of matrix management both within and external to the home-enterprise will create whole new views and definitions of the very terms used so liberally throughout the book: *enterprise, network,* and *organization.* Business literature already experiences this phenomenon.
- Plan for continuing education and lifetime learning. Seek out professional groups that have an interest and whose members are doing research in some of the problems facing the enterprise, and work with them.

WHAT BUSINESS IS I/T IN?

Recently, one consultant spoke of how quickly businesses are changing and used as an example a company that changed its answer to the above question from the brewery business to the pub business to the real estate business. The company brewed beer, hence management thought of themselves as being in the brewing business. After careful analysis, they found that brewing beer was incidental to their real—and very profitable—business of owning and operating pubs. Further analysis of the pub sites revealed that the company undervalued the land in its financial reports, the land being significantly more valuable than the pub itself. Only then did they begin to focus on the management of their greatest asset—the land.

The assessment of business value associated with I/T spending is complex because the context in which it occurs is both dynamic and multifaceted. The reason? The business value of I/T flows from the manner of its use—not the formula for its funding—not altogether unlike the pub sites. Its ultimate business value is not how much it costs but how its usefulness can be leveraged. Unfortunately, superior management skills and a solid track record of past performance by I/T doesn't ensure the existence of business value, either, despite the criticality of these skills when building parallel strategies coordinating business and I/T transformation. Thus, achieving optimum business value from I/T flows from a mutuality of vision, goals, and achievements.

Parallel business and I/T strategies are vital to the successful creation of the next-generation enterprise and to the creation of business value.

What I/T needs to do is to understand what kind of transformation service business it is really in. What services are I/T trying to provide and what are its critical service elements? What are the things that I/T absolutely needs to track so that it can be as flexible as possible? What constitutes success, and how does I/T know if it has done a good job? How can it do a better job?

Today's enterprise is a partnership of organizations within the business working toward a common goal, and this partnership is the unifying theme of *Strategic Transformation.* As the focus of new management paradigms and emphasis shift from controlling to contributing, both business and I/T struggle to define new meanings and yardsticks for performance in the competitive arena and within the business itself. For I/T to succeed in contributing—much less measuring—its value to the business, partnership and teamwork becomes absolutely critical. Perhaps the best designation for this decade is the decade of value and partnership, for they are the signatories to success in the turbulent competitive environment.

At the same time that I/T struggles with the issues surrounding contribution of business value, there is greater diversity among its competitors' business cultures. Not only are there more multinational companies, each is shaped by different imperfect competitive models (e.g., Japan, U.S., U.K., and Germany). All are competing in the same market, yet choose—or are even forced by prevailing regulations—to implement different sets of business practices and to embrace different value systems. This raises the stakes for all professionals to become increasingly multidisciplinary—to both understand and contribute to their own organization and to appreciate the competition, with a view towards understanding and ferreting out new paradigms and best practices to employ.

There will always be an inevitable allure to redesign, automate, and be done with it. In a transforming enterprise, being done never happens. Transformation represents the real time enterprise, and static strategies and strategic planning methodologies don't suffice, nor do inflexible information systems and information availability. For all areas of business, service and quality standards are constantly improving, best practices are constantly evolving, and new paradigms are constantly being discovered and applied. Organizational and business processes are continually changing. Employee relationships and responsibilities to the organization concerning empowerment, loyalty, and learning are constantly evolving. Continuing, constant innovation and improvement are the underlying strategies behind enterprise transformation, and it is the responsibility of the I/T organization to be a full partner by transforming itself, enabling the rest of the enterprise to effectively pursue its strategies.

Appendix I

PART I. ASSESSING NEW
MARKETPLACE DYNAMICS

Today's economic and competitive forces are creating a dynamic new business environment, one requiring enterprises to transform themselves to sustain current competitive positions. The globalization of markets, the impact of evolving political realignments, and the demographic and lifestyle changes that affect both the labor force and market definition are significant elements in this change. However, each enterprise responds to these forces differently, due largely to their unique core competencies and their differing perspective of stakeholder values, resulting in unique solutions to market change.

In "Corporate Transformation: Amalgams and Distinctions," Dr. Barbara Blumenthal, Temple University, and Dr. Philippe Haspeslagh, Professor of Business Policy at INSEAD (Fontainebleau France), observe emerging patterns in the transformation process and suggest some guidelines for managing these critical change processes. Citing well-known examples, they provide the first steps in conceptualizing the transformational enterprise and its competitive strategies.

When reading "Corporate Transformation" and thinking about the differences between the approaches taken by a Motorola, General Motors, or General Electric—and the leaders and corporate culture they possessed before initiating transformational activities—we gain our first appreciation of a new business paradigm. Copy cat, follow the leader marketing strategies may be successful to recapture temporary market segments. However, transformational success requires crafting a unique set of strategies based upon current core competencies and corporate culture, while simultaneously creating a management culture that easily manages sets of contradictory values, strategic shifts, and continuing ambiguities.

"Market Forces Shaping the Competitive Environment" provides a view of three conflicting forces (political realignments, demographic trends, and environmental awareness) and the impact of each in North America, Greater Europe, and The Pacific.

Corporate Transformation: Amalgams and Distinctions

Barbara Blumenthal
and
Philippe Haspeslagh

INTRODUCTION

As competitive pressures intensify in industry after industry, executives in the United States and Europe dream of creating an enterprise for the twenty-first century in which strategies evolve quickly to take advantage of each shift in the competitive arena; managers make decisions quickly; employees are empowered and contribute a multitude of good ideas; the organization is at once lean and agile while wielding the clout of a large firm. For most firms, the gap between its current capabilities and this ideal are enormous. Most corporate giants are crumbling under the weight of their heritage, because the structures, processes, and cultures that have shaped their success also have created the sclerosis that is making them increasingly less competitive. Alert to the challenge, management scholars offer advice on strategic renewal, the role of transformational leaders, and managing transformations and cultural change. The issues are complex and can be approached from a variety of perspectives, providing a fertile breeding ground for academic gurus and a major business opportunity for consultants.

Managers have turned for guidance to a number of well-known examples that in the 1980s successfully transformed themselves, including the success stories of GE, Motorola, Ford, British Airways, and even the Finnish Ahlstrom. Of equal interest are the failures of Sears and GM to change rapidly enough as well as the unfolding stories of IBM, Phillips, and DEC. These firms have faced a wide variety of challenges in very different competitive environments and have used substantially different approaches to confronting their problems. Nevertheless, a close review of these and other cases reveals interesting patterns in the amalgam of corporate transformation and provides the basis for a number of distinctions and lessons on managing such change processes:

- Not all Periods of Significant Change are Transformational.
- Don't Confuse the Ingredients of Transformation With the Blend.
- Most Transformations are Still Stop-Gap Measures.
- Many Transformation Recipes are Possible.
- Successful Transformation Need not Focus on Issues of Competitive Strategy.
- There is More Than One Way to Approach Strategic Transformation.
- As Always the Key is to Adopt the Ideology That Fits.
- It is Easier to Start a Transformation Than to Finish it.
- Transforming People May Be More Difficult Than Transforming Organizations.
- The Need To Transform Never Ends.

NOT ALL PERIODS OF SIGNIFICANT CHANGE ARE TRANSFORMATIONAL

While advice on managing strategic change has interested academics for years, we believe there is a subtle, yet important, difference between change and transformation. Due to the current passion for calling any type of change that occurs in an organization transformational, it is important to offer some definition for *transformational* so that lessons can be drawn from appropriate analogies.

While there are many possible definitions, we suggest that a corporate transformation requires a change that is both vast in scope and in depth. A litmus test is whether the behavior of the vast majority of the individuals in the organization has been significantly changed. A wide variety of new behaviors may be necessary to meet the challenges of the market place, such as acting upon global thinking, cooperating across functions, greater willingness to challenge managers, or greater sensitivity to customer needs. Regardless of the desired behavior, creating a change in behavior is difficult and requires a concerted and persistent effort from management.

While some strategic changes require new behavior by managers and employees, others do not. British Airways changed its strategy in the mid-1980s to become more marketing- and customer service-oriented. This led to extensive training to change the way all employees perform their job. During the first two years every employee and manager attended a "Customer First" seminar. This was closely followed by a program aimed at managing people, first targeted to senior managers. British Airways is currently in the fourth round of Customer First seminars, which are designed to continually reinforce the message.

Mergers are typically important strategic moves that can drastically reshape an organization, yet they do not always imply a transformation. Even a horizontal merger of equal size partners, such as SmithKline and Beecham, while requiring enormous changes to individual roles and sense of identification, did not initially produce a new way of working throughout the firm. Three years after the merger, however, SmithKline Beecham is beginning to examine new ways to compete that take full advantage of the combined strengths of the firm. This transition could very well transform the firm in a more fundamental, although less dramatic, way than the merger itself.

DON'T CONFUSE THE INGREDIENTS OF TRANSFORMATION WITH THE BLEND

In reviewing overall transformation efforts, it quickly becomes apparent the differences in competitive situations, identified problems, leadership style, and intervention used make comparisons nearly impossible. However, if one looks at the various activities within an overall transformation effort, one can identify four broad categories of processes at work. They are Portfolio Restructuring, Dramatic Operational Improvement, Strategic Transformation, and Corporate Self-Renewal.

Portfolio Restructuring

Restructuring the corporate portfolio, albeit not transformational in itself, is often addressed early in the overall transformation process. Management audits its portfolio of businesses and decides which businesses to stay in, sell, or enter. Such decisions can be based on an analysis of the firm's core competencies and the possible synergy's within the portfolio as well as current performance criteria and the historical position of particular businesses within the firm,

Dramatic Operational Improvement

Dramatic operational improvement is a transformation process whose goal is to achieve a quantum improvement in the firm's efficiency often by reducing costs, improving quality, reducing development time, or improving service. Improvements are achieved by reengineering business processes, restructuring roles and responsibilities, and redefining performance standards and measurements, thereby transforming the way people work.

Strategic Transformation

Strategic transformation is a process that seeks to regain a sustainable competitive advantage by redefining the business objectives, creating new competencies and harnessing these capabilities to meet the new market opportunities. While setting a new strategic direction has an intellectual component, strategic transformation requires organizational and behavioral changes to effectively define and implement the new strategy, because old strategies must be unlearned and new competencies developed.

Corporate Self-Renewal

Corporate self-renewal are efforts by top management to instill a management approach that is able to anticipate and cope with change whenever major market shifts occur. Firms typically attack unwieldy structures, eliminate bureaucracy, and speed up decision processes to induce new behaviors throughout the firm, such as facing reality and setting aggressive performance targets. The ability for self-renewal also depends on developing managers who can initiate and lead change efforts as needed.

MOST TRANSFORMATIONS ARE STILL STOP-GAP MEASURES

Among the firms that have had the most difficulty reacting to the need for change and implementing effective transformations over the past ten years are some of the household names of world industry, firms with long histories of success and dominant market positions. Rather than adjusting gradually to the changed competitive environment, these firms have let an ever-increasing gap develop between actual and required competitiveness, staying comfortable with satisfactory underperformance until suddenly confronted with a performance crisis. It seems that success, if left unchecked, can lead to a condition we call "Success Sclerosis," caused by a combination of arrogance, excessively bureaucratic structures, and slow decision processes.

As a minimum, a transformation seeks to close the competitive gap. But for firms suffering from Success Sclerosis, Corporate Self-Renewal is crucial to creating a more fundamental transformation. As adaptability becomes a more important competitive weapon in a variety of industries, many firms can benefit from continuous improvement, organizational learning, and innovation. Particularly for firms facing turbulent environments, adaptability may be more important than the choice of strategic direction.

Yet the need for Corporate Self-Renewal is often not high on the list of priorities as management first moves to stem the losses and avert disaster. Once Strategic Transformation and Operations Improvement efforts have helped avert a crisis, management enthusiasm for addressing the more difficult issues often wanes. Yet solving the immediate performance issues can help prepare the organization for long-term adaptability. Clearly a fat and unaccountable organization cannot adapt and that to be constructive, entrepreneurship needs to be channeled.

Corporate Self-Renewal is the most difficult transformation process, which explains why it is uncommon and not understood well enough. The examples of GE and Ford illustrate that the process must be owned by the chief executive officer (CEO) and pushed over a period long enough to create a fundamental change in behavior in the management ranks. Jack Welch at GE has been at it for over a decade years and expects the process to require until the year 2000. Sir Colin Marshall at British Airways argues that the pressure must be kept on for one generation of employees.

MANY TRANSFORMATION RECIPES ARE POSSIBLE

There is enormous variety to the combination and sequence of transformation processes, even for firms that essentially face the same issues. Executives from both GM and Ford toured Japanese factories in the late 1970s and early 1980s and were impressed by what they saw. Both firms realized that improving quality and reducing their costs were essential, but they had different ideas about how to accomplish those objectives. GM's primary concern in the 1980s was to invest in technology, while Ford focused its efforts on improving the way the organization functioned and on changing its culture to empower employees. While this is of course a simplification of a wide range of changes that occurred in each firm, the efforts from top management to direct the transformations were strikingly different.

Not only CEOs but academics and consultants bring different perspectives to a firm's situation and often disagree on which levers to pull and which processes to emphasize. For some, the key to any transformation is leadership. The first intervention is to identify change agents and prepare these managers as leaders of the coming change efforts. Others emphasize the intellectual agenda so that strategic issues are dealt with up front and remain the central focus. For many, the starting point is much less important than creating momentum, so that new behaviors become common throughout the firm.

While there is enormous variety, at the same time some patterns are discernible. For example, while it may be more intuitive to resolve strategic issues before attacking operational improvements, the reverse is quite common. Management frequently attacks the most pressing problems first, such as costs or quality. Once the firm has caught up with its competitors, more fundamental strategic issues may be revealed. Even with a competitive cost position, the firm may find itself quite vulnerable to competitor's actions and must then begin to create sources of lasting competitive advantage.

Another common pattern emerges because managers tend to pull those levers that they can reach first. A favorite change is structure, particularly at the top of the organization, coupled with shuffling managers in senior positions. The next target is often process changes, which can be initiated from the top, but are designed and implemented bottom-up. The important role played by middle management attracts attention only at a later stage, when the top-down structure and bottom-up processes have failed to create radical change in behavior.

A SUCCESSFUL TRANSFORMATION NEED NOT FOCUS ON ISSUES OF COMPETITIVE STRATEGY

Issues of competitive strategy are not always central concerns in a transformation. Occasionally, a firm does not face a strategic dilemma. The trends in the industry may be clear and the basis of competitive advantage secure, but the firm has grown fat and happy, and operational improvements are called for. A second explanation is that issues of competitive strategy can be attacked indirectly by raising performance goals, by revamping the strategic decision process, and by creating leaders in the business units who can deal effectively with strategic issues as they arise.

The transformation of GE, which began in 1981, did not focus directly on issues of competitive strategy in its major business units. To begin with, corporate portfolio issues were in the forefront from 1981 until 1985, as Jack Welch established performance criteria and grappled with which businesses to "close, fix or sell." Corporate provided some helpful hints to managers looking for the answers—productivity improvements, cost reductions, reducing bureaucracy, and establishing a global position were frequently on the agenda.

The revolution was really about corporate self-renewal, introducing sweeping changes to the role of management by pushing managers to face reality, accept criticism, engage in open communication, make fast decisions, and accept responsibility for those decisions. Because these changes provided the context the question of how to create a lasting competitive advantage could be addressed effectively in each business unit.

The indirect approach to strategic issues, taken by GE, was possible because of the capabilities that already existed in the firm. GE managers were well versed in the finer points of strategic thinking, competitor analysis, and the virtues of strategic planning. Welch addressed only those points that were lacking. Thus, borrowing a page from Welch's book might prove disastrous in another firm. For many firms, analyzing the business's competitive position and anticipating competitors' moves are not well understood concepts and are not practiced. For such firms, emphasizing the intellectual agenda might be a better starting point.

While there were some businesses in GE's portfolio such as consumer electronics and small appliances that presented difficult issues of competitive strategy, GE decided to sell them rather than to fix them. Unlike most firms in the midst of a transformation, GE began its transformation effort before it was in financial difficulty, with many of its large businesses in excellent competitive shape, and with the luxury of being able to sell off less competitive businesses without depressing the firm's financial performance.

For other firms, issues of competitive strategy are front and center. IBM and Sears cannot diversify themselves out of their current problems and must face up to a number of difficult strategic dilemmas. For such firms, a process of strategic transformation that directly addresses the intellectual agenda is necessary.

THERE IS MORE THAN ONE WAY TO APPROACH STRATEGIC TRANSFORMATION

When a firm faces an impending crisis due to an outdated competitive strategy, the first order of business for top management is to resolve the firm's strategic dilemma. The overall transformation effort takes on a very different character and presents different challenges for top management, depending on how and when the strategic issues are resolved.

An increasingly popular approach is strategic framing in which top management defines the firm's strategic intent rather than a detailed strategy and creates an ambition for the firm that is significantly beyond its current capabilities. At the same time, management must identify the core competencies in which the firm must invest to reach its ambition. While the strategic intent and core competencies provide a general direction for the firm, middle management plays a critical role because they are responsible for creating initiatives and experiments and developing competencies. Reaching clarity on the firm's strategy is a gradual top-down/middle-up process and is intertwined with the implementation of the new capabilities.

To use a strategic framing approach requires substantial changes for most firms, from the way managers think about strategy, to the way investments are funded, as well as the relative role of top management and middle management. The overall transformation effort begins, not with a resolution of the strategic issues, but the creation of new organizational capabilities that enable the process to work.

In many ways a transformation using this approach promises to be messy and difficult to manage, but in many situations it presents the only real hope of destroying one set of organizational capabilities and creating new ones. Galvin and Fisher used this approach at Motorola, where the firm's ambition led it back into consumer electronics and created world class competencies in key technologies. At the same time, middle managers influenced strategy with initiatives such as the Iridium Project, which is the launch of a massive network of lower-orbit satellites. And continuous experimentation with multiple approaches has played a large role in shaping the reality of the new strategy. The appropriate response to the dilemma of localization and globalization, for example, was tested in different ways in various countries.

Nor have all the traditionalists caved in. They continue to hold that there is nothing intrinsically wrong with the traditional top-down process of strategic decision-making in which alternatives are reviewed and a choice is made and implemented. The key, they argue, to the quality of the decision, is to involve those who are close to the facts and who will be responsible for implementation. One solution is a cascade of strategic decision-making workshops involving successive levels of management, each of which leads to shared commitments to a course of action. Charles Mackay, Inchape's new CEO, is using this approach to further refocus and ensure continued growth of his diversified marketing and services firm. The task requires above all some clear decisions on which activities to focus, and some creative solutions on how to build competitive advantage in what are essentially fragmented and simple industries. Most of all it requires a process that generates commitment to carry through the decisions that were adopted.

Entrepreneurial championing represents yet another approach, which, while similar to strategic framing, assumes an even more minimalist view of the role of top management. Here the real change agents are middle managers, and top management's role in this middle-up-down process is to foster a competitive process of winners and losers with little or no direction from the top. The failure to clarify strategy is not viewed as a lack of leadership, but as proof that those closest to the market are driving initiatives and that the market will ultimately determine strategic direction. Proponents of this view have long seen Ken Olsen from Digital as the example of this style of leadership and point to the entrepreneurial networks within the company as the cornerstone of the firm's strategic transformation.

The risk of entrepreneurial championing, of course, is that without direction from the top, empowerment can lead to unproductive infighting and wasted resources. It may also be inappropriate where large investments are required. Such an approach may be useful during short periods of turbulence because several strategic directions are being tested or for small ventures that do not depend on the rest of the firm.

AS ALWAYS THE KEY IS TO ADOPT THE IDEOLOGY THAT FITS

Clearly there is no one best way to tackle the strategy gap. The process is often shaped by the tradition of the company's culture or the style of top management. In our view, how companies go about solving their strategic dilemmas should reflect the reality of their environment. More specifically it depends on how clear the answers can be to the direction that needs to be taken and how obvious the steps are that will take one there. In many industries the complexity of industry changes, the multitude of evolving technologies, the myriad feasible combinations of product/market positions and competence investments has rendered the old strategic decision-making framework obsolete.

The strategic answers for a company like IBM, for example, are not at all obvious. Its past formula for success, charging high prices and securing 70 percent profit margins from a customer base locked into proprietary systems, is no longer sustainable now that these customers can switch to open systems. The search for other formulas, or strategies that can generate comparable profit margins, is likely to prove futile, except in limited niche markets. The question is which of IBM's many strengths will be relevant in the changing world of I/T. What advantages can be derived from its sheer size, market recognition, competencies, and (dwindling) financial resources? The only answer may be to try a variety of markets and approaches and only later to chase and dedicate resources to what works. Even if IBM can identify priority products and markets, to succeed will require creative thinking, experimentation, and adaptation over time. In such circumstances, the strategic framing approach is clearly superior to classic strategic decision-making.

The danger of top management failing to take responsibility for clear strategic direction, however, is as great as the danger of imposing unilateral decisions. For example, a company like IBM may not want to bring premature closure on a strategy for interfacing with the customer in areas like services or systems integration. In contrast, it would be foolish to lack clear direction or support divisive internal competition in businesses like disc drives, printers, or other businesses in which clear choices and consistent implementation are called for.

Not only do the various businesses of a single firm require very different approaches to strategic transformation, the same business does need a different approach at various points in time. The art of strategic leadership consists in knowing when to hold out on making a choice despite conflicting calls for clarity, when to provide a broad strategic framework, and when to decide and insist on a clear strategy.

IT IS EASIER TO START A TRANSFORMATION THAN TO FINISH IT

Top management plays a crucial role at the beginning of a transformation. Sometimes a CEO, such as Sir Colin Marshall, is the one who recognizes the need for change, articulates a vision, initiates appropriate change processes in various units, and pushes the organization mercilessly toward the vision. In other cases, the transformational drive originates in a regional or business unit. The origins of the newly competitive Xerox, for example, largely stem from an awareness and ideas imported to the United States that had first been adopted in the European Rank Xerox, in turn from lessons learned in the Fuji-Xerox joint venture. At some point leadership from the top is required to broaden and deepen the efforts. In the case of Xerox, David Kearns got the whole management committee to immerse itself in the fundamentals of total quality management, to become, in turn, the teachers to the next levels.

Middle management, however, is the key to finishing the transformation. For changes to stick, middle managers must be affected in large numbers. When the driven and charismatic CEO retires, dramatic changes in the way things are done can quickly revert back to form if middle management is not solidly converted to the new approach. Yet, creating real change in the roles and behavior of middle management presents perhaps the most difficult challenge for transformation leaders. Middle management is frequently also called on to make some of the most painful adjustments in the organization. As management levels shrink and spans of control increase, an entirely new approach to management may be called for, where responsibility exceeds authority and the ability to coach and facilitate become critical. Middle management are also those that have to endure the largest uncertainties in the transformation process, being caught in a limbo in which the old rules have been shattered and the new ones are slow to come forth.

It is difficult to find interventions that reach middle managers in large enough numbers to be effective. In 1989, after eight years of discussing and cajoling managers to embrace new values and change their management behavior, Jack Welch began "Workout" as a device to reach this group. The Workout meetings, held in each plant or location in the company, use a format in which employees can challenge management, make suggestions for improvements, and solve problems as a group, while giving managers a quick lesson in listening. Workout has enabled GE to "break through the wall" and obtain the kind of improvements in productivity that had been so elusive.

TRANSFORMING PEOPLE MAY BE MORE DIFFICULT THAN TRANSFORMING AN ORGANIZATION

Frequently, organizational changes demand a different set of skills or behavior of managers. While coaching from top management and management development efforts can help many managers adjust to their new roles, there are always some managers who are either unable or unwilling to adapt. Senior managers, and particularly the "barons" who run autonomous businesses, are often the hardest to reach. They have been the most successful under the old rules. Having contributed the most to the past, they may feel they have the most to lose from the future. Senior managers who pay lip service, yet are silently resistant to the new ways, have slowed many a transformation effort to a dead halt. If left in place, the change process in those pieces of the organization is greatly diminished. Many CEOs have said, with the benefit of hindsight, that they did not move quickly enough to remove senior managers who resisted efforts to change.

In most of the firms regarded as examples of successful transformation, a closer look reveals that the cast of characters shows many new faces. One of the most painful decisions for Jack Welch was to remove some of GE's senior managers, including a few who were put into their positions by Welch himself. At British Airways the shift to a marketing orientation revealed that some managers were ill-suited to the new environment and had to be moved aside. And as the Finnish Ahlmstrom went through various steps in its strategic transformation, those who held so strongly to the earlier strategy that they were willing "to die for it," indeed had to be let go.

THE NEED TO TRANSFORM NEVER ENDS

The final phase in any transformation process is to institutionalize changes so that the firm can return to a period of relative stability. Adaptability, then, is not a state of continuous flux or chaos in which important elements of the organization are changed at will. Rather it depends on reaching a new state in which structures and processes more easily accommodate changes and in which managers more easily recognize and act on the need for incremental as well as fundamental change.

Some organizations, such as 3M or HP, are born with a genetic code or set of values, which support self-renewal and do not need a transformation to create this capability. Yet even these firms require transformation on a periodic basis to deal with shifts in the competitive environment. Behavioral shifts may be needed when a firm moves from producing a full product line to a narrow one; from being a domestic to a global competitor; from being a centrally run global business to a set of strong domestic businesses with global coordination; from being a technology-driven firm to one with a stronger customer focus. Each shift in strategy can lead to a shift in structure, roles, systems, processes, performance measures, and of course, management behavior.

Ultimately the difficulty and cost of these adjustments are reduced as organizations learn to change, and managers become more professional at handling the ambiguity created by these changes. Organizations indeed represent a set of paradoxes that must be managed simultaneously, such as an internal focus and external focus, initiative and control, flexibility and stability. Excellent managers are able to understand these organizational paradoxes and to manage a set of contradictory values. These managers have learned to deal with strategic shifts and can play a variety of roles, from monitor and director to facilitator and coach, and can make shifts as needed by the environment. By investing in the development of middle level managers and by promoting the value of change, organizations ultimately develop something like a shock absorber so that strategic shifts can be more easily accommodated.

A successful transformation is one in which management has succeeded in institutionalizing behavioral change. Of course, other factors being equal, a firm that is skilled at managing the transformation process will show better financial performance in the long run than a firm that is not. But fundamental changes are likely to be disruptive, and it is misleading to look at short-term performance as evidence that the changes are working. At the same time, a downturn is not a sign that the transformation has failed. Ford's recent losses should not be interpreted as a sign that the fundamental changes—employee involvement, quality first, and cross functional teams—have not had a positive impact on the firm's competitiveness.

In fact, there is no guarantee that Ford's next Taurus will be hot or that GE will create the next breakthrough jet engine. But given the massive changes that have taken place, the odds may be in their favor.

Market Forces Shaping the Competitive Environment

Marilyn M. Parker

Identification of the trends that impact the enterprise and its definition of the market place is key to creating alternative strategies for successful business transformation. Power shifts based upon nationalism, regionalization, and globalization create new market dynamics and have a profound effect on how the enterprise defines itself. Simultaneously, significant demographic shifts are occurring. The populations of the three leading economic and industrial powers (U.S., Japan, Germany) are graying rapidly, whereas the massive global teenager population resides in Third World countries. This impacts the enterprise product mix, geographical market definition, and labor source and necessitates an adoption of new business cultures (such as business federations, offshore and/or offsite workplaces) to maintain and/or improve competitive position. Additionally, an increasing emphasis on environmental protection creates its own set of market dynamics for the enterprise at a local, national, and international level.

Cosmonaut Sergei Krikalev spent 311 days in space with his partner. Upon returning to earth in March of 1992, he entered a new world. The country and space agency that sent him into space no longer existed, and his hometown of Leningrad had a new name, St. Petersburg. *The Wall Street Journal* described the cosmonaut as an "odd victim of politics."[1] Cosmonaut Krikalev may have been the first unusual political victim to achieve global recognition, but he will not be the only individual to experience the consequences of major political realignments in this era of radical change. Indeed, it isn't even necessary to leave the earth's atmosphere to see it.

Europe is coming together as never before. The European community is the world's most advanced and promising experiment in transnationalism. The Free Trade Agreement, initially between the United States and Canada, grows, and on the far side of the Pacific, the booming economies of Southeast Asia are increasingly tying themselves to Japan. Yet at the same time that we see unprecedented economic cooperation among nations, we see equally strong protectionism movements motivated by ethnic unity and national and economic interests. Europe, in spite of its focus on economic unity, is breaking apart as never before. Within a year, the U.S.S.R., Yugoslavia, and Czechoslovakia became geographic history. Nor is North America immune: voters in both northern and southern California see sufficient economic reason to split the single state into two, and Staten Island voters favor leaving New York City. Further to the North—and even after the October 1992 "no" vote— many in French Quebec sustain a level of enthusiasm for declaring independence from English-speaking Canada.

These conflicting market-defining dynamics have a profound effect upon how an enterprise defines its market, work force, competitors, and suppliers—necessary elements in the development of business strategy. In this article, we will examine three of the conflicting forces at work in North America, Greater Europe, and the Pacific: political realignments, demographic trends, and environmental awareness. Each play a significant role in the unique shaping of its enterprise strategies and competitive environments, thus creating unique competitive models or brands of capitalism.

CONFLICTING FORCES FOR GLOBALIZATION, REGIONALIZATION, AND PROTECTIONISM

In the coming years, the tension between liberal and protectionist trade policies will become as definitive to government and business direction as the struggle between capitalism and communism during the Cold War. But society has a history of being protectionist, so where and how did this recent liberalization trend begin?

The current climate of interest in globalization probably began in 1947 with the initiation of the first agreement under the General Agreement on Tariffs and Trade (GATT). GATT was a collection of many small agreements, added to over the last quarter century, whose aim was to reduce the barriers impeding the worldwide import and export business. GATT supported the concept of true globalization: one giant free-trade zone. Successive rounds of negotiations, diligently conducted since 1947, pushed down tariffs from 40 percent to 4 percent in member countries. The 1992 round of GATT negotiations, referred to as the Uruguay Round (so named for the talks' original venue in the mid-1980s), is of particular interest to American business. It addressed—for the first time—new areas of commerce (about one-third of the world economy), including banking, telecommunications and insurance services, and intellectual property rights relating to patents and software protection. These are all areas in which U.S. firms could compete effectively if unhampered by the foreign equivalent of "Buy America" laws.

Trade liberalization activities also occur outside GATT in the form of regional agreements such as the North American Free Trade Agreement (NAFTA) and the European Union (EU). Some believe that promoting regionalism through accords like NAFTA and the EU is the fastest way to create free trade worldwide, because reaching any accord with GATT involves long and cumbersome negotiations. Regional pacts spread the philosophy of freer trade by showing how increased local trade leads to economic growth. Others believe that trading groups influence local customers to ignore low-cost producers outside the region. Instead, they purchase from friendly low-tariff producers within the bloc. The true protectionists will argue that any reciprocal trade agreements cause unemployment at home.

Change in trade policy is evident on all fronts. The GATT negotiations support the move toward globalization, while the emergence of NAFTA and EU strongly support moves toward regionalization. Concurrently, new restrictions via tariffs and antitrust legislation provide evidence of protectionist activity. There are no clear winning or losing trends. If GATT—which became the World Trade Organization (WTO) in 1994—continues to grow, regionalization in North America and the Pacific will give way to globalization, just as nationalism has already given way to regionalization in Western Europe under the EU umbrella. If, on the other hand, the international support for WTO and WTO-like activities begin to wither, just the opposite could happen. The three regionally and culturally focused groups could evolve into internally open but externally closed trading fortresses.

Regional Accords

North America.   NAFTA grew out of an already existing Free Trade Agreement (FTA) between Canada and the United States, and links the United States and Canada with Mexico, with an underlying agenda of encouraging the European Union to eliminate trade barriers against North American NAFTA partners. Latin American leaders envision NAFTA as the vehicle to create a single market stretching from Alaska to Antarctica. Through new Latin and South American investment policies, privatization is becoming a part of its systematic economic reform. Privatization efforts have attracted local investment and new capital to the region.

Latin America, with a population of 400 million, represents the fastest-growing export market and the brightest prospect for exports and growth for the United States. Unfortunately, there is also a negative side. Latin poverty touches the United States through migration, political upheaval, debt default, and ecological devastation. Unlike the Asians, or even the ex-communists, the Latin's face the challenge of educating and training its huge economic underclass. Somehow, they must parlay its liability of poor into an asset.

Efforts by the Caribbean Community (Caricom) to create a common market in the 1995 time frame are hampered by uncertainty over the establishment of a customs union—a fundamental for creating a common market. Caricom, with a market of 5.5 million people, consists of thirteen English-speaking countries of the region, including Belize in Central America, the Bahamas, and Guyana in South America. The community, established in 1973, has the objective of strengthening the member economies through increased regional trade and of providing a common approach in trade negotiations with third countries.[2] While Caricom's progress towards trade liberalization lags behind that of other groups in Latin America attempting common markets (e.g., the Central American Common Market and the Andean Pact), its leaders remain optimistic. In 1994, the thirteen member countries of Caricom decided to apply to join NAFTA, and in a parallel move, established a new regional group, the Association of Caribbean States (ACS). ACS is the forerunner of a trading bloc to encompass close to 40 nations in the Caribbean basin with a combined population of 200 million people and an estimated gross national product of $500 billion. How the ACS bloc will ultimately interface with the NAFTA trading bloc and what the role and impact will be of individual ACS member nations who become NAFTA signatories, is currently unclear.

Greater Europe: Economies everywhere have been moving closer to each other since the mid-1940s. Successive trade talks lowered tariffs and other barriers to trade. A trend toward greater dependence on trade, especially between other European countries, caused the formation of a new European economy, the European Economic Community (EEC), in March of 1957. Intra-European trade grew rapidly between the European Community's six original members (Belgium, France, Holland, Italy, Luxembourg, and West Germany). For a brief time in 1965, France boycotted the community but rejoined under the "Luxembourg compromise" in January of 1966. From 1966 through 1985, the EEC began to enlarge, adding Britain, Denmark, Greece, Ireland, Portugal, and Spain as members. Economic cooperation increased, and interest grew in the economic convergence of currencies. In 1979, the European Monetary System (EMS) was established to create a European zone of exchange-rate stability. The system promoted intra-European trade and helped member governments fight inflation.

The EEC dropped its middle initial and became known as the European Community (EC), and by the beginning of the 1990s the members were highly integrated economies and moved forward on two fronts:

- They moved to create a single, common market. Objectives of the single market are to eliminate frontier controls, initiate public procurement, and denationalize financial services. By removing frontier and passport controls, there are no more delays involving customs inspection. It becomes possible to divert resources to more profitable activities. This forces national suppliers to compete with nonnational suppliers, a direct cost reduction. By removing the existing national barriers to competition, the cost of financial services in retail banking and insurance declines.

- The members moved to create an Economic and Monetary Union (EMU), and with it the european currency unit (ecu), a single currency for the community to eliminate the significant transaction cost associated with trading in member country currencies. The European Commission estimates that its businesses convert about six trillion ecus ($7.7 trillion) from one currency to another each year. This amounts to about ten billion ecus ($12.8 billion) in conversion charges.[3] Additionally, significant savings in accounting costs accrue to business. Target for conversion to the ecu is 1997.

Europe possesses other economic advantages in addition to the EC, which evolved into the European Union or EU in 1993. Europe's greatest asset is its capacity to grow. Its geographical position allows it to forge effective trade alliances with two existing trading blocs—the European Free Trade Association (EFTA), a confederation of Western European countries that do not belong to the European Union, and Central Europe. The combined blocs would include at least 25 countries and 450 million people by the year 2000.

Like Latin America, privatization is being used to attract new investment in Central Europe, the former Soviet Union Republics, and most notable in the European Union, Britain. Britain privatized its British Telecom and British Gas and published plans (late 1991) to privatize its railroad, British Rail. The Treuhandanstalt, set up in 1990 to privatize the economy of East Germany, sold the first 3,000 businesses to firms in Eastern Germany and to members of the European Union, EFTA (European Free Trade Association), and NAFTA.[4]

Three things could slow or even prevent the European economic explosion: a flood of refugees from countries formerly in the Soviet Union; a more costly than anticipated German reunification; and continuing ethnic conflicts in Central Europe. The first two are problems that specifically impact Germany. Refugees flooding into Germany could slow reunification if funds necessary to support unification were diverted to assist the immigrants. Finally, any ethnic conflicts in Central Europe will not only slow the development in Central Europe but will also have a ripple effect in the European Union and EFTA by reducing market potential.

The Pacific.   There has been nothing as dramatic as the fall of the Berlin Wall, but the map of the Pacific is quietly realigning just as significantly as Europe's. While Europe and North America struggle with economic issues, Asia prepares for its next economic leap fueled by trade, investment, and technology links between countries. Consider some facts about the Pacific Rim:

- Six of the ten world's largest ports are in Asia, together with the six largest banks.
- The combined gross national product (GNP) of the region equals that of Europe and is three-quarters the total for North America.
- Asian dependence on the U.S. market is fading. Intra-Asian exports make up over 40 percent of the total external trade of Asian nations, and intra-Asian trade is growing at twice the pace of trade with North America, and four times as fast as Asian trade with Europe.[5]

This is happening despite the political, cultural, and infrastructure barriers to regional cooperation. No long-standing formal structures to promote regional investment and trades exist, even the Association of Southeast Asian Nations (ASEAN) lacks a clear charter for the promotion of trade. Even so, the intraregional trade of Asia is greater than Europe, with its quarter-century history of trade alliances via the European Union.

Japanese investment is the primary driver of this rapid expansion. Its investment has grown in all four newly industrialized countries (NICs)—Hong Kong, South Korea, Singapore, and Taiwan—and it has increased investment in the ASEAN 4, the four largest ASEAN economies (Indonesia, Malaysia, the Philippines, and Thailand). Associated with this investment is a manufacturing-based transfer of technology valued at $1 billion. The result? Production of many Japanese-manufactured goods now flow from these countries, resulting in closer business ties for these 8 countries with Japan.

Japan foresees leadership exercised through economic means, causing a policy dilemma that goes straight to the heart of its most fundamental economic strategies. The problem is how to make its success acceptable to the rest of the world and continue to grow, without triggering retaliatory actions, given the cultural differences that make it different from Europe or North America. These critical differences are:

- An educational system that produces literate workers: They have an ability to adopt and adapt technology originating from abroad. They exhibit a capacity for hard work, and they have verbalized national policies and action plans, with a commitment to make them work. These forces combine to create a work force that tends to be loyal, stable, and capable of maintaining high quality and productivity.

- Strong, positive, government and industry ties: This results in an environment that nurtures and protects industry. (As a by-product, it may hinder or prevent the successful entry of a newcomer.) Most notable among its government agencies is the Ministry of International Trade and Industry (MITI), an influential and positive force in the 1950s and 1960s. It arranged low-cost loans and provided access to foreign exchange, tax reduction, and protection from foreign competitors. MITI successfully targeted Japanese industries based upon economic and technical criteria and the national interest.[6] Today, MITI cannot influence the private sector as it once did, but still is a force foreign businesses consider.

- Stakeholder values putting producers, not consumers, in the economic drivers' seat: Japanese businesses tend to view profits as necessary to nation-building, using profits for further investment and expansion, not dividends. Stock prices or the quarterly balance sheet rarely drive managerial decisions, and they tend to invest resources for long-term gain, not short-term profit. The primary source of capital equity comes from institutional investors, who are still somewhat subject to the influence of MITI.

- Vertical integration through *keiretsu: Keiretsu* is an intercompany-group relationship allowing risk-sharing, access to capital and technology, and shared learning. These linked companies protect each other from takeover and minimize transaction costs. Companies excluded from the *keiretsu* have trouble competing and are often effectively shut out of the market. Foreign law generally prohibits practices like these, thus making the Japanese domestic market difficult to penetrate.[7] Where the U.S. Department of Justice antitrust enforcement extends to collusive practices by foreign companies in their home markets, MITI philosophy and U.S. unfair competition laws are at odds.

A large, informal Asian trading bloc, with Japan as its core, is a growing reality. It already has the financial, technological and human resources to be a self-sustaining regional economy, yet faces the same uncertainties as North America and Europe—that of worldwide blocs, conflicts of value systems, protectionism, latent nationalism, perceived strength of monetary systems, and environmental concerns. Still to be defined is the economic role that an economically evolving China is to play.

Political Realignment and the Telecommunications Industry

If one were to single out one event that symbolizes the importance of the role of modern communications in creating the global village, it would be the role that the transmission of faxes and computer networks played during the Chinese pro-democracy student protests. While the official news agencies in China were subject to censorship and delays in the release of the happenings at Tiananmen Square, the Chinese students kept in touch with their peers outside the country by using telecommunications technology. In the early hours of the protest, this was the only source of information to the outside world.

At a conference in Prague in 1990, the U.S. political analyst Albert Wohlstetter delivered a paper entitled "The FAX Shall Make You Free." He said that dissidents in the then U.S.S.R. used the explosive growth of Western technology to end the isolation that made resistance seem hopeless. In the Western world, personal computers and modems, faxes, and satellites have been a powerful engine driving innovation and economic growth, creating world markets and reducing costs and uncertainties.[8] Yet in the same time-frame, the lack of communications infrastructure in the Soviet sphere prevented the installation of even the simplest banking system: electronic fund transfers were impossible, and bankers and businessmen were carrying money in suitcases to complete banking transactions and payrolls.

Because of the ready availability of satellite, cellular, digital, and fiber-optic technology, locations with inadequate or nonexistent telephone service can make up lost ground quickly. The pace of technology advances allows most developing countries to leap frog a generation of communications technology. In 1993 virtual telephone service with 1,000 electronic mailboxes became available to three cities in Mexico (Tijuana, Mexicali, and Ensenada). Citizens get their own number and confidential voice mailbox and by calling from any public telephone they retrieve messages left by other callers.[9] This provides instant hookup in areas in which more expensive telephone installation may take months or years.

The technology is available, the cost is right, and borders are coming down. Growth of communications business, however, isn't just limited to the less developed nations. Telephone companies in the larger trading blocs are also going global. Three major forces are at work.

- Global industries need global communications services: Computer data and e-mail require it. Customers with offices abroad are becoming more demanding about the type of telephone service they want. They want the ability to choose one source for all their services. They do not want to use their own resources to patch and manage networks out of different national services. To provide global customers with one-stop service, telephone companies will need to either build their own networks abroad or form alliances with foreign companies.

- Future vision: Japan's Nippon Telegraph & Telephone Corp. (NTT) is investing heavily in digital switches and fiber-optics and expects to complete installation of a fiber-optic network to every Japanese home, school, and business by 2015.[10] Singapore has installed a state-of-the-art network to attract global investment. The United States talks about the information superhighway and legislated the High Performance Computing Act to stimulate investment by private companies. The European Union is talking about an equally ambitious European Nervous System, linking its governments and research establishments. The basis of all these initiatives is the belief that the first step toward competing effectively in the future is the ability to network with others and share information and ideas.

- Deregulation and privatization: As more and more governments around the world deregulate telephone industries, competition and opportunity increase. Japan and Britain began privatizing their telephone monopolies in the 1980s. The U.S. government compelled AT&T to break itself into long-distance and local telephone firms in 1983, and Canada allowed competition in its long-distance telephone service in 1992.

Nowhere is the globalization of the industry more evident than in the European Union. In 1987, the European Union adopted a plan to abolish government monopolies on data transmission and e-mail. In 1992, it initiated guidelines for opening satellite and mobile communications and for private data networks. Next is the deregulation of voice service, which accounts for 90 percent of all European telecommunications traffic. As a direct result of deregulation, U.S. telephone services are entering the market as soon as it is open, providing competition for the Continent's Post, Telephone, and Telegraph (PTT) monopolies-in-transit. In Portugal, Pacific Telesis won licenses for cellular phone and paging systems, and Sprint runs a European data network from London.

The biggest opportunities for the newcomers (foreign or domestic) seem to be in an area where the existing PTT companies showed little interest: that of transborder communications. In Europe, transborder communications are expensive. (A five-minute call from Paris to Barcelona, about 500 miles away, costs $4.20, while between New York City and Charleston, South Carolina, about the same distance, a call of the same duration costs $1.10.[11]) As a result, a group of eleven national railroads open its private networks to public use, Daimler Benz sells capacity on its satellite, and Sweden's Kinnevik is developing cellular systems.[12] They all see potential profits through exploitation of already existing networks.

This new activity revitalized existing PTTs. Many are investing in fiber-optics, adding services, and cutting prices. They are forming alliances to create new voice and data networks. Others are following the example of France Telecom, who bought a stake in private data networks in Britain, Germany, and Italy and replaced outdated analog switches with digital ones.

Perspectives on Political Realignment

The proof of political realignments through the conflicting forces of globalization, regionalization, and protectionism is here. Evidence is there every time we pick up a newspaper or watch the news on TV, if we are sensitive to it. The fuel of some realignments are economic forces, and for others, ethnicity. Occasionally, a natural disaster in the form of an earthquake or flood, or a famine in a Third World country, makes the news and causes a change in the global economic balance. There are subtle shifts every day, and they are there for us to see, evaluate, and act upon.

How will the United States react if it cedes its role of world leader to another nation? What will the political and economic repercussions be? Could terrorist activity impede economic growth in the European Union? Will the shared common culture between the European Union and North America lead to an economic world composed of two trading blocs: a European Union-North American bloc versus a Japanese-Asian bloc? For any of these issues, there are economic consequences for today's business. We must take a closer look at what new market truth or new business paradigm could result and determine how we can best respond to the change and maintain business viability.

Political and market realignments, like earthquakes, just don't happen. Along a fault line, the earth moves a tiny fraction of an inch every day. We only pay attention when the jolt occurs, and then we must rely on previously made plans. The same holds true for business. Precursors of major jolts in business activity give forewarning. It is up to us to understand what those signals are, monitor them for change, and build business strategies and plans accordingly.

CONFLICTING FORCES IN DEMOGRAPHIC AND LIFESTYLE CHANGE

The world population is aging, however, the industrial countries are aging far more rapidly than the Third World, and many, such as Germany and Japan, are aging even more rapidly than the United States. Aging alters lifestyles, the nature and makeup of the work force, the goods and services wanted and needed, and the public policy choices made on a wide variety of issues, from lifelong education to health care. Meanwhile, many Third World countries have huge young populations that are beginning to move into their adult years, including many with little prospect of employment. The aging of industrial societies offers an interesting counterpoint to the rising economic, military, and political power of the populous youth in the Third World.

We see the cost of college education rise; the return of apprenticeships in Europe; the economic importance of Latin America; the demographic pressures creating havoc in Japan; and the rise of fundamentalist Protestantism fueling capitalism in countries in which Catholicism and socialism once flourished. We observe the melding of rural, suburban, and urban populations and environments that is creating new social patterns. We see the traditional family disappear, replaced with new social forms.

We also hear about underground and gray economies proliferating around the world, which not only casts national economic data in doubt but siphons off profits from legitimate businesses. In Germany, for example, many Eastern European skilled workers work *off the books* for subcontractors, making less pay than German workers and having no legal rights. A worldwide example is the growth in size of the underground economy supporting illegal drug activities. Estimates of the gray economy's size in the United States alone represent from 15 to 30 percent of its GNP.[13] That would place it in the same range as the size of the aboveground GNP of Canada. One can only speculate about the global scope and competitive repercussions.

Today, every industrial economy is undergoing rapid change. Changes in age structure, family composition, income distribution, social groups, migration, and rates of growth present a demographic pattern that impacts every major issue on the government policy and business strategy agenda. The net effect suggests future conditions significantly changed from those of the past or present. To cope with and profit from these developments, businesses must view them from new perspectives because these future conditions are sharply at odds with most prevailing government policies and business strategies.

Regional Forces

North America.   Three major demographic trends are occurring in the United States today.

- Negative growth: The American population will level off and begin to decline about the middle of the next century, even allowing for substantial immigration. The population is growing older: people live longer, and families have fewer babies.
- Growth of ethnic diversity: In the twenty-first century, America will have a new ethnic profile. The prospect of having a Hispanic, Asian, or African American in the White House is plausible. If current trends continue, at sometime during the next century, non-Hispanic whites will join African Americans, Hispanics, and Asians as a minority of the total U.S. population, leaving no clear majority.[14]
- Social change: American households today differ from the past. The number of single-person head-of-households increased and the number of married households and household size decreased.

Even though these are important domestic trends, the United States represents only a fraction of the world's population. In the future, this population share shrinks even further. As a result, the United States becomes increasingly vulnerable to global demographic forces over time.

Immigration.   Foreign immigration is a substantial force in forming the cultural heritage of America. It is not generally viewed as an administrative tool to initiate and carry out economic or social reforms. The policy supports the reuniting of families and provides for political sanctuary. Even so, immigration represents a vast infusion of labor and technical and entrepreneurial skills into the U.S. work force. As a whole, the United States is far more open to newcomers than any country in the world. Immigration has always been a source of fresh energy and change, and each generation seems to take on its own attitudes toward education, personal rights, religion, and family and social values.

Immigration is not without problems. There are conflicts between different newly immigrated groups, as well as conflicts between the recent arrival and the citizenry, as each tries to climb the economic ladder. The immigration policy of the United States also exacerbates an already existing problem: a problem of education and professional skills. There is little emphasis on targeting the skilled and educated for immigration. As a result, the United States can't count on a brain gain through immigration. Quite the opposite: Some immigrant groups seem to resist learning English, which in some states has already created a bilingual culture. One example is California, where the non-Hispanic white majority will become a minority by the year 2000 in greater Los Angeles and in the state by 2010.[15]

Aging.   The American population is growing older. Slow labor-force growth, combined with greater economic pressures on both business and older workers, will reverse the trend toward early retirement by the end of this decade. Companies will retain older workers to meet skill shortages and to lower private pension costs. Public and private pension systems are likely to move to later retirement provisions to keep the systems financially sound—exerting pressure on workers to stay on the job longer, with some predicting the standard retirement age to increase to 68 by the year 2000.[16]

Social Structure.   The idea of a typical family or household makeup is increasingly obscure. Consider the two presidential candidates in the 1992 elections. The candidates (George Bush and Bill Clinton) and their wives exemplify how the family structure is changing. Today, households made up of working couples, single parents, three generations, and retired children taking care of elderly parents are part of the recognized social fabric.

With the rise of single-parent and working-parent households, schools are rethinking and reformulating their role in society regarding health screenings, extended day care, and adult education. At the same time, other schools are turning to year-round school in response to budget cuts to better utilize existing facilities. In doing so, they compound the problem by creating additional scheduling and day-care burdens for families with two or more school-age children.

Another social change has been a slow migration to the rural areas. Three factors contributed. First, many activities supporting manufacturing and service moved out of the urban areas and into rural areas. This occurred for the same reasons as other U.S. commercial activities moved offshore: to achieve cost savings. Second, the resort industry grew, primarily in the less-populated areas. Third, after retirement, some people seek a slower pace and move from the city.

Necessary for further revitalization of rural areas is educational reform; the application of new information technologies to transform the workplace; and an investment in building and maintaining infrastructure—from roads to telecommunications linkages. In a recent article, a noted futures researcher suggests the strong role that information technology plays in a rural revival movement and posits four scenarios.[17]

- Business as usual: This scenario assumes that no major change in the economy occurs, and there are no substantial government policy interventions. The most active areas of the rural economy (large-scale farming, tourism, trucking, and food processing) invests heavily in innovations in information technologies. The rural infrastructure, weakened by rising costs and lack of new subsidies, forces the use of new information technologies to achieve maximum efficiency in transportation, energy, and manufacturing. The drive toward greater efficiency applies to labor productivity, but because low-skilled rural labor is relatively cheap, the drive to apply automation is weak.
- Women find work, men do not: In this scenario, information technology investment in office work doubles nationwide, and the advances trickle down into the rural workplace. The service and information economy move low-skilled work out of the urban office, and employs the rural female work force. Advances in expert systems and related technologies bring new work into the information-industry sector and ease the needs for extensive training.
- Information technology attracts: Telecommuting becomes a way of life for an increasing portion of the work force. The small-community lifestyle and less expensive real estate draws telecommuters to rural areas that are close to an urban fringe.
- Rural communities revive: In the final scenario, information technology moves out of the office, onto the road, and into the home. Portable, handheld, mobile, laptop, and miniature computers outdistance the desktop workstation. Networks proliferate, telecommunications accommodate distant work sites, and I/T revives rural America. As information technology pervades education, it becomes less necessary for students to be on-site, creating new day-care problems for working parents.

The world of the twenty-first century will be far more complex than today, as global technological and economic interdependence grows. At the very time that the international challenge increases, America becomes defined by an older generation. The changing nature of the rural economy, associated with the increasing importance of I/T helps achieve the economic diversity necessary for a stable economy.

Greater Europe. Europe, too, faces similar economic consequences relating to its aging population, immigration policies, and social structures.

Immigration. Probably the greatest peril to Germany and the rest of the EU economies is the position they take on migration. Germany is a magnet for refugees from Central Europe and the former Soviet Union because it has the most liberal immigration laws. Continued unrest may force Central European governments to abandon free market reforms. If this happens, waves of impoverished refugees would flood into Germany.

Aging. The world's average population age is 24 years. Currently, half the EU's population is over 34, and because of low birthrates, it will age quickly.[18] As Europe becomes a continent of old people, its politics and economics will alter. Lobbies for lower inflation, larger pensions, sterner crime control, better health services, and more reliable public transport will grow.

Social Structure. Germany's problem with immigration and migrant labor is really an all-European one. It's just that Germany is the first member of the European Union to address and begin to evaluate the social and economic consequences. German labor policy affects its business strategy. Facing soaring labor costs and taxes, German companies have begun to move some of their production to the United States. Lower wages are one incentive. Another incentive is the potential of a vast, integrated market created through free-trade negotiations among Canada, the United States, and Mexico. Examples are plentiful: Benckiser bought fragrance-maker Coty from Pfitzer for $440 million; Deutsche Bank increased its lending to top U.S. corporations; and Siemans completed the buy out of telecommunications-maker Rolm from IBM.[19] In an even bolder move, BMW built a manufacturing facility in Spartanburg, South Carolina, the first German luxury full-scale automobile manufacturing facility in another country, where it produces cars 20 percent more cheaply than in Germany. Like other German manufacturers, including Mercedes-Benz, BMW doesn't think it can compete anymore from a domestic base that has the shortest workweek, longest vacations, and highest business taxes in the industrialized world.

In the EU countries (excluding Britain and the Netherlands, which have large private-sector pension funds), the tradition is to pay the higher proportion of retirement costs through public funding. If unchanged, it is impossible to sustain some current public sector pension plans. Germany has some special problems in this arena, too. Firms save for its employees retirement by establishing reserves and deduct reserve contributions from taxable profit. Reserves traditionally have one great attraction: the employers decide how to invest them, thus reserve funds can further business aims through purchased stakes in friendly companies. This web of cross-shareholding shields firms from hostile takeover and breeds strong producer-supplier relationships, creating family economies that are difficult for an outsider to break into. This will change, because as workers retire and funds diminish, it becomes harder to hold onto the friendly shareholdings. Finally, German law requires firms to raise pensions in line with inflation—a liability unaccounted for in reserves. As German unification fuels inflation, this indexing becomes increasingly costly.

Europe faces a choice. It can head for slower economic growth with an aging population while trying to keep the newcomers out. Alternatively, it can face the problems of absorbing a growing number of foreigners. The economic fallout associated with immigration could potentially occupy Europe for a generation or more.

The Pacific. In economic terms, Japan could be the next world leader. However, its economy, for all its stunning success, has serious flaws: inflated real estate values, lavish subsidies to farmers, and a history of low domestic consumption.

Immigration. The Japanese strategy on immigration is completely different from those of the United States or Europe. Japan is a highly homogeneous society. It retains its historical tradition of racial exclusivity and treats its relatively small population of immigrants as permanent outsiders. Few ever obtain Japanese citizenship. When its extraordinary economic growth brought rising wages and labor shortages, it responded by exporting capital and technology. Japan dispersed physical production to Taiwan, Korea, Singapore, and Latin America. It moved physical production, design, and service industries to the United States and Europe. Japan consistently rejects immigration of any sort.[20]

Aging. As the Japanese grow in wealth, they became healthier. Their life expectancy overtook that of the United States in 1982. In 1990, 11 percent of Japan's population were age 65 or over. It was younger than Europe or the United States.[21] By 2010 18 percent will be over 65, making it the grayest part of the industrialized world. A 1986 International Monetary Fund (IMF) study showed that Japan's social security costs of 15 percent of its GNP were the lowest of the seven largest world economies. By 2010, the same study projected Japan's costs to rise to 26 percent of GNP. The burden of caring for this unparalleled crop of elderly people could seriously shrink Japan's high savings' rate and slow its productivity growth. Because Japanese firms don't have long-established pension funds, meeting those costs cut into profits and wages. Already, pension contributions add $87 to the cost of each Honda automobile manufactured.

Japan's law is like Germany's law in this respect: the employer sets up reserves. As a result, they use funds to support business strategy by purchasing minority ownership in related companies. Like Europe with its family economy, the strong producer-supplier relationships and the *keiretsu* are the result in Japan. As workers retire, the availability of Ministry of International Trade and Industry (MITI)-directed institutional investment funds shrink. Japanese businessmen, like their European counterparts, will find it harder to continue holding the minority ownership stakes.

Social Structure. Japanese business suffers from a three-way pressure: workers want to work fewer hours; trading partners want Japanese business to be less aggressive in capturing markets; and shareholders (or stakeholders) want a greater return-on-investment as they grow older.

- Workers: Workers want to work fewer hours and have time for leisure activities. In response, some companies are changing. For example, Omron, a manufacturer of automation controls, introduced sabbatical leaves for its middle managers, to be used to pursue a hobby or outside interest.[22]

- Competitors: Competitors clearly want the Japanese to be less aggressive in identifying and capturing markets. For Japan to have free access to EU and North American markets, it must offer quid pro quo, free access to its domestic markets.

- Shareholders and Institutional Investors: Institutional investors will need to withdraw funds to pay pensions, and when this occurs, they won't be able to wait for long-term payoffs on their investments. In the economic weekly magazine *Toyo Keizai,* Japanese economist Richard Koo predicts that companies will have to increase prices or withdraw from unprofitable lines of business if they are to meet investors' expectations.[23] Because institutional investors are increasingly free from MITI and regulatory control by the government, which directed past investments toward supporting national development, companies must change to ensure future access to capital funding.

The nation must restructure its economy not only to accommodate the shareholders demands for a higher return on their investments, but also to satisfy the workers, eager to enjoy the prosperity that they created. To respond to these pressures, Japanese business needs new paradigms for the twenty-first century, and the end result may be to raise prices and abandon the market-share strategy. In 1992, Akio Morita, the Sony chairman, stated that Japan must do some fundamental rethinking—somehow reinventing itself "to blend with the prevailing attitudes and practices of international business."[24] What he called for is far from easy—it means that Japan must reform deeply ingrained cultural attitudes toward work, leisure, and the world outside.

Business Impact of Demographic and Lifestyle Change

The role of the United States for the last half-century has been to stabilize and provide momentum for the international economic system. The United States accomplished this through applying a combination of population, economic, and political weight. Japan has half the population of the United States, and the newly unified Germany has about one-third the population of the United States. It is unlikely that either could amass enough political and economic weight to exercise world economic leadership alone. Because the populations of both countries are aging more rapidly than that of the United States, it is even less likely. What are the consequences? A U.S. Committee for Economic Development study shows that unless the international economic system finds a new center of gravity and a new formula for leadership, the likelihood of instability increases.[25] The reason is that today's demographic trends tend to increase costs more than expand capabilities of the industrialized nations. Within these nations, there is an increasing age consciousness concerning spending on programs for the old and the young. Increased ethnic diversity appears to be reinforcing the inclination for people to identify with narrower personal and group interests at the expense of broader common goals. Will the progressively aging populations, when confronted with increasingly vigorous and technically skilled populations abroad, engage that world? The alternative is that they may draw steadily back into themselves, expressing a preference for consumption and relative comfort and security over investment.

The three leading industrial nations are going through integrational stress. The United States is still integrating into its culture the civil rights movement and the diminishing difference in occupations between men and women. Germany is reintegrating its eastern and western halves. Japan is integrating a new social personality with its competitive business character. Additionally, these countries are experiencing stress from the growing integration of the global economy. This means new levels of competitiveness, new definitions of comparative advantage, and new modes of economic specialization for countries and regions within them. Concurrently, newly industrialized countries (NICs) emerge from the Third World. South Korea, Taiwan, Hong Kong, and Singapore recognize that they must act quickly to join the huge European and North American markets before trade barriers go up. The NICs promise to change the face of world trade in manufactured products with a skilled work force available at lesser cost. This process accommodates and accelerates the gradual transformation of the older industrialized nations into service industry economies. For the European Union, Japan and the United States, this means entering a new phase of international specialization and competition.

Will the U.S. industrial leaders influence legislation to make immigration procedures more selective? Alternatively, will business sufficiently reengineer its processes to compensate for the changing composition of the work force? Will Germany be able to absorb the influx of immigrants, therefore reducing its labor costs and increasing its world-class competitiveness? Will Japan make the cultural adjustments necessary to maintain competitiveness and, in the process, develop a world strategy that all will follow? Business management must know which trends are most critical to the success of their enterprise and monitor for early warning signs that signal a change in direction. Unfortunately, these directional signals come from all sides. Both the consequences of the aging work force and the evolving immigration policies determine the environment in which national policy is formulated: policy formulation in the individual national movements supporting globalization, regionalization, and protectionism. It is most clearly evident in Germany, where an open immigration policy requires massive expenditures for social services—expenditures that would otherwise go to unification efforts. Yet to solve the unemployment problem and fuel German industry, necessary elements in providing the funding for social services to support the aging population, it needs a large skilled working population. How Germany balances these two forces will determine its economic future.

The leading economic nations of today are aging rapidly. At the same time, the field of competition is an increasingly global economy, in which information, technology, and finance is more mobile than ever. And so are the people. A young, skilled work force energizes any economy; the older work force provides a source of experience and a potential economic base. The industrialized nations will each create its own unique economic destiny through its public policy and business strategy.

The combination of an aging work force and the increasing pressures of a global economy will result in new national public policies. As a consequence, both domestic and international business strategies will require reconceptualization and reformulation.

CONFLICTING FORCES FOR ENERGY AND ENVIRONMENTAL CONSERVATION

It's only been in the last twenty years that most companies and individuals have given much thought to the environment—whether it took the form of being concerned about the economic effects of overfishing coastal waters, polluting streams and waterways, or conserving energy. In the case of energy, consuming it was a nonissue because of its relatively stable price. That attitude ended with the oil-price shocks of 1973–1974, and of 1979, which pulled up other energy prices in its wake. By 1986, prices had dropped back to about their 1973 level, but we didn't return to treating energy consumption as a nonissue. The reason was the growing awareness of the lasting effects of environmental pollution.

Any internationally acceptable solution regarding energy production and consumption implies a sharing of the carbon budget. If developing countries need a bigger share to accommodate their growth, the rich countries need to accept less. Over the next two decades, the populations of developing countries will increase by about 2 billion—countries where energy use is currently the lowest. (The average person in a developing country uses the equivalent of one or two barrels of oil a year; the average European and Japanese, an equivalent of ten to thirty; the average American, forty.)

Coal, the greatest climatic offender, is economically important to two of the most populous countries: India and China. Combined, they sit on over one-third of the known coal reserves.[26] These governments control the energy supplies and set the prices. In India, prices are about 40 percent of the global average; in China, about half that of India. Generating electricity to meet subsidized demand has severe environmental consequences: the world's most polluted air is in China's Shenyang and Xi'an. By 2020, China alone will account for 20 percent of the world's carbon-dioxide output. Add India, and the total rises to 30 percent. To persuade either China or India to leave their coal in the ground, an alternative source of energy must exist. That source of energy must have three characteristics. First, it has to be cheaper than coal, especially for capital cost. Second, it has to be easier to use. Third, it must be environmentally friendly.

What energy alternatives do we have? The political difficulties of siting new nuclear plants have increased since Chernobyl. Capital costs of a new facility are large, as are the expenses of decommissioning. Hydroelectric development isn't popular with environmentalists in some countries, and it usually involves the cost of relocating people. Solar power is still relatively expensive and experimental. Even more experimental is the search to find an inexpensive and efficient way to commercially produce hydrogen, the cleanest-burning of all fuels, although many experts think that this will be the twenty-first century energy solution for the environment. Thus, we have no ready alternative to offer the Chinese and the rest of the developing nations. Until we do, the Americans, Japanese, and Europeans must take the leadership role to develop policies to encourage the development of environmentally friendly technology; to reduce consumption of *dirty* energy; and to create and commercialize a new, clean, inexpensive source of energy for the world to use. This, in conjunction with international agreement is the best way to solve environmental problems that transcend national borders.

Regional Activities

North America.   Conservation of power is igniting an energy revolution in the United States. In 1991, some 200 utilities invested $2 billion into 1,300 conservation programs.[27] In 1993, new national standards required many refrigerators to use 20 to 40 percent less energy, and in 1995, similar rules apply to washers, dryers, and other appliances. Builders are using simple but important technologies to construct homes that heat for $1 a day. Designers incorporate technologies that take 50 percent less energy to light, heat, and cool commercial buildings. Trend-setting states like California plan to reduce gasoline consumption through incentives and penalties to encourage mass transit, car pools, and walking.

This interest in boosting energy efficiency has resulted in the development of demand-side management projects by electric utilities. The idea grew out of a campaign against the Pacific Gas and Electric Company (PG&E) by the Environmental Defense Fund (EDF). The EDF argued that promoting conservation was cheaper than building new power stations, yet it had the same effect. Any utility customers' interest is in keeping warm or cool or running their appliances. It's not in buying kilowatts.

The question of how to persuade a utility to sell less of its product was to decouple profits from sales volume. States where environmental pressure is strongest became pilot sites for regulatory changes. These regulatory changes make it more profitable to invest in energy conservation and efficiency than to supply more power. California was the first state to take this approach, allowing utilities to earn a return on their investments in programs such as energy audits and rebates on energy-saving appliances that create negawatts, or conserved power. By 1992, nineteen states enacted regulatory changes to support the negawatt concept.

States are also starting to require utilities to factor the cost of environmental damage into the cost of power production. In California, where the process of calculating environmental cost is just beginning, the price assigned wind power is 15 percent lower than that for energy from traditional sources. The idea behind environmental least-cost pricing is to levy a *paper penalty* on relatively dirty forms of fuel to reflect its environmental costs. This paper penalty is part of the cost calculations that utilities must submit to their regulatory agency. It forces utilities to look at cleaner fuels when adding new sources of power. Besides California, New York, Massachusetts, and Nevada require this adder, using market forces rather than regulations to keep the environment clean.[28]

The National Environmental Act, passed in 1969, set deadlines for reaching air quality standards. It legislated progressively tightening standards. Initially, federal agencies issued compliance goals and then mandated the acceptance methods for achieving the goals. Because there was no strong, built-in incentive for industry to do better than the standard, a revision of The National Environmental Act in 1990 tried to rectify the situation, bringing federal standards closer to those of California. Companies can now meet pollution goals by whatever means they have. If, through technology investment, it produces less pollution than its permits allow, it may sell its unused permits to other businesses. This provides business with an incentive to cut pollution below government regulations. It also provides so-called dirty industries a way to continue functioning until they find a way to reduce their pollutant by-products through purchasing allowances from cleaner industries. The results of this particular scheme are being watched with interest in other countries.

This illustrates the different, and sometimes conflicting, roles that the state and federal governments play in American business. The role of the federal government is traditionally one of laissez faire, using antitrust enforcement to ensure market access. It doesn't set national agendas for industry either, as have the Japanese and German governments. Therefore, tougher measures at the national level, such as sharply higher gasoline taxes and more stringent auto-fuel-economy standards, aren't the rule. (Both of these measures would, by the way, force Detroit to design more efficient cars, and would, as a result, make them more competitive with the Japanese and European products.) As a consequence, there is no direct incentive from the federal level to develop tools, technologies, or products to sell in a global market. Conversely, the state and local governments, concerned with regional issues, address them as such. They create and support initiatives to benefit their own region.

Greater Europe.   The EU countries set targets for the reduction of sulfur dioxide in the 1988 Large Combustion Plants directive. The EU, active in areas of common interest, gave initial approval to levy a tax on carbon dioxide-producing fuels. This ultimately increases the price of natural gas about 30 percent and coal about 60 percent.[29] The net effect is to spur businesses and individual consumers to conserve energy. Additionally, the European Union helps finance development of clean technologies, such as 100-percent recyclable cars and low-polluting power generators. Aware of the contamination of industrial sites, the European Union began development of a position that starts with the recognition that plans need to address the past environmental damage.[30]

Some European countries provide incentives by funding initiatives for development of environmentally-friendly products and industries. The French TGV, a 186 mile-per-hour train, attracts passengers that would normally fly. The train, developed as a direct result of government subsidy, provides a technologically advanced product to a worldwide market. Additionally, the imposition of a waste tax to fund the development of advanced waste-treatment plants is a French initiative that promises to create an entire export industry for the country. Concurrent with the French activities, Britain anticipates the market value for its environmental products to be $50 billion by the year 1995. There, the government set up a $20 million fund to support innovations in recycling and in environmental monitoring and reduction of waste from manufacturing processes. It gives farmers grants up to 50 percent of the cost of building new slurry and silage storage facilities to cope with farm waste.[29] Finally, Europe's greenest nation is Germany, although it didn't start that way. After the various U.S. Clean Air Acts in the 1970s, Germany did little until the early 1980s when it saw its forests dying. It imposed limits for sulfur dioxide and nitrogen oxides so stringent that only the most modern technology could meet them. There, commercial banks grant low-interest loans for pro-environment projects, and the complete phase out of chlorofluorocarbons in 1993 is two years ahead of most countries.

One area in which the European Union is not leading policy coordination is in recycling. The individual governments are legislating with only one thing in common: they place the responsibility of making recycling work on individual companies, not local authorities. The companies must take responsibility not just for their products, but also for what happens to the products at the end of their lives. Countries are already legislating regulations that will force manufacturers to take back and recycle their products, including automobiles, batteries, and electronic parts in computers. This will change the way European companies operate in the future and will impact product design, product manufacture, and location of sale.

Let's examine Germany, the European equivalent to California's environmental activism. When the issue of one-trip drink containers came up, the result was Parliament's packaging ordinance of April 1991, requiring retailers to take back packaging from customers, manufacturers to retrieve it from retailers, and packaging companies to reclaim its materials from the manufacturers. The packaging companies must then recycle to avoid heavy deposit levies on their products. Some 400 German businesses and multinationals banded together to form the Duales System Deutschland (DSD) and organized nationwide recycling of household waste packaging. After packaging, electronic components and automobiles were next.[31] Manufacturers had to set up networks to receive and recycle electronic components by the end of 1993. The legislation specifies a free market approach to recycling—companies themselves must find ways to reuse old products, so that industry, not the government, bears the cost.[32] As part of this movement, Volkswagen became the first automobile supplier in the German market (and in the world) to guarantee that vehicles were returnable at the end of their lives. The initial guarantee is for the 1992 model Golf onward. Volkswagen plans to gradually extend the guarantee to earlier models.

Although other European countries and companies are following Germany's example, generally they have less aggressive goals. Eventually, in the interests of a single market, the European Union will have to introduce similar legislation whether it uses the German legislation as a springboard or as a blueprint.

The Pacific.   Two decades ago, Japan's major cities suffered from the same problem as did the Los Angeles Basin: photochemical smog from automobile and factory emissions. Japan then suffered through two oil crises that sent prices soaring and created shortages. The Japanese government enacted legislation to foster energy efficiency, creating a long-term effect on industry initiatives. It fostered green technologies spanning a broad range of industries, forming a new global export environmental market. The Japanese lead both the United States and Germany in pollution technology for basic industry, and the Japanese Association of Industrial Machinery predicts a $12 billion market by the year 2000 for Japanese company's environmental products. These products include waste incinerators, air-pollution control equipment, and water-treatment devices.

As part of a far-reaching national policy, MITI created its "New Earth 21" blueprint. The purpose of the blueprint is to try to vastly reduce carbon dioxide emissions by the end of the next century. To support this project, MITI supports the Research Institute of Innovative Technology for the Earth. Another MITI-backed series of exotic projects dedicate effort to the development of a commercially viable process to manufacture hydrogen, the most promising clean-burning fuel. The government is spending about $4 billion a year to broaden the country's environmental skills. MITI targets the development of integrated systems that minimize waste and create new markets. It is making a major effort to develop and export pollution control gear and expertise. This focus is paying off for MITI. For example, researchers at the Japanese Atomic Energy Research Institute, Chubu Electric Power Company, and Ebara Corporation work on a joint project to convert sulfur and nitrogen oxides (the chief causes of acid rain) to ammonium sulfate and nitrate for fertilizers.[33] Japan licensed research groups in the United States, Poland, and Germany to use the technique.

Other areas of environmental technology are exportable, too. Japan has technology for such things as low-emission incinerators for solid and liquid waste, the recycling of heat and waste products in the steel industry, sewage control and sludge-treatment equipment for heavy industry, and the removal of sulfur and nitrous oxides from the stacks of steel and electric-power plants. Although interested in exporting Japanese technology to North America and Greater Europe, Japan's top priority is the Pacific market. The government earmarked Official Development Assistance (ODA) funds to subsidize environmental projects there. In 1991, for example, MITI proposed bundling aid projects aimed at energy development in China, Malaysia, and Indonesia with ODA subsidies for Japanese environmental equipment purchases.

Closing Perspective

Nuclear generating facilities are aging. As we begin decommissioning, do we have an alternative energy source? We know our current business culture couldn't survive in a low- to zero-emission operating environment. How and what must we change today to maintain competitiveness tomorrow? These are not easy questions, nor are there any easy answers.

Political trends (globalization, regionalization, and protectionism), demographic trends (aging and immigration), and greening trends (energy and environmental conservation) have important implications, but even more significant is how they interact with one another to influence future competitiveness. These close relationships between trends aren't always easily recognizable, and the power and direction of trends are sometimes easy to ignore, resulting in political and business constituencies focusing on their own narrowly defined priorities. These constituencies frame the policy and strategy debates, and define the actions based on its own agendas. The result is to make small, incremental adjustments in reaction to immediately noticeable business or political pressures, rather than to rethink the conceptual assumptions and strategic implications. It's questionable that this technique will ensure much future success if continued, for the magnitude of change today requires questioning assumptions and implications with the goal of creating a more sustainable, globally competitive enterprise.

PART II. ENABLING ENTERPRISE TRANSFORMATION WITH I/T

In Part I, we focused on the new market place of international competition and traced a few of the global trends that affect businesses today. One of these trends relates to energy and the environment. Today there is an increasing emphasis on environmental protection at all levels—the incident at Chernobyl provided a vivid reminder to everyone that environmental damage doesn't stop at political or geographic boundaries. Consequently, this heightened social awareness—coupled with increased legislative activity and regulatory reform ensuring environmental safety—is creating new markets for some products and restricting or eliminating markets for others. Building upon the market dynamics identified in Part I, business has already begun to identify new paradigms that are necessary to transform itself into a new competitive form with new focus. The transformation paradigms for addressing these changes include mass customization; service, quality, and integrity; and business process and organizational reengineering—paradigms having particular relevance to both current and future I/T activities.

Chapter 12 introduced the reader to Southern California Edison Company, a large investor-owned electric utility operating in Southern and Central California. This is a company that consistently acts like a leader. It was the first utility to institute scenario planning as part of its strategic planning process. It is committed to creating partnerships with its customers to increase productivity, improve product quality, and meet California's high environmental standards. It uses energy-efficient technologies and offers an increasing array of energy-efficient services. It is a key player in the emerging wholesale power market. But perhaps more importantly, it understood the opportunities of the increasing domestic (out of physical service territory) market and the growing international privatization of utilities and thus restructured itself in the mid-eighties to take advantage of these growing markets. As a result, by 1992, SCEcorp had more earnings from nonutility businesses than any other electric utility holding company in the United States.

In "Coping with Business and Technological Change," Michael L. Mushet, the lead author and general manager, Power Systems Management Division, Southern California Edison, provides an insight into the evolution and future direction of the I/T function within a business dominated by a management prizing leadership skills. Becoming an equal partner in planning the business strategy, a goal not yet achieved in many organizations, is assumed in this I/T function. Being given the responsibility for the management of a new and vital business initiative is perhaps another future goal for I/T organizations who wish to become equal business partners. Again, this is a goal already achieved by the SCE I/T function. Why this I/T organization is so different from most, and what its vision of the future is, requires thoughtful consideration by both business and I/T management.

Coping With Business and Technological Change

A Brief Case Study of the Electric Utility Industry

Michael L. Mushet
with
Marilyn M. Parker

INTRODUCTION

The utilities business is, without a doubt, a unique one. With roots that go back over one hundred years, electric utilities have provided virtually the same product, created by the same means, distributed in the same fashion to the same customer set for five generations. Today the United States has an electric power industry that provides a level of quality and service second to none in the world. The utilities achieved this level of service without notoriety or fanfare, for the most part, measuring progress using megawatts, kilowatt hours, and BTUs/kilowatt, terms little understood by the general public. Nonetheless, growth was meteoric, the industry rock solid, and their widow's and orphan's stock a mainstay of retirement funds. Driven by engineering technology and with information technology as a friend, electric utilities grew and prospered.

Recently, however, the industry has faced a set of challenges totally different from those of the past. These changes have taken several generic forms: political/environmental, societal, financial, and technological. More and more, utilities are turning to information technology to help them meet their new challenges. This is good news and bad news. Never has there been a richer set of information technology choices from which to pick and never before has there been the level of confusion about those choices. This article briefly reviews the nature of the electrical utility business, followed by the more recent history of the Southern California Edison Company (a subsidiary of SCEcorp). It then presents an approach to developing and delivering an I/T support structure to meet the needs of the corporation for the next decade.

THE ELECTRIC UTILITY INDUSTRY

It is instructive to review a little about the nature of the electric utility business. This will help put into perspective some of the rationale presented later. There are several aspects to explore. They are the nature of the product, the obligation to serve, the business characteristics, and the operation of modern power systems.

Nature of the Product

The main product (from the customers' perspective) of electric utilities is truly unique. It is its intangibility that creates a wrinkle that promulgates itself through the operation of the business. It is the only product that gets created, distributed, and consumed in the same instant. This nature creates an environment similar to the traditional just-in-time inventory of normal manufacturing industries—except that the factory floor spreads out over thousands of square miles. The safety aspects of the product have put the responsibility on the utilities to have complete control over it—from creation to a point of delivery at the customer's residence, store, factory or other point of consumption. The delivery of the product is in synchronization with all other product deliveries—to the fraction of a second. A matter of a few thousandths of a second can be enough of a disruptive effect to blackout major sections of a city or state. (As an example, the January 1994 Northridge earthquake in southern California caused electric service disruptions as far away as Oregon due to a momentary fluctuation of SCE energy flow into the Northwest power grid.)

Obligation to Serve

The second unique characteristic of electric utilities is the obligation to sell product to anyone anywhere in their service territory. Through the establishment of a franchise, the utility must connect customers even if the cost of connection is cost-prohibitive in a normal business environment. Operating through rights of eminent domain and its own rights-of-way, the utility will run electrical service to all who ask. In addition, this happens in a fashion, that to a majority of customers, is extremely reliable. There is seldom if ever a doubt that the lights will go on when the customer throws the switch. (Some customers even take the position that it is too reliable—they would accept less reliability for less price.)

Business Characteristics

The third characteristic to explore is the business nature of electric utilities. The high level view of the utility would show an extremely capital intensive business. This capital investment spreads over hundreds or thousands of square miles. In the past, many viewed the utility as a giant financial machine for raising money to invest in expensive capital equipment. This equipment would have a useful life of several decades, paid for through the collection of rate-payer money for electrical service provided. All of these transactions would have the oversight of a utilities commission that had varying influence and control depending upon the state. This regulation is the price the utility paid for the privilege of being a monopoly within its service territory. There was no competition. For many years the utilities enjoyed this status of regulated monopoly. They had a captive customer base for whom they created, distributed, and sold product. In the case of investor-owned utilities, management used the profits to expand the system and repay shareholders through dividends. Municipal or federal utilities returned the profits to users in the form of reduced rates. In many of these environments, I/T supported the coordination of the mechanics of running the electrical network, supported the billing process for thousands or millions of customers, and assisted in the general administrative work of the utility.

The Operation of Modern Power Systems

A modern power system consists of four major components. They include the functions of generation, transmission, distribution, and system operations.

Generation. Utilities either create product or purchase it from other connected utilities. The more traditional way of creating product is to convert some hydrocarbon into electrical energy through the process of burning coal, oil, or gas, using the resulting heat to create steam. The steam spins a steam turbine connected to an electrical generator, creating the electricity. Nuclear power plants utilize the heat of fissionable heavy elements to create the steam. Hydroelectric units utilize falling water to turn generators directly; wind generators work on a similar principle. More exotic means consist of high-technology solar and geothermal processes.

Utilities purchase power from other utilities through various forms of purchase/sale agreements. With high-voltage transmission lines, the utilities transmit power hundreds or thousands of miles to meet customer demand. Using sophisticated control schemes, the selling utility raises its generation to exceed its current load. Almost simultaneously, the purchasing utility lowers its generation, thus causing the electrical current to flow to its area's customers. (All of this occurs in the matter of a few seconds.) These purchase/sale agreements occurred as a result of a variety of external issues such as anticipated demand, weather, generation status, and water availability.

In the past, the utility would generate a majority of the power used to serve its customer base. This is no longer the case at many utilities. Through numerous changes in state and federal regulation, utilities have seen a continued erosion of their market share as enhanced electrical technology has allowed third parties to sell electrical energy indirectly to the end customer. Indeed, many large customers are starting to install equipment to meet their own electrical needs and to sell any excess back to the utility. The utility, due to regulation, must purchase this power at top dollar—regardless of the current needs of their other customers. To keep the instantaneous balance of generation and demand load, utilities must curtail their own generation to accept that of these third parties. Extensive use of information technology assists in this balancing act.

Regardless of the source of the energy, it must exactly match the profile of the demand. The demand will track to m-shaped curves that peak just before and after noon and drop off to a small percentage of their maximum in the evening hours. The peaks of the *m* will vary with weather and season. Some utilities peak in the winter, others in the summer. It is the shape of the curve, however, that causes problems. What it means is that the utility must have enough capacity to meet the peaks yet let the equipment lay idle during the off-hours. Large utility steam generators take several days to come on-line so extensive planning is necessary to guarantee their availability when required. In addition, these devices do not operate efficiently while idling. Engineered to be at peak efficiency when operating at near-maximum power output, running them at lower settings wastes fuel and increases their relative output of emissions.

It is this area that has recently caused the most problems to many utilities. While there have been, and will continue to be, concerns about environmental issues of generation, it is the availability of high-efficiency, relatively low-cost generation capability that is changing the nature of the business. In much the same way that personal computers broke the mold of large central mainframe processors, new high-tech generation (e.g., the fuel cell) is causing electric utilities to reevaluate their model of large, central power generation facilities. Faced with aging and less efficient equipment, utilities must compete in a manner that maintains their financial viability as well as their commitments to preserve the investment their rate-payers have made in the older equipment.

Information technology supports initiatives involving such things as system efficiency monitoring, work flow planning, and maintenance management. The bulk of the technology is usually used outside the station proper for system operation and dispatch.

Transmission.   The transmission network is the mechanism for bulk power delivery by the utility. Relying on high-voltage technology, the utility transforms electrical energy from a relatively low generation voltage to a much higher voltage, minimizing electrical losses in the transmission lines. It then lowers the voltage before delivery to the distribution system.

The transmission system is a real battleground. Rights-of-way are becoming more difficult to obtain as the population encroaches on the once out-of-the-way locations used for transmission corridors. Environmental concern for wildlife has heightened making siting even more difficult. The most critical issues, however, will clearly prove to be those associated with access to this network. As more third parties enter the generation business, they and their potential customers are asking for the right to utilize the capability of the lines—sometimes at the expense of the utility—to serve the native load of the utility. Taken to the extreme, this means that third-party competitors building new energy-efficient generating facilities and exercising their right to equal access to the utility-owned transmission system could relegate current utilities to becoming primarily transmission and delivery managers. This also suggests an increasing likelihood of future intrastate and interstate price wars to sell electricity.

Within the transmission system, I/T supports engineering design and operation and maintenance management.

Distribution.   The distribution system provides the point of contact with the customer. Its purpose is to take power from the bulk system and provide delivery at the voltage appropriate for customer needs. It is the distribution system with which most people are familiar. Typically consisting of thousands of miles of underground cables and vaults and overhead wires on poles, it is under constant attack from everything from errant tree limbs and cars to mylar helium balloons. The distribution system for most utilities is an expensive, high maintenance, but necessary proposition.

While there is usually a high degree of information intensity for meter reading, billing, and customer information, this area is usually the least automated of the three major utility components. It is ripe with opportunity.

System Operation.   The systems operation components are really the brains behind the operation of the utility. Serving as production control, the systems control component schedules generation and purchases of electricity, manages the use of the transmission network, and provides overall coordination of all electrical system functions down to the distribution level.

I/T has always played a key role in this area. Using communications lines to feed sophisticated control algorithms with necessary generation and transmission data, the system operation component keeps the proper balance of generation and demand load while meeting financial and regulatory commitments.

System Summary.   A typical distribution of total electrical system investment is about 49 percent in generation; 17 percent in transmission; 31 percent in distribution; and 3 percent in the more general categories.

The Stages of the Electric Utility Business in the United States

In their book *Public Utilities,* Ferris and Sampson posit that the economic role of public utilities in American capitalism is a very distinctive one: that the services provided by public utilities are essential for economic growth and development.[34] They state that no economy can progress very far without what economic growth theorists call *social overhead capital.* There are several types of social overhead capital, however, the one of most interest to us is a flexible and reliable power source. Further, they point out that there have been a number of stages in the development of the public utility industry. These stages include:

- The promotional stage: Working with crude technology, early utilities were small and often subsidized by grants of money and land to meet the tremendous capital intensive needs of the utility business.
- The competitive stage: An eager society promulgated a competitive environment that lacked controls. Prices were high; service often not the best. Cities started to exercise their franchise rights.

- The monopolistic stage: During this phase most utilities merged into citywide monopolies as cities recognized that competitive franchises were not effective in such capital intensive enterprises.
- The regional stage: In this stage, utilities expanded into regional or even statewide service territories. They adopted extensive controls designed to ensure the rights of the consumer and began efforts to improve efficiency and service levels while delivering a reduction in rates.
- The cooperation stage: In this stage, utilities started to cooperate at broader levels to improve their reliability and service levels. They initiated interconnections and purchasing agreements, creating an electrical system greater than the sum of its parts.

A number of changes have occurred since Ferris and Sampson published their book in 1984. Collectively these changes have created a new stage; one that may mark the most dramatic effects on the power industry.

Significant Drivers in the Public Utility Model

There are several major drivers in the electrical utility industry. These drivers set the stage for and act as the prime movers for almost all utility strategies and policies. They include:

- The social/environmental drivers: The last several decades have seen a greatly heightened awareness of societal and environmental issues. This influenced the utilities in matters ranging from facility siting, environmental impact studies, and special rate consideration for certain sectors of the rate base.
- The political/regulatory drivers: New regulatory implications accompanied the explosive growth of population and industry over the last few decades. Safety and environmental concerns about nuclear energy, air and water quality, and preservation of wildlife resulted in more stringent regulations. Additionally, open access to formerly private transmission facilities prove to be difficult to manage and regulate.
- The financial drivers: The utility business is extremely capital intensive, with electric utilities at the high end of the scale.
- The technology drivers: Without a doubt, technology has had the most profound effect on the utility business. The most influential has been the progress made in generation capability. Here, utilities made substantial progress in lowering the price points of generation. More and more, equipment such as combined cycle generators and fuel cells are sounding the death knell for a central power station model. Customers, migrating to a model of distributed generation, serve their own distributed loads. The combination of these factors alone will forever change the nature of the electric utility business.

THE SOUTHERN CALIFORNIA EDISON COMPANY

"The history of the Southern California Edison Company reflects a proud tradition of service performed by dedicated and creative people. In 1886, Edison's first ancestral utilities supplied a rudimentary service to a few dozen customers. From these beginnings, far-sighted pioneers worked to produce a reliable supply of electricity to light the homes and streets, run the electric railroads, power the factories and businesses, and irrigate the fields and orchards of southern and central California." Howard P. Allen, former president, chairman and chief executive officer of SCEcorp.

Financial and Demographic Snapshot

SCEcorp is a publicly held California holding company created in the mid-eighties that is the parent organization to Southern California Edison Company (known as SCE or Edison) and a collection of other subsidiaries known as the Mission companies.

SCE is a large electric utility chartered by the state of California to provide electrical service to major portions of the southern section of the state. The service territory includes mountain, desert, and marine environments. Like other electric utilities, SCE is capital intensive. The basic demographic information includes:

- Revenue: US$7.7 billion
- Employees: 16,000
- Customers: 4.1 million
- Sales: 75,600,000 KWh
- Service Area: 50,000 square miles

SCE's capital investments consist of 55 generation units powering 9,700 miles of transmission lines connecting almost 900 electrical substations. Customers receive service through 3,880 distribution circuits on 1.5 million power poles. Total generation investment is $8.1 billion; transmission is $1.09 billion; substations amount to $2.35 billion; and distribution equipment is $3.98 billion.

The Mission companies include Mission Energy, a major developer and investor in energy related projects; Mission Finance, providing a wide-range of financial backing for a variety of investments; and Mission Land, involving a nationwide real estate program.

Nature of the People

It is probably the employees that distinguish SCE more than any other thing. As you might expect in a company with over a century of operation, the company is rich with tradition. Rated as one of the top one hundred places to work in the United States, the employees have a proud heritage and are proud of themselves, their accomplishments, their innovations, and their company. While it is changing now, in many respects the work force had been paramilitary in its structure and chain of command. Driven perhaps by the needs of safety, a majority of the company's operation was proceduralized. In an environment like this, one would expect stability as the norm, with change stifled. However, this has not been the case.

SCE counts many engineering firsts among its accomplishments. It was the first company to use steel towers to transmit high voltage current; the first to explore the Colorado River searching for hydroelectric power; the first to use nuclear power to feed the commercial power grid; and the first to harness the hydroelectric power of the High Sierra with the Big Creek project. From a business perspective, SCE was the first U.S. utility to have its stock listed on non-U.S. markets; the first to issue bonds in nondollar denominations (Japanese Shogun bonds); and the first to create a major independent power producing profit-driven, nonregulated competitor in its subsidiary company, Mission Energy.

It is not uncommon to have several family generations with company roots. A majority of middle and senior management have worked their way up through various positions within the company. The company has an organization known as the Diamond Club for employees with over twenty-five years of service. Its membership is large and its meetings well attended.

In the past, the company had little need for a strategic plan. The planning it did have was genetic, guided by the basic principles of "Good Service, Square Dealing, and Courteous Treatment" established by then president John B. Miller in 1905. It is now clear that this heritage has in some ways worked against current strategic planning initiatives. While not large from a staffing perspective, it has still proven difficult to move the thinking of a large group of employees at a pace that meets the expectations of the company's new chief executive officer.

The Business

Through the Seventies.   As with other utilities, SCE spent the early years focused on expansion of the service territory. The employee base grew with the acquisition of other smaller companies throughout this period. The thirties saw the development of major hydroelectric facilities at Hoover Dam and in the High Sierra. During the sixties, the company undertook major construction of fossil fueled plants and the initiation of its first major nuclear plant. At the same time, they developed major transmission corridors from Southern California to the Pacific Northwest. The company continued to pride itself on its engineering prowess and created a major organizational unit dedicated to engineering and construction.

Business in the Eighties.   The eighties saw several significant changes in the company. Changes in federal regulations and increased competition from independent power producers caused the company to rethink and broaden its approach to contributing to the overall earnings picture.

The Mission Companies.   In 1985, SCE reorganized its structure into a holding company, SCEcorp. Subordinate to this holding company is the Southern California Edison Company and several subsidiary companies operating under the Mission banner. By creating these subsidiaries, it could leverage the resources of the company in ways that would maximize the return to the shareholder through promising profit-making ventures unencumbered by the regulatory concerns of the various public utility commissions. At the same time, it could still honor the compact the company has with its rate-payers, successfully insulating the regulated activities (and fixed return on investment) from the unregulated (higher risk, higher reward) activities. There are currently three active Mission companies.

- Mission Energy: Mission Energy, with fewer than 500 employees, is a $2 billion company dedicated to being the leader in the long-term development, ownership, and operation of independent power production and co-generation facilities domestically and internationally. The company owns 1,507 megawatts of generation capacity in thirty operating domestic and foreign projects, enough power to serve 750,000 customers. If Mission Energy were a standalone company, it would rank as number 157 in the Fortune 500 list.

- Mission First Financial: Mission First Financial, with over three quarters of a billion dollars in assets, is an investment subsidiary whose primary focus is energy-related investments. The company's passive investment strategy effectively complements Mission Energy's active involvement in developing, owning, and operating power projects. In the last five years, Mission First Financial's earnings have grown at an average annual rate of 21%.

- Mission Land: Mission Land owns and operates almost $500 million of industrial parks, primarily in Southern California. In 1991, SCEcorp decided not to pursue real estate development as one of its core businesses and to exit the business in an orderly way over the next three to five years.

The Merger.   SCEcorp throughout its history had been a composite of other companies. Built through succeeding layers of merger and acquisition, its last merger was with California Electric Power in the mid-sixties. Because each utility is a regulated monopoly in its own service territory, the only way to expand is to link up in some fashion with another utility.

Conservation Initiatives.   Although most consider utilities one of the larger stationary sources of air pollution, they are not. Vehicles account for an order of magnitude higher level than utilities. SCE, in its environmentalist role, continues to exhibit leadership by winning a number of environmental awards. By combining state-of-the-art engineering and innovative unmarketing techniques such as conservation-friendly fluorescent lights, swimming pool pump timers, and energy-efficient refrigerator rebates, SCE continuously demonstrates consideration for the community and the ecosystem as a whole.

Financial Creativity.   One measure of the success of a utility is the ability to generate funds for capital investment programs. Because SCE's earnings are determined by the amount of its capital programs that are part of its rate base, it is extremely important to its financial viability to open its funding programs to the widest range of markets. They exercised financial creativity on several occasions, for example, SCE was the first utility to issue Shogun bond issues in nondollar denominations. These bonds opened up the previously unreachable Japanese market as a source of funds.

Qualified Facilities.   A number of changes in energy legislation took place during this period. Some of this legislation served to somewhat minimize the monopolistic status previously held by utilities. The legislation allowed the creation of qualified facilities (QFs). Regulators allowed QFs to generate electricity for purchase by the utilities at market value, in spite of the utilities' ability to generate the electricity at a lower rate. As both the utility and the QF worked their way through the nuances of this type of arrangement, they initiated a large number of contracts. While it did develop energy capability, many would argue that it did so at the expense of the ratepayer. In any event, it set the stage for the nineties, when questions of retail wheeling and open access to transmission would prove to be a major issue of contention. Additionally, in the later part of the decade, many large industrial concerns began to explore the concept of cogeneration; where they were able to generate more electricity than they required and were able to sell the excess back to the utility. This too proved to be stage-setting for the nineties.

Business in the Nineties and Beyond.   It was during this period that the company began to reinvent itself in earnest. The bulk of this work unfolded under the guise of strategic planning.

Strategic Planning.   In 1990 the former chairman and chief executive officer retired, creating opportunities for a new executive team. The new team quickly got down to the business of developing and institutionalizing a new vision for itself. Working closely with a variety of management consultants, the team attempted to assess the direction and approach that would allow it to be competitive in the business environment of the next decade.

The team established a strategic focus consisting of Competitive Performance, Customers, Community/Environment, The SCE Team, Regulators, and Shareholders. These focus points had specific strategies and goals. They were:

Competitive Performance.   Strategy: SCE will aggressively benchmark and manage costs in all areas to ensure competitiveness and provide superior customer value.

   Goals:

1. Competitive Rates: Keep system average rate increases below the level of inflation. Meet or beat competitive price levels in each major customer segment.
2. Competitive Production and Acquisition Costs: Meet or beat competitive power production and acquisition costs.
3. Operating Income: Increase utility revenues to benefit customers and shareholders.

Customers.   Strategy: The operative term is *value.* SCE will differentiate services to enhance customer value, increase customer satisfaction, and build market share of customer's energy solutions.

Goals:

1. Satisfaction: Measure and continuously enhance value in each major customer segment.
2. Energy Efficiency: Provide enhanced customer value by delivering cost-effective energy efficiency services, including 10 billion KWhs of conservation by year 2000 and 5 billion KWhs of source-fuel-efficient electrical solutions by the year 2000.

Community Environment. Strategy: The operative term is *leadership.* SCE will seek to be a corporate leader in helping to solve the region's dual challenges of economic competitiveness and environmental quality.

Goals:

1. Regional Leadership: Lead the partnership with customers, communities, and governments to achieve integrated solutions to the challenges of economic competitiveness and environmental quality.
2. Environmental Leadership: Demonstrate industry leadership by continuously improving the environmental performance of operations.

The SCE Team. Strategy: The operative term is *excellence.* SCE will develop a team with the skills, creativity, and enthusiasm to achieve the competitive performance strategy. SCE will eliminate the unnecessary work and establish systems and practices that make it easy to identify results expected, measure progress achieved, and reward results attained.

Goals:

1. Employee Partnership: Commit the resources to develop and attract both employees and employee teams that can excel in a competitive environment and reward demonstrated excellence.
2. Diversity: Maximize the value of diversity by meeting or exceeding the SCE Comprehensive Equal Opportunity Pledge.

Regulators. Strategy: The operative term is *shared purpose.* SCE will seek to develop a sense of shared purpose and common objectives with the regulators. SCE will ensure that the policies advocated are carefully developed, well coordinated, effectively communicated, and based on a shared view of the utility's role in the future energy marketplace.

Goals:

1. Purpose: Demonstrate mutual respect and shared purpose when dealing with regulators.
2. Leadership: Lead in energy policy-making.
3. Management: Manage all aspects of the business to eliminate disallowance for imprudence.
4. Explore New Ideas: Explore innovative regulatory mechanisms that contribute to the region's vitality and SCE's long-term business outlook.
5. Excellence: Excel in fulfilling all regulatory commitments.

Shareholders.   Strategy: The operative term is *value*. SCE will enhance share-holder value by earning the authorized return, eliminating write-offs and disallowance, and maintaining the AA bond rating. SCE will seek additional earnings' opportunities that do not materially increase risk.

Goals:

1. Maintain Earnings: Earn the authorized return on rate base.
2. Expand Earnings: Seek to expand earnings as allowed for energy-efficient services, regulatory incentives, and other selected opportunities.
3. Maintain Ratings: Maintain AA bond rating.

Report Card.   The above strategies and goals were the second in a series. After the first round, management created a report card that clearly identified to all where the company did poorly and where the company did well. For the most part, SCE met its goals. It did well in most areas although some results were inconclusive. Disappointments occurred in the areas of performance to shareholders and the loss of SCE's AA bond rating—a result of a regulatory decision of the California Public Utilities Commission (PUC). This reporting vehicle will probably be an ongoing measure of success.

All in all, it was the feeling of the chairman that ". . . we must realize that we have a long way to go. We are a good team. And we'll continue to be, if we think boldly, act with urgency and focus on results to achieve our corporate vision of being a great company that provides business and regional leadership."[35]

PLANNING A MERGER

Few business processes are as disruptive as a merger. A merger strips a business to the core in a way that never presents itself in a normal business operation. It forces the opportunity to reevaluate mission, policy, function, objectives, and resource deployment as two business entities restructure into one. Possibly more important, from the human perspective, it challenges the mettle of all the employees as they search the newly emerging corporate identity for the stability they once knew.

This section describes the merger planning process of two large investor-owned Southern California electric utilities. The planning process extended over a two-year period. During that time, the two companies jointly developed a transition plan to address total integration of all facets of the business. That process provided a wealth of knowledge about the ins and outs of planning for a large restructuring. This paper, while legally prohibited from discussing business detail, describes the strategies and structure of the planning process.

Background

Earlier, we discussed how SCEcorp evolved through succeeding layers of mergers and acquisitions. Immediately south of SCE's service territory, and extending to the Mexican border lay the San Diego Gas and Electric Company, a utility with a similar history. Also one hundred years old, it was the product of a number of prior mergers and acquisitions. Its staff had a much more informal and open culture than that at SCE. The officers would often walk the halls, conversing with company employees from all areas of business activities. They even had a more relaxed dress code than that of SCE, a code more in keeping with the casual atmosphere of the city of San Diego.

In the late eighties, an opportunity presented itself to further extend the customer base and service territory of SCE. San Diego Gas and Electric (SDG&E), the utility to the south, about one quarter the size of SCE, expressed public interest in merging with an out-of-state utility. SCEcorp felt that the public would receive better service if it were to merge with SDG&E and after lengthy discussions persuaded the SDG&E board to abandon the out-of-state plan and vote for an SCEcorp merger. In late 1988 and early 1989, after a number of rounds of negotiations, the respective boards of the two major investor-owned utilities agreed to a $2.4 billion merger or pooling of interests to form what would have been the largest electric utility in the United States.

The merger plan was not without its detractors. Simultaneous to its announcement there erupted an acrimonious battle that involved the city of San Diego, the state attorney general, dozens of intervenor groups, and the PUC. SCE argued that they could easily provide needed power to an energy-poor San Diego area while maintaining, on balance, air quality throughout the service territory.

Immediately following the approval by the two boards, a small group of employees started the transition planning process. Within a few short weeks, over a thousand employees became engaged at one level or another in developing the road map for the restructuring and integration of the two companies.

The Case-in-Chief (CIC) was the vehicle for presenting the vision of the merged company. The CIC was the major guiding document for the merger process. It contained the definitions of the costs and benefits of the proposed merger. The two companies submitted the CIC to the various regulatory agencies as the joint utilities proof of the value of the merger. It identified at a unit by unit level the derivation of the benefits—where they occurred and why. In total, the CIC reflected over $1.7 billion of benefit over a ten-year period, along with providing guaranteed lower rates to current SDG&E customers and improving both service and air quality.

General Planning Strategy

Management recognized at the onset that a simple, but powerful strategy needed to be formulated and communicated to all the employees in both companies. So, early on, the focus was to develop a number of major strategies for the transition planning process. These were:

- Transition management: The I/T management team would lead the effort. The SCE executive vice president who had lead responsibility for the merger process made the decision. He based it on the fact that I/T management had a *Swiss neutrality,* would take a systems approach to the effort, and had ongoing relationships with all areas of the company.

- Plan ownership: The people responsible for implementing the plan would develop it.
- Organization: SCE organization would predominate. This was reasonable due to the large size differential between the two companies.
- Business policy: SCE business policy would predominate. This also made sense due to the size difference between the two organizations. SCE operated in areas broader than SDG&E, while SDG&E's territory was similar to parts of SCE's. The operative word, however, was predominate. Where it made good business sense to follow SDG&E's policy, it would.
- Personnel equality: Each employee, regardless of original company, would receive the same treatment concerning selection for positions in the merged company.
- Filing compliance: The transition plans would be in conformance to the CIC filing.
- Layoffs: No individuals would be laid off as a result of the merger. They might have to relocate (at company expense), but they would receive a job at comparable level and salary.

Together, the technical aspects of the merger were relatively simple since, while the organization and policies were different, the fundamental business functions were quite similar. These fundamental functions pervaded both organizations and served as the basic foundation or building blocks to the creation of the new structure.

Plan Concepts: General

One of the key pacing items during the development of the transition plan was the ongoing approval hearings. These hearings occurred over many months and used the CIC as the primary evidence document. It was the CIC that described the rationale and benefits for the merger. Completion of this document occurred early on—shortly after a due diligence process. Now, with the benefit of weeks and weeks of additional time, detailed planning was taking place, and it would have been easy for organization planners to specify components of the plan that could be at odds with the CIC. This, of course, would jeopardize the integrity of the CIC and potentially the whole merger. Planners were cautioned to be mindful of the CIC contents as they proceeded into their planning process. Divergence from the CIC would occur only after a great deal of careful consideration.

Plan Concepts: Products

To help the planning teams in their task, it was decided to provide a reasonably complete definition of the expected outcome of the planning process. Detailed descriptions were created for all the plan components. The transition management team adopted specific project planning tools and document formats. The components to be produced included a Gantt chart of all activities; projections of capital, expense, and staff requirements; organization charts; facilities requirements; major business issues and resolutions; procedural and systems changes; and a list of assumptions and risks. These products were packages in a plan with the following table of contents:

Plan Table of Contents.   To aid those involved with the planning process and establish a method to integrate thousands of activities, a standard pro forma plan was developed. This plan consisted of the following four major sections.

Introduction.   The Introduction consisted of Mission/Objectives, defining the overall mission of the department and jurisdiction statements that clarified its charter; Strategy/Policies, identifying the basic strategies, principles, and policies under which the plan was developed; Constraints, documenting such things as corporate commitments, regulatory conditions, timing, etc.; and Assumptions, stating the assumptions about the business or other conditions that must exist to support the transition plans.

Future Organization Functions and Operation.   This section described the future organization. Utilizing organization charts and narrative, the step by step process of moving to a merged organization was described. Job functions and titles were referenced in the Human Resources Interdepartmental Plan.

Transition Activities.   These activities utilized a standard Gantt format and standard task codes to identify the timeline of all relevant transition activities.

Measurement.   The final section described how they intended to measure and track plan adherence. Although the planning teams were each allowed a great deal of freedom in defining their plan and its constituent activities, they had to describe how they were to measure progress.

Plan Concepts: Players

Organization Planning Teams.   Seventeen Organization Planning Teams formed the backbone for the planning process—one for each major functional area. Each team consisted of representatives from the various departments and was co-led by organization coordinators, one from each utility. These coordinators served as the primary interface with other organizations.

Selected by officers of each utility, their charter was the responsibility to produce a plan unique to that organization. Although constrained by general guidelines, each team was free and encouraged to make accommodations necessary for its organization. The teams' purpose was to develop the various components of the transition plan and equally important, they were to help secure employee buy-in to the end product. Throughout the planning period, the individual teams held several dozen meetings at SCE's Rosemead headquarters, in San Diego, and half-way in between.

Interdepartmental Service Teams.   While the Organization Planning Teams focused inward and addressed issues that were specific to their organization, there were numerous issues that came up that crossed organizational boundaries and required resolution. The major service functions of Accounting, Facilities, Personnel, and Systems were identified and coordinators were assigned from both utilities. They were to address issues that are broader in scope and have impact on all other areas.

These teams consisted of representatives from Controller's, Human Resources, Information Services, and Facilities Management. The purpose of each team was the support of organizational planning teams, the coordination and resolution of policy issues, the overall plan coordination of particular service functions, and the development of interdepartmental plans.

Transition Planning Committee.   The Transition Planning Committee (TPC) served as the overall coordination point for plan development and as a forum for issues and policies that needed special attention. The TPC was a small group that consisted of officers and senior managers representing both staff and line functions from both companies. Their role was to provide the senior management officer interface; to conduct issue follow-up and resolution; to integrate the transition plan; to provide implementation planning and transition management; and to review and approve the transition plan.

Executive Review Boards.   The Executive Review Boards (ERB) consisted of three executives from each company. There was one ERB for each SCE/SDG&E organizational group. They assured executive management recognition and assessment of key transition issues. ERB participants were executives from both companies aligned organizationally, much like the Organization Planning Teams. Organization coordinators brought status and issues before their respective ERB.

The specific purpose of the ERB was major issue resolution; ensuring that all issues received a fair hearing; reviewing appropriateness of resolved issues; assessment of transition planning status; ensuring interdepartmental coordination and transition plan review and approval.

Synchronizing the Process.   As planning was underway, it became clear that synchronization of all the activities in all the plans would be a major issue. Various teams were proceeding at different speeds based on factors such as organization size and number of differences in operational practice. The tactic was to do the work in two steps or phases rather than trying to complete all the development and synchronization work at one time. The first phase would consist of completed project plans as had been specified, but the primary focus would be on the individual plan itself.

The second phase would be a refinement of the earlier one and would have prime focus on the planning interaction between groups. This would allow any phase one steps to proceed without delay. Priority for phase two integration consisted of several aspects: benefits, logical sequence, merger agreements, regulatory actions, and personnel policies.

A key priority, of course, was the ability of the plan to deliver the benefits outlined in the CIC. Further sequencing occurred by logically arranging the activities. For example, facilities modifications had to occur before staffs could combine. The Merger Agreement established by both boards defined certain requirements that had to be considered during the planning process. The regulatory process likewise established certain requirements. These were usually in the environmental impact area. And, lastly, it established certain policies for the treatment of personnel. An example in this area would be the proper handling of a situation in which a married couple worked for the merged company. One would not be asked to relocate without the other.

The Planning Process

It was realized from the onset that Transition Management could not plan for every eventuality nor could it answer all the possible questions raised by the various teams during the planning process. They developed a framework for policy development that established some ground rules for team direction. The framework proscribed a range of responses and formality depending upon the universality of the policy. For instance, high-level matters would be planned and guidance provided for divisional and some section level issues. The rest was the responsibility of the local teams to determine.

The overall approach was a systems-based one. This provided a logical basis upon which to do the analysis and allowed a rational basis for resolving some of the more emotional laden issues. The general process has eight steps:

1. Enumerate major business areas.
2. Decompose areas into functions. In many cases, the information systems provided the framework for this.
3. Augment with manual systems.
4. Identify major business policy issues.
5. Map San Diego systems to function.
6. Identify business policy differences.
7. Initiate required systems changes.
8. Create plan products.

The People Issues

A great deal of time and effort went into personnel considerations. It was important to keep the employees from both companies informed—especially critical due to the protracted period between the announcement of the merger and the final decision of the PUC. There were three formal mechanisms developed to aid the communication process:

1. "Keeping Current": This was a publication jointly developed and reviewed for dissemination to the employee population of both companies.
2. Visits to SCE: Hundreds of SDG&E employees came to SCE for a three-day familiarization program. This was a mix of formal presentation by SCE managers and a shadowing process by which SDG&E employees would spend a day with a counterpart at SCE.
3. Visits to SDG&E: This was the same program as above, but in reverse.

These programs were augmented by the normal interaction created by numerous cross-company visits conducted by the various departments as they went about their planning process. All of these communication programs received excellent review by everyone involved and helped allay many of the fears of SDG&E employees.

The PUC Decision and Lessons Learned

In the end, the PUC decided that the merger was not in the public interest and prohibited its consummation. While certainly not pleased with the outcome, SCE did use the opportunity to closely analyze their operations and use that analytic exercise to further strategic planning efforts that followed.

After three years of work and planning, what was learned? For certain, a degree of humility. There was such a high degree of intensity and determination expended during the planning period that the disapproval of the merger was a shock and a feeling of profound loss for those employees closely related to it. This was especially evident in both companies on the day the common PROFS network was permanently disabled. However, other lessons were by-products of the planning process—lessons that have proved invaluable for both current and future planning efforts outside the breadth of a merger.

- People considerations are a high priority. Although unanticipated at the onset, teams spent more time on people issues than any other matter. Each tried hard to be candid and open about what was taking place and why. On a person by person basis, as one met the other, barriers came down.
- You can have too much time to plan. Many people expressed the desire to finish planning and press on to the doing.
- Communications are critical. This cannot be stressed enough. Teams did all they could to broadcast to all employees the status of the planning and approval process. It was important that not only should these communications be timely, accurate, and detailed, but they also require delivery to both employee groups at the same time to emphasize the equitable nature of the effort. Management failed to synchronize the release of material on one occasion and learned the hard way. Equally important was to be sure that the planning process had engendered within it mechanisms to create one-on-one opportunities between the two employee groups.
- A systems approach removes much of the politics. By approaching the task from a systems perspective, Transition Management was able to short circuit a number of political agendas.
- There is a strong need for clear organization of the planning process that has involvement of all sides. Everyone needs to feel a sense of ownership in the plan. This is true in other endeavors and proved again in our environment.
- Establish basic principles up front. These really end up being the rules of the game and require statement up front. Transition Management found that this minimized a lot of wasted effort.
- Rely on the experience of others. Seek the advice of others who have done similar things.
- Be ready for the cultural exchange. Even though the merger did not take place, the SCE culture and the SDG&E culture were each changed in the direction of

the other. It is clear from observations within the company and from discussions with SDG&E employees that SCE has become more open and less formal, while SDG&E has taken on a heightened sense of analytic review. Both are clearly better for the exchange.

In retrospect, there was no magic in what was done or learned. The concepts discovered are really just common sense and part of any good book on business management. Perhaps that is the greatest lesson. While approaching the effort as new and unique, it really was not. Both management and teams would have to have done all that they did, but could have taken comfort in the notion that they were doing the right things as they did them.

Many people toiled in this effort. For even twenty-year veterans, it was more than 10 percent of their work career; for others, much more. What everyone took away from participating in this process was a broader understanding of our own company and a greater appreciation of the importance of human interaction.

THE I/T ORGANIZATION

Perhaps to the surprise of both the business and technology management readers, the responsibility for the transition management associated with the proposed merger between SCEcorp and SDG&E was the responsibility of the I/T management within SCE. The management of a merger is a significant responsibility in any enterprise, so it is particularly important to understand the history and development of the I/T organization within SCE, and how it became such a respected business partner, equal to the challenge of managing this vital business initiative.

Through the Seventies

Throughout the seventies, the key focus was on the optimization of technology. Each step taken by the data processing organization, as it was called, was expected to improve the cost performance of the computers or those who programmed them. After an extensive study, the company made a major break from Honeywell processors to IBM. Several years were spent in training the people and rebuilding the infrastructure to support this new computing base.

A strong service ethic drove the departmental units. The client (internal customer) was always right. There was little sense of corporate accountability in the selection and application of the technology. Each service unit within the data processing organization was attached to a specific client and met all of that client's needs.

The company had just liberated data processing from its roots in the financial part of the company and merged it with an engineering programming group to create a new organization chartered with the mission to either build or rebuild the company's major business applications. It was at this time that a number of major legacy systems were spawned dealing with corporate accounting, employee records, and payroll— along with the ongoing quest for a new customer information system. The real-time computing group in the operations area had just embarked on the development of a new digital system to manage the electrical system. This replaced an overworked and undercapable analog system for doing generation dispatch and control.

Major achievements during this period included the development of a base architecture for use in all future on-line applications. A great deal of investment was made in communications in specific support of the operation of the power system and the then new Customer Information System.

Technology in the Eighties

The eighties saw a wholesale attempt to retool the staff. These were the halcyon days of structured methodologies. In an attempt to improve the productivity and effectiveness of the technical staff, SCE embraced structured programming, but discovered, as did many other companies, that the programming was only a small portion of the job. So began the movement upstream—improving both the programming specifications and the structured design training began in earnest. It soon became clear that this too was not enough, and structured analysis became the training buzzword of the day. All the while, the search was for more refined techniques, better tools, and ways to train more quickly. Standards took on a more important role in all aspects of work. However, the focus was still internal to what now became known as information services. The overall feeling was that Information Services could deliver the most value by doing what it was already doing, but faster.

The major thrust was an increasing use of the IBM transaction processing software known as the Customer Information Control System (CICS). SCE created a set of development practices and programming tools known as generalized architecture (GA). These concepts allowed the on-line products to share a common look and feel—making development and use easier. GA was a precursor to IBM's System Application Architecture (SAA). During this period, dozens of CICS applications were developed using these techniques.

CICS took on the status of an art form. Whatever was done was with CICS. It seemed that the first major specification each client had was *the application must be on-line.* It was the only real tool the Information Services staff had, so every problem had this as an integral part of the solution.

Management realized that there were more clients than Information Services had technical staff and that some means needed to be developed to meet the burgeoning computer demands. Through the auspices of a user computer center (UCC), management allocated an entire processor to client organizations to do their own thing. Trained by the UCC in tools such as SAS and FOCUS and accessing the system through the TSO operating system, the clients achieved a level of control and satisfaction. The Information Services staff were not sure if they were pleased that the client was happy or worried that they now had competition. At the introduction of the personal computer (PC) in 1982, Information Services viewed it as an interesting toy. The UCC fostered the use of the new PC and loaned them to interested executives. The Information Services staff largely dismissed them as not being a real computer and as such, little effort was made to learn about them or to understand their potential.

The introduction of PC technology did more to intrigue the more technically oriented client. It created tension with regular system developers. When SCE created the UCC to support the PC and other non-mainstream technologies, the focus was on the end user, not the developer. Questioning how this upstart technology could ever compete with chilled water solutions, many developers dismissed it out of hand as a passing fad. Those who did not were relegated in the early years to conducting their investigations into the PC's capabilities on their own time. Their support of the legacy systems had higher priorities.

San Onofre, SCE's large nuclear power plant located on the beach in San Diego county, required a major commitment of Information Services support. For the first time, a large contingent of Information Services personnel relocated to a remote field location.

Information Services continued to be fundamentally disconnected from business at a strategic level. The business, however, was running on momentum. The need to change course was not part of the vision. So the corporation and Information Services continued with business as usual, focusing on productivity improvements rather than fundamental change. Indeed, the Information Services department was already awash with change, but it was technology-driven rather than stemming from business need.

Technology in the Nineties and Beyond

There has been a major change in the focus of Information Technologies, as we now call it. Just as the company was in the process of reinventing itself, so was Information Technologies. The nascent notion of linking Information Technology to the business strategy is coming to full bloom. Driven by a vision for the decade, the function is coming to a more complete understanding of itself and its role in the company.

As a service organization, the department provides for the needs of other organizations by doing those things that the client department either cannot or does not want to do for itself. This concept, however, is changing. As Information Technology becomes more and more a part of the fabric of client organizations, an increasing number of clients find that to further their own needs, it is imperative that they take charge of their own I/T. As a result, to continue to add value, the Information Technologies department must assess its resources and plan how to channel them into new and innovative services. Information Technologies, role is no longer to do the information technology for the company, rather it is to ensure that SCE expends any Information Technologies dollar in a manner consistent with the overall direction of the corporation. This creates an interesting tension between client accountability in the more traditional sense and the newer view of corporate accountability.

The SCE Information Technologies vision calls for a split between those services that are purely infrastructure and those that are client-specific. The infrastructure components relate to the communications network and the processor support. The client-specific component is preparing itself for redistribution to client control. In this way, clients who are themselves embarking on reengineering through the strategic planning process and who depend on application software to closely match their business process and policy, are completely in control of the resources necessary to do so.

This step has already been taken in the area of SCE's Customer Systems. The general manager from Information Technologies who was responsible for their system support reports directly to the vice president of customer service along with his complete staff. These individuals were combined with the customer service employees who had systems accountability to create a staff over 150 strong.

This move to client-controlled software is not without risk. We anticipate that several issues will need resolution on an ongoing basis. These include:

- The staff itself: The Information Technologies technical staff, like those of other organizations, has a strong affiliation with their profession—perhaps stronger than that with the company. The care and feeding of the professional staff is a critical concern. The company must meet their training, development, and progression needs if it is to be successful in its notion of distributed Information Technologies staffs.
- The need for staff fluidity and flexibility: As departmental software efforts wax and wane, there is a continuing need to be able to match the project's needs with resource availability. In a traditional human resource environment, such moves are difficult and time consuming.
- The requirement for conceptual integrity of development efforts: System interface points must link together in a seamless fashion. Users of multiple systems must be able to readily understand the user interface of the various systems. To the extent possible, they should seem as if developed by a single mind. While standards and guidelines will help in this effort, it will take a conscious effort by all project teams.

Information Technologies management is working closely with senior business managers to ensure that the technology properly links to the business strategy. A software project ranking mechanism provides specific measures as to how closely proposed software investments support the strategic and tactical direction of the corporation.

Major efforts for the nineties include the redevelopment of a flexible customer information system. Coupled with the ability of providing greater support to our customer interface needs will be applications to facilitate energy consumption reduction programs and methods of improving the efficiency and effectiveness of our field crews. Major systems for generation, transmission, and distribution will also focus on productivity issues. The department will continue to operate as a data processing factory, but it will also maintain the nucleus for spinning off distributed technical staffs to address the needs of individual lines of business.

By far the most ambitious undertaking is that underway in improving SCE's communications capability—SCENet. SCENet is a major enhancement to SCE's data and voice communications facilities. This system, based on a combination of fiber-optic cable, microwave, satellite, trunked radio, and spread spectrum packet technologies will provide seamless, high-speed communications throughout all the SCE service territory. This electronic highway will link SCE to its facilities and operating equipment, its suppliers, and its customers, providing profound new capability to meet business needs through the decade.

The nineties will see a continued demand for decreases in costs. Management anticipates that these decreases will flow from new technologies such as client-server computing, object oriented techniques, and enhanced business interactions such as outsourcing. The Information Technologies organization is already actively exploiting these methods and others to hone its skills and to continue to provide increasing value to the corporation.

PART III. EMERGING VENUES FOR I/T LEADERSHIP

As a result of enterprise transformation, new application concepts receive significant attention from business management in their effort to implement and strengthen new strategies. Concepts and initiatives involving mass customization, service, quality and value, and organizational and business process redesign are the frequent targets at the individual enterprise level, requiring new and diverse information technology support. The focus of these new strategies falls into four major areas:

- Anywhere, anytime offices, involving a redefinition of office work, office workers, and office automation.
- Information empowerment, providing more and improved information to those collegial relationships with the enterprise (employee-colleagues, suppliers and customers).
- Agile enterprises, involving physical organizational redesign, restructuring, and business process redesign that creates new enterprise forms with ready ability to move quickly and with ease to take advantage of evolving marketplace opportunities such as mass customization.

- Networked enterprises, where I/T is revolutionizing not just the internal structures and control systems of the enterprise, but, through network linkages, the shape and nature of external constituency relationships.

What underlies each of these strategies and resulting initiatives is the issue of quality of results and the role of I/T.

Because the quality movement began in manufacturing, it has been slow to transfer and grow in the many of the services industries. Historically, I/T organizations within these industries (the service within the service enterprise) have viewed their role as more of a participant rather than the provider or facilitator of process change—a view that must change if transformation is to be successful.

In "Value and Service in the Retailing Industry," the author submits a short comparative overview of the diversity of strategies implemented by retailers, with a focus on Nordstrom and its customer service.

Value and Service in the Retailing Industry

Marilyn M. Parker

INTRODUCTION

The retailing industry offers an interesting spectrum of the value relationships of price, service, and product quality. Nordstrom, the Seattle-based retailer, is world renowned for its customer service. Customers of a Nordstrom store shop there because of quality service, yet these very same service- and quality-conscious consumers also shop at wholesale clubs like Price Club for items other than high-quality fashion apparel. Here, they expect no service at all. These same consumers then justify the premium price, relative to common bank cards, of an American Express card on the basis of the diverse services offered. The retailing industry defines itself by a series of unique business niches and Nordstrom, the wholesale clubs, and American Express have each created its own in the American market.

THE NORDSTROM STORY

Nordstrom is the leading fashion specialty retailer in the United States. The company offers the largest selection of high-quality fashion apparel and shoes for men, women, and children. Merchandise ranges from contemporary classics to the latest designer lines.

Background

John W. Nordstrom founded the company in 1901 as a shoe store in Seattle, Washington, and in 1929 Nordstrom's three sons took over the management of the store. Selling shoes is a service-intensive business: salespersons must be willing to identify a customer's needs and tastes, locate the shoes, and try them on the customers' feet. Style, price, fit, and the patience of both the customer and salesperson are all key to a successful sale. What they learned about retailing from selling shoes, along with innovative merchandising and customer service, helped them survive the depression years of the 1930s.

After the depression they began expansion in the Seattle area only to face new challenges in the 1940s. During World War II, shoe rationing occurred because of the great shortages of materials. Aggressive marketing combined with building a solid rapport with suppliers and customers during rationing ensured their continued success. By 1960 it had grown to be the largest independent shoe retailer in the United States, and the downtown Seattle store was the largest shoe store in the nation.

By the end of 1963, Nordstrom purchased Best's Apparel fashion specialty stores and diversified into the apparel industry, and the third generation of Nordstrom's joined the business. Three grandsons of the Nordstrom founder ran the company by committee, rotating the title of president among themselves during an impressive growth period, boosting revenues from about $600 million in 1982 to $3.2 billion in 1991.[36]

Responding to fierce price-cutting and consolidation in the retail industry, the executives began easing Nordstrom's upscale image by offering more lower-priced merchandise. Because the company wants to keep its reputation for high-quality goods and top-notch service, it's selling more of its own private-label shoes and clothing, computerizing inventory control, refocusing advertising on value-priced merchandise, and studying the possibility of opening discount outlets.

Forays into new markets will keep testing their ability to duplicate Nordstrom's service-oriented culture. The company's balance sheet remains strong, its sales are double the department-store average, and its return on equity was second-highest in the department-store industry (after May Department Stores) in 1991. Seven of Nordstrom's fourth generation are working their way up through the ranks. In the family tradition, each started in the business by waiting on customers.

Their challenge today is an interesting one: How do you apply an ethic that thrived in small towns and tightly knit neighborhoods in a world in which companies count their customers in the millions? Will a value that held sway in the rural village survive in the global village? To some extent, Nordstrom is proof that it can when the ethic is service and quality.

Organization

Nordstrom believes in a highly decentralized structure. Those closest to the customer are most essential to its success. The company encourages sales and sales support people to initiate and implement new ideas. Store buyers and regional managers make many decisions on the spot. Management's goal is one of support, working closely with their customers, salespeople, and manufacturers to guarantee the finest service and quality merchandise at the best prices.

The Nordstrom family likes to describe their business organization chart as an upside-down pyramid, with them on the bottom. They shun executive perquisites, such as having private secretaries. Their small offices are identical in size.

Nordstrom, with 40 percent of its shares still in family hands, creates a strong corporate culture fueled by large commissions for salespeople and a long tradition of promoting only from within, breeding intense loyalty among the employees. Nordstrom salespeople are responsible for servicing all customers' needs. They keep track of sizes, preferences, and special events, making exchanges credits and refunds. They stand behind their merchandise, and dissatisfied customers are a rarity. Their trademarks include personal thank-you notes to customers.

Philosophy

Since its founding, Nordstrom's guiding philosophy has been its founder's: Offer the customer the best service, selection, quality, and value.

This philosophy of unequaled service, quality, and commitment to value, along with the high standards of the people they employ, has contributed tremendously to Nordstrom's growth throughout the western United States and Alaska and is the reason they can enter new market areas with confidence.

It's interesting that while Japan Air Lines developed a training program to teach politeness and markets it, Nordstrom doesn't. They learn how to run the cash register, are given a brief lecture of the company's history, and proceed directly to the sales floor. Nordstrom says that they just take care to hire nice people.

Central to the Nordstrom merchandizing philosophy is a strong belief in an individualized approach to fashion. Each Nordstrom store tailors itself to reflect the lifestyles of customers in the surrounding area. It showcases a wide selection of shoes, apparel, and accessories in a variety of distinctive *shops* that are rich in color, texture, and design.

A Service Story of Mass Customization

Everyone that shops even occasionally at Nordstrom has their own service story. The author—with hard-to-fit feet—wears Ferragamo shoes exclusively for business. A few years ago, while in Florence, the Italian corporate home of Ferragamo, I went to the showroom to stock up on shoes. Upon discovering home was in the United States, the Italian manager suggested Nordstrom since, according to the manager, Nordstrom has an even wider selection available than any of the Ferragamo-owned salons in Europe. The Ferragamo manager was right. When I returned, I called the nearest store, talked to the assistant buyer, McCurtis Kelley at the Costa Mesa (California) store, and discussed my mismate requirements. I've purchased all my shoes from Nordstrom ever since. At the beginning of the season McCurtis telephones to determine my requirements (colors, styles, etc.). As the shoes arrive at the store, they are mismated at no charge and shipped to me. Anything I don't like, I mail back. Even though I've now relocated to the East Coast—and McCurtis moved to become buyer at the Nordstrom South Bay Galleria—I still buy all my shoes from McCurtis Kelley.

Catalyst in Retailing

Nordstrom has been a catalyst for many in the retailing industry. After years of concentrating on keeping costs low and luring customers with constant rounds of sales, large department and apparel stores increasingly see competent service from an efficient, empowered sales staff as the key to success in an increasingly competitive retailing environment. When Nordstrom planned to open a store in Chicago in 1991, Marshall Field, an established retailer in Chicago, began to improve its service. It reduced to less than two minutes—from more than ten—the average amount of time it takes a salesperson to approach a customer. When Nordstrom unveiled its East Coast Tysons Corner store, R. H. Macy ripped up its just-built dressing rooms and redid them to match Nordstrom's more spacious ones. In California, where Nordstrom opened twenty-one stores over a eleven-year period, more established rivals like Macy's and The Broadway began to imitate Nordstrom strategies, such as putting salespeople on commission, a step to foster more helpful attitudes in their employees.

Nordstrom has earned a reputation for exceptional customer service, value, and quality. At Nordstrom, friendliness, courtesy, and a sincere desire to help is the rule rather than the exception.

NO-FRILLS SHOPPING: THE WAREHOUSE CLUBS

Another facet of value and service puts a greater emphasis on price. Just as Nordstrom's cachet is outstanding service, warehouse clubs offer a compelling alternative: high-quality merchandise at minimal markups and services. Members lift items right off the shipping pallets and shelves without sales help. Payment is in cash.

These warehouse clubs have an annual membership fee and cater to small-business owners and individuals with steady incomes. Goods range from office furniture and supplies, personal computers, television sets, small appliances such as coffee-makers, frozen and canned foods, and paper goods. Price Club, founded in San Diego in 1976, was the first warehouse club in the United States. Other successful U.S. warehouse clubs, generally regional, are Costco Wholesale, which carries extensive lines of fresh food, including a bakery on the premise, and Sam's Wholesale Club, owned by Wal-Mart.

AMERICAN EXPRESS: SERVICE VERSUS VALUE?

The strategy for the American Express charge card was to deliver an upscale product that enabled the company to charge customers and merchants more because it offered outstanding service. What was right for the 1980s isn't working well in the value-oriented 1990s. American Express (Amex) has to compete with a horde of competitors offering all manner of special deals, discounts, rebates, and other features. The most visible result of the competition: Amex lost customers in droves, with cards in force dropping by 500,000 in each of the first three quarters of 1992.[37]

Although it still markets itself as a premium product, it is signing up lower-end merchants. Amex used to be a high-priced card with high-perceived value, only for the most affluent. They clearly step back from that by announcing that the cardholders could use the card at Kmart.

In a six-page memo to 53,000 Amex employees entitled "Elements of our Strategic Vision," the company describes ambitious plans to earn 100 percent of customers' plastic spending. The basic idea is to offer cardmembers a variety of ways to pay for virtually all their purchases—charge card, revolving credit, and perhaps even debit.

American Express has good news mixed with bad. Amex management blames the decline in cardholders on its difficulty in continuing to attract new customers rather than the more serious problem of cardholders simply canceling their cards. There is also some growth in the spending per cardholder, due largely to its Membership Miles program, which, like similar features offered by other card companies, gives frequent flyer miles. On the other hand, one obvious problem is simultaneously cutting costs while trying to maintain its world-class global service. Another is the employee layoffs that phased through 1994. Only time will tell whether these initiatives worked.

PART IV. TRANSFORMING I/T

In Parts II and III, we focused on new application concepts important to business management involving anywhere, anytime offices; information empowerment, providing better information in support of team efforts and other collegial relationships; and agile and extended enterprises, involving physical organizational redesign, restructuring, and business process redesign, and evolving network linkages, changing the shape and nature of external constituency relationships. In Part IV, we focused on the consequences of these changes to I/T organizations and how they must reposition and reengineer their own infrastructure and business processes to provide appropriate customer focus, to deliver value to the enterprise, to create technology infrastructures that allow future flexibility, and to support and strengthen core competencies.

In Organizational Restructuring and Process Reengineering, Lynwood Walker describes the initiatives that one business organization, AGT Limited and it's Network Systems group, took to better position itself in the market. This is an excellent case study involving technology downsizing, outsourcing, decentralization and recentralization, and strategic alliances— what they did and why they did it, what worked and what didn't. Although the business executive may find the section on technology downsizing somewhat technical, it is important from the perspective of understanding what and how I/T can facilitate business change.

Change surrounded the Network Systems group. The enterprise itself was undergoing restructuring stemming from a privatization initiative and moving from a government-owned and operated utility into a private sector commercial (competitive) enterprise environment. Simultaneously, the enterprise stakeholders were changing, market definitions were undergoing reexamination, and internal organizations were restructuring. What became key to the success of the I/T organization (Network Systems) and its efforts were a variety of initiatives—team effort being one. Treating outside vendors and end users as partners in development broke down organization and communications barriers. Facilitating special cross-department activities through groupware, along with empowering and redefining the organization and its structure increased collaborative and cooperative efforts within the company. The responsible director was pro-active, energetic, and enthusiastic and made sure that all affected functions were fully informed and on board. In this paper, Walker also explores the rationale behind AGT Limited's decision to outsource some of their I/T functions; their definition and development of "core competencies" and "critical skills" and how they became a part of the decision-making process; and the inclusion of the "customer" in all major stages of the process—all critical to transformation. During the process that he describes, Walker was Systems Planning Advisor, AGT Network Systems.

"Business Value," by Robert J. Benson offers an in-depth discussion of the subject.

Organizational Restructuring and Process Reengineering

Lynwood Walker

INTRODUCTION

Until 1990, AGT Limited was a Crown Corporation owned and operated by the government of the Province of Alberta, Canada. The province sold half of its interest in AGT and its affiliated companies to the Canadian public in September of that year to establish TELUS Corporation in what was the largest single share offering in Canadian history. Approximately one year later, the province announced a second offering of most of the remaining shares still held by the province.

AGT Limited is the major subsidiary of TELUS Corporation, accounting for over 90 percent of total revenues. AGT Limited is the leading long-term supplier of telecommunications services in Alberta and the third largest telecommunications supplier in Canada. In 1991, its 1.1 million network access lines generated over 391 million long distance messages carried over a network spanning more than 18 million kilometers.

TELUS Corporation's total 1991 assets (after depreciation) exceeded CDN$3 billion, and their net income exceeded CDN$180 million (CDN$1.33 per share) on total operating revenues of CDN$1.2 billion. At the time, TELUS Corporation employed approximately 10,200 staff with an aggregate annual payroll of more than CDN$450 million.

The transformation of AGT Limited from a public to a private corporation has meant dramatic changes in several key areas:

- Increased accountability for fiscal performance
- Change in regulatory bodies from provincial to federal jurisdictions
- Changes in labor codes from provincial to federal jurisdictions
- Preparation for competition in key market segments formerly operated as a monopoly

Taken together, these fundamental changes in the nature and function of the organization reflected the changes occurring within AGT Limited's various systems organizations. The major initiatives listed below were undertaken largely in parallel in only one twelve-month period:

- Technology Downsizing: Implementation of a 150-node LAN by the Network Systems group with growth planned to over 300 nodes within one year, largely displacing an equivalent number of mainframe office systems devices.
- Outsourcing: Development and implementation of plans to outsource mainframe and personal computer (PC) services to ISM Alberta Limited, a joint venture between TELUS Corporation, IBM Canada Limited, and ISM Limited.
- Decentralization/Recentralization: Implementation of Customer-Focused Service groups in Network Systems to serve distinct business functions.
- Protecting Critical Skills: Delegation of workload assignment and tracking to peer-level teams in Network Systems.
- Strategic Alliances: Planning and implementation of an Operations Development Alliance to leverage common systems development efforts taking place in other Canadian telecommunications service suppliers.
- Global Office: Testing and implementation of products to link the office systems of AGT Limited with major suppliers and alliance partners across Canada.

In this paper, we will examine the history and impact of each of these change forces within AGT Limited—specifically the Network Systems group—in more detail. One must be careful to note, however, that these changes are not taking place independently but have an impact on each of the others.

TECHNOLOGY DOWNSIZING

What Did We Accomplish?

The Network Systems group in AGT Limited consisted of 175 staff who were responsible for planning, developing, and maintaining 115 application systems on various mainframes, VAX, PDP, TANDEM, and PC platforms. In addition, they were responsible for operation of two major data centers as well as an extensive network interconnecting the data centers with various terminal and equipment sites around the province of Alberta. The data centers house the VAX, PDP, and TANDEM processors and related peripherals as well as the network support facilities. One Network Systems data center is in Calgary, the other is in Edmonton. Corporate Information Systems provided all mainframe operations and SNA network support from their own data centers until they transferred these services to ISM Alberta Limited in January of 1993.

AGT appointed a new director for Network Systems in October of 1991 as part of a general reorganization. By the end of October, the incoming director stated his desire to have full LAN services operational throughout Network Systems by the end of 1991 or, at the latest, the first quarter of 1992.

At the time this vision was announced, approximately 120 of the 175 Network Systems staff relied on mainframe office services accessed via 327X monochrome terminals. Only 55 had personal computing devices on their desks—and 30 of those were in the data centers. The remaining 25 were a mixed bag of CAD and mapping workstations, VAX development workstations, and a small number of PCs connected to a TANDEM platform for support of a specific application. A small number of other PCs did exist in the department—they were standalone devices shared among work-group members. Staff frequently had to reserve time on these devices—and were almost never allowed more than a half-day at a time.

By the end of November 1991, a team consisting of representatives from Systems Planning, Systems Operations, and Corporate Information Systems had defined the network topology, selected the equipment vendor, ordered equipment for the first phase of the implementation, and begun planning the second stage.

December of 1991 saw arrival of 46 new PCs and the start of floor wiring in both cities. In January of 1992, the floor wiring was complete for all nodes and installation of the new PCs and printers began, as well as conversion and reallocation of remaining devices to individuals. Changes were also complete to the boot servers in each of the two cities to perform all the LAN file and printer management functions.

By the end of February, approximately 110 Network Systems staff had full access to LAN-based and mainframe office systems through PC devices on their desktop. The remaining 30 or so were active by the end of May of 1992. These activities were further complicated by the move of the director and 25 of his staff to a newly renovated floor during the summer of 1992 that necessitated the disconnection, moving, and reconnection of the affected PC printers and network facilities.

By the end of that summer, all Network Systems staff had access to most LAN-based office services, regardless of whether they operated on a PC, Macintosh, or VAX workstation device.

Announcing the Vision

Beyond Mere Messaging. The vision outlined in October of 1991 went far beyond the ability to merely compose and address text messages across the network. It included in its scope such lofty goals as compound documents, interactive groupware, document management features, and, eventually, full multimedia capabilities including sound, motion, and live action video.

The initial implementation included basic compound document capabilities through integrated, graphically oriented word processing, spreadsheet, and presentation graphics packages for installation on each PC. This was to be followed in mid-1992 with integrated groupware and document management services. The third stage, originally slated for late 1993, would include the multimedia service extensions necessary for sound, motion, and live action video.

Existing Office System Services.   Corporate Information Systems provided basic office system services via four PROFS mainframe hosts serving a total of 7,700 users throughout the corporation. The basic vehicle for interpersonal communication in this environment was the PROFS Note to which a user could attach a text-only document. Alternatively, end users could create and mail documents using only electronic "buck slips" for routing and minor annotation.

The PROFS environment provided many other services as well:

- A complete directory of all TELUS/AGT Limited employees including location, title, account codes, manager/subordinate reporting, and PROFS location/ID/ nickname.
- Corporate and departmental news services.
- Templates for corporate and departmental forms, including letterheads.
- Document management and version control (e.g., draft versus final).
- Individual and group calendars, activity lists, and other time-management aids.
- Distribution lists at the corporate, departmental, and individual level.
- Access to corporate policies and procedures via the reference library.
- Access to various gateways for ENVOY messaging, fax service, and so on.

Comprehensive as these services were, they suffered from a number of limitations:

- PROFS is text-only. Users could not include graphical material in a note or document other than crude block diagrams or the company logo (which I/T transformed into a PROFS symbol equivalent to a character).
- The mainframe terminals employed by the vast majority of users were monochrome 327X devices with no color or graphic display capabilities.
- Most document creation and editing utilized the Document Composition Facility (DCF), which involved placing specialized formatting "tags" throughout the document to indicate bolding, centering, or other text attributes.
- Hard copy output was restricted to black-and-white, with a limited set of type styles and sizes available.
- Document exchange with PCs was awkward at best—and impossible for most.
- Usage of the PROFS systems had grown to the point at which capacity limitations were adversely affecting response time and even the time it took to get a new user ID authorized and implemented.

Everyone viewed these limitations as significant hurdles to providing and effectively communicating information within Network Systems as well as between Network Systems and its user community.

Basic LAN Office Systems Features.　The core functions envisioned for the LAN-based office system were as follows:

- PC-based, integrated word processing, spreadsheet, and presentation graphics for every staff member
- Integrated file and printer services for the entire department including access to color as well as monochrome output devices
- Transparent gateways to the PROFS office system for communication with the rest of the company
- Centralized, professional administration and backup of all LAN services

Additional requirements for specialized applications such as project management and desktop publishing were also noted for some individuals based on their current job responsibilities.

Document Management in a LAN World.　With the advent of the LAN, it was also apparent that mere filing was not enough to provide adequate control over document creation, editing, distribution, annotation, and approval. The company needed sophisticated tools to manage the "electronic paper trail" as the myriad correspondence, reports, and other documents floated around the LAN environment. This capability was essential if the LAN-based office system was to authorize and distribute financial reports and other sensitive documents.

Groupware.　Network Systems had evolved into a highly motivated team environment that was quite distinct from many of its counterparts in the rest of the company. It was essential therefore that appropriate capabilities be provided on the new office system to help these teams work cohesively. Features such as integrated project management, time reporting, and calendars were necessary to its overall success.

Additional features were defined to quickly define and implement automated business processes in the LAN environment. This was an essential step to replacing the paper- and forms-based processes currently employed.

Distributed Graphical Documents.　Any documents in this new environment had to be capable of incorporating graphical components as necessary, from simple logos to complex illustrations and even photographs. Furthermore, they had to be capable of color output to screens, slides, transparencies, or paper when appropriate.

The Future—Compound Documents and Multimedia.　The LAN-based system had to be capable of incorporating and filing these graphical components as well as maintaining links to the original information as needed for automatic updating and reporting.

As the rate of multimedia expands in the business world, so too must the ability of the LAN-based office system to keep pace. So-called live documents that incorporate text, graphics, sound, motion, and even video images must be readily available to the LAN-based system user.

Maintaining the Corporate Linkage

Network Systems was (and still is) a distinctive organization within AGT Limited. The emphasis on cross-functional teams, facilitative leadership styles, and group problem-solving has helped it to lead the way in many aspects of AGT Limited's changing corporate culture.

It was recognized early on, however, that Network Systems must still continue to interact intensively with the rest of the company if it is to contribute to the success of the organization as a whole. The company also acknowledged that extensive support from corporate departments and managers was a requirement for the LAN to be implemented within the needed time frame.

To that end, four key decisions were made even before the project commenced:

1. Commitment to Corporate Standards and Policies

   The project would adhere to all known Corporate Standards and Policies in force at the inception of the project. The project would use corporate standard equipment wherever possible. Additionally, the project would follow corporate policies and processes concerning orders, authorizations, purchasing, and budget control. Personal intervention and "expediting" work through the process was often necessary—and even encouraged. Deviations from the process were unacceptable unless both of the affected directors knew of and agreed with the change.

2. Leveraging Corporate Service Agreements

   The project would attempt to take advantage of current procurement and service agreements with existing suppliers. This was to ensure that minimal additional support, training, or even vendor qualification would be necessary to execute the project.

3. Linking to Corporate Office System Offerings

   It was absolutely essential that the LAN-based office system provide transparent gateway access to corporate office applications on either PROFS or other corporate LAN solutions. This was to ensure the maintenance of effective communications with the rest of the corporate organization.

4. Obtaining and Keeping Corporate Support

   Perhaps the most critical task of all was to obtain and keep the support of Corporate Systems management and staff needed to execute the project. Network Systems was about to ruffle some organizational feathers by insisting on carving a new path into what had been exclusively the domain of the Corporate Systems organization. Consequently, significant efforts were made to keep all parties involved with (and part of) the process as much as possible.

   Liaison staff were assigned with the responsibility for shepherding paperwork through their respective departments. Specialists from both sides met frequently to iron out difficulties and to report progress in each of their respective areas. Even the respective directors spent a lot of extra time keeping each other informed and grappling with any issues unresolved at lower levels.

Making and keeping commitments in these four critical areas proved to be a key foundation for future project success.

Implementation

The implementation process followed a traditional, albeit compressed, process common to most systems projects. Requirements were defined, equipment ordered and configured, the network wiring completed, and everything connected together. Once the predetermination was complete, many of the remaining stages overlapped. For example, floor wiring was completed while the equipment was assembled and shipped, and some equipment was undergoing final configuration and installation in parallel with the data center changes.

Predetermination.   The critical question asked during all stages of the predetermination stage was "What have we already got in terms of equipment, experience, and vendor support that we could leverage into an effective solution?" The answers to this question usually provided the simplest and most effective means of defining the network topology, nodes, PC equipment, software packages, and even the floor wiring to be used.

There were, of course, equipment budget restrictions. This dictated the ultimate limit for network nodes for installation in the first wave. Adjustments in service budgets for installation time, network facilities, and data center operations reflected the requirements imposed by this project. Workloads were rebalanced to allow for the additional load imposed by the LAN project.

After much debate, the decision was made to purchase all PC equipment from a single vendor for the initial phase. The regular PC supplier was unable to provide the type or quantity of workstations desired so the company selected a reputable vendor already involved in other aspects of the project.

All aspects of the predetermination were conducted by a team of specialists from both Corporate Information Services and Network Systems. Membership on the team changed as the work progressed. While the preliminary discussions involved primarily management and the systems planning community, the final configurations, quantities, and milestones involved negotiations between technical specialists from the affected areas as well as from equipment and software suppliers when required.

Bulk Ordering.   Having the major vendors on board early was a significant advantage. After completing the determinations of approximate quantities, they advised their production and inventory staff to get ready. Once agreeing on the final numbers and prices, they started reserving units, time, and even trucks to ensure on-time delivery. All this activity took place well before receipt of the actual order.

Corporate Information Services provided the vendor with the AGT Limited standards concerning installation of the software packages. This information enabled the vendor to ship the units with most of the software preloaded and configured for immediate use. All that remained was for AGT Limited and network vendor staff to assemble and test the units and install the network driver software. They were then ready to attach to the network as soon as the wiring activity was complete.

Prebuilt Foundation.   Much has been said already about leveraging existing standards and equipment to obtain the most effective solution for the problem at hand. The project team attributed much of its effectiveness to the fact that it didn't have to go out and spend endless days researching network topologies, protocols, vendor credibility, or PC configurations. During this time the director's motto was "Don't study the question if you already know the answer."

Management was advised that standards were in place for many aspects of the project. Their decision: "Use them, don't invent something new!" When told that all four office buildings affected by the project were prewired with a backbone LAN/WAN, they quickly agreed to use it rather than something new and untested. The software was chosen based on corporate standards and ease of use to enable document exchange with other corporate PCs.

Data Center Service Organization.   Another significant contributor to the success of the project was that Network Systems already operated two medium-size data centers, one each in Calgary and Edmonton. The staff in these centers were familiar with the backbone LAN/WAN already in place as well as with much of the server and administration functions that would later become their responsibility. They too were able to leverage existing vendor support agreements to get the incremental start-up training they needed to provide more in-depth support.

The data centers were prepared in other ways. They were already responsible for security and administration on the backbone LAN so adding the Network Systems users was not a big stretch. Neither was it difficult to include the LAN server and associated files in the regular backup and disaster recovery plans for each center. This freed the user community from having to deal with these more mundane but nonetheless critical functions.

Planning—Now That We've Got It, What Do We Do With It?

The rapid deployment of the initial LAN configuration had left little time to consider its impact on the day-today operation of Network Systems and vice versa. Consider, for example, the basic issue of storage management on the LAN. Under the PROFS regime, users had access to only a relatively small amount of personal storage space. All circulating documents in either draft or final versions were held in "Main PROFS Storage," often for years. There was no apparent control or capacity limitations to this service (at least to the average end user).

On the LAN, however, it was different. Every staff member with a LAN-attached PC initially got four distinct network drives. Each individual had their own personal "D:" drive reserved for network configuration and start-up information. In addition, they received an "M:" drive for their exclusive use that no one else had access to. Each person within a given section shared access to a common "L:" drive for section-level files. Finally, all Network Systems staff had access to a common "N:" drive, intended for files that needed sharing across various organizational boundaries.

Difficulties arose, however, when it became apparent that the "N:" drive was the only vehicle for sharing information between cross-functional team members from different sections. The number of directories and files on "N:" increased so rapidly that normal file management, storage, and retrieval became tedious and frustrating. The solution was to create other network drives for each of the known interest groups. For example, the management team had their own "P:" drive for confidential files. Other teams received their own logical drives to minimize the load on the common "N:" drive.

None of these assignments required installation of additional hardware. They were simply a form of "access control list" to different directories and files stored on a shared storage space. Each logical drive shared the same total capacity. Files added to one logical drive caused a reduction in apparent capacity of each of the remaining logical drives.

Another area that required attention was the planning and coordination of hardware and software upgrades. Individuals were still placing upgrade orders with the Order Control group in Communications Services. Unfortunately, Communications Services was in no position to tell if the affected PC was part of the LAN configuration or not. Consequently, a few staff members would obtain software versions that were out of sync with the rest of the organization. Only a few others could read or update their documents or spreadsheets. The help desk personnel and others responsible for support of the application were caught off guard when these individuals requested help on a new feature. Finally, some upgrades were not fully compatible with existing display driver or network driver software. This, in turn, led to frustration in some cases—and complete application failure in others. The solution was to assign a dedicated order coordinator to ensure the planning and execution of upgrades in a coordinated fashion.

Finally, more planning was necessary to clarify the vision for subsequent development of the LAN environment. It was no longer adequate to provide only file sharing and printer services. Management, planners, and technical specialists began looking at the next generation of LAN services—multiplatform independence and basic groupware applications.

The Second Wave

Completion of the first phase of the LAN implementation occurred in late February of 1992. Planning was already underway for extension of the LAN to the remainder of Network Systems. Primary considerations were those individuals without PCs that got missed on the first round as well as those with Macintosh or workstation devices.

A third category of need was also identified—the several staff that spend significant portions of their time traveling between cities. Their PCs of choice were laptops.

There were no provisions in the original implementation, however, for connecting laptops to the network.

Who Got Missed on the First Round?   There was still approximately thirty staff without PCs at the end of the first stage of implementation. Implementation and activation of these nodes were somewhat simpler than the original because the regular corporate supplier was now able to provide appropriate desktop models with the right power and size combinations. The cubicles had all been wired for the LAN in the initial stage, so all that remained was to order the appropriate quantities, configure them, and arrange for installation. The experience gained in the initial stage proved beneficial in enabling rapid configuration and customization of each node to meet the needs of the person receiving it.

Mac's, Workstations, and Laptops—Tying Up the Loose Ends. There were still some significant technical issues to resolve. Network Systems had to wait for the software companies to develop network driver software for the Macintosh devices. Initial beta releases didn't work as well in the Network Systems environment as was first hoped. It was only after several iterations of testing and working with the software developers that the final commercial product was approved and implemented.

The workstations had to rely on a PC emulation unit in the data center that gave them access to the office LAN functions as if they were a "normal" PC node. Unfortunately, they were still unable to use their workstation word processors, databases, or graphics programs to exchange information with regular PC nodes elsewhere in the network.

Staff using laptop PCs received full-size color screens, regular size keyboards, and external LAN driver units at their normal desk or office. In addition, at least one empty cubicle in each city was similarly equipped for use by visiting staff. When traveling, all that was necessary was to detach the laptop from its auxiliary equipment, pack it into a briefcase, and reattach it at the other end. All files stayed intact, access control was uniform between sites, and the employee was able to work enroute if they chose—without loss of data or cumbersome upload/download processes.

Extended Office Features

Network Systems began planning for the next extension of the office LAN even while implementation of the second wave was underway. The original vision was an integrated office environment with provision for rapid prototyping and implementation of office systems applications. Since Corporate Information Services was facing similar decisions concerning the rest of the organization, it decided to pool resources and come to a joint solution.

Trial of Groupware Products.   There appeared to be at least three distinct schools of thought among groupware vendors. One company took the approach that groupware applications were distinct entities in their own right. It therefore built a standalone application within which one could develop and maintain any number of custom office applications—primarily around document creation, editing, distribution, and approval functions.

The applications developed within the framework of this environment were interesting on their own but could not interact with other standard office packages except to act as an envelope for distribution of the final products. In addition, the need for a multitude of dedicated servers conflicted with the operational and administrative goals of the Network Systems LAN environment.

Another company saw the role of groupware to be one of extending and enabling existing packages to perform electronic distribution functions. This solution maximized the utility of existing products, yet it didn't appear to be as adept at creating new office applications or managing document flows through the organization.

A third company sought to replace the underlying graphical user interface with a more advanced, "Object Oriented" version. The decision for abandoning this option was made on strategic grounds—new releases of the existing software were expected to provide many of the advantages of this product without moving to a new vendor and complicating end-user support. In addition, the electronic distribution features resided on unique servers—their own brand naturally, with which neither Network Systems nor Corporate Information Services had any significant experience.

In short, the immediate answer from the vendors was "Sorry, we're not quite there yet!" No single vendor had the right combination of application integration, ease of application development, document management features, distribution management, and multiplatform server software. The decision: We have little choice but to wait for this product area to mature somewhat.

Network Extension Via Standard Mail and Directory Services. The initial LAN configuration provided only a mainframe gateway to the PROFS office environment. Once logged onto PROFS, an authorized user could then use external ENVOY and fax gateways to send text-only documents and messages to external contacts. It was still not possible to forward PC-formatted documents via PROFS except "as is"—with no display or printing capabilities. This function was for the occasional uploading and downloading of files, particularly when the information needed to be in another city or building.

The growth of the corporate LAN environment posed its own problems. While both groups used the same PCs, there were no means of exchanging files, documents, or even messages between the two worlds other than by manual disk "sneaker-net." It was at this time that corporate was considering implementation of X.400 addressing gateways to enable more efficient access to these various communities of interest.

The original intent was that X.400 addressing software in each of the respective LAN environments would package mail destined for the other LAN. The packaged mail would then be sent via the mainframe gateway to a central mail server that would then repackage it, translate the routing if necessary for the destination, and forward it back through the mainframe gateway for final delivery.

This was all well and good until someone realized that each transaction would require handling up to eleven times between origin and destination. This overhead was unacceptable and the specialists worked on an alternative solution.

Network Systems plans also included incorporation of X.500 standard directory services. At the time, this standard was still very much in embryo and had not been implemented commercially. Again, Network Systems was forced to wait until stable commercial products could be developed.

All the while this was going on, much of the Corporate Information Services planners' time was being spent supporting the team working on a more critical project—the outsourcing of mainframe computing services to ISM Alberta Limited. It gradually became apparent that little would happen until after the outsourcing had been completed. The remainder of the X.400 and X.500 implementation was put on hold until mid-1993, by which time the transfer to ISM would be complete and stabilized.

The Third Wave—Incorporating Multimedia Features

The final frontier faced by Network Systems in its LAN implementation is the wide-scale incorporation of multimedia features such as video and graphic presentations, sound annotation of documents and presentations, and eventually live action video on desktop computers.

Already the first signs have begun to appear. A few PCs are now equipped with CD-ROM readers for access to multimedia reference works and clip-art libraries. The large meeting room used for major presentations has a video projector driven by a LAN-attached PC and presentation graphics software that displays short animation sequences or "flicks." Color scanners are now available elsewhere in the company should the need arise to import photographs or illustrations for office applications. The incorporation of multimedia functions will occur as soon as the business need becomes apparent and affordable technology becomes available to reliably service each need.

Formalization

The speed with which the LAN was implemented caused some work to be left by the wayside. Among these items were formalization of LAN standards, training requirements, and end-user support responsibilities.

Standards.   Standards were adopted in several areas such as LAN naming conventions, backup and recovery procedures, user access control, and LAN file management. In most cases, the technical specialists were able to propose reasonable solutions in quick order—again paying close attention to the axiom "If you already know the answer, don't study the question!"

Training.   Initial LAN training for most users consisted of a one-day introduction to basic LAN functions such as changing passwords, activating printers, and the like. Some office application training was also available through the System Education section of Corporate Information Services. The majority of users, however, received training at the "School of Hard Knocks" with their peers as tutors and advisors when the going got tough. Fortunately, the consistency of the user interface and printer controls made it fairly easy for most to get off to a quick start.

Other Support Issues.   The biggest hassle faced by the user community was trying to figure out who to call for help. If the corporate help desk was called, they didn't know about the network or the PCs. If the PC vendor received the call, the user often didn't have the support agreement numbers and other information necessary to initiate a service call. Finally, if the Network Systems help desk received the call, they could restore printer queues but had to send someone out from the data center if that failed to resolve the problem.

After recognizing this problem, essential contact information was printed on business card-size tags and affixed to the front of the system unit. These cards showed a single number that all users could contact. The staff answering these calls would then look after dispatching the correct resources from corporate, the vendor, or within Network Systems to resolve the problem.

What Worked

Without question, the greatest single factor contributing to the successful implementation of the Network Systems LAN was the high degree of senior management commitment. The director outlined the vision, organized the major players, ensured that funding was available and approved, made sure his peers in other affected departments were aware and supportive, and resolved conflicts as they arose. Without his energy and enthusiasm, the project would have shifted to the back burner in favor of other pressing demands.

The next biggest factor was the teamwork between the various affected groups. While this was nothing new for most staff from Network Systems, the team approach to problem solving was a new experience to many staff from outside the department. This approach helped to break down organizational and communications barriers to make the project a success. Bringing the vendors in during formative discussions also helped to clarify options, quantities, and intentions.

The urgency of the initial deadlines also contributed by eliminating any allowance for posturing, lobbying, extensive studies, or other negative or delaying tactics. There was only just enough time to do the job once, so it was necessary to do the job right the first time.

Implementation.   The actual implementation got off on the right foot by bringing the vendors in early. They knew what was going on, how much was needed, and when it needed delivery. Having the PCs arrive preconfigured also resulted in significant time savings at little additional cost.

The other significant implementation factor was that the network backbone was already in place. Data Center staff already had experience with installation and configuration as well as operation of basic network elements. This experience was then leveraged into the full-scale LAN implementation.

Standards.   Having standards in place for basic components simplified the choices considerably, thereby accelerating the speed of the decision-making. Using corporate standard PC platforms and software packages also enabled Network Systems to gain the most benefit from existing support and training services available from other departments in the corporation.

Room for Improvement

There are always some things that could be done a little better, no matter how success-ful the project. This project was no exception. The single biggest weakness was that the support organizations lagged somewhat behind the actual implementation of the network. This is not surprising when one considers that many of the same people were responsible for both aspects of the project.

Although a LAN administrator position was defined and approved, it was not staffed at the end of 1992. This left many administrative issues hanging until the prob-lems (such as "N:" drive congestion) became a virtual crisis. Only then was some lim-ited action taken to provide an interim solution.

The absence of a LAN administrator was also apparent in issues such as upgrade order control, definition of user support contacts, and coordination of training with implementation of the network.

Adhering to Corporate Timetable.

The other significant hurdle was that Network Systems found itself out on the "bleeding edge," far ahead of the corporate plan for LAN implementation. While it forced the corporation to accelerate its thinking somewhat, it also thrust Network Systems into the forefront of office LAN development in the organization. Much of the original vision remains unfulfilled because software developers haven't yet built the necessary components to complete the framework.

Should Network Systems have waited for eventual implementation of the Cor-porate Plan? The general consensus, at least within Network Systems, is an emphatic "No!" Implementation of the LAN has already proved a significant catalyst in the move toward cross-functional teams. Information moves faster and more reliably than ever before. Staff regularly employ graphs, charts, and illustrations to communicate more effectively. Having the LAN in place has enabled Network Systems staff to posi-tion themselves for the future—to provide advanced application solutions based on the potential of this new technology rather than on the restrictions of the old.

OUTSOURCING

AGT Limited announced its intent to investigate the potential outsourcing of its main-frame systems operations functions in the first quarter of 1992. The investigation moved through three distinct phases: a proposal was submitted in early June, feasibil-ity testing occurred over the summer, and detailed definition of the outsourcing con-tract completed in late November. The contract was ratified at the end of November and came into force on January 1, 1993.

Why Outsource?

AGT Limited is currently the major subsidiary of TELUS Corporation—accounting for over 90 percent of its total assets and revenue. TELUS has been seeking diversified business opportunities to lessen its dependence on the telecommunications marketplace for long-term growth. Outsourcing the mainframe system operations functions provided just such an opportunity. Not only would TELUS and AGT both gain through the lower cost of mainframe computing services, TELUS would also gain a foothold in the mainframe systems services market. The company would offer these services to other companies in the Alberta marketplace resulting (hopefully) in additional profitable returns to TELUS.

A secondary benefit is that the outsourcing of mainframe systems operations would enable AGT to focus its attention on its core business—telecommunications. Taking the complex issues surrounding mainframe and desktop services out of the top management process means that more attention can be paid to decisions directly affecting the core business. This will enable faster reaction to changing market conditions that are the key to survival in the current business market.

The third significant benefit is of course the reduced cost of obtaining mainframe and desktop computing services. AGT Limited would no longer have to directly support the hundreds of staff that were responsible for everything from the actual operation of the mainframe systems to provision and maintenance of personal computing devices and mainframe terminals. In addition, the actual costs of mainframe and desktop computing were significantly lower under the outsourcing contract than when they were under internal control.

Planning for Outsourcing

There were three distinct stages anticipated for implementation of an outsourcing agreement. A proposal was first created that outlined the potential benefits of outsourcing and recommended an outsourcing strategy. This stage took several months to complete but involved only senior I/T managers plus a few senior planners.

The second stage involved a detailed feasibility testing of the proposed strategy. Costs and benefits were examined for several alternative arrangements. The most effective combination of outsourced services and expected costs were then selected for the final stage, detailed definition of the outsourcing contract. I/T staff from AGT Limited performed the feasibility testing. Detailed definition of the outsourcing contract was a joint effort between the selected outsourcing partner (ISM) and the I/T staff from AGT Limited.

Implementation of the Outsourcing Agreement

There were a number of major elements to consider in the implementation of outsourcing at AGT Limited. Among them were:

- Division of responsibilities
- Financing
- Staffing
- Handing over the keys

- Ensuring continuity
- What worked
- Room for improvement

Discussion of each of these elements follows.

Division of Responsibilities.   Traditional agreements have given the out-sourcing provider responsibility for installation and maintenance of the internal networks and data centers of the "host" organization. This has proven to be a major benefit in many firms, but was not viable in the AGT Limited environment. AGT Limited's primary products are telecommunications and network services, with at least three layers of networks in use at AGT Limited. The largest by far is the switching and facility network that is the basis for all the services sold by AGT Limited. The second layer is a monitoring and control network with its own systems, facilities, data centers, and dedicated end-user equipment. There is a growing trend for major customers to have access to this network so that they may control their own internal networks carried on AGT Limited facilities. Finally, there is the traditional mainframe and PC-based office system network that is used for more than traditional data processing applications. This third layer has its own mainframe data centers, and LANs, and services approximately 7,000 of AGT Limited's 10,000 employees.

There was never any question of whether the switching and facility network should remain under the control of AGT Limited. It was also agreed that the office network, the associated data centers, and end-user equipment should be the responsibility of the outsourcing agency, ISM Alberta Ltd. The debate largely centered on what to do with the middle layer—the monitoring and control systems. On the one hand, there might have been some cost savings arising from the consolidation and operation of data centers under ISM Ltd. The disadvantages, however, outweighed any potential cost savings that might occur:

- The middle network is essential for the monitoring and control of the service network. Data centers are located in high-security buildings. System and network outages are dealt with on a priority basis by highly trained specialists. It was felt that AGT Limited would lose some credibility with its major customers if it did not retain the ability to monitor and control its own service network.
- AGT Limited did not want a third party inserting itself between AGT Limited and its customers. Several major customers have AGT Limited facilities and end-user equipment on their premises for monitoring and controlling their own internal telecommunications networks. It doesn't make a lot of sense to have customers call ISM Alberta Ltd. to fix a problem on a network connection whose use is to monitor AGT Limited's service network. This would give ISM a foothold that would enable them to market their own network management tools and facilities—thereby draining revenue away from AGT Limited. As ISM's net-

work grows, it may also offer its own services in direct competition with those available from AGT.

In the end, AGT decided to retain control of the monitoring and control network as well as the associated data centers and customer premises equipment.

A second issue was the question of deciding how to coordinate service requests between the two organizations. ISM was not set up to cope with a multitude of requests flooding it from every corner of the province. It established a control help desk facility to coordinate trouble reporting and other end-user service requests. Requests for additional applications, storage space, and other longer-term issues were first coordinated through a liaison group in AGT Limited before forwarding them to ISM for implementation. This helped ensure a minimization of overlap and that consistent documentation accompanied each request.

Financing.   The outsourcing company was eager to hammer out a long-term contract—effective for a least ten or more years. AGT Limited, on the other hand, was less willing to commit itself for this extended period. A compromise was reached whereby the master agreement is effective for at least the first five years with options to renew. In addition, the list of services provided by ISM Alberta Limited is subject to more frequent renegotiation and costing is renegotiated annually.

Staffing.   Approximately 250 AGT Limited staff performed duties to be taken over by ISM Ltd. Because the outsourcing negotiations were taking place at the same time as a significant work force downsizing, this group got special attention. First, AGT allowed ISM Alberta Ltd. to select the staff it needed from the available pool. Those employees not offered a position with ISM received sixty days to find another position in AGT Limited. Those that were unable to find one received the same severance package as was offered to the remainder of AGT Limited. Of the 250 original staff, approximately 180 received offers for positions with ISM. Although a few found positions elsewhere, most of the rest took advantage of the severance package.

Handing Over the Keys.   Finally, the fateful day arrived. On January 1, 1993, ISM Alberta Limited took over mainframe and office system PC applications and services. The PROFS office system quickly choked as the remainder of the staff returned from their Christmas vacations and tried to access all 7,000 mailboxes simultaneously. The senior managers at ISM were probably wondering what they had gotten themselves into! Things got back to normal within a week or so, however, and life continued much as it had before the transfer to ISM.

Ensuring Continuity.   While the physical transition itself went off fairly smoothly, there was a considerable effort going on behind the scenes to ensure the maintaining of service continuity through the coming months and years as new applications were implemented and obsolete ones were retired from service. Planners that were helping to define the ISM requirements participated in development and implementation of a Corporate Systems tactical planning process. This helped to ensure that appropriate linkages were maintained so that the planning process could continue.

These same representatives also assisted with development and presentation of the first Corporate Tactical Plan for Systems Development. As several of these players transferred to ISM, they carried with them the knowledge gained during the development of the plan.

Finally, as the various Divisional Systems groups in AGT Limited have developed their own tactical plans, they have included representatives from the AGT Limited liaison group, as well as ISM Limited planners and senior management, in the distribution and presentation of the finished products. This helps to keep all the players informed and enables the fullest possible coordination of planning and development efforts.

What Worked.   There were several aspects of this transition that are worth highlighting:

- AGT Limited, because of its existing network infrastructure, had the vision of establishing a new business venture—not just unloading a financial burden. It sought out competent partners and has begun to establish itself through ISM Alberta Limited as a credible player in the systems outsourcing services market.
- The transition to ISM Alberta was negotiated at several distinct levels, much as systems are developed. A general proposal was developed first, followed by feasibility testing. Only after the concept was proven feasible from economic and technical perspectives was authorization given to proceed with detailed definition and implementation of the outsourcing agreement.
- Employees of AGT Limited were kept informed of the intent and progress of the outsourcing negotiations through periodic bulletins on the office system news service as well as by articles in the company newspaper. Staff groups directly affected by the transition were often briefed in person by members of the negotiating team. This helped all employees to understand what was happening, why it was necessary to take this approach, and what implications it held for them personally, professionally, and economically.

Room for Improvement.   The original estimate for this transition suggested that it could be done in six months or less. In fact, it wound up taking nearly twice that long to do it properly. This caused frustration on both sides as they struggled in vain to meet impossible deadlines. Perhaps the timetable was appropriate for a pure outsourcing agreement. It wasn't recognized at the time, however, that this was also the start of a new business venture—which complicated the planning somewhat. Add to that the issues of staff selection and placement for the new organization, and it was no wonder that the original schedule was wholly inadequate!

DECENTRALIZATION/RECENTRALIZATION

A Brief History of Network Systems in AGT Limited

Network Systems was formed in 1986 as an amalgamation of isolated systems groups that served the interests of various operations and engineering organizations in AGT Limited. This took place as part of a general corporate reorganization that saw the engineering and operations divisions of the company consolidated under a single senior vice president.

The fundamental reason for this consolidation was to ensure that applications were built in an integrated fashion to satisfy the requirements of both communities. AGT recognized it could no longer afford duplicate data entry or awkward manual processes for conveying information from one system to another. The consolidation also mirrored the business organization in which a single division was responsible for all aspects of delivering and maintaining telecommunications network services to AGT Limited's customers.

Another reorganization in 1990, just before AGT Limited was privatized, saw the operations portion of Network Services split away from the engineering side of Network Services. It was recombined with customer service and billing groups to form the Customer Services business unit. Network Systems continued to provide development, support and data center operating functions for the new Customer Services Operations organization.

There were some conflicts, however, with another system group in the Customer Services organization. This second group was initially responsible for trouble ticketing and force management applications that required extensive interaction with the network surveillance and diagnostic systems developed and maintained by Network Systems. After several months of discussion and debate, management decided to transfer those applications and the associated staff to Network Systems who in turn transferred responsibility for service-oriented applications back to the Customer Services Systems organization.

Late 1992 saw the activation of a strategic alliance between AGT Limited and several other telecommunications companies across Canada. The Operations Development Alliance or ODA was established to promote the development and implementation of common applications across Canada for network surveillance, control, diagnostics, and even customer assignment. The overall aim was to reduce the cost of redundant development and support efforts, thereby making these companies more competitive. As a member of this alliance, AGT contributes a significant number of Network Systems staff to these joint projects.

Customer Focus Groups

Today, Network Services is responsible for approximately 120 application systems running on mainframe, minicomputer, and desktop platforms. The 155 staff are not split along traditional organizational lines, however. The traditionally separate development and support organizations combine into "Customer Focus Groups" that are responsible for the systems requirements of a business function, not a specific customer organization.

These high-level business functions were derived using standard enterprise modeling techniques. This has proved vital to the efforts of Network Services and Customer Services management to reduce the amount of redundant information floating around the organization. For the first time, a single team was responsible for coordinating all the systems relating to management of staff workload, real-time control of the network, or activation of software-based customer services.

The composition of these Customer Focus Groups varies over time depending on the nature of the activities being performed and the relative priority of the activities with respect to the total Network Systems work load. Staff members report to an administrative manager that is responsible for salary and benefit administration, documentation of performance reviews, and so on. They also report to a functional manager that heads up one of the seven Customer Focus Groups. The role of managers is primarily that of process owner, as opposed to the traditional planner, director, or controller. It is the functional managers' responsibility to act as primary liaison with their peers in the various organizations served by Network Systems. They are also responsible for coordination of the work between each of the several project or support teams within their jurisdiction.

Day-to-day project management issues are generally dealt with inside the affected project team rather than at the managerial level. Definition and staffing of work items are primarily the responsibility of a group called the Operating Plan Management Team or OPMT. The OPMT is composed of representatives from each Customer Focus Group and meet on a regular basis to plan and coordinate the work load for Network Systems based on current business priorities and available staff skills.

The OPMT reports progress and issues on a regular basis to a second group called the Systems Portfolio Management Team or SPMT. The SPMT is not another Network Systems management team. Rather, it is made up of directors of each of the customers' groups served by Network Systems. It is this group of senior customer representatives that has the final word on the work load and priorities for Network Systems. This forces the various customer organizations to come to some sort of agreement on the true priorities for systems development and support. It also enables them to support and promote the resulting work plans and associated budgets.

Critical Success Factors.   The single most important factor in the establishment of the Customer Focus Groups was getting and keeping the staff involved, informed, and motivated. These changes had the potential to plunge Network Systems into total chaos if handled improperly. It was essential therefore that everyone be brought on board quickly. Staff worked with managers to define the initial focus groups. Staff took on responsibility for keeping each other informed about progress made by the study team. Organizationwide communication sessions shared and promoted the focus team concept. Opinions and ideas were sought from throughout the organization.

The spirit of cooperation and consensus-building helped to solidify ownership of the new organization by all of its participants, staff and management alike. This was (and still is) a radical departure from the norm for most of AGT Limited. For the first time a major chunk of the company was taking ownership of its organization, mandate, and work flow management right from the grass roots level.

Of course, none of this would have been possible without the foresight and trust of the director of Network Systems. It took a great deal of courage to stand aside and let the staff define their own organization. It also took a great deal of work to build trust among his peers in the division and to build support among the various client communities. The ongoing intensive support by the Network Services Human Resources group was also instrumental in implementing these concepts within Network Systems and in maintaining credibility throughout the rest of the organization.

Client support existed because the clients themselves were a vital part of the process. Client representatives worked with Network Systems to define and obtain approval for the enterprise model that served as the basis for the new organization. Clients also began to see these new teams as being more effective in meeting their needs because of the integration of development and support functions. Finally, it is the customers themselves who determine the priorities for Network Systems and therefore the composition and work load of each of the various focus teams.

The Importance of Being Earnest: The Role of Team Skills, Peer Reviews, and Other Interpersonal Skills. It was recognized quite early in the transition to the new team environment that traditional interpersonal skills bred in a traditional hierarchical organization would not suffice. Management decided that everyone in Network Systems would undergo specialized training in team skills such as arriving at consensus, giving and receiving constructive feedback, and so on. In addition, several staff took more advanced training in meeting facilitation and/or facilitative leadership to help keep the rest of the organization on track and keep the process moving.

A significant milestone in maturity of the new Network Systems organization came as several teams began conducting their own peer reviews. This occurred at first on an experimental basis with assistance from the Network Services Human Resources professionals. As the groups became more adept at peer reviews, Network Systems facilitators from outside the group replaced the human resource facilitators. It should be noted that those teams conducting peer reviews have volunteered to do so. Several groups that don't feel ready to take this next step have not been pressured to do so.

The general consensus among the participants is that the peer reviews are both more immediate and more relevant than those conducted in the past by their managers. To be effective, however, the peer review requires a significant investment of time from every participant. Preparing for, conducting, and documenting the results of a complete team peer review can easily take upwards of five working days per team member. Multiply that by the number of team members and the time lost to more productive activities soon escalates. A careful balance has to be maintained between the need for self-examination and the need to accomplish significant work on behalf of the teams' clients.

It is also important to maintain a balance for those members who may be on multiple teams. Each team has to be willing to accept input from others as to each members' overall contribution to the organization. In the end, it is generally each staff members' primary team affiliation that determines who actually conducts the review.

Much of the Customer Focus Group process has simply evolved as various teams experimented with alternative methods for getting the work done. This led to some inconsistencies when customers were dealing with different teams in Network Systems. This resulted in yet another team being established—to take the best of what has evolved to date, document it, and establish it as standard practice in the Network Systems organization.

Summary.   The major factor in the success of Customer Focus Groups has been the continual involvement of the Network Systems staff in defining all aspects of the implementation and evolution of the concept. It has built ownership, commitment, and a desire to succeed far beyond what normal reorganizations ever attain.

A second major factor was that the new organization was based on a common model developed and understood by both Network Systems and its clients. This enabled both groups to work towards a common understanding within a consistent frame of reference.

The third critical success factor was the unwavering support of the director and the human resources facilitators. When the director was appointed to another position in AGT Limited, he went to considerable trouble to ensure that the incoming director understood what was taking place and would not interfere with the natural course of events.

The biggest impediment to the change process was its own success. When staff started to see results in one area, they wanted to start changing a second. After the first year there were so many teams analyzing various aspects of the Network Services organization and processes that most staff were continuously bombarded by changes, both real and proposed. This was when it was decided to document the best of the changes to date in a single forum and to stabilize the process somewhat. This has resulted in more effort being placed in implementing a few high-quality suggestions instead of merely interesting ideas.

A second hurdle was that few organizations have attempted this degree of restructuring in so short a time. Having few road maps meant that discussions often led down blind alleys, with associated penalties in cost, confusion, and delays.

The third major issue was the amount of staff that this change effort took away from real work being done on real systems for real customers. Customers were becoming increasingly frustrated with Network Systems staff being unavailable for extended periods of time. It was only through the efforts of the managers and the director that the customers were able to realize that the long-term gains in efficiency, productivity, and responsiveness were worth the initial cost of the transition.

A New Process for Manpower Planning

There were concerns raised by both staff and management about apparent inconsistencies in the way that work was allocated to staff. In some cases, the staff were canvassed for volunteers. In others, management assigned work without necessarily being aware of all the implications. In many cases, little attention was paid to the skills or aspirations of those being asked to do the work.

A Staff Placement Initiative Team consisting of Network Systems management and staff as well as a human resources representative was established to formulate a consistent process for work load allocation. The team sought to first understand the multidimensional relationship between the work, the staff that were available to do it, the skills needed and available, and the career needs and aspirations of the staff. The team held brainstorming sessions with all staff and managers to collect their impressions of the current process as well as their ideas for improvement. From these sessions, it was determined that the best place to start improving the process was to document the skills and aspirations of the Network Systems staff.

They began in the Fall of 1992 to devise a way of assessing the current skill levels of Network Systems staff. A pilot group was selected with representatives from all levels in the organization and with widely varied backgrounds. The pilot group was then asked to complete and comment on a proposed skills inventory questionnaire. The results were then discussed in a joint session with the pilot group and the Skills Inventory Project Team.

The initial emphasis was on technology-based skills—being able to operate, administer, or maintain various processors, peripherals, and network configurations. The majority of the pilot group, however, found that these skills were irrelevant to the successful execution of their job functions. It was generally felt that more value would accrue through a debate on critical skills needed in the organization than through building prototype inventory tools for collection of irrelevant data.

What Are Critical Skills?   There appear to be at least three critical skill areas that need assessment:

- "Soft skills" such as interpersonal communication, decision-making, facilitative leadership, and team skills.
- Process skills including an understanding of customer business processes as well as the processes used for defining, building, and supporting systems.
- Technology-based skills for various segments of the business such as office systems, minicomputer platforms, and mainframe languages.

It is not enough to merely ask whether the skill is present. Skills can be practiced at many different levels of responsibility. Most individuals perform some form of time management, for example. This does not provide a reliable indication that they are capable of (or even want to become capable of) time management on a project or team basis. Another person may perform work load planning for a team but not have any experience in planning the overall work load for the directorate. The level of proficiency should also be taken into account as well as the aspirations of the employee.

It is also important to keep the skills' identification at a reasonably high level. Because many skills are transferable between devices, platforms, or processes, it adds little value to identify each hardware subassembly, language dialect, or administrative process. There are a couple of caveats to this general rule. If an organization is making a transition to a specific platform or software version, it may wish to specifically identify the target so that both individuals and the organization can measure their distance from it. Space should also be provided for individuals to list skills and experience outside the defined bounds of the organizational requirement. This will enable the organization to capitalize on experience gained in outside endeavors that could lead to improved performance on the job.

Linking Resource Planning to Business Objectives.   Another dimension to the issue of work load assignment is that the work to be done should directly contribute to the business objectives of the organization. Network Systems has employed a process for determining the relative business, technical, and economic value of project activities since 1988. Basically, the process involves devising a set of measurement criteria based upon published objectives, assigning appropriate weighting factors to each criterion, and assessing each project against them. Each project is awarded points according to its contribution towards achieving the objectives. The projects are then listed in order of total points. The higher the point score, the higher the relative priority of the project. This process evolved from foundation work by Parker, Benson, and Trainor in their book *Information Economics.* (More information on the evolution and application of information economics theory in Network Systems is provided in the commentary article for Part Five that follows.)

Although the project-level work was measured fairly consistently, there was still a significant amount of work that was not project-related such as ongoing maintenance and support of existing applications. A similar process was devised for these activities based on criteria that were adapted for the purpose. For the first time, staff, managers, and customers could compare the value of maintaining an existing application versus diverting effort towards building a replacement.

The same processes are used throughout the tactical and operational planning stages. At the tactical level, work is roughly allocated to a given Customer Focus Group. The Operating Plan Management Team then reviews the tactical allocations, refine them as needed, and then seek actual staff to do the work. Once suitable volunteers are found (or assigned as a last resort), the detailed operating plans for each focus group are ratified by both Network Systems management and senior customer representatives.

AGT Limited has also implemented a number of options for staff with significant aspirations or commitments outside the company. These options include conversion to a regular part-time position, formal job sharing agreements, educational leave, and self-funded leave. These options allow AGT Limited to retain highly skilled and motivated employees while maximizing the employees options for personal growth and a balanced lifestyle. Interested employees are provided with detailed information on the purpose and policies of each option as well as a recommended process for investigation of its suitability from the perspective of the employee, AGT Limited, and AGT's customers.

The regular part-time option is available where the demands of the position are less than regular full-time work. The employee must work at least 50 percent of the hours of a full-time job and is still eligible for benefits, training, and career development. Job sharing, on the other hand, is a voluntary agreement between two employees to share the responsibilities and salary of one full-time position.

Educational leave is a partially paid (25 percent of salary) leave of absence for employees wishing to pursue full-time studies relating to AGT's business. The studies must lead to a certificate, diploma, professional designation, or degree. AGT Limited pays the costs of tuition and books and provides employment during major school breaks. AGT also guarantees reemployment upon completion at the employee's former level. The maximum leave is four years, but intervals as short as three months can be accommodated.

Self-funded leave is a partially paid leave of absence that the employee funds in advance by payroll deferral. This option is for those employees seeking "time out" to balance family needs, participate in community service, attend courses, or take an extended vacation. This leave can be for periods of six months to one year. The employee would typically defer 20 percent of their salary for four years and receive 80 percent of their regular salary in the fifth year while away from work. Salary deferrals of between one-tenth and one-third are allowed for a one-year to five-year period, and held in a trust fund until paid out during the leave period.

What Worked.   The largest single contributor to the success of resource planning efforts in Network Systems has been the inclusion of the customer in all major stages of the process. Senior customer management define the business and financial objectives. Systems work is prioritized based upon those objectives, and the prioritized list ratified and finalized by senior customer management. Finally, senior customer management reviews and approves specific near-term work plans. The customers even worked with Network Systems to define the process, offering many suggestions that have been incorporated into the current model.

Next in overall importance is the application of consistent prioritization criteria to all development work (and later support work) being undertaken by Network Systems. These enable both the systems and customer communities to measure the value of applications between functional areas, thereby neutralizing many of the turf wars fought in the past.

Establishing a formal linkage between the tactical and operating plans provided the necessary framework for detailed planning without redefining tasks already established in the tactical plan. This not only shaved weeks off the time needed to make the transition, it also provided a common basis for understanding throughout Network Systems and the affected customer groups.

The last significant factor is the management of work by peers. This was instrumental in the establishment of the team environment in Network Systems. Work was no longer assigned by individual managers but incorporated into a coherent plan by a team representing the total scope of Network Systems activity. This enabled individuals and project teams to directly view their contribution to the success of the organization. The proximity of the peer contacts also provides a ready feedback mechanism should problems be encountered that require adjustments to the work plans.

Room for Improvement.   The current process is fairly unique to Network Systems and its customers. As such, the linkage to the corporate planning process is tenuous at best. The success of the linkage is heavily dependent upon the skill and the awareness of the planners in Network Systems. They have to find out when the new objectives are available, collect them, incorporate them in the process, and make systems and client communities aware that the new objectives exist. Further work is necessary to incorporate this resource planning model across the company so that the linkage to corporate processes and objectives-setting becomes much more consistent and automatic.

The existing process is designed to work within an annual planning cycle. This, however, is inadequate to meet the rapidly changing business needs of the organization. The process needs simplifying, streamlining, and automating where feasible to maximize the flexibility of resource assignment without inducing unnecessary "churn" in work load planning. In other words, it needs to be ongoing in nature rather than tied to a fixed annual period.

STRATEGIC ALLIANCES

AGT Limited is no stranger to the concept of strategic alliances. It has been a member of an alliance of major Canadian telecommunications companies for many years. The Telecom Canada organization, as it is known, consists of employees of the various member companies "on loan" for periods of two to three years at a stretch. Telecom Canada is responsible for development and coordination of products and services that cross operating boundaries. It also allocates the revenue from intercompany long distance billings among the members based on their respective call volumes and capital investment in network equipment.

As a member of Telecom Canada, AGT Limited participated in the formation of a strategic alliance with MCI to facilitate the design and provisioning of cross-border telecommunications services. A secondary motive was to preempt the possibility of MCI forming an alliance with Unitel, the major competitor to Telecom Canada in the Canadian market. There was also the expectation that the American telecommunications giant AT&T would not even consider dealing with a minuscule young upstart like Unitel, thereby locking Unitel out of the lucrative cross-border services market. It took only a few short months, however, for this assumption to be proven wrong. It took less than one year after the Telecom Canada-MCI announcement for Unitel and AT&T to formulate a similar alliance.

A third major alliance is with other Canadian telecommunications companies—this time for joint development and support of computer systems for trouble detection, resolution, and emergency control of the joint telecommunications network. This Operations Development Alliance is staffed by systems development and support staff from within each ODA member company. The difference between this organization and Telecom Canada is that the employees remain at their normal location instead of being relocated to Ottawa.

Project teams are being established based on an agreed list of high-priority projects. Attempts are being made to leverage the experience of companies in specific areas wherever possible by allocating a single project to one development or support group. This team would then undertake to develop and maintain the specified application on behalf of all the member companies.

Business Value

Robert J. Benson

More often than not, there is a real gap between I/T management and business management. Symptomatic of the business value gap is when business management says:

- I/T isn't responsive to real business requirements.
- I/T has no clear business vision for the next major steps.
- I/T values aren't the same as enterprise business values.
- I/T has technical managers hiding behind their technology.

I/T is very visible. Its costs escalate and it is often the single largest cost pool senior managers see. The good news: Many I/T organizations can point to real success. Projects become operational. Operations are satisfactory, with increasingly good reliability. First-line users are relatively content: new workstations offer productive tools and services, training is appropriate to user needs, and user support organizations are active in responding to problems. Yet the gap remains when it comes time to consider large new investments in I/T. The senior I/T executive often doesn't feel like a full member of the business team, and the senior user managers are lukewarm in their support for what's needed in subsequent I/T action plans.

I/T management knows there are real challenges ahead. Process reengineering is merely one of them, and additional investments in needed infrastructure including systems development automation are necessary. The business value gap can prevent management acknowledgment and understanding of the investments required. Worse yet, the size of the investments—particularly for infrastructure and complex applications such as reengineering—keeps getting bigger.

ESTABLISHING BUSINESS VALUE

Investment in I/T, by itself, doesn't guarantee improved enterprise performance; there's something else, something additional involved in those companies that truly do achieve improved business performance. Key factors are, most often, the strategy of the particular enterprise and its possession of the core competencies to carry it out and the overall health of the industry it is in. Those looking at service sectors make a similar argument. Here, the argument is that investment in I/T has produced little discernible improvement in service worker productivity, particularly in the banking industry. Banks with large I/T investments show no better return-on-assets than those with smaller ones. Here, the reason is that while investments in I/T allow banks to cut

488

costs and drive the design of its future products, it does something else. It lowers the barriers to entry into its retail business of nonbank competitors (e.g., credit cards issued by AT&T and General Motors, auto loans issued by automobile manufacturers, residential mortgages issued by credit unions), placing pure banking in a shrinking market.

It's no wonder that there's a value gap between business management and I/T itself. This gap has two related elements. The first is the disbelief managers express about the real business value contributed by both business and I/T on joint costs and new development projects. Management expresses disbelief with aggregate value and with specific projects. The second is that I/T may not be addressing all the business needs that exist, and there is a lack of focus on the issue of what business value really is. This latter problem, of course, feeds the first one. Even without it, the first problem is serious enough. Consequently, it is important to develop a mutual understanding of what business value is and how to achieve it.

PROBLEMS OF VALUE

A telecommunications infrastructure is a good example of an I/T investment that may make it possible for an enterprise to achieve important business goals. For example, an enterprise might use a communication network to offer new products and services, increase the level of service it offers to customers and suppliers, and enable internal changes such as reduced cycle-times and increased productivity in business processes. The real question is: "Should they?" Should an enterprise make the considerable investment in software and hardware necessary to accomplish such goals?

Whether these goals are important to an enterprise is one set of issues. Another is whether extensive use of telecommunications networks is the best approach to achieving enterprise goals. Answers to both depend on a clear link between the technology solution to the enterprise business goals and enterprise management plans and objectives—its strategic vision. That is, it is necessary to define the business grounds on which enterprise managers can agree that a communications technology investment is the wisest application of scarce enterprise resources.

This is not a new problem. Managers have made decisions about I/T, particularly computer hardware and software, for fifty years. What makes the problem especially vexing now is the nature of communications technologies, in particular the technologies offering easily used networking within and between organizations. Because the capability of networking business organizations together—linking business processes, linking customers to suppliers, linking partners in strategic alliances and collaborative relationships—raises important new challenges to management. Addressing them requires new ways to think about the process whereby the enterprise plans, organizes, manages, and justifies I/T. Further, the very act of considering that there are fundamental—and perhaps irreversible—shifts in the economic base of competition (national to trading bloc or global markets; manufacturing shifts to the newly industrialized countries; nations that are current economic leaders shift from a manufacturing base to service, information, or technology-dominated economic base) require developing a new business mind-set for decision-making for both business and technology.

Impact of I/T

I/T has immense capabilities to change how business functions. One only has to use an airline or visit a rental-car desk to observe, in some detail, how these businesses have changed over the last few years. The collection of products and services these firms offer their customers is determined very much by the information technology they employ and the communications networks they use to deliver them throughout the world. On the other hand, does all this have real economic value? That is, have past investments in I/T produced benefit to the enterprises making them? Should an enterprise invest in I/T for future economic value? And, if so, how much? How can an enterprise determine the answer for its specific situation? These are, of course, complex questions, and illustrate just one dimension of the issues open to discussion.

The concluding section of Chapter 10 states that I/T is a prime enabler of business change once business commits itself to the reengineering process. However, I/T—especially communications networks and enterprisewide computing activities—changes the business itself not only in economic and competitive terms, but also in the way the enterprise manages itself and its various information technologies. I/T stands as an enabler of basic and fundamental improvement in business behavior and business performance. Adopting effective management solutions to the problems this creates is necessary to attaining the appropriate change in enterprise performance and to realizing the business value of I/T, in general, and communications technology, in particular.

The problems largely revolve around management attitudes toward allocating scarce resources to I/T. I/T can be expensive, and with infrastructure investments like networks, somewhat distant from real business benefits. Senior management always has a limited amount of money available, and this creates a real need to understand why they should invest more in I/T versus more marketing personnel or on developing more distribution channels or on whatever other investment alternatives may exist. At the same time, it isn't completely clear that previous large investments in I/T produced any real value. When the disruptive aspects of change are added—the whole point of modern I/T is to change how a business organization functions—the conditions exist for a lessening of management willingness to invest in I/T opportunities if there is no perceived achievement of lasting business value through such investments.

Evolutionary Aspects of I/T

It's informative to look at the evolution of I/T over the last half century. For the first thirty years the emphasis was on technology management—and the major challenges focused on getting the technology to work reliably. I/T management practices evolved to ensure proper technology implementation and operation. Systems development methodologies, change management methods, data administration, and communications network management emerged largely as ways to reduce the unreliability of I/T in the enterprise.

In parallel, I/T emerged as a centralized resource for the most part. The I/T organization became the center of technology management and technical innovation, particularly because the technology itself had centralizing characteristics. On-line systems, enterprisewide corporate systems, corporatewide communications networks, and single-image corporate databases are good examples of technology applications with these characteristics. Of course, PCs (and the related defensive measures I/T organizations used such as information centers) focused some attention on the users and on decentralizing technologies. The 1980s also focused on these matters, including the emergence of end-user tools (e.g., query languages, relational databases). Now, the 1990s offers even more of the same: communications is a critical technology that further enables enterprise management to respond to an organization's latent tendencies to disperse information technologies throughout the enterprise. Local networks, enterprisewide networks, and nationwide networks serve to make the information dispersion easier to accomplish—easier to move information within and among enterprises, its components, and collaborators.

The foregoing is, essentially, a technical view of the impact of computing and communications in the enterprise—and it is easy to look at the issues as a technology management matter. The real impact, however, is in business and organizational terms. The prospect—and in many existing cases, the reality—of widespread communications capabilities accelerates the need to address the business management issues.

MANAGEMENT ISSUES SURROUNDING I/T

If nothing else, past experience in managing I/T solved most of the hard technical problems. Generally, technology works, it's reliable, and it delivers the technical promises. Delivering business value, however, requires solutions to problems created by an organization's use of technology. Management faced these sorts of problems from the beginning and evolved a range of solutions. However, modern technology that transforms the enterprise and changes how it does business creates a whole new set of problems and management impacts. They are:

- Cross-organizational impact: I/T crosses organizational lines within the enterprise and among multiple enterprises.
- Investment impact: I/T requires clear, business-based investment justification.
- Performance impact: Any effective justification for I/T links to improvements in business performance that are measurable.
- Impact on I/T management: Realizing business value (e.g., harvesting the benefits) changes the I/T management job.

Cross-Organizational Impact

Over the last few years, I/T applications became more complex. Twenty years ago, application delineation was by departmental lines and functional lines. Justification and value were issues in a relationship with a single manager responsible for a specific function or department—often an overhead unit. Consequently, I/T grew to serve the users' needs and—essentially—to reduce expenditures for the overhead units. This is important but it certainly is not the basis for true value—where the basis is improving the business performance of the various lines of business and strategic business units. Additionally, by having a history of working primarily for the overhead units, it carries the burden of being considered a cost, not an asset of the enterprise. This is no surprise when one considers the historic bias towards serving masters in an overhead arena.

There is much discussion on reengineering, cross-functional business processes, integration of business activities, and collaborative enterprises. Communications and networking technologies enable these changes. However, as organizational lines blur or cross, the value and justification of computing become a more subtle issue for the hierarchical organization. At the very least, finding an effective sponsor for I/T costs when the benefits spread themselves over many organizational units—or, in the case of virtual enterprises, multiple enterprises—is more difficult. The same is also true for those organizations becoming more fluid and horizontal through workteams and employee empowerment. Additionally, the benefits themselves become more difficult to define, forcing I/T managers to deal increasingly with intangibles. They deal with the idea that I/T value doesn't come from cost reduction alone, and they find that it is much more difficult to quantify benefits in business terms that are intangible (e.g., customer satisfaction, cycle-time reduction, improved quality).

The ideas of key business process (Chapter 10) provide important clues here. The basic enterprise model consists of a customer requesting a product or service and the enterprise producing it. This model describes the fast food restaurant, the aircraft manufacturer, the lawyer's office. From the perspective of business management, I/T should make the internal enterprise processes more timely, less costly (for example, collapse the business process that produces each key variable to the customer by ten times in cost or time or both), and more valuable to the customer by providing information or improved services and quality.

This simple example shows why I/T raises the stakes, for it becomes possible for the enterprise to employ communications networks to both collapse cycles (e.g., reducing the communications time among the tasks needed to complete the customer request) and to control the many participants in the production process (e.g., just-in-time manufacturing processes that employ many suppliers of critical product elements). The capability for doing this is competitively important—and equally important to the ways the enterprise controls and manages its development of processes and supporting information technologies. This is cross-organizational, indeed multiorganizational, in ways that subvert the old ways of managing information technologies. It creates enormous new management challenges, requiring new management approaches and skills. One of these is performance-based, value-based management of I/T.

Cross-organizational Impact: I/T crosses organizational lines within the enterprise and among multiple enterprises, making it more difficult to plan, justify, implement, and manage.

Investment Impact

I/T is expensive. The multiorganizational character, which blurs the specific justifications for each organizational unit, makes financial justification more difficult. Of course, this is not a new problem, for managers have been making investment decisions about computers ever since their development. Generally such decisions reflect business-driven choices made by managers—sometimes many managers—and the choices they make are between many alternatives. Computations such as return-on-investment (ROI) are helpful if they are consistent and done for all alternative choices in compatible fashion.

However, financially derived computations intended to reflect the linkage between I/T investments and business goals miss the main point—that the investments are intended to achieve business goals that have a broader base in time and product than can be credibly reflected in current-period financial measures (e.g., increased customer satisfaction, market share, product quality). That these business goals have ultimate financial importance to the enterprise is unquestioned, yet management doesn't have the tools to calculate the exact financial impact in advance. Consequently, it needs methods to connect I/T investment to the achievement of business goals, particularly with investments in infrastructures such as a national or international communications network. Among other attributes, such methods need to provide industrial-strength management consensus-building on the business value of I/T because what management believes about the value of I/T is critical to its justification and development.

I/T can be the single most visible and costly corporate support activity in the enterprise, and for many, I/T is not only the largest, but also the fastest growing line item in the budget. Yet line and senior management do not believe in the value of I/T. To them, I/T costs appear high at the same time that low-cost technology is available in the form of local computers and client-server networks that, more often than not, bypass the central I/T organization (Chapter 10). For everyone, money is tight. As a result, business management needs the ability to link I/T costs to the business values of the enterprise. Any relevant approach to this problem has two requirements.

- Business management must be able to define—and subsequently measure—business performance improvement.
- Business management must agree to and establish the linkage between business performance and I/T.

Business management needs to concentrate on both efforts, because the hardest problem I/T management faces is getting business agreement on value and the potential value resulting from a particular I/T investment. Until everyone understands both what the linkage between a potential I/T investment is and what realizing a potential improvement in business means, business is not getting the most from its investments.

The justification and valuation of I/T are already well-known problems. Most solutions employ a variation of cost-benefit techniques and to a considerable extent I/T organizations have well-developed methods for justifying I/T projects. Typically, the larger the enterprise is, the more elaborate these methods become.

However, two areas are particularly difficult. First, modern I/T projects result in hard-to-quantify benefits such as quality, customer satisfaction, and competitive benefits. Analysis of these sorts of proposed I/T projects probably does not result in measurable economic impact (e.g., projects that add to customer satisfaction or to service quality) in standard ROI or present value terms. Second, investment in I/T to create or add to I/T or enterprise infrastructure (e.g., large-scale networks, application development infrastructure) produces benefits bound up in the I/T projects and applications that use them. The justification of such second-order projects do not cleanly demonstrate measurable business benefit. Given that I/T investments compete for management attention and support with other possible investments, the difficulties associated with these two areas can be important to resolve effectively. Whereas we describe these two difficulties using terms associated with justification, we could just as easily describe them in terms of linkage—that is, I/T management's goal is to create projects (investments) in I/T closely linked to enterprise business objectives.

> *Justifying and valuing I/T projects that lack clear-cut computations, and I/T infrastructure projects that lack clear-cut economic impact, signify difficulties in achieving linkage to business planning.*

We need a management method to determine the value of enterprise investments in I/T. A business value approach answers questions that managers have about I/T retrospectively, and "Am I getting my money's worth from I/T?", and prospectively, "Should I invest in I/T?" and "What should my priorities be?" The two questions relate, because in both, the value results from linking I/T to business activities. Management recognizes value by linking I/T investments to business goals of the enterprise and its components.

> *Investment Impact: I/T requires clear, business-based investment justification based upon the contribution to business value.*

Performance Impact

The focus on value has grown recently. A number of companies in the United States and Europe have adapted a business-value approach to better focus investment needs. Based on their experience, value—and linkage to business objectives—has become a dominant business theme. This interest in the business value approach has, thus helped develop a better understanding of the value of I/T.

In one sense, the result is simplistic: The value of I/T derives from the improved performance I/T provides the enterprise and its component parts. As an example, an order-entry system has value when it improves productivity or customer satisfaction to the point that it improves market share—assuming this is important to the enterprise. In another sense, this result forces a better understanding of the ways an enterprise articulates to itself the things that are important—and the consequent ways an I/T project links to these things. This fuller understanding encompasses the following areas:

- Value is an extension of management planning. Value isn't isolable from the management processes that define priorities and set objectives for the enterprise itself.
- Value, to be recognized and articulated, requires measurement.
- Value is relative (not absolute) and is a function of time. Value isn't isolable from measurements. The basis of value is business performance improvement.

These principles evolved during the experiences of applying business value to the investment justification for I/T. At the same time it is important not to abandon or downgrade the concepts of ROI—the concepts of cost-benefit analysis and measurable economic benefits. The basis of business value is economic impact, and the concepts of value and linkage are necessary to deal with the difficulties involved, the nature of modern I/T benefits, and infrastructure investment justification.

The basic principle of business-based investment justification is that investments in I/T aren't justified solely by ROI or present value but by the overall value to the enterprise. This value results from improvement in overall performance and competitive position for the enterprise. In this sense, the information technology itself has little intrinsic value in the business domain. Rather, its value lies in the application of the technology that causes change in business performance. Therefore, any value of information technology derives from the capability it affords the I/T organization to deliver its services to the business units, whereas the basis for value contributed to the business domain is the information and services actually delivered. From the technology perspective, the basis of the viability of the investment is the project resources available compared to the resources needed to successfully develop and implement the project (see Figure IV-1). For I/T organizations that use some form of chargeback to users, this translates into a cost-recovery analogous to a revenue stream for a business unit. To be viable, the cost recovery must be sufficient to cover all potential costs including items such as training, changes to development methodologies, and temporary reductions in productivity due to introduction of new technology, that is, the costs associated with the (temporary) loss of enterprise equilibrium. Even if an I/T organization does not use a chargeback process, the problem

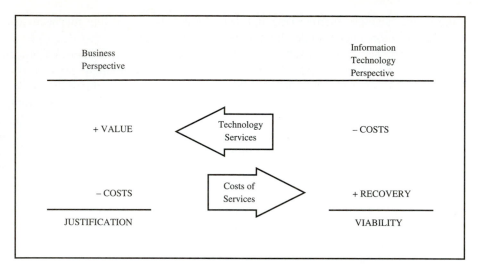

Figure IV-1   Relationship between Business and I/T Perspectives.

remains: Does it have the necessary resources, such as time and personnel, to over-come project hurdles?

> *The justification for I/T is the balance of value and cost assigned to the business, mea-sured by the business organization in business terms, whereas the basis of viability is the value of the I/T to the I/T organization, compared to the cost of using the technology for the service organization.*

This is an important shift in perspective because it redefines the purpose of information systems organizations and I/T. I/T is not primarily to serve user needs per se. Rather, I/T exists to add value to the business unit—to improve the functioning of every unit, including those internal to the enterprise as well as those that deal with customer mat-ters. Information is valuable—I/T adds value to the enterprise—when the performance of the business unit improves. Value occurs when those measures of customer choice, quality, and financial performance change for the better. Information with no direct link to such change is valueless. By extension, I/T and information systems organiza-tions with no linkage are also valueless.

One critical point about business performance: The achievement of measure-ments depends very much on the character of the business unit. More specifically, three clusters of business types exist. A business unit that primarily manufactures tan-gible products, such as automobiles or consumer goods, concerns itself with attracting customers, manufacturing and delivering products, and in so doing, performs prof-itably in financial terms. A business unit that primarily provides services, such as a hospital, lawyer, or fast food unit, also concerns itself with attracting customers, but has a just-in-time, customer-response focus rather than a manufacturing and delivering focus. Finally, an organization that is nonprofit or government in nature, including utilities and similar organizations, doesn't concern itself with attracting customers so much as adequately serving those that it is required or mandated to service. These organizations have a capacity and access focus.

Governing the choice of measurements of performance—and consequently the contribution of I/T to its improvement—are the characteristics of the business and the business unit for each enterprise. Consequently, information has value if it moves the measures of performance. A key way to move the measures is to provide full information about the customer and enterprise performance concerning the customer to the key actors in the enterprise.

Jointly, the I/T user and the I/T professional are capable of defining the appropriate performance measurements that represent value to the business. These performance measurements fall into the general categories of customer choice (such as market share), service and quality (such as product returns), financial (such as profitability), and timely response (such as time-to-market for new products or time-to-respond to new requirements). Hence information systems and technology planning concentrates on linking the information systems goals to the cause-and-effect the information system has in moving these measures. With this linkage, the information produced then has value, and should be the basis of investment by management.

Performance impact: Any effective justification for I/T requires linkage to improvements in business performance.

I/T Management Impact

The problems of achieving business impact with I/T, complicated by the cross-organizational aspects and imperatives to link I/T investments to business performance, stress technology management. Instead of managing technology—the traditional view of their role in the enterprise—technology managers must put on a business hat to be effective.

Over the years, I/T evolved largely as a single organization within an enterprise, supplying information and information systems services (e.g., development and operations) to individual operating units. As a consequence, I/T organizations became monolithic organizations, applying common methods and single large systems solutions to the complex businesses it served. This paradigm is based on a technology management perspective of the role I/T organizations are to play in the delivery of information systems and services to the business organizations.

Business also evolved in functional terms with hierarchical management and organizational forms. This means that the I/T organization evolved in ways that tend to optimize its relations with the business hierarchical forms (e.g., to business functions, departments), and the management patterns evolved from technical management. As businesses entered this decade, the common I/T paradigms were:

- Technology is characterized by specialized management functions.
- Critical mass and economy of scale are essential factors.
- The I/T organization should optimally serve the needs of the organizational units of the enterprise and develop appropriate methods and tools to do so.

This optimization was a natural outgrowth of I/T desires to serve user requirements. Additionally, it's an outgrowth of the evolution of systems themselves, which originated as single-department systems. I/T first created systems for the accounting department, for the human resources department, for the marketing department—all representative of the organizationally defined business function. (Early portfolio analysis ideas illustrate this. The enterprise is described in terms of the Anthony Triangle and business functions mapped onto that triangle. This is comparable to mapping systems onto an organizational hierarchy.)

The approach remains acceptable in organizations where information systems support remains bounded by single organizational units. If I/T develops systems for well-defined and separate organizational units—for example, the accounting department or the engineering department—then the drive to optimizing the I/T organization to match the business organization is the appropriate direction to take. Some of the actions that can occur include:

- Adoption of departmental computing platforms.
- Dispersing the systems development group into the functional departments.
- Reliance on traditional systems development methods and/or adoption of new techniques on dispersed platforms, where the decision affects the single department individually.

Hence, an enterprise can adopt a mix of approaches. However, the basic principles by which the enterprise manages I/T break down under current business and technology changes. These conditions attack the hierarchical view in both business and technology organizations. In particular, the challenges appear when either systems cross organizational boundaries or when business requirements are significantly different across those organizational boundaries. A good example is the current activities associated with reengineering key business processes. In these cases, the basic assumption of the central I/T organization—that it exists to manage and deliver technology-based services to the enterprise—requires a new set of assumptions.

In business, the hierarchical organization as the sole arbiter of plans, business strategy, and performance, is giving way to the recognition that many of these matters are more effectively addressed by considering new organizational frameworks. These frameworks use terms like *process* (e.g., the enterprise's customer billing process), activity (e.g., the enterprise's marketing activity), and line of business (e.g., the enterprise's consumer products line of business).

Impact on I/T management: Realizing business value (e.g., harvesting the benefits) changes the I/T management job and the I/T organizational structure.

Without consistently linking to business performance, I/T becomes irrelevant. With a credible and demonstrated link to business performance, I/T is an enormously powerful tool for business managers to improve the performance—its strength and vitality—for their responsible organizations.

COMPETITIVE VERSUS PERFORMANCE VIEW OF VALUE

Managers often view information as a tool for significantly changing enterprise competitive opportunities. One vision focuses on customer information used to drive subsequent marketing and service opportunities.

- A retailer might collect sales information, analyze it, and then tailor marketing strategies to the specifics of customer interests.
- A computer vendor might collect all customer orders and provide important information about the pattern of computer purchases to not only its own management but to the management of its customer or enterprise. Alternatively, the vendor might be able to implement variable pricing or service schemes based on complete customer information on all sales made throughout the customer's enterprise. Another vision targets the use of information to control or guide supplier activities in ways that add value to the customer.
- A corporate travel organization might offer cumulative ticket savings based on patterns of purchase from the customer enterprise.
- A food supplier might target special marketing initiatives based on patterns of purchases or aid the food retailer in better use of shelf space.

In these cases, management looked to the information itself as a vehicle for altering the nature of the services offered its customers. Information becomes part of the service product itself, particularly where the enterprise can do things that its competition can't. This use of information—a strategic use—still has measurable impact as defined by market share, customer retention, and customer satisfaction. What is different, primarily, is the way the strategic opportunities come about. In this case it's vision: How can information add to the value the enterprise provides its customers? How can information strengthen the enterprise capability to offer new capabilities, services, or support to the customer? When these questions have answers, information has value in the same way enterprise products have value.

I/T has a major role to play in transforming the business enterprise. Much of the basis of the appeal is the competitive environment. For example, an enterprise may find it critical to reduce its order-to-delivery or product-development-to-market cycle-times, and information technology creates most of this competitive impact. Its realization is a complex matter of many ideas. The business vision itself, encompassing product, services, relationship to customers, and internal organization, is obviously critical. At the same time, the exact manner of the development and deployment of I/T, including change management, cost justification, and management commitments to the process, is equally critical, and the process involves a multiple-step connection of concepts and practices. The implementation stages may well involve new technologies (e.g., CASE) and operational technologies (e.g., client-server). Additionally, the connection of the development stages is itself difficult—the connection between business vision and the deployment of I/T involves considerable issues of value and justification as well as business management changes. Finally, it's also more complicated in that the ideas and concepts and practices in each area do not effectively talk to each other (except as asserted in methodologies like information engineering). The four impacts (cross-organizational, investment, performance, and management) are parallel activities and developmental processes; much like overlaying ill-fitting templates upon the enterprise itself.

ROADMAP TO DELIVERING BUSINESS VALUE

The authors have observed the management of I/T in a number of U.S. and European companies, which led to several conclusions about I/T organization and management practices relating to, first, the achievement of business value, and second, the approaches to justifying large-scale infrastructures such as national networks and other aspects of large-scale communications. The issues raised here, namely the problems of multiple organizations, complicated by the value gap and other management disconnects, often create unfortunate consequences. For the typical large organization, the I/T organization starts to become frozen in place. There is a disconnect with management in explaining what's possible or what's happening. Management sees huge unresponsive costs, which leads to a focus on cost as compared to business contribution. For managers of technology, complexity overwhelms. Enterprises consider the dismantling of its central I/T organization with a sense of confusion and lack of clear direction. I/T professionals don't know what they should be doing. The following problems characterize this situation:

- Enterprise management lacks an objective, comprehensive, business-based view about information technology—about the business-based value of I/T.
- I/T professionals lack the tools and methodologies to give the objective, comprehensive, business-based views to enterprise management.
- I/T professionals need the business-based tools and methodologies to enrich the partnership with their user managers, to give the objective, comprehensive, business-based view about the business value of I/T.
- I/T may not be willing to take the necessary steps to implement the required changes.

This last point is key, because to achieve the lasting impact of I/T requires fundamental change. This change focuses on identifying new ways of measuring and recognizing value, along with how I/T management represents that value to senior managers. More broadly, the changes go to the heart of improving the way to organize, plan, and manage I/T.

We described a number of management issues associated with achieving business value through using I/T. Communications, and in particular, national and global communications networks linking enterprisewide computing activities, are a particularly powerful form of such technologies. They enable the dispersion of information technologies throughout the enterprise, linking business processes within and among enterprises and generally making it possible to use information effectively to manage, to give better service to customers, and to improve the quality and desirability of products.

Notwithstanding these technologies, there remains a twofold problem in justification and measurement. First, there are still I/T functions that have yet to put a process in place to justify its proposed investments and subsequently measure the effect of these actual investments on the business values or outcomes of the I/T actions. Second, to successfully face the challenge of this decade—creating the next generation enterprise—I/T organizations must develop and justify investment programs for I/T using scenario planning to support the various business strategy scenarios so that it will have the appropriate architectures and platforms, critical skills, and applications necessary when the business needs occur.

PART V. PLANNING I/T AND ENTERPRISE TRANSFORMATION

The nature of transformation requires new approaches to planning for both the various business and I/T organizations within the enterprise. In Part V, we introduced a new contextual framework within which transformational planning can occur, including the recognition and subsequent definitional development of transformational value and risk criteria and justification and measurement criteria. By using The Seven Questions Methodology for Transformation Planning (Chapter 13), Information Economics (Chapter 14), and justification criteria linked to the development of new measurement criteria and systems (Chapter 15), we link the establishment of the transformation mission and strategy to the development and financial justification of specific action plans to the development of appropriate measurement systems. This is a tall order for any enterprise, especially as we begin to weave together all the objectives, initiatives, and desires discussed earlier—those of improving service and quality, focusing on the customer, empowering the organization, making the enterprise more agile, and improving overall performance for the stakeholders. This is particularly difficult for most I/T organizations, in that consistently delivering and measuring demonstrable value has not been a significant part of its traditional culture. Where can an I/T organization start?

In "Managing Change in a Performance-Driven Organization Using Information Economics," Lynwood Walker concludes his description of what went on at AGT Limited during the period that he was Systems Planning Advisor, AGT Limited Network Systems, with a focus on how they introduced, used, and subsequently fine-tuned the information economics concept. The point of this paper is twofold. First, it demonstrates that the concepts underlying Information Economics are valid. Secondly, it demonstrates that there is no one right way, right tool, or right methodology that can be simply "plugged in" and used with guaranteed results. This latter point is the most important when planning for transformation because every enterprise is unique, requiring a unique plan for transformation. This is the underlying premise of the entire planning philosophy presented in *Strategic Transformation and Information Technology*.

Walker presents the use of Information Economics at AGT Limited, following it through four stages: the theoretical analysis, evaluating whether or not this was a reasonable approach for AGT planning; tracing it through from the perspective; the pilot evaluation, where it was introduced to the organization at minimal risk; the customization of the concepts and methodology to the specific needs of the enterprise; and finally, the standardization and institutionalization of the process as a means of improving resource allocations. From his previous paper, we know that this was accomplished in an enterprise experiencing significant turmoil involving its strategic transformation.

"Stakeholder Values and Structural Change" and "Evergreen Environmental Consultants" supplement Chapters 12 and 13.

Managing Change in a Performance-Driven Organization Using Information Economics

Lynwood Walker

INTRODUCTION

Once business value(s) of alternative I/T plans are established, the values are effective for both planning and controlling I/T costs and for use in determining future I/T strategies. This paper focuses on the linkage of business value to I/T strategy, with accompanying examples from industry, that of AGT Limited, introduced in the preceding section.

Network Systems at AGT has changed in the last three years from a traditional hierarchical organization to one that is largely team-driven, customer-focused, and governed by total quality (TQ) management principles. The processes and criteria employed to define and manage the portfolio of work have likewise evolved from the traditional (Those who yell the loudest get their work done) to a sophisticated combination of joint prioritization by customers, value assessment of existing applications, and resource allocation by empowered workteams.

The objective-setting process for AGT Network Systems commences with senior management commitment to corporate and divisional objectives for the coming year. These are then transformed into organizational and personal objectives for Network Systems staff through a series of intensive reviews that result in individuals and teams taking ownership of realistic and appropriate objectives. Network Systems employs a multistage process to define realistic work plans and to obtain the necessary consensus and commitment from customers and their management. This process includes obtaining and documenting internal and external work requests, prioritizing the work, linking the work to corporate planning efforts, obtaining customer agreement with proposed work plans, and transforming high-level plans into specific commitments for Network Systems workteams.

The use of information economics in AGT Limited's Network Systems directorate evolved through four distinct stages: theoretical analysis, a pilot evaluation, customization to the specific needs of Network Systems, and finally standardization of the process within the Network Services business unit. Each of these stages dictated a parallel evolution in the organization of the evaluation and approval teams, the mechanics of the approval process, and, of course, the assessment criteria themselves.

EVOLUTION OF THE ORGANIZATION

The year was 1988. The Systems Planning section of Network Systems took upon itself the task of bringing some rationality and coherence to the systems development program.

Projects were being presented to steering committees and approved with little or no discussion of the impact on the rest of the development program. Although various methods of prioritizing projects had been tried in the past, they were basically one-shot affairs, designed more to demonstrate compliance with fiscal objectives than to truly measure the relative priority of all projects in the systems development portfolio.

Responsibility for getting the investigation underway fell to one of the senior planners in the section. He surveyed the literature from various sources and attended the Enterprise-wide Information Management (EwIM) conference that year in St. Louis, Missouri. It was at this conference that he obtained a copy of the basic text on the information economics technique written by Marilyn Parker and Robert Benson, with Ed Trainor, and published by Prentice Hall.

Shortly after his return, he was appointed acting section manager (a "temporary" assignment lasting more than two years). Another senior planner (the author) received the assignment to test the suitability of the technique within the Network Systems environment. The textbook recommendations were formulated into a pilot version of a questionnaire. The planner surveyed the existing development projects using this questionnaire and presented the results to the Network Systems Steering Committee in the fall of 1989. This steering committee consisted of the senior vice president for the business unit plus the assistant vice presidents and directors that reported directly to him.

The steering committee reviewed the results with some skepticism—the numbers were wrong, the project order didn't reflect the true business need, and so on. They were then asked to ignore the numerical results of the pilot surveys for a moment and listen to their debate. For the first time they were actually discussing the relative merits of all the projects at the same time and adjusting the priority of each based on overall business value. The process had passed the first hurdle.

The steering committee volunteered director-level delegates from each of the major interest groups to assist Systems Planning in customizing the basic technique to meet the needs of the business unit. Representatives from Strategic Planning, Marketing, Network Provisioning, Network Operations, and Finance joined Systems Planning and Systems Development to provide wide-ranging expertise on business, financial, and systems issues that could affect development priorities. This group was called the Systems Portfolio Management Committee or SPMC. Eventually, it not only had responsibility for defining the criteria, but also for evaluating the list of projects and for compiling the initial prioritization recommendations.

After the success of the first SPMC-driven planning cycle in 1990–1991, much of the work fell to delegates of the original SPMC members to maintain. By late 1992, a team consisting mostly of first and second-level managers from across the business unit made an initial prioritization of the candidate projects. The priorities were finalized and approved by the directors in a single joint session. The steering committee took itself out of the systems project approval decisions for all but the largest projects. It concentrated instead on overall funding and business objectives.

EVOLUTION OF THE APPROVAL PROCESS

There were three major thrusts in the evolution of the systems project approval process for Network Systems:

- Simplification of the process itself.
- Delegation of approval authority to lower levels in the organization.
- Coordination of the approval process with the company business planning cycle.

Each of these is discussed in further detail in the subsections following.

AGT Limited, like many other major organizations, followed the traditional "waterfall" model for systems development. The initial proposal was followed by a feasibility testing stage. If the project was economically viable, it went through definition, design, and ultimately construction. Progression from one stage to the next was dependent on obtaining formal approval, generally at the vice presidential steering committee level. This was a major bottleneck since there were severe constraints on the amount of time available for discussion.

Several changes were made to simplify and streamline the process. First, all projects at the proposal (or conceptual planning) stage were prioritized according to the established criteria. Only those projects of sufficiently high priority won authorization to proceed to the next stage. This general vetting replaced the general feasibility testing done under the old process. The project team then undertook the detailed definition of the project, followed by detailed project costing and scheduling. These time and dollar commitments, once approved, became the benchmarks for measuring project and team performance through the remainder of the activities. Designing and building the system were combined into a single construction stage with no intermediate approvals required. Provision was made, however, for periodic reviews of project performance and redefinition or rebudgeting if the work was exceeding time or money allocations.

Approval levels were lowered as well, bringing them into line with those for other capital construction projects. The director of Network Systems, in conjunction with the director(s) of the affected client community, could approve systems projects up to $500,000—a substantial improvement over the old limit of $10,000. Focus Team leaders in Network Systems could unilaterally approve projects costing up to $10,000 so long as they did not adversely impact existing commitments. These limits dropped considerably if the project or activity had not been previously reviewed and prioritized by the Systems Portfolio Management Committee. This provided a significant incentive to get all the work defined in the general portfolio in time for the annual review by the committee.

The third major improvement was integration of the systems planning and prioritization processes with the overall corporate business planning cycle. The call for systems projects was issued early in the calendar year. Near the end of the first quarter, the Systems Portfolio Management Committee reviewed and prioritized the resulting "wish list." The resulting list was ratified by the steering committee in a single annual review a month or so later. Once approved, the prioritized list formed the basis for staff allocations and planning estimates that made up the Medium Range Financial Plan submitted to Corporate Finance at the end of the second quarter. As project requirements became better known, more accurate staff, technology, and dollar estimates were incorporated into the short-term operating plan that, in turn, was the basis for setting department and section budgets in the final quarter of the year. The end of the year was also the time for setting personal and project team objectives for the coming year. These too had to be related to the prioritized list of work ratified earlier in the year.

EVOLUTION OF ASSESSMENT CRITERIA

The three original pilot categories for assessment criteria enabled study participants to measure project value based on business, technical, and economic merit. These three categories have remained constant even though the criteria within each have changed somewhat. The subsections following will trace the evolution of the criteria used in each of these categories.

Business Value Assessment

A combination of no less than five individual criteria provided the basis for the original business value assessment:

- Strategic Match—Did the project align with business objectives?
- Competitive Advantage—Did the project provide a significant competitive advantage?
- Competitive Response—Did the project respond to strategic initiatives by competitors?
- Management Information—Did the project provide company management with significant information on company health or operations?

- Project and Organizational Risk—Was the organizational impact of the project known and fully understood by all the players?

Each of these criteria was scored from 0 to 5 based on their relative contribution. The scores were then multiplied by weighting factors based on the relative importance of the criteria. The total business value score was the sum of the weighted scores for the individual criteria.

The steering committee had two principal objections to this approach:

1. The criteria names and evaluation were foreign to the Network Systems environment.
2. The weighting factors obscured any relationship between the individual criteria's scores and the resulting business value total.

The second-generation business value criteria were much simpler. A ranked list of the ten highest priority business objectives was obtained from senior management at the conclusion of their annual planning session. Each objective was given a point value from one to ten based on its position in the list. Each project was then awarded points based upon the objective to which it most directly contributed. The second stage of the evaluation awarded additional points based on the degree of contribution towards achievement of the objective in question. The sum of these two assessments was the total business value of the project.

There were problems with this approach too, however. The most important objective on the list was not ten times more important than the least, despite what the numbers suggested. Modifying the initial results with the second factor only distorted the values even further.

The third-generation business criteria used the same list of ten business objectives. This time, however, the senior managers were asked to indicate the relative priority of each item on the list. They gave the top four objectives the same scores as before—counting down from a maximum of ten points. The middle two objectives were judged approximately equal but somewhat lower in value than those preceding and were assigned a value of five points each. The last four objectives were thought to be of equal, but lesser, importance, and were awarded values of two points each.

The critical lesson here is not what points were assigned to each objective, but rather that it was the senior business managers that were determining the relative importance of each objective. It was the business community that defined the importance, not the systems community.

The latest step on this evolutionary path incorporated the results of the general corporate objective-setting process as opposed to that of a single business unit. A general company reorganization had dispersed Network Systems clients over three business units. The prioritization process therefore required modification to accommodate the business objectives of their home areas.

The corporate planning process also changed. Senior executives worked together to compile a list of specific business objectives for the company as a whole.

Each one also developed a series of objectives for his specific areas. Many of these objectives related directly to those on the corporate list. Others, however, were specific to the needs of their own organization.

It was impossible to prioritize the seventy-five or so individual objectives that developed during this exercise. The Systems Portfolio Management Committee therefore took a very democratic approach. All objectives were assumed to be of equal value to the company. The significant issue for systems projects was the degree to which they supported the objectives. This then became the sole business value determinant.

The ten points available for business value scoring were split—five points were available for contribution to corporate objectives, the other five for contribution to the objectives of the business unit sponsoring the project. The same point scale was used for both assessments. Projects received the maximum of five points if they directly achieved the whole of the business objective. Lesser points were awarded if the project directly or indirectly achieved a major or minor portion of the objective.

This method had a simple, yet elegant, approach for recognizing the higher value of certain major business objectives. The truly significant objectives in the corporate list were often repeated in the lists of the affected business units. Systems projects that contributed directly to the achievement of these objectives effectively received double points. Those projects that could only demonstrate indirect relationships at either or both levels received substantially lower scores.

Additional Business Criteria

Impact on Customer Service.   AGT's major business processes were structured from the inside out towards the customer. At the core were the various administrative processes and systems such as Accounting, Payroll, Inventory Management, and so on. Next came the fundamental plans that outlined the basic network configuration and technology over the medium to long term. Marketing then defined the specific services offerings for the network, and engineering provisioned the network components and software translations to make the service available. Finally, individual customers were connected to the services and AGT moved into the maintenance and billing mode.

Feedback from senior managers on the effectiveness of the prioritization process indicated that there was a need to assess the impact of systems projects on service provided to AGT's bill-paying customers—not the next group in the business process. Unfortunately, this chain of business processes is upside-down from the customers' perspective. The customers were understood to have three main concerns (listed in order of importance):

1. Do the services I have today work?
2. Am I being accurately billed for use of those services?
3. Can I change what I have or get more?

Customers will rarely know (or care) if there is an outage or error in the payroll system or long-range planning systems. On the other hand, service disruptions or billing errors are immediate grounds for frustration, complaints, and other negative interactions with the company. An evaluation criterion emerged that mirrored the concerns of the customer. A maximum of five points were awarded in this category (out of the total of thirty possible points) according to the following scale:

Points	Description
0	The system has no discernible impact on bill-paying customers.
1	The system is required for planning new network configurations.
2	The system is required for planning new service offerings.
3	The system is required for provisioning new services or network components.
4	The system is required in order to assign or activate new services.
5	The system is required for maintenance and/or billing of existing services.

Project Preparedness

The prioritization process developed by Network Systems was gaining wider acceptance throughout AGT Limited. A team was established at the corporate level to consolidate the planning effort of the central IS organization with those of the five Divisional Systems groups. This team adopted the latest generation of prioritization criteria, as outlined above, for their own process. They added one other criteria to the business value segment: the issue of Project Preparedness. In other words, each project was to be assessed on how prepared the project team and sponsoring management were to undertake the project.

Again, the adjudication was kept as simple as possible. A maximum of five points were awarded in this category. One (1) point was awarded for each positive response to the following questions:

- Is the technology known and understood?
- Are trained staff available to work on the project?
- Are the project scope and boundary well defined?
- Is there a committed sponsor for the project—at the director (or higher) level?
- Will the project last less than one year?

The addition of these criteria brought the total number of points awarded for business value up to twenty—out of thirty-five possible points available in all categories. This trend reflects the overall intent of the process—to lessen the importance of tangible dollar returns in favor of rewarding low-risk contribution to business objectives and improvements in customer service.

Technology Value Assessment

The evolution of the technology value assessment process has paralleled that of the business domain. The original pilot assessment used a base of four criteria, each of which could receive up to a maximum of five points:

1. To what degree did the project match existing or planned IS architectures?
2. What degree of uncertainty was present in the project definition and scope?
3. To what degree was the technology known and understood by the project team?
4. What risks did the project pose to the existing IS infrastructure?

The raw scores were then weighted and summed to determine the overall technological value of the project. As was the case in the business side discussed earlier, this was too cumbersome a process. There were too many factors to assess and the use of weighting factors obscured any meaning the original numbers may have held.

The second-generation criteria were simpler. A maximum of five points were awarded out of a possible twenty-five. Two points were awarded if the project demonstrated data and/or process integration with existing applications. Two additional points were awarded if the project was known and identified in the systems plan issued earlier that year. Finally, a single point was added if the project built on standard technologies already supported by the organization.

The third generation was simpler yet. By this time Network Systems had built a comprehensive model of the enterprise that it served. This model also provided a future view of the business systems required to facilitate the consolidation of various business processes. The Technology Value Assessment criteria were changed to reflect the importance of this new plan. From that point on, all projects were evaluated based on their contribution towards the attainment of that ideal. A maximum of five points were still available, but they were awarded according to the following scale:

Points	Description
0	The project did not contribute to the target enterprise architecture.
1	The project was part of the architecture, but its priorities and/or prerequisites were undefined.
2	The project was part of the architecture, but it was not a prerequisite, nor was it linked to other projects with more direct contributions.
3	The project was part of the architecture, but it was not a prerequisite, it was only loosely linked to other projects with more direct contributions.
4	The project was part of the architecture, not as a prerequisite but closely linked to other projects that were prerequisite.
5	The project was an integral and prerequisite component of the enterprise architecture.

The only change in recent times is that the list of eligible architectures has expanded beyond the enterprise level to include computing architectures and infrastructure technology where applicable. A project that can demonstrate its prerequisite value at any of these three levels receives the maximum point score.

EVOLUTION OF ECONOMIC VALUE ASSESSMENT

No significant systems projects are undertaken in Network Systems (or most other organizations) without some consideration being given to the economics of the project. Economic assessment criteria therefore form the vital third leg of the prioritization process.

The initial pilot prioritization process suggested the use of two economic criteria—the traditional net present value (NPV) and payback period—measures known and understood throughout most of the organization. In this initial stage, the NPV, expressed in millions of dollars, became the raw score. A project with an NPV of $1 million got 1 point, an NPV of $2.5 million scored 2.5 points, and so on. On the payback side, the raw payback (in years) was divided into the number five—since five years was the longest desired interval. A project with a payback of one year would receive a base score of five points while one with a payback of 2.5 years would receive only two points. Multiplying both the NPV and payback scores by weighting factors brought them into line with the weighted scores from the other categories.

While senior executives applauded the use of company-standard economic indicators, they felt that the use of weighting factors obscured any meaning that lay in the original numbers. As with the other criteria, some simplification was in order.

In retrospect, the pendulum probably swung too far the other direction. The entire economic value assessment in the second iteration of the process hinged on a single factor—the project NPV. There was an NPV computed and recorded for every project in the development portfolio. The project with the highest NPV was awarded five points. The NPV of every other project was divided into the highest NPV and the result multiplied by five. For example, a project with an NPV that was half of the highest NPV in the portfolio would receive 2.5 points.

This approach too had its problems, the most significant of which was that relying solely on the NPV as an economic indicator ignored the investment or time needed to achieve the theoretical payback. In addition, a single large project dramatically skewed the results with its huge numbers. This huge NPV caused the remainder to appear essentially equivalent in overall priority, which was certainly not the case.

The pendulum swung back towards center on the third evolution of the process. NPV information was still used, but in a couple of different ways. Every project undergoing the economic value assessment had to first demonstrate a positive NPV. In other words, the company had to eventually recoup the cost of the undertaking. Any project that failed this hurdle criterion received zero points for economic value and sat out the rest of the evaluation.

Those projects that passed the initial hurdle were assessed on two economic indicators—a profitability index and the payback period. The profitability index, or PI as it became known, was computed by dividing the NPV of the project by its one-time development costs. This provided a relative measure of the anticipated return against the development cost and served to minimize the adverse impact of large projects on the rest of the evaluation. For example, a project with an NPV of $12 million but a development cost of $10 million would have a PI of 1.2. A smaller project with an NPV of only $1 million but a development cost of $500,000 would have a PI of 2.0, indicating a higher return per dollar invested.

The project with the highest PI received five points. The raw index scores for each of the other projects were divided by the highest one and the result multiplied by five to obtain the final PI score. This had the effect of actively ranking the projects against each other—not against some arbitrary scale devised for the "ideal" project.

The payback period was evaluated in a straightforward, linear fashion. Projects with a payback period of less than one year received five points. Those with a payback between one and two years received four points, and so on. Any projects with a payback period of greater than five years received zero points for this portion of the economic assessment.

There are a few important points to note about the evolution of the fiscal criteria. First, they were developed by senior financial advisors based on the business objectives in place at the time. Second, the base numbers used in the evaluation are part of the standard business case preparation for systems projects in the organization. Senior managers and project teams alike are familiar with the basic economic indicators and their computation. In addition, most business cases for projects seeking formal approval to proceed with construction were already audited by these same financial advisors to ensure compliance with standard company practices. The effective combination of these three factors lent considerable credibility to the results of the prioritization effort.

Summarizing the Results

Changes were also made in the summarizing and reporting of the prioritization results. The pilot evaluation produced a single ordered list, in descending order, based on the total scores for each project. When the approval process itself was shortened to only three stages, it was decided that projects at similar stages should be evaluated against each other, not necessarily against the entire portfolio. The following categories were therefore established:

- Projects Currently Under Construction
- Projects Seeking Construction Approval
- Projects Seeking Detailed Planning Resources
- Projects Seeking Concept Planning Resources

Evaluation of projects currently under construction was not used as a hammer to shut down lower-value projects that were already underway. In fact, it was recognized that there were significant commitments to these projects and that they still had to be finished, documented, and handed off to support groups in a professional manner. To do otherwise would mean that few projects would ever be completed and the credibility of the organization (and the company) would suffer tremendously. This list was used instead as information for senior managers so that if there were major changes in business direction or dramatic changes in project scope or budget, the relative priority of projects in this group could be compared and decisions made accordingly.

The projects seeking construction approval were those that had completed detailed planning, costing, and scheduling of their project. The project scope, budget and schedule were treated as fixed commitments by the project team. The business cases for these projects were either built or audited by senior financial advisors within the business unit both as a reality check and to ensure compliance with standard costing and related policies.

Those projects seeking resources for detailed planning were really in competition for the relatively few business and process analysts available in Network Systems. It was recognized that a solid definition of project requirements was the key to meeting commitments in later stages and delivering a quality product. The latter stages of projects in this group also required skilled financial analysts and project planners to define the project commitments for the construction stage.

The most basic prioritization group consisted of all those projects being proposed by the client community as being worthy of attention by Network Systems. This is where the initial vetting took place—only those projects with the highest overall priority were generally successful in obtaining the business analysts needed to help scope out their respective projects.

There are two other segments of the general portfolio that are reported for information purposes but are not actively prioritized. The first is a list of rumored projects—those in very early, almost embryonic, stages of conceptualization. This list might include future systems requirements highlighted at business planning meetings, long-range plans from strategic alliance partners, or plans from other business units within the company that may require assistance from Network Systems. The second segment contains a list of projects that were either completed and passed on to support staff or dropped from the list at the request of the originators. This provides a sort of audit trail that enables both client groups and Network Systems staff to ascertain why a particular project no longer appears on one of the active prioritization lists.

Other Reports

There were two other reports presented to senior managers when they ratified the prioritized list. The first was a graph that contrasted the number of projects that were thought to contribute to a particular business objective, contrasted with the number that actually did. This enabled the senior managers to see which of the objectives were subject to the most misinterpretation and to redefine them in more meaningful terms. The second report was a diagram depicting the agreed-to business model of the enterprise overlaid with the names of projects affecting each of the eleven major business processes. This diagram enabled the senior managers to see which business processes were attracting the most attention—and whether there was any significant overlap between projects.

KEY LESSONS

There have been several key lessons learned through the evolution of information economics as a prioritization tool in Network Systems:

- The prioritization of systems projects is most effective when the client community does it—not by the systems group on their own. This draws clients into the systems program and helps develop a sense of ownership. The payoff for systems comes when it comes time to draw on these same clients for assistance during definition and development of the project. Clients tend to be much more willing to support the systems effort when they understand the overall importance of the project. The systems group may wish to facilitate the process, as was the case with Network Systems, but ultimately, it has to be the client community that decides what is truly important to the organization.

- The criteria used must be relevant to the objectives of the organization. There should be a direct and positive association with published business plans developed and approved by senior managers in the organization.

- The process must be as simple as possible to ensure that each criterion has a visible impact on the final scoring of the project. On the other hand, it must not be so simple that it ignores important areas or is perceived as some mechanical "cookie cutter" that only favors a specific type of project.

- The criteria used for prioritization should examine each project from a number of perspectives—business, technical, and economic factors are but three of many possibilities. For some businesses, and especially governmental agencies, the social and/or political impact of the project may warrant consideration. For others, environmental impact may be sufficiently important to justify its being included in the list of project criteria. Each organization must determine for itself the group of criteria that represent a balanced perspective.

- Senior client managers must have an opportunity to review the numerical results of the prioritization process and to perform final adjustments to the prioritized list. This will enable them to fine-tune the list based on their own understanding of business priorities—perhaps based on factors not originally included in the prioritization criteria. This accomplishes at least two things: the senior managers work together to ratify the list—thereby building unified support for the result; and any refinements they make point to areas for improvement in the criteria so that the process will closer approximate reality in the next iteration.

- Projects that are competing for similar resources should be prioritized against each other and not necessarily against every other project in the portfolio.

Information economics can be an important tool in determining the relative priority of a group of projects. The effort put into drawing the customer into the process and defining a concise, relevant, and equitable set of evaluation criteria will be directly reflected in the credibility and usefulness of the results.

SUMMARY

The two commentary articles describing the changes in AGT Limited's Network Systems directorate serve to illustrate the complex nature of today's business environment. Here was an organization steeped in the bureaucratic traditions of civil service that transformed itself from within to meet the challenges of the competitive marketplace.

Not only was the company facing competition from the outside, the Network Systems group was facing internal competition as well. Competition for scarce funding, staff, and other resources were significant factors that triggered the need for change. Network Systems was also facing competition from its own customers—many of whom had the skills necessary to build at least rudimentary applications to meet their own needs.

Network Systems had to demonstrate its competence in building and maintaining sophisticated applications. More importantly, it had to demonstrate its ability to build and maintain effective relationships with internal and external clients. If it was going to meet the needs of its client's it had to demonstrate that it understood those needs in the first place. If it was going to be viewed as a useful service, it had to be willing to serve its client's needs and not pursue obscure technical objectives.

A wise person once remarked: "People won't care how much you know until they know how much you care." Perhaps this is the greatest lesson of these two articles. If any I/T organization is going to build or maintain credibility within its own organization or with the organization's customers, it must focus at least as much attention on its client relationships as it does on the applications or technology it provides.

The I/T organization must go out of its way to understand the client's business. It must be sensitive to the priorities and objectives of its clients. It must be willing to meet the client on the client's own turf, to explain it's activities in the client's own language, and to work with the client through the client's own evolution. Only then will it be an effective facilitator of strategic transformation in the enterprise.

Stakeholder Values and Structural Change

Marilyn M. Parker

A significant driver for change is the enterprise stakeholder. The role and power of each class of stakeholder varies not only by enterprise, but by culture, making every business transformation unique in its problem-set. Stakeholder power structures determine the individual values and agendas of the enterprise, and as stakeholder values change, they are reflected by new business values and strategies—and may exacerbate even larger structural changes in the national and global economy.

Over time, the differences in the external capital market and the differences in stakeholder values have caused four distinct versions of capitalism to develop: those of the United States, Germany, the United Kingdom, and Japan. As the world of business becomes more global, these different capitalistic cultures, combined with economic structural shifts (e.g., the growth of service, information, and technology-based activities) adding even additional stress, conflict with each other. Out of this conflict will emerge a new form of global capitalism, because working with different assumptions becomes untenable (and noncompetitive) over the long term.

Japan, according to Sony's Akio Morita, achieved its competitiveness by keeping margins and prices low over long periods, constantly searching for volume to provide the cash flow.[38] This resulted in skimping the other stakeholders of Japanese companies in favor of the customer. Japan, he states, must fashion a new corporate attitude, rebalancing stakeholder interests, and becoming more compatible with the Western versions of capitalism.

Western capitalism may have to fashion new corporate attitudes, too, but in the opposite direction. More earned surplus needs to go back to the customer by way of lower margins and lower return on projects. To do this, we must create a new role definition for the shareholder: perhaps shifting from owner to financier, and rethinking expectations and motivations. Typically, shareholders invest because they expect a competitive return. If they receive less than the market rate, they will switch their holdings into enterprises where they will get it. Some Western enterprises are already attempting to reshape the shareholder role by influencing expectations. Most begin by formally listing their priorities in the annual shareholder reports, putting customers and employees ahead of shareholders in their stakeholder priorities. At the same time, these same enterprises are taking pains to educate the shareholder about their long-term strengths and plans.

Corporate governance is also at issue. The Anglo-American versions of capitalism grew out of the owner-manager model early in this century. Increasingly, it's become more difficult to align the interests of those who own a company and those who run it. In the United States, we characterize the 1980s as a period of hostile takeovers, when executives, wanting to protect their positions and maximize their pay, pitted themselves against shareholders determined to maximize profits flowing to them. The 1990s ushered in a series of proxy battles. At the annual general meetings, incensed shareholders battled escalating executive pay, and the Japanese, who earn less and pay a sharply higher tax rate, asked why executives in America make so much money while corporate performance slips. In Japan, top managers expect to take voluntary pay cuts when a company gets into trouble, and executive pay cuts occur before eliminating lower-level positions.[39] Even the Japanese government officials' made an issue of U.S. executive compensation during the 1993 Structural Impediments Initiative talks aimed at lowering major trade barriers in both countries. The Japanese argued that overpaid American executives, preoccupied with short-term results, added to the worsening U.S. international competitiveness.

An additional trend that brings focus to the issue of corporate governance is the increasing concentration of shares in the hands of investing institutions. This causes two conflicting forces. Some fund managers are investing proportionally in the companies that make up share indices, thus locking big shareholders into longer-term stakes. Alternatively, other managers try to move in and out of many companies, spreading the risk, and maximizing the short-term profitability measures.

Differing stakeholder values, conflict over corporate governance, and differing capital markets all shape the structures of capitalism. No matter which variation of competitive structure under discussion, the real purpose of a business is to provide quality goods and services to customers, to provide the capacity for quality lives and work for its employees, and to provide a reasonable return-on-investment for the shareholder. In this paper we examine how each version of capitalism fulfills this purpose, and how structural changes embodied in the global economy create new stakeholder values.

ENTERPRISE STAKEHOLDERS

Enterprise stakeholders are all the organizations or individuals, existing inside and outside the enterprise, that directly affect its actions. In Chapter 1, we discussed the enterprise view of the world and depicted it in Figure 1-1. We discussed global, social, and economic forces and how they define the enterprise view of the marketplace. We also discussed how, given the specific resources of the enterprise, the enterprise will define and position itself in the marketplace. These are not one-way forces. Each is a potential stakeholder of the enterprise.

It is the responsibility of the enterprise to treat each of its stakeholders equitably. The responsible enterprise serves all stakeholders by increasing their ability to pursue objectives more efficiently and effectively.[40] Enterprise stakeholders include its employees, shareholders, banks, suppliers, customers, government, and debtors.

- Employees: Employees are enterprise stakeholders. Because the enterprise exchanges money for work to create a product or service, employment is the principal means to distribute income in industrialized societies. The product of labor is becoming increasingly an intellectual rather than a physical one. The asset base of the enterprise shifts from equipment and production lines to the intellectual assets of its employees. Similarly, the product of management is becoming more critical as management reformulates enterprises to prepare for new competitive environments. This reformulation is changing the relationships and priorities of the other stakeholders.

- Shareholders and other owners: Shareholders and other types of owners furnish money to the enterprise with an expectation of receiving it back at some future date. Shareholders expect a return on their investment through appreciation of stock value, payment of dividends, and increased profitability.

- Banks, financial institutions, and other lending agencies: Banks and other financial agencies also furnish money to an enterprise with an expectation of receiving it back at some future date. Banks and financial agencies expect a repayment of loans, along with scheduled payments of interest in the interim. Bankers and other lenders may also participate in the running of the enterprise—a practice common in Europe and Japan, but prohibited by law in the United States. Because an American bank can't own equity in nonfinancial companies or underwrite securities, it has less influence and a more distant relationship with borrowers than does its foreign counterparts, exerting limited influence in the development of strategy, direction, and functioning of the American enterprise. The only way that this group exerts influence is to either withhold funding or to supply it at a favorable rate.

- Suppliers: The enterprise exchanges money for goods and services furnished by suppliers. Enterprises can have a variety of relationships with their suppliers, ranging from one-time or casual relationships, to highly integrated, long-standing relationships. An example of a highly integrated relationship is a paint manufacturer who formulates paint on-site for the truck and automobile manufacturer. Another example is an on-site information systems organization staffed and managed by an outside organization. European and Japanese enterprises are more likely to have major supplier representatives on its boards because it views long-term, reliable relationships as ways to cut costs as business partners learn from and help one another.

- Customers: The enterprise exchanges goods and services for money from its customers. Like suppliers, enterprises can have a variety of relationships with its customers. They can range from one-time, casual relationships to highly integrated, highly interdependent relationships.

- Governmental agencies: The enterprise exchanges money for goods and services from government. It receives services such as water and power, fire and police protection. The enterprise also receives regulation from the government and may choose to lobby to change the regulations if it feels the regulations are detrimental to the enterprise. In Japan, authorities permit cartels to keep out foreign competitors and to foster cooperative research and development. Japanese ministries are active partners in long-term development as compared to the United States, where these types of close activities between the government and private industry are generally prohibited.

- Debtors: Completing the list of stakeholders is the debtor. The enterprise, if it is a bank or other lending agency, exchanges money for future repayment with another enterprise. A supplier-debtor expects prompt payment of invoices, and a bond-holder expects payment upon bond maturity.

Of the seven corporate constituencies or stakeholders, three are critical to build a corporate culture for success: customers, shareholders, and employees. In a study by Kotter and Heskett, firms whose cultures seem consistently to produce long-term economic success share one fundamental characteristic: the managers do not let the short-term interests of shareholders override all else, but care equally about all the company's stakeholders.[41]

A strong corporate culture per se can just as easily be an obstacle to change as it is a factor of success. Too strong a culture can lead to corporate arrogance and insularity. What makes a corporate culture a competitive weapon, rather than a liability, is a proper balance between stakeholder relationships. Only when managers care about the legitimate interests of shareholders do they strive to perform well economically over time. In a competitive industry, this is only possible when the managers take care of their customers. In a competitive labor market, that is possible only when managers take care of those who serve the customers: the employees. This type of thinking went out of style in the 1980s in America when many firms paid so much attention to the short-term interests of its shareholders that customers and employees seemed forgotten.

Each version of capitalism typically prioritizes the interests of the shareholder, the customer, and the employee differently. Governments and other regulatory agencies evolve to support and protect its own business culture. As global markets evolve, all participants will be challenged to seek new definitions of fair competition and the role of the enterprise.

Stakeholder Values and Business Culture

North America.   The United States attempts to run capitalism without capitalists. Companies traded on the New York Stock Exchange are about 50 percent owned by financial institutions, such as mutual funds, pension funds, and insurance companies. By federal law, this group may not be hands-on owners. The institutions face strict state and federal rules that effectively limit how much of any single company they can hold. They do not put their executives on boards of directors, because this would give them inside information not available to small shareholders. Such shareholders have no choice but to be short-term speculators, buying and selling shares based on quarterly profits. For them, the takeover wars are the only route to superior performance. Without board representation, they cannot be active builders who seek to strengthen a company's long-run competitive position.

An international study conducted in 1991 ranked business firms of twenty-three nations on their ability to take the long view, and the results ranked American firms twenty-second. Only the Hungarians were worse than the United States.[42] International differences are also reflected in equity markets. U.S. and U.K. companies live in fear of their shares being traded instantly if they fall out of favor with investors.[43] The overall result is that self-interest drives Anglo-Saxon capitalism. These cultures believe this system is best because it champions free trade.

Greater Europe.   In Europe, family ownership makes many current enterprises very stable. In Italy, for example, only 7 of the top 200 companies listed in Milan have over half its shares in public hands.[44] Many EU nations want to preserve the systems that consider stakeholder interests of family ownership, employees, and continuity.

- Employee rights: Germany and the Netherlands have active supervisory boards, strong unions, and Worker's Councils. Belgium relies on Worker's Councils to protect employees as stakeholders.
- Shareholders' rights: Voting rights protect shareholders' rights. Germany and the Netherlands have additional protection mechanisms related to management elections and who can participate in them.
- Market structure: Equity ownership, cross-holdings among enterprises, and controls of financial information and family attitudes are tools to ensure continuity in the enterprise.

Germany.   In Germany, Deutsche Bank owns 10 percent of the shares in more than seventy companies, including 28 percent of the largest company in the country, Daimler-Benz.[42] Among Germany's one hundred biggest firms, the ten largest banks directly own 10 to 25 percent of forty-eight companies, 25 to 50 percent of forty-three others, and over 50 percent of the remaining nine. Where shareholdings are significant, bank representatives sit as company directors. Germany also boasts permanent, well-informed, and involved customers. The negative aspect of this system is that it is difficult to withdraw capital when the company isn't going in the right direction, and it has little concern for the smaller shareholder.

There is not a strong equity culture in Germany. There are only about 4.2 million shareholders in Germany, about 5 percent of the population. In contrast, there are 12 million shareholders in the U.K. and 51 million in the United States, in both cases about 21 percent of the population.[45] So few Germans participate in the equity market for the following reasons:

- Cultural aversion to speculation: Memories of the great inflation of the 1920s and the political consequences tend to make them averse to speculation and financial excesses of any kind.

- Businesses aren't managed to benefit shareholders: The concept of shareholder value—of managing the business for the benefit of the shareholder—is rare. German law requires that managers put the long-run interests of the company ahead of those other parties.

- Limited role of the German stockmarket: Only about 600 companies are listed (compared with 1,950 in the smaller economy of the U.K.), and all but about 50 of these are under the control of family shareholders or the German banks and insurance companies. Companies rarely turn to the market as a source for new capital, relying instead on relationships with commercial banks.

- Domestic institutional investing is not well developed: Pension funds and insurance companies invest comparatively little in German shareholdings. Germany's insurance industry averages between 5 to 15 percent of its reserves invested in stocks, with the rest of reserves in government bonds. This is just the opposite of the U.S. and U.K. markets, and it hinders the development of a large equity market.

- Insider dealing: There was a number of insider dealing cases in the early 1990s. Insider dealing became illegal at the end of 1992, as part of a new regulatory regime. Although these initiatives target international institutional investors, they may ultimately bring private individuals back into the market.

In March 1993, Daimler-Benz, Germany's biggest industrial company, announced that it was to become the first German company to list its shares on a U.S. stock exchange—a move that promises to have a significant impact on the German investment culture. Combined with Germany's struggle with unification requiring a large source of private capital, foreign investors are leading the way in insisting that financial returns match the risk of holding equity and openly question the wisdom of the long-standing links between companies and financial institutions.

United Kingdom.   The Archbishop of Canterbury set off a maelstrom in the U.K. by criticizing companies' narrow focus on maximizing stockholder value, which is the effect of English business law. The Archbishop, Charles Handy, and U.K. stockholders began rethinking the purpose and standards of business. Handy, visiting professor at the London Business School and noted author, answered the comments of the Archbishop of Canterbury by calling for a shift in thinking about the priorities and purpose of capitalism.[38] Now that communism and centrally planned economies are no longer a common opponent, he believes that the old answer of enhancing shareholder value with all of its implications of efficiency, customer service, shrewd investment, and personnel policies may no longer be the *raison d'être* for a capitalistic enterprise.

The U.K. debate on corporate governance traditionally centered on better auditing, more shareholder activism, and curbs on dictatorial management. The Committee on Financial Aspects of Corporate Governance, chaired by Sir Adrian Cadbury (the former chairman of Cadbury Schweppes), introduced a new level of dynamics into the corporate governance discussion when it published its draft report in May of 1992. Cadbury introduced a code of best practices that include the following proposals:

- Non-executive directors: Pick non-executive directors by a formal selection process. They must be approved by the whole board. They should be able to seek outside professional advice, at company expense, if necessary. Shareholders should approve all directors' contracts every third year.
- Board authority: Divide authority between a chairman and a chief executive. Board structures combining the two roles require a leader of non-executive directors.
- Leader of non-executive directors: An appointed leader of the non-executive directors will provide a balance in concentration of executive power in companies that combine the roles of chairman and chief executive officer.
- Audit and remuneration committees: Companies should have audit and remuneration committees made up of non-executive directors. They should disclose most details of directors' pay. Audit committees should meet at least once a year with external auditors without the presence of executive directors.
- Interim audit statements: Prepare and issue interim audits. Rotate audit partners. Protect auditors who alert authorities to suspected fraud from legal action.[46]

These suggested changes provide shareholders with more information. The problem with the suggestions is that they rely heavily on non-executive directors to improve corporate governance and leave open the issue of enforcement. Also, while the Cadbury committee believes that cleaner relations with auditors will improve disclosure, there are limits to what clean accountancy can accomplish. In the real world, it's difficult for auditors to catch problems in time to solve them, and rarely do they catch fraud in an appropriate time frame. The cause of poor corporate performance is failing strategy, incompetent management, or both.

Remedying all these ills still leads back to the boardroom, and institutions in the U.K. have not committed themselves to manning the boards of the companies in which they hold minority positions, and legislation prevents institutions in America from taking positions.[47] Decades of modern capitalism have yet to yield a perfect model. The question is how many more decades of messy experimentation will be necessary to evolve one.

The Pacific.   Japan places most emphasis on maintaining market share to safeguard jobs in companies and their suppliers. Return-on-investment, the first priority of the Anglo-Saxon culture, ranks in ninth place in Japanese capitalism's order of preference.[43] The Japanese brand of competition is more concerned with collective good.

The Japanese seem to have broken down the us versus them barriers that plague the worker-management relationships in U.S. and European companies. The finance-dominated capitalism forgets that the business organization consists of people and can function no better than they do. Business today depends largely on intellectual property, and Japanese managers believe that the company's employees, not its machines, are its most important assets. Japanese companies train their employees, generally guarantee them job security, and offer career paths that grow as the company grows.[48] The benefits to this approach are a highly trained work force that is more productive; a multiskilled work force that is more flexible; and a job-secure work force that is more open to innovation and change.

The biggest problem, from the perspective of the Japanese competitor, is that the prices of Japanese-made products tend to be lower than the products of comparable Western manufacturers. This has many causes, including cost reduction, higher quality, cost of capital, and the benefits of modern manufacturing facilities. But there is also an aspect peculiar to the Japanese—their attitude regarding market share—mentioned earlier.[49] A Japanese company tends to first set a price that aims to gain market share, and then tries to cut costs and profits according to the price—an approach opposite of German, Britain, and U.S. enterprises.

Japanese employee working conditions are also less favorable than those of its global competitors. Japanese workers put in 200 more hours-per-year than the Americans, and 500 more than the French and Germans. Employee compensation as a percentage of corporate profits is much lower, so they have less earning power, and less purchasing power. Shareholders also receive a considerably smaller dividend payout ratio as compared to that of Western counterparts. And vendors may often fare less well because Japanese manufacturers quite often exercise control over the parts' suppliers for contractual conditions like delivery deadlines and prices.

Competition based on market share, as in Japan, is fundamentally different from competition based on profitability, as in the West. Companies can improve profits without necessarily hurting their rivals. Companies cannot increase market share without hurting their rivals. Hence, no matter what might happen in the future, over the short period of time, competition will remain stiff, and any rebalancing will come slowly.

Changing the Concept of Free Enterprise

Every culture has evolved its own ethic of fairness in competition. Trade barriers protected domestic competitors from outsiders, and domestic regulations proscribed local practices. The issue now is how and where to establish some consistency to create a global competitive ethic.

Principal-Agent Relationships.   Modern economics identifies a serious incentive issue as the principal-agent problem. First, how do corporate boards ensure that executives serve the interests of the shareholders? Second, how do managers get workers to put forth their best efforts?

American capitalism solves the first problem beautifully. Huge stock options and other financial incentives make the interests of executives and shareholders almost as one. When that fails, corporate raiders stand by ready to buy up companies whose incompetent or opportunistic management depresses stock market values. As a last resort, shareholder activist groups initiate actions for changing corporate governance.

The Japanese specialize in solving the second principal-agent problem—motivating the work force—by making its employees both principals and agents. Managers begin their careers on the factory floors. Aggressive pursuit of corporate growth, even when it is unprofitable, guarantees a level of job security and provides attractive career ladders for employees.

Fluid and Dedicated Systems of Capital.   Both the United States and United Kingdom have strong, fluid equity cultures. The fluid system of capital has two important advantages. It is more flexible and responsive, therefore better at reallocating capital rapidly from unprofitable industries to profitable ones. It's also better at financing new industries. The problem with this type of equity base is that it's not good at aiming enough investment at protecting a firm's competitive position in existing businesses.

Unlike the United States and United Kingdom, Germany and Japan have a dedicated equity culture. In Japan, for example, other companies hold between 65 and 80 percent of any company's shares. Companies hold shares in companies they do business with.[43] The principal goal of executives in these enterprises is to secure a firm's long-term competitive position.

In the dedicated capital systems of Japan and Germany, the dominant owners are not agents who invest for others like U.S. pension plans. The primary investors are banks and other institutions, and families that hold large stakes for a long time. All have greater interest in long-term appreciation, the incentive to monitor long-term progress, and because they are able to assume board positions, they have better access to inside information. Japan and Germany have permanent, well-informed, and involved investors, however they have less flexibility to withdraw capital when a company is on the wrong track and less regard for small shareholders compared to the U.S. and U.K. systems.

MOVING TOWARDS A NEW VIEW OF FREE ENTERPRISE

When we examine the current activities in America's free enterprise system, we find dissatisfaction with current corporate governance. Disenchanted shareholders no longer believe that the boards of directors are adequately representing their interests and believe that executive management is putting their personal interests above those of the other stakeholders of the enterprise, including the other employees. Shareholders are still technically the owners of America's biggest firms, but state and federal laws that protect executives and workers from shareholder intervention have effectively disenfranchised them. The Council on Competitiveness recommends change, as does the Securities and Exchange Commission.

Examining the free enterprise system in the U.K., we find much the same type of dissatisfactions. Here, the Cadbury committee recommends a voluntary code of ethics.

Germany, by comparison, lacks a strong equity culture, and has less concern for smaller shareholders. Because of high labor costs and strength of labor unions, German manufacturers are moving production out of their country, yet the supporting legal corporate code remains unchanged. Finally, Japan and its elder statesman of business, Akio Morita, also see room for improvement. Shareholders receive little pay-out for their investments, and workers want a better quality of life.

Today, many Japanese businesses serve as world role models, creating new best practices and new world standards, while still other Japanese businesses have lackluster performance and fail. The same is true for U.S., Germany, and U.K. businesses. All operate within competitive cultures that evolved over time, and in competitive contexts providing limited shelter from political and social changes, where each country's legal code defines, supports, and reflects its past competitive culture. These cultures served each country until enterprises began to compete in the expanded marketplace.

The four major competitive models—those of the United States, Germany, Japan, and the United Kingdom—are imperfect in the global market, and each country's business leaders study their world-class competitors to learn new paradigms for success. Japanese manufacturers, with their traditions of lifetime employment, begin to abandon these social contracts to sustain global competitiveness and, in this aspect, move closer to the U.S. model. Germany, who's traditional economic model favors tight linkages with government, banking, and labor unions over those with stockholders, finds that it must rethink this emphasis if it wishes to have access to a strong equity market—as exists in the United States—for funding economic expansion. The United States, whose competitive model reflects an adversarial relationship between employee and employer, adopts the Japanese teamworking concept to improve quality, and whose government espouses a free market economy, ponders a new role of establishing a national agenda to create a world-class information superhighway—not unlike Germany, Japan, and Canada. And the United Kingdom continues to struggle under the burdens of a costly social system that hinders global competitiveness, while debating the ethical role of the enterprise in society, in search of its own solution. As the era of globalization proceeds and everyone begins competing for the same customer, these competitive cultures will become remarkable in their similarities rather than in their differences.

Prepare for significant changes in the rules of fair competition. Trade agreements usher in new, more globally-defined rules of competition.

Evergreen Environmental Consultants

Marilyn M. Parker

SERVICE CATEGORIZATION GRID

In Chapter 6, we introduced some of the problems in measuring quality of service, where the service was an added value associated with a manufactured product. Here, we discuss service businesses and categorize them by the degree of labor intensity and degree of customization of the product. From this, we develop a service categorization grid (Figure V-1) that includes:

- Service utilities: Characterized by low labor intensity, low customization services from organizations like airlines, banks, and data centers.
- Service shops: Including low labor intensity, high customization services from organizations such as auto repair, or an I/T help desk.
- Mass services: With high labor intensity, low customization service offerings including most retail establishments, education, and for I/T, a Communications Software Development Group.
- Service professionals: Furnishing high labor intensity, high customization services of doctors, lawyers, and consultants.

This is also a valid approach for I/T, because it is essentially a group of services, businesses or lines of service, each requiring its own strategies, organizational forms, performance (business value contribution) measurements, critical service elements, and staffing.[50]

Service Utility

The service utility has a low degree of labor intensity and a low degree of ability to customize the product. For many electric companies, there is little customization—when the switch is on the customer gets electricity and when the switch is off the customer doesn't. A customer may see a representative of the utility company only once during the life of the service—when opening the account—and there is no continuing interaction with the company unless the bill is paid in person.

Other industries in this quadrant include banks and fast food. Banks have a selection from a fixed repertoire, but with personalized service it provides some feeling

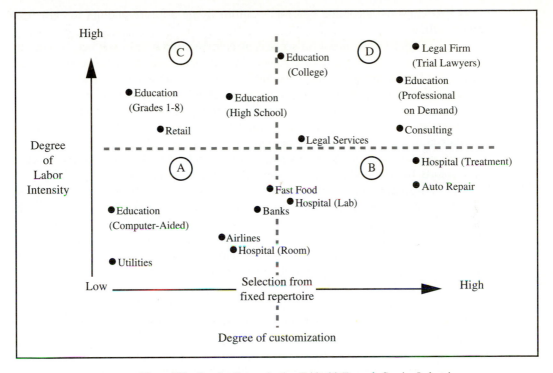

Figure V-1   Service Categorization Grid with Example Service Industries.

of choice. Fast food is a bit more labor intensive than banks or airlines but is still a selection from a fixed repertoire.

The airline is a service that has low labor intensity and moderate customization—a selection from a fixed repertoire. Unless chartering an airplane, choosing becomes limited to a selection from a fixed schedule of services. The airlines publish their schedules periodically and the Official Airline Guide (OAG) publishes the composite of all airline schedules.

Along with these standardized services come very standard and rigid organizational hierarchies and responsibilities. The only thing that softens the interaction during service delivery is a friendly interchange with the employee. The number of interactions—the number of hamburgers sold, or the number of new bank accounts opened—is the way the business measures its success. Employees must do their jobs in very standard ways—the business organization cannot tolerate inconsistent quality in the food, nor can it tolerate the bank teller using innovative bookkeeping, or a pilot ignoring the flight plan and schedule. They must understand and execute standard operating procedures.

The consumer must also believe that the individual carrying out the procedures will follow the prescribed protocol, for example, the bank teller depositing the funds correctly, the pilot following the flight plan as filed, and the IRS agent applying consistent guidelines during an audit. Incidents of bankers that embezzle and commercial pilots that consume alcoholic beverages before flying are rare enough to earn front page headlines.

The service utility measures success by cost, number of interactions, friendly interchange, facility utilization, and scheduling. Its strategies to achieve success are built around standard operating procedures, economies of scale, rigid organizational hierarchy, high employee execution skills, and technology penetration and utilization.

Service shop: The service shop has the same low degree of labor intensity as the service utility, however it begins to customize the service delivered. Examples include hospitals and automobile repair. Although there is a variance in the training required, the service itself is unique to the patient or automobile. The deliveries of the services are standard, like a blood test, an electrocardiogram, or a brake job.

If we decompose a hospital into its various functions or lines of service (LOS), the LOS have different kinds of service measurements and emphasis. For example, the hospital room itself is in the utility grid. The only differentiation might be a private versus a semi-private room or a room in intensive care (and these rooms are not interchangeable). The hospital lab represents a selection from a fixed repertoire and is more labor intensive. The hospital treatment itself is even more selective, more customized, and more labor intensive.

How do measures of success change as we move from standardized services to customized services? First, there is a change relating to effectiveness of size. Previously, the emphasis was on economies of scale (the bigger the better and the cheaper). The issue now becomes the size of the group and the required mix of skills necessary to provide the service. Are there enough doctors to cover twenty-four hours a day, seven days a week? Are there enough nurses given the number of beds in the hospital? A particular specialty of the hospital (orthopedics) or hospital wing (intensive care) increases service levels. (Duke Hospital, one of the top five hospitals in the United States, discovered that by having only specialty medical groups and excluding family practice services, it wasn't staying cost-competitive. In 1994, it announced a restructuring of its services, a planned reduction of 1,500 employees over two years, and a planned $70 million reduction in budget.) Facility utilization is also an important factor. Just ask any hospital administrator about bed utilization or a hotel manager about room utilization!

There is an increased interaction with the consumer and a greater emphasis on quality of interaction. Employee skills in the service shop require some level of professional interchange and a level of diagnostic skills rather than the execution skills of the service utility. Whether it is an automobile in for a tune-up or a family member in for surgery, there is a level of diagnosis.

The service shop, therefore, focuses its measures of success on the following characteristics: customization of process, effectiveness of size, increased service, quality of interaction, facility utilization and scheduling, and technology penetration and utilization. Its strategies to achieve success relate to assuring professional interchange, a mixed diagnosis and execution of standard services, and building employee identification and loyalty to the firm.

Mass Service

Mass service offers the more standardized services, but with a higher degree of labor intensity, including retailing, and many educational functions. For example, primary grades 1 to 6 have a high degree of labor intensity but a fairly standardized product. Ask grade school teachers and they will talk about lesson plans and standardized tests in which students must demonstrate a level of competency at the end of each school year. Students in secondary school have elective subjects, picking from a predetermined menu. College is also a selection against a fixed repertoire, however, it is higher on the grid due to smaller classes and special study's groups.

Professional, on-demand, education involves a high degree of labor intensity and high customization, whereas computer-aided education doesn't. Within many large organizations there is a mix of these two types of education, and the practice is to offer computer-aided education almost exclusively—an example of just-in-time education—supplementing it with specialized, tailored training.

How do we measure the type of service (mass services) delivered in this quadrant? There are still standard operating procedures, economies of scale, and the emphasis on cost control. These are the same as the service utility, but there is a different emphasis—an emphasis on hiring and training personnel. This results from needing different kinds of employees with different sets of skills to act as a team and to provide the service. The qualities of elementary school principals are different from the teachers, just as the qualities of maintenance programmers are different than those of a software consultant. Again, there is an emphasis on scheduling and utilization, along with rigid organizational hierarchies and responsibilities. The employee skills require mixed execution and diagnosis—for example, teachers must identify students with special problems and attempt to resolve them within the classroom, or the shoe salesman must match the unique requirements of each customer for size and style to the shoes available from current inventory if the store doesn't allow special orders.

Service Professionals

The service professional includes legal, consulting, and medical services. There is a high degree of interaction with the consumer in the process of delivering the service and a high degree of customization of the service itself. For all practical purposes, all services (solutions) are unique.

Legal services separate into various lines of service. There are legal office chains specializing in different kinds of cases (divorce, personal injury, and the like). Everything is highly computerized, and the practice won't accept cases outside its specialization. Its actions are similar to a utility providing a standard service within a specialization, applying measures of success related to economies of scale. This is a very different type of legal service as compared to a trial lawyer. The trial lawyer represents a purely customized process, with employee skills requiring a professional interchange and quality of interaction and a heavy emphasis on diagnostic skills. There is heavy emphasis on hiring and training personnel, maintaining a low turnover of employees, and work force scheduling and utilization.

The characteristics of delivering services by the professional focus on customization of process, effectiveness of size, increased service, quality of interaction, hiring and training, work force scheduling and utilization, and multiple location control. Critical employee skills are ones of professional interchange and diagnosis.

From this perspective, what are the characteristics of the I/T business and what are the lines of service (LOS) within I/T? How does the previous discussion of the service industry help an I/T professional? Is there any relevance to I/T problems?

EVERGREEN ENVIRONMENTAL CONSULTANTS

The senior partners of Evergreen Environmental Consultants (a fictitious name), providing a wide range of environmental consulting services, wanted to increase revenues by increasing the hours billed by the professionals and the number of retainer contracts. They also planned to increase the client-base types as a hedge against an anticipated drop in number of special projects being undertaken in the public sector. Previously, the firm specialized in providing environmental services to state and local government agencies. Due to a recent move by many agencies to have in-house environmental experts, the work load would gradually drop if the practice didn't begin to diversify. The partners knew that these changes in strategy could temporarily disrupt the revenue stream generated by some of their best professionals who, by assisting the senior partners in developing new contractual relationships, would be billing less. This redirection of professional effort would create a (hopefully temporary) revenue shortfall. The senior partners asked the I/T organization to develop a support strategy to reduce overall I/T expenditures to compensate for the projected drop in revenue.

Using the service categorization grid, the I/T planners at Evergreen identified and classified the lines of service (LOS) within I/T as Systems and Applications Development, I/T Internal Consulting Services, End-User Information Services (EUIS), Data Delivery, Communications, and Operations. They classified Operations and Communications as a service utility; Systems and Applications Development as mass services, Data Delivery as a service shop, and I/T Internal Consulting Services and End-User Information Services as consulting (see Figure V-2). It became evident that the half a dozen or so measures of I/T performance and single strategy currently in use were simply not sufficient to plan for the new operating environment, since different qualities and characteristics surrounded each of the I/T businesses.

Operations and Communications, the planners decided, are service utilities because they exhibit economies of scale, emphasis on utilization, and use standard operating procedures. To maintain lights out or unmanned computer operations required standard operating procedures, availability of resources, and utilization of those resources. The rest of the I/T activities ranged from a selection from a fixed repertoire to a high degree of customization, and tended to be higher in the degree of labor intensity. This created a problem—the thing that Evergreen's I/T group measured the most

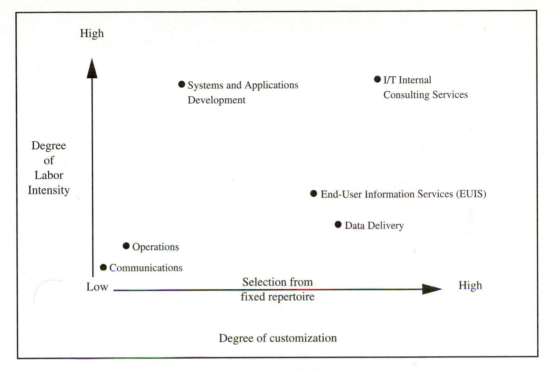

Figure V-2   Services Categorization Grid with I/T Lines of Service.

(and the best) was machine utilization and availability, yet it represented success in only one of the I/T lines of service, and it certainly didn't measure the quality of service, which was an issue even before the budget cut.

When the I/T planners examined the End-User Information Services (EUIS) lines of service within this same context, they discovered a number of things (see Figure V-3). The four functions that were most important to this LOS were Consulting, Training, PC Workstation Support, and Package Acquisition. The only difference between them (from the perspective of categorization) was the degree of labor intensity in providing the services. Because EUIS represented the largest single budget item (for personnel costs) within I/T, the planners focused on it.

The planners attempted to translate these EUIS activities into strategy and concurrently move from internally (I/T provider) driven standards and measurements to externally (environmental consultant) driven standards and measurements in hopes of providing higher quality service. I/T proposed a change in Package Acquisition requiring a move from a large number of vendors offering many diverse applications packages to fewer vendors with targeted applications specialties.

When a new environmental consultant joined the group, they often brought along some personal software that I/T provided an interface for or integrated into the system. I/T eliminated support for this type of assistance. This, they reasoned, created a standard approach and eliminated some current problems with data exchange. With

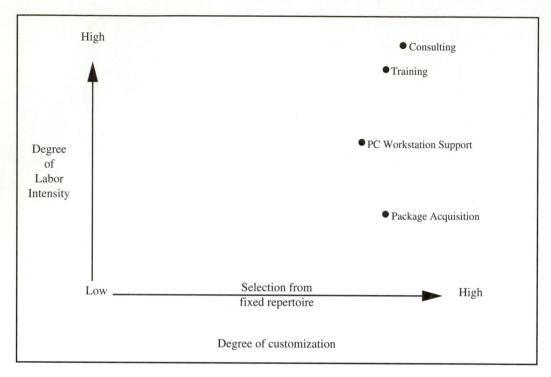

Figure V-3   Services Categorization Grid with End-User Computing Lines of Service.

fewer vendors and applications packages to support, I/T required less labor for the total effort.

When they examined the consulting activities occurring ad-hoc in EUIS and compared them to the chartered activities of the I/T Internal Consulting Services, the planners recommended that consulting be coordinated under the umbrella of EUIS. By doing this, they could better leverage staff expertise.

Next, they turned to PC workstation support strategy, which tied to the training strategy. They wanted to increase the amount of end-user specialized training, thus making the environmental consultants more competent and ultimately reducing the labor required for PC Workstation Support. The I/T planners felt this investment would provide long-range (and greater) returns. The strategy to this point was twofold:

- Move towards a subset of approved vendors.
- Increase the specialized training for the end users so they would become more self-sufficient.

The planners then examined the provider-driven measures for EUIS. They wanted to change the package acquisition measurements to focus on interrelated packages requiring less support, thus reducing package failures (measured in man-hours and un-recoverable investment dollars). They made similar changes to the measurements in other functions.

The overall strategy was to move from customization to standardization. They were trying to drive down the total man-hours for EUIS and make the remaining more effective within measurement criteria meaningful to business management. In this way, I/T could demonstrate that it was providing new business value.

The I/T strategy for Evergreen sounds reasonable, but does it help achieve the new business strategy? At first glance it appears to be inconsistent. Cost is important during a significant change in business strategy, but so is the support of the professionals that generate revenue. However, the I/T organization adhered to the financial constraints for new investments, and felt the strategy was appropriate.

After I/T presented its strategy, the senior partners began questioning how this new strategy affected the consultants. They asked if the EUIS strategy would have a negative impact on the business strategy to increase the number of hours billed per professional. The answer was, unfortunately, affirmative. The strategy moved less expensive I/T support effort from the technology domain into the business domain and forced the professionals—the consultants who were directly generating the revenues—to be more self-sufficient. The partners then asked whether or not the I/T strategy created a business organizational risk in trying to support the new objectives of EUIS. Again, the answer was yes. Following this strategy, I/T created a new business organizational risk involving both revenue generation and staff morale.

By moving toward a subset of approved vendors for software, the partners found that EUIS reduced their risk of failure. But, they continued to probe, will the EUIS strategy to reduce software options have a negative effect on the business strategy to move from a single- to a multiple-client type base? This was possible if the software chosen eliminated any business options deemed critical by the partners. Does this create another new business organizational risk while supporting the performance measures for I/T services? The answers to these questions were unclear to the senior partners.

If you were a senior partner in this firm, what would you do? After a lengthy discussion during the monthly business meeting, they—although suspecting it before—knew they could no longer plan any of the business functions in a vacuum. By tweaking one (reducing the I/T budget), they created repercussions (both positive and negative) throughout the organization. The senior partners discovered the problem of trying to maximize equilibrium while introducing change (dysfunction) into the enterprise.

Evergreen Environmental Consultants received a significant amount of its revenues from retainer fees. That meant—at least for the interim—that whether the consultants billed hourly or not, the firm would still maintain a reduced but stable revenue base. Perhaps, the partners reasoned, instead of trying to increase the number of hours billed per professional, a better approach might be to focus primarily on creating the ability to service more clients on retainer, thus increasing the potential retainer revenue base.

Although unhappy with the prospect of increased business organizational risk introduced by the I/T strategy, the senior partners of the firm decided to endorse it and make it part of the overall business strategy. This meant that some previous work would be off-loaded from I/T and moved to the 200-plus junior partners and associates, forcing up the level of competency, proficiency, and technology requirements for all business professionals. The senior partners made this decision because they felt that any future competitive advantage required some degree of technology proficiency. After having previously invested in I/T in computer organization facilities, training, subscriptions to computerized databases and other services, they decided to use this move to a higher technology skill level as a kind of litmus test. They wanted all the members of the firm to step up to the technology-related parts of their profession now, rather than moving an inch at a time.

The first year of operating under the new strategy was difficult. Both I/T and environmental consulting lost staff due to frustration, long hours, and the unwillingness or inability to change. However, within three years of deciding upon the new strategy, the combined consulting and retainer revenues almost tripled, coupled with an approximate 50 percent increase in the number of consultants. The move effectively doubled the revenue-generation capabilities of the consultants, and Evergreen management attributed much of the newly generated revenue to the innovations of the EUIS group. EUIS introduced and supported an anywhere-anytime office environment allowing the consultants to spend more time in the field, thus facilitating an increase in billing hours. Additional communications linkages with clients allowed consultants to carry and effectively service an increased number of clients on retainer. There was also an unexpected benefit when the two I/T consulting groups consolidated: for the first time, the I/T consultants had a unified view of the overall enterprise requirements. Taking a lesson from I/T consulting, the senior partners made I/T planning an integral part of the business strategic planning, and started working together to identify new advantages to exploit.

What happened here? Changing market conditions required a new business strategy—announced to I/T as a budget cut. I/T planning responded by developing a strategy for each of its LOS and concentrated its efforts on the most labor-intensive, customized product delivery function—EUIS. Not only did I/T develop a viable strategy, but they developed the strategy around standards and measures important (therefore meaningful) to the business and the user. Through carefully controlling (defining, choosing, and maintaining) EUIS-supported software, the EUIS emphasis shifted from individualized hand-holding, training, and maintenance activities to focused systems enhancements, focused end-user training, and technology scanning activities, benefiting the entire organization. As a result, Evergreen became the first environmental consulting group to effectively implement the anywhere-anytime office with the remote retainer relationship, providing the company with a significant, albeit temporary, competitive edge.

PART VI. PERFORMING WHILE TRANSFORMING

In the book, we began by examining the dynamics of international competition and how these dynamics force business enterprises to transform themselves to remain competitive in this new environment. Characteristics of this new enterprise include an increasing customer focus, providing improved quality, value, and services through business process reengineering initiatives that incorporate the concepts of empowerment, flexibility, and constant change. Furthermore, we found that these enterprise changes have significant impact on the I/T organizations that support them. These organizations must not only support the enterprise effort involving quality, value, service, and process reengineering initiatives, but it must simultaneously integrate these same concepts and philosophies into its own technology and organizational infrastructure.

Previous papers have touched on a number of these issues. Blumenthal and Haspeslagh explored the various forms that transformation can take, Cannon discussed the role of quality in an information technology organization, and Walker wrote at length about the transformation initiatives within AGT Limited. In "New Technologies and New Services," Dr. Jon Thorhallsson introduces another theme—that of innovations in business and technology that create new work practices and lead to advances in business. These generate new needs which in turn lead to more technological progress. Specifically, he focuses on the technological progress and innovation necessary when applying I/T to combat the competitive forces the enterprise is facing. For the first time, we see the I/T organization as a true business partner. Here, I/T abandons its protective coloration and role of a support organization and grapples with the real issues of understanding competitive strengths and weaknesses of the enterprise (whatever it is), creating strategies and products that will improve overall competitive performance. In this role, leadership, risk, and reward become mandatory as I/T defines and executes its own strategic transformation.

Dr. Thorhallsson is associate professor of information technology at The University of Iceland and is also managing director of SKYRR, the state and municipal data center in Reykjavik. "New Technologies and New Services" is based upon a presentation given by Dr. Thorhallsson at The Academy of Local Government Information Science as part of its International Workshop in Marathon, Greece.

"National Defense and the Age of Uncertainty," by Lt. Col. Robert T. Morris, United States Air Force, provides a fitting close to the book. The restructuring of the U.S. defenses have a profound political and economic impact felt globally. Shifting global alliances, a proliferation of weapons capable of mass destruction, the exploitation of technology to achieve combat information dominance, and weaponry and tactics requiring new core competencies have all contributed to the new military mandate for performing while transforming.

New Technologies and New Services

Jon Thorhallsson

Information and information systems have brought about social transformation—the transformation from industrial society to information society. Now we hear that we are heading towards a new kind of a society, the so-called knowledge society. Technology has not been the only pace setter for this transformation. Technology has of course played its part, and played it very well indeed, but business has had an important role to play as well. Therefore, the real pace setter, if we have to name one, is innovation, both technological and business innovation, and its tremendous dynamics of interaction.

In this context of innovation, every information system has five components. First, there is a business goal stating what is to be accomplished by a particular information system. Second, there are the work practices for the people using the system and working towards that goal. Furthermore, every information system includes the components of information (the formatted data, text, pictures, and sounds), people (the people who enter, process, and use data), and information technology (the hardware and software that process data)—the third, fourth and fifth components. These are starting points for analyzing or designing almost any information system and understanding its role in innovation.

Regarding the dynamics of interaction between business and technological innovation, we observe that the current state of information technology enables current work practices and is also the starting point of innovations. Shortcomings in an industry's work practices reveal needs, opportunities, and risks. These needs and opportunities in turn motivate the search for technological improvements such as enhanced data capture technology through scanners or advancement in telecommunications through satellites. In turn, the innovations eventually become widespread, and the cycle continues with the search for business opportunities.

Business needs and the technology itself are the two driving forces. As the current technology itself evolves, it provides a platform for developing even more powerful technologies. In turn, these new technologies enable advances in both industry's work practices and technology itself. These mutually reinforcing phenomena ensure rapid future change.

Applying information systems is not just a technical task. Major successes and innovations in applying information systems arise from business needs and opportunities. Let us take a little closer look at this by examining some of the present business trends related to information systems:

- Greater pervasiveness of computers
- Convergence of computing and communication
- Greater automation of work
- More value residing in information
- New forms of organization and management
- Faster pace of business
- Accelerating global competition
- Gradual acceptance of global standards

Business trends related to information technology have a counterpart in technological trends related to information systems. These include:

- Increasing speed and capacity of electronic components
- Greater availability of digitized information
- Greater portability of electronic devices
- Greater connectivity
- Greater ease of use
- Continuing inability to automate common sense

Both the business and the technological trends constantly interact and generate the dynamics of business and technology innovation mentioned earlier. There will not be any real advancement without both, because business needs technology and technology needs business. Their constant interaction leads to the synergy that brings us the real advancement in structure and shape of society—from industrial to information, and from an information to knowledge society.

Let us now reflect upon our own situation and our particular environment, the local government. Thus far, we have been referring exclusively to business, business trends, and technology, and technological trends as related to business and the dynamics of innovation between business and technology. But how does this concern local government? What have the dynamics of business and technology got to do with local government? Everything, we contend!

Why should there be any difference? Business is business and those responsible for local government should always act as if it were a business driven by costs, benefits, service, and quality. Therefore, everything we said about business also applies to local government. We—all of us—are a part of the dynamics of business and technological innovation. We can also refer to it as the dynamics of local government business and technological innovation. The trends are the same, and the issues to be dealt with are the same.

Let us look at the trends again. We said they included a greater pervasiveness of computers, a convergence of computing and communication, and a greater automation of work. We also said there would be more value residing in information, new forms of organization and management, a faster pace of business, accelerating global competition, and a gradual acceptance of global standards.

All these trends are also visible in local government, even the acceleration of global competition. On a lesser global scale, the Nordic Kommunedatas (a group of individual data centers, each representing the computing arm of its respective country government) are facing the option of competing against each other—the Icelandic Kommunedata competing against Sweden's or Norway's Kommunedata. On a larger global scale, we may face an environment in which we will be competing against a company providing processing services, and because of its location in an entirely different time zone and its available work force, it is able to offer its capacity in an around the clock fashion at a low price.

Therefore, our conclusion remains: Local governments are a part of the business community, like it or not. There is nothing special about us. What is good for business is good for us, and what is good for us is good for business.

If we are one of them, let's stop worrying about how to beat them. We can also stop viewing ourselves as a special case. Therefore, we can stop the fruitless and infinite search for our own special identity. One of the advantages of adopting this point of view is that we can apply all the wisdom and all the advice coming out of the academic circles to our situation and our particular environment.

So for the moment, let us adopt this position. What are the new technologies businesses face today? And what are the technological trends business has to cope with and consider? One of them is the merging of old and new technologies. First, consider the new technologies of imaging, electronic data interchange, artificial intelligence, expert systems, executive information systems, multimedia, virtual reality, and downsizing. Now consider the merging technologies of e-mail, fax, voice mail, view mail, computers, communications, television and telephone switchboards. How should Kommunedatas react?

If we are willing, at least for the moment, to view ourselves as a business and behave like a business, one option is to look and see how our role model, that is, the business, reacts in a situation such as this. Do we examine it theoretically, practically, or both? Let us examine at least one academic model to gauge the reaction of business to new technologies and merging technologies.

In *Competitive Strategy: Techniques for Analyzing Industries and Competitors,* Michael Porter introduced his model of competitive forces.[51] In the model, he surrounds the strategic business unit or enterprise by the outside competitive forces of potential new entrants (where one assesses the relative ease of others entering the market), the bargaining power of suppliers and buyers (where one assesses the strength/weaknesses of outside relationships and the channels of distribution), and the threat of substitute products or services (where one assesses the dynamics of the market itself).

Porter developed his model for use in the manufacturing industry, but it has been extended to include the service industry as well. In such a setting, I/T and the I/T department are assigned the role of being a supporter to the main business line, whether it is fish in Iceland, automobiles in Sweden, paper in Finland, oil in Norway, or food in

Denmark. However, in the case of the Kommunedatas, I/T is the strategic business unit. It is the only line of business. Consequently, in our industry I/T plays a double role, that is, it is not only the business line, it is also supports it. In spite of this double role, why should Porter's model not be equally applicable to the Kommunedatas?

His model, among other things, defines the forces of competition acting on a strategic business unit. Besides defining the forces of competition, he also discusses the impact of those same forces and consequent implications. Subsequently, other authors like Cash, McFarlan, and Mckenney discuss the potential use of I/T to combat those competitive forces.[52] For example:

- Threat of new entrants: This force implies potential dedication of new capacity and resources by the new entrant. The enterprise already established in the market might consider using I/T to create entry barriers based upon economies of scale, switching costs, product differentiation, or access to distribution channels.
- Buyers' bargaining power: If the buyer is in a strong position, they may dictate lower prices, higher quality, and specialized services. The enterprise might apply I/T to create product differentiation (the mass customization of product) or through just-in-time delivery increase switching costs for customers or create new entry barriers for competitors.
- Suppliers' bargaining power: If the supplier is in a strong position, the implication to the enterprise may include lack of control over price, quality, and services. I/T may be of assistance in creating a threat of backward integration.
- Threat of substitute products or services: While this may limit the potential return-on-investment or create an artificial cap on prices, I/T may help improve price/performance or redefine the products and services to make them unique.
- Traditional rivals within the industry: The existing competitors in the industry compete based on price, product, distribution, and service. We may use I/T to create differentiation in each of these areas.

The interesting point is that in our case we are looking at using I/T to combat forces of competition on I/T itself! Let us now examine the impact of competitive forces on the Kommunedatas.

Threat of New Entrants

With the recent rampage of deregulation and outsourcing, new entrants are knocking on our customers' doors. In fact, all of us are indeed potential competitors. But there are others as well. Outsourcing companies like EDS and IBM are good examples. To be more precise, IBM has formed outsourcing subsidiaries in all Nordic countries with the exception of Iceland. Consequently, IBM is not only one of our major suppliers, but also a formidable competitor.

There are also newcomers—small specialized companies—sometimes even a one-product company who tries to discover a small niche to occupy. And not so incidentally, in some instances the personnel are former employees of ours. What are some potential uses of I/T to combat these competitive realities?

- We can sometimes provide economies of scale by resource integration consolidation of data centers.
- By providing integrated tightly coupled solutions, it becomes more difficult for a new entrant to find a niche, a niche big enough to make it worth the effort for the customer to leave everything else behind.
- By differentiating our products by providing solution packages in such a size and shape that makes it difficult for our competitors to imitate.
- We can make more use of our networks to distribute our services and products. However, not every network will do. It has to be something more than the mere infrastructure most European national telephone and telegraph companies provide and is available to everybody, including our competitors. What is necessary is a value added network with the added value provided by us.

Buyer's Bargaining Power

We all hear the same complaints from buyers of our services, that is, our customers. They complain about not getting enough value for their money. Also, big customers expect a better deal than smaller ones. How can we use I/T to combat this force?

- We do (or at least did) not provide open systems, thus increasing switching costs.
- We have differentiated ourselves by providing total integrated solutions in an area with broad focus.
- We have raised entry barriers by becoming value added service companies.

Bargaining Power of Suppliers

We all probably have in one way or the other experienced the stronghold IBM has (or had) on us, both in hardware and system software. What are the avenues open to us here?

- We have switched or threatened to switch to alternative hardware suppliers, Amdahl or NAS, or gone for used equipment.
- The situation for system software is similar because we have a choice between DB2, Adabas, Datacom, Oracle, among others. MVS is probably the only piece of software where we have no real choice of an alternative. (We all know the prices IBM charges for MVS!)

- Some of us have left the IBM mainframe environment altogether and moved to different platforms.

Threat of Substitute Products or Services

Our customers do not only look to us for services, they also look elsewhere. The forces of deregulation in the European Community force them to do so. They have no choice. We have been a part of their value chain for a long time and that certainly counts for something, but not everything. We will now have to compete for the position in their value chain that we previously took for granted and enjoyed. That is something new to us.

What must we do to earn ourselves a permanent seat, at least for now?

- We can improve price/performance by moving, for example, towards more automation, by economies of scale, and by moving to different platforms.
- We can also redefine products and services, for example, integrate systems and integrate services, offering solutions instead of systems and services.

CONCLUSIONS

We can conclude that this discussion has revealed absolutely nothing that suggests that the Kommunedatas are different from business in any way. Furthermore, by accepting that fact, we have lots of options available to us to fight off the competition that is all around us.

Let us return to the earlier question of new technologies and merging technologies. What should we do about them? How should we react? Well, how would business react? Let us view this considering Porter's theory. We identified new technologies (imaging, electronic data interchange, artificial intelligence, expert systems, executive information systems, multimedia, virtual reality, and downsizing), and merging technologies (e-mail, fax, voice mail, view mail, computers, communications, television and telephone switchboards). We can put both new technologies and merging technologies to work for us, not against us, by including them as part of our strategy to use I/T to combat the competitive forces, for example, to the threat of new entrants, to reduce the buyer's bargaining power, and to reduce the threat of substitutive products or services, as outlined in the examples above. This is far from easy, but if private business can do it, so can we!

National Defense and the Age of Uncertainty

Lt. Col. Robert T. Morris

Just as water retains no constant shape, so in warfare there are no constant conditions . . . He who can modify his tactics in relation to his opponent, and thereby succeed in winning, may be called a heaven-born captain.[53]

INTRODUCTION

The Chinese military philosopher Sun Tzu noted in the fourth century B.C. that victory goes to the warrior who adapts to changing conditions. Whether applied in business or warfare, the writings of Sun Tzu in *The Art of War* speak to the challenge of competing in today's global environment. For the U.S. Armed Forces, shifting geopolitics and fiscal demands are forcing a rethinking of national defense objectives, strategy and possibilities that are unprecedented in modern military history.

The restructuring of U.S. defenses will continue to have profound political and economic impact. Hundreds of thousands of volunteer service members, civilian employees, and their families have already felt the effect. From 1991 to mid-1994, the Defense Department reduced its full-time military and civilian force from 3,058,725 to 2,543,595, a cut of more than 510,000 jobs. Those losses were more than double the combined reductions that occurred at IBM, AT&T, and General Motors in the same period.[54] By 1994 the Air Force operated with half the money and a third fewer people than it did in the mid-1980s, and the Navy sailed fewer than 400 ships, the smallest number since 1939.

However, dissolution of the Warsaw Pact and the fall of communism did not eliminate the need for a combat-ready force. Despite the reductions, U.S. Armed Forces remained fully engaged across the globe, operating transport ships and planes in 180 countries in 1993.[55] Far from a tranquil world, the bi-polar strategic environment gave way to multi-polarity, ethnic strife, regional disputes, and the threat of proliferation of weapons of mass destruction. The high tempo of modern military operations required a fresh strategy and force structure that was wholly different from the military that helped win the Cold War.

CULTURAL SHIFT: PREPARING FOR CHANGE

Transformation within the military demanded fundamental cultural change in every uniformed service. Speaking of cultural shift in his own service, former Air Force Chief of Staff General Merrill A. McPeak said, "We all recognize that our organizational behavior is driven by shared values and experiences, unspoken, even unacknowledged conclusions about our past, that give us our institutional identity." As a result, cultural shift was particularly difficult for the Air Force because the only identity the service had known sprang from Army Air Corps strategic bombing of World War II. According to General McPeak, a kind of vertigo or aimlessness infected some airmen when culture failed to match reality:

> (The Air Force) didn't do any strategic bombing, at least not of the type envisioned by our founding fathers. This was because during the era of the independent Air Force, we have not had to fight an all-out war with an industrialized state . . . So, from the beginning, we had this concept of independent strategic bombing, and, over time, this concept got more and more out of sync with our real world experience, which seemed to require a different kind of organization, training, doctrine, requirements—in other words, a different culture.[56]

The result was a new concept called "Global Reach, Global Power," a framework that stepped beyond historic origins in strategic bombing to capitalize on the force projection characteristics of modern air power. It was the first step toward a revised mission statement and reorganization of forces to meet new-era threats.

Army Chief of Staff General Gordon Sullivan termed it an *intellectual change,* but the result was the same: a revision of Army doctrine, organization, force mix, tactics, and training. "We saw that the world had changed and we determined that the Army had to change, to adapt to the challenges of a 'new world order.' We knew that intellectual change must lead physical change," General Sullivan said. With publication of *Field Manual 100-5: Operations,* the Army shifted doctrinally from a forward-based force prepared for land battle in Europe or Asia to a "force projection Army," primarily based in the United States and adapted for rapid mobility anywhere on the globe.[57]

Likewise, the Navy's 1992 white paper, "From the Sea," outlined a vision for Navy and Marine Corps operations that shifted emphasis from global battle with a Soviet Navy to projecting American sea power to any regional crisis or contingency. "This strategic direction . . . represents a fundamental shift away from open-ocean warfighting on the sea toward joint operations conducted from the sea," the white paper said. "The Navy and Marine Corps will now respond to crises and can provide the initial, 'enabling' capability for joint operations in conflict—as well as continued participation in any sustained effort."[58] Parenthetically, this was the scenario during the initial phase of the Haiti operation in 1994, where a Navy aircraft carrier provided transportation to Army helicopters and an operations base for them as well.

These were difficult transitions for every service. In the tradition-rich armed forces, fundamental change comes only after prolonged and frequently public debate. Press coverage centered on "roles and missions" issues and perceived interservice rivalry to protect time-honored turf. The *Washington Times* reported a "bureaucratic feeding frenzy" as each service positioned for programs, missions, and hardware.[59] Admiral Paul David Miller, then commander-in-chief of US Atlantic Command, caused "military traditionalists to break out in rashes with a succession of proposals for mixing and matching forces in exotic new ways," one newspaper said.[60] But this coverage only alluded to the main point: the changes going on inside the Pentagon were fundamental, not incremental, and more revolutionary than evolutionary. Amidst the turmoil, and certainly as a result of the Gulf War experience, consensus was reached on the central point: That each service brings core competencies in land, sea, and air operations to the battlefield, and that these forces must train and fight under a single theater commander, regardless of the uniform worn. As an island nation with global interests, the new-world strategy of power projection cemented the need for a unified force. The days of a separate Army, Navy, and Air Force were gone forever.

REORGANIZATION AND PHYSICAL CHANGE

Metamorphosis toward unification began slowly but finished with a torrent of change after the Cold War. In World War II, theater commanders were first assigned the missions and forces to wage war. Despite the challenges of new technology and limited lines of communication and supply, the American way of war became joint warfare, conducted by theater commanders—not the services. After passage of the National Security Act of 1947, service leaders met at Key West, Florida, to clarify and delineate service-specific functions and laid the foundation for the services as we know them today.[61] Nearly forty years later, Congress legislated the next major change through the Goldwater-Nichols Defense Reorganization Act of 1986. The act strengthened authority of combatant commanders and created a professional track for officers specializing in joint warfare—requiring new matrix management skills, with their promotions and career paths carefully monitored.

The demise of the Soviet Union was the clear opportunity to further refine and unify the military. As a result, former chairman of the Joint Chiefs of Staff, General Colin L. Powell, wrote in his 1993 report on roles and missions that "more changes have occurred in the U.S. military in the past three years than in any similar period since the National Security Act of 1947."[62]

First, nuclear forces were fundamentally reorganized. Nuclear weapons were removed from Army and Marine Corps arsenals. The Strategic Air Command was eliminated—an almost unbelievable event to thousands of bomber and missile crews who had stood alert through the Cold War. All strategic nuclear weapons—bombers, missiles, and submarines—were placed under a unified commander, either an Air Force or Navy four-star at the newly created Strategic Command at Offutt Air Force Base in Nebraska. In 1991, President Bush took all strategic bombers and missiles off alert for the first time since the 1950s.

The Armed Forces destroyed their chemical weapons and increased involvement in missions such as assisting law enforcement agencies in drug interdiction. U.S. Atlantic Command greatly expanded its mission to assume responsibility for joint training and force packaging of Continental U.S.-based forces. With this move, according to General Powell, "Unification of the Armed Forces, which began in 1947, would at last be complete."

The new security environment prompted the Bottom Up Review directed by former Secretary of Defense Les Aspin in 1993. This collaborative study blended service doctrine, acquisition policy, and fiscal reality to lay a foundation for military force structure in the modern era. A steering group including the Office of Secretary of Defense, the Joint Staff, and service leadership analyzed new-era dangers, revised defense strategy, and outlined new planning assumptions and force structure. The study identified four national security threats:

- Dangers posed by existing nuclear weapons and the proliferation of weapons of mass destruction, including nuclear, biological, and chemical weapons.
- Regional dangers, including aggression by major regional powers and the dangers posed by smaller, internal conflicts based on ethnic or religious divisions and state-sponsored terrorism.
- Dangers to democracy and reform in the former Soviet Union and worldwide.
- Economic danger to U.S. national security, which would result through failure to build a prosperous, competitive, growing economy.

The last two threats to U.S. security (dangers to democratic reform and the nation's economy) were clearly beyond the scope of traditional military response. The military-dominated paradigm to contain communism was over. A new definition for national security embodied the essence of American values: creating a world in which free market economics and democratic principles could thrive. Military capability, a robust economy, and the advancement of democracy were viewed as mutually supportive. The Armed Forces would contribute in part through smaller, less expensive forces to allow domestic investment for national prosperity.

Those forces would have to be flexible, mobile, and designed for quick, decisive victory. The legacy of Vietnam and the War Powers Resolution of 1978 ended the likelihood of U.S. military forces engaged in protracted wars of attrition.[63] Public opinion, live news coverage, and abhorrence for casualties raised concern over the morality of war as an instrument of national policy. American wars of the future would have to be fought with speed, precision, and minimum casualties to achieve sharply defined military objectives. These objectives would be diverse, including nuclear deterrence, traditional use of force and operations other than war, such as peacekeeping and humanitarian missions. The new military would be called to confront unpredictable, unknown threats across the globe.

The recommended structure to meet these dangers was a "lean, mobile, high-tech force," Aspin said. Compared to fiscal year 1990 levels, this plan recommended cutting Army divisions from 18 to 10; Navy ships from 546 to 346; and active Air Force wings from 24 to 13. Because the Marine Corps was already tailored for expeditionary missions, the report recommended minimal end-strength reductions from 197,000 in 1990 to 174,000. Marine Reserve end-strength was virtually untouched, settling at 42,000. These forces, along with Reserve and National Guard equivalents, were deemed capable to fight two "major regional contingencies" nearly simultaneously. The goal was to maintain enough flexibility to deter an aggressor while U.S. forces were involved in another operation. Strategic airlift, sealift, and logistics would be critical to rapidly deploy and sustain combat-ready units. To enhance these smaller conventional forces, the Bottom Up Review also recommended prepositioning of Army equipment and supplies around the globe, acquiring modern precision-guided munitions and improving National Guard and reserve force readiness.

In 1994, with review of conventional forces complete, Secretary of Defense William J. Perry announced results of the first comprehensive review of nuclear forces in fifteen years. The Nuclear Posture Review (NPR) recommended adjustments to "reflect the changed political situation at the end of the Cold War and the reduced role nuclear weapons play in U.S. security."[64] Compared to 1988 levels, the U.S. nuclear stockpiles would be reduced 71 percent by 2003, with no new strategic systems planned or under development. The requirement to continue a viable nuclear deterrence was clear: states of the former Soviet Union had not implemented reductions under the START I Treaty, and START II had yet to be ratified. Because of the uncertain political and economic future within former Soviet states, Perry concluded that "deeper reductions beyond those we made in the NPR would be imprudent at this time . . . The results of the NPR strike an appropriate balance between showing U.S. leadership in responding to the changed international environment and hedging against an uncertain future."[65]

IMPERATIVES FOR THE FUTURE

The only thing known with certainty is how little we know about the future. U.S. military forces must be ready to respond with innovation to unspecified threats whose time, place, and nature are not yet known. The chairman of the independent, Congressionally-mandated Commission on Roles and Missions, John White, said he was operating on the assumption that "someplace over the horizon, there is a significantly greater threat to our interests than we see around us today. I don't know where it is; I don't even know what it is. Assuming it exists . . . you want the institutions to continually adjust so that they're ready for it."

Adjusting the military for the age of uncertainty has yielded a few trends. The United States will seek to build alliances and coalitions where they serve economic and military interests—an approach equivalent to strategic alliances and joint ventures formed by competitive corporations. Once engaged, U.S. military forces will rely increasingly on information technology to win combat information dominance on the battlefield. That technology will come largely from the commercial sector as the military reforms acquisition practices and invests in dual-use technologies to achieve security goals. (In effect, this reverses the flow of federally funded high-tech research and development-based products by NASA and other governmental agencies to domestic products. In the future, the government expects to benefit from commercial research and development-based products.) All this will occur while ensuring force readiness for a variety of new missions.

Alliances and Coalitions

The United States will continue to pursue international relationships to project influence and promote cooperation in a broad range of security issues. These include short-term, multinational coalitions formed during crisis, such as those in Desert Storm in 1990 and the Haiti crisis in 1994, that provide immediate political support and international leverage for U.S. diplomatic, economic, and military initiatives. Other alliances, such as the North Atlantic Treaty Organization (NATO) and North American Aerospace Defense Command (NORAD), have become central tenets of U.S. security strategy, just as GATT and NAFTA are to U.S. economic competitiveness strategy.

NATO remains a crucial venue for U.S. leadership in trans-Atlantic affairs. President Clinton pursued through NATO a series of initiatives to promote economic and security ties with former nations of the Warsaw Pact. Twenty-one countries, including Russia, subsequently joined the Partnership for Peace. Military training between NATO and Partnership member nations began in 1994, including joint peacekeeping operations between American and Russian soldiers in the southern Urals. In support of NATO commitments, the United States retains in Europe its most significant remaining overseas military presence. Humanitarian airlift into Bosnia-Herzegovina and operations to halt the spread of conflict in Yugoslavia demonstrate the continued importance of U.S. leadership in NATO.

Similarly, the United States will seek to continue the NORAD agreement, which must be renewed with Canada by 1996. The threat of air attack on North America has greatly diminished, but both nations still demand the right to control anyone flying in their nation's airspace (including those who would attempt to smuggle drugs). Peacetime air sovereignty operations will continue with or without NORAD, but it is difficult to conceive how each nation could do it more effectively or at less cost on their own. Additionally, NORAD continues to monitor ballistic missile launches anywhere in the world, and this information provided early warning of Scud attacks and cueing of Patriot missile batteries protecting Allied Forces during the Gulf War.

Information in Warfare

Early warning of missile attack is but one example of the torrent of information flowing into the modern battlefield. Just as business demands instant communications in the global economy, the military exploits technology to achieve combat information dominance. Whether that information is intelligence, surveillance, weather, navigation, or communication support, commanders rely on instantaneous information for situational awareness and battlefield decisions. Increasingly, that information comes from space—satellites that provide information ranging from multispectral imagery to near real-time warning of ballistic missile attack. As in sea and air control, commanders must now consider the issue of space control—how to ensure friendly use of space while denying adversaries the same advantages. Because the United States does not operate anti-satellite weapons, campaign planners must devise other ways to deny enemy use of space, including signals jamming and targeting of ground relay stations. Joint warfare is a battle of speed, precision, and information—making space support to the warfighter critical in high-tempo operations.

Integration of Military and Commercial Technologies

Defense budgets will no longer support a separate national defense industry. The military-industrial complex provided technology that gave U.S. Forces the advantage over numerically superior Warsaw Pact forces through the Cold War, and planners will continue to rely on upgraded systems to counter the diversity of weapons and threats that the military will face in the future. The difference is that the military will acquire technology based on commercial and international standards, with military-unique, performance-driven specifications added only as required. (With the increased commercial emphasis on mass customization, state-of-the-art military products should also become less costly to produce.) The Defense Department has aggressively sought dual-use technologies, serving both defense and commercial needs, that stimulate private industry and enhance the relationship between a strong domestic economy and national security. Further, this saves the Defense Department procurement dollars through economy of scale and the rapid pace of technology development within the commercial sector. Deputy Secretary of Defense John Deutch said that "we can no longer afford the extra cost of maintaining a defense-unique technology and industrial base. Second, we find in many fields vital to defense that commercial demand—not defense demand—is driving technological innovation."[66] Deutch cited a $500-million investment in commercial development of high-resolution flat panel displays, the type commonly seen in laptop computers. Reliable, rugged displays that can fuse massive data will serve commercial as well as military applications in aircraft, on ships and in the field. Integrating the defense base in national industry ensures U.S. dominance in defense technologies even when the military can no longer afford to be the lead investor. As the military learned to fight as a unified team, it is learning to procure in synchronization with U.S. industry.

Readiness

High operating tempos highlight concerns about continued readiness of the force to fight. Patriot missile crews and AWACS (airborne warning and control) aircrews were deployed over 200 days in 1994, and some Marine and Army units deployed to new contingencies within days or months of return from others.[67] Army Chief of Staff General Gordon Sullivan noted the average soldier was spending 140 days away from home each year. As the military assumes new, nontraditional missions such as peace-keeping and humanitarian operations, national leadership must carefully weigh every request for use of military forces. Government must strike a prudent balance to invest in competing demands of operations and maintenance, training, modernization, and quality of life programs like health care, housing, and pay. Historically, the United States has done a poor job of managing military drawdowns—the military equivalent of industry downsizings. Secretary of Defense William Perry noted that within five years of World War II, U.S. forces were driven from the Korean Peninsula, and the Vietnam drawdown resulted in the aptly named hollow army. "As we reduce the force we have to maintain our commitment to readiness and effectiveness so that whatever our force size, person for person and unit for unit it is the most effective force any-where in the world," Perry said.

CONCLUSION

The U.S. Armed Forces have adjusted doctrine, structure, and tactics to meet chal-lenges of the new era, just as industries have done.

- The redirection of national resources toward domestic needs, the shift from bipolar to multipolar threats, and the emergence of an array of new information technologies forced a fundamental rethinking of service culture. Industry faces a similar problem in rethinking its organizational culture and how it must change to improve competitiveness.

- A revised strategy of power projection for response to regional threats led to physical reorganization of forces designed for mobility, speed, and precision. There are parallels in industry. Industry has adopted new organizational models to increase organizational agility, it has focused on reducing cycle-time, and it has embraced quality throughout the process.

- Joint warfare doctrine strengthened command structures and unified land, sea, and air elements for joint combat operation. Again, similar parallels exist with industry participating in joint ventures and strategic alliances (globally and do-mestically) to exploit perceived windows of opportunity.

- Downsizing and reorganization proved to be painful, yet necessary steps toward structuring a military prepared for a different world. So too is industry taking similar steps to prepare for its new competitive environment.

Despite the difficulties, the challenges must be met. As Air Force General Merrill A. McPeak said: "Reinvention amounts to a break with the past, a transformation. What emerges at the end is something new in the same way that a butterfly is not just an improved caterpillar; it is an entirely different creature."[56] By embracing innovation and change, the U.S. Armed Forces will continue rising to the security demands of the future.

Appendix II

STRATEGIC VALUES

Strategic Match

Strategic match focuses on the degree to which an initiative supports or aligns with the enterprise or line of business (LOB) stated strategic goals. The scores range from zero (having no linkage to stated business strategy goals) to five (having a direct linkage). Enterprises should develop their own unique descriptions for gradations between these two extremes. A sample set follows.

0. The initiative has no direct or indirect relationship to the achievement of any stated enterprise, LOB, or departmental strategic goals.

1. The initiative has no direct or indirect relationship to the achievement of any stated enterprise, LOB, or departmental strategic goals, but will achieve greater operational efficiencies.

2. The initiative has no direct or indirect relationship to the achievement of any stated enterprise, LOB, or department strategic goals, but the initiative is a prerequisite to another initiative (or initiatives) that achieves a portion of an enterprise, LOB, or departmental goal.

3. The initiative has no direct or indirect relationship to the achievement of any stated enterprise, LOB, or departmental strategic goals, but the initiative is a prerequisite initiative (a necessary precursor) to another initiative (or initiatives) that does achieve an enterprise, LOB, or departmental strategic goal.

4. The initiative directly achieves a portion of a stated enterprise or LOB strategic goal.

5. The initiative directly achieves a stated enterprise or LOB strategic goal.

Competitive Advantage

To include competitive advantage as a strategic value, the enterprise must develop an assessment definition gradation that will accurately reflect the chosen strategy implementation. One company used the following criteria in support of its strategy of cost leadership.

0. The initiative does not support increased competitiveness of the enterprise or LOB concerning alternate products. It has little or no impact on the cost of sales. Alternatively, the initiative is for internal use only and does not directly improve the competitive position of the enterprise or LOB by increasing operating efficiency.

1. The initiative indirectly improves competitive positions of the enterprise or LOB by improving operating efficiencies. It has no impact on the effectiveness of the sales operation.

2. The initiative directly improves competitive position of the enterprise by improving operating efficiencies in a key strategic area. The initiative does not directly impact the sales force effectiveness in competing against alternate suppliers.

3. The initiative has some degree of impact on the ability of the sales force to compete with alternate suppliers. Or, it materially reduces the cost of sales so that the product is marginally more competitive.

4. The initiative will measurably improve the ability of the sales force to compete against alternate suppliers. Or, it materially reduces the cost of sales so that the product is moderately more competitive.

5. The initiative will measurably improve the ability of the sales force so that there is a high probability of materially impacting the enterprise or LOB competitive position concerning alternate suppliers. Or, the initiative will reduce the cost of sales in a key competitive market such that the enterprise and/or LOB will gain an increased market share.

Competitive Response

Competitive response measures the degree to which failure to do the system will cause competitive damage to the enterprise. For I/T initiatives, competitive response looks at the timely implementation of projects as a possible preemptive move to prevent the competition from gaining a foothold. The assessment of value ranges on the low side if postponing the project for a year won't affect competitive position. On the high side, postponement of the project will result in competitive disadvantage to the enterprise, loss of competitive opportunity, or curtailment of existing activities. Intermediate values reflect the more balanced potential. A financial services company, highly dependent upon I/T support for integrating new product offerings into its current product menu, developed the following competitive response descriptors.

0. The initiative can be postponed for at least twelve months without affecting competitive position; or existing approaches can produce substantially the same result and will not affect competitive position.

1. The postponement of this initiative does not affect competitive position, and minimal labor costs are expected to be incurred to produce substantially the same result.

2. The postponement of the initiative does not affect competitive position; however, labor costs may escalate to produce substantially the same result.

3. If the initiative is postponed, the enterprise remains capable of responding to the needed change without affecting its competitive position; lacking the initiative, the enterprise is not substantially hindered in its ability to respond rapidly and effectively to change in the competitive environment.

4. The postponement of the initiative may result in further competitive disadvantage to the enterprise, or in a loss of competitive opportunity, or existing successful activities in the enterprise may be curtailed because of the lack of this initiative.

5. The postponement of the initiative will result in further competitive disadvantage to the enterprise, or in a loss of competitive opportunity, or existing successful activities in the enterprise must be curtailed because of the lack of the proposed initiative.

Management Information for Critical Success Factors

Management Information for critical success factors is an assessment of an initiative's contribution to management's need for information concerning critical activities, for example, activities directly involved in the realization of the enterprise mission, as distinguished from support and accounting activities. A natural gas utility selling and delivering product to domestic households uses the following descriptors to assess its initiatives involving management information for critical success factors.

0. The initiative is unrelated to improving management information in support of defined critical success factors (CSFs) or related key activities of the enterprise. The information does not have an impact on decision-making.

1. The initiative will not affect CSFs or related key activities, but does provide some information that impacts decisions made by supervisors or managers.

2. The initiative improves the timeliness or quality of information used in one of the key activities or CSFs, but is not expected to impact decisions made by managers or vice presidents.

3. The initiative provides new information for a key activity or CSF that will impact decisions made by a manager.

4. The initiative provides significant new information for two or more key activities or CSFs that will impact decisions made by vice presidents in the future.

5. The initiative provides significant new information for two or more key activities or CSFs that will impact decisions currently made by vice presidents.

STAKEHOLDER VALUES

Stakeholder values flow from initiatives that contribute to the successful execution of overarching enterprise strategies that enhance broad stakeholder interests and represent directional or transformational change.

Service and Quality

While the service and quality strategies are unique to every enterprise, the following is a generic description ready for tailoring to a specific enterprise strategy:

0. The initiative is unrelated to the improvement of any key service or quality measurement. Postponement of a year has no competitive consequences.

1. The initiative is unrelated to the improvement of any key service or quality measurement, but it has a positive impact on minor customer interfaces. Postponement of a year will probably not affect competitive position.

2. The initiative is unrelated to the improvement of any current or proposed key service or quality measurement, but it has a positive impact on major customer interfaces that may improve customer image. Postponement of a year will not affect competitive position substantially.

3. The initiative indirectly relates to the improvement of a key service or quality measurement because it is essential to precursor activities as a building block and will improve customer image. Postponement might result in a slight competitive disadvantage.

4. The initiative is essential to improving key services or quality measurements in the future, and may cause some current improvement, and will immediately improve customer image. Postponement will result in some competitive disadvantage.

5. The initiative is essential to improving key services or quality measurements in the current period and is necessary to maintain customer image. Postponement will result in competitive disadvantage or loss of competitive opportunity.

Service and quality initiatives, as noted in Chapter 8, have a synergistic effect enterprisewide and require a long-term continuous commitment to improvement.

Environmental Quality

Although the environmental issues are unique to each enterprise, the following represents a set of illustrative descriptors that one may tailor to a specific enterprise, its products, and its operating environment:

0. The initiative is unrelated to any specific environmental impact (positive or negative). Postponement of a year has no competitive consequences.

1. The initiative is unrelated to any specific environmental impact (positive or negative), but it has a potential emotional (or real) impact on stakeholders. Postponement of a year will probably not affect competitive position.

2. The initiative relates indirectly to a specific environmental issue, and has a potential to create a positive image for the enterprise because of its perceived emotional (or real) impact. Postponement of a year will not affect competitive position substantially.

3. The initiative relates indirectly to a specific environmental issue and is a precursor to a key environmental initiative with a high emotional (or real) impact. Postponement might result in a slight competitive disadvantage.

4. The initiative is essential to improving corporate environmental quality in the future and may contribute some current improvement. It may be a future mandate because of its emotional (or real) impact. Postponement will result in some competitive disadvantage.

5. The initiative is essential to improving corporate environmental quality in this current period, or may be a mandate, or it will establish industry leadership. Postponement will result in competitive disadvantage or loss of competitive opportunity.

Agility Learning and Empowerment

Agility learning and empowerment can (and eventually will) change task-time allocations, necessitating business process redesign and/or job redesign and require different skills for the staff. Agile, flexible, learning organizations of the future build on the empowerment initiatives of today. The following illustrates a sample set of descriptors for agility learning and empowerment.

0. The initiative can be postponed for at least a year without affecting competitive position; or existing systems, procedures and core competencies can produce substantially the same result and will probably not affect competitive position.

1. The postponement of this initiative will probably not affect competitive position and minimal labor costs are expected to be incurred to produce substantially the same results.

2. The postponement of this initiative will probably not affect competitive position substantially; however labor costs will escalate to produce substantially the same results, exposing fragile but minor core competencies.

3. The postponement of the initiative results in the enterprise remaining capable of responding to needed change without affecting its competitive position, but costs will escalate. Lacking the agility and empowerment initiative, the enterprise becomes hindered in its ability to respond rapidly to a change in competitive environment, due to weakening minor or major core competencies.

4. Postponing the initiative may result in competitive disadvantage or in a loss of competitive opportunity. Existing successful activities in the enterprise may degrade due to a lack of agility and empowerment and loss of a major core competency.

5. Postponing the agility learning and empowerment initiative will result in competitive disadvantage to the enterprise or in a loss of competitive opportunity. A loss of two or more major core competencies forces the curtailment of existing successful activities.

Agility learning and empowerment focus on making both the employees and the business processes more flexible, intelligent, and more adaptable to change.

Cycle-Time

Cycle-time focuses on all elements in the process from establishing an innovative culture that stimulates new product ideas through their successful development, production, and delivery to the customer at a time that meets or establishes a new industry standard or best practice. A sample set of descriptors follow.

0. This initiative is unrelated to any time improvements in the successful development, production, or delivery of products or services by or to this enterprise and its customers, suppliers, or collaborative units. Postponement of a year has no competitive consequences.

1. This initiative is unrelated to any time improvements, per above, but does improve the competitive position of the enterprise by improving operating efficiencies that relate to competitive performance. Postponement of a year will probably not affect competitive position.

2. This initiative is unrelated to any time improvements, per above, but does improve operating efficiencies in a key strategic area. Postponement of a year will not affect competitive position substantially.

3. This initiative provides some degree of time improvements and moderately improves the competitive position of the enterprise. Postponement might result in a slight competitive disadvantage.

4. This initiative provides a moderate degree of time improvements and substantially improves the competitive position of the enterprise to a level of (time) responsiveness beyond most competitors. Postponement will result in some competitive disadvantage.

5. This initiative provides a high degree of time improvements and greatly improves the competitive position of the enterprise by providing a level of (time) responsiveness unmatched by competitors. Postponement will result in competitive disadvantage or loss of competitive opportunity.

Mass Customization

Mass customization (Chapter 5) requires the ability to more quickly produce an ever greater variety of products through customization. Niche markets and a flexible product line require business processes, organizational design, and information systems designed with heterogeneity in mind. Sample descriptors for mass customization follow.

0. This initiative is unrelated to any mass customization in the design, development, production, or delivery of products or services by or to this enterprise and its customers, suppliers, or collaborative unit. Postponement of a year has no competitive consequences.

1. This initiative is unrelated to any mass customization activities, per above, but does improve the competitive position of the enterprise by improving temporary development, production, or other operating efficiencies that relate to competitive performance. Postponement of a year will probably not affect competitive position.

2. This initiative is unrelated to any mass customization activities, per above, but does temporarily improve current development, production, or other operating efficiencies in a key strategic area. Postponement of a year will not affect competitive position substantially.

3. This initiative facilitates some degree of mass customization, per above, and moderately improves the competitive position of the enterprise. Postponement might result in a slight competitive disadvantage.

4. This initiative facilitates a moderate degree of mass customization, per above, and substantially improves the competitive position of the enterprise to a level of responsiveness beyond most competitors. Postponement will result in some competitive disadvantage.

5. This initiative facilitates a high degree of mass customization, per above, and greatly improves the competitive position of the enterprise by providing a level of customization unmatched by competitors. Postponement will result in competitive disadvantage or loss of competitive opportunity.

Strategic I/T Architecture

Strategic I/T Architecture evaluates the degree to which the initiative aligns with the overall I/T strategies. While each enterprise tailors its own scoring system, a starting point for evaluating the strategic I/T architecture component might look something like the following.

0. The initiative is unrelated to the I/T plan or blueprint. Postponement of a year has no competitive consequences.

1. The initiative is a part of the blueprint, but it has no defined priority. Postponement of a year will probably not affect competitive position.

2. The initiative is part of the blueprint and has a low financial payoff; it is not a prerequisite to other blueprint projects nor is there any linkage to other prerequisite projects. Postponement of a year will not affect competitive position substantially.

3. The initiative is an integral part of the blueprint and has medium financial payoff; it is not a prerequisite to other blueprint projects but loosely linked to other prerequisite projects. Postponement might result in a slight competitive disadvantage.

4. The initiative is an integral part of the blueprint and has a high financial payoff; it is not a prerequisite to other blueprint projects but is closely linked to other prerequisite projects. Postponement will result in some competitive disadvantage.

5. The initiative is an integral part of the blueprint and is one requiring early implementation; it is a prerequisite project to other blueprint projects. Postponement
   will result in competitive disadvantage or loss of competitive opportunity.

COMPETITIVE STRATEGY RISKS

Business Strategy Risk

Business strategy risk reflects the level of the success of the business strategy itself,
given the market dynamics, enterprise dynamics, and timing. One manufacturing organization uses the following descriptors to classify the business strategy risk.

0. The initiative reflects a strategy that is successful for the industry leaders. It is
   an industry standard practice and a necessary cost of doing business. No long-
   term external force (political realignment, regulatory group, demographic shift,
   etc.) will affect the initiative.

1. The initiative represents a level of change accepted as incremental improvement
   by suppliers and/or consumers. No long-term external force (political realignment, regulatory group, demographic shift, etc.) is likely to affect the initiative.

2. The initiative represents differentiation from industry leaders. Although initially
   disruptive, suppliers and/or consumers will recognize long-term benefit. No
   long-term external force (political realignment, regulatory group, demographic
   shift, etc.) is likely to nullify the long-term benefit of the initiative to the supplier and/or consumer or the short-term benefit to the enterprise.

3. The initiative represents medium risk. It requires moderate change in supplier
   and/or consumer relationships but relationships are strong. A well-defined product or market exists. A long-term external force (political realignment, regulatory group, demographic shift, etc.) is likely to nullify the long-term benefit of
   the initiative to the supplier and/or consumer, but not the short-term benefit to
   the enterprise, which may weaken the currently strong relationship.

4. The initiative requires moderate change in supplier and/or consumer relationships that are weak or relatively new. Moderately defined market, but new to the
   enterprise. A long-term external force (political realignment, regulatory group,
   demographic shift, etc.) may nullify any benefit of the initiative. Alternatively, a
   market may develop, but not sufficiently enough to sustain the initiative.

5. The initiative represents a high risk. It requires significant competitive strength
   to force change associated with supplier or customer relationships, supplier and
   distribution channels, ordering or inventory or pricing practices, business and industry practices. Or, there is no clearly defined emerging or existing market, or
   the existing market collapses due to a previously unrecognized long-term external force (political realignment, regulatory group, demographic shift, etc.). Or,
   this initiative may exacerbate long-term external force (political realignment,
   regulatory group, demographic shift, etc.) forcing withdrawal from market.

Business strategy risk focuses on the longer term risk surrounding competitive strategy and change in the market environment due to political realignments, demographic trends, or regulatory trends.

I/T Strategy Risk

I/T strategy risks reflect the level of potential impact on long-term I/T strategy as a whole, including architecture and platform (closing off future options), systems interdependencies (incompatible but similar systems in other business functions), business strategy (mergers, acquisitions and divestitures), business environment change (industry restructuring, deregulation, etc.), equilibrium, and critical skills. This dimension focuses on the volatility of the industry environment and the accommodations that the enterprise must make as a result of being forced by others or by its own initiatives. A utility company currently uses the following descriptors for assessing its I/T strategy risk.

0. Architecture and platform are open and accurately reflect long-term business strategy and enterprise form. No interdependencies or incompatibilities exist that would nullify I/T scenarios built to support the set of current business scenarios.

1. Known interdependencies and incompatibilities, but they affect only the less likely identified future scenarios. No new core competencies required.

2. Known interdependencies and incompatibilities, but they affect only the moderately likely identified future scenarios. Current core competencies can strengthen and cope with new requirements.

3. Known interdependencies and incompatibilities, but they affect only minor areas of the most likely identified future scenarios. Required core competencies are weak.

4. Known interdependencies and incompatibilities, affecting at least one major area of the most likely identified future scenario. Required core competencies are obtainable externally.

5. Implementation of architecture or platform or lack of core competencies will exclude significant future identified options. Existing systems and/or applications are incompatible; or investment not reflective of current business strategy. Alternatively, majority of interdependencies and incompatibilities are unknown. They will restrict future business and I/T options because strategy assumes no change in industry or enterprise structure.

I/T strategy risk focuses on the competitive strategy risk involved as a result of changing business structures, including alliances, joint ventures, and virtual corporations, and the necessity to support the enterprise as it adjusts to the new demands of the marketplace.

ORGANIZATIONAL STRATEGY RISKS AND UNCERTAINTIES

While competitive strategy risks are externally based and externally focused, organizational strategy risks and uncertainties have an internal enterprise focus. They in-

clude business organization risk, I/T definitional uncertainty, I/T technical and implementation risk, and I/T services delivery risk.

Business Organization Risk

Business organizational risk reflects the level of sophistication of the various business
organizational components involved.

For an I/T initiative, business organizational risk is an assessment of the degree
to which an I/T project depends on new or untested non-I/T corporate or line of business skills, management capabilities, or experience. For example, a business unit that
installs online terminals to interface to its customers runs the risk of lack of acceptance—upsetting (or further upsetting) the current degree of equilibrium between the
organizational units.

While an initiative may look attractive and the technical skills may be available,
an unacceptable level of risk may still be associated with the initiative if other required
skills are missing. This category also focuses on the extent to which the organization
is capable of carrying out the changes required by the initiative, that is, the user/busi-
ness requirements. This does not include the I/T technical organization, which is measured under the category of I/T infrastructure.

0. The business domain organization has a well-formulated plan for implementing
   the initiative. Management is in place and processes and procedures have documentation. Contingency plans exist for the initiative, there is an initiative champion, and the product or competitive value added is well defined for a well-
   understood market.

1 through 4. Values for 1 to 4 apply to situations requiring a blending of elements
   of preparedness with elements of risk. See the following checklist as a guide.

	Yes	No	Not Known
Well-formulated business domain plan	____	____	____
Business domain management in place	____	____	____
Contingency plans in place	____	____	____
Processes and procedures in place	____	____	____
Training for users planned	____	____	____
Management champion exists	____	____	____
Product is well-defined	____	____	____
Well-understood market need	____	____	____

For each "no" or "not known", .5 point may be added.

5. The business domain organization has no plan for implementing the proposed
   system. Management is uncertain about responsibility. Processes and procedures are undocumented. No contingency plan is in place. There is no defined
   champion for the initiative. The product or competitive value added is poorly defined. There is no well-understood market.

As organizations and business processes evolve, the actual existing skill levels may not match the level anticipated (or required). Business organization risk focuses on the shorter-term risks inherent in business process redesign and organizational restructuring.

I/T Definitional Uncertainty

Definitional uncertainty reflects the level of stability of the receiving environment. Essentially another measure of risk, this dimension relates an initiative's potential to reach objectives to the degree to which they can be specified. An example illustrating the gradations from 0 through 5 follow.

0. Owner/user has clearly defined requirements. They are firm and are approved. Specifications are firm and approved. Investigated area is straightforward. High probability of no changes.

1. Owner/user has moderately firm requirements defined. Specifications are moderately firm. No formal approvals. Investigated area is straightforward. Low probability of nonroutine changes.

2. Owner/user has moderately firm requirements defined. Specifications are moderately firm. Investigated area is straightforward. Reasonable probability of nonroutine changes.

3. Owner/user has somewhat firm requirements defined. Specifications are moderately firm. Investigated area is straightforward. Changes are almost certain almost immediately.

4. Owner-user does not have firm requirements. Specifications are not firm. Area is quite complex. Changes are almost certain, even during the project period.

5. Owner/user has unknown requirements. Specifications are unknown. Area may be quite complex. Changes may be ongoing, but the key here is unknown requirements.

I/T definitional uncertainty, along with the remaining I/T technical and implementation risk and I/T services delivery risk focus on implementation and delivery risks.

I/T Technical and Implementation Risk

Technical and implementation risk assesses an initiative's dependence on new or untried technologies, which may involve a single technology or a combination of new technical skill sets, hardware, or software tools. Technical and implementation risk reflects five risk components in any I/T project: (1) skills required, reflecting the critical skills level necessary versus available for management and staff; (2) hardware dependencies, reflecting the hardware necessary versus what is currently available and/or in use; (3) software dependencies (other than application software), assessing straightforward versus significant advances in state of the art; (4) application software, reflecting commercially available or currently existing versus new state of the art, even if done through subcontracting; and (5) application dependencies, reflecting the level of complexity of implementation, including the length of the project, new technologies, the accuracy of estimates, and the complexity of the implementation organization. An example of the gradations from 0 through 5 follows.

Scores From Below

A. Skills required are available in the technology domain.   _____
B. Dependency on specific hardware not now available.   _____
C. Dependency on software capabilities not now available.   _____
D. Dependency on application software development.   _____
E. Application Implementation dependencies.   _____

Total (A + B + C + D + E)/5 = Rating

A. Skills required

  0. No new skills for staff, management. Both have experience in projects of similar nature.
  1. Some new skills for staff, none for management.
  2. Some new skills required for staff and management.
  3. Some new skills required for staff, extensive for management.
  4. Extensive (new) skills required for staff, some for management.
  5. Extensive (new) skills required for staff and management.

B. Hardware dependencies

  0. Hardware is in use in similar application.
  1. Hardware is in use, but this is a different application.
  2. Hardware exists and has been tested, but not operationally.
  3. Hardware exists, but not used yet within organization.
  4. Some key features are not tested or implemented.
  5. Key requirements are not now available in I/T configuration.

C. Software dependencies (other than application software)

  0. Standard software, or straightforward or no programming required.
  1. Standard software is used, but complex programming is required.
  2. Some new interfaces between software are required, and complex programming may be required.
  3. Some new features are required in operating software, and some complex interfaces between software may be required.
  4. Features not now supported are needed, and moderate advance in local state of the art is required.
  5. Significant advance in state of the art is required.

D. Application software

  0. Programs exist with minimal modifications required.
  1. Programs are available commercially with minimal modifications, or programs available in-house with moderate modifications, or software will be developed in-house with minimal complexity.

2. Programs are available commercially with moderate modifications, or in-house programs are available but modifications are extensive, or software will be developed in-house with minimal design complexity but moderate programming complexity.
3. Software is available commercially but the complexity is high, or software will be developed in-house and the difficulty is moderate.
4. No package or current in-house software exists. Complex design and programming are required, with moderate difficulty.
5. No package or current in-house software exists. Complex design and programming are required, even if contracted outside.

E. Application Implementation Dependencies
   0. No new skills required. Small, simple, straightforward application, taking a short time to develop. Comparable applications exist in enterprise.
   1. Moderate size application. Comparable applications developed with little difficulty. Some skill development necessary. Estimates are straightforward.
   2. Advanced programming techniques required. Comparable applications in enterprise done with moderate difficulty. Moderate size of application and time length of application appears reasonable.
   3. Small state-of-the-art advances required. Comparable application exists within enterprise but done with difficulty. Some complex design and programming required. Size of application or length of time to implement is significant. Somewhat difficult to estimate.
   4. Moderate state-of-the-art advance required. Comparable application may exist, but outside the enterprise. Complex design and programming are required, with moderate difficulty. Moderately large organization and time span required to implement. Moderately difficult to estimate.
   5. Significant advance in state of the art is required. No comparable application exists. Complex design and programming are required. Large application, difficult to estimate, requiring large staff to implement.

I/T technical and implementation risk focuses on the short-term organizational risks evolving around existing skills, hardware and software dependencies, application software dependencies, and application implementation dependencies.

I/T Services Delivery Risk

The assessment of I/T infrastructure risk is essentially an environmental assessment, assessing the degree to which the entire I/T organization is both required to support the project (e.g., the degree of nonproject technical support investment necessary) and the degree to which it prepares to do so. An initiative that requires the support of several functional areas is inherently more complex and difficult to supervise, and it depends on factors that may not be under the control of the I/T project manager. An example gradation for I/T services delivery risk follows.

0. The initiative uses existing services and facilities. No investment in I/T prerequisite facilities (e.g., database management) required; no up-front costs not directly a part of the project itself anticipated.

1. This initiative requires a change in one element of the computer service delivery system. The associated up-front investment other than direct project costs is relatively small.

2. This initiative requires small changes in several elements of the computer service delivery system. Some up-front investment is necessary to accommodate this initiative. Some later investment for subsequent integration of this initiative into the mainstream of the I/T environment may be necessary.

3. This initiative requires moderate changes in several elements of the computer service delivery system. Some up-front investment is necessary to accommodate this initiative; some later investment for subsequent integration of this initiative into the mainstream of the I/T environment will be necessary.

4. This initiative requires moderate change in elements of computer service delivery, and in multiple areas. Moderate to high up-front investment in staff, software, hardware, and management is necessary to accommodate the initiative. This investment is not included in the direct project cost, but represents I/T facilities investment to create the needed environment for the initiative.

5. This initiative requires substantial change in elements of computer service delivery, and in multiple areas. Considerable up-front investment in staff, software, hardware, and management is necessary to accommodate the initiative. This investment is not included in the direct project cost, but represents I/T facilities investment to create the needed environment for the initiative.

I/T services delivery risk focus is on the short-term organizational risks for the computer service delivery.

Notes and Suggested Readings

Chapter 1

Notes

1. See "Welcome to the Revolution," *Fortune* 128, 15 (December 13, 1993), 66-78. All rights reserved by Fortune.

2. The American Management Association and, in particular, Management Centre Europe (the European Headquarters of the American Management Association International) periodically offer conferences that focus on global competition. Contact Management Centre Europe, rue Caroly 15, B-1040 Brussels (Belgium), telephone 32/2/516.19.11.

3. Burt Nanus, *Developing Visionary Leadership: Securing the Future*. "Visionary Leadership: Creating a Compelling Sense of Direction for Your Organization," p. 174. Copyright 1992 Jossey-Bass Inc., Publishers. Code 9273

4. See "The Search for the Organization of Tomorrow," *Fortune* 125, 20, May 18, 1992, 92-98. All rights reserved by Fortune.

5. See "Culture Shock at Home: Working for a Foreign Boss," *Business Week* 3192, December 17, 1990, 80-84 for an in-depth discussion of the topic.

6. Adapted from "The high price of social cohesion," *Financial Times* (London), February 28, 1994, p. 13, col. 1-8. Also monitor both the *Financial Times* (New York and London) and *The Wall Street Journal* (New York) for current information.

7. The figures were provided by a noted economist, but were not verified by the author.

8. Adapted from "Help promised for multimedia development," *Financial Times* (London), January 7, 1994, p.4, col. 1-2.

9. Reprinted by permission of *Harvard Business Review*. "The New Society of Organizations" by Peter F. Drucker, September-October 1992, 95-104. Copyright © 1992 by the President and Fellows of Harvard College; all rights reserved.

10. See, for example, *The Wall Street Journal* (New York) for current trends.

11. Reprinted by permission of *Harvard Business Review*. "Think Like the Customer: The Global Business Logic" by Rosabeth Moss Kanter, July-August 1992, 9-10. Copyright © 1992 by the President and Fellows of Harvard College; all rights reserved.

12. "Business in the 21st Century," *The Futurist* 26, 2 (March-April, 1992), 13-17. Information is reproduced with permission from THE FUTURIST, published by the World Future Society, 7910 Woodmont Avenue, Suite 450, Bethesda, Maryland 20814.

Suggested Readings

"Business in the 21st Century," *The Futurist* 26, 2, March-April 1992, 13-17.

The Economist Year Book: 1992 Edition (London: The Economist Books, Ltd., 1992).

BURT NANUS, *Visionary Leadership* (New York: Jossey-Bass, 1992).

OECD Economic Outlook 56. For information write to OECD, 2, rue Andre'-Pascal, 75775 PARIS CEDEX 16, France (Paris: Organization for Economic Co-operation and Development, 1994).

KENICHI OHMAE, "The Global Logic of Strategic Alliances," *Harvard Business Review*, March-April 1989, 143-154; and *The Borderless World: Power and Strategy in the Interlinked Economy* (New York: Harper Business, 1990).

MICHAEL E. PORTER, *Competitive Advantage: Creating and Sustaining Superior Performance* (New York: The Free Press, 1985); and The Competitive Advantage of Nations (New York: The Free Press, 1990).

ROBERT B. REICH, "Who Is Them?," *Harvard Business Review*, March-April 1991, 77-88.

JERRY M. ROSENBURG, *The New Europe: An A to Z Compendium on the European Community* (Washington D.C.: The Bureau of Nation Affairs, 1991).

PAUL J. H. SCHOEMAKER, "How to Link Strategic Vision to Core Capabilities," *Sloan Management Review* 34, 1, Fall 1992, 67-81.

Chapter 2

Notes

1. Adapted from "Home is where the office is," *Financial Times* (New York), August 16, 1993, p. 8 col. 1-5. *The Financial Times* (New York and London), *The Wall Street Journal* (New York), and *The Economist* periodically publish supplements on this and other related business and technology topics.

2. Adapted from "At home in the office," *Financial Times* (New York), March 9, 1994, p. 9 col. 1-4. *The Financial Times* (New York and London), *The Wall Street Journal* (New York), and *The Economist* periodically publish supplements on this and other related business and technology topics.

3. "The Eternal Coffee Break," *The Economist* 323, 7749 (March 7, 1992), 71.

4. Adapted from "Sit where you like," *Financial Times* (New York), September 30, 1992, p. 10 col. 2-7.

5. Adapted from "BT managers could work from home," *Financial Times* (New York), September 1, 1992, p.6, col. 1-4. Also, see "The Office Is A Terrible Place to Work," *Business Week* 3352, December 27, 1993, 46, for an in-depth discussion of this topic.

6. "The Virtual Organization," *The Futurist* 28, 2, March-April 1994, 9-14. Information is reproduced with permission from THE FUTURIST, published by the World Future Society, 7910 Woodmont Avenue, Suite 450, Bethesda, Maryland 20814.

7. Adapted from "Carriers take the IT route," *Financial Times* (New York), September 3, 1992, p. 10, col. 7.

8. *Computerworld* is an excellent resource for material of this type. For example, see "Utility to Save $1.6M with Pen Computing Plan," *Computerworld* 26, 21, May 25, 1992, 35. Copyright 1992 by Computerworld, Inc., Framingham, MA 01701.

9. See "Big Brother, Pinned to Your Chest," *Business Week* 3279, August 17, 1992, 38, for an in-depth discussion of this topic.

10. "The Delight of Digital Maps," *The Economist* 323, 7751, March 21, 1992, 69-70. Also see "Intelligent Sidewalks," *The Futurist* 26, 5, September-October 1992, 6. Information is reproduced with permission from THE FUTURIST, published by the World Future Society, 7910 Woodmont Avenue, Suite 450, Bethesda, Maryland 20814.

11. See "Where Am I? Ask A Satellite," *Business Week* 3270, October 26, 1992, 116, for an in-depth discussion of this topic.

12. See "But are they useful?" *The Wall Street Journal* (New York), November 16, 1992, sec. R, p. 14 col. 1-6. Paraphrased information reprinted by permission of The Wall Street Journal, © 1992 Dow Jones & Company, Inc. All Rights Reserved Worldwide.

13. "Tomorrow's Phones: Portable, Pocket-sized, Powerful," *John Naisbitt's Trend Letter* 11, 19, October 1, 1992, 1-3. Published by The Global Network, Washington D.C.

14. Advertisement, *The Economist* 324, 7783, October 31, 1992, 57-60.

15. See "In the Friendly Skies: Coffee, Tea—and Microprocessors," *Business Week* 3290, October 26, 1992, 90, for an in-depth discussion of this topic.

16. See "More Than a Cash Machine: ATMs for the Jet Set," *Business Week* 3290, October 26, 1992, 115, for an in-depth discussion of this topic.

17. See "American firms send office work abroad to use cheaper labor," *The Wall Street Journal* (New York), August 14, 1991, sec. A, p. 1, col. 6. Paraphrased information reprinted by permission of The Wall Street Journal, © 1991 Dow Jones & Company, Inc. All Rights Reserved Worldwide.

18. Shifting operations abroad to help cut costs is a particularly popular practice in the airline industry.

19. *Computerworld* is an excellent resource for material of this type. For example, see "Electronic Meetings: No More ZZZ's," *Computerworld* 26, 37, September 14, 1992, 109. Copyright 1992 by Computerworld, Inc., Framingham, MA 01701.

20. See note 12 in this chapter.

21. See "Not-nearby doctor helps agile robot perform surgery," *The Wall Street Journal* (New York), March 4, 1994, sec. B, p. 7, col. 4-5. Paraphrased information reprinted by permission of The Wall Street Journal, © 1994 Dow Jones & Company, Inc. All Rights Reserved Worldwide.

22. Adapted from "Don't shoot the messenger," *Financial Times* (New York), September 24, 1992, p. 9, col. 1-6.

23. See "Rolm Delivers Voice Mail to the Deaf," *Business Week* 3245, December 23, 1991, 84f, for an in-depth discussion of this topic.

24. *Computerworld* is an excellent resource for material of this type. For example, see "Feds Seek EDI Contracting Solution," *Computerworld* 26, 37, September 14, 1992, 109. Copyright 1992 by Computerworld, Inc., Framingham, MA 01701.

25. *Computerworld* is an excellent resource for material of this type. For example, see "EDI Still Takes Time," *Computerworld* 26, 40, October 5, 1992, 75-80. Copyright 1992 by Computerworld, Inc., Framingham, MA 01701.

26. Adapted from "Making tracks in the freight industry," *Financial Times* (New York), November 5, 1992, p. 11, col. 6-7.

27. Adapted from "E-mail moves away from mainframes," *Financial Times* (New York), October 13, 1992, p. III, col. 1-8.

28. Adapted from "Acquiring new tricks," *Financial Times* (New York), September 8, 1992, p. 15, col. 2-5.

29. *Computerworld* is an excellent resource for material of this type. For example, see "Catch a Ride on the Fax Wave," *Computerworld* 25, 14, April 8, 1991, 53. Copyright 1991 by Computerworld, Inc., Framingham, MA 01701.

30. See "Extra! Extra! Hot Off The Faxes!," *Business Week* 3245, December 23, 1991, 84e, for an in-depth discussion of this topic.

31. *Computerworld* is an excellent resource for material of this type. For example, see "Imaging Cures Hospital's Paper Woes," *Computerworld* 26, 26, June 29, 1992, 74. Copyright 1992 by Computerworld, Inc., Framingham, MA 01701.

32. *Computerworld* is an excellent resource for material of this type. For example, see "No Image Problem—Sales Set to Take Off," *Computerworld* 25, 51, December 23, 1991-January 2, 1992, 46. Copyright 1992 by Computerworld, Inc., Framingham, MA 01701.

33. Adapted from "Worth watching: satellites to guide ambulance service," *Financial Times* (New York), May 13, 1994, p. 14, col. 6-7, and note 21 in this chapter.

Suggested Readings

WILLIAM H. DAVIDOW and MICHAEL S. MALONE, The Virtual Corporation: Structuring and Revitalizing the Corporation for the 21st Century (New York: HarperCollins: 1992).

ROBERT JOHANSEN, Groupware: Computer Support for Business Teams (New York: The Free Press, 1988).

PRAMODE K. VERMA (editor), ISDN Systems: Architecture, Technology and Applications (Englewood Cliffs NJ: Prentice-Hall, Inc., 1990).

ROBERT H. WATERMAN, JR., Adhocracy: The Power to Change (New York: W. W. Norton & Co., 1992).

Chapter 3

Notes

1. "Ye Olde Computerised Networke," *The Economist* 321, 7734, November 23, 1991, 66.

2. "Information Empowerment: Power to the People Through Automation," Critical Technology Report C-4-1, Chantico Publishing Co., Inc., 1991. For information about this publication, contact The Information Management Forum, 4380 Georgetown Square, Suite 1002, Atlanta, Ga., 30338.

3. Many publications on collaborative technologies focus on the technology issues to the detriment of the quality relationships necessary to make the use of technology a success. See Chapter 8, where this topic is discussed at length.

4. See "Consumers in the Information Age," *The Futurist* 27, 1, January-February 1993, 15-19. Information is reproduced with permission from THE FUTURIST, published by the World Future Society, 7910 Woodmont Avenue, Suite 450, Bethesda, Maryland 20814.

5. Adapted from "From feudalism to federalism," *Financial Times* (New York), October 19, 1992, p. 14, col. 1-7.

6. Adapted from "Whither the IT department?" *Financial Times* (New York), September 17, 1992, p. 12, col. 7-8.

7. Adapted from "Making 'fast tracks' more empowering," *Financial Times* (New York), July 10, 1992, p. 24, col. 1-7.

8. See "Software Even A CFO Could Love," *Business Week* 3291, November 2, 1992, 132-135, for an in-depth discussion of this topic. *Computerworld* is an excellent resource for material of this type. For example, see "AI makes mark in corporate world," *Computerworld* 26, 20, May 18, 1992, 87-92. Copyright 1992 by Computerworld, Inc., Framingham, MA 01701.

9. "White-collar Computers," *The Economist* 324, 7770, August 1, 1992, 57-58. Also see "Smart Programs Go To Work", *Business Week* 3255, March 2, 1992, 97-105, for an in-depth discussion of this topic.

10. Frito-Lay is one of the legendary leaders in the use of I/T to further competitive advantage, along with American Airlines, USAA, and American Hospital Supply (now Baxter).

11. See "Where Neural Networks Are Already At Work," *Business Week* 3291, November 2, 1992, 136-137, for an in-depth discussion of this topic.

12. See "Chaos Hits Wall Street—The Theory, That Is," *Business Week* 3291, November 2, 1992, 138-140, for an in-depth discussion of this topic.

13. See "Software That Can Dethrone *Computer Tyranny*," *Business Week* 3260, April 6, 1992, 90-91, for an in-depth discussion of this topic.

14. *Computerworld* is an excellent resource for material of this type. For example, see "IDC White Paper: Executive Information Systems," insert in *Computerworld* 26, 42, October 19, 1992. Copyright 1992 by Computerworld, Inc., Framingham, MA 01701.

15. *Computerworld* is an excellent resource for material of this type. For example, see "IDC White Paper: Sales Force Automation," insert in *Computerworld* 26, 50, December 7, 1992; and "The Hardest Sell," *Computerworld* 27, 38, September 20, 1993, 125-127. Copyright 1992 by Computerworld, Inc., Framingham, MA 01701.

16. *Computerworld* is an excellent resource for material of this type. For example, see "Two Ready for the Next Generation," *Computerworld* 26, 23, June 8,1992, 77. Copyright 1992 by Computerworld, Inc., Framingham, MA 01701.

17. Adapted from "Waging war against the paper chase," *Financial Times* (New York), October 29, 1992, p. 9, col, 5-7.

18. Reprinted by permission of *Harvard Business Review*. "Information Partnerships—Shared Data, Shared Scale" by Benn R. Konsynski and F. Warren McFarlan, September-October 1990, 114-120. Copyright © 1990 by the President and Fellows of Harvard College; all rights reserved.

19. "Information Empowerment: Power to the People Through Automation," Critical Technology Report C-4-1, 32-33, Chantico Publishing Co., 1991. For information about this publication, contact The Information Management Forum, 4380 Georgetown Square, Suite 1002, Atlanta, Ga., 30338.

Suggested Readings

THOMAS H. DAVENPORT, MICHAEL HAMMER, and TAUNO J. METSISTO, "How Executives Can Shape Their Company's Information Systems", *Harvard Business Review*, March-April 1989, 130-142.

MAX DEPREE, *Leadership Jazz* (New York: Currency Doubleday, 1992).

RICHARD TANNER PASCALE, *Managing on the Edge: How the Smartest Companies Use Conflict to Stay Ahead* (New York NY: Simon & Schuster, 1991).

JAMES H. SNIDER and TERRA ZIPORYN, *Future Shop: How New Technologies Will Change the Way We Shop and What We Buy* (New York: St. Martin's Press, 1992).

Chapter 4
Notes

1. "When it Pays to Think Big: The Extended Enterprise," *IBM Directions*, June 1988, 3-5.

2. *Computerworld* is an excellent resource for material of this type. For example, see "MRP II: Out with the old . . .," *Computerworld* 26, 23, June 8, 1992, 73-77. Copyright 1992 by Computerworld, Inc., Framingham, MA 01701.

3. Reprinted by permission of *Harvard Business Review.* "How Networks Reshape Organizations—For Results" by Ram Charan, September-October 1991, 104-115. Copyright © 1990 by the President and Fellows of Harvard College; all rights reserved.

4. See "Messaging: The Global Payoff," *Business Week* 3210, April 20, 1992, 48-49, for an in-depth discussion of this topic.

5. Reprinted by permission of *Harvard Business Review.* "Strategic Intent" by G. Hamel and C. K. Prahalad, May-June 1989, 63-76. Copyright © 1990 by the President and Fellows of Harvard College; all rights reserved.

6. Information reprinted from "Beyond Business Process Redesign: Redefining Baxter's Business Network" by James E. Short and N. Venkatraman, *Sloan Management Review* (34, 1, Fall 1992), pp. 7-21, by permission of publisher. Copyright 1992 by the Sloan Management Review Association. All rights reserved. *Computerworld* is also an excellent resource for material of this type. For example, see "EDI cures ills of hospital supply procurement," *Computerworld* 28, 20, May 16, 1994, 63-66. Copyright 1994 by Computerworld, Inc., Framingham, MA 01701. Additionally, see "Hospitals Attack a Crippler: Paper," *Business Week* 3359, February 21, 1994, 104-106, for an in-depth discussion of this topic.

7. See "Meet The New Revolutionaries," *Fortune* 125, 8, February 24, 1992, 94-101. All rights reserved by Fortune.

8. *Computerworld* is an excellent resource for material of this type. For example, see "Internet Tapped for Global Virtual Publishing Enterprise," *Computerworld* 26, 12, March 23, 1992, 69. Copyright 1992 by Computerworld, Inc., Framingham, MA 01701.

9. Adapted from "High-tech future for food retailers," *Financial Times* (New York), May 18, 1992, p. 3, col. 5-8, and "Tying the Knot," *The Economist* 331, 7863, May 14, 1994, 73.

10. "I Want It Now," *The Economist* 323, 7763, June 13, 1992, 78-83.

11. See "3M Run Scared? Forget About It," *Business Week* 3231, September 16, 1991, 59-62, for an in-depth discussion of this topic.

12. See "Big Rail Is Finally Rounding the Bend," *Business Week* 3239, November 11, 1991, 128-129; and "Electronic Teamwork that Makes Shipping Overseas Smooth Sailing," *Business Week* 3327, July 12, 1993, 140, for in-depth discussions of these topics. *Computerworld* is also an excellent resource for material of this type. For example, see "Railroads reroute," *Computerworld* 27, 30, July 26, 1993, 57. Copyright 1993 by Computerworld, Inc., Framingham, MA 01701.

13. Adapted from "A freer flow of goods," *Financial Times* (New York), March 12, 1993, p. 9, col. 3-6; and "Airfreight: Just in Time," *Lufthansa Bordbuch*, September/October 1992, 72-74. *Computerworld* is also an excellent resource for material of this type. For example, see Also see "Logistics providers enable *virtual* firms," *Computerworld* 28, 29, July 18, 1994, 28. Copyright 1994 by Computerworld, Inc., Framingham, MA 01701.

14. See "Northwest sues American alleging predatory pricing," *The Wall Street Journal* (New York), June 15, 1992, sec. A, p. 5, col. 5-6. Paraphrased information reprinted by permission of The Wall Street Journal, © 1992 Dow Jones & Company, Inc. All Rights Reserved Worldwide.

15. See "Oh, What a Lovely Fare War," *Business Week* 3272, June 19, 1992, 37, for an in-depth discussion of this topic.

16. See "The Airlines Are Killing Each Other Again," *Business Week* 3269, June 8, 1992, 32, for an in-depth discussion of this topic.

17. See notes 14 and 16 in this chapter.

18. *Computerworld* is an excellent resource for material of this type. For example, see "Inside Lines: Fly the Crowded Skies," *Computerworld* 26, 23 (June 8, 1992), 110. Copyright 1992 by Computerworld, Inc., Framingham, MA 01701.

19. See note 14 in this chapter.

20. See "Why Air Fares Are Sure To Go Up," *Fortune* 125, 20, May 18, 1992, 12. All rights reserved by Fortune.

21. Information under copyright 1992, USA Today, "USA snapshots: Calling for cheap airfares," *USA Today*, June 6-8, 1992, sec. B, p. 10, col. 1. Information reprinted with permission.

22. See note 15 in this chapter.

23. Adapted from "A revolution on the runway," *Financial Times* (New York), May 7, 1992, p. 14, col. 4-8.

24. "Banking on a Big Bird," *The Economist* 326, 7793, January 9, 1993, 5. Also see "Betting On The 21st Century Jet," *Fortune* 125, 16, April 20, 1992, 102-117. All rights reserved by Fortune.

25. "Now for the Really Big One," *The Economist* 327, 7854, March 12, 1994, 73-74. See "Reinventing Boeing," *Business Week* 3307, March 1, 1993, 60-63, for an in-depth discussion of this topic. Also see "Can Boeing Reinvent Itself?," *Fortune* 127, 5, March 8, 1993, 66-73. All rights reserved by Fortune.

26. Adapted from "Seducer eyes a double prize," *Financial Times* (New York), January 6, 1993, p. 8, col. 1-3.

27. F. Warren McFarlan, "The External Opportunity," *IBM Directions*, June 1988, 7-9.

28. Alvin Toffler, *Power Shift: Knowledge, Wealth and Violence at the Edge of the 21st Century* (New York: Bantam Books, 1990), 178-179, 186.

29. SELECTED EXCERPT from THE VIRTUAL CORPORATION by WILLIAM H. DAVIDOW and MICHAEL S. MALONE. Copyright © 1992 by William H. Davidow and Michael S. Malone. Reprinted by permission of HaperCollins Publishers, Inc.

30. Peter F. Drucker, *Managing for the Future: The 1990s and Beyond* (New York: Truman Talley Books/Dutton, 1992), 10-11.

Suggested Readings

RUSSELL L. ACKOFF, *Creating the Corporate Future: Plan or Be Planned For* (New York: John Wiley & Sons, 1981).

JOEL ARTHUR BARKER, *Future Edge: Discovering the New Paradigms of Success* (New York: William Morrow and Company, 1992).

CHRISTOPHER A. BARTLETT and SUMANTRA GHOSHAL, *Managing Across Borders: The Transnational Solution* (Boston: Harvard Business School Press, 1989).

MARK F. BLAXILL and THOMAS M. HOUT, "The Fallacy of the Overhead Quick Fix," *Harvard Business Review* 69, 4, July-August, 1991, 93-101.

WILLIAM H. DAVIDOW and MICHAEL S. MALONE, *The Virtual Corporation: Structuring and Revitalizing the Corporation for the 21st Century* (New York: HarperCollins, 1992).

STAN M. DAVIS, *Future Perfect* (New York: Addison-Wesley Publishing Company, 1987).

STAN DAVIS and BILL DAVIDSON, *2020 Vision: Transform Your Business Today to Succeed in Tomorrow's Economy* (New York: Simon & Schuster, 1991).

PETER F. DRUCKER, *Managing for the Future: The 1990s and Beyond* (New York: Truman Talley Books/Dutton, 1992).

R. EDWARD FREEMAN and DANIEL R. GILBERT, JR., *Corporate Strategy and The Search for Ethics* (Englewood Cliffs NJ: Prentice Hall, 1988).

CHARLES HANDY, *The Age of Unreason* (Boston: Harvard Business School Press, 1989); and "Balancing Corporate Power: A New Federalist Paper," *Harvard Business Review* 70, 6, November-December 1992, 59-72.

JOHN P. KOTTER and JAMES L. HESKETT, *Corporate Culture and Performance* (New York: The Free Press, 1992).

BURT NANUS, *Visionary Leadership: Creating a Compelling Sense of Direction for Your Organization* (San Francisco: Jossey-Bass, 1992).

KENICHI OHMAE, "The Global Logic of Strategic Alliances," *Harvard Business Review* 67, 2 March-April 1989, 143-154; and *The Borderless World: Power and Strategy in the Interlinked Economy* (New York: HarperCollins, 1990).

RICHARD TANNER PASCALE, *Managing on The Edge: How the Smartest Companies Use Conflict to Stay Ahead* (New York: Simon & Schuster, 1991).

PETER SCHWARTZ, *The Art of the Long View: Planning for the Future in An Uncertain World* (New York: Doubleday Currency, 1991).

JAMES A. SENN, "Electronic Data Interchange," *Journal of Information Systems Management* 9, 1, Winter 1992, 45-53.

EILEEN C. SHAPIRO, *How Corporate Truths Become Competitive Traps: How to Keep the Things that "everyone knows are true" from Becoming Roadblocks to Success* (New York: John Wiley & Sons, 1991).

ALVIN TOFFLER, *Power Shift: Knowledge, Wealth and Violence at the Edge of the 21st Century* (New York: Bantam Books, 1990).

ROBERT H. WATERMAN, JR., *Adhocracy: The Power to Change* (New York: W.W. Norton & Co., 1990).

Chapter 5
Notes

1. See "Japan's New Personalized Production," *Fortune* 122, 9, October 22, 1990, 132. All rights reserved by Fortune.

2. *The Structure of Scientific Revolutions*, by Thomas S. Kuhn (New York: New American Library, 1986), provides another view of the transformation process.

3. From *Future Edge* by Joel Arthur Barker, © William Morrow and Company, 1992, 192-193. By permission of William Morrow and Company, Inc.

4. Stanley M. Davis, *Future Perfect* (Reading MA: Addison-Wesley, 1987), 157. © by Stanley M. Davis. Reprinted by permission of Addison-Wesley Publishing Co., Inc.

5. David Garwood and Michael Bane, *Shifting Paradigms: Reshaping the Future of Industry* (Atlanta GA: Dogwood Publishing Co., 1990), 80-82.

6. Stanley M. Davis, *Future Perfect*, 169.

7. From B. Joseph Pine II, *Mass Customization: The New Frontier in Business Competition* (Boston Mass: Harvard Business School Press, 1993), p. 171-212.

8. See "American Express: Service that Sells," *Fortune* 120, 11, November 20, 1989, 80-94. All rights reserved by Fortune.

9. See "Computers by Mail: A Megabyte Business Boom," *Business Week* 3265, May 11, 1992, 93-96, for an in-depth discussion of this topic.

10. "Trail Blazer," *The Economist* 320, 7725, September 21, 1991, 82.

11. "AT&T to sell phone numbers to last a lifetime," *The Wall Street Journal* (New York), April 29, 1992, sec. B, p. 1, col. 6. Paraphrased information reprinted by permission of The Wall Street Journal, © 1992 Dow Jones & Company, Inc. All Rights Reserved Worldwide.

12. See "MCI's Winning Pitch," *Business Week* 3206, March 23, 1992, 36, for an in-depth discussion of this topic.

13. See "Congratulations On Your Big Earnings Increase!," *Business Week* 3279, August 17, 1992, 58, for an in-depth discussion of this topic. *Computerworld* is also an excellent resource for material of this type. For example, see "American Greetings puts cards on PCs," *Computerworld* 28, 29, July 18, 1994, 40, and "Hallmark offers do-it-yourself cards," *Computerworld* 27, 24, June 14, 1993, 52. Copyright 1993, 1994 by Computerworld, Inc., Framingham, MA 01701.

14. Mohsen Attaran, "Flexible Manufacturing Systems," *Journal of Information Systems Management* 9, 2, Spring 1992, 44-47. Notes reprinted from "Information Systems Management" (New York: Auerbach Publications), © 1992 Warren, Gorham & Lamont. Used with permission.

15. See "Brace for Japan's Hot New Strategy," *Fortune* 126, 6, September 21, 1992, 62-74. All rights reserved by Fortune.

16. See "Moving Past the Assembly Line," *Business Week* Special Edition: Reinventing America, 1992, 177-180, for an in-depth discussion of this topic. Computerworld is also an excellent resource for material of this type. For example, see "Can America win the wardrobe wars?," *Computerworld* 28, 4, January 24, 1994, 67-72. Copyright 1994 by Computerworld, Inc., Framingham, MA 01701.

17. "Agile Manufacturing," *The Futurist* 28, 2, March-April 1994, 11. Information is reproduced with permission from THE FUTURIST, published by the World Future Society, 7910 Woodmont Avenue, Suite 450, Bethesda, Maryland 20814.

18. Adapted from "Avoidable problems," *Financial Times* (New York), September 24, 1992, p. 23, col. 1-8.

19. Adapted from "New name for an old idea," *Financial Times* (New York), September 24, 1992, p. 24, col. 1-3.

20. See "The New Realism In Office Systems," *Business Week* 3270, June 15, 1992, 128-133, for an in-depth discussion of this topic.

21. Reprinted from "Interactive Marketing: Exploiting the Age of Addressability" by Robert C. Blattberg and John Deighton, *Sloan Management Review*, (33, 1, Fall 1991), 5-14, by permission of publisher. Copyright 1991 by the Sloan Management Review Association. All rights reserved.

22. See "What the Leaders of Tomorrow See," *Fortune* 120, 1, July 3, 1989, 48-62. All rights reserved by Fortune.

23. Adapted from "Ain't no mountain high enough," *Financial Times* (New York), January 11, 1993, p. 8, col. 1-5.

24. "Ambitious," *The Economist* 323, 7755, April 18, 1992, 74-75; and "When they think they're investing, the sale's easier," *Forbes* 152, 11, November 8, 1993, 342-343.

25. Adapted from "The Prospect of a Swatch Car," *Financial Times* (New York), May 7, 1992, Special Survey: Switzerland, VI.

26. Stanley M. Davis, *Future Perfect*, p. 140-190.

27. *Computerworld* is an excellent resource for material of this type. For example, see "Financial services firms move in parallel," *Computerworld* 26, 41, October 12, 1992, 28. Copyright 1992 by Computerworld, Inc., Framingham, MA 01701.

28. Stanley M. Davis, *Future Perfect*, p. 152.

Suggested Readings

ALFRED D. CHANDLER, *The Visible Hand: The Managerial Revolution in American Business* (Cambridge: The Belknap Press of Harvard University Press, 1977).

PETER F. DRUCKER, *Managing for the Future: The 1990's and Beyond* (New York: Truman Talley Books/Dutton, 1992).

JOSEPH B. FULLER, JAMES O'CONOR, and RICHARD RAWLINSON, "Tailored Logistics: The Next Advantage," *Harvard Business Review* 71, 3, May-June 1993, 87-98.

B. JOSEPH PINE II, BART VICTOR, and ANDREW C. BOYNTON, "Making Mass Customization Work," *Harvard Business* Review 71, 5, September-October 1993, 108-119.

B. JOSEPH PINE II, *Mass Customization: The New Frontier in Business Competition* (Boston: Harvard Business School Press, 1993).

Chapter 6
Notes

1. See the extensive list of books that follow as Suggested Readings.

2. Stephen L. Yearout, "The International Quality Study Reveals Which Countries Lead the Race for Total Quality," *The Journal of European Business* 3, 4, March/April 1992, 27-30.

3. Stephen L. Yearout, "The International Quality Study Reveals Which Countries Lead the Race for Total Quality," p.30.

4. See "10,000 New EC Rules," *Business Week* 3282, September 7, 1992, 48-50, for an in-depth discussion of this topic.

5. "Standards Become Trade Issue," *The Futurist* 26, 5, September-October, 1992, 51-52 Information is reproduced with permission from THE FUTURIST, published by the World Future Society, 7910 Woodmont Avenue, Suite 450, Bethesda, Maryland 20814.

6. See "International Standardization," *Fortune* 126, 10, November 2, 1992, 133-142. All rights reserved by Fortune.

7. Adapted from "Uruguay deal boosts world standardization," Financial Times (New York), February 4, 1994, p.5, col. 6-8. Also see "Want EC Business? You Have Two Choices," *Business Week* 3288, October 19, 1992, 58-59, for an in-depth discussion of this topic.

8. Michael J. Timbers, "ISO 9000 and Europe's Attempts to Mandate Quality," *The Journal of European Business* 3, 4, March/April 1992, 14-25.

9. See "Making Quality More Than A Fad," *Fortune* 125, 10, May 18, 1992, 12-13. All rights reserved by Fortune.

10. See the extensive list of books that follow as Suggested Readings.

11. See "Quality does count, GAO finds in study of firms program," *The Wall Street Journal* (New York), June 4, 1991, sec. A, p. 6, col. 2. Paraphrased information reprinted by permission of The Wall Street Journal, © 1991 Dow Jones & Company, Inc. All Rights Reserved Worldwide.

12. See "Going for the Glory," *Business Week* Quality 1991, October 25, 1991, 60-61, for an in-depth discussion of this topic.

13. See "Mexico's Total Commitment to Quality," *Fortune* 126, 10, November 2, 1992, 87-103. All rights reserved by Fortune.

14. See note 11 in this chapter.

15. See "Value Marketing," *Business Week* 3239, November 11, 1991, 132-140, for an in-depth discussion of this topic.

16. This is one of the more popular legends that make up the Saturn story.

17. "Japan, At Your Service," *The Economist* 319, 7677, October 20, 1990, 83-84.

18. "Help Lines Abound—Aid May Be Just a Call Away," *John Naisbitt's Trend Letter* (Washington D.C.), October 29, 1992, 4-5. Published by The Global Network, Washington D.C.

19. Valarie A. Zeithaml, *Defining and Relating Cost, Perceived Quality, and Perceived Value*, (Cambridge Mass: Marketing Science Institute, 1987), Report 87-101; and Valarie A. Zeithaml, Leonard L. Berry, and A. Parasuraman, *Communication and Control Process in the Delivery of Service Quality*, (Cambridge Mass: Marketing Science Institute, 1987).

20. Adapted from "U.S. comes top in services output," *Financial Times* (New York), October 13, 1992, p. 6, col. 5-8.

21. See note 14 in this chapter.

22. See "Real Thoughts on the Virtual Corporation," *Business Week* 3307, March 1, 1993, 7, for an in-depth discussion of this topic.

Suggested Readings

RAFAEL AGUAYO, *Dr. Deming: The American Who Taught the Japanese About Quality* (New York: Carol Publishing, 1990).

KARL ALBRECHT, *At America's Service: How Corporations Can Revolutionize The Way They Treat Customers* (Homewood Ill.: Dow Jones-Irwin, 1988).

KARL ALBRECHT and RON ZEMKE, *Service America! Doing Business In the New Economy* (Homewood Ill.: Dow Jones-Irwin, 1985).

LEONARD L. BERRY, DAVID R. BENNETT, and CARTER W. BROWN, *Service Quality: A Profit Strategy for Financial Institutions* (Homewood Ill.: Dow Jones-Irwin, 1989).

KEN BLANCHARD and SHELDON BOWLES, *Raving Fans: A Revolutionary Approach to Customer Service* (New York: William Morrow and Company, 1993).

DAVID W. COTTLE, *Client-Centered Service: How to Keep Them Coming Back for More* (New York: John Wiley & Sons, 1990).

PHILLIP B. CROSBY, Quality Is Free: The Art of Making Quality Certain (New York: New American Library, 1979); Quality Without Tears: The Art of Hassle-free Management (New York: New American Library, 1984); The Eternally Successful Organization: The Art of Corporate Wellness (New York: McGraw-Hill Book Company, 1988); and Let's Talk

Quality: 96 Questions You Always Wanted to Ask Phil Crosby (New York: McGraw-Hill, 1989).

JOHN A. CZEPIEL, MICHAEL R. SOLOMON, and CAROL F. SURPRENANT, *The Service Encounter: Managing Employee/Customer Interaction in Service Businesses* (Lexington Mass: Lexington Books, 1985).

GEORGE DIXON and JULIE SWILER, *Total Quality Handbook: The Executive Guide to the American Way of Doing Business* (Minneapolis: Lakewood Books, 1990).

JOSEPH B. FULLER, JAMES O'CONOR, and RICHARD RAWLINSON, "Tailored Logistics: The Next Advantage," *Harvard Business Review* 71, 3, May-June 1993, 87-98.

DAVID A. GARVIN, *Managing Quality: The Strategic and Competitive Edge* (New York: The Free Press, 1988).

ROBERT E. GRASING and MICHAEL H. HESSICK, *Achieving Quality in Financial Service Organizations: How to Identify and Satisfy Customer Expectations* (New York: Quorum Books, 1988).

JOHN GUSAPARI, *I Know It When I See It: A Modern Fable About Quality* (New York: American Management Association, 1985); and *The Customer Connection: Quality for the Rest of Us* (New York: American Management Association, 1988).

BRUCE R. GUILE and JAMES BRIAN QUINN, editors, *Technology in Services: Policies for Growth, Trade, and Employment* (Washington D.C.: National Academy Press, 1988).

JAMES L. HESKETT, *Managing in the Service Economy* (Boston: Harvard Business School Press, 1986).

V. DANIEL HUNT, *Quality in America: How to Implement A Competitive Quality Program* (Homewood Ill.: Business One Irwin, 1992).

J. M. JURAN, *Juran on Planning for Quality: An Executive Handbook* (New York: The Free Press, 1988); *Juran on Leadership for Quality: An Executive Handbook* (New York: The Free Press, 1989); and J*uran on Quality by Design: The New Steps for Planning Quality into Goods and Services* (New York: The Free Press, 1992).

PETER K. MILLS, *Managing Service Industries: Organizational Practices in a Postindustrial Economy* (Cambridge Mass: Ballinger Publishing Company, 1986).

PRICE PRITCHETT, *Service Excellence* (Dallas: Pritchett and Associates, Inc., 1989).

HAL F. ROSENBLUTH and DIANE McFERRIN PETERS, *The Customer Comes Second and Other Secrets of Exceptional Service* (New York: William Morrow and Company, 1992).

LINDA SILVERMAN GOLDZIMER with GREGORY L. BECKMANN, *"I'm First" Your Customer's Message To You* (New York: Rawson Associates, 1989).

RON ZEMKE and CHIP R. BELL, *Service Wisdom: Creating and Maintaining the Customer Service Edge* (Minneapolis: Lakewood Books, 1989).

RON ZEMKE with DICK SCHAFF, *The Service Edge: 101 Companies That Profit From Customer Care* (New York: New American Library, 1989).

VALARIE A. ZEITHAML, A. PARASURAMAN and LEONARD L. BERRY, *Delivering Quality Service: Balancing Customer Perceptions and Expectations* (New York: The Free Press, 1990).

Chapter 7
Notes

1. See "Management's New Gurus," *Business Week* 3281, August 31, 1992, 44-52, for an in-depth discussion of this topic.

2. See "Thriving In A Lame Economy," *Fortune* 126, 7, October 5, 1992, 44-54. All rights reserved by Fortune.

3. Stephen L. Yearout, "The International Quality Study Reveals Which Countries Lead the Race for Total Quality," *The Journal of European Business* 3, 4, March/April 1992, 27-30.

4. J. Richard Hackman and Greg R. Oldham, *Work Redesign* (Reading Mass: Addison-Wesley, 1980). © 1980 by Addison-Wesley Publishing Co., Inc. Reprinted by permission of the publisher.

5. Reprinted with the permission of Simon & Schuster, Inc. from the Macmillan College text *End-User Information Systems: Perspectives for Managers and Information Systems Professionals* by Elizabeth A. Regan and Bridget N. O'Connor. Copyright © 1994 by Macmillan College Publishing Company Inc.

6. See "The Dumbest Marketing Ploy," *Fortune* 126, 7, October 5, 1992, 88-94. All rights reserved by Fortune.

7. Adapted from "Consumers slow to put their hands in pockets," *Financial Times* (New York), August 9, 1994, p 15, col. 4-7. Also see "Your Digital Future," *Business Week* 3282, September 7, 1992, 56-64, for an in-depth discussion of this topic.

8. Adapted from "Nuts and bolts of giving power to the people," *Financial Times* (New York), September 21, 1992, p. 14, col. 5-6.

9. See Richard Tanner Pascale, *Managing on The Edge:* (New York: Simon & Schuster, 1990). © 1990 by Richard Pascale. Reference by Permission of Simon & Schuster, Inc.

10. See "Putting A Damper On That Old Team Spirit," *Business Week* 3264, May 4, 1992, 60, for an in-depth discussion of this topic.

11. See "The Lessons GM Could Learn For Its Supplier Shakeup," *Business Week* 3281, August 31, 1992, 29, for an in-depth discussion of this topic.

12. "IBM says buyouts will trim 40,000 jobs," *The New York Times* (New York) September 30, 1992, sec. C, p. 1, col. 3-5. Copyright © 1992 by The New York Times Company. Reprinted by permission.

13. Adapted from "GM plans mutual aid scheme with suppliers," *Financial Times* (New York), November 16, 1992, p 17, col. 2-6.

14. Adapted from "A new car industry set to rise in the east," *Financial Times* (New York), September 24, 1992, p. 15, col. 2-6.

15. Adapted from "Old Rover learns new Japanese tricks," *Financial Times* (New York), Weekend October 10/October 11, 1992, sec. II, p. I, col. 1-7.

16. "Unipartners," *The Economist* 323, 7754, April 11, 1992, 67.

17. See "How to Steal the Best Ideas Around," *Fortune* 126, 8, October 19, 1992, 102-106. All rights reserved by Fortune.

18. See note 2 in this chapter.

19. "The Lean Enterprise Benchmarking Project," *Andersen Consulting*, 2 Arundel Street, London WC2R 3LT (January 15, 1993).

20. Adapted from "British fail to make the grade," *Financial Times* (New York), January 8, 1993, p. 8, col. 1-5.

21. Reprinted by permission of *Harvard Business Review*. An excerpt from "Technology Fusion and The New R&D" by Fumio Kodama, July-August, 1992, 70-78. Copyright © 1992 by the President and Fellows of Harvard College; all rights reserved.

22. "Management Brief: Food for Thought," *The Economist* 324, 7774, August 29, 1992, 64-66.

23. Pieter M. Ribbers, "Strategic Vision, globalization, and the Office Systems," *Proceedings of the Eleventh Annual Office Systems Research Conference*, March 6-8, 1992, San Antonio, Texas, p.5.

Suggested Readings

"Assignment: Re-engineering," *Computerworld* 26, 45, November 9, 1992, 71-73.

WILLIAM H. DAVIDOW and MICHAEL S. MALONE, *The Virtual Corporation: Structuring and Revitalizing the Corporation for the 21st Century* (New York: HarperCollins, 1992).

DANIEL MORRIS and JOEL BRANDON, *Re-engineering Your Business* (New York: McGraw-Hill, 1993).

ELIZABETH REGAN and BRIDGET O'CONNOR, *End-User Information Systems: Perspectives for Managers and Information Systems Professionals* (New York: Macmillan Publishing Company, 1994).

PIETER M. RIBBERS, "Strategic Vision, globalization, and the Office Systems," *Proceedings of the Eleventh Annual Office Systems Research Conference*, March 6-8, 1992, San Antonio, Texas.

RICHARD J. SCHONBERGER, *Building A Chain of Customers: Linking Business Functions to Create the World Class Company* (New York: The Free Press, 1990).

Chapter 8
Notes

1. John P. Kotter and James L. Heskett, *Corporate Culture and Performance* (New York: The Free Press, 1992), 11-12; 145-49. Adapted with the permission of The Free Press, a Division of Simon & Schuster Inc. from CORPORATE CULTURE AND PERFORMANCE by John P. Kotter and James L. Heskett. Copyright © 1992 by Kotter Associates, Inc. and James L. Heskett.

2. "The Team Dream," *The Economist* 324, 7725, September 5, 1992, 69.

3. Reprinted by permission of *Harvard Business Review*. An excerpt from "The New Society of Organizations" by Peter F. Drucker, September-October 1992, 96. Copyright © 1992 by the President and Fellows of Harvard College; all rights reserved.

4. Raymond Miles and Charles Snow, "Causes of Failure in Network Organizations," *California Management Review*, 34, 4, Summer 1992, 53-72. Copyright © 1992 by The Regents of the University of California. Reprinted from the "California Management Review," Vol. 34, No. 4. By permission of The Regents.

5. See "Balking U.S. automotive suppliers talk of giving up business with car maker," *The Wall Street Journal* (New York), November 2, 1992, sec. A, p. 6, col. 1-2. Paraphrased Information reprinted by permission of The Wall Street Journal, © 1992 Dow Jones & Company, Inc. All Rights Reserved Worldwide.

6. See "Hanging in there," *The Wall Street Journal* (New York), December 1, 1992, sec. A, p. 1, col. 6. Paraphrased Information reprinted by permission of The Wall Street Journal, © 1992 Dow Jones & Company, Inc. All Rights Reserved Worldwide.

7. "Why Networks May Fail," *The Economist* 325, 7780, October 10, 1992, 83.

8. Adapted from "A meeting of minds," *Financial Times* (New York), October 25, 1993, p. 9, col. 1-4; and "The risk of sleeping with the enemy," July 16, 1993, p. 9, col. 5-7.

9. See "Motorola, Toshiba near pact to develop chip for high-definition television sets," The

Wall Street Journal (New York), December 11, 1990, sec. B, p. 1, col. 3. Paraphrased Information reprinted by permission of *The Wall Street Journal,* © 1990 Dow Jones & Company, Inc. All Rights Reserved Worldwide.

10. See "GM plans to sell cellular phones via car dealers," *The Wall Street Journal* (New York), January 11, 1990, sec. B, p. 1, col. 3. Paraphrased Information reprinted by permission of The Wall Street Journal, © 1991 Dow Jones & Company, Inc. All Rights Reserved Worldwide.

11. Adapted from "Shaken Europe's pillar of strength," *Financial Times* (New York), September 28, 1992, p. 14, col. 3-7.

12. Other typical alliances and joint ventures include Motorola and Protexa (a cellular-phone joint venture) and Exabyte with Sony and Kubota.

13. "The West Is Won," *The Economist* 320, 7720, August 17, 1991, 70-72.

14. See both "The Age of Consolidation" *Business Week* 3235, October 14, 1991, 86-94 and "Do Bank Mergers Make Sense?" *Fortune* 124, 3, August 12, 1991, 70-71 for additional in-depth discussions regarding mergers and acquisitions.

15. See the follow-on article to the preceding note, "When Mergers Make Sense," *Fortune* 125, 13, June 29, 1992, 85.

16. Peter F. Drucker, *Managing for the Future: the 1990s and Beyond,* (New York: Truman Talley Books/Dutton, 1992), 276-277.

17. "Squeezing Out Profits," *The Economist* 324, 7776, September 12, 1992, 90.

18. Adapted from "Shaken to the core," *Financial Times* (New York), August 18, 1992, p.12, col. 3-7.

19. Adapted from "When head office goes native," *Financial Times* (New York), December 2, 1992, p. 11, col. 1-7.

20. "The Company that likes to obsolete itself," *Forbes* 152, 6, September 13, 1993, 139-144. For additional background material, also see "Keeping Motorola on a Roll," Fortune 129, 8, April 18, 1994, 67-78. Finally, see "Motorola: Training for the Millennium," *Business Week* 3364, March 28, 1994, 158-163, for an in-depth discussion of the topic.

21. "A Knowledge-Based Canada: The New National Dream," *Information Technology Association of Canada*, January, 1993.

22. Adapted from "All change for a successful corporate revolution," *Financial Times* (New York), October 23, 1992, p. 17, col. 1-7.

Suggested Readings

CHRISTOPHER A. BARTLETT and SUMANTRA GHOSHAL, *Managing Across Borders: The Transnational Solution,* (Boston: Harvard Business School Press, 1989).

WILLIAM H. DAVIDOW and MICHAEL S. MALONE, *The Virtual Corporation: Structuring and Revitalizing the Corporation for the 21st Century* (New York: HarperCollins, 1992).

R. DONALD GAMACHE and ROBERT L. KUHN, *The Creativity Infusion: How Managers Can Start and Sustain Creativity and Innovation* (New York: Harper & Row, 1989).

CHARLES HANDY, "Balancing Corporate Power: A New Federalist Paper", *Harvard Business Review* 70, 6, November-December 1992, 59-72.

PAUL HERSEY and KEN BLANCHARD, *Management of Organizational Behavior: Utilizing Human Resources* (Englewood Cliffs NJ: Prentice-Hall, Inc., 1992).

LARRY HIRSCHORN and THOMAS GILMORE, "The New Boundaries of the "Boundary-less" Company," *Harvard Business Review* 70, 3, May-June 1992, 104-115.

RALPH H. KILMANN, INES KILMANN and associates, *Making Organizations Competitive: Enhancing Networks and Relationships Across Traditional Boundaries*, (San Francisco: Jossey-Bass, 1991).

RAY MARSHALL and MARC TUCKER, *Thinking For A Living: Education and the Wealth of Nations* (New York: BasicBooks, 1992).

DANIEL MORRIS and JOEL BRANDON, *Re-engineering Your Business* (New York: McGraw-Hill, 1993).

BURT NANUS, *Visionary Leadership: Creating A Compelling Sense of Direction For Your Organization* (San Francisco: Jossey-Bass, 1992).

KENICHI OHMAE, *The Borderless World: Power and Strategy in the Interlinked Economy* (New York: Harper Business, 1990).

MICHAEL E. PORTER, editor, *Competition in Global Industries* (Boston: Harvard Business School Press, 1986).

PETER M. SENGE, *The Fifth Discipline: The Art and Practice of the Learning Organization* (New York: Doubleday, 1990).

EILEEN C. SHAPIRO, *How Corporate Truths Become Competitive Traps: How to keep the things that everyone knows are true from becoming roadblocks to success* (New York: John Wiley & Sons, 1991).

BENJAMIN B. TREGOE, JOHN W. ZIMMERMAN, RONALD A. SMITH, and PETER M. TOBIA, *Vision in Action: Putting a Winning Strategy to Work* (New York: Simon and Schuster, 1989).

Chapter 9
Notes

1. Adapted from "Firm foundations," *Financial Times* (New York), December 29, 1992, p. 7, col. 1-7.

2. "Looking back ... and ahead," *John Naisbitt's Trend Letter* (Washington DC), October 15, 1992, p. 3-5. Published by The Global Network, Washington D.C.

3. See "The Challenge of Corporate Leadership in a Changing Europe," *Business Week* 3392, January 25, 1993, 97-100, for an in-depth discussion of the topic.

4. Information reprinted from "How Can Organizations Learn Faster? The Challenge of Entering the Green Room" by Edgar H. Schein, *Sloan Management Review* (34, 2, Winter 1993), pp. 85-92, by permission of publisher. Copyright 1993 by the Sloan Management Review Association. All rights reserved.

5. Peter M. Senge, *The Fifth Discipline: The Art & Practice of the Learning Organization,* (New York: Doubleday, 1990).

6. Information reprinted from "Organizational Learning—The Key to Management Innovation" by Ray Stata, *Sloan Management Review* (30, 3, Spring 1989), pp. 63-74, by permission of publisher. Copyright 1989 by the Sloan Management Review Association. All rights reserved.

7. "When technology heightens office tensions," *The Wall Street Journal* (New York), October 5, 1992, sec. A, p. 12, col. 3-6. Paraphrased information reprinted by permission of The Wall Street Journal, © 1992 Dow Jones & Company, Inc. All Rights Reserved Worldwide.

8. *Computerworld* is an excellent resource for material of this type. For example, see "Get Out There And Innovate!," *Computerworld* 26, 25, June 22, 1992, 139. Copyright 1992 by Computerworld, Inc., Framingham, MA 01701.

9. "Work-school apprenticeships," *John Naisbitt's Trend Letter* (Washington D.C.), February 4, 1993, p. 1-3. Published by The Global Network, Washington D.C.

10. Adapted from "German workers go back to school to get ahead," *Financial Times* (New York), September 25, 1992, p. 11, col. 1-7.

11. Adapted from "The classroom moves closer to the workforce," *Financial Times* (New York), September 29, 1992, p. 21, col. 1-3.

12. *Computerworld* is an excellent resource for material of this type. For example, see "Honoring thy Messenger, Japan-style," *Computerworld* 26, 15, April 13, 1992, 87-89. Copyright 1992 by Computerworld, Inc., Framingham, MA 01701.

13. Rotational assignments and working on cross-functional teams, although accepted in Japan and Europe, still remain the exception in many of the largest U.S. companies. See William G. Ouchi, Theory Z: How American Business Can Meet the Japanese Challenge (pp. 32;58), © 1981 by Addison -Wesley Publishing Co. , Inc. Reprinted by permission of the publisher.

14. See "How Sony Keeps The Magic Going," *Fortune* 125, 8, February 24, 1992, 76-84. All rights reserved by Fortune.

15. *Computerworld* is an excellent resource for material of this type. For example, see "The Information Integrator," *Computerworld* 26, 36, September 7, 1992, 91-92. Copyright 1992 by Computerworld, Inc., Framingham, MA 01701.

16. Paul R. Hessinger, "I/T Paradigms for the 1990s," Critical Technology Report No. C-5-1, Chantico Publishing Co., 1991. For information about this publication, contact The Information Management Forum, 4380 Georgetown Square, Suite 1002, Atlanta, Ga., 30338.

17. Adapted from "Survival of the best qualified," *Financial Times* (New York), February 10, 1993, p. 10, col. 6-7; and April 25, 1994, p. 10, col. 4-7.

18. *Computerworld* is an excellent resource for material of this type. For example, see "Don't Let IS Become Your CEO's Ball and Chain," *Computerworld* 27, 7, February 15, 1993, 27. Copyright 1993 by Computerworld, Inc., Framingham, MA 01701.

19. Hugh W. Ryan, "Can IS Avoid Marginalization?," *Journal of Information Systems Management* 8, 3, Summer 1991, 57-59. Notes reprinted from "Information Systems Management" (New York: Auerbach Publications), © 1991 Warren, Gorham & Lamont. Used with permission.

20. Information reprinted from "The Withering Away of the IS Organization" by John Dearden, *Sloan Management Review*, (28, 4, Summer 1987), pp. 87-91, by permission of publisher. Copyright 1993 by the Sloan Management Review Association. All rights reserved.

21. *Computerworld* is an excellent resource for material of this type. For example, see "Deere's Faraway IS Solution," *Computerworld* 27, 7, February 15, 1993, 76. Copyright 1993 by Computerworld, Inc., Framingham, MA 01701.

22. Peter F. Drucker, *The Post-Capitalist Society* (New York: HarperCollins, 1993).

23. See "Libraries shift from books to computers," *The Wall Street Journal* (New York), February 8, 1993, sec. B, p. 4, col. 3-5. Paraphrased information reprinted by permission of The Wall Street Journal, © 1993 Dow Jones & Company, Inc. All Rights Reserved Worldwide.

24. SELECTED EXCERPTS from POST-CAPITALIST SOCIETY by PETER F. DRUCKER. Copyright © 1993 by Peter F. Drucker. Reprinted by permission of HarperCollins Publishers, Inc.

Suggested Reading

THOMAS H. DAVENPORT, MICHAEL HAMMER, and TAUNO J. METSISTO, "How Executives Can Shape Their Company's Information Systems," *Harvard Business Review*, March-April 1989, 130-142.

"Developing an IT Education Plan," *I/S Analyzer* 30, 9, September, 1992.

STEPHAN H. HAECKEL and RICHARD L. NOLAN, "Managing By Wire," *Harvard Business Review*, September-October 1993, 122-132.

Chapter 10

Notes

1. See "The Modular Corporation," *Fortune* 127, 3, February 8,1993, 106-115. All rights reserved by Fortune.

2. Selected excerpt from *The Virtual Corporation* by William H. Davidow and Michael S. Malone. Copyright © 1992 by William H. Davidow and Michael S. Malone. Reprinted by permission of HarperCollins Publishers, Inc.

3. See "The Virtual Enterprise," *Business Week* 3304, February 8, 1993, 98-103, for an in-depth discussion of this topic.

4. "The Global Firm:R.I.P.," *The Economist* 326, 7797, February 6, 1993, 69.

5. From *Shifting Gears: Thriving in the New Economy* by Nuala Beck. Copyright © 1992 by Nuala Beck. Published by HarperCollins Publishers Ltd.

6. Technology scanning has played an important role in the success of Southern California Edison (see Appendix I).

7. See "Borden's breakup with Meiji milk shows how a Japanese partnership can curdle," *The Wall Street Journal* (New York), February 21, 1991, sec. B, p. 1, col. 1-3 for additional examples. Paraphrased Information reprinted by permission of The Wall Street Journal, © 1990 Dow Jones & Company, Inc. All Rights Reserved Worldwide.

8. Regan, Elizabeth A.; Jalowski, Edward; Walker-Johnson, Yvonne; and Slade, S. Alan, "Managing Technological Change: Bringing Productivity Gains to the Bottom Line," *Proceedings of the Tenth Annual Office Systems Research Conference*, March 1-3, 1991, pages 19-41; and a telephone conversation with E. Regan on 3/13/91.

9. For further information about the IBM/Washington University Joint Study of Enterprise-wide Information Management, including availability of case studies, working papers, or software, contact *Key Strategies and Solutions Inc.*, 402 North Casey Key Road, Osprey FL 34229 or send a FAX to 813-966-1567. Along with the working papers, two books have been published. *Information Economics* (Englewood Cliffs NJ: Prentice-Hall, 1988) is available in bookstores or through IBM Mechanicsburg, #S365-0001. *Information Strategy and Economics* (Englewood Cliffs NJ: Prentice-Hall, 1989) is also available in bookstores and through IBM Mechanicsburg, #S365-0002.

10. Research is currently being conducted on Key Business Processes by Bob Blanchard, Consultant, Raleigh NC; Andy Boynton, Professor, Darden School of Business, University of Virginia; Gerry Jacobs, Consultant, Raleigh NC; and Bart Victor, Professor, School of Business, University of North Carolina–Chapel Hill.

11. "Information Technology Strategy: Drivers in the 1990's," a presentation at Palisades, NY, in April 1991 by Bruce J. Rogow, Gartner Group, Stamford, CT.

12. All too often, systems fail for lack of proper consideration of learning curves related to new technology combined with the requirement to change corporate culture.

13. *Computerworld* is an excellent resource for material of this type. For example, see "Bend me, Shape me," *Computerworld* 25, 1, December 24,1990/January 1, 1991, 14. Copyright 1991 by Computerworld, Inc., Framingham, MA 01701.

14. "Why Not Farm Out Your Computing," *Fortune* 124, 12, September 23, 1991, 103-112. All rights reserved by Fortune.

15. Global office systems impact corporate and local culture, as well as technology. See Chapter 2 Notes for related material, along with the following publications, including *Computerworld*, the *Financial Times* (New York and London), *The Wall Street Journal* (New York), and *The Economist*. They periodically publish supplements on similarly-related business and technology topics.

16. *Computerworld* is a good source for periodic updates on the subject.

17. *Computerworld* is an excellent resource for material of this type. For example, see "U.S. companies find outsourcing a sensible way to go international," *Computerworld* 26, 15, April 13, 1992, 79. Copyright 1992 by Computerworld, Inc., Framingham, MA 01701.

18. Many of the leading consulting groups have newsletters on technology developments and practices, and are a good source of state-of-the-art thinking in such areas as client/server applications, migration strategies, etc.

19. Letter from Wm. C. Harenburg, Consultant, Triadigm International, Los Angeles, Ca. to M. Parker, dated March 18, 1993 regarding adding value to Client/Server applications.

20. See note 18 in this chapter.

21. *Computerworld* is an excellent resource for material of this type. For example, see "Smooth client/server takeoff at United," *Computerworld* 26, 19, May 11, 1992, 68. Copyright 1992 by Computerworld, Inc., Framingham, MA 01701.

22. See "Putting PCs Where Mainframes Used to Reign," *Business Week* 3263, April 27, 1992, 106, for an in-depth discussion of this topic.

23. *Computerworld* is an excellent resource for material of this type. For example, see "The New Centralization," *Computerworld* 26, 17, April 27, 1992, 85-88. Copyright 1992 by Computerworld, Inc., Framingham, MA 01701.

24. Information reprinted from "Systems Delivery: Evolving New Strategies" by John F. Rockart and J. Debra Hofman, *Sloan Management Review*, (33, 4, Summer 1992), pp. 21-31, by permission of publisher. Copyright 1992 by the Sloan Management Review Association. All rights reserved.

25. *Computerworld* is a good source for periodic updates on the subject.

Suggested Reading

"A Job for Life: A Survey of Management Education," *The Economist* 320, 7696, March 2, 1991, 26 pages appearing as a supplement between pages 52 and 53.

R. J. BENSON and M. M. PARKER, "ENTERPRISE-WIDE INFORMATION MANAGE-MENT: An Introduction to the Concepts," IBM LASC Report G320-2768, 1985.

CHARLES HANDY, *The Age of Unreason* (Boston: Harvard Business School Press, 1990).

JANET J. PALMER, "The Effect of Culture Upon Office Systems Offshore," *Proceedings of the Tenth Annual Office Systems Research Conference*, March 1-3, 1991, pages 54-61.

WALTER B. WRISTON, "Technology and Sovereignty," *Foreign Affairs* 67, 2, Winter 1988/89, 63-75.

Chapter 11

Notes

1. Cafeteria scenario developed in conversations between the author and R. J. Benson, Washington University, and James A. Senn, Georgia State University. Marilyn M. Parker and James A. Senn, "Strategic Transformation and Business Value: The I/T Connection," *Canadian Information Processing/Informatique Canadienne*, May/June 1992, 13-16.

2. *Computerworld* is an excellent resource for material of this type. For example, see "New Year: It's High Time for an IS Makeover," *Computerworld* 26, 1, January 6, 1992, 55. Copyright 1992 by Computerworld, Inc., Framingham, MA 01701.

3. See "Why the Fed May Redefine the Money Supply," *Business Week* 3323, June 14, 1993, 22, for an in-depth discussion of this topic.

4. See "A Sweeping Prescription for Corporate Myopia," *Business Week* 3273, July 6, 1992, 36-37, for an in-depth discussion of this topic.

5. "The Best Companies: Scrambling to the top," *The Economist* 320, 7723, September 17, 1991, 21-24.

6. See "America's Best Wealth Creators," *Fortune* 128, 16, December 27, 1993, 64-76, for more information. All rights reserved by Fortune.

7. From *Shifting Gears: Thriving in the New Economy* by Nuala Beck. Copyright © 1992 by Nuala Beck. Published by HarperCollins Publishers Ltd. Knowledge ratio, 127; Return on Knowledge Assets, 141: Peak-to-Growth ratio, 149; Patent-to-Stock-Price ratio, 152; Research-to-Development ratio, 153-4; Research and Development-to-Patent ratio, 153-4; Technology Spending ratio, 155; Credit Access ratio, 157; Credit Electricity index, 157; Insider Funding ratio, 157; Global Penetration ratio, 158; Revenue Per Voting Share ratio, 160.

8. See "A New Tool for Managing Costs," *Fortune* 127, 12, June 14, 1993, 124-129. All rights reserved by Fortune. Also see *Computerworld* for periodic updates on this subject.

Suggested Readings

MICHAEL T. JACOBS, *Short-Term America: The Causes and Cures of our Business Myopia* (Boston: Harvard Business School Press, 1991).

JOHN KOTTER and JAMES HESKETT, *Corporate Culture and Performance* (New York: The Free Press, 1992).

CYNTHIA A. MONTGOMERY and MICHAEL E. PORTER, editors, *Strategy: Seeking and Securing Competitive Advantage* (Boston: A Harvard Business Review Book, 1991). (This is a collection of relevant of HBR articles.)

DANIEL MORRIS and JOEL BRANDON, *Re-engineering Your Business* (New York: McGraw-Hill, Inc., 1993).

MICHAEL E. PORTER, *Competitive Advantage: Creating and Sustaining Superior Performance* (New York: The Free Press, 1985).

DAVID R. VINCENT, *The Information-Based Corporation: Stakeholder Economics and the Technology Investment* (Homewood Ill.: Dow Jones-Irwin, 1990).

The following publications discuss the topic of business value at length.

BELA GOLD, "Charting A Course to Superior Technology Evaluation," *Sloan Management Review* 30, 1, Fall 1988, 19-27.

MARILYN M. PARKER, ROBERT J. BENSON, and H. E. TRAINOR, *Information Economics: Linking Business Performance to Information Technology*, (Englewood Cliffs NJ: Prentice-Hall, 1988).

MARILYN. M. PARKER, H. EDGAR TRAINOR, and ROBERT J. BENSON, *Information Strategy and Economics: Linking Information Systems Strategy to Business Performance,* (Englewood Cliffs NJ: Prentice-Hall, 1989).

JAMES A. SENN, "The Business Value of Information Technology," Executive Brief, Society for Information Management, Chicago, Ill., Summer 1991.

JOHN K. SHANK and VIJAY GOVINDARAJAN, "Making Strategy Explicit in Cost Analysis: A Case Study," *Sloan Management Review* 29, 3, Spring 1988, 19-29.

PETER B. B. TURNEY and BRUNE ANDERSON, "Accounting for Continuous Improvement," *Sloan Management Review* 30, 2, Winter 1989, 37-47.

Chapter 12

Notes

1. Peter Schwartz, *The Art of the Long View: Planning for the Future in an Uncertain World* (New York: Doubleday, 1991). Permission by DOUBLEDAY, a division of Bantam Doubleday Dell Publishing Group, Inc.

2. For help in building an initial set of scenarios or modifying an already existing set, the following sources might be helpful: *The Economist Year Book: (current year) Edition* (London: The Economist Books, Ltd.). Also recommended is the *OECD Economic Outlook (current edition)*. For information write to OECD, 2, rue Andre'-Pascal, 75775 PARIS CEDEX 16, France (Paris: Organization for Economic Co-operation and Development, 1994). *The Futurist* provides a futures view of society and business, and is published by the World Future Society, 7910 Woodmont Avenue, Suite 450, Bethesda, Maryland 20814.

   Two books that might assist in developing a "scenario mindset" include *Crystal Globe: The Haves and Have-Nots of the New World Order*, by Marvin Cetron and Owen Davies (New York: St. Martin's Press, 1991), and *The Art of the Long View*, by Peter Schwartz, (New York: Doubleday Currency, 1991).

3. "When Gray Is Golden," *The Futurist* 26, 4, July-August, 1992, 16-20. Information is reproduced with permission from THE FUTURIST, published by the World Future Society, 7910 Woodmont Avenue, Suite 450, Bethesda, Maryland 20814.

4. "Wall Street Courts the Small Investor," *The Economist* 323, 7762, June 6, 1992, 85-86.

5. See "Los Angeles," *The Wall Street Journal* (New York), Centennial Edition, December 31, 1990, sec. A, p.15, col. 1-2. Paraphrased Information reprinted by permission of The Wall Street Journal, © 1990 Dow Jones & Company, Inc. All Rights Reserved Worldwide.

6. "Can LA Still Make It," *The Economist* 324, 7717, July 27, 1991, 59-60.

7. See "Latin America's Newest Capital City: Miami," *Business Week* 3233, September 30, 1991, 120-122, for an in-depth discussion of this topic.

8. "A Power for Good, A Power for Ill," *The Economist* 320, 7722, August 31, 1991, Special Survey 3-30.

9. "Whose World Is It, Anyway?," *The Economist* 323, 7761, May 30, 1992, Special Survey 1-24.

10. "A Power for Good, A Power for Ill," *The Economist* 320, 7722, August 31, 1991, Special Survey 3-30.

11. See "Conservation Power," *Business Week* 3231, September 16, 1991, 86-92, for an in-depth discussion of this topic.

12. Source material and suggestions for this section, including "Planning for Uncertainty," were contributed by Southern California Edison Company (Rosemead, CA).

13. *Computerworld* is an excellent resource for material of this type. For example, see "Tool lets managers 'play out' scenarios," *Computerworld* 28, 18, May 2, 1994, 42. Copyright 1994 by Computerworld, Inc., Framingham, MA 01701.

Suggested Readings

CHRISTOPHER A. BARTLETT and SUMANTRA GHOSHAL, *Managing Across Borders* (Boston: Harvard Business School Press, 1989).

MARVIN CETRON and OWEN DAVIES, *American Renaissance* (New York: St. Martin's Press, 1989).

STAN M. DAVIS, *Future Perfect* (Reading Mass: Addison-Wesley, 1987).

STAN DAVIS and BILL DAVIDSON, *2020 Vision* (New York: Simon & Schuster, 1991).

PETER F. DRUCKER, *Managing for the Future* (New York: Truman Talley Books/Dutton, 1992).

R. SCOTT FOSLER and others, *Demographic Change and the American Future* (Pittsburgh: University of Pittsburgh Press, 1990).

AL GORE, *Earth In the Balance: Ecology and the Human Spirit*, (Boston: Houghton Mifflin, 1992).

GARY HAMEL and C. K. PRAHALAD, *Competing for the Future* (Boston: Harvard Business School Press, 1994).

AUSTIN H. KIPLINGER and KNIGHT A. KIPLINGER, *America in the Global '90s: The Shape of the Future–How You Can Profit from It*, (Washington D.C.: Kiplinger Books, 1989).

KENICHI OHMAE, *The Borderless World: Power and Strategy in the Interlinked Economy*, (New York: Harper Business, 1990).

MICHAEL E. PORTER, *Competition in Global Industries* (Boston: Harvard Business School Press, 1986), and *The Competitive Advantage of Nations*, (New York: The Free Press, 1990).

PETER SCHWARTZ, *The Art of the Long View* (New York: Doubleday Currency, 1991).

Chapter 13
Notes

1. The following books cover in detail the initial Seven Questions and Information Economics methodologies: Marilyn M. Parker, Robert J. Benson, and H. E. Trainor, *Information Economics: Linking Business Performance to Information Technology*, (Englewood Cliffs NJ: Prentice-Hall, 1988); and Marilyn M. Parker, H. Edgar Trainor, and Robert J. Benson, *Information Strategy and Economics: Linking Information Systems Strategy to Business Performance*, (Englewood Cliffs NJ: Prentice-Hall, 1989). For information about the Joint Study or the strategic transformation methodology enhancements, write to *Key Strategies and Solutions Inc.*, 402 North Casey Key Road, Osprey, FL 34229, or FAX: 813-966-1567. For information about *The Beta Group*, write *The Beta Group*, 6810 Pershing Avenue, St. Louis, MO 63130.

2. Marilyn M. Parker and Robert J. Benson, "Applying Service Management Principles To Information Systems Organizations: An Introductory Discussion", Center for the Study of Data Processing, Working Paper Series (WP 88-21), vol. 3, no. 1, Washington University in St. Louis, 1989.

3. See "Look! No wires!" *The Wall Street Journal* (New York), February 11, 1994, sec. R, p. 1-28. This is a special section on telecommunications and its impact on daily life. Paraphrased Information reprinted by permission of The Wall Street Journal, © 1994 Dow Jones & Company, Inc. All Rights Reserved Worldwide.

4. Adapted with the permission of The Free Press, a Division of Simon & Schuster Inc. from COMPETITIVE ADVANTAGE: Creating and Sustaining Superior Performance by Michael E. Porter. Copyright © 1985 by Michael E. Porter.

5. Bruce J. Rogow, "Information Technology Strategy: Drivers in the 1990s," Gartner Group, Inc., Stamford, CT, 1991.

6. Marilyn M. Parker and Scott B. Barker, "Organizational and I/T Design: Planning for Compatibility", unpublished paper, Los Angeles Scientific Center, IBM Corporation.

7. For information about *The Helix Group, Inc.* and *HelixPLAN*, write to *The Helix Group, Inc.*, 14105 Allison Drive, Raleigh NC 27615.

Chapter 14

Notes

1. See "Business school plans index of customer satisfaction," *The Wall Street Journal* (New York), September 1, 1994, sec. A, p. 2, col. 5. Paraphrased Information reprinted by permission of The Wall Street Journal, © 1994 Dow Jones & Company, Inc. All Rights Reserved Worldwide.

2. For detailed discussions of underlying philosophy and specific calculation techniques, see Marilyn M. Parker, Robert J. Benson, and H. E. Trainor, *Information Economics: Linking Business Performance to Information Technology*, (Englewood Cliffs NJ: Prentice-Hall, 1988), available in bookstores or through IBM Mechanicsburg, #S365-0001; and Marilyn M. Parker, H. Edgar Trainor, and Robert J. Benson, *Information Strategy and Economics: Linking Information Systems Strategy to Business Performance*, (Englewood Cliffs NJ: Prentice Hall, 1989), also available in bookstores and through IBM Mechanicsburg, #S365-0002.

3. Adapted with the permission of The Free Press, a Division of Simon & Schuster Inc. from COMPETITIVE ADVANTAGE: Creating and Sustaining Superior Performance by Michael E. Porter. Copyright © 1985 by Michael E. Porter.

Suggested Readings

GEOFF HOGBIN and DAVID V. THOMAS, Investing in Information Technology: Managing the Decision-Making Process (London: McGraw-Hill, 1994).

MARILYN M. PARKER, ROBERT J. BENSON, and H. E. TRAINOR, Information Economics: Linking Business Performance to Information Technology (Englewood Cliffs NJ: Prentice Hall, 1988).

MARILYN M. PARKER, H. EDGAR TRAINOR, and ROBERT J. BENSON, Information Strategy and Economics: Linking Information Systems Strategy to Business Performance (Englewood Cliffs NJ: Prentice Hall, 1989).

Chapter 15
Notes

1. For detailed discussions of underlying philosophy and specific calculation techniques, see Marilyn M. Parker, Robert J. Benson, and H. E. Trainor, *Information Economics: Linking Business Performance to Information Technology*,(Englewood Cliffs NJ: Prentice Hall, 1988), available in bookstores or through IBM Mechanicsburg, #S365-0001; and Marilyn M. Parker, H. Edgar Trainor, and Robert J. Benson, *Information Strategy and Economics: Linking Information Systems Strategy to Business Performance* (Englewood Cliffs NJ: Prentice Hall, 1989), also available in bookstores and through IBM Mechanicsburg, #S365-0002.

2. Reprinted by permission of *Harvard Business Review*. An excerpt from "The Balanced Scorecard—Measures That Drive Performance" by Robert S. Kaplan and David P. Norton, January-February 1992, 71-79. Copyright © 1992 by the President and Fellows of Harvard College; all rights reserved.

3. "Your Company's Most Valuable Asset: Intellectual Capital", *Fortune* 130, 7, October 3, 1994; and "Mr. Learning Organization", *Fortune* 130, 8, October 17, 1994, 6-28. All rights reserved by Fortune.

4. SCEcorp 1991 Annual Report (Rosemead, CA), 6-28.

5. See Marilyn M. Parker, H. Edgar Trainor, and Robert J. Benson, *Information Strategy and Economics: Linking Information Systems Strategy to Business Performance* (Englewood Cliffs NJ: Prentice Hall, 1989), 9-13.

6. PPG Industries, Inc. 1992 Annual Report (Pittsburgh, PA), 2-7.

7. Stephen R. Noble, Robert J. Benson and Marilyn M. Parker, *Business Value Analysis: Measuring the Value of Information Technology into the 21st Century*, currently unpublished paper.

8. See "Rating R&D: How Companies Get the Biggest Bang for the Buck," *Business Week* 3326, July 5, 1993, 98, for an in-depth discussion of this topic.

9. "The price of everything, the value of nothing," *The Economist* 328, 7822, July 31, 1993, 63.

10. "A Green Account," *The Economist* 328, 7827, September 4, 1993, 69.

11. "Life ever after," *The Economist* 329, 7832, October 9, 1993, 77, and "The price of everything, the value of nothing," *The Economist* 328, 7822, July 31, 1993, 63.

12. "The Wonders of Workflow," *The Economist* 329, 7841, December 11, 1993, 80.

13. "Barefoot into PARC," *The Economist* 328, 7819, July 10, 1993, 68.

14. "America's Best Wealth Creators," *Fortune* 128, 16, December 27, 1993, 64-76. All rights reserved by Fortune.

Suggested Readings

ROBERT S. KAPLAN and DAVID P. NORTON, "The Balanced Scorecard—Measures That Drive Performance," *Harvard Business Review*, January-February 1992, 71-79; and "Putting the Balanced Scorecard to Work," *Harvard Business Review*, September-October 1993, 134-147.

Chapter 16
Notes

1. From B. Joseph Pine II, *Mass Customization: The New Frontier in Business Competition* (Boston: Harvard Business School Press, 1993), p. 16.

2. Reference reprinted with permission of Rawson Associates, an imprint of Simon & Schuster, Inc. from THE MACHINE THAT CHANGED THE WORLD by James P. Womack, Daniel T. Jones, & Daniel Roos. Copyright © 1990 James P. Womack, Daniel T. Jones, & Daniel Roos and Donna Sammons Carpenter.

3. Anne Turner, "Adding Business Value: Changing the Change Agents," *Canadian Information Processing/Informatique Canadienne*, May/June, 1992, 16-18.

4. Austin H. Kiplinger and Knight A. Kiplinger, *America in the Global '90s: The Shape of the Future—How You Can Profit from It* (Washington D.C.: Kiplinger Books, 1989), pp. 71-77; 167-168.

5. "Answer Me," *The Economist* 324, 7769 (July 25, 1992), 79-80.

6. Adapted from "Avoidable problems," *Financial Times* (New York), September 24, 1992, p. 23, col. 1-8.

7. Reprinted by permission of *Harvard Business Review*. "Reengineering Work: Don't Automate, Obliterate" by Michael Hammer, July-August 1990, 104-112. Copyright © 1990 by the President and Fellows of Harvard College; all rights reserved. Also see Richard Tanner Pascale, *Managing on The Edge:* (New York: Simon & Schuster, 1990). © 1990 by Richard Pascale. Reference by Permission of Simon & Schuster, Inc.

8. See "Management's New Gurus," *Business Week* 3281, August 31, 1992, 44-52, for an in-depth discussion of this topic.

9. Tom Peters, *Liberation Management: Necessary Disorganization for the Nanosecond Nineties* (New York: Alfred A. Knopf, 1992). Copyright © 1992 Alfred A. Knopf Inc.

10. Information reprinted from "Toward a Definition of Corporate Transformation" by Barbara Blumenthal and Philippe Haspeslagh, *Sloan Management Review* (35, 3, Spring 1994), pp. 101-106, by permission of publisher. Copyright 1994 by Sloan Management Review Association. All rights reserved.

11. See "The Search for the Organization of Tomorrow", *Fortune* 125, 20, May 18, 1992, 92-98. All rights reserved by Fortune.

12. Peter M. Senge, Charlotte Roberts, Richard B. Ross, Bryan J. Smith, Art Kleiner, *The Fifth Discipline Fieldbook: Strategies and Tools for Building a Learning Organization* (New York: Currency Doubleday, 1994), 275-278, 457.

13. Marilyn M. Parker and James A Senn, "Strategic Transformation and Business Value: The I/T Connection," *Canadian Information Processing/Informatique Canadienne*, May/June, 1992, 13-16.

Suggested Readings

ROGER E. BOHN, "Measuring and Managing Technological Knowledge," *Sloan Management Review* 36, 1 (Fall 1994), 61-73.

See the Special Section on "The Management of Change" in *Harvard Business Review* 71, 6, November-December, 1993, for the following articles: Roger Martin, "Changing the Mind of the Corporation," 81-96; Tracy Goss, Richard Pascale, and Anthony Athos, "The Reinvention Roller Coaster: Risking the Present for a Powerful Future," 97-108; Jeanie Daniel Duck, "Managing Change: The Art of Balancing," 109-118; Gene Hall, Jim Rosenthal, and Judy Wade, "How to Make Reengineering Really Work," 119-133; and Steven E. Prokesch, "Mastering Chaos at the High-Tech Frontier: An Interview with Silicon Graphic's Ed McCracken," 134-145.

Appendix Notes

Market Forces Shaping the Competitive Environment

1. See "Odd victim of politics," *The Wall Street Journal* (New York), February 5, 1992, sec. A, p. 1, col. 7. Paraphrased Information reprinted by permission of The Wall Street Journal, © 1992 Dow Jones & Company, Inc. All Rights Reserved Worldwide.

2. Adapted from "Tariff Row Spoils Caribbean Community Spirit," *Financial Times* (New York), April 30, 1992, p. 7, col. 2; and "Caribbean states take step nearer new trade bloc," July 5, 1994, p. 6, col. 1-2.

3. "One Europe, One Economy," *The Economist* 321, 7735, November 30, 1991, 54-55.

4. "The Global Rush to Privatize," *Business Week* 3236, October 21, 1991, 49-56, for an in-depth discussion of this topic.

5. "The Pacific Century: Europe Can't Stop It," *Business Week* 3192, December 17, 1991, for an in-depth discussion of this topic. This is a Special Supplement.

6. "What's Good for Japan Isn't Necessarily Good for the US," *Business Week* 3232, September 23, 1991, 23, for an in-depth discussion of this topic.

7. "Japan Takes a Good Hard Look at Itself," *Business Week* 3252, February 17, 1992, 32-35; and "There Are Capitalists, Then There Are the Japanese," 3182, October 8, 1990, 21, for an in-depth discussion of this topic.

8. See note 3 in chapter 13.

9. After Operation Desert Storm, cellular technology replaced the damaged telephone equipment in the Mid-East. Also see note 3 in chapter 13.

10. "The Fruitful, Tangled Trees of Knowledge," *The Economist* 323, 7764, June 20, 1992, 85-88.

11. "Competition on the Line," *The Economist* 323, 7763, June 13, 1992, 17-18.

12. "BRR-RING! America Calling," *Business Week* 3268, June 1, 1992, 98-101, for an in-depth discussion of this topic.

13. "Business in the 21st Century," *The Futurist* 26, 2, March-April 1992, 13-17. Information is reproduced with permission from THE FUTURIST, published by the World Future Society, 7910 Woodmont Avenue, Suite 450, Bethesda, Maryland 20814.

14. From DEMOGRAPHIC CHANGE AND THE AMERICAN FUTURE, by R. Scott Fosler, William Alonso, Jack A. Meyer, and Rosemary Kern, pages 6-18 , © 1990 by University of Pittsburgh Press. Reprinted by permission of the University of Pittsburgh Press.

15. Fosler, *Demographic Change*, 201-222.

16. "And Fewer Workers Could Mean Later Retirement," *Business Week* 3239, November 11, 1991, 26, for an in-depth discussion of this topic.

17. "Reviving Rural Life," *The Futurist* 26, 2, March-April 1992, 21-28. Information is reproduced with permission from THE FUTURIST, published by the World Future Society, 7910 Woodmont Avenue, Suite 450, Bethesda, Maryland 20814.

18. "The New Europeans," *The Economist* 321, 7733, November 16, 1991, 65-66.

19. "The Exodus of German Industry Is Under Way," *Business Week* 3267, May 25, 1992, 42-43, for an in-depth discussion of this topic.

20. Fosler, *Demographic Change*, 23-39.

21. "Ride the Wave," *The Economist* 323, 7764, June 20, 1992, 19-21.

22. "The Lure of Leisure," *The Economist* 323, 7757, May 2, 1992, 81.

23. "The Global Rush to Privatize," *Business Week* 3236, October 21, 1991, 49-56, for an in-depth discussion of this topic.

24. "Japan Just May Be Ready To Change Its Ways," *Business Week* 3250, January 27, 1992, 30, for an in-depth discussion of this topic.

25. Fosler, *Demographic Change*, 158-177.

26. "A Power for Good, A Power for Ill," *The Economist* 321, 7722, August 31, 1991, Special Survey 3-30.

27. "Conservation Power," *Business Week* 3231, September 16, 1991, 86-92, for an in-depth discussion of this topic.

28. "Making Clean Energy Sweeter to Utilities," *Business Week* 3222, July 15, 1991, 136, for an in-depth discussion of this topic.

29. "The Green Giant? It May Be Japan," *Business Week* 3253, February 24, 1992, 74-75, for an in-depth discussion of this topic.

30. Adapted from "Stuck with the Bill," *Financial Times* (New York) May 6, 1992, p. 12, col. 1-6.

31. Reprinted by permission of *Harvard Business Review*. "How Europe's Companies Reposition to Recycle" by Frances Cairncross, March/April 1992, 34-45. Copyright © 1992 by the President and Fellows of Harvard College; all rights reserved.

32. "A Power for Good, A Power for Ill," *The Economist* 320, 7722, August 31, 1991, Special Survey 3-30.

33. "The Green Giant? It May Be Japan," *Business Week* 3253, February 24, 1992, 74-75, for an in-depth discussion of this topic.

Coping with Business and Technological Change

34. Martin Ferris and Roy Sampson, *Public Utilities* (Prospect Heights, Illinois: Waveland Press, 1984).

35. John E. Bryson, *A Report on 1992 Goals and Results, SCEcorp 1992 Annual Report*, Rosemead, California.

Value and Service in the Retailing Industry

36. "Nordstrom's Gang of Four," *Business Week* 3270, June 15, 1992, 122-123, for an in-depth discussion of this topic.

37. "Less-Than-Fantastic Plastic," *Business Week* 3292, November 9, 1992, 100-101, for an in-depth discussion of this topic.

Stakeholder Values and Structural Change

38. Adapted from "Priorities and purpose at the heart of capitalism," *Financial Times* (New York), May 12, 1992, p. 19, col. 1-4.

39. See "Compensation gap," *The Wall Street Journal* (New York), December 30, 1991, sec. A, p. 1, col. 7. Paraphrased Information reprinted by permission of The Wall Street Journal, © 1991 Dow Jones & Company, Inc. All Rights Reserved Worldwide.

40. Much has been written about shareholder values, especially the changing orientation of European corporations. Good sources for those interested in this topic is *The Economist* and the *Financial Times*.

41. "The Caring Company," *The Economist* 323, 7762, June 6, 1992, 75.

42. Lester Thurow, "Let's Learn from the Japanese," *Fortune* 124, 12, November 18, 1991, 183-186. All rights reserved by Fortune.

43. Adapted from "Economist identifies culture clash," *Financial Times* (New York), June 9, 1992, p.13, col. 1-3.

44. "Europe's Corporate Castles Begin to Crack," *The Economist* 321, 7735, November 30, 1991, 67-68.

45. Adapted from "Why the Germans fight shy of shares," *Financial Times* (New York), May 23-24, 1992, Weekend, p. V, col. 1-4, and "Learning to Love Equity," *The Economist* 328, 7818, July 3, 1993, 71-72.

46. "Cadbury Speaks," *The Economist* 323, 7761, May 30, 1992, 76.

47. "In Search of Better Boardrooms," *The Economist* 323, 7761, May 30, 1992, 13-14.

48. See "How Japan Puts the 'Human' in Human Capital," *Business Week* 3239, November 11, 1991, 22, for an in-depth discussion of this topic.

49. See "Morita's message to Japan will take time to sink in," *The Asian Wall Street Journal* (New York), August 24, 1992, p. 12, col. 1-4. Paraphrased Information reprinted by permission of The Wall Street Journal, © 1992 Dow Jones & Company, Inc. All Rights Reserved Worldwide.

Evergreen Environmental Consultants

50. Marilyn M. Parker and Robert J. Benson, "Applying Service Management Principles To Information Systems Organizations: An Introductory Discussion", Center for the Study of Data Processing, Working Paper Series (WP 88-21), vol. 3, no. 1, Washington University in St. Louis, 1989.

New Technologies and New Services

51. Michael E. Porter, *Competitive Strategy: Techniques for Analyzing Industries and Competitors* (New York: The Free Press, 1980).

52. James I. Cash, Jr., F. Warren McFarlan, and James Mckenney, *Corporate Information Systems Management: The Issues Facing Senior Executives* (Homewood, Ill.: Irwin, 1992).

National Defense: Preparing for the 21st Century

53. Sun Tzu, *The Art of War* (New York: Dell Publishing, 1988), edited by James Clavell.

54. IBM reduced 85,000 employees; AT&T 83,500; and GM 74,000.

55. Testimony by Gen. Ronald R. Fogleman, USAF, commander in chief of US Transportation Command, before the Defense Subcommittee, House Appropriations Committee, April 20, 1994.

56. General Merrill A. McPeak, "Reinventing the Air Force." Speech delivered to the Air Force Association, Washington DC, September 14, 1994.

57. "Coping with Ethnic Conflict in an Unstable World." Speech by Gen. Gordon R. Sullivan, USA, before the Institute for Foreign Policy Analysis, Washington DC, August 2, 1994.

58. "From the Sea: Preparing the Naval Service for the 21st Century," Department of the Navy White Paper, September 1992, 1.

59. "Armed forces battle each other for roles," reported by Rowan Scarborough in *Washington Times*, September 15, 1994, 1.

60. "Military's Rapid Switch In Haiti: A Tactical Win for Joint-Force Planner," reported by John F. Harris in *Washington Post*, September 28, 1994, 21.

61. The National Security Act of 1947 formalized the Joint Chiefs of Staff as a permanent body, established the Department of the Air Force, and ultimately provided transition from the Department of War to the Department of Defense.

62. Chairman of the Joint Chiefs of Staff Report on the Roles, Missions, and Functions of the Armed Forces of the United States, February 1993, vi.

63. Among other provisions, the War Powers Resolution authorized Congress to pull troops from hostilities within 60 to 90 days unless Congress extended the deadline, declared war, or could not convene.

64. Secretary of Defense William J. Perry as quoted in a Department of Defense news release, "DOD Review Recommends Reduction in Nuclear Force," September 22, 1994.

65. Ibid.

66. "Future Technology May Work, But That's Not Enough." Speech by Deputy Secretary of Defense Mr. John Deutch at Northeastern University, June 18, 1994.

67. "Readiness Problems Graver than DoD Admits–Thurmond," *Defense Daily*, October 5, 1994, 20.

Index

A

Abbott Laboratories, 75
Aberdeen Harbour Board, 192
Acquisition, 33, 64, 173–76, 192, 198, 434–36, 533–34, 548, 550
Action planning, 287, 311
Active badge, 33
Activity-based costing (ABC), 255, 336
Adaptability, 184, 297, 350–52, 394, 400
Adding value, 132–33
Agile Manufacturing Information System (AMIS), 105
Agile manufacturing systems, 102
Agile production, 101
Agility, 6, 10, 22, 88–89, 102–7, 112, 184, 209, 293, 313, 322–24, 329–30, 346, 354, 370, 375–76, 552, 557–58
Aging as a constituency, 262
AGT Limited (and Alberta Government Telephone), 98, 189, 257, 459–87, 503–17, 537
Air France, 80, 163
Airbus, 84, 86
All Nippon Airways, 85
Alldays Peracock, 192
Allen-Bradley, 59, 367
Alliances, 6, 9, 17, 67, 71–72, 74, 87–88, 103, 159–60, 164, 169, 172–75, 184, 189, 192, 205, 214, 216, 218–23, 232, 264, 288, 293, 296, 299, 313, 324, 326, 330, 370, 383, 406, 409–10, 459, 462, 486, 489, 538, 549–50, 552, 561
America West Airlines, 82
American Airlines (AA), 37–38, 65–66, 68, 71, 82–83, 87–88, 106, 132, 295, 438
American Express, 56–58, 60, 68, 97, 106, 367, 453, 456
American Gas Association (A.G.A.), 120, 124
American Greetings CreataCard, 96
American Hospital Supply, 66, 73
American Management Association, 38
American National Standards Institute (ANSI), 119
American Quality Foundation, 115
Americans with Disabilities Act, 31, 41
Analog Devices, 200
Andersen Consulting, 77, 157
Anheuser-Busch, 83
ANSI, 119–20
Apple, 30, 149
Applications development, 228, 235, 532
Applications maintenance, 235
Apprenticeship, 204
Armenia, 40
Artificial intelligence, 54–56, 541, 544
ASAP and ASAP Express, 73–76

Asea, 371
Asia, 12, 41, 85, 131, 176–77, 181–82, 265, 267, 402, 406, 546
Association of American Railroads, 79
AT&T, 46, 83, 96, 98–99, 105–6, 250, 265, 367, 409, 486, 489, 545
Australia, 29, 37, 52
Austria, 52
Auto Trends, 52
Autodesk, 250
Automobiles, 47, 52, 112, 132–34, 146, 210, 270–71, 351, 421, 496, 541
AutoPrint Instant Print Vending Machine, 99
Avis, 83
Ax'ent, 84

B

Balanced Scorecard, 343–44, 351, 361, 385
Baldrige, 121, 123, 128–29, 131, 170, 183
Bane, Michael, 95
BankAmerica, 176–77
Bankers Trust, 354
Banking, 10, 34, 36, 66, 87, 114, 116, 132, 136–38, 176–79, 211, 247, 262–63, 293, 358–59, 367, 403, 405, 408, 452, 488–89, 527

Bankruptcy, 83, 87, 92
Barbados, 37
Barker, Joel, 93
Barnevik, Percy, 371
Baxter Healthcare, 66, 71, 73, 86,
    89, 103, 368
Baxter Travenol, 66, 73
Beck, Nuala, 252–54, 357–58
Bell Canada, 234
BellSouth, 109
Benchmarking, 119, 131, 141,
    156–58, 368–69
Benson, Robert, 189, 221, 286, 460,
    484, 488, 506
Bergen Brunswig, 75
Berghaus, 107–8, 111
Best practice(s), 94, 104, 109–10,
    117, 119, 125, 141, 158,
    193–95, 216–19, 226, 235–36,
    248, 309–10, 323, 346, 361,
    368–69, 381, 386–87, 524,
    527, 558
Beta Group, 286, 304
Bethlehem Steel, 249–50
Biases, 200, 214
Biotechnology, 111–12
Blattberg, Robert C., 106
Blaupunkt, 34
Blue Cross/Blue Shield, 48
Blumenthal, Barbara, 1, 389, 391,
    537
BMW, 3, 12, 414
Boeing, 36, 38, 71, 84–88, 104, 149
Boise Cascade, 75, 78
Borden, 219
Borderless enterprise, 169
Borderless organizations, 216
Boston Consulting Group, 101, 142
Bowen, David, 150
Brazil, 182
Bridgestone/Firestone, 11
British Aerospace, 86
British Airways, 85, 391–92, 394,
    400
British International Freight Associa-
    tion (BIFA) and BIFAnet, 43,
    67, 71, 79–80, 87
British Petroleum, 207, 250
British Telecommunications (BT),
    31, 98, 250, 406
Brown Boveri, 371
BSO/Origin, 354
Buick, 153
Burlington Coat Factory, 202
Burlington Northern, 78
Business architecture, 9, 67, 296
Business competencies, 75–76

Business investment profile, 335–40,
    351
Business model(s), 219–20, 515
Business network, 70, 73–76, 148,
    214, 304, 368–69
Business organization risk, 313, 327,
    330, 358, 562, 563
Business partner, 7, 21–23, 48, 238,
    255, 258, 286, 375–80, 445,
    538
Business process redesign, 22, 42,
    50, 58, 68, 73–76, 113,
    141–43, 148–49, 160–63, 203,
    206, 303, 313, 327, 358, 369,
    373, 377, 451, 459, 563
Business process reengineering, 95,
    151, 311–13, 322, 343, 382,
    537
Business processes, 1, 6, 10, 14–15,
    42, 46, 48, 50, 61, 73, 76, 79,
    110, 117, 141–43, 148, 152,
    164, 178, 182, 203, 207, 211,
    214, 217, 220–23, 229, 233,
    237, 275, 286, 291, 293, 295,
    303, 317, 322–24, 327,
    347–48, 358, 361, 370–71,
    377–78, 385, 387, 393, 438,
    459, 465, 483, 489, 492, 498,
    501, 510, 512, 515, 558, 563
Business scope, 73–74
Business strategy risk, 313, 325–26,
    330, 356, 560–61
Business value, 22–23, 54, 123, 189,
    205, 214–15, 234, 237–48,
    251–55, 285–88, 293, 295,
    297–98, 303, 309, 332–33,
    342, 345–50, 357–58, 372,
    374–83, 386, 460, 488–95,
    499–501, 505–11, 528, 535
Business-based financial values,
    312–14, 350
Business-I/T credibility gap, 241
Buy-outs, 179

C

Cadbury Committee, 524–26
Cadillac, 153
California, 9–10, 13, 15–16, 27, 30,
    45, 55, 176, 250, 267, 272–75,
    277, 279, 283, 291, 346, 352,
    403, 412, 419–21, 426–28,
    433–35, 438, 455
Campbell, Van, 174
Canada, 11, 47, 52, 98, 116, 140,
    184–85, 234, 252, 260,
    268–70, 309, 402–4, 409, 411,

    414, 461–62, 479, 486–87,
    505, 527, 550
Canadian Imperial Bank of Com-
    merce, 344–45
Canadian Information Technology
    Sector Advisory Committee,
    184
Capacity to innovate, 14
Capital, 7, 32, 66, 89, 101–2, 138,
    142, 147, 154, 159, 176, 182,
    184–85, 211–14, 249–51, 268,
    270, 274, 315, 334, 344–45,
    351, 381, 404, 407, 415–18,
    428, 431–35, 440, 486, 507,
    518–19, 522–26. Also see
    index for customer capital,
    human capital, intellectual
    capital, and structural capital.
Cardiff Business School, 157
Carnation, 11, 15
CAT scans, 40
Cathay Pacific, 37, 80
Cellular telephone(s), 29, 63,
    149–50, 172
CellularOne, 98
CEN, 118–19, 121
Central America, 404
Chaos theory, 55, 58–59
Charan, Ram, 72, 172
Chase Manhattan, 176
Chemical Banking, 177
Chernobyl, 268, 274, 418, 425
Chiat/Day, 31
Chicago, 32, 83, 92, 106, 455
Chief Financial Officer (CFO),
    57–61
Chief Information Officer (CIO), 53,
    68, 205–9, 246, 285, 293–94
China, 7, 12, 14, 19, 37, 261, 270,
    408, 418, 422
Chrysler, 133, 152, 156
Circuit City, 50, 106–7
Citgo Petroleum Corp, 45
Citibank, 66, 71, 88, 296
Citicorp, 172, 176–77
Clamshells (McDonald's), 160–61,
    354
Client relationships, 144, 517
Client/server, 203, 226, 229–34, 493,
    500
Colgate-Palmolive, 249
Collaborative enterprise, 214
Collaborative technologies, 50
Collegial relationships, 26, 50, 54,
    143, 451, 459
Command and control, 54, 68, 105,
    151

Commercial banking, 176
Committee for Standardization, 118, 121
Competitive advantage/competitive-ness, 3, 5–6, 9–12, 42–45, 55, 70–75, 86–88, 94, 100, 102, 105, 108, 112, 117, 119–24, 128–29, 131, 152, 156, 158–59, 169–72, 181, 184–86, 191, 196, 206, 208–13, 218, 237–38, 240, 248–49, 269, 291, 308–12, 318–20, 324, 329–30, 335, 351–52, 361, 365–67, 370, 376, 393–97, 401–7, 416–17, 422, 430, 436–37, 456, 489, 508, 518–21, 525–27, 541–43, 550, 552, 554, 558–59
Competitive jockeying, 75
Competitive response, 309, 312, 318, 320, 324, 329, 352, 508, 554
Competitive strategy risks, 313, 325, 327, 330, 356, 560, 561
Complementary applications, 316–17, 350
Computer-aided design (CAD), 64, 104, 204
Computer(s), see pen computers, personal computers, portable computers
Connectivity, 43, 229, 540
Conoco, 180
Consensus-driven, 340, 360
Consortia, 87–88, 249
Consumer Electronics Show, 13
Consumer Reports, 52
Continental Airlines, 83
Continental Holding Co., 45
Continental Insurance Co., 39
Continuous improvement, 11, 14, 21, 122, 139, 143, 154, 169, 343, 365, 370–77, 394
Contribution circles, 156
Core competencies, 4, 6, 14, 76, 87, 89, 146, 173, 184, 191–97, 203, 211–15, 226–27, 233–39, 249, 275, 283, 295, 301, 341, 351, 354–60, 365, 370–71, 375–77, 384, 389–90, 393, 396, 459–60, 488, 538, 547, 557, 561
Core environment, 275
Core values, 167, 201–2
Cornell University, 30
Corning, Inc., 169, 174
Corporate culture, 29, 91, 105, 164–73, 182–84, 193, 201–2,

228, 249, 277, 361, 371, 389–90, 454, 466, 521
Corporate form(s), 213–14
Council on Competitiveness, 249, 252, 526
Covia, 82
Crandall, Robert, 82–83
Cray Research Inc., 112, 250
Creation Station, 100
Creativity, 88, 167, 184, 206–7, 281, 435–37
Critical mass, 9, 176, 184–85, 235, 268, 302, 375, 498
Critical Success Factors (CSFs), 290–91, 294, 304, 312, 318, 320–21, 324, 329, 352, 555
Crosby, Phillip B., 125, 127
Cross-functional teams, 39, 54, 81, 116, 142, 167–68, 191, 194, 226, 236, 371, 376–77, 466, 469, 474, 492
Cross-industry alliances, 71
Crysel, 130
Cuba, 265, 267
Culture, 4, 7, 9, 15, 18, 22, 29, 39, 68, 91, 102, 105, 116, 145, 154, 164–71, 173, 177, 181–87, 193–94, 197, 199–202, 205, 207, 217, 226, 228, 231, 246, 249, 252, 260, 264, 277, 304, 321, 323, 329–30, 348, 355, 358, 361, 371, 389–90, 395, 398, 410, 412, 417, 422, 439, 444, 454, 466, 504, 518, 521–27, 546, 552, 558. See also Corporate culture; I/T culture
Cummins Engine, 45, 151
Customer capital, 345, 351
Customer choice, 243–44, 496–97
Customer perspective, 137, 343, 351–52, 356
Customer service, 18–19, 45–46, 56–57, 62–63, 68, 99–102, 106, 114, 124, 126, 138, 142, 150, 165, 179, 191, 209, 211, 229, 236, 241, 317, 378, 383, 392, 448, 452–53, 456, 479, 510–11, 523
Customer-driven planning, 6
Customized catalysts, 111–12
Customized chips, 111–12
Customized service, 78, 86
Customized solutions, 48, 376
Cycle time, 129, 313, 322–24, 329–30, 345, 355, 558
Czech Republic, 12

D

Danish Steel Works, 354
Data Discman, 149
Database(s), 11, 34, 40–41, 44, 51–52, 61, 64–65, 84, 97, 99, 106, 112, 149, 207, 218, 229, 232, 250, 324, 329, 381, 470, 491, 536, 566
Davidow, William H., 89
Davis, Stan, 94–95, 111
De-loading, 148
De-skilling, 93–94
Dearden, John, 210
Decentralization, 182, 189, 206, 234, 236, 299, 459, 462, 479
Decentralized organizations, 72, 298–99
Decision rooms, 38
Dedene, Guido, 340
Deere & Company, 211
Deighton, John, 106
DelaSalle, Pierre, 340
Dell Computer, 39, 98, 133
Deloitte & Touche, 101
Demand articulation, 159–60, 279–80
Deming, W. Edwards (Deming Award and Deming Prize), 123, 125, 128–30
Demographic change, 1, 2, 4, 16, 34, 98, 132, 197, 247, 260–62, 266–67, 277, 291–93, 313, 326, 389–90, 402–3, 410–12, 416, 422, 433, 560–61
Department of Commerce, 119
Department of Defense, 64
Deregulation, 79–80, 86–87, 133, 138, 184, 278, 280, 326, 409, 542, 544, 561
Detroit Edison, 33, 250
Deutsche Aerospace, 86
Development of standards, 235
DHL, 33, 80
Dictionary, 64, 229
Discontinuous change, 7, 283, 345
Digital Equipment Corp. (DEC), 112, 391
Disney World, 34, 84
Distribution channel, 6, 87, 148, 311, 322, 324–25
Distribution channels, 5, 16, 70, 87, 146, 247, 310, 326, 490, 542, 560
Dole Foods, 135
Domesday 2000 and New Con-sumerism, 51

Domesday Book, 49
Dominican Republic, 37, 228, 265
Dow Chemical, 174, 344
Dow Corning, 174
Downsizing, 10, 14, 17, 41, 43, 142, 164, 177, 189, 192, 197, 201, 206, 225–26, 234, 296, 364, 370, 459, 462, 477, 541, 544, 552
DRI McGraw-Hill, 12
Drucker, Peter, 13–16, 89, 168, 178, 211
DTK Computer, 265
Du Pont, 121, 172, 180–81, 223, 250
Dun & Bradstreet, 192
Dunkin' Donuts, 35
Dynamic harmony, 384
Dynamic stability, 378, 382–84

E

E-mail, 10, 18, 43, 45, 73, 77, 214, 252
Eagle peanuts, 83
Early warning (signals), 166, 193, 225, 255, 262, 268, 275–77, 291, 302, 341, 357, 366, 377, 382, 384, 417, 550
Earthquakes, 21, 262, 410
Eastman Kodak, 75, 100, 121
EasySABRE, 87
Echocardiograms, 40
Economic base, 14, 16, 19, 371, 418, 489–90
Economic indicators, 58, 185, 246–51, 309, 513–14
Economic value added (EVA), 251
Economy (economies) of scale, 75–76, 86, 94, 101, 110, 134, 142–43, 178, 226, 264–65, 366, 498, 530–32, 542–44, 551
Economy (economies) of scope, 75, 86, 101, 143
EDF, 161, 419
EDS, 226–27, 354, 542
Education, 12–14, 17, 19, 68, 126, 130, 133, 169, 204, 212, 228, 262, 264, 292–93, 330, 361, 366, 372, 375, 385, 410–13, 472, 528, 531
Electromation, 152
Electronic bulletin, 39, 80
Electronic bulletin boards, 39
Electronic bunkers, 11, 28
Electronic Data Interchange (EDI), 42–45, 73–81, 91, 140, 152, 195, 202–3, 214, 235, 324,

343, 351, 374
Electronic funds transfer, 235
Electronic home shopping, 78
Electronic immigrants, 36
Electronic mail, 10, 30, 36–44, 60–62, 71–73, 149, 203, 214, 235, 283, 355, 409, 541, 544
Electronic point of sale (Epos), 77
Employee buy-outs, 179
Empowered workers, 21, 375
Empowerment, 6, 10–11, 18, 21–22, 26, 49, 50–55, 58, 63–70, 89, 91, 150–51, 154, 160, 169, 173, 182, 187, 191, 195–97, 212, 220, 226, 234, 236, 295, 303, 313, 322–24, 329–30, 354, 361, 370–76, 387, 397, 451, 459–60, 492, 537, 557–58
EN 29000, 122
England, 33, 51, 112, 192
Enterprise agility, 22, 370
Enterprise environment, 276, 460
Enterprise-wide Information Management (EwIM), 221–22, 506
Environmental damage, 161, 268, 354, 419–20, 425
Environmental quality, 10, 160, 162, 268, 313, 321–24, 329–30, 342, 353, 367, 437, 556, 557
Eo Inc., 46
Ernst & Young, 115, 131, 143, 205
Europe, 2, 7, 9, 12, 41–42, 77–80, 86, 99, 107–8, 118–19, 121, 124, 150, 153–55, 163, 174, 181–82, 203–4, 260–62, 265–70, 292, 309, 354, 390–91, 402–11, 414–15, 420–22, 455, 494, 520, 522, 546, 550
European Currency Unit (ecu), 175, 250, 405
European Union (EU), 3–4, 7–10, 71, 81, 118–19, 121–24, 131, 174–75, 260–62, 267, 270, 292, 312, 366, 403–6, 409–10, 414–17, 420–21, 522, 544
Evergreen Environmental Consultants, 258, 290, 294, 303, 504, 528, 532, 535
Excel Logistics, 81
Executive information systems (EIS), 49, 60–61, 236, 541, 544
Expert systems, 54–57, 61, 103, 413, 541, 544
Exxon, 250, 268

F

Fanuc, 159
Fax, 17, 35, 41–47, 73, 92–93, 105, 118, 149, 162, 203, 283, 355, 366, 408, 464, 471, 541, 544
Feasibility and priority issues, 288
Federal Express (FedEx), 11, 32, 61, 79–81, 135, 150, 355
Feedback channels, 144
Feigenbaum, Armand, 125, 127–28
Fetal monitoring, 40
Fidelity, 264
Financial justification, 212, 218–19, 286, 334, 343, 493, 503
Financial kiosks, 28, 36
Financial Times, 53, 108
Finland, 30, 541
Fisher, Alfred J., 153, 397
Flex-N-Gate, 152
Flexibility, 6, 10, 21–22, 51, 67, 72–73, 94–95, 101–2, 137, 148, 168, 172, 174, 187, 193, 216, 218, 220, 233–34, 290–91, 293, 305, 341, 352, 368, 374, 378, 400, 448, 459, 486, 526, 537, 549
Flexible manufacturing, 78, 96, 100–101, 325, 356, 367–68
Flexible manufacturing systems (FMS), 100
Florida, 40, 82, 84, 95, 118, 265, 547
FMC, 63
Food and Drug Administration (FDA), 42
Ford, 21, 143, 154, 365
France, 2, 80, 138, 163, 389, 391, 405, 410
Frito-Lay Inc, 56
Fuji Heavy Industries, 85
Functional organizations, 298, 314, 342
Future Perfect, 111
Future Shock, 88
Fuzzy logic, 55, 59–60

G

Gartner Group, 223
Garwood, David, 95
Gateway 2000, 97–98, 133
Gemeentekrediet Van Belgic, 340
General Agreement on Trades and Tariffs (GATT), 4, 8, 15, 403–4, 550
General Electric (GE), 30, 43, 59, 67, 170, 172, 250, 368, 389–96, 399–401

General Electric Information Services (GEIS), 43, 67
General Foods, 74, 135
General Mills, 135
General Motors (GM), 3, 153–54, 156, 158, 167–68, 170–72, 391, 394–95
General Motors Credit Card, 88
General Safety, 153, 170
Genetic engineering, 111–12
Georgia, 40, 263, 368
Germany, 3–4, 11–12, 14, 18, 107, 116, 118–19, 138, 154, 163, 180, 203–4, 247, 251, 260–61, 267–70, 386, 402, 405–6, 410–11, 414–17, 421–22, 518, 522–23, 526–27
Ghoshal, Sumantra, 193
Global Business Network, 304
Global competition, 9–10, 21, 24, 87, 105, 140, 169, 221, 296, 540–41
Global economic bases, 6
Global economy, 11, 89, 119–20, 132, 135, 169, 180, 217, 260, 269, 366, 417–18, 518–19, 550
Global environment, 5, 115, 277, 545
Global Information Systems (GIS), 18, 34, 112
Global manager, 9–10
Global mindset, 181–82
Global office, 187, 462
Global Positioning Systems (GPS), 33–34, 47
Global teenager, 4, 402
Global workforce, 6, 17
Global workplaces, 4
Globalization, 3, 8–11, 86, 169, 182, 186, 292, 371, 383, 389, 397, 402–4, 409–10, 417, 422, 527
Graphic user interface (GUI), 232
Great Atlantic & Pacific Tea Company (A&P), 11, 147
Great Britain, 518
Greenfield sites, 155
Grocery trade, 77
Groupware, 28, 38–39, 71, 148, 229, 252, 460, 463, 465, 469–71
GTE, 30, 192

H

Hackman, J. R., 143
Hallmark, 100, 355, 358
Hamel, Gary, 73
Hammer, Michael, 369, 477, 514

Hand-writing recognition programs, 150
Harenburg, W. C., 229–30
Harvard Business Review, 15, 65, 72
Harvard Business School, 87, 101
Haspeslagh, Philippe, 2, 389–91, 537
Hayek, Nicolas, 108–10
Healthcare, 46–48, 66, 70–74, 76, 86–87, 89, 97, 103, 116, 250, 293, 368, 410, 552
Heavyweight team(s), 167–68, 183
Helix Group, 304
Herman Miller, 142, 150
Hertz, 35, 83
Heskett, James, 165, 521
Hewlett-Packard, 3, 168, 265
High involvement, 10, 18, 150
Hilton hotels, 106
Hirayama, Tomoshi, 206
Hokkaido, 262
Holiday Inn, 84
Holland, 30, 163, 250, 405, 522
Holography, 111–12
Home shopping, 44, 78
Home-work, 28
Honda, 154, 156, 415
Hopper, Max, 65
Horizontal organizations, 6, 10, 18, 21, 169, 210, 223, 298, 333, 375–76, 392, 492
Hotdesking, 28, 30–31
House of Windsor Collection, 81
Hughes Aircraft, 172
Hughes, Louis, 154
Human capital, 345
Hungary, 7
Hyatt hotels, 106
Hypermarkets, 77

I

I/T charter, 6, 22, 186, 191, 203–4, 207, 210, 212, 293
I/T-based financial values, 312, 316, 350
IBM, 22, 31, 40, 66, 96–97, 112, 121, 133, 165, 171, 182, 210, 221, 234, 250, 286, 340, 354, 357, 367, 391, 396, 398, 414, 445–46, 462, 542–45
Icahn, Carl, 83
IDC, 62
Imaging, 29, 46–47, 64, 75, 81, 148, 264, 541, 544
Immigration, 4, 10, 15, 247, 260, 262–68, 283, 411–17, 422

Imperial Chemical Industries, 180
Incremental change, 28, 283, 345
India, 3, 19, 37, 119, 211, 228, 270, 418
Industry foresight, 281–82
Infiniti, 132
Information Economics, 257–87, 303–4, 311, 322–33, 338–43, 351, 360, 385, 484, 503–6, 515–16
Information empowerment, 22, 26, 49–50, 52–55, 58, 63, 65–70, 89, 91, 160, 187, 195–97, 212, 226, 295, 303, 322, 324, 371, 374, 451, 459
Information integration, 205–8, 295
Information management, 50, 53, 205, 221, 264, 286, 506
Information partnerships, 66–67
Information politics, 53
Information superhighway, 7, 13, 17, 19, 367, 409, 527
Information utility infrastructure, 225
Information-related technologies, 1, 6, 371
Informational networking, 54
Infrastructure investments, 383, 385, 490
Inmarsat C, 45
Innovation, 6, 11, 50, 86, 89–91, 101, 108–9, 129, 141, 159, 161, 166, 169–70, 182–85, 193, 200, 203, 206, 215, 254, 299, 330, 343, 345–46, 352, 357, 369–70, 372, 375–77, 387, 394, 408, 491, 525, 538–40, 549, 551–52
Innovative applications, 29, 44, 311, 317–18, 350
Input-process-output (IPO), 354
INSEAD, 2, 193, 389, 391
Intellectual assets, 19, 193–94, 197, 249, 344–45, 351, 361, 375, 380, 383, 385, 520
Intellectual capital, 344–45
Intelligent Body Assembly System (IBAS), 101
Intelligent systems, 49, 54–56, 59, 69
International courier(s), 32
International Electrotechnical Commission (IEC), 119, 121
International Mobil Machines, 172
International standardization, 117–18, 121
International Standards Organization (ISO), 81, 119–24, 140

Internet, 18, 33, 76–77, 87, 263, 367
Interoperability, 48, 53, 208, 217, 374, 376, 383
Investment prioritization, 220
Iowa, 40
Ireland, 37, 228, 405
IRIS, 35
Italy, 77, 107, 118, 130, 163, 265, 405, 410, 522

J

Jamaica, 37, 228, 265
Japan/Japanese, 3–4, 10–15, 18–19, 30, 35, 40, 59, 72, 80, 85–86, 93–94, 101–4, 108–9, 116, 118–19, 121, 125, 128–30, 133–34, 138, 143, 151–59, 167–68, 171, 174, 181, 204–6, 219, 247, 261–62, 267–70, 292, 309, 366–67, 386, 394, 402–3, 407–11, 415–22, 434, 436, 455, 518–21, 524–27
JC Penney, 202
Job involvement, 150
Johnson & Johnson (J&J), 75
Joint Computer-Aided Acquisition and Logistics Support (J-Cals), 64
Joint ventures, 72, 103, 172–73, 192, 262, 293, 299, 313, 326, 550, 552, 561
Jones, Daniel, 158
Juran, Joseph M., 125–27
Just-in-time, 16–17, 42, 71–80, 86–87, 100, 102, 104, 108, 133–34, 146, 152, 154, 156, 247, 292, 310, 343, 361, 374, 378, 428, 492, 497, 531

K

Kantor, Rosabeth Moss, 15
Kao Corp., 101
Kaplan, Robert, 343
Kawasaki Heavy Industries, 85
Kearney, 101
Keiretsu, 152, 156, 171, 174, 309, 407, 415
Key business processes, 73, 76, 141, 178, 182, 214, 217, 220–23, 233, 275, 348, 385, 498
Key Strategies and Solutions, 286, 304, 453
Kinder Care, 283
Knowledge, 11, 13–14, 16, 49, 53, 55–57, 60, 62–63, 67, 69, 88–90, 93, 104, 131, 142, 151, 160, 168–69, 173, 184–85, 191,

193–96, 198–205, 207, 209, 211–12, 214–15, 220, 229, 236, 248, 252–53, 295, 299, 304, 338, 340, 345–46, 356, 358, 360, 366–67, 370, 372, 374–77, 381, 438, 478, 539–40
Knowledge ratio, 253, 345
Knowledgeable relationships, 49
Kodak, 53, 75, 100, 121
Komatsu, 11
Konsynski, Benn R., 66–67
Kotter, John, 165, 521
Kraft General Foods Inc., 74
Kroger, 147
Kuhn, Thomas, 93

L

L. L. Bean, 106, 157
Labor force, 4, 6, 13, 19, 31, 211, 389
Latin America, 7, 163, 261, 265–66, 404, 406, 411, 415
Lawler, Edward, 150
Leading economic indicators, 246–48, 251, 309
Lean manufacturing, 153–55, 163, 186
Lean production, 101–2, 158, 366
Learning organizations, 168, 191, 198, 200, 253, 323, 365, 370, 372, 557
Lehigh University's Iacocca Institute, 103
Lenders, 309, 520
Life-cycle analysis (LCA), 354
Lifelong learning, 184–85, 212, 372, 385
Lifetime employment, 14, 18, 527
Lightweight teams, 167
Linkage, 88, 163, 221, 223, 239, 242–43, 246, 286, 318, 323, 339–40, 351, 375, 378–79, 383, 466, 485–86, 493–97, 505, 553, 559
Literacy, 212, 228
Local area network(s) (LANs), 43–44, 214, 230, 235
Lockheed, 96, 98
Logistics, 64, 75, 81, 91, 294, 549
London Business School, 208, 250–51, 523
Longines, 110
Lorenz, Christopher, 53, 108
Los Angeles, 21, 30, 93, 176, 261, 264–66, 268, 273, 286, 412, 421
Lotus Notes, 39
Lufthansa, 80

M

Madras, 211
Magellan Systems, 34
Malone, Michael S., 89
Management dashboard, 332–33, 340–41, 343, 353, 357, 359, 385
Management information, 72, 241, 312, 318, 320–21, 324, 329, 339, 352, 508, 555
Management information for CSFs, 312, 318, 320, 324, 329, 352, 555
Managing alliance relationships, 218
Managing security, 218
Managing surprise, 198
Manufacturing, 3, 10, 12–15, 19, 39, 56, 59, 64, 71–72, 77–81, 86, 89, 92–96, 99–110, 115, 117, 123, 125, 127, 129–30, 132, 134–35, 137, 140, 145, 147, 151, 153–56, 158–60, 163–64, 168, 182–87, 192, 215, 244, 247–48, 251–54, 262, 264–65, 270–71, 273, 300, 325, 341, 351–53, 356, 367–69, 407, 413–14, 421, 428, 452, 489–90, 492, 496–97, 525, 541, 560
Maps, 34, 482
Market dynamics, 22, 113, 262, 290–91, 325, 330, 402, 425, 560
Market environment, 5, 239, 276–77, 326, 561
Market redefinition, 6, 325
Market value added (MVA), 251
Market-driven, 120, 159, 169, 172, 221
Marketplace dynamics, 1, 389
Marriott, 84
Marubeni, 46
Mass customization, 15, 22, 27, 92–100, 108, 110–12, 154, 160, 170, 186, 191, 197, 218, 255, 310, 313, 322, 324, 329–30, 354–56, 367, 376, 382, 425, 451, 455, 542, 551, 558–59
Mass production, 10, 15, 21, 89, 92–95, 98, 100–102, 104, 107–8, 110, 143, 153–54, 158, 169, 254–55, 310, 313, 333, 356, 365–67
Massachusetts Institute of Technology (MIT), 34, 158, 198, 202

MassMutual Life Insurance Company, 220
Matrix organizations, 301
Matsushita, 46, 92, 151, 250
Matsushita, Konosuke, 151
McDonald's, 35, 132, 134, 150, 160–62, 203, 250, 354
McDonnell Douglas, 86
McFarlan, F. Warren, 66–67, 87–88, 542
MCI, 96, 98–99, 486
McKinsey, 78, 137
Meiji Milk, 219
Memorial Sloan-Kettering (MSK), 46–47
Mendel, Perry, 262
Mercedes Benz, 12, 110–11, 414
Merger(s), 9, 54, 108, 137, 139, 164, 169, 173–77, 192, 195, 232, 264, 326, 392–93, 435, 438–45, 561
Merrill Lynch, 53, 264
Mexico, 3, 9–10, 12, 19, 128, 130–31, 140, 260–61, 265, 270, 283, 404, 408, 414
Miami, 9, 45, 265–67
Microsoft, 22
Miles, Raymond, 33, 104, 170, 264, 272, 409, 428–29, 431, 433, 457
Military strategy, 13
Minitel, 80
Mitsubishi Heavy Industries, 85
Mobile workers, 31
Modular corporate forms, 213
Monsanto, 180–82, 353
Morgan Stanley, 12
Morio, Minoru, 206
Morris, Robert T., 147–48, 250, 364, 538, 545
Motorola, 22, 121, 151–52, 168–70, 172, 180, 182–84, 203, 330, 357, 368, 389, 391, 397
Multi-disciplinary, 104–5, 305, 360, 374, 386
Mushet, Michael, 426–49

N

Nanus, Burt, 16–17
National Bicycle Industrial Company, 92, 96
National Car Rental, 226
National Defense, 13, 364, 538, 545, 551
National Institute of Science and Technology, 159

National Labor Relations Act of 1935, 151
National Labor Relations Board (NLRB), 151–52
NationsBank, 176
NCR, 112
NEC, 130, 134
NEC Tohoku Ltd., 130
Negawatt, 248–49, 419
Neill, John, 155
Nestle Enterprises, 11
Network management, 235, 280, 476, 491
Networked enterprises, 27, 70, 169, 255, 452
Networking infrastructure, 68
Networking problems, 171
Networks, 6, 11, 17–19, 21, 35–36, 40, 43–48, 55, 58, 66, 70–72, 77–78, 81, 89, 98, 104–5, 134, 138, 148–50, 163, 169, 171, 177, 186, 201–3, 214, 226, 229–30, 233, 235, 282, 324, 366, 370, 375–76, 385, 397, 408–10, 413, 421, 476, 489–94, 500–501, 543
Neural networks, 55, 58
Nevada, 40, 419
New Consumerism, 51–52, 75
New paradigms, 4, 29, 93–94, 191, 237, 255, 365, 371–72, 375–76, 386–87, 416, 425, 527
New technology-to-technology spending ratio, 252, 350
Newton, 149
Niche markets, 94, 110, 283, 324, 367, 398, 558
Nike, 170
Nintendo, 17
Nissan, 101, 132, 154
Nissho Awai, 80
Non-standard interfaces, 48
Nordstrom, 22, 114, 165, 452–56
North American Free Trade Agreement (NAFTA), 3, 8–9, 12, 15, 140, 260–61, 264–66, 268, 366, 403–6, 550
North Carolina, 40
Northern Telecom Ltd., 149
Norton, David, 343
NSF International, 120

O

O'Connor, Bridget, 145
Ocean Carriers' Electronic Access Network (OCEAN), 79–80, 546

Office automation, 30, 65, 72, 101, 451
Office Systems Research Association (OSRA), 204
Offshore workers, 37, 228
Ohno, Talichi, 156–57
Okuma Corp., 101
Oldham, G. R., 143
Oldsmobile, 153
Olivetti Research Laboratory, 33
Omega, 110
OnCall EDI, 75–76, 91
Operating costs, 71, 315
Operation Desert Storm, 40
Organizational design, 4, 18, 202, 297, 299, 301, 324, 558
Organizational environment, 11, 275–76, 299
Organizational interdependencies, 217
Organizational models, 1, 10, 68, 205, 216, 371, 552
Organizational redirection, 14
Organizational restructuring, 50, 164, 189, 236, 311, 313, 322, 327, 364, 377, 382, 459, 461, 563
Organizational structures, 6, 13, 48, 141, 341, 369
Organizational transformation, 1, 6, 29
Orlando, 34, 266
Otis Elevator Co, 59
Output-based added value (OVA) analysis, 250–51
Outsourcing, 17, 54, 81, 88, 164, 169, 177–79, 189, 192, 195–97, 210–11, 214, 218–21, 223, 225–29, 234–35, 237, 275, 277, 295–96, 330, 383, 449, 459, 462, 472, 474–78, 542

P

PacifiCare Health Systems, 207
Paradigm(s), 4, 22, 29, 50–51, 89, 92–99, 110, 112–13, 130, 158–60, 164–65, 168, 184, 186, 191, 237, 249, 254–55, 285, 310, 313, 333, 363, 365–69, 371–72, 375–77, 386–89, 410, 416, 425, 497, 527, 548
Parallel processing, 111–12
Parking tickets, 32
Pascale, Richard, 186

Patent-to-stock-price, 253, 357
Peak-to-growth, 253, 357
Pen computers, 33, 150
Pentagon, 34, 103, 547
Personal Communication Networks
   (PCN), 35
Personal computer(s), 19, 30, 33, 38,
   40, 43–45, 47, 65–66, 97–98,
   100, 105, 112, 130, 133, 150,
   229, 328, 368, 408, 430, 446,
   456, 491
Personal Digital Assistants (PDA),
   149
Personal pagers, 29
Pet, 15, 355, 360
Peters, Tom, 371
Pfitzer, 97, 414
Pharmacies, 87
Philippines, 37, 40, 228, 407
Phillip Morris, 148, 250
Phillips Electronics NV, 34
PhoneMail, 41
Physical assets, 19, 375
Physicians, 29, 40
Piecework, 155
Pillsbury, 135
Pioneer Electronic Corp., 34
Pittiglio Rabin Todd McGrath, 355
Pittsburgh, 36
Plan Do Check Action (PDCA)
   Cycle, 126, 130
Planned change, 22
Pocket communication service
   (PCS), 43, 65, 149, 229
Point-of-sale (POS), 96, 103, 134,
   162, 202
Poland, 7, 78, 422
Polgar, Elod, 340
Politics of information, 53
Pontiac, 153
Portable computer(s), 30, 32, 62
Porter, Michael, 252, 269, 293, 302,
   304, 319, 541–42, 544
Postindustrial economies, 13
PPG Industries, 249, 346–47, 353
Prahalad, C. K., 73
Praxair, 180
Pre-transformation issues, 288, 290,
   293, 295, 297, 302
Presentation formats, 200–201·
Problem-solving teams, 151, 374
Process-driven, 95, 222
Proctor & Gamble (P&G), 78, 147,
   354
Prodigy, 66
Product intelligence, 193
Prototyping, 103, 470

PTT, 41, 409
Publishing, 76–77, 87, 121, 465
Puerto Rico, 265
Purchased Input Concept Optimiza-
   tion with Suppliers (PICOS),
   153

Q

Quaker Oats, 147
Quality, 1, 6, 10, 15–16, 22, 26, 32,
   38–39, 42, 47–51, 59–63,
   68–70, 74, 77–79, 86, 93–95,
   101–10, 113–47, 151–62,
   169–71, 178–79, 182–84, 187,
   191–92, 195, 201, 208–11, 214,
   218, 220–23, 228–29, 232,
   235–38, 240, 243–44, 250–51,
   262–63, 268, 270, 273–77, 286,
   294–95, 304, 309–10, 313,
   317–18, 321–24, 329–30, 339,
   341–42, 345–47, 351, 353–54,
   356, 367, 369–71, 373–74,
   376–77, 381–84, 387, 393–95,
   397, 399, 401, 407, 420,
   425–27, 432, 437, 439, 451–56,
   482, 492–97, 501, 503, 505,
   515, 519, 525–33, 537, 540,
   542, 552, 555–57

R

Rado, 110
Rail carriers, 78
Railinc, 79
Railroads, 46, 71, 78–80, 86, 409,
   433
Rapid prototyping, 103, 470
Rationalization, 61, 141, 143
Recentralization, 189, 234, 459, 462,
   479
Redesign, 6, 22, 39, 42, 46, 48, 50,
   58, 68, 73–76, 107, 113,
   141–45, 148–53, 157, 160–63,
   186–87, 191–92, 195–96, 203,
   206, 214, 223, 229, 237, 293,
   303, 313, 316–17, 323, 327,
   358, 369–70, 372–73, 377,
   386, 451, 459, 557, 563
Reengineering, 14, 22, 28, 61, 64,
   95, 141–42, 147, 151, 163,
   165, 182, 187, 189, 213, 215,
   220–21, 237, 242, 296, 311,
   313, 322, 333, 343, 347, 358,
   368–69, 372, 378, 382, 393,
   425, 447, 459, 461, 488, 490,
   492, 498, 537
Regan, Elizabeth, 145

Regulatory environment, 13, 282
Relationships, 1, 3, 13, 15, 17,
   26–27, 30, 49–50, 52, 54, 57,
   70–75, 86, 88, 106, 115, 133,
   139, 143–45, 148, 150,
   152–53, 162, 168–70, 173–74,
   187, 198, 203, 208, 216–18,
   225, 236, 260–61, 269, 275,
   281, 285–86, 292, 298, 303,
   309, 317, 326, 336, 345–50,
   366, 378, 384, 387, 414–15,
   422, 439, 451–53, 459, 489,
   510, 517, 520–25, 532, 541,
   550, 560
Renaissance Strategy Group, 304
Research and development-to-patent,
   254, 357
Research-to-development, 253–54,
   357
Retail banking, 137–38, 176, 405
Retailing, 77, 114, 132–33, 138, 192,
   247, 366, 452–55, 531
Return-on-investment (ROI), 311,
   315, 318, 334, 342, 350, 494,
   495
Reuters, 77
Ricoh, 129
Rightsizing, 225–33
Risk, 15–16, 76, 85, 104, 108, 111,
   170–73, 185–86, 218, 220,
   224, 231, 233, 250, 257, 277,
   296, 304, 308–16, 320,
   325–37, 340, 343, 352,
   356–59, 367, 372, 375–76,
   383, 397, 407, 435, 438, 448,
   503–4, 509, 511, 519, 523,
   535, 538, 560–66
Road-warriors, 32
Robert Bosch GmbH, 34
Robots, 29, 92, 94, 100–101, 367–68
Rogow, Bruce, 223
Rolm Co., 41
Rotational assignments, 205–9, 376
Rover, 154–55, 158
Royal Dutch Shell, 11, 250
Russia, 7, 550
Rymer, John, 67

S

SABRE, 65, 82, 87, 296
Safeway, 147
Saflex, 181
Sainsbury, 78, 91
Sales force automation (SFA), 49,
   61–63, 368
Satellite office, 30

Satellite tracking, 34
Saturn, 132–33, 167–68
Satyam Computer Services Ltd., 211
Savage, Charles, 168
Scenario planning, 87, 257–61,
    277–84, 290–91, 301, 304,
    311, 325, 333, 340, 357, 360,
    366, 371, 377, 384, 426, 501
Schein, Edgar, 198
Schneider National, 79
Schwartz, Peter, 260
Schwinn, 92
Sears, 31, 66, 192, 250, 391, 396
Security Pacific, 176–77
Seiyaku, Tanabe, 125
Self-managed teams, 151
Senge, Peter, 199
Service and quality, 6, 15, 22, 116,
    139, 151, 160, 187, 275, 277,
    294–95, 309, 313, 321–24,
    329–30, 339, 342, 353, 377,
    382–83, 387, 454, 497, 503,
    540, 556
Seven Questions Methodology, 257,
    285–89, 294, 304, 311, 331,
    360, 503
Shearson Lehman, 58
Sheraton, 141
Siemens, 45, 121, 414
Singapore, 18, 35, 37, 407, 409, 415,
    417
Skandia Assurance & Financial Ser-
    vices, 344–45
Skoda Automobile Co., 12
Smart cards, 42, 47
Smart materials, 21
Sneakerware, 232, 374, 376
Societe Suisse de Microelectronique
    et d'Horlogerie (SMH),
    108–11
Sociocultural, 16
Sony, 11, 34, 149, 205–6, 416, 518
South America, 8, 265, 404
Southern California Edison
    (SCEcorp), 27, 250, 272–84,
    346, 426–49
Soviet Confederation of Independent
    States, 78
Spatial database, 34, 112
Special purpose teams, 151
Spiegel, 55
Stakeholder value(s), 18, 251, 295,
    303, 308, 312–13, 317,
    321–22, 329, 341, 353, 389,
    407, 518–21, 555
Stakeholders, 7, 10, 143–45, 249,
    251, 254, 308, 310, 317–18,

323, 330, 332, 341–48,
    352–53, 356, 359, 373, 415,
    460, 503, 518–22, 526, 556
Stalk, George, 101
Standards, 9, 43–44, 75, 81, 98,
    113–31, 139–40, 145, 157–58,
    183–85, 210, 214, 217–18,
    221, 223, 226, 228, 235, 255,
    268–72, 277, 294, 323, 369,
    373–74, 378, 387, 393,
    419–20, 426, 446, 448, 455,
    466–68, 472–73, 523, 527,
    533, 536, 540–41, 551
Stata, Ray, 200–201
Steelcase, 81
Steering committees, 217, 506
Stockholders, 83, 144, 166, 200,
    249, 251, 309, 342, 346, 350,
    353, 523, 527
Strategic alignment, 221
Strategic alliance(s), 6, 67, 74, 87,
    164, 169, 172, 175, 184, 189,
    192, 205, 214, 288, 299, 324,
    330, 370, 459, 462, 479, 486,
    489, 515, 550, 552
Strategic elements, 279–80
Strategic I/T architecture, 322–24,
    356, 559
Strategic insourcing, 153, 171
Strategic intent, 4, 14, 73, 211, 370,
    378, 385, 396
Strategic match, 312, 318–19, 324,
    329, 351, 508, 553
Strategic planning, 5–6, 88, 157,
    208, 216–17, 222, 227, 271,
    286–88, 302, 305, 314,
    317–20, 324, 335, 379, 384,
    387, 396, 426, 434, 436, 444,
    447, 506, 536
Strategic standardization, 119
Strategic transformation, 23–24, 38,
    48, 73, 75, 165, 180, 193, 212,
    257–58, 286–87, 317, 322,
    324, 331, 370, 386, 392–400,
    504, 517, 538
Strategic values, 312, 317–18, 324,
    329–30, 553
Structural capital, 345
Structural change, 77, 184, 246, 249,
    254–55, 258, 504, 518
Substitutive applications, 316
Success factors, 14, 287–93, 304,
    320–21, 335, 352, 366, 385,
    480, 555
Supermarket branch banks, 36
Supermarkets, 15–16, 36, 78,
    156–57

Supplier relationship, 87
Suppliers, 3, 6, 16, 26, 36, 45, 47,
    49–50, 52, 66, 70–78, 84, 86,
    103–5, 108, 112, 121, 123,
    125, 129, 131, 134, 147, 148,
    151–53, 157, 161–62, 168–72,
    179, 196, 198, 203, 277, 282,
    309, 319, 324, 326, 343, 371,
    375–76, 381, 383, 403, 405,
    449, 451, 453, 462, 466–67,
    489, 492, 520, 524–25,
    541–54, 558, 560
Supply chain management, 42
Supreme Court, 152
Sustaining transformation, 295, 317,
    369
Swatch Collector Clubs, 109
Swatch products, 108–11
Sweden, 52, 107, 371, 409, 541
Swiss, 11, 15, 56, 107–9, 202, 439
Swissair, 37–38
Switzerland, 107–10, 260, 340, 371
Syncordia, 98
Systems and applications mainte-
    nance, 235
Systemshouse, 234

T

Taiwan, 181, 261, 265, 407, 415,
    417
Taylor, Frederick, 354
Team productivity, 39
Teamsters Union, 152
Teamworking, 167–69, 183, 186,
    527
Technology environment, 236
Technology fusion, 40, 158–60, 163,
    168, 182, 184, 268
Technology roadmaps, 183
Technology scanners, 183, 216, 382,
    384
Technology scanning, 216–17, 231,
    382–83, 536
Technology spending, 252, 345,
    350
Technology strategy, 88, 148, 160,
    227
Telecommunications devices for the
    deaf (TDD), 41
Telecommuting, 28, 31, 413
Telemedicine, 40, 47
Telex, 45, 73
Tesco, 77, 91
Texaco, 58, 250, 265
Texas, 40, 176, 204, 267, 273
Texas Instruments, 273

Textile Clothing Technology Corp., 103
Thailand, 15, 407
The Fifth Discipline, 199
Thorhallsson, Jon, 302, 363, 537–39
3M, 77, 400
Time-based competition, 370
Time-to-market, 104, 105, 118, 143, 184, 193, 236–37, 241, 310–11, 317, 322, 352, 369–70, 497
Timex, 53
Toffler, Alvin, 88
Tools and techniques, 186, 229, 235, 281, 304
Toshiba, 170, 172
Total Quality Management (TQM), 122–23
Toyota, 11, 101, 152–58, 172, 250
Tracking system, 234, 381
Trade loading, 146–47
Trade unions, 154, 156, 163
Trans World Airlines (TWA), 82–83
Transformation, 1, 5–6, 9, 14, 21–29, 38, 48, 50, 73, 75, 88–89, 113, 126, 147, 164–65, 179–80, 183–89, 191, 193, 196–99, 202, 212, 215–16, 221, 223, 236–37, 241, 257–59, 285–91, 293, 295–98, 302–3, 305, 311, 317, 322, 324, 330–33, 341, 357–59, 365, 369–70, 372–73, 378–402, 417, 425, 451–52, 460–61, 503–5, 517–18, 537–39, 546, 552
Transformation issues, 288–98, 302
Transformational activities, 333, 345, 389
Transforming enterprise, 7, 21, 24, 189, 293, 368, 372, 378, 386
TRAXON, 80
Triadigm International, 229
Trimble Navigation Ltd., 34
Trucking, 45, 79–81, 87, 138, 213, 320, 413
TRW, 30
Turnstone, 81
Twentieth Century, 102, 261, 264

U

UL, 120
Uniglobe, 83
Union Carbide, 180
Union Pacific, 79, 144
Union Pacific (UP), 79
Unipart, 154, 155–58, 162
United Airlines, 36, 82, 85, 234
United Auto Workers Union, 168
United Kingdom (UK), 31, 47, 51, 77, 107, 154–55, 157–58, 180, 210, 386, 527
United Parcel Service (UPS), 11, 29, 32–33, 61, 79–80, 85–86, 97, 178, 290, 355
United States, 4, 109, 364, 402, 404, 407, 409–10, 422, 427, 431, 433, 439, 453, 455, 545–46, 551–52
Upstream values, 348
US Council on Competitiveness, 249
US Pentagon, 34
US Supreme Court, 152
USAA, 63
USAir, 82
Utility worker, 32

V

Value added, 251, 354, 543, 562
Value Chain, 135, 302, 304, 363, 544
Value-added partner, 74
ValueLink, 74–76
Vanderbilt University Medical Center, 74
Venkatraman, N., 74–75
Venture capital, 185
Vertical hierarchies, 169
Videoconferencing, 31, 38, 40, 72
Virtual corporation, 89, 105, 215
Virtual enterprise(s), 6, 71, 81, 214, 370, 375, 492
Virtual office, 11, 62
Virtual organizations, 71
Virtual sales offices, 62
Virtual teams, 168
Virtual workgroups, 71
Visionary Leadership, 16
Voice mail, 40–41, 203, 252, 292, 541, 544
Voice messaging, 40–41
Voice processing systems, 41
Voice recognition, 367
Volkswagen, 110, 421
Volmac, 250
VW, 12, 110

W

Wagner Act, 151–52, 163, 167
Wal-Mart, 165, 456
Walker, Lynwood, 189, 257, 459–61, 504–5, 537
Warner Custom Music, 96
Washington University, 221, 286, 488
Waste Management, 74, 86
Waste Management Inc., 74
West Virginia, 40
Western Union, 45
Whirlpool, 56
White collar jobs, 12
Window of opportunity, 13, 67, 217, 320
Workflow, 43, 148, 229, 354, 355
Workgroup, 43, 49, 145
Workplace, 10, 17–19, 28–30, 48, 53, 184–85, 203, 322, 413
Workplaces, 4, 17, 26, 28, 402
Workspace 21, 29–30
Workteams, 122, 191, 193, 370, 492
World Trade Organization (WTO), 4, 8, 12, 404
Wygod, Marty, 76

X

Xerox, 53, 56, 121, 129, 131, 156–57, 355, 399

Y

Yachiyo, Kogyo, 155
Yoji, Akao, 130

Z

Zadeh, Lofti A., 59
Zero defects, 126–27
Zero pollution vehicles, 272, 282
Zero-defect production strategies, 154